PARADISE AT WAR

Books by Radha Kumar

The Republic Relearnt: Renewing Democracy in India, 1947–2024
A Gender Atlas of India
Making Peace with Partition
Divide and Fall?: Bosnia in the Annals of Partition
The History of Doing: Movements for Women's Rights and Feminism in India, 1800–1990

Books edited by Radha Kumar

Negotiating Peace in Deeply Divided Societies: A Set of Simulations
Bosnia-Herzegovina: Between War and Peace (Josep Palau)

PARADISE AT WAR

A POLITICAL HISTORY OF KASHMIR

RADHA KUMAR

ALEPH BOOK COMPANY
An independent publishing firm
promoted by *Rupa Publications India*

First published in India in 2018 by
Aleph Book Company
7/16 Ansari Road, Daryaganj
New Delhi 110 002

Published in paperback in 2024

Copyright © Radha Kumar 2018, 2024

All rights reserved.

The author has asserted her moral rights.

The views and opinions expressed in this book are the author's own and the facts are as reported by her, which have been verified to the extent possible, and the publishers are in no way liable for the same.

No part of this publication may be reproduced, transmitted, or stored in a retrieval system, in any form or by any means, without permission in writing from Aleph Book Company.

ISBN: 978-81-970811-9-4

1 3 5 7 9 10 8 6 4 2

Printed in India

This book is sold subject to the condition that it shall not, by way of trade or otherwise, be lent, resold, hired out, or otherwise circulated without the publisher's prior consent in any form of binding or cover other than that in which it is published.

Kashmir, the Lyric

O best of kings, the goddess Uma is also Kas'mira.
An enchanting lake for six generations of our aeon,
  It became a beautiful land in this generation.

O protector of men! Earth's hallowed spaces are all here.
Starred with hermitages, sweet in summer and winter,
  It augurs good fortune.

Impregnable,
Innocent of the fears of defeat,
Rich in cow, horse and elephant,
  It is free of famine.

Graceful as a temple where gentlewomen pray,
It is free of evil serpents, tigers, buffaloes or bears.

Always celebrant,
Where the bow twangs and Vedic chants resound,
  It throngs with sportive and joyous crowds.

—*Nilamata Purana*, sixth to eighth century[1]

The land of Kashmir is blessed like the land of Syria,
Fruit trees and shade trees, wondrous streams and soaring mountains,
  Are found here.

This land was settled by the Prophet Solomon,
His genies turned it into a fertile flowering garden.

Allah's friends and followers make their home here,
This land is without equal, the place of spirits and angels.

—Baba Daud Khaki, sixteenth century[2]

CONTENTS

Preface to the Revised Edition   ix

1. A Wonder That Was Kas'mira   1
2. The Rise of Politics   21
3. Twin Partitions   45
4. A Lion in Winter   78
5. Between Wars: 1965–1971   112
6. Two Decades of Relative Quiet?   140
7. Benazir, Rajiv and Their Successors   171
8. The Siege of Hazratbal   187
9. 'The Sky is the Limit'   197
10. Gujral's Short Foray   207
11. Sada-e-Sarhad   216
12. Kargil: Pakistan's Implausible Deniability   225
13. The NDA's Annus Horribilis   237
14. The Rise of Jihad   246
15. Suddenly in 2000   259
16. New Beginnings   281
17. The Peace Process, 2004–2008   290
18. Intifada, 2010   317
19. 'Talking to the People'   332
20. 2016 and After: Losing Kashmir?   396
21. A Doom Only Partially Foreseen   417

Afterword   425
Acknowledgements   427
Notes   428
Bibliography   458
Index   461

PREFACE TO THE REVISED EDITION

Since the independence of India and Pakistan, Jammu and Kashmir has faced four wars of varying lengths as well as a protracted insurgency that resurges sporadically. The first war was a by-product of the 1947 Partition of India, and its outcome was the de facto partition of the princely state of Jammu and Kashmir in 1949. Sixteen years later, it faced another India–Pakistan war, followed in less than ten years by a third war, and then an insurgency from the late 1980s to the mid-2000s, punctuated by a smaller war in 1999. In other words, neither Indian nor Pakistan-held Jammu and Kashmir have experienced an extended period of stability over the past seventy-five years.

Devastation by war is not unfamiliar to Jammu and Kashmir's people—the region has undergone waves of conquest, empire, and colonialism. But where other regions gained peace dividends after the end of empire, Jammu and Kashmir did not. Its history has remained one of fiercely contested battles for power that were triggered externally as well as internally.

This book has been written at a particularly difficult time for Jammu and Kashmir, one in which options for peace, nurtured between 2002 and 2013, were definitively closed. How far this closure affects the former state's future prospects will only be judged in hindsight; nor can I predict how many fresh layers of complexity it has added for peacemakers to come, though I can predict that their task is infinitely more difficult now. For anyone attempting to chronicle the political history of Jammu and Kashmir, the endeavour is inevitably riddled by inaccuracies of perception as well as fact. I apologize for mine.

Chapter 1

A WONDER THAT WAS KAS'MIRA

A Kashmiri political scientist once said to me, 'You cannot discuss Kashmir, or the Kashmir conflict, without starting with history.' I was puzzled: what did the region's ancient or medieval history have to do with a conflict that began after the partition of India in 1947? It was only when I started researching this book that I found that many contemporary threads of the conflict—and, more importantly, its solution—lead back in time.

Internally, the valley's particular form of religious syncretism, which is so different from the demographic pluralism of Jammu or the 'living together separately' model of Ladakh, is rooted in the opening centuries of the first millennium CE. Kashmir was amongst the earliest regions of the Indian subcontinent to record its history, and through the ages, Kashmiri historians and mythologists preserved much of the culture as it developed. The traditions that were anchored through retelling were not unbroken: Kashmir too fell under a series of empires as well as a rapid succession of dynasties, each of which left its imprint. But the philosophical underpinnings of Kashmiri tradition were relatively undisturbed, perhaps because it was at the periphery of empire and few ancient empire-builders treated peripheries as bulwarks. The beliefs that Kashmir and Kashmiris are exceptional, that they are guardians of the religious sites of all faiths, that the pursuit of knowledge requires engagement with every view, that the military is an inferior occupation—a view shared by India's nineteenth-century social reformer Swami Vivekananda—remain strong even today, though they are increasingly under threat.

Externally too, the region's horizons have not altered in any major way despite the changing geopolitics of the region. Neighbours continue to play make-or-break roles in the state.

Afghanistan's leaders, who once ruled Kashmir, no longer seek control or influence there. Yet, events in Afghanistan continue to fall out on Kashmir, largely because of Pakistani activism in both regions. Attacks from modern Pakistan, which includes the ancient territories once called Dardistan, have increased, but only to the extent that there are shorter lulls between attacks than there were centuries ago. While Iran is less prominent than ancient Parthia, it continues to sway Shias in the state politically and Kashmiri elites culturally. China is no longer a potential ally for Kashmir, since it occupied a large part of the state's territory after the 1962 India–China War and became a stakeholder in the Kashmir conflict. Tajikistan and Uzbekistan, once of some significance for both trade and cultural exchange, may regain those ties if plans for connectivity take off. Kashmiri leaders lobby for inclusion in emerging regional road and rail networks that will revive the relations they built during the ancient Silk Route period, in a more peaceable neighbourhood than there was then.

No wonder any discussion on Kashmir has to begin with history, however mythologized some of it may be.

◆

For ancient Hindus, Kashmir was a sacred geography to which humans were introduced by divine intervention. The *Nilamata Purana,* also known as *Kasmira Mahatmya,*[1] was regarded as one of the texts in the Vedanta, a body of scriptural literature that combines myth and legend with what may have been real-life events and often interprets one through the other. It describes the Kashmir valley as originally one vast lake, home to the gods Shiva and his wife, Parvati, but it also refers to the valley itself as Uma, another name for Parvati, turning it into a place *to* worship as well as a place *of* worship.

This vast lake, says the *Nilamata,* was drained at the order of the sage Kashyapa, grandson of the god Brahma, by cutting a rock gorge at Varahmula, which is Baramulla today. It gradually separated into large and small lakes when the divine clan of Nagas, who were protagonists in the epic Mahabharata, and other fortunate mortals settled there. 'Because water called Ka² was taken out by Balarama the plough-wielder from this country, so it shall be called Kas'mira in this world.'[3] A paradise to live in, with soaring mountains and flowering orchards, the goddesses Sati, Saci, Ganga, Aditi, Yamuna, Diti and Karisini all took the form of rivers flowing through it. 'The water of Vitasta [today's Jhelum] mixed with that of Sindhu [Indus] is like milk mixed with nectar, beauty combined with elegance, and knowledge combined with good nature.'[4]

Descendants of the sage Kashyapa, whose wife Kadru gave birth to the Naga clan, the *Nilamata*'s writers saw Kashmiris as guardians of the sacred 'who perform sacrifices and are engaged in self-study and contemplation, virtuous ascetics well-versed in the Vedas.'[5] Their life sounds idyllic, if unreal; protected by the formidable mountains that surround it, Kas'mira had never been conquered and its people were free from fear. The valley echoed with the sounds of lutes and drums, religious chants, dance and theatre in an unending round. 'One should feast in the company of friends and should play to one's content.'[6]

Yet, if they failed to follow the edicts of their founder-king Nila, retribution would descend on them in the form of 'floods, excess of rain, drought, famine, deaths, untimely death of the king, and dreadful punishments'.[7] Just such an eventuality was described in the Mahabharata, written a thousand years earlier, with Kashyapa's two wives falling out and turning their children, the Nagas, and the great bird Garuda, into sworn enemies. To trump his foes, Garuda brought the Nagas the nectar of immortality but prevented them from swallowing it, and a series of disasters followed. The Naga chiefs fell out, their people were massacred, their king, Gonanda I, besieged the god Krishna in Mathura and was killed by Krishna's brother, while Krishna himself killed Gonanda's son, Damodara I, in Gandhara, which comprised present-day Kandahar and Kabul in Afghanistan together with Pakistan's Khyber–Pakhtunkhwa and Swat. A repentant Krishna anointed the dead king's wife, Yasovati, the new ruler of Kashmir, because 'the goddess Uma [was] the same as Kas'mira'.[8]

Whether these myths constituted imaginative interpretations of actual alliances and conflicts between rulers of the time is debatable, though it would be aetiologically unsurprising given Kashmir was a Hindu kingdom during the Mahabharata period. It became a part of the Buddhist Mauryan empire between the third and first centuries BCE. The Emperor Ashoka founded the beautiful city of Srinagari in the third century BCE, some twenty kilometres from today's capital Srinagar, abutting its suburb Soura. Modern Srinagar dates back to the seventh century and is in fact built on the site of the sixth-century royal capital Pravarapura, mentioned in the Chinese annals of the Tang dynasty. The modern city took the older Ashokan name.[9]

Buddhism flowered in Kashmir under Ashoka, who dispatched hundreds of monks from Gandhara to spread the faith, at the same time building a Shiva temple at Vijeshwari to support what was then the religion of the majority. Vijeshwari is now Bijbehara in Anantnag district, the constituency of former Chief Minister Mufti Mohammad Sayeed from 2002–15.

Buddhism continued to blossom in close proximity to Hinduism under Ashoka's son and grandson, as well as under the Kushana kings who captured Kashmir from the Mauryan empire in its decline. The Kushanas are believed to be of Turkic origin and possibly belonged to the Xinjiang and Gansu regions of modern China. Folklore has it that the Kushana king Kanishka hosted the Fourth Buddhist Council in the first century at Harwan, today's Shalimar Garden in Srinagar. The council drew 500 Buddhist and Hindu scholars from all over the region, including China, to codify Sarvastivada, the precursor to Mahayana Buddhism.

First under the Mauryas and then the Kushanas, Kashmir's horizons stretched across the Indian subcontinent, from Magadha in the southeast, comprising modern Odisha and parts of Bengal, to Malwa or modern Rajasthan in the southwest. In modern-day Pakistan, they covered Gandhara to the north and the lands of the Dards in the northwest, comprising Chitral, Gilgit and Kohistan in Swat, Gurez in Baltistan and parts of northern Punjab, and Mehrgarh or today's Balochistan in the west. Beyond the subcontinent, they reached further west to Palmyra in Syria and Parthia or Persia, which is present-day Iran; north to Bactria, lands in the Amu Darya or Oxus basin including parts of Afghanistan, Uzbekistan and Tajikistan, through Sindh and northeast to China.

Ancient China loomed large on Kashmir's security map as a potentially powerful bulwark against the western and northern kingdoms that sought to conquer the valley. The Kushanas saw a common bond with China, born of religion as well as geopolitical circumstance. Buddhism spread to China from Kashmir as well as from east India, and both Kashmir and China faced threats from Persia and the Tibetan empire. To strengthen trade, Kanishka built land routes to join the ancient Silk Road from China, one branch of which ran along the border of Kashmir from the kingdom of Kapisa, part of modern-day Afghanistan, and another through Kashmir, Ladakh and central India, exiting on to the west coast of India. Kashmir exported shawls, indigo and coral to Central Asia, Russia and Europe through these routes. Forced to repel repeated attacks on his lands from Persia, the Kushana King Vasudeva (historians debate whether this was Kanishka's predecessor Vasudeva I or successor Vasudeva II) sent an embassy to the Wei emperor in China to seek military aid between the first and second centuries, when China too sought allies against Persia.

China was not the only ally that Kashmir's rulers sought against Persia—they sent a delegation to Emperor Augustus in Rome too. There was a flourishing sea trade between the Kushanas and the Romans and, according to the sixth-century historian Procopius, ancient Kashmiris sought a trade alliance with ancient Romans against Persia: 'About the same time [ca. 550] there came from India certain monks; and when they had satisfied Justinian Augustus that the Romans no longer should buy silk from the Persians, they promised the emperor in an interview that they would provide the materials for making silk so that never should the Romans seek business of this kind from their enemy the Persians, or from any other people whatsoever.'[10]

Nor was Persia the only threat against which ancient Kashmiris sought alliances. The expansive Tibetan empire, with its push to the west, was a danger to both China and Kashmir, said the envoy 'U-li-to' who was sent to the imperial Tang court in the mid-eighth century by Kashmir's King Lalitaditya of Magadha.[11] King Lalitaditya, the envoy added, together with his ally Yasovardhan of Kannauj in central India, had successfully repulsed the Tibetans from territories to the north of Kashmir, including Ladakh, and closed all five routes into Kashmir and onwards into the Gangetic plains. He then invited a 200,000-strong Chinese auxiliary force to base itself on the shores of the lake Volur, or Wullar Lake today. Since the Chinese had just defeated the Tibetans in Po-liu (present-day Baltistan), he explained, this would cement an alliance of two victorious rulers.

The Chinese emperor greeted U-li-to and his delegation with pomp and fanfare. Lalitaditya's older brother, King Chandrapida, had sought to bring Kashmir into the Chinese sphere of influence three years earlier, when the Arab general Muhammad-bin-Qasim conquered neighbouring Sind and Multan from their Hindu rulers. Fearing bin-Qasim would attack Kashmir next, Chandrapida sought military support from the Tang emperor. China was itself facing threats from Arabs and Turkmens, having expelled Tibetans from the Silk Road basin, but at this point the emperor contented himself with sending a formal letter recognizing Chandrapida as the king of Kashmir. In the event, Chandrapida was able to deter the Arabs without Chinese aid.

Three years later, when U-li-to visited bearing Lalitaditya's request, the Tang emperor decided to aid Chandrapida's brother. Though he did not send the troops U-li-to sought, the Chinese military supported Lalitaditya in his campaign to expand his territories to Central Asia, Afghanistan and Punjab, helping him restructure his army and introduce heavily-armed cavalry units with new types of armour.[12]

Unlike the author(s) of the *Nilamata Purana*, the tenth-century Arab historian al-Biruni saw the tall mountains that surrounded Kashmir as a barrier rather than a defence. Lamenting the brutality with which Mahmud of Ghazni conquered large tracts of northern India, al-Biruni remarked that he had driven 'Hindu sciences' to the citadel of Kashmir, thus denying the rest of the world access to them. Though Mahmud twice attacked Kashmir and was turned back by its then queen, Didda, to al-Biruni Kashmir's mountains bred insularity. The Kashmiris, he said, 'are particularly anxious about the natural strength of their country, and therefore take always much care to keep a strong hold upon the entrances and roads leading into it. In consequence, it is very difficult to have any commerce with them.'[13] Over the years, he continued, Kashmiris had grown unwelcoming of outsiders. 'In former times they used to allow one or two foreigners to enter their country, particularly Jews, but at present they do not allow any Hindu whom they do not know personally to enter, much less any other person.'

Under Queen Didda, the entry of non-Kashmiris was forbidden, but her reign was brief. Perhaps al-Biruni's view was jaundiced by her short-lived edict, or perhaps ancient Kashmiris welcomed ideas more freely than they did people. At a time when Buddhism was in decline across most of India, the *Nilamata Purana* used Hindu and Buddhist concepts interchangeably, including cosmology, and prescribed that Gautama Buddha's birthday should be celebrated with a grand festival. Close to 500 years later, the first history of Kashmir to be written, the twelfth-century *Rajatarangini* or *River of Kings* by the historian Kalhana, listed a long line of monarchs who built both Buddhist and Shaivite shrines and monasteries. Kalhana himself, according to his translator, the Indologist Aurel Stein, was a Shaivite Brahmin as well as Buddhist, though he displayed more admiration for Buddhists 'who do not feel anger even against the sinner, but in patience render him kindness'.[14] Shaivite Brahmins were Kalhana's own dominant community and Buddhism had again begun to be attacked in Kashmir, as it was 400 years earlier in the sixth century, when the 'White Hun' Toramana from the steppes of Central Asia, who had established his authority along the Amu Darya and conquered Persia, wrested Kashmir.

Vanquishing the Buddhist kingdoms that had ruled the northwest of the Indian subcontinent for 800 years, King Toramana's son, Mihirakula, established his capital in western

Punjab, in what is now the Jhang district of Pakistan, home to the sectarian terrorists of the Lashkar-e-Jhangvi, and then sought to expand southwards. Despite Mihirakula's cruel reputation for persecuting Buddhists—he was said to favour Brahmins—it was ironically a Kashmiri ruler who offered him sanctuary when his expeditions south to Malwa and Magadha were repulsed and he was driven back north. While living on the Kashmiri king's hospitality, Mihirakula organized a coup to conquer Kashmir.[15] Fittingly, he later committed suicide. Ancient Kashmiris clearly saw themselves as hospitable even to enemies; it was fate that brought these enemies to their just deserts.

Yet, al-Biruni's comments also reflect a shrinking of Kashmir's horizons that began in the ninth century, when the empire that Lalitaditya built began to crumble. Kashmir's own Karkota dynasty, founded by Lalitaditya's grandfather, Durlabhavardhana, conquered the territories surrounding Kashmir from Afghanistan to Punjab. They also ventured further south to establish connections as far as present-day Tamil Nadu, Karnataka and Kerala. After Lalitaditya's grandson, Jayapida, died, there was a line of short-lived Karkota kings who lost most of the lands bordering Kashmir and were replaced by the Utpala dynasty in the mid-ninth century. The ninth-century Utpala king, Avantivarman, sponsored new technologies, such as engineering, that were being developed in Girnar, Bhojpur and Vijayanagara. While the latter constructions aimed at water conservation in the plains through reservoirs, Avantivarman's engineer, Suyya, focused on mountain river regulation, building dams, embankments and new river beds to steer the course of the Vitasta (Jhelum) and irrigate the valleys it flowed through. As a result of this boost to agriculture, the price of rice, according to Kalhana, fell from 200 to 36 dinnaras per khari (roughly eighty kilograms).[16] The city Suyya founded, Suyyapur, 'a town resembling heaven', is today's Sopore.[17]

Rising to power at a time when Kashmiri territories had shrunk and its feudal lords were at war within, Avantivarman's first efforts aimed at internal consolidation, which, said Kalhana, he achieved so successfully that he was able to bring the pursuit of knowledge back to Kashmir and, like many of the kings that preceded him, build a new city named Avantipura, home today to an army base and the Islamic University of Kashmir. His son tried to recapture Kashmir's erstwhile lands unsuccessfully, but did found his own city, Shankarapura, now called Pattan.

Kashmir's inward turn continued during Kalhana's time, which saw intense infighting between royal contenders for the throne, so much so that Kalhana remarked bitterly that Kashmiris, including soldiers, fled every offensive even if it was only by a gang of 'resolute robbers', and that Kashmir's people welcomed every change of ruler, even if the contender was known to be worse than the king he replaced. Whether this characterization of Kashmiris existed before Kalhana is unclear, but it continued into the twentieth century. Writing in 1900, Kalhana's translator Stein commented, 'We read of Kasmir armies which disperse at the sight or even the rumour of a resolute foe, of rival forces which both tremble in fear of each other...Murder by a few resolute ruffians in the royal palace is usually followed by a general stampede of guards, courtiers, ministers, and troops. The uncompromising realism with which Kalhana paints such scenes leaves no doubt as to the estimate which experience had led him to form of his countrymen's military valor.'[18]

Surveying this history, I was struck by how contemporary al-Biruni and Kalhana's observations seem, though I wonder whether that is because Kashmiris themselves draw attention to the traits the two writers singled out. Kashmiris *are* insular insofar as they see themselves as an exclusive community defined by birth and culture. At the same time, they welcome trade and the exchange of ideas with their neighbours and the wider world. These twin features are as much a part of being Kashmiri as are a lyrical pride in the valley's beauty—which is as strong in the twenty-first century as it was in the sixth—and, at least until recently, a deep pride in the valley's history of religious and philosophical enquiry as the foundation of its pluralism.

Just like Kalhana in the twelfth century, contemporary Kashmiris cite historical observation to exemplify root characteristics of their being, stretched back over time as an unbroken continuum, in stark contrast to most other Indians (except Bengalis), who cite history mostly to justify prejudice. As the Kashmiri historian Parvez Dewan says, 'Even today, Kalhana's name, and that of his multi-volume *Rajatarangini*...pop up in middle class conversation in Kashmir with the same regularity as Shakespeare does elsewhere, i.e., at least once a week.'[19] Both in the 1990s and in the 2010s, Kashmiri friends repeated Kalhana's self-deprecating observations about their capacity to fight and recommended I read him as well as Stein and the British civil servant Walter Lawrence. Less noted was the Kashmiri appetite for peace that Gandhi so appreciated during partition.

Whether Kashmir's young share this pride in Kashmir's history is unclear; the generation of the 2010s appears to have lost it. As the Kashmir valley enters its thirtieth year of conflict, one cannot help noting that the great cities founded by the ancients—Srinagar, Baramulla, Sopore, Bijbehara, Pattan—are today strongholds of slash-and-burn militancy. The angry young people that I met in 2010–11 were either unaware of or impatient with the valley's pre-conflict history, unlike the 1980s generation of guerrillas that I had got to know during the peace process years of 2000–08. One reason might be that the Pandit teachers of the valley fled during the armed insurgency of the 1990s that targeted Hindus as well as political parties, government and security installations. As a result, the 2010s generation did not learn their history. Yet, it could equally be that even if the present generation were to be taught this history, they would reject it as yet another ploy to bind Kashmir to India. This break and shift in historical narrative is further explored later in the book; for now, we return to a quick chronicle of the past.

♦

Official Islam came to Kashmir through Ladakh in the fourteenth century when Prince Lhachen Gyalbu Rinchen of Baltistan conquered the kingdom and converted.[20] Ten thousand Kashmiris converted along with Rinchen, renamed Sultan Sadruddin, in a public ceremony; Dewan says that Islam was adopted as the official state religion under him. Described as a 'lion among men' by the fifteenth-century historian Jonaraja, who took on Kalhana's mantle, Rinchen died within three years of becoming Kashmir's new ruler. His vizier, Shah Mir, originally from Swat, won the throne sixteen years later, founding a 200-year dynasty.

Shah Mir and his sons were better known for administration and infrastructure than for patronage of religion. The former slashed taxes and the latter founded new towns and built bridges, including at Sopore. It was under the fourth and fifth rulers of the Shah Mir dynasty, Sultans Qutbuddin and Sikander, that Islam multiplied. The revered scholar-priest, Mir Syed Ali bin Shahabuddin Hamadani, popularly dubbed Shah-e-Hamadan, brought Sufi Islam to Kashmir in the late fourteenth century, after spending some years in Gilgit fleeing Timur's brutalities in Khorasan, which then covered most of eastern Iran, northern Afghanistan and parts of Turkmenistan. In Kashmir, he persuaded the ruler, Qutbuddin, to enforce the Sharia,[21] divorce his Hindu wife and adopt Islamic dress. He is said to have converted 37,000 people, and the 700 Syeds he brought with him converted many thousands more.

Qutbuddin's successor, Sikander, with his military commander-in-chief and later prime minister, Suhabhatt Malik Saifuddin, were generous funders of Islamic art and enquiry. Scholars and saints from Central Asia and Khorasan flocked to Kashmir. Under the influence of Hamadani, Sikander and Suhabhatt embarked on an Islamic purification mission, banning alcohol, prostitution and gambling. Though they built two great hospices—the Khanqah-e-Mu'alla, dedicated to Hamadani, and the Khanqah-e-Faiz Panah at Tral—as well as the Jamia Masjid in Srinagar, they were said to have destroyed scores of temples, including the great temples in Martand, Bijbehara, Ishabar (near Srinagar's Nishat Garden), Triphar (at the foot of the Mahadeva mountain) and Baramulla district. They also imposed jizya, a tax on non-Muslims, a practice followed by the Ottoman empire and the Taliban. Hindus were so persecuted that there was an exodus of Pandits from the valley; Sikander came to be known as the 'But Shikan' or idol-destroyer, though some contemporary Kashmiri historians believe that it was his prime minister, Suhabhatt, who was the chief villain. Moreover, argued Khalid Bashir Ahmad, Sikander's persecution of Brahmins was no greater than that of previous monarchs, including Hindus.[22] Ahmad's argument is not entirely persuasive since the examples he gives of previous persecution are mostly of looting of temples, not jizya or forced migration, nor of course does an earlier persecution cancel a later one, but his overall point, that all Kashmiris suffered under one or other ruler, is well taken.

Hamadani and his son Mir Mohammad, who belonged to a Sunni order that revered the Sufi saint Hazrat Ali, apparently disapproved the targeting of Hindus and cautioned Suhabhatt against it,[23] but Kashmiri Pandits returned to the valley only during the rule of Sikander's successor, Sultan Zain-ul-Abidin. Seeking competent administrators for the government, which his predecessors had weakened to the point of a drained exchequer, Zain—who was named Budshah or great king by his grateful subjects—encouraged the return of Pandits, appointing several to influential posts and rehabilitating them with lands that were newly reclaimed through building a system of canals called Zainagirs.

Though he did not abolish jizya, Zain slashed the tax to a minimal amount. He proclaimed Persian the official court language but encouraged Persian and Sanskrit scholars to translate widely revered texts into each other's languages. Partly as a result of this, Persian writers drew a similar sacred geography for Islam in Kashmir as had the ancient Hindu texts before them. Quoting the sixteenth-century author of *Rishinama* (Chronicle of Saints) Baba Daud Khaki, historian Chitralekha Zutshi noted how Khaki's Islamic imagery drew from the *Nilamata Purana*, using the same metaphors for its beauty but attributing it to different founders.

In the same period that Zain encouraged cross-pollination of Sanskrit and Persian literature, a devotional-mystical strand of Islam, unique to Kashmir, was born through Sheikh Nooruddin Wali of Kaimoh, near Srinagar. Combining elements of the Hindu spiritual tradition with Islam, Sheikh Nooruddin was dubbed 'Nund Rishi' by his Hindu and Muslim followers alike. While influenced by

Hamadani and the Sufi saint Shamsuddin Iraqi—who sought to reinstate Hamadani's 'true' Islam against the Shia variant and expanded Kashmir's horizons further west to Iraq—Nooruddin also revered his contemporary, the Shaivite poetess Lalleshwari or Lal Ded, asking in one of his verses to be granted the same depth of spiritual understanding that she had. Unlike the Sanskrit or Persian writers who cast the land as sacred geography, Lal Ded's vakh or sayings in Kashmiri focused on inward transformation. One of her most quoted poems went:

> Siva is all-pervading and present in each particle,
> Never differentiate between a Hindu and a Muslim,
> If you are shrewd and intelligent, know yourself,
> There lies acquaintance with God.[24]

Five centuries later, when the guerrilla-turned-Gandhian, Yasin Malik, leader of the Jammu Kashmir Liberation Front (JKLF), sought a symbol for his new politics, he chose Lal Ded to signify commitment to Kashmiriyat or the culture and practice of being Kashmiri. Like Lal Ded, her contemporary, the haunting singer-songwriter, Habba Khatoon, wrote in Kashmiri. Both women left their husbands, but while Lal Ded became a mystic and ascetic, Habba Khatoon is said to have remarried Yusuf Shah Chak who was imprisoned by Akbar. His descendant, Yakub Shah, was the last monarch of an independent Kashmir.[25]

Akbar annexed Kashmir to the Mughal empire in the late sixteenth century. The annexation was sought and welcomed by Khaki, amongst others. Khaki and his cohort hoped that the Mughals would curtail the system of begar under which peasants had to till land in exchange for daily food. They were disappointed. The kingdom remained under Mughal rule for the next 200 years. Akbar and his descendants waxed lyrical about the beauties of the valley, but it continued to be governed by a series of good, bad and indifferent governors, the worst of whom encouraged begar and further stretched already expansive tax regimes. When Akbar's son, Jahangir, ascended the throne, he found the then governor had imposed such rigorous and all-encompassing taxes on the people that he had to publicly proclaim their rollback in an order that was inscribed in stone on the gateway of the Jamia Masjid in Srinagar.[26]

With his famous couplet on Kashmir—'If there be a paradise on earth, this is it, this is it, this is it'—Jahangir built palaces and created parks, including the Shalimar Garden in Srinagar. But he also reintroduced begar and banned marriage between Hindu men and Muslim women. His son, Shah Jahan, revoked Jahangir's order on begar and revived Islamic arts, in particular literature and calligraphy, along with his son, Dara Shukoh, a scholar who spent many months in Kashmir translating the Bhagavad Gita. Now poets from Persia and calligraphers from Central Asia flocked to Kashmir, but Shah Jahan's second son, Aurangzeb, who imprisoned his father and killed his brother, returned to religious persecution, of Shias as well as Hindus.

◆

As the Mughal empire entered its decline in the eighteenth century, the Afghans under Ahmed Shah Durrani succeeded in conquering Kashmir, which shifted from one set of governors to another, with the chief difference being that the Afghan governors were even more brutal and expropriative than their Mughal predecessors. Having initially welcomed the Afghan conquest of their state, just as they had welcomed the Mughal conquest earlier, Kashmiris hoped for better when Maharaja Ranjit Singh of Punjab wrested Kashmir in 1819. They were once again disappointed to find that a change of rule at the top did not result in substantive reform on the ground. Thirty years later, Ranjit Singh's own appointed governor, the Dogra Gulab Singh, colluded with the British to defeat the Sikhs.

The Treaty of Amritsar was signed on 16 March 1846, barely a week after the Treaty of Lahore under which the defeated Sikh empire ceded to the British all its territories between the rivers Indus and Ravi. Seven days later, the British sold Kashmir and Ladakh, which Ranjit Singh had conquered less than three decades earlier, to Gulab Singh, now titled maharaja, for the princely sum of ₹75 lakh (7.5 million), with the proviso that he would acknowledge 'the supremacy of the British Government'.[27] 'How cheap the sale,' the poet Iqbal was to later comment. Kashmir's new maharaja, in his turn, founded a new Dogra dynasty that ruled for a hundred years.

The 1846 treaty bound Gulab Singh and his heirs to contribute troops for any British military engagement in adjoining hill territories. In return, Britain would defend Gulab Singh's kingdom and would not intervene in his administration. Or so they said. Less than two years later, as the British contemplated embarking on a Second Anglo-Sikh War, Governor General Sir Henry Hardinge warned Gulab Singh, 'In no case will the British Government be the blind instrument of a Ruler's injustice towards his people and if, in spite of friendly warnings, the evil of which the British Government may have just cause to complain be not corrected, a system of direct interference must be resorted to which, as Your Highness must be aware, would lower the dignity and curtail the independence of the Ruler.'[28]

Did the British government never intend to honour the terms of the 1846 treaty or was this a sudden shift in policy—and what necessitated it?

The nineteenth century was a period of intense jockeying between Britain and Russia for control over access to Central Asia and its legendary wealth of resources. It gave rise to the Great Game in the 1830s, a time when imperial Russia had expanded its footprint to the Kazakh and Turkmen emirates. Intended to create secure trade routes to Central Asia for British commerce at the height of its growth, as well as a buffer zone between Russia and Britain's Indian empire, the Great Game initially focused on Afghanistan, Punjab and Sindh, the territories through which protected routes would have to run. But feuding Afghans and Punjabis—each with an eye on the other's territory—demanded alliances against each other. With an infinitely richer and stronger Punjab as an immediate neighbour to British India, then run by the East India Company, the British spurned Afghan offers of alliance. When the visit of a Russian envoy to Kabul raised suspicions that the ruler of Afghanistan was flirting with the Russian government, the British India government went to war. The First Anglo-Afghan War (1839–42) lasted three years and ended with British defeat.

British attention then turned to Sindh and Punjab. Sindh was conquered in 1843. Punjab was roiled by conflicts of succession following the death of Ranjit Singh in 1839, and its army became a parallel force called the Sikhs' Dal Khalsa (Army), with units raised by landowners multiplying its strength from 29,000 to 80,000. Alarmed by the presence of a rapidly growing military force on the border, the British army deployed forward posts on the eastern banks of the river Sutlej, which in turn led the Sikh army to suspect nefarious intention. A classic security dilemma played out when the Sikh army crossed the Sutlej in 1845, culminating in the First Anglo-Sikh War in which the Sikh kingdom was defeated. Governor General Hardinge himself accompanied the troops.

Gulab Singh played a major role in helping the British to victory in the First Anglo-Sikh War. Seeing a loyal ally in him, the British government sold him the valley, arguing that British capacities would be overstretched if they tried to integrate it as a princely state. But neighbouring Punjab did not settle under the new dispensation of a British Resident and, in 1848, the Second Anglo-Sikh War broke out, which the British again won. In April 1849, the British annexed Punjab, and bordering Kashmir grew in strategic importance. Though Gulab Singh aided them in the Second Anglo-Sikh War, too, the British could no longer afford a vulnerable flank in Kashmir. At the same time, they could not visibly expand their influence over Kashmir's internal affairs without violating the 1846 treaty.

The British government consolidated both administrative and military control over the bulk of territories this side of the Himalayas by the late nineteenth century. The best way to keep watchful control, Delhi advised London, was to post a British political officer at the maharaja's court, as in other princely states.

Gulab Singh resisted and the British authorities decided not to challenge him. He was the largest princely contributor of troops to the British army and had expanded the frontiers of the state to Gilgit, and both Hunza and Nagar paid him tribute. Allowing him a degree of independence was a small price when he kept the frontier safe for British India at no cost.

Gulab Singh's successor, Ranbir Singh, was not so lucky. Writing to Maharaja Ranbir in 1873, the then governor general Lord Northbrook proposed, 'In view of the important position of Your Highness's territories on the north-western frontiers of British India, the increasing importance attached to political affairs in Central Asia, the necessity of obtaining early and reliable information of all that takes place beyond the Himalayan passes, the mischief caused by the circulation of false and exaggerated rumours from those quarters, and the close relations which will, His Excellency in Council trusts, be established with Yarkand, it appears to His Excellency in Council to be advisable that a British Resident should remain permanently at the Court of Your Highness. This alteration of the present arrangements is made for reasons relating to the external relations of British India, and the Viceroy has no intention of interfering more than heretofore in the internal affairs of Kashmere.'[29]

Though Ranbir resisted in his turn, he accepted a watered-down 'Resident' post, allowing the British to station an Officer on Special Duty at his court as well as in Gilgit, which he had reconquered in 1860 after Gulab Singh had been forced to give it up. But neither the maharaja nor the ruler of adjoining Chitral cooperated with the British representative in Gilgit, who reported directly to Delhi, and the post was closed in 1881. British pressure on Ranbir Singh increased rather than abated after the closure. Viceroy Lytton had hoped to develop an alliance with the Afghans that would provide a buffer between Imperial Russia and Britain's Indian empire, but talks with the Afghan ruler, Sher Ali, failed, leading to war in 1878 and another British defeat.[30] The spotlight was back on Kashmir as the British frontier.

When Ranbir Singh fell into a protracted illness and it became clear that he would soon die, the British seized the opportunity to revive the idea of stationing a political agent in the state. In May 1884, the Earl of Kimberley, then secretary of state for

India, empowered Viceroy Ripon to appoint a British Resident irrespective of heir apparent Pratap Singh's wishes, saying 'whether regard be had to the condition of the country, to the character of the Prince into whose hands the Government will shortly pass, or to the course of events beyond the border, which has materially increased the political importance of Kashmir, the appointment which you request a discretionary authority to make appears to be not only desirable but necessary. Your Excellency in Council is therefore, at liberty to proceed in the matter as you may think proper at any time after the death of Maharaja Ranbir Singh, taking care meanwhile that strict secrecy is observed as to your intentions.'[31]

To British surprise, Maharaja Pratap proved as resistant to accepting a British Resident as his predecessors had been, saying that such a step would lower 'me in the eyes of my subjects and in the estimation of the public' even before he could prove himself 'equal to the onerous and responsible duties of a good ruler'.[32] His plea was not accepted and Colonel Oliver St John, who was Officer on Special Duty, was promoted to Resident. In 1888, St John sent a scathing report that Maharaja Pratap was incapable of fulfilling the promises he had made to curb corruption and provide justice.[33] The next year, in March 1889, Pratap Singh was forced to abdicate on the grounds that he had been in secret communication with Russian agents seeking to undermine Britain's Indian empire. Ironically, British representatives were themselves in negotiation with Russian envoys at the time to identify a buffer zone between Russian territories and Britain's Indian empire. In fact, the two governments agreed a series of frontiers between their empires from 1873 to 1895.

The first act of the British government following Maharaja Pratap's abdication was to revive the Gilgit post of Officer on Special Duty in July 1889. Pratap Singh was reinstated with limited powers in 1891, when journalists proved that the accusation against him, of collaborating with the Russians, was based on forged letters. In return for reinstatement Pratap Singh had to accept a Council of Regency to which he would be subordinate, and which would in turn be subordinate to the British Resident. The council was set up at St John's suggestion. He was now the ruler of the state in all but name.

This quiet coup did not pass unnoticed, nor was it easily accepted. Maharaja Pratap garnered a great deal of support from other Indian princes, whose families had intermarried with his and who feared their fate was presaged in his. Jammu and Srinagar too abounded with conspiracy theories of British intention. Under these twin pressures, and considering that they had already violated the 1846 treaty provisions, the British moved to restore some of the maharaja's powers. In 1905—the same year that he partitioned Bengal into Hindu- and Muslim-majority territories—Viceroy Curzon abolished the Council of Regency. But Pratap Singh remained subordinate to the Resident, without whose approval he could not formulate the state's annual budget or appoint senior officials.[34] All decisions on administering the frontier regions—Gilgit and Ladakh—were also to be submitted to the Resident.

◆

By the end of the nineteenth century, and chiefly as a result of British intervention, two arcs of separation had been set in motion that were to dog Jammu and Kashmir through the next century. The first, a structured Hindu–Muslim rift, described in the next chapter, dragged the state into the divide and rule politics of British India and then into partition. The second, a dual-key system of governance, with a titular head in the state while real power was exercised by Delhi, became a grievance that has persisted to this day—especially since Delhi's actions were predominantly guided by security concerns. British government representatives were military officers throughout the fifty-plus years that Britain exercised power over the state, with an eye towards threats across the border.

Externally, too, a new line was drawn between the state and adjoining areas. Even though Kashmir's geopolitical horizons have altered only very little over the centuries, Britain introduced a new threat from Russia and turned China into a potential threat rather than a potential ally as before. Imperial Russia had not figured in the Kashmiri calculus up to this point and did not in fact advance to the frontiers of Kashmir. But Soviet Russia was to play an influential role in the conflict over Kashmir post-partition. The Chinese threat became a reality with the 1962 India–China War and the conquest of the mountain plateau, Aksai Chin, in Ladakh.

Chapter II

THE RISE OF POLITICS

In the popular Kashmiri narrative, the Dogras are reviled for a cruel and autocratic rule that discriminated against both Muslims and the valley. Kashmir's last dynasts are said to have imposed even more far-reaching taxes than the empires that preceded their rule, promoted Hindus above Muslims, especially in their army, and ridden roughshod over dissent.[1] The accusations are only partially true. Maharaja Gulab Singh's rule over the valley lasted a mere eleven years; he died in 1857. But in those eleven years he continued the wide-ranging taxes of his predecessors and added more—for example, on shawl weavers whose output was his chief source of income. Discovered by Empress Josephine of France at the turn of the eighteenth century, the Kashmiri shawl became an essential European fashion accessory by the mid-1850s, and the taxes imposed by Gulab Singh drove an estimated 4,000 Kashmiri weavers to flee to Punjab.

On the plus side, Gulab Singh also took several steps that benefited his state. He reorganized the tax structure, controlled rice prices and established administration in the valley, which had been left largely to governors till then. Admittedly, Pandits occupied far more government posts than Muslims in the valley, but they had done so for centuries, and indeed grew as a community of administrators under the popular king Zain-ul-Abidin.

In Jammu, the narrative was quite different. Maharaja Gulab was a descendant of the most popular monarch of Jammu, Ranjit Dev, who ruled from the mid- to late-eighteenth century and turned Jammu into a booming kingdom that offered shelter to refugees fleeing persecution in neighbouring lands. Gulab Singh had been governor and then raja of Jammu and adjoining fiefdoms under the Sikh kingdom for over two decades before he purchased the valley. According to contemporary accounts by European visitors, he proved an able administrator who equally respected his Hindu and Muslim subjects.[2] He had high-level Muslim advisers and Muslim generals in his army.

What cast itself as a Hindu–Muslim divide was actually more a Jammu–valley competition that arose with the expansion of the state. Gulab Singh's tenure as maharaja was the first time that Jammu and its neighbouring areas, including Mirpur, Bhimber, Kishtwar, Rajouri and Poonch, were integrated with the valley under a single rule. Though many of these fiefdoms, Kishtwar and Rajouri for example, had long provided a retreat for beleaguered Kashmiri rulers, and their royal families had intermarried, they had remained semi-independent until Gulab Singh took them over. He also conquered Ladakh in 1834 and Skardu in 1840, initially for the Sikh kingdom; the acquisition of Kashmir brought his new state to the borders of Gilgit. The Muslims in his employ, from high to low, were mostly drawn from Jammu and the adjoining fiefdoms that he had ruled for twenty-five years already.

Gulab Singh's successor, Maharaja Ranbir, was a Persian scholar who introduced Unaani medical practice to the state. His trusted general, Zorawar Singh, further expanded the frontiers of the state with the conquest of Gilgit in 1860. Within the state, Ranbir Singh built the Jhelum Valley Road and the Banihal Cart Road linking Jammu and Kashmir, which is today a national highway and a lifeline for supplies from mainland India to the valley. Across state borders, he began construction on a Srinagar–Rawalpindi road to connect the valley with British Punjab, which was completed by his successor, Maharaja Pratap. In 1897, Pratap Singh built the Jammu–Sialkot rail line and named the town through which it entered Ranbir Singh Pura.

Integration was not painless. Historically, it was the first time that Kashmir's population and ruling dynasty belonged to two different faiths. The Dogras were Hindu and, unlike previous periods, this time the valley's people did not convert to the religion of their new monarchs. It was also the first time—after Queen Didda's brief reign in the tenth century—that the valley was ruled by someone from Jammu. And it was the first time the kings' chief home was outside the valley.

A sense of being discriminated against began to grow in the Kashmir valley. It soon acquired a communal overtone, spurred in part by the politics of identity that had begun to sweep British India and in part because Gulab Singh and his son Ranbir endowed temples and promoted Hindu arts and literature along with the Dogri language in Jammu. In fact, Muslims as well as Hindus spoke Dogri and there were Muslim as well as Hindu Dogras (the former were Hindu converts from the sixteenth and seventeenth centuries). Though Dogra officers increasingly populated the maharaja's army, many of them were Muslim. Ranbir Singh's son Maharaja Pratap himself observed Eid and was said to halt his chariot in respect whenever the call to azaan (prayer) was heard. Census records show that the proportion of Muslims in Jammu grew under Dogra rule between 1911 and 1941, from 60.6 to 68 per cent in Reasi, 39 to 43.6 per cent in Udhampur and 29 to 31 per cent in Kathua.[3] But Srinagar had to share its status with Jammu, which became a part-time capital of the expanded state.

Ironically, Maharaja Ranbir Singh's efforts to develop connective infrastructure between the state and British India also backfired. Though food prices were at their lowest during his reign, new and easy access enabled his subjects to discover that they paid three times higher taxes than in neighbouring Punjab. The famine of 1877 sealed Kashmiri resentment. It was unrelated to the Great Famine that swept south and central India in the same year, in which over 5 million died due to the British export of a record 320,000 tons of foodgrain from India. The Kashmir famine was internally caused, by unseasonal August rains that destroyed much of the valley's crops, but it inflicted almost as much damage proportionally. Tens of thousands died in the absence of adequate relief from the maharaja. Since the famine affected the valley alone, this failure, too, was chalked up to Ranbir Singh's perceived preference for Jammu Hindus over valley Muslims.

From what few sources are available, it seems that the Dogra dynasty was tagged anti-Muslim only in the late nineteenth century, when the British decided to depose Maharaja Pratap. The British policy of religious divide and rule in India had already begun, following the 1857 rebellion within the British Indian Army. First applied to the reorganization of the army in 1859, it was soon extended to internal politics. As the acting Viceroy and Lieutenant Governor of the North Western Provinces, Sir John Strachey, commented, 'The existence side by side of the hostile creeds was one of the strongest points in our political position in India.'[4]

While Ranbir Singh was tagged anti-Muslim retrospectively, Pratap Singh was tagged even before he began his rule. In 1884, anticipating Ranbir Singh's death, the Earl of Kimberley, then Britain's secretary of state for India, lamented the incumbent's poor character, distinguishing between 'the present Hindu ruling family' and 'the Muhammadan population' and saying that British intervention on behalf of the latter had 'already been too long delayed'.[5] In 1905, while announcing the restoration of Pratap Singh's powers, Viceroy Curzon admonished, 'You rule a State in which the majority of your subjects are of a different religion from the ruling caste, and in which they are deserving of just and liberal consideration.'[6]

Kashmir had been victim to communal policies before, but only rarely, and chiefly under empire. The Hindus and Muslims of Jammu saw themselves as Jammuites first; Kashmiri Muslims retained their ancient Hindu caste groupings and both Hindus and Muslims in the valley saw themselves as Kashmiris first. Britain's attempt to divide and rule undercut these dual identities and failed initially, only to put down roots when representative politics made their ingress into the state.

The new winds of change, freedom and democracy that swept the Indian subcontinent from the early nineteenth century came late to the princely state, especially the Kashmir valley, which had grown intellectually isolated during its oscillations between monarchy and empire. It was, ironically, the much-reviled Dogra monarchy—in tandem with Britain's Indian empire, and mostly under its pressure—that initially curtailed the state's isolation, though only partially. Brought into contact with the politics of the subcontinent through education in the early twentieth century, young Kashmiris began to dream of escape from—or at least the reform of—Dogra feudalism. Initially their demands were relatively modest—for more equitable access to education, employment and representation—but Maharaja Pratap and his successor, Hari Singh, responded with measures that were seen as too little too late.

In fact, Maharaja Pratap began his tenure with far-reaching reforms, abolishing forced conscription, slashing taxes[7] and effecting a land revenue settlement under the popular British civil servant Sir Walter Lawrence. Pratap Singh built hospitals and embanked rivers, decentralized administration, established the judiciary and introduced higher education to Kashmir with British support, setting up a college each in Jammu and Srinagar. But only the more educated Hindu and Pandit minorities were able to take advantage of new employment and educational avenues; the majority of Kashmiris were still poorly schooled Muslims who worked the land. In 1912, Maharaja Pratap issued instructions that government jobs should be reserved for 'mulkis' or natives, an effort to open employment for Muslims.[8] Once again it proved to be an opportunity that educated Pandits and Rajputs were best placed to use. As late as 1931, according to British records, Hindus and other educated minorities held the overwhelming majority of government jobs. There were 120 non-Muslims as to 4 Muslims in customs, 150:9 in education, 33:4 in the judiciary, 113:35 in revenue, 186:13 in the treasury and 71:12 in the police. Only the constabulary showed some sort of balance, perforce: 799 non-Muslims as to 662 Muslims.[9]

For much of his rule Pratap Singh was preoccupied with battling the British for control over the state. Beginning in 1889, he was still fighting in 1919 to be able to requisition up to ₹20,000 per annum to entertain visiting dignitaries without having to seek the approval of the British Resident, as well as to have some authority—after the British Resident—over policies to be adopted by his government. Though Pratap Singh won these small concessions, the bigger concession of power to make decisions affecting the state's frontier he lost. While he did get to be the final authority over domestic policy, it was a triumph of form over substance. He was simultaneously warned that he would have to obey the Resident on 'all important matters'.[10]

In 1916, Maharaja Pratap invited the British Education Commissioner to suggest reforms in the state, but his recommendations were poorly implemented, if at all. In 1924, again under British prodding, he set up the Jammu and Kashmir State Council in an effort to improve administration, but gave priority to security considerations, presumably with British approval. The commander-in-chief of the maharaja's troops had the power to supervise 'Political matters affecting the peace and good Government of the State'.[11]

The measure had immediate negative results. Just months after the commander-in-chief was given his new powers, a week-long silk workers' protest in Srinagar in July was put down by the maharaja's troops. His predecessors, Gulab Singh and Ranjit Singh, had similarly dealt with shawl workers. Later that year, a group of eminent citizens submitted a memorandum to Viceroy Reading asking for increased Muslim representation in state employment, which he forwarded to the Kashmiri ruler. Two of the signatories were banished and others dismissed. Pratap Singh died the year after, in 1925, and Maharaja Hari Singh began as an absentee ruler. He was in the throes of a sex scandal in Britain that his peers suspected was entrapment by the British government.

Soon after Hari Singh's ascension to the throne, Kashmiri Pandits launched a 'Kashmir for Kashmiris' movement, seeking jobs, freedom of the press and the right to association. Though he had rejected the Muslim demand for more jobs six months earlier, Hari Singh partially accepted the Pandit demands in 1927, issuing an order reserving jobs in public services for 'state subjects', which created four classes of Kashmiri citizens:

> Class I: All those who lived in the state before Maharaja Gulab Singh's takeover in 1846 or settled there before 1886.
>
> Class II: All those who settled in the state before 1924 and owned property there.

Class III: All those who had a residence permit and acquired property in the state.

Class IV: Companies registered in the state in which the Maharaja's government had a financial interest or that had convinced the government of their profitability.[12]

The order defined and codified the instructions of Maharaja Pratap in 1912, but this time neither Kashmiri Pandits nor Muslims benefited. Instead, the number of Dogras in the public services swelled. Only Rajputs—by definition Dogras and a small minority of migrants from Rajasthan mostly settled in Poonch—were allowed to bear arms. When Maharaja Hari Singh decided that Jammu would henceforth be the permanent instead of rotating state capital, resentment in the valley hit a fresh peak. Though it did not go so far as to challenge the monarchy at this point, it soon did.

In any case, the monarchy was weakened by the power-sharing arrangement that Maharaja Gulab Singh had agreed to in 1846, under which the British government reduced the king's authority to domestic rather than security policy. Gulab Singh at least won a royal title and relative freedom in domestic policy. Had Hari Singh been as astute in the ways of empire as his ancestor, he may have been able to stave off or limit further British encroachment. His efforts to do so were, unfortunately, ill-judged. He succeeded in terminating the post of British Resident that his predecessor Pratap Singh had been forced to accept, but in doing so he antagonized his far more powerful overlords and ended up inviting greater British intervention.

Even had he played the British better, however, the extent of Hari Singh's room to manoeuvre is debatable. Paradoxically, Kashmir had gained greater strategic importance with the decline of the Great Game by the 1920s. Having lost their renewed bid to create a buffer for India in Afghanistan, the 'graveyard of empires', British policymakers felt it all the more important to ensure control over Kashmir. Though Pratap Singh agreed to allow a British Resident in Gilgit, a strategic frontier, and Hari Singh left both frontier and foreign policy to the British government, British officials judged the latter unequal to the task of securing Muslim loyalty to the empire. Or perhaps they found it more rewarding to pit his Muslim subjects against Hari Singh; the tactic garnered them direct Muslim support rather than through the maharaja. In 1929, Hari Singh's political adviser, Sir Albion Banerjee, appointed on the advice of the British India government, resigned, issuing a press statement in which he accused the maharaja's administration of having 'no sympathy with the people's wants and grievances'.[13]

Hari Singh appears to have fallen victim to the gap between perception and reality. He was a better ruler than his opponents—chiefly British administrators—alleged. He abolished forced labour or begar as well as untouchability, banned child marriage, prostitution, polygamy and polyandry, made the giving and taking of dowry or bride price a punishable offence, introduced modern banking and promoted Kashmiri trade and crafts. He continued the open-door policy of Ranjit Dev, which his forefathers had also followed, under which Jammu became a refuge for those fleeing persecution or hardship in neighbouring states to its northwest. At his coronation he declared, 'Providing justice for all is my first Dharma [ethic].'[14]

But Hari Singh was unable to read the pulse of his people, or perhaps of any people. His son, Karan Singh, described his father as formidable, aloof and meticulous. Even had he been more approachable, however, he was hemmed in by British and courtly advisers. His actions suggest he was more committed to social and economic than political reform. At any rate, he allowed it to seem as if he undertook political reform only under British pressure. It was a costly mistake.

By the early twentieth century, the young of the state had begun to organize themselves. A slew of associations sprang up—the Anjuman-i-Nusrat-al-Islam, Anjuman-i-Hamdard Islam, Young Men's Muslim Association, Reading Room, Yuva Sabha, Dogra Sabha—some of them devoted to social reform and others to political, including ethnic, rights. Three leaders emerged from these organizations that were to have a lasting impact on the state:

Chaudhry Ghulam Abbas of Jammu, and Sheikh Abdullah and Mirwaiz Yusuf Shah of the Kashmir valley.

Born into a well-off Jammu family, members of the Gujjar caste that had converted to Islam en masse, Abbas founded and became the first president of the Young Men's Muslim Association when he was eighteen. 'A youthful age, an emotional personality and indifference to education were great excuses for national service,' he wrote deprecatingly in his autobiography, *Kashmakash* (dilemma).[15] In fact, he was a lawyer who was offered the position of a sub-judge but refused, preferring politics. Despite his admitted lack of interest in education, he started out as a reformer who helped build schools for uneducated Muslims. Like many other Jammu Muslims, he celebrated both Hindu and Muslim festivals. While in jail—imprisoned by Maharaja Hari, along with Abdullah and most other young Muslim leaders—he read commentaries on the Quran and the Bhagavad Gita.

Also a Gujjar, Abdullah was born into a shawl merchant's family in Soura, next to Srinagar, and originally came to public attention for his sonorous Quran chant, from which he transitioned to passionate political orator. His conscience was first stirred as a child, according to his autobiography, *Aatish-e-Chinar* (The Blazing Chinar),[16] when he saw the wretched condition of shawl weavers. In Aligarh and then in Lahore, where both he and Abbas did graduate studies, he absorbed socialism as well as ideas of independence and was influenced by the poet and political activist Iqbal, whom he met there, though he did not share Iqbal's vision of a Muslim homeland carved out of British India. Tutored by a Sufi scholar, the Islam he imbibed was the syncretic philosophy of Nund Rishi, who had in turn drawn from Lal Ded. It was not only his sonorous voice that attracted; he had extraordinary charisma, as his contemporaries noted, amounting to what seemed like a physical force, drawing those around him into his orbit. Photographs show him and Abbas, when in their twenties, as tall, strapping and dreamy-eyed young men, each wearing the famous Kashmiri hat of Karakul lamb (now banned for cruelty to a rare species).

Mirwaiz Yusuf Shah was the hereditary head priest of the

Jamia Masjid in Srinagar—a position he inherited in 1931—and a signatory to the memorandum presented to Lord Reading in 1924. His family had been involved in Islamic education since the early years of the century, founding the Anjuman-i-Nusrat-al-Islam and Islamia schools in Srinagar. Unlike Abbas and Abdullah, who received secular education, Shah studied at the religiously conservative Darul Uloom in Deoband. He graduated in 1924 and returned to the valley, intending to set up a local branch of the Gandhi–Ali inspired Khilafat Movement to protest the dismantling of the Ottoman empire. His early sermons at the Jamia Masjid sought to rid Kashmiri Islam of its Hindu and Buddhist influences; he revised the syllabus of the Anjuman schools in the same vein. Unlike the many photographs of Abdullah and Abbas, the few photographs available of Shah show a small and rather sad man with the traditional turban of a religious leader.

At the beginning, all three leaders were united in their quest for Muslim rights, founding the All Jammu and Kashmir Muslim Conference in 1932, but they soon parted company. Shah departed in the mid-1930s and Abbas some years later. Both aligned with Jinnah's Muslim League, while Abdullah aligned with Gandhi and Nehru's Indian National Congress.

In a way, the parting was presaged. Two opposing ideas of India had emerged by the 1920s, which crystallized in the 1930s. The first, that India was a pluralist whole, united by aspirations for democracy, freedom and safety of religious practice. The second, that India was composed of two distinct nations, Hindu and Muslim, which each demanded self-rule. As a princely state, Kashmir was on the fringe of this development. In 1930, Iqbal, presiding over the Muslim League session in Lahore, called for an autonomous northwestern state in British India. His demand was made at a time when the British government was considering limited self-rule for India. The 1927 Simon Commission and 1930 Round Table Conference both discussed whether and how to reconstitute British India as a federation. Kashmir was not included in Iqbal's proposed state, which was to comprise the Muslim-majority areas of Sindh, Baluchistan and the North West

Frontier Province (NWFP). In fact, Iqbal, who was of Kashmiri descent, opposed the inclusion of princely states in an Indian federation on the grounds that this would prolong despotic rule over Muslim subjects since the majority of princes were Hindu.[17]

The year 1931 was a watershed one for the state, with spiralling protests that led to a clutch of reforms. An alleged abuse of the Quran by a Hindu constable in Jammu prison on 8 June became the trigger for a campaign led by the Young Men's Muslim Association in which Abdullah made his debut as a public speaker, introduced by Shah. Two weeks into the campaign, the maharaja invited Muslim representatives to discuss community grievances. The Young Men's Muslim Association decided to elect its representatives through a public meeting that included Abbas, Abdullah and Shah. The venue was the Khanqah-e-Mu'alla, the shrine built for Hamadani in the late fourteenth century. At the meeting, a fiery young Pathan named Abdul Qadir stood up and exhorted Kashmiri Muslims to overthrow the monarchy, with sticks and stones or their bare breasts if need be.

Qadir worked for a British army officer and was a follower of Syed Jamaluddin al-Afghani, the founder of the nineteenth-century Salafi movement that sought to modernize Islam and unite all Muslims under a single Sunni caliphate that would, however, recognize the sovereignty of Persia over the Shia. First courted and then expelled by the Ottomans from Turkey and Egypt, al-Afghani had collaborated with the British in the late nineteenth century. Though Afghanistan's rulers no longer sought to influence Kashmir, it seems its religious leaders did. The goal of an Islamic caliphate that some young Kashmiris began to fight for in the 2010s dates back to 1931.

Qadir was arrested by the maharaja's troops, imprisoned and eventually sentenced to life. On 13 July, the date on which his verdict was to be announced at an in-camera trial in prison, several thousand Kashmiris assembled at the prison gates to demand an open trial and verdict session. When they refused to disperse at the order of the maharaja's prime minister, troops opened fire, killing twenty-one and wounding scores more. Crowds carried the dead bodies to burial in the graveyard attached to the shrine of Khwaja Bahawuddin Naqshbandi in Srinagar, which has since then been known as the Mazar-e-Shuhada (Martyrs' Graveyard).

In protest against the killings, Abdullah's Reading Room party called for a shutdown across the state, and at a public meeting at the Martyrs' Graveyard announced that 13 July would be commemorated as Martyrs' Day, symbolic of the Kashmiri struggle for freedom. Abdullah and Abbas, along with three others, were arrested and imprisoned; they were only released after three weeks of public protest. Unrest persisted and was exacerbated by their arrests. In the aftermath of the firing, there were allegations of widespread looting of Muslim shops by state troops, assisted by the British Indian Army, and of Hindu and Sikh shops by Muslim mobs. The British Resident reported sporadic communal attacks on Hindus and Sikhs in south Kashmir and bordering areas of Jammu through 1931 and into 1932.

Outraged by the 13 July firing, on 25 July, the head of the Ahmadiyya in Punjab, Hadhrat Mirza Bashiruddin Mahmud Ahmad, invited a group of sympathetic Muslims of whom Iqbal was a member, to set up a Kashmir Committee. The committee declared that 14 August would be observed as Kashmir Day and organized protests across India against oppression in the valley. Thousands attended the public meeting in Srinagar to demand punishment for officials responsible for the firing. The next day, eleven of their leaders, including Abdullah and Mirwaiz Yusuf, met Maharaja Hari Singh with a memorandum of grievances. On 26 August, they signed an agreement with the maharaja's prime minister that pledged their fealty to the monarch. In return, Prime Minister Koul agreed to release political prisoners, reinstate employees who had been sacked and suspend harsh police measures.[18] The terms were widely regarded as humiliating, but Abdullah limited the damage by announcing he would give the maharaja's administration two months to fulfil its commitments, and embarked on a valley-wide village tour. He was rearrested and imprisoned on 21 September.

A new wave of protests broke out in Srinagar and south

Kashmir to which the maharaja responded by giving his police and troops emergency powers. According to the contemporary activist and commentator, Prem Nath Bazaz, 'It was easy for the police to report anyone as a turbulent man, get him summarily tried and convicted... One hundred respectable and grown-up men (*sic*) were sentenced to flogging' in public. Shopian became a town with 'no law'[19] from which hundreds fled or went into hiding.

Once again, a Jammu–valley divide surfaced, this time between Abbas and Abdullah. Abbas accused Abdullah of ignoring the people of Jammu and neglecting the sacrifices in Mirpur, Kotli and Rajouri where as many as 1,000 men allegedly lost their lives in communal protests in November 1931 but were not included in Kashmir's list of martyrs. In fact, that list was of those killed on 13 July, not after.

Alarmed by persistent and spreading unrest, Maharaja Hari Singh declared an amnesty on his birthday, 5 October, and withdrew emergency powers. The next month, he appointed a four-member commission to look into Muslim grievances, led by B. J. Glancy of the British Indian Civil Service. The commission recommended that control over religious shrines, many of which had been appropriated to the state by the Mughals, be handed back to their respective communities, a 'fair' share of government jobs be apportioned to all communities, along with concessions in land revenue and the expansion of primary schools and enrolment of Muslims in the Education Department.

Hari Singh accepted the recommendations and issued a detailed set of orders for their implementation, adding the stern rider that officials who did not implement his decision properly would lose their decision-making powers. At the same time, he empowered a Constitutional Reforms Commission, again under Glancy's chairmanship, to recommend steps to democratize the monarchy by creating a legislative assembly or Praja Sabha. A central legislative assembly had been set up in British India following the 1919 Government of India Act, also known as the Montagu-Chelmsford Reforms. The Congress boycotted the legislative assembly elections during the 1920s under Gandhi's non-cooperation programme, but in 1932 decided to field candidates in the forthcoming election.

The Constitutional Reforms Commission's political recommendations did not have as easy a passage as the Glancy Commission's social recommendations. Though there was close to consensus on establishing a Praja Sabha that would represent Jammu, Kashmir, Ladakh and Gilgit with reserved seats for Hindus, Muslims and Sikhs, there was little agreement on the proportion of nominated and elected members or its composition. Protection for non-state subjects was another sore point. In the end, Glancy decided to forward his recommendations alone. They defined the powers of the assembly to pass laws subject to the approval of the maharaja and, following the lines of the 1919 Government of India Act, laid down a limited franchise in which only taxpayers, property holders, government or ex-government servants and matriculation graduates would be allowed to vote. Women were disallowed on the grounds that the majority Muslims would oppose votes for women.

The most contentious issue, however, was the composition of the Sabha. Glancy proposed a total of 60 members of which 33 would be elected, 22 nominated (at least a third of them non-official) and 5 would be ex-officio members from the maharaja's cabinet, appointed by him. Elected seats would outnumber nominated ones.

Glancy's recommendations included separate Hindu, Muslim and Sikh electorates. Of the 33 elected seats, 20 would be reserved for Muslims, 11 for Hindus and 1 each for Sikhs and Buddhists. Regionally, Jammu and the valley would have 15 seats each, Ladakh would have two and Gilgit one. The relative populations cited in the report were 1.37 million in Jammu, 1.55 million in Kashmir, 150,000 in Ladakh and 32,000 in Gilgit. The demographic composition was 54 per cent Muslim to 46 per cent Hindu in Jammu and 96 per cent Muslim to 4 per cent Hindu in Kashmir, but Glancy used the principle of weighted representation for minorities.[20] His report did not include the breakdown of Muslims, Buddhists and Hindus in Ladakh.

Lacking consensus among members of the commission, Glancy

recommended that a franchise committee finalize his proposals. The franchise committee submitted its report in 1933. The size of the assembly was expanded to 75, but its composition was altered to give nominated rather than elected members the majority, with 33 elected, 30 nominated and 12 ex-officio members. In other words, 42 out of 75 members would be pro-government. To compensate, the committee increased the number of elected Muslim seats to 21 and reduced elected Hindu seats to 10. It also suggested that the Muslim and Buddhist seats in Ladakh and Gilgit be nominated rather than elected due to the challenge of holding elections in such a large, mountainous, thinly populated and widely dispersed terrain. Finally, it set a minimum number of 32 for Muslim elected and nominated seats (excluding ex-officio nominees) and a maximum of 25 for Hindu seats. Thus, it gave primacy not only to the authority of the monarch but also to religious and ethnic identities.

Upholding Glancy's disenfranchisement of women, the committee commented wryly, 'We have a representation from the local branch of the All India Women's Conference, and some of our Hindu witnesses have favoured women's suffrage. But it is obvious that the majority of the population would not welcome this and we must add the practical consideration that the inclusion of women voters in any large number would increase the administrative difficulties of the first election.'[21]

Abdullah protested against the franchise committee's weightage in favour of nominated members, but contested the 1934 election on the grounds that some representation was better than none. By this time, the Muslim Conference had split; a division that several analysts saw as inevitable given that Abbas's constituency was chiefly among Sunni Muslims in the Jammu province, many of whom were Dogra, Abdullah's amongst Sufi-influenced pluralist Muslims, valley youth and peasants, and Mirwaiz Yusuf Shah's among conservative urban Sunnis.

However, the first split between the valley leaders was on its way. Shortly before the 1934 election, a breakaway faction led by Shah founded the Azad Party Muslim Conference, leaving

Abdullah in undisputed leadership of the original party. The 1934 election campaign in the valley was built around Abdullah and Shah. It was projected as a battle between the lion and the goat, with Abdullah dubbed lion and his opponent goat, a seemingly contemptuous reference to the long beards of the devout. The lion swept the state, winning the bulk of reserved Muslim seats—the goat lost all. The highly limited powers of the Praja Sabha had one positive result: both Muslim and Hindu legislators united in displeasure at how toothless it was. Abdullah's success was repeated in the 1938 election, this time with a scattering of Hindus and Sikhs also voting for his party.

Yet, the Muslim Conference did not have easy going. Abdullah's combination of pluralist Islam and socialism, the first of which he grew up with and the second of which he absorbed during his student days at Aligarh and Lahore, did not sit well with many, especially the external supporters of Muslim rights in Kashmir. In 1937, Punjab's Ahmadiyya withdrew their support for the Muslim Conference. Hamadani's followers, who had remained with Abdullah against Shah, also withdrew. Abbas, with his base in Jammu, drew away from Abdullah after the Muslim League's Lahore session in 1940, and formally split the National Conference soon thereafter.

The combination of pluralist Islam and socialism did, however, endear Abdullah to Nehru and through Nehru to the Indian National Congress. Himself a socialist, Nehru opposed the 1935 Government of India Act that extended the franchise to more Indians, but only in British India. The Congress Working Committee adopted a resolution recognizing that the people in the princely states had 'an inherent right to Swaraj', pledging its support 'in their legitimate and peaceful struggle for the attainment of full responsible government'.[22] Nehru also urged Kashmiri Hindus to support the Muslim Conference after the 1931 firing and its communal fallout. Enthused, Muslim Conference democrats celebrated the fiftieth anniversary of the Congress in the valley, adopting in their turn a resolution assuring the Congress of Kashmiri support in the fight for freedom. Non-Muslims began to join them. In May 1936, when the Muslim Conference held public meetings across the state in favour of extending the franchise and creating fully elected institutions, the chairs of the meetings in Srinagar, Jammu and Poonch were either Hindu or Sikh.

Abdullah and Nehru first met in January 1938 at the Lahore railway station. The two men took an instant liking to each other, so much so that Nehru, who was on his way to Peshawar to meet Khan Abdul Ghaffar Khan, invited Abdullah to join him and Abdullah agreed. Deeply struck by Nehru's vision of an inclusive and democratic India, and by Ghaffar Khan's economic and spiritual approach to reform for Pathans as well as his commitment to the all-India freedom movement, Abdullah returned to Srinagar determined to continue efforts to secularize politics in the valley. He stopped at Amritsar en route to give a press conference at which he expressed his resolve to keep Kashmir out of the polarized politics of the Punjab. He had warned Kashmiris against being swayed by communal Punjabi politicians through the 1930s.

A host of urban and rural labour associations had grown under Abdullah's patronage in the mid- to late 1930s. Now he contemplated opening the Muslim Conference to Hindus, Sikhs and Buddhists, partly on Nehru's advice. In June 1938, the Conference's Working Committee decided to amend the party's constitution in order to admit non-Muslims. On 5 August, the Muslim Conference rallied for 'responsible government', a Congress slogan adapted for Jammu and Kashmir. Hindu and Sikh members of the Kashmiri Pandit Yuvak Sabha, local Congress Committees and the Hindu Progressive Party participated in considerable numbers, and several eminent Hindus addressed the rallies. Twenty days later, on 24 August, party leaders released a manifesto titled 'The National Demand', in which they called for the maharaja's government to be accountable to the Praja Sabha and the latter's powers to include approval of the annual state budget. The Praja Sabha, the pamphlet said, should comprise only elected leaders and there should be full adult franchise along with joint rather than separate electorates (again a Congress demand; the League was in favour of separate electorates). The manifesto had first appeared several months earlier in the Abdullah-Bazaz newspaper *Hamdard* (fellow feeling) and was much criticized by conservative Muslims and Hindus. The former argued that the Muslim Conference was 'a tool' of the Congress and the latter that it would bring in Muslim-majority rule. Despite these criticisms, the manifesto was affirmed at a mammoth public meeting at Hazratbal shrine the next day, 25 August 1938.

The signatories to the manifesto were arrested soon after, along with most of the top leadership of the conference and hundreds of its cadre as well as those of Bazaz's Hindu Progressive Party. Though the Congress sent a deputation to the maharaja's government seeking their release, the maharaja's prime minister, Gopalaswami Ayyangar, refused. At the same time, Hari Singh issued a proclamation amending the 1934 Constitution Act, which increased the number of elected members of the Sabha to forty, made the office of the deputy president of the Sabha an elected one, laid down that a non-official member of the Sabha would be appointed as deputy secretary to the government, and gave the Sabha limited powers to vote on the state budget.

Once again, Hari Singh responded with too little too late. In February 1939, the Congress-led All India States' People's Conference adopted a resolution that expressed 'its solidarity with the people of Jammu and Kashmir State in their struggle for responsible government' and gave 'its support to their National Demand which embodies changes in political and constitutional liberties which are immediately necessary... This Conference in particular condemns notification 19-L, which in effect normalizes a state of Martial Law in the State and enacts the rule of military and police. This notification confers powers of arrest and internment of political workers by Sub-Inspectors of Police and military officials, powers of search without warrant, of confiscation of property, of the flogging of political workers, fines and long terms of imprisonment without proper trial. Such an enactment is an offense to all civilized canons of legislation and government.'[23]

Despite his growing opposition to the monarchy, Abdullah and his party, along with the Congress, sought the princes' support for reform through the 1930s. Most princes, however, failed to accept his invitation. Though Maharaja Hari Singh may have suspected the Muslim leadership's intention or strength in 1931, when they pledged fealty to him along with demands for change, he was presented another golden opportunity for rapprochement. In March 1939, Abdullah declared in his address to the Punjab State People's Conference, 'The struggle in the States is not as much against the Princes as against the Political Department of the Government of India and against British imperialism.'[24] Fighting his own lonely battle against British encroachment, here was a chance for Hari Singh to make common cause, but he rejected it and perhaps did not even recognize it for what it was—an olive branch.

In April 1939, the General Council of the Muslim Conference moved a resolution to rename the party the National Conference and open its membership to men and women of all religions and castes. On 11 June, after a marathon debate, the resolution was adopted at a special session of the Muslim Conference, with 175 out of 178 delegates in favour. Abbas was one of the four members of the party's working committee—all from Jammu—who had initially voted against the resolution in 1938 on the grounds that Hindus would join the party only for opportunist reasons. Despite his reservations, however, Abbas now voted for the change of name.

Though the overwhelming majority of delegates had voted in its favour, the resolution roused the ire of several party leaders and cadre, who held separate conventions in Srinagar on 13 June and again on 17 June, at which they decided to establish a unit of the Muslim League in the city. According to newspaper reports, members of the meeting said that 'Gandhi and Nehru could not be the leaders of Muslims as they were enemies of Islam', and that the 'Congress was leading the people towards agnosticism'.[25] What's more, they added, Muslims and Hindus were separate communities and 'Hindus would not offer their cooperation as their interests were linked with the present Government; Kashmiri

Muslims could not afford to lose the sympathy of the Muslims of the Punjab', thus repudiating Abdullah's warning against Punjab's communal politics. With the support of Mirwaiz Yusuf Shah and his party, the dissidents were able to mobilize large public support, holding a mass meeting on 29 June at the Jamia Masjid in Srinagar, which the Mirwaiz headed.

Meanwhile, Hari Singh continued to tinker with constitutional reform. In September 1939, he repealed the Constitution Act of 1934 and promulgated a new Act that ratified the proclamation of 1938 but expanded the Praja Sabha's oversight of the state budget. The National Conference, Azad Muslim Conference and local Muslim League were united in their criticism of the Act, which failed to address the key demands for full adult franchise and a fully elected legislature. To be fair, neither provision was offered anywhere in British India or the princely states. The Azad Muslim Conference and the League unit, however, added a communal twist, saying 'the existing constitutional provisions did not have any opportunities of (Muslim) political participation' and therefore rendered Muslims 'politically subservient to the Hindus in the State'.[26]

A few months later, following discussions with League leaders, the other two organizations dropped the debate about constitutional reform. The Muslim League had watched the Muslim Conference–Congress rapprochement first with dismay and then with outrage. When Jinnah visited the valley in 1936, two years before Nehru, his goal was to canvass Abdullah. The first meeting between the two began well, with Jinnah agreeing that the Muslim Conference must cultivate minorities. But when he visited again some years later,[27] Abdullah asked how his party could ally with the League. They were a party of landlords and seen as being, therefore, more partial to the princes. His was a party that opposed the monarchy. Jinnah departed, fulminating that Abdullah was impossible to work with and that he was undermining the Muslim cause in India. The League had in any case turned its attention to Mirwaiz Yusuf Shah and Ghulam Abbas. According to a contemporary report, both were 'castigated by the League leaders for having acquiesced in the dissolution of the Muslim Conference and having...pushed the Muslims of Kashmir into the Congress fold'.[28] League leaders urged Abbas and Shah to focus on the 'new battle' for the creation of Pakistan, in which 'the Kashmiri Muslim would have a place of pride' and abandon the struggle for constitutional reform in the state.

In May 1940, when Nehru and Ghaffar Khan visited Srinagar, they were received rapturously by the National Conference and its cadre, but Muslim Conference workers pelted brickbats and stones at the boats carrying the Congress leaders down the Jhelum. Nehru's speech, calling on Kashmiri Hindus to join the National Conference in its quest for political reforms, garnered wide support, but it also deepened the schism between conservatives and bridge-builders in the National Conference. Shortly after the Congress leaders left Srinagar, Choudhry Hamidullah, leader of the National Conference's parliamentary wing in the Praja Sabha, resigned from the party. Ten of the twenty-one party members of the Praja Sabha left with him, vowing to resuscitate the Muslim Conference.

But reviving the Muslim Conference took considerable time and effort. Shah's supporters toured the state urging the Muslim Socialist Conference and League units to sink their differences with the Azad Muslim Conference and unite under a new Muslim Conference. In Jammu, they pleaded with Abbas to join, but his dislike for Shah and his supporters led him to refuse initially. It was only in June 1941 that a refitted Muslim Conference was launched by Abbas, Hamidullah and Shah, from the Jamia Masjid in Srinagar. Abbas was declared president of the party. Its seven-point agenda stated that Hindus and Muslims were two separate nations and political power should be transferred to the Muslim majority in Jammu and Kashmir.

The battle lines were drawn, but not without internal fissure. The Muslim Conference was able to consolidate large groups of Muslims in Jammu, most notably in Poonch and Mirpur, leading to a sharp decline in the National Conference's support there. In Kashmir, where Abdullah held sway, they were not so successful, until a new twist was added in 1942 when the British government sent a Cabinet Mission under Sir Stafford Cripps to discuss a new constitutional order for India. In his submission to the Cripps Mission, Prime Minister Ayyangar declared the state's support for a united India that included the princely states. Though this was a position that Abdullah also held, neither he nor his party could concur with a representative of the Dogra monarchy, especially since many Kashmiris held Ayyangar personally responsible for tough security measures against protesters.

Members of the National Conference who were unhappy with the growing alliance between their party and the Congress voiced the suspicion that, when push came to shove, the Congress might support the maharaja. Abdullah's criticism of the Cripps Mission was carefully crafted with these views in mind. He stressed the right of 'the peoples of the Indian States to self-determination including the right to join a future federation of India or remain out of it'. He also emphasized 'the right of the State to secede from the Union after a State had joined it'.[29] Soon after, he launched a 'Quit Kashmir' movement along the lines of the Congress's Quit India Movement, demanding that the 1846 Treaty of Amritsar be abrogated and Dogra rule end. He was arrested in June 1946 and remained imprisoned until the partition of India in August 1947.

Mirwaiz Yusuf opposed the Quit Kashmir Movement on the grounds that it undercut the League's call for Pakistan. This was Jinnah's position too—he called it a movement 'organized by some malcontents'[30]—and the League used this opposition to woo Maharaja Hari, an attempt that failed. Abbas did not oppose the League's policy but did not join it either. He too was a votary of the League but, like Abdullah, he was deeply steeped in local culture and put local aspirations first. Instead he pushed the Muslim Conference to demand a democratic constitution for the state, and was arrested and imprisoned in 1946. Lodged in the same jail, Abbas and Abdullah discussed the possibility of joining forces deep into the night but failed to agree.

After 1948-49, both Abbas and Shah made their homes in

Muzaffarabad, the chief town of Pakistan-administered Kashmir.*
Abbas was there due to a prisoner exchange under the 1948 India–Pakistan ceasefire agreement. It seems several political leaders pled with Abdullah to prevent the exchange of Abbas, but Abdullah refused. Sadly, though the two leaders shared a similar vision of democracy for the state, they were divided by the Jammu–valley rift.

The first half of the twentieth century thus saw intense political change in Jammu and Kashmir. Beginning with the tussle between the British and the Dogras, which yielded both benefit and loss to the maharaja's subjects, it ended in a three-way confrontation—between the maharaja and the National Conference supported by the Congress, between the National Conference and the Muslim Conference supported by the Muslim League, and between the Muslim Conference and the 'Hindu' maharaja.

Yet, the period also saw crucial initiatives that have defined Kashmir's status post-partition. The state subject order passed by Hari Singh mutated into a 'Kashmir for Kashmiris' approach that has become the bedrock of Kashmiri demands through the decades, for both those that seek to remain with India and those that seek independence. Indeed, it also remains a sore point in the territories of the former princely state held today by Pakistan, where it has been observed mainly in the breach. As a vice-chancellor from Muzaffarabad told me in 2006, he and many others saw the India–Pakistan peace process as a bargaining chip to gain more autonomy from the Pakistani government and military. 'Both countries are vying for our favour. We see it as an opportunity to achieve more freedom for our people.'

---

*Pakistan divided the areas of the former princely state which it held into two entities, 'Azad Kashmir' and Gilgit-Baltistan, with very different political and administrative systems. As 'Azad Kashmir' is not recognized by any countries other than Pakistan and Turkey, the term has not been used in this book. The two entities together are referred to as Pakistan-held territories of the former princely state or Pakistan-held territories; the region that Pakistan calls 'Azad Kashmir' is referred to as Pakistan-administered Kashmir or the statelet; and the regions of Gilgit and Baltistan are referred to by the pre-2009 name of Northern Areas where relevant and post-2009 as Pakistan-administered Gilgit-Baltistan or Gilgit-Baltistan.

The Jammu–valley divide, which first surfaced with expansion and integration in the late nineteenth century, acquired a further layer of Muslim Conference–National Conference enmity with the rise of politics in the first half of the twentieth century. By the late 1940s, it had become a regional-cum-communal-cum-political separation and was to become the fault line along which Jammu was partitioned in 1949. Post-partition, it put forth two further offshoots—a Ladakh-valley rift and de facto separation between two parts of the former princely state under Pakistani control—the Jammu and valley districts of Poonch, Mirpur and Muzaffarabad as one entity, and Gilgit-Baltistan as another.

Chapter III

TWIN PARTITIONS

By 1947, the state had been dragged into the politics of British India and the quest for independence was steadily moving towards division. Indeed, the India–Pakistan conflict over Kashmir has often been described as 'the unfinished business of partition'.[1] The phrase is especially popular with Pakistani politicians; most Indian politicians and Kashmiri nationalists say or used to say, with critically different motives, that there is no connection between the Kashmir conflict and the partition of India. Strictly speaking, they are right, though they also miss the point. The princely states were not parties to the partition of India in 1947. But they were drawn into the clutch of partition-related issues when the British gave them only the right to choose whether to accede to India or Pakistan, not of independence.

While the choice was relatively easy for the Hindu- and Muslim-majority princely states that bordered India or Pakistan, it was very difficult for Jammu and Kashmir. Overall, the state had a Muslim majority and a border with Pakistan, but it was ruled by a Hindu maharaja. It also had a border with India, albeit no more than a shoestring.

Jammu and Kashmir's case was further complicated by its demography, which was a patchwork of ethnically concentrated districts interspersed with mixed ones. Strongly resembling a cauliflower head, the upper floret of the state was bisected by the Kashmir valley that ran from its west down to its southwest, with the tribal lands of Gilgit and Hunza to its north and Baltistan to its northeast, Ladakh to its east and Jammu to its south. Broadly speaking, the northern regions of the state were majority Shia and the valley at its centre was majority Sunni. The vast mountainous tract of Ladakh in the state's east, bordering Tibet, was predominantly Buddhist, but had the Shia majority region of Kargil in its west, providing the only connection between the Sunni valley and Buddhist Ladakh.

Jammu province in the state's south, the most heavily populated of its regions, was mixed Hindu, Muslim and Sikh. Muslims constituted a majority in the province—in 1941, Jammu's population was 61 per cent Muslim, 37 per cent Hindu and 1.5 per cent Sikh—but its minority figures were large enough to significantly influence both policy and communal reaction on the ground. Three out of Jammu province's seven districts, Jammu, Kathua and Udhampur, were Hindu majority. Another three, Poonch, Mirpur and Reasi, were Muslim majority. Poonch and Mirpur were overwhelmingly Muslim, whereas Reasi, the third Muslim-majority district, was far more mixed, as were the Hindu-majority districts.

Pakistan's leaders assumed that Britain would weigh in on its side in the Kashmir accession race. Kashmir, said Jinnah, 'was in his pocket'. Its accession to Pakistan would be an extension of the underlying principle of the 1947 partition that contiguous Muslim-majority territories would go to Pakistan. The state's economy was deeply dependent on west Punjab; its roads and rail led to Sialkot and Rawalpindi, which were allocated to Pakistan. But Britain, having already taken sides to the extent of supporting partition, was now looking for a speedy exit. The boundary demarcated by Sir Cyril Radcliffe in August 1947, as part of the agreement to partition India, allowed a workable route between the state and India from Jammu's Kathua district through Gurdaspur in eastern Punjab. Accession to India became feasible as a result, though still less so than Pakistan.

The award to India of three of the four subdivisions or tehsils of Gurdaspur, which had a bare Muslim majority of just over 50 per cent, shocked the Muslim League, who attributed it to Governor General Mountbatten and his perceived bias towards Nehru. Mountbatten and Nehru were certainly good friends, as were Lady Mountbatten and Nehru. And Jinnah's insistence on becoming governor general of Pakistan himself, instead of accepting

Mountbatten as governor general of both new countries, was taken as a personal slight by Mountbatten. But Mountbatten also told the maharaja in June 1947 that the Congress would accept the state's accession to Pakistan, if he so chose—an offer that many avowedly Hindu leaders took as a sign of his bias towards Pakistan.

Radcliffe's own explanation for awarding Gurdaspur to India cited physical infrastructure as the main reason. The three tehsils allotted to India lay on the eastern bank of the Ravi where it crossed Punjab, whereas the fourth, awarded to Pakistan, was on the western bank. The headworks for the canals irrigating Amritsar were in eastern Gurdaspur, and the railhead connecting India to eastern Punjab was in Pathankot, the sole Hindu-majority tehsil of Gurdaspur. The only feasible road connection from India to Kashmir, via Jammu, also ran through Pathankot.

Concern for Sikhs was an additional reason for the award. Drawing a rough draft of the division of British India in February 1947, then Viceroy Wavell awarded the whole of Gurdaspur to India, saying 'Gurdaspur must go with Amritsar for geographical reasons and Amritsar being [the] sacred city of Sikhs must stay out of Pakistan.'[2] The fact that Gurdaspur district also hosted the headworks for the canals that irrigated the Lahore district was 'awkward', he added, but then there was no perfect solution given the demography of the Punjab, with its interspersed Muslim, Hindu and Sikh settlements.

With accession to India now feasible, many—including Mountbatten—assumed the Hindu maharaja would lose no time in pledging his state to India. But Hari Singh deeply disliked the Congress, which would inevitably rule independent India just as the Muslim League would rule Pakistan. The Congress supported his adversary Abdullah; by contrast, the League attempted to woo him. On the other hand, he was a Hindu king—what powers would he have in a Muslim homeland? Though he signed a Standstill Agreement with Pakistan in August 1947 that would allow previous arrangements such as road and rail access to markets in west Punjab to continue, he toyed with the idea of independence even as the British government disapproved this option for princely states.

Hari Singh hoped to agree on a status for Jammu and Kashmir akin to that of Switzerland, which would combine independence for the princely state with neutrality in times of neighbourhood war. Abdullah, too, spoke of a Switzerland model for the state, but he also sought an end to monarchy, an option that Hari Singh would not consider. A last opportunity for common cause between the two went the way of previous opportunities—nowhere.

While Hari Singh dithered, a rapid sequence of events in the state forced his hand. Months before the declaration of partition, the state was already fraught. From March to April 1947, when massacres started to mount in bordering Punjab, Hindu and Sikh refugees from the Sialkot and Rawalpindi regions of west Punjab began to pour into Jammu province, bringing horrific tales of communal attack that might spill over the border. By late September, there were as many as 130,000 refugees in the province, 65,000 of them in Jammu city alone. According to an eyewitness political leader, Krishan Dev Sethi, minorities of every religion began to move from Jammu's mixed districts even before the announcement of partition, but the devastating Hindu–Muslim and Muslim–Sikh riots that consumed Jammu and its districts broke out only after partition.[3]

As one of the main points of entry for refugees from northwest Pakistan, Poonch was the first of Jammu's districts to experience communal outbreak. A stronghold of the Muslim Conference, with a 90 per cent Muslim and 6 per cent Hindu population, Poonch bordered Punjab's Rawalpindi to its north, where gruesome Muslim-Hindu-Sikh violence took place. Poonch was also an exit point for Muslims from Jammu migrating to Pakistan, though the bulk of such migrations happened in late 1947.

There was already trouble brewing in Poonch over a double-tax regime and, in the spring of 1947, its people mounted a no-tax campaign. Poonch had a semi-autonomous status within Jammu province. It had its own minor monarch, a distant cousin of Hari Singh's, who had reluctantly accepted Maharaja Hari as overlord, only to find that the latter converted Poonch into a district of the province, a decision that the British government upheld when appealed to by the raja.

Poonchis had to pay two sets of taxes: one to the raja and one to the maharaja. Resentment against double taxes flared after the end of World War II, when demobilized soldiers returned to their homes. Poonch and Mirpur had been major suppliers of troops to the British Indian Army; it is estimated that the two districts alone might have provided as many as 60,000 troops. Given their combined population was just over 800,000, this meant a whopping 15-20 per cent or one in five men in Poonch and Mirpur were recently returned soldiers. With few provisions for jobs or welfare by the British government—even the sanctioned per capita grant for demobilized soldiers was unpaid—they too had to suffer high taxes. But, having experienced a far better standard of living in the army, they did not tolerate the burden as passively as their families. Visiting Poonch in April 1947 on a tour to assess the ground situation, Hari Singh was 'impressed and alarmed' on being greeted by 40,000 former British Indian Army veterans in Rawlakot.[4] Their anger grew when the frightened maharaja refused to recruit them to four new battalions that he had approved to expand state forces, and further increased when, in July 1947, he decreed that they would have to hand in their weapons. Simultaneously, the maharaja's army beefed up its garrison in Poonch, with mainly Hindu and Sikh soldiers.

Anger was joined by threat, and some Poonchis began to band into guerrilla groups, acquiring weapons through Pakistan from the great arms bazaars in the NWFP. They included the Muslim Conference activist Sardar Ibrahim Khan, later to become the first 'president' of the statelet of Poonch, Mirpur and Muzaffarabad, which was named 'Azad Kashmir' by the rebels,[5] and former soldier of the British Indian Army Sardar Abdul Qayyum Khan, then twenty-four years old, who claimed to have organized a 50,000-strong militia in the Bagh tehsil of Poonch. The guerrillas included deserters from the maharaja's army as well as demobilized soldiers of the British Indian Army. They were supported by regiments of the Pakistan Army (serving soldiers who opted for the Pakistan Army after independence). Ibrahim and Sardar

Qayyum would lead politics in Pakistan-administered Kashmir for the next fifty years.

Poonch erupted after independence. On 14 August, which had been designated Kashmir Day by Iqbal and his Kashmir Committee, 'Pakistan Day' was widely celebrated in the district. In tehsils like Bagh, there were Muslim attacks on Hindus and Sikhs, with allegations of indiscriminate firing by the maharaja's troops that killed 500 Muslim civilians. Spreading communal violence, according to government sources, 'compelled' the state's army 'to deal with it with a heavy hand'.[6] By then, intelligence was trickling in that armed guerrillas from across the border planned an insurrection, and Hari Singh's officers had recorded cross-border raids for some weeks already. According to his son, Karan Singh, 'reports from the frontier areas of Poonch and Mirpur as well as the Sialkot sector started coming in which spoke of large-scale massacre, loot and rape of our women by aggressive hordes from across the borders'.

By end-August, guerrilla leaders claimed that the entire district, barring Poonch town, was in rebel hands, though these comprised local gangs rather than a coordinated force. The district's Muslim officials and troops joined the rebels en masse. On 2 September, officers in the maharaja's army were issued shoot-at-sight orders. In the ensuing weeks, entire villages were destroyed. 'I recall the grim atmosphere that began to engulf us as it gradually became clear that we were losing control of the outer areas,' said Karan Singh.[7]

According to Sardar Ibrahim, he now moved to unify local guerrillas under a central command, the 'Azad Army', based in the Pakistani hill station Murree, with communication lines provided by the Pakistani government. By end-September, local insurrections had combined into a battle between state troops and 'Azad Army' units with aid pouring in from the Mehsud and Afridi Pashtun tribes in the NWFP.

The NWFP's political configuration had radically restructured just two months earlier. Under Ghaffar Khan, the ruling Khudai Khidmatgars and their supporters had wished to accede to India, but the province lacked physical access without connecting through Jammu and Kashmir. Even if the maharaja had pledged to accede to India in June 1947, as Mountbatten wished him to, it is difficult to imagine that Jinnah would have accepted an outcome that left Pakistan semicircled by India. He was already complaining about the 'moth-eaten' Pakistan that partition would bring.[8]

The Congress had more or less abandoned claim to the NWFP, deeply disappointing Ghaffar Khan, but the British government nonetheless ordered a referendum on which new country its people wished to join. Ghaffar Khan's Khudai Khidmatgars boycotted the referendum because their demand for independence as a third option was not accepted, and it yielded an overwhelming vote in favour of Pakistan. Less than 15 per cent of the province's population was eligible to vote and only half of the registered electorate voted. In other words, the referendum represented the views of less than 8 per cent of the population. Following the referendum, Ghaffar Khan's government was dismissed and a Muslim League government headed by Abdul Qayyum Khan (not to be confused with the guerrilla leader from Poonch, though also of Kashmiri descent) was appointed.

Contemporary accounts describe a concerted effort to mobilize Pashtun guerrillas for a Kashmir jihad after the ouster of the Khudai Khidmatgars, led by two soldiers of the Pakistan Army, Colonel Akbar Khan and Major Khurshid Anwar, and facilitated by Qayyum Khan. Their efforts bore fruit and, on 21 October, several thousand Pashtun tribesmen invaded Muzaffarabad on a mission to capture Kashmir. They travelled in a convoy of trucks armed with rifles, grenades, mortars and Mark V mines diverted by Akbar Khan from regular Pakistan Army supplies. Jinnah denied official government support for the invaders, described in a typical orientalist way as 'raiders' by the Indian and state governments, and the British commander of the Pakistan Army, General Frank Messervy, almost certainly did not know of Khan and Anwar's actions. But Prime Minister Liaquat Ali Khan, senior members of the Muslim League and at least some Pakistan Army officers, both British and Pakistani, certainly colluded.[9] Jinnah is said to have heard rumours of the plan in mid-October but refused to be briefed on the rumours because he wanted 'to have his conscience clear'.[10] Anwar, in fact, accompanied the tribesmen as a military adviser reporting to Akbar Khan, who in turn was in regular touch with Liaquat Ali.

The Muzaffarabad invasion came as a culmination of deteriorating relations between the governments of Jammu and Kashmir and Pakistan. Hari Singh had continued to attempt peace with Pakistan in the months following partition, right up to October 1947, with diminishing results. In late August, the rail link from Sialkot to Jammu ceased to operate, causing acute shortage of food and essential supplies to the state. The maharaja's government saw this as an economic blockade intended to pressure him to accede to Pakistan. Jinnah's reply was that truckers feared to risk communal attack when passing through Punjab to Sialkot. Acerbic telegrams flew back and forth between the Kashmiri and Pakistani administrations through September, when Hari Singh finally gave up hope that an agreement could be reached on reviving the rail service. In late September, the maharaja turned to Nehru, who promised to find a way to send supplies through the Radcliffe awarded Pathankot-Kathua route, and the dirt track that existed was rapidly metalled. Slowly but surely, Pakistani actions began to push Jammu and Kashmir towards India.

Hari Singh was not yet ready to discuss accession with Indian leaders. But he did begin backchannel negotiations with the Congress through Meher Chand Mahajan, who became his prime minister some weeks later, on 15 October 1947. Mahajan had been a member of Radcliffe's Boundary Commission for the Punjab in August and was recommended to the maharaja by Sardar Patel. Nehru, however, set a number of conditions for accession, including the release of Abdullah and his participation in the state's government. Abdullah was released on 29 September, but giving him and his party a role in the state's administration was a step too far for the maharaja, who continued to drag his feet on accession.

Alienated from both the Congress and the League, Hari Singh

fell back on his own Dogra community. At the same time, he also considered allying with a third group, one that supported his monarchy, the Hindu chauvinist Rashtriya Swayamsevak Sangh (RSS). Founded in 1927, the RSS had opened a branch in Jammu in 1940 and the valley in 1944, but did not garner much support until partition in 1947. According to Balraj Madhok, founder of RSS branches in Jammu and the valley, Hindu alarm was triggered when, on 15 August, the Pakistani flag flew from every post office in the state. Actually, the flag-flying was inadvertent—the state's post offices fell under the Sialkot headquarters, which was awarded to Pakistan, and on the day of independence, all government institutions of the two new countries hoisted their respective national flags.

Hari Singh was quick to intercede and the flags were removed, but in an already polarized situation, the damage had been done. The RSS began to attract volunteers from amongst Hindus in the state as well as Hindu and Sikh refugees and, because the RSS was not an electoral party, a new political party was founded in November 1947, the Praja Parishad, led by eminent Dogras.

Rumours of an impending Pakistani attack had begun to circulate in the state days before the Muzaffarabad invasion. Information collected by the RSS in mid-October, said Balraj Madhok, described a plan under which Kashmir would be invaded from Abbottabad through Muzaffarabad on 22 October, Muslim officers and troops of the maharaja's army would join the invaders and Srinagar would be captured by 25 October. He took this information to the then chief of staff of the maharaja's army and on 23 October, 'at dead of night', Hari Singh asked Madhok if he could muster 200 volunteers to defend Srinagar. The next day, Madhok's volunteers were taken to the army's Badami Bagh compound, given weapons and trained in their use.[11]

Madhok appeared to think that his information was news to the government. In fact, Nehru had already warned of an impending Pakistani attack in late September, writing to Patel on 27 September that reports from the state indicated that the Muslim League in Punjab and the NWFP were making preparations to invade.[12] The invasion would take place before the onset of winter when snow cut off the state, in late October or at the latest, the beginning of November. Patel took Nehru's warning seriously enough to instruct the Indian Army to be ready to supply the maharaja with whatever arms and ammunition his troops requested. But the acting British commander of the Indian Army, General Lockhart, ensured that the arms requested by the maharaja were not sent. He had been instructed to withhold by his superior, General Claude Auchinleck, then Supreme Commander of all British forces in India and Pakistan. Lockhart also suppressed intelligence received from his Pakistani counterparts about an impending infiltration by tribesmen. It was at this point that Patel began to support the state's accession to India, having earlier been non-committal.

Madhok also misread the importance of his volunteers to the maharaja, who formally requested Indian military support on 24 October, the day the Poonch rebels announced that they had formed a 'Provisional Government of Azad Kashmir', comprising Poonch and Mirpur in Jammu and Muzaffarabad tehsil in the valley. Muzaffarabad, said Hafizullah, a contemporary chronicler of the invasion, had been cleared of 'all Sikhs, Dogras and RSS cutthroats'.[13]

Patel was in favour of sending troops to the state immediately, but Mountbatten insisted the maharaja accede to India first. Otherwise, he said, Pakistan would point to the presence of Indian troops as a reason for sending its own army in. Two days later, on 26 October, Hari Singh signed an Instrument of Accession to India, and the next day, Indian soldiers arrived in Kashmir. Pakistan did react to the arrival of the Indian Army in the state as Mountbatten had predicted but the maharaja's accession to India made no difference. On hearing that Indian troops had been sent in, an enraged Jinnah ordered the Pakistan Army to Kashmir. His chief of general staff and deputy commander-in-chief of the Pakistan Army, General Douglas Gracey, refused, and was backed by his superior, Commander-in-Chief General Frank Messervy. General Auchinleck had instructed that British officers would have to stand down in the event of an India–Pakistan war. Procedurally,

Gracey and Messervy toed a fine line since Jinnah was Governor General of Pakistan and they were bound to obey his orders. But they also prevented Jinnah from folly. The maharaja had not invited Pakistani military aid, and sending Pakistani troops in without his request would have constituted an act of war.

Abdullah was with Nehru when the news of accession arrived. He still preferred the Switzerland model as did the maharaja, he confessed to Nehru, but he supported Hari Singh's request for India's defence of the valley and had himself come to Delhi to urge it. Though accession had been agreed, there was still debate in the Indian cabinet about sending in the army. According to Field Marshal Sam Manekshaw, then an officer who sought instruction on deploying troops, Nehru initially agonized but pulled himself together when Patel said sternly, 'Jawaharlal, do you want Kashmir, or do you want to give it away?'[14] Nehru was already considering taking the issue of Pakistani invasion to the UN, as was Mountbatten, but the urgent requirement for defence of the state took priority. On 27 October, Indian troops were airlifted to the valley.

They were almost too late. In truth, they escaped losing the valley by a hair's breadth. The invaders, facing little if any resistance from the thinly-strung maharaja's troops whose Muslim soldiers had deserted, made rapid progress towards Srinagar, using the Rawalpindi-Murree-Muzaffarabad-Baramulla route, and killed an estimated 22,000 villagers on the way, most of them Muslim. The 'Azad Army' would have reached Srinagar before Indian troops landed, and perhaps taken it, had it not been for Brigadier Rajinder Singh, commander of the maharaja's forces, who held them off at Uri for a crucial forty-eight hours by blowing up the bridge from Muzaffarabad. Ordered by Hari Singh 'to hold the enemy at Uri at all costs and to the last man',[15] Rajinder Singh had with him a column of around 100 troops, and lost his own life at the end.

Though the invaders succeeded in erecting a makeshift bridge and crossing the river, the time that Rajinder Singh and his few troops bought proved invaluable. Led by Anwar, the 'Azad Army' conquered Uri and Muzaffarabad on 24 October and reached

Baramulla on 25 October. Here, one of the worst massacres of Hindus, Muslims and Christians took place. Not even the St Joseph's convent and hospital staff were spared. Eyewitnesses at the convent and hospital said the tribesmen segregated the women and children from the men, the children from the women, and shot all the men as well as some of the women. In the town, according to eyewitness accounts again, they raped women indiscriminately, and 'shrieks of terror and agony of those girls resounded across the town'. The two days they spent killing, raping and plundering in Baramulla included the auction of kidnapped girls.[16]

By the time the 'Azad Army' advanced from Baramulla to Pattan, the first Indian Army contingents had landed. Their immediate task was to secure the Srinagar airport for troops and supplies, followed by securing Srinagar city and building a bridgehead between the city and Pattan, which the invaders had occupied. Within a few days, the Indian Army drove the 'Azad Army' from Pattan. Baramulla was rescued on 8 November and Uri on 10 November. Military analysts suggest that Indian troops could have recaptured Muzaffarabad and then Poonch in mid-November; instead, they secured Poonch town but did not advance to the remaining areas of Poonch and Mirpur, where retreating tribesmen and local guerrillas thronged.

Why did Indian troops not push further to recapture Poonch, Muzaffarabad and Mirpur? The contingent reason might have been logistical. Their first and arguably only feasible window was in November, said former Pakistani Major Agha Humayun Amin.[17] But November was when winter began to set in. To recapture those areas, a considerable ground and air attack would have been required, both difficult to muster in a season of snow and sleet. Indian troops had sizable Pakistan-backed militias to contend with, that had much easier access to supplies and engaged in a series of flanking operations through December. They had the additional task of rescuing stranded garrisons of the maharaja's army as well as beleaguered minorities. Moreover, by end-1947, General Gracey decided that the risk of Indian penetration into Pakistan from Poonch was too high to keep Pakistani troops out and from December, Pakistani troops were stationed on the Poonch, Mirpur and Muzaffarabad borders.

By this time, Nehru was convinced that Indian forces would need to enter Pakistan if they were to cut off the invaders' lines of reinforcement and supplies. 'The invasion of Kashmir is not an accidental affair resulting from the fanaticism or exuberance of the tribesmen, but a well-organized business with the backing of the State,' he wrote to Mountbatten on 26 December.[18] He met with concerted resistance, including not so veiled threats from British prime minister Clement Attlee, Governor General Mountbatten and—most importantly—the British Army, from Supreme Commander General Auchinleck to the British commanders of the Indian Army, Generals Bucher and Lockhart.

The Indian Army did make plans to counter-attack in the spring when snows melted, but by then the 'Azad Army' had more than doubled in both men and materiel. Localized battles dragged on until the summer of 1948—Rajouri fell and was recaptured, large chunks of Poonch went from hand to hand, Uri fell for a second time and was again recaptured—by which time the Indian Army controlled the bulk of territories east of the Pir Panjal range that traversed from north to south of the western section of the state, while Pakistan controlled the bulk of territories to the west and northwest of the range.

Poonch and Mirpur had already been ethnically cleansed of their Hindu and Sikh minorities. The latter had a larger minority population than the former—close to 20 per cent of Mirpur's population was Hindu or Sikh. By late November, there were concerted attacks to drive them out, just as there had been in Muzaffarabad. On 25 November, the day that Mirpur fell to the 'Azad Army', there was a massacre of Hindus in which as many as 25,000 might have died. Of the roughly 13,000 that survived, the bulk fled to Jammu.

Uri was jointly rescued by Indian troops and National Conference volunteers. Appointed 'emergency administrator' for Kashmir on 30 October, Abdullah rallied his cadre to defend the valley against the invaders. The National Conference's support for the Indian Army was another shock to the Pakistani government. Jinnah had sent emissaries to court both the maharaja and Abdullah after the latter's release at the end of September. While they threatened the maharaja with 'dire consequences' if he did not accede to Pakistan, they were more conciliatory with Abdullah. But they did not offer support for his demand for representative government before accession, nor did they share his vision of a plural Kashmir. They, too, had to choose between the Muslim and National Conferences. The two parties could no longer work together.

Jinnah and his cabinet appear to have adopted a peculiar carrot-and-stick policy towards Kashmir throughout the conflict. The Pakistani government's notion of a carrot was more sour than sweet—it comprised threat rather than benefit. In mid-August, they sought to coerce the maharaja into acceding through an economic blockade. From end-September through late October, they courted Abdullah and Hari Singh unsuccessfully without lifting the blockade. While courting the two leaders in October, some of the top Pakistani leaders actively supported the Poonch uprising and Muzaffarabad invasion, including recruitment for the 'Azad Army' through Maulana Maududi's radical madaris—others did little to discourage it. The stick came as an extreme version of the carrot; when pressure and diplomacy failed to win the state, members of the Pakistani government and its armed forces turned to military means, using non-state actors. The strategy was a first glimpse of what was to be repeated over and over again: Pakistan's use of non-state actors in a low-scale and protracted jihad to wrest Kashmir.

The Muzaffarabad invasion marked a turning point in the state. Until then Hari Singh had hoped against hope to make his state a sovereign country that would be bound to neutrality. Indeed, as late as 12 October, his deputy prime minister declared in Delhi that, 'Despite constant rumours, we have no intention of joining either India or Pakistan... The only thing that would change our mind is if either side decide to use force against us.'[19] Ten days later, the poet Faiz Ahmed Faiz echoed his warning. Then chief editor of the *Pakistan Times*, Faiz said when news of the invasion broke, '[E]verything was lost... There ended the chance of Kashmir's accession to Pakistan.'[20] Oddly enough, Hari Singh took the same view regarding his monarchy. Fleeing Srinagar late at night on 25 October, he remarked grimly, 'We have lost Kashmir.' Both proved to be right.

While the Poonch and valley wars took centre stage, Jammu slipped into intense ethnic conflict. Communal tensions had started to build as early as the spring of 1947 in the districts bordering Sialkot, where the most brutal ethnic cleansing of partition took place. Sialkot had a large Sikh minority as well as a slightly smaller Hindu one. It was, like Poonch, an exit point for Hindu and Sikh refugees from west Punjab, many of whom arrived injured when refugee transports were attacked. It was also an entry point for Muslim refugees streaming in from east Punjab with their own heart-wrenching tales of murder, rape and plunder.

Sporadic Hindu–Muslim violence had already begun in September in districts such as Kathua, which was 68.5 per cent Hindu and 31 per cent Muslim, Udhampur (56 per cent Hindu and 44 per cent Muslim), Jammu (58 per cent Hindu and 40 per cent Muslim) and Reasi (31 per cent Hindu and 68 per cent Muslim). It was spurred partly by the influx of refugees and the unspeakable horrors they had endured, partly by inflammatory statements from across the border, often made by Kashmiri leaders who had moved to Pakistan, and partly by the Pakistani government's inimical actions.

Attacks on Muslims spiralled into a rampage with the involvement of Hindu and Sikh refugees and support from the maharaja's troops. Deputy Director General of Intelligence G. C. Bali reported to Nehru from Jammu that the Dogra and Rajput soldiers of the army were 'torching villages like rioters, abducting women and raping them. The silence of the Maharaja and people in power here was only emboldening them.'[21] In Jammu city, it was alleged, RSS volunteers organized arms training for Hindu and Sikh guerrillas.[22] Jammu city, like many others in India, was divided into Hindu, Muslim and Sikh neighbourhoods, making each more vulnerable.

The most brutal attacks, however, were in Muslim-majority Reasi, which was cut off from Muslim-majority Poonch and Mirpur by Hindu-majority districts. Eyewitnesses later told how 500 to 600 armed men arrived from Jammu at the outskirts of Reasi town on 4 November 1947. Prominent citizens, who had formed a peace committee in the town tried to persuade the mob to leave, but instead they murdered the three Muslims in the committee and spared the lone Hindu. In the days that followed, thousands of Muslims were killed. One survivor estimated that almost the entire Muslim population of Reasi town, numbering around 8,000, lost their lives.[23]

Muslims began to stream out of Jammu province, in many cases helped along by the maharaja's troops who offered a safe passage to the state border. The offer proved hollow in several instances, when refugees under escort were killed by Hindu guerrillas that intercepted their convoy. In December, it was reported that there were over 200,000 Muslim refugees from Jammu in Pakistan and, in mid-1948, this figure swelled to 400,000.

By the end of the Jammu conflict, the province had undergone large demographic change, mostly due to the expulsion of minorities. The Hindu and Sikh population of Pakistan-administered Kashmir was estimated to have fallen from 12.5 per cent to under 1 per cent, according to the 1951 Pakistan Census, which showed that only 0.09 per cent Hindus and Sikhs remained. Though the 1951 census of India did not cover the state due to its disturbed conditions, the 1961 census reported that the Muslim population of Jammu district had fallen to one-third of what it was in 1941, while other districts saw a fall of around 17 per cent. Overall, Jammu province lost close to a third of its Muslims while Pakistan-administered Kashmir lost almost all of its Hindus and Sikhs.

Looking back, it is astonishing that Jammu did not fall into a full-fledged civil war as Bosnia did fifty years later in similar communal and geopolitical circumstances. Analytically, the intensity of violence in the province was entirely predictable; the history of ethnic conflict reveals that the more ethnically mixed the region, the greater the likelihood of a prolonged and brutal war once it starts. With a Muslim population of just over 60 per cent and a Hindu population of just under 40 per cent in 1941, Jammu province was set for internecine violence when faced with the choice of affiliation to India or Pakistan.

Caste and tribe were additionally complicating factors. The three major communities in Jammu province were Hindu Brahmin, Muslim Gujjar and both Hindu and Muslim Rajput. In addition to its 78,000 Muslim Rajputs and 63,000 Gujjars, Poonch had an equally large community of Sudhans (74,000), who claimed descent from Afghan Pathans and led the Poonch revolt for accession to Pakistan. The chief Muslim communities in Mirpur, which saw the largest massacre of Hindus and from which almost all Hindus were expelled, were Jat (103,000) and Rajput (69,000).[24]

In the Hindu-majority districts, by contrast, there were five or more substantial communities. Of Jammu's 300,000-strong population, one-fifth were Muslim Gujjar, another fifth Hindu Brahmin, and over a sixth were Rajput (19,000 Muslim and 36,000 Hindu). Scheduled Castes (SC) constituted close to a quarter of the population. Around 3 per cent were Muslim Jat, with the same proportion of Hindu Mahajan. Almost a third of Udhampur's Hindu population were Rajput and over a tenth were Brahmin, with another tenth SC. Around a quarter of its 44 per cent Muslim population was Gujjar while another 5 per cent were Muslim Rajput, and the remainder were Kashmiri Muslim. Udhampur was the only one of Jammu's Hindu-majority districts to have a substantial Kashmiri Muslim population of 59,000. Of the 68 per cent Muslim population of Reasi, where the most intense Hindu attacks on Muslims occurred, more than two-thirds were Muslim Gujjar and around 15 per cent Muslim Rajput, with another 15 per cent Kashmiri Muslim. An almost equal number of Rajputs were Hindu. The bulk of Reasi's 31 per cent Hindu population was Brahmin.

These figures suggest that Gujjars, despite their large numbers, rarely led communal attacks. Had they done so, their sizable population would have caused a far greater number of Hindu deaths. Conversely, it would appear that Hindu and Muslim

Rajputs, both minority populations, along with Muslim Sudhans, were prime actors in the Hindu–Muslim wars of ethnic expulsion.

One reason why communal conflict in Jammu did not spiral into full-fledged civil war might have been the presence of neutral troops of the Indian Army. Though they were focused on driving back the invaders, rioters feared that once the Indian Army had turned the tide of that war, they might turn their attention to ending internecine conflict in the province.

An equally, if not more, important reason might have been the presence of Abdullah and the National Conference, both committed to defending all communities uniformly. As Gandhi noted, the valley remained remarkably free from the communal conflict that swept Jammu—in fact, it stood in stark contrast. The monarchy's days were already numbered: though Maharaja Hari had acceded to India, the Congress was pledged to end princely rule and three of its chief leaders—Gandhi, Nehru and Patel—backed Abdullah. This widely known eventuality was almost certainly an initial contributor to the communal violence by Hindus and Sikhs in Jammu. As we have seen in other ethnic conflicts—whether Ireland, Bosnia or Sudan—when faced with sweeping political change, each community sought to establish territorial control by changing the demographic facts on the ground. But anticipation that the National Conference would soon come to power may also have been a factor in the violence dying down. With Abdullah at the helm, communal violence would likely be severely punished.

Chroniclers of the Jammu violence also blamed the Muslim Conference. Abbas was in prison and most of the leadership of the party had already crossed the border to Pakistan. Those who remained in Jammu were second and third-rung. Abdullah was rightly seen as a valley leader who was relatively rootless in Jammu because Jammu Muslims tended to support the Muslim Conference rather than the National Conference. Without Abbas, there was no one to speak for Jammu Muslims. It was at this point, when Jammu's Muslim leaders were in prison, that Sardar Ibrahim emerged as a leader. But he was unable to win acceptance as spokesman for Jammu Muslims.[25]

Meanwhile, the war dragged on. In November, the state was attacked on another flank, through Gilgit, which had traditionally been of strategic importance and continued to be. Wars and peace, Buddhism and Islam, had all come to the valley through Gilgit via Ladakh. It was the gateway to Afghanistan, China and Central Asia, where the three great mountain ranges of the Himalayas, Karakoram and Hindu Kush converged, forming a natural security barrier for the valley. No wonder Maharaja Gulab and his successor had sought to conquer it, and the British had sought to control it.

Gilgit was divided into two parts under the British: the Gilgit Agency, which the British administered, and Gilgit Wazarat, administered by the maharaja but leased to the British in 1935. Both were part of the maharaja's state and were returned to Hari Singh on 1 August 1947, after the British government decided to withdraw from its Indian empire, leaving Gilgit's Muslims in fear of what Dogra rule might bring. Their fears multiplied when Hari Singh sent a governor to Gilgit who was both credulous and complacent, and were successfully played upon by Major William Alexander Brown, then commander of the Gilgit Scouts, an armed force that the British had raised in 1913 after pressuring Maharaja Pratap to allow a British Agency there.

Inspired by T. E. Lawrence's deeds in Arabia, Brown saw an opportunity in Gilgit's volatile situation. By his own account, he foresaw disaster if Britain left Gilgit's fate to be decided with that of the rest of Jammu and Kashmir. The British government, he said, did not recognize that such inaction would allow the Soviet Union to drive a strategic wedge between India and Pakistan, and the only way to prevent this from happening was for Gilgit to become an 'Agency' under the Pakistani province of NWFP. British officers, according to him, were already pro-Pakistan; far more had opted to stay with the Pakistan Army than with the Indian Army. Moreover, he said, 'I considered that the whole of Kashmir, including Gilgit Province, should unquestionably go to Pakistan in view of the fact that the population was predominantly Muslim. Partisan, traitor, revolutionary, I may have been, but... my sentiments dictated that if the Maharaja acceded to India, then I would forego all allegiance to him and I would not rest content until I had done the utmost in my power to ensure that not only the Gilgit Province joined Pakistan, but the whole of Kashmir also.'[26] His sentiments did not, apparently, dictate that he should not continue to draw pay from the maharaja while working against him.

The rulers of fiefdoms in Hunza and Nagar were already inclined towards Pakistan, Brown found; they would help in the struggle for Gilgit and beyond, to 'the whole of Kashmir'. He and his junior colleague, Captain Mathieson, accordingly planned an operation they called 'Datta Khel', which loosely translates as 'the game of veritable intelligence'. On the date chosen by Brown, he would put the governor and his staff 'under protective custody', herd Hindus and Sikhs into refugee camps, cut telephone cables, take over the wireless system, establish his own administration and send a message to the Pakistani government that Gilgit had revolted in favour of accession to Pakistan. Mathieson, meanwhile, would check whether the Muslim soldiers of the maharaja's troops that were stationed in neighbouring Chilas would desert to their side. If they would not, the Scouts would mount a lightning night attack on their barracks.

The Muslim Scouts, said Brown, were already hostile to the maharaja and, in October 1947, they began talking of revolt—but Brown had been talking of it since August–September. While secretly steering rebellious Scouts and the progress of their brewing revolt, he allowed Governor Ghansara Singh and Maharaja Hari Singh to remain in ignorance of the severity of the threat. Indeed, he persuaded Ghansara to ignore the maharaja's instruction to arrest a suspected ringleader of the revolt. British interests came first, he said, even if few in the British government held a similar view of what these were.

Abetted by Brown, who described with great relish the solemn ceremony by which they filed out to revolt on 31 October after taking an oath of loyalty on the Quran, the Scouts arrested Governor Ghansara Singh and his staff, and hoisted the Pakistani flag on 1 November. The first two steps of Datta Khel were completed and within days the next four steps were taken. Then Brown discovered that the interim administration he had appointed was planning, along with some Scouts, to establish a sovereign state of Gilgit-Astore. An independent state did not fit his plans—a strong Pakistan under British influence served much better than a small state sandwiched between Pakistan and far more powerful China—and he sent a secret telegram to the authorities in Pakistan inviting them to take over. Within two weeks, Gilgit was under Pakistani governor Sardar Muhammad Alam, previously a tehsildar in the NWFP. Gilgit was a windfall for the Pakistani government.

The battle widened. In order to protect Gilgit from Indian counter-attack, Brown said, Skardu, the chief town of Baltistan, would have to be captured else Indian troops could use it as a base. On the other side, the Kashmiri and Indian governments feared that if Skardu fell, Pakistani forces would have entry to Ladakh and from there to the valley and Jammu. In late November, the maharaja ordered a small contingent of troops to the town. Marching through snow, the force arrived in early December. Soon after, guerrillas from Gilgit, Hunza and Nagar led by Pakistan Army officers laid siege to Skardu. Though the maharaja's army sent troop reinforcements in February and again in April, their numbers were too small to withstand the siege, at 200 versus 3,000 or more. Starved, the maharaja's troops eventually surrendered. The Pakistan Army officially entered the war in May 1948.

In July 1948, the Gilgit and Hunza Scouts, led by Lieutenant Shah Khan of the Pakistan Army, captured the Zoji La pass that connected Kargil to Leh by road, thus blocking Indian land access. In August, Skardu, Kargil and Drass fell. The first Indian counter-attack to recapture the pass by land was unsuccessful. General Cariappa, then Western Army commander, with Major General Thimayya, then general officer commanding of the 19th Infantry Division, turned to a combined land, water and air stealth attack using cavalry and sapper regiments. Dismantled tanks were moved in parts from Srinagar up through Ladakh and winched across river bridges. A mule track from Baltal to Zoji La was hastily converted into a motorable road, and on 1 November, armoured

Indian regiments surprised the numerous but relatively thinly-armed Pakistani forces, to recapture the pass. The air attack, which demanded extraordinary skill given the narrow mountain passes, was launched soon after and joined with ground attack to force Pakistani troops back to Drass and then to Skardu. The Indian Army recaptured Kargil and Drass by end-November 1948, but Skardu remained under Pakistani control.

Inexplicably, the Indian government decided to halt its troops after the recapture of Kargil and Drass despite protests from army commanders on the ground. Military planners had debated the issue of where and when to end the war for the past six months. Between the spring and summer of 1948, there were lengthy arguments over whether the Indian counter-attack should stop at Kargil or press on to recapture Skardu and even Muzaffarabad. Nehru's private secretary Dwarkanath Kachru, a Kashmiri Pandit who had been sent to report from the state, wrote a series of letters to Nehru from April to December 1948 that suggest military strategists were divided on the issue. In April, he reported that Cariappa, influenced by the British commander-in-chief of the Indian Army, General Bucher, was of the opinion that 'we should give up Gilgit and Skardu and hold onto Ladakh which is easy to keep and defend'.[27] In July, however, Kachru reported that Thimayya, the commander in the field, believed that if his request for further troops was accepted, Skardu could be recaptured and 'we may in the very near future find ourselves in the occupation of Muzaffarabad and a substantial part of Poonch Jagir'.

On the ground, stressed Kachru, Indian Army officers and troops said they were constrained by Delhi's caution in prosecuting the war. The Government of India, they felt, was overanxious to avoid casualties. This anxiety, however, risked a long-drawn war that was not necessary. At that moment, Pakistan Army troops were at the rear of the tribal guerrillas. They did not wish to lead from the front because it could precipitate 'open conflict with the Indian Army' and the Pakistani government's denial of official engagement in the war would be shown as hollow. 'This weakness of the Pakistani government's position should be taken advantage of and our troops should be ordered to go ahead,' Kachru concluded.

In December, when instructions were issued to halt the Indian advance, Kachru wrote, '[A]fter discussions with Sheikh Abdullah, Bakshi [Ghulam Mohammad] and senior Army officers, I...am personally convinced that the recapture of Kargil has committed us to the capture of Skardu because in order to hold the frontier illaqas [regions] of Ladakh and Kargil and to give the necessary security to the civil administration and the people, it would be necessary for us to liquidate the enemy pockets between Skardu and Ladakh and between Skardu and Kargil.' Parts of Skardu such as Khaplu, he added, were already in revolt against Pakistan and their rulers would aid an Indian advance. India could then consolidate lines of communication from Gurez as far as Burzil, which would 'be easy to defend and maintain even in the event of a possible division'. Moreover, stopping at Mendhar in Poonch would not sufficiently secure Jammu. 'I would have actually suggested a full blast advance towards Muzaffarabad,' he concluded, 'because looking at the whole scenario from the approaching ceasefire, which seems to be inevitable, it would be very advantageous to us if we have already reached and consolidated along the points and lines which we will ultimately demand.'

Did Kachru realize that his recommendations would be anathema to the British, whose chief aim was to contain the Kashmir conflict while maintaining Pakistan's claims? Though the British government had decreed at partition that no British soldiers would serve as combatants in an India–Pakistan conflict—even as the two new armies' commands remained in British hands—British officers of the Pakistan Army, who outnumbered their counterparts in the Indian Army by a factor of 3:1, had already entered the Kashmir war in support of their Pakistani troops. In contrast, no British soldier of the Indian Army fought in Kashmir throughout the sixteen-month-long conflict.

By May 1948, Britain's Commonwealth Relations Office was aware that three Pakistani regiments were fighting in Kashmir, accompanied by at least a dozen British officers of whom two were named, Lieutenant Colonel Milne and Captain Skellon. Though the officers had violated orders, the British government decided to hush the issue. As Sir Terrence Shone, then Britain's High Commissioner to India, put it, if India had asked for British troops to stand down in Kashmir, it would have crippled the Pakistan Army since their only competent officers were British. Bucher was informed by Gracey about the presence of British soldiers in Kashmir, but he pressured the Indian government to keep silent, simultaneously counselling against Thimayya's proposals for an advance. Meanwhile, Britain's high commissioner to Pakistan, Sir Laurence Barton Grafftey-Smith, reported that Gracey strongly opposed the proposal of a stand-down 'with no effect of HMG's [His Majesty's Government] delicate position on him'. In the event of a confrontation, Grafftey-Smith added, he was 'at a loss to suggest [an] effective, secure course of action to ensure Gracey's loyalty'. Rather than risk Gracey flouting Britain's two-pronged strategy to build Pakistan as a security partner while strengthening economic ties with India, Britain's Foreign Office resolved to counter an Indian request for stand-down 'with all the arguments we can muster'.[28] Nehru asked Attlee to order a stand-down three times—in July, August and December 1948—but was turned down each time, even though a stand-down would have hastened a ceasefire.

The writing on the wall was clear but, despite rejection by the British government, Nehru did not withdraw or overturn the instructions to halt. Patel agreed with Bucher that the drain on the army, if Thimayya's strategy was followed, would be great. The 'Azad Army' now numbered 35,000, and Patel had to factor in the possibility that the Indian Army might have to enter the princely state of Hyderabad, whose Muslim ruler was considering accession to Pakistan while his Hindu subjects were in favour of acceding to India. In any case, the dynamics of the conflict had already changed and, advised by Mountbatten, Nehru went to the UN. Mountbatten had floated the idea of a UN-organized plebiscite or referendum on accession as early as the summer of 1947.

Nehru took the issue of Pakistan's Kashmir invasion to the UN on 1 January 1948. In April, the UN appointed a Special Commission for India and Pakistan, and in July, the commission visited Jammu and Kashmir. There was urgent pressure on India and Pakistan to agree to a ceasefire, which ultimately transpired on 1 January 1949. Had Nehru withstood British pressure and allowed the war to progress in December, as Kachru had suggested, perhaps the state that remained with India would have been stronger and less vulnerable to cross-border attacks. Like Thimayya, Kachru understood the importance of establishing facts on the ground.

But time was short. Over a year into the war, neither side had won a decisive victory. De facto, the state of Jammu and Kashmir stood divided between Indian and Pakistani-held territories. Punjabi speakers underwent a second communal separation, this time in Jammu province; Balti and Shina speakers underwent their first, with Skardu under Pakistani rule and Kargil under the maharaja. Within a year of the end of the British empire, the Indian subcontinent had suffered a double partition: the first the division of British India and the second a division of the princely state of Jammu and Kashmir. This second partition, too, occurred under British aegis.

♦

It is now widely recognized that Nehru made a cardinal mistake in taking the issue of the Kashmir invasion to the UN. The UN had only been founded in October 1945 and had little track record of acting against aggression, as India requested, and even less of solving international disputes. At only six months old, India's government did not have strong or deep relations with the governments of the five permanent members of the UN Security Council—the US, Britain, France, China and the USSR—except for Britain, with whom relations were already strained and soured further as the Kashmir conflict progressed. Like Pakistan, India itself was still plunged in communal conflict, its leaders shattered by the assassination of Mahatma Gandhi that occurred four weeks after Nehru went to the UN.

Had he lived, would Gandhi have been able to steer Nehru through the quagmire that ensued? We have only one speech of his to go by, made on 4 January 1948, three days after Nehru's telegram had been submitted to the UN Secretary-General. 'You may ask if I approve of the union government approaching the UNO,' he said, 'if I had my way I would have invited Pakistan's representatives to India and we could have met, discussed the matter and worked out some settlement.' Were the two countries to agree a solution, he concluded, the 'big powers in the UNO' would have no option but to endorse it.[29]

The Indian government did try Gandhi's way periodically from 1949 onwards but with little success, for a variety of circumstantial reasons that are discussed in the next chapters. Undoubtedly, the entry of the UN made the search for a resolution more rather than less difficult, as the engagement of third parties without the will or capacity to impose a settlement tends to do, especially if they have a selfish stake. It was a time of massive post-war global reorientation, from imperial to ideological standoffs, and the five permanent members of the UN Security Council each had their own interests to defend. India, Pakistan and the Kashmir conflict were of indifferent consequence to most of the permanent members. They were paramount only for Britain.

British strategists were already looking to shape a new world order in which their security interests would lie with Pakistan rather than India. The Yalta conference of February 1945, where Roosevelt, Churchill and Stalin agreed to set up an institutional body to manage international peace and security, took place eight months before the UN was founded, and was spearheaded by Britain. While agreeing to set up the UN, the three leaders also agreed to Churchill's brainchild—the division of Europe into Atlantic and Soviet spheres of influence. The Indian subcontinent must act as a boundary to curb Soviet influence, British representatives argued, and Pakistan would be a more reliable partner than India. Nehru talked of neutrality between the Atlantic alliance and the Soviets, British officials told their US counterparts. On the other hand, Pakistan's government 'repeatedly' expressed willingness to play the country's 'full part in defensive preparations against Communism'.[30]

By 1947, members of the British government openly discussed the importance of Pakistan to their security requirements, first as a bulwark against Soviet expansion in Asia, second as an ally in the Middle East, where British mandates were due to expire or pass to UN Trusteeship, and finally as a conduit to Central Asia, where British commercial interests were set to expand. Britain's military chiefs were especially dedicated advocates. The 'future of Kashmir', declared Auchinleck, 'must be understood, interpreted, and settled' in the context of the 'defense of the Commonwealth against the USSR'. India's actions, he added, created discontent in an area of 'vital strategic importance'.[31]

The ongoing civil war in the British mandate of Palestine was another consideration. When victorious Jews declared the independent state of Israel in May 1948 and immediately plunged into war with neighbouring Arab states, British embassies in the Middle East were instructed to remind Arab governments that Britain had facilitated the creation of a Muslim state in India and London 'would always come to Pakistan's help',[32] as if the creation of one Muslim state would compensate for the loss of another. The Pakistani acquisition of Gilgit, many British policymakers agreed, was essential to promoting Pakistan's loyalty to Britain. Major William Alexander Brown may have acted independently of the British government in leading Gilgit to revolt and accession to Pakistan, but in 1948, he received an OBE for his services there and also the Sitara-e-Pakistan.

Going by British records, Britain's manipulation of the UN Security Council was both incessant and adroit. Though their ambassador to the UN was Alexander Cadogan, the British government sent a special envoy to handle discussions on Kashmir at the council. Britain, they said, was uniquely qualified to advise on Kashmir as no other member of the council had the same or any depth of knowledge. Yet, Cabinet Minister for Commonwealth Relations Philip Noel-Baker, to whom the charge was entrusted, had never served in India. He had dealt with the Kashmir conflict from London since 1947. The choice was clearly strategic. Unlike Mountbatten and several of his colleagues at the Commonwealth Relations Office, Noel-Baker had few doubts that Pakistan was key to British influence against the Soviets and in the Middle East. Britain, he felt, would have to push the UN to seek a political settlement between India and Pakistan on Kashmir instead of the Pakistani withdrawal that India had asked for, even if this meant alienating India. Any other action, he said, would have 'grave consequences for our relations with Pakistan'.[33]

The UN Security Council Resolution of 20 January 1948 (UNSCR 39, S/654), which was moved by the Belgian President of the Council, Fernand Van Langenhove, reflected the British position. It set up a three-member commission on the 'India–Pakistan Question' to look into issues that both countries had raised, dismissing India's request for Pakistani withdrawal under Chapter VI, Article 35 of the UN Charter. Article 35 enabled any member-state to alert the Security Council to situations that might endanger international peace.

While India's presentation focused on the invasion and Pakistan's role in it, Pakistan's spokesman, Foreign Minister Zafrullah Khan, questioned the validity of Kashmir's accession to India and argued that the Muslim-majority state should rightfully go to Pakistan, considering the principle that partition was based on and the likely desire of its Muslim people. By including these issues, the resolution shifted emphasis from military aggression to political dispute. Commenting on it, Noel-Baker was self-congratulatory: 'The fact that Van Langenhove is largely guided by us is not known…and we take every precaution to ensure that it is not known.'[34]

By April, Noel-Baker was able to move the goalposts further on accession, an issue that US representatives had flagged in conversation with him and other British interlocutors. The accession was legal, US representatives said, so why should the issue be reopened through a plebiscite? Unfortunately for Nehru, under Mountbatten's influence, he had himself allowed the accession to be questioned when he included the assurance that India would 'refer to the will of the people' once peace returned to the state, in his letter to the UN seeking Pakistani withdrawal. Even so, Nehru's reference was to accession to India. Noel-Baker, on the other hand, turned the UN Security Council to believe it should be on accession to India or Pakistan. The US's Truman administration cavilled. As late as November 1948, the ardent cold-warrior John Foster Dulles, then acting leader of the US delegation in the Security Council, complained that the 'present UK approach [to the] Kashmir problem appears extremely pro-GOP [Government of Pakistan]'. But in the end, the US supported a Noel-Baker orchestrated resolution in April (UNSCR 47, S/726).

The April resolution, which was voted on paragraph by paragraph instead of being adopted as a whole, went much further than the January one. It dealt cursorily with the Indian complaint by asking the Pakistani government to 'use its best endeavours' to ensure the withdrawal of tribesmen and any Pakistani nationals who had 'entered the state for the purpose of fighting'. The Pakistani government was also asked to prevent any intrusion or aid for intruders. Notably, there was no reference to the British officers of the Pakistan Army fighting in Kashmir. Once the Government of India and UN representatives were satisfied that the invaders were withdrawing, the resolution continued, the Indian government would be asked to progressively reduce troops, leaving behind only as many as were necessary for the conduct of a free and fair plebiscite.

Then followed a long list of conditions for the plebiscite, all directed at the Indian government since they would be in control of the state. Not a single clause of the resolution addressed the state government; it was as if the maharaja did not exist. At the same time, the April resolution also treated the Indian government as a sort of trustee to execute the instructions of the plebiscite administrator (to be appointed by the UN). Worst of all, it included a clause stating that the UN Commission could call upon either Indian or Pakistani troops to keep the peace if they felt the situation warranted additional forces.

Though the validity of the Instrument of Accession was not

questioned in the April resolution, several of its clauses cast implicit doubt. The fact that all the plebiscite requirements were made of India indicated that the Security Council accepted the accession as valid. However, the inclusion of Pakistan in the plebiscite indicated the council saw accession to India as temporary. Moreover, the council appears to have paid little attention to the clauses of the Instrument of Accession, which restricted India's role to foreign affairs, defence and communication. Under these terms, the Government of India could not comply with the resolution's requirement for free and fair conditions to be created for a plebiscite—that was for the state government to do.

Legally, there were no grounds to challenge the accession to India, though detractors, especially in Pakistan, argued that if the Instrument was signed after Indian troops had landed in the valley, that is, on 27 October instead of the day before, then the presence of the Indian Army would be in violation of Kashmir's sovereignty. In international law, however, there was nothing that prevented one sovereign state, as Kashmir briefly was in the period between Indian independence and accession, from requesting and getting military support from another sovereign state. This the maharaja had done on 24 October.

Nor did the Instrument refer to conditional or temporary accession, or make accession subject to the will of the people. In itself, it was a final and binding deed.

Morally, on the other hand, there was a problem. Nehru and Mountbatten both qualified the Instrument by stating that accession to India would be put to public affirmation once the invaders had withdrawn and order was restored. Though the document clearly stated a permanent accession, and neither the Indian cabinet nor parliament resolved that it was temporary, the fact that the Indian prime minister and governor general had both stated that it would be subject to the will of the people left a question mark over it.

Ultimately, both governments rejected the April resolution—India because the plebiscite terms questioned the maharaja's accession to India, and Pakistan because it required giving up their military gains in Poonch, Mirpur, Baltistan and Muzaffarabad, not to mention relinquishing Gilgit, at least temporarily. When the UN Commission, now expanded to five members, finally visited in the summer of 1948, they found that there was such a gulf between the Indian and Pakistani positions that no compromise was possible. In frustration, said Josef Korbel, the Czechoslovak member of the commission, they suggested that the division of Jammu and Kashmir was the only available option. Such a division, he added, would have to be 'based largely on ethnical principles, though giving due consideration to economic, geographical and strategic needs'.

When Korbel broached the possibility of partitioning Kashmir with Pakistani leaders, telling them that the Indian government might be amenable, he met a resolute no. India might have eastern Jammu, then Governor General Ghulam Mohammad said, but the rest of the state, which was Muslim majority, must go to Pakistan. In fact, Mountbatten had had his adviser V. P. Menon draw up a possible partition plan for Kashmir in June 1948, and Nehru had mentioned partition as one of four options to Sheikh Abdullah as early as 1947, but there is little evidence that the Indian government would have backed a UN-brokered division at this point. Certainly, Ghulam Mohammad's position was a non-starter. 'Once again, the Commission was thwarted,' Korbel concluded.[35]

He might have added, and so was Pakistan, even if the thwarting was self-inflicted. For an Indian historian, this is a revisionist point to make, but if the Pakistani government had accepted Korbel's partition idea for Kashmir, with its 'ethnical principles', they might have gained more of its people and territory. When the war finally drew to an end in mid-1949, both India and Pakistan retained the territories they held militarily in late 1948.

Failing to negotiate a permanent solution through partition, the commission's spotlight moved to a more achievable task, the cessation of hostilities. The August 1948 resolution, proposing a truce between India and Pakistan, provided some relief to India. It stated that the presence of Pakistani troops in Jammu and

Kashmir 'constitutes a material change in the situation since it was represented by the Government of Pakistan before the Security Council', and requested the withdrawal of Pakistani troops as well as Pakistani nationals and tribesmen.[36] Local authorities would administer the territory evacuated by Pakistani troops under the surveillance of the commission, the resolution added, until a solution was agreed between India and Pakistan.

According to Korbel, the resolution was intended to pressure the Pakistani government into a solution. It omitted the call for a plebiscite, saying instead that 'upon acceptance of the truce agreement', the two governments would begin consultations with the commission 'to determine fair and equitable conditions whereby such free expression [of the Kashmiri will] will be assured'. By January 1949, however, when India and Pakistan began to inch towards a ceasefire, the plebiscite was back on the table, again with the proviso that it would be held only after Pakistani troops, nationals and tribesmen had withdrawn.[37]

The two countries eventually signed a UN-brokered ceasefire agreement in July 1949. The agreement established a line that divided the princely state, leaving Pakistan in control of Poonch, Mirpur and Muzaffarabad and the Northern Areas of Gilgit, Hunza, Nagir and Baltistan. The rest of the princely state of Jammu and Kashmir remained under India's control. Monitored by UN military observers, the ceasefire line grew into a de facto partition of the state and a new boundary between India and Pakistan.[38]

Based as it was on existing military controls on the ground, this partition of Kashmir did not reach the Muslim-majority Kashmir valley except for its Muzaffarabad district. Rather, it divided the former fiefdoms of Poonch and Mirpur in the province of Jammu to create a separate Muslim entity[39] and transferred Gilgit from one long-distance rule (the maharaja with Britain) to another (Pakistan). But it also divided the thus far undivided Baltistan, leaving stranded families on either side. And the communal upheaval that had accompanied the war in the Jammu province and Muzaffarabad left a lasting imprint on the polity of the two regions.

The ceasefire line was supposed to be temporary. But, as

discussed earlier, neither country could agree to the UN proposals for settlement. In the event, talks foundered on the interim arrangements themselves. India rejected Pakistan's proposal of international administration for Kashmir—which the UN was neither in a position to provide, nor inclined to. And Pakistan rejected India's proposal to reunite Kashmir under its anti-monarchist leader, Sheikh Abdullah, fearing that his closeness to India's Congress party would prejudge the dispute. He had already appeared on behalf of India at the UN. Pakistan did not withdraw its troops and nationals, and the plebiscite was never held.

In any case, the UN resolutions were solely recommendatory. Under Chapter VI, Article 35, they were also restricted to finding ways to end the war. The only binding element to come out of the Security Council parleys and the work of the UN Commission was the 1949 ceasefire agreement. In 1951, after the UN Commission wound down, the UN's involvement was restricted to a UN Military Observer Group in India and Pakistan (UNMOGIP), which continued to monitor the ceasefire line, increasingly feebly.

◆

Korbel's account of the work of the UN Commission provides a wry footnote. He and his fellow members visited Delhi, Karachi, Srinagar and Baramulla alone. They did not visit Jammu, Ladakh, Gilgit, Baltistan, Poonch, Muzaffarabad or Mirpur (though a military subcommittee did visit the last two). In Karachi, they met the leaders of Pakistan-administered Kashmir, Ghulam Abbas and Sardar Ibrahim—at a tea party, arranged so as to not offend the Indian government.

In other words, just as Abdullah instituted the now all too common tactic of political mobilization following Friday prayers, so the UN Commission instituted the practice of foreign delegations visiting the valley alone as the core site of conflict. And the Pakistani government took on the limp practice of meeting Kashmiri dissidents—now from the valley—at tea parties. The latter is surely history repeating itself as farce.

Chapter IV

A LION IN WINTER

On a fine May afternoon in 1967, a young girl called Jayashree Apparao began her daily walk around the Kodaikanal Lake. A few paces ahead, she saw a tall man wearing a distinctive hat made of a tightly curled fur that she later discovered was karakul lamb. Intrigued, the girl ran up and introduced herself, then walked the rest of the way around the lake with the tall man. He was from Kashmir, he told her, and wistfully described the grandeur of his snow-capped mountain home, the shimmer of its blue-green lakes, its towering wide-leafed trees, its red saffron and pink lotus fields.

For the rest of the summer, the twelve-year-old girl and the sixty-year-old man took a daily walk around the lake, he telling her fables of his land and she defending hers. One conversation she remembers was about a Kashmiri lion. 'There are no lions in Kashmir,' she said, fresh from her Indian fauna class. 'Not all lions are four-legged,' he replied. Foxed, the girl repeated that there were no lions in either Kashmir or Kodaikanal, but her new friend persisted. 'What does a lion do when he is caged far from home?' Now she was on firmer ground. The king of the jungle had friends who set him free, she said, and told him the parable of the lion and the mouse that chewed through his net. 'And what if this Kashmiri lion has lost his friend?' the old man said sadly, then changed the subject.

The next summer when Jayashree returned to Kodaikanal, her friend was no longer there. Finding her disconsolate, her parents enquired and discovered the old man was Sheikh Abdullah, the 'Lion of Kashmir'. Jayashree never saw him again and did not know that her friend had been interned in Kodaikanal when they met, nor that this was his third imprisonment in independent

India. Nor did she realize until much later that the lion he had referred to was himself, and the friend he lost, Nehru.

For many Kashmiris, what happened to Abdullah defined the troubled relationship with India that marked the next fifty years. For many Indians, what Abdullah had done just before being arrested for the third time, on a trip to Pakistan, was another proof of his divided loyalty that had shown itself as early as 1953. Abdullah went to Pakistan with Nehru's blessing, apparently to discuss the idea of a confederation between India, Pakistan and Jammu and Kashmir, but was turned down. Suspecting this was a way to surreptitiously bring Pakistani Muslims back into the Indian fold, Pakistani general Ayub Khan rejected his proposal. Abdullah was rearrested within a year of his return, months before a second India–Pakistan war over Kashmir broke out.

According to Abdullah's confidantes, he had sounded Nehru out on the confederation proposal and received the green light; however, there is nothing in Nehru's papers to indicate whether this was true. But the event did indicate one truth that had dogged Kashmiris since the independence of India and Pakistan: Kashmiris were both sandwiched and divided between the two countries when it comes to emotional loyalties.

◆

What happened in the years following the 1949 Kashmir war? As it petered to a halt, and even before the ceasefire line was formally agreed, the leaders of India and Pakistan, along with the leaders of Jammu and Kashmir, began to change the status of the kingdom, which was now divided into two parts.

Trouble began in Pakistan-administered Kashmir soon after the UN held its first debates on 'The India–Pakistan Question'. In 1948, the Pakistani government formed the Ministry of Kashmir Affairs to liaise with the statelet's administration. Its first priority was to handle the 35,000-strong 'Azad Army'. From mid-1948 onwards, large sections of the militia began to be integrated into the Pakistan Army,[1] seemingly against the will of the statelet's defence minister who argued that they could as well be demobilized and return to farming. The issue was a contentious one. While overseeing a ceasefire agreement in July, and demanding the withdrawal of Pakistani troops and tribesmen in August, the UN Commission was prepared to permit 'Azad Army' forces to remain. According to Sardar Ibrahim, the commission had 'military balance' in mind.[2]

Against this position, India's foreign secretary, Sir Girija Shankar Bajpai, presented a four-step plan to implement the UN Commission's August resolution. Step one was the ceasefire, which had already been achieved. Step two was to disband the 'Azad Army', leading to step three, which was enabling the return of refugees and the internally displaced. Step four followed thereafter: to ascertain the will of the people by a plebiscite or referendum, or any other means.

The four steps were implied in the ceasefire agreement of July 1949, with critical divergences. Bajpai's step two was further sub-divided by the UN negotiators. Pakistanis and tribesmen had to withdraw in step one, followed by Indian troops' reduction in step two. The UN resolutions did not spell out the return of refugees and the internally displaced, a startling omission. Pakistan did not agree to either the UN or the Indian proposals for demilitarization, and none of the recommended measures were implemented. US Admiral Chester Nimitz, who oversaw the ceasefire agreement, stepped down as the plebiscite administrator after failing to persuade the two countries to move to demilitarize the state.

In the meantime, there was the question of whether the UN Commission would recognize the ad hoc government that presided over Poonch, Mirpur and Muzaffarabad. The three areas had always been separately administered; now Muzaffarabad town, once part of the valley, was established as the capital of the statelet. Mirpur too, like Poonch, had been a fiefdom that paid tribute to the maharaja, but was made a district of the new statelet. Gilgit and Baltistan, which were administered partly by Britain and partly by the maharaja, were considered formally to be part of the statelet but were already under direct Pakistani administration.

Originally Abbas and Sardar Ibrahim, along with other leaders of the Poonch rebellion, formed a 'War Council' administration in Pakistan-administered Kashmir that declared its sole objective was to liberate Jammu and Kashmir. Throughout 1948, they lobbied hard, with backing from Pakistan's foreign minister Zafrullah Khan, for the UN Commission to recognize the War Council as at least a de facto if not de jure representative of the Kashmiri people. In July 1948, Ibrahim protested to members of the commission that his government would not 'accept any settlement to which they are not a party, and that Pakistan, though keenly interested in the future of Jammu and Kashmir', could not bind or 'commit them to any course of action without their prior approval'. According to Ibrahim, Korbel replied in September that the commission had 'gone as far as it could' by accepting them as local authorities and they could not 'lose sight of the fact that the state of Jammu and Kashmir still exists as a legal entity'[3] whose sovereignty had to be respected.

Muhammad Ali Jinnah died in the same month. Ibrahim remarked that though he was the Quaid-e-Azam who had created Pakistan, he did not offer the same support to the statelet's administration and their aspiration to accede to Pakistan, perhaps because Pakistan would then have to give up its claim to the whole of Jammu and Kashmir. If the Indian government could embed the Instrument of Accession in the Indian and state constitutions without winning back the rest of the princely state, Ibrahim asked, why was the Pakistani government chary of following suit with the areas under Pakistani's control? Legally, however, the accession deed maintained India's claim because it was the maharaja of undivided Kashmir who had acceded to India. What was a sore point for Ibrahim would not hold in international law, as Korbel's account of the UN mission amplified (see previous chapter).

The real culprit in Pakistan, according to Ibrahim, was the Ministry of Kashmir Affairs. Categorizing its creation as Pakistan's 'first blunder', Ibrahim accused its minister M. A. Gurmani of 'playing havoc' with the movement to 'free Kashmir' until it was 'finally liquidated to the satisfaction of bureaucrats in Pakistan'.[4]

Presumably, this bitter comment was an indirect reference to the agreement that Gurmani negotiated with the statelet's government in April 1949 in Karachi, which Ibrahim did not discuss. The agreement ceded Gilgit and Baltistan to direct rule by Pakistan through a political agent, reminiscent of the post of the British Resident in Kashmir, and restricted the powers of the statelet's government to local administration. The portfolios of defence, foreign affairs, refugee issues and the powers to negotiate a Kashmir settlement were allocated to Pakistan.

The agreement was propelled by a January 1949 UN Commission resolution, which laid down that the provisions of the August 1948 resolution would be implemented after the ceasefire between India and Pakistan. Territories held by Pakistan would be vacated and administered by local authorities under the supervision of a 'plebiscite administrator' appointed by the commission. In other words, the statelet's War Council would have to go.

In March 1949, the Muslim Conference passed a resolution authorizing its 'Supreme Head' to appoint a president for Pakistan-administered Kashmir. The move paved the way for the April 1949 agreement which formalized already existing relations between Pakistan and the Pakistan-administered parts of the former princely state. Despite his qualms at the handover of leadership to Pakistan, Ibrahim signed the April agreement.[5] Ghulam Abbas, who headed the Muslim Conference, had appointed him president of the statelet in March. The two other signatories were Abbas and M. A. Gurmani for the Government of Pakistan. The 1949 agreement has been the steel frame of relations between the statelet and Pakistan to this day.

Though Abbas and Ibrahim worked closely together in 1948, rifts between them developed soon after the 1949 agreement. As a leader from Jammu province rather than Poonch district, Abbas was respected by Jinnah, had networked his way into the Punjabi elite of Pakistan and was backed by the large Muslim refugee community from east Punjab. His focus was on Jammu and Kashmir and he thought electoral politics in the statelet would distract from the battle to win the whole of the state, or so said his critics. Sardar Ibrahim, on the other hand, was a lawyer and former member of Maharaja Hari Singh's assembly, who pushed for elections in Pakistan-administered Kashmir. A district leader from Poonch, he was torn between the overarching battle and the need of the local people for administration. He had far greater support on the ground than Abbas since he was rooted in the clan politics of Poonch and Mirpur. As analyst Ershad Mahmud put it, Ibrahim's militarily powerful family and 'sudden rise to the top position made him a hard bargainer and inflexible with reference to his contemporaries'. The Abbas–Ibrahim power struggle, Mahmud pointed out, reduced their influence over Pakistan's Kashmir policy and 'made them junior players in the corridors of the Ministry of Kashmir Affairs'.[6]

In May 1950 Ghulam Abbas sacked Ibrahim's government, leading to a mass uprising demanding that the Muslim Conference restrict the powers of its Supreme Head to appoint the government, and hold elections based on adult franchise. In response, the Ministry of Kashmir Affairs, in consultation with Abbas, framed new 'rules of business' in December. Instead of allowing an elected government, the new rules expanded the powers of the Supreme Head. He would now appoint the council of ministers as well as the president, and no fresh legislation could be passed without his approval. Commenting on the 'intrigues and counter-intrigues' that led to this new dispensation, historian Yousaf Saraf said, '[The] Abbas group was straining every nerve to deprive the Azad government of as much power as possible. It also seemed to suit the convenience of...M. A. Gurmani, Minister Without Portfolio who was in charge of Kashmir affairs [and] had his permanent office at Rawalpindi. He was playing one group against the other.'[7]

A year later, in 1951, the Pakistani government applied the Pakistan Army Act directly to what remained of the 'Azad Army', saying they 'needed to be put on a regular footing' and 'brought under some code of military discipline'.[8]

The move followed hard on the heels of an attempted coup against the Liaquat Ali administration, led by Akbar Khan, now major general and chief of general staff in the Pakistan Army and the same man who had been a key organizer of the Kashmir invasion. The coup attempt, known as the Rawalpindi Conspiracy, was supported by Pakistani communists, among them Faiz Ahmed Faiz. It was spurred by discontent at Ali's acceptance of UN mediation in the Kashmir conflict, the continuing presence of British officers in the army that restricted promotions of Pakistani officers, as well as the broad public perception that Ali's administration was corrupt and inefficient. Military suspicion of Ali's intentions had already been sown a year earlier, when he signed the Delhi Pact of April 1950 with Nehru, for the return of refugees, abducted women and looted property, de-recognition of forced conversions and protection of minority rights. Both countries agreed to set up national minorities' commissions to implement the Delhi Pact.

Though the pact did not trigger a coup attempt in India as it had in Pakistan, it was opposed in India too, with a member of Nehru's cabinet, Syama Prasad Mookerjee, resigning in protest.

Ali was tipped off to the coup attempt, and its chief leaders and supporters, including the poet Faiz, were arrested and imprisoned. Most of them were pardoned and released in 1957. Akbar Khan went on to become head of national security under Zulfikar Ali Bhutto in 1971. Ghulam Abbas resigned as head of the Muslim Conference in 1951 to protest the arrests. Liaquat Ali was assassinated soon after, in October 1951, by an Afghan who had been stripped of his nationality and was living in the NWFP, first in the pay of the British and then of the Pakistani authorities. Gurmani, the man whom Ibrahim excoriated, went on to become interior minister in the successor government to Ali.

In the years to follow, Pakistan treated the statelet as formally separate and temporarily under its protection in international forums, but integrated its population through the labour market, and its politicians ran shop from Islamabad, while a Pakistani governor, generally a retired colonel, managed the statelet. In 1952, the 'rules of business' were again revised, giving the Ministry of Kashmir Affairs further powers. While the Supreme Head of the Muslim Conference continued to appoint the president and council of ministers, it was now mandatory for him to get the ministry's approval for all appointments, from the president to the heads of the government departments and judiciary. Local political groups protested, seeking to be allowed to elect their government. But when the Pakistani authorities finally accepted their demand, elections were restricted to those who swore an oath of allegiance to Pakistan, dissident politicians were regularly jailed, and there was little freedom of speech and no civil society to speak of. Pakistan treated Gilgit and Baltistan, lumped together as the Northern Areas, more openly as protectorates; they were run by the centre via a governor and had no elected government or administration.

◆

On the Indian side of the ceasefire line, Jammu and Kashmir's fortunes underwent a series of twists and turns. In March 1949, Maharaja Hari Singh formed an interim administration for the state, headed by Sheikh Abdullah, who was appointed prime minister. Through his order, Hari Singh became a constitutional monarch, but only briefly. In late June, under pressure from Abdullah, Nehru and Patel, Hari Singh left the state for 'a few months', appointing his son, Karan Singh, Regent.[9] Karan Singh was only eighteen at the time and had just returned from college in the US. Writing about the sudden onus upon him, he described his father's resentment at the corner he had been pushed into and his own excited trepidation at the duties he would now undertake.

Though the young Regent and the middle-aged Abdullah began cordially, rifts soon appeared. The first of them was over Abdullah's land redistribution programme, which originally offered the landlords no compensation. It was later grudgingly amended at Indian intercession. Abdullah had promised 'land to the tiller'[10] under the Naya (new) Kashmir manifesto that he, Bazaz and others issued in 1944. Now that he was in power, he moved fast to fulfil his promise. His redistribution programme, supported by Karan Singh, profoundly altered the economy of the valley as well as Jammu, where it exacerbated Dogra and Hindu fears of

National Conference rule. But Karan Singh insisted on consulting the Government of India on whether compensation should be offered to landlords, which garnered an angry response from Abdullah, who underlined that under the Instrument of Accession, land redistribution was a domestic policy issue and the Indian government had no jurisdiction in this matter. In Karan Singh's words, he and Abdullah differed in that 'he [Abdullah] looked upon himself as a Kashmiri who happened to find himself in India and I considered myself to be an Indian who happened to find himself in Kashmir'.

Their next tussle was over the election of a constituent assembly to determine the future of the state. India's own constituent assembly, elected in 1946, adopted a paragraph on the accession of Jammu and Kashmir as Article 306A of its draft constitution in October 1949. Article 306A was incorporated into the Constitution of India as Article 370, a special and temporary or transitional provision, in January 1950. It proposed a special status for Jammu and Kashmir in the union, along with internal autonomy for the state. Indian jurisdiction was limited to the three areas specified in the Instrument of Accession: defence, foreign affairs and communications.

Procedurally, the follow-up was for Article 370 to be adopted in the constitution of Jammu and Kashmir, for which the state would have to appoint a constituent assembly. Abdullah wanted the assembly to be elected following a proclamation from the Regent, but his father instructed Karan Singh not to sign, since he, Hari Singh, was still ruler of the state. Eventually, Karan Singh issued the proclamation after the Indian government intervened in Abdullah's favour.

Abdullah's National Conference swept the board in Kashmir's first election. The Jammu-based Praja Parishad that had been founded in November 1948 boycotted the election because the union and state governments rejected their demand for the monarchy to be preserved untouched. Praja Parishad members also alleged that state election officials had rejected many of their candidacy papers on the specious grounds of being incomplete.

For the first time in a hundred years, state power moved into the hands of Muslims. Hearing of impending constitutional change, however, the UN Security Council issued a resolution in March 1951 affirming the disputed nature of the state and calling for a plebiscite to be held even though, strangely, it had paid no attention to the agreement between Pakistan and Pakistan-administered Kashmir of two years earlier. The resolution asked India and Pakistan to find a way out of their deadlock over demilitarization of Jammu and Kashmir. It added that if both countries failed to agree, their governments should accept arbitration by the International Court of Justice.

Abdullah's opening speech to the assembly indirectly referred to this resolution. 'Finally we come to the issue which has made Kashmir an object of world interest, and has brought her before the forum of the United Nations,' he said. 'This simple issue has become so involved that people have begun to ask themselves after three and a half years of tense expectancy, "Is there any solution?" Our answer is in the affirmative.'[11]

If two issues were tackled first, he went on, the solution would follow: 'Firstly, was Pakistan's action in invading Kashmir in 1947 morally and legally correct, judged by any norm of international behaviour? Sir Owen Dixon's verdict on this issue is perfectly plain. In unambiguous terms he declared Pakistan an aggressor.'

An Australian who had been appointed the UN's Representative to India and Pakistan in 1950 after Admiral Nimitz stepped down as plebiscite administrator, Dixon came close to achieving a tenuous agreement between India and Pakistan. Building on the partition idea that the UN Commission floated back in 1948, Dixon proposed a restricted plebiscite in the Kashmir valley. Ladakh, he proposed, would be assigned to India, Poonch, Mirpur, Muzaffarabad, Gilgit and Baltistan to Pakistan, and the remaining districts of Jammu divided between the two countries, with its Muslim-majority districts west of the Chenab going to Pakistan.[12]

Despite their distaste for the communal principle on which India had been partitioned, the Indian cabinet seems to have been prepared to accept Dixon's partition-cum-plebiscite proposal as a starting point. Nehru and Liaquat Ali held a marathon discussion under Dixon's aegis, in which Ali remained non-committal but let it be known that it could be floated as India's proposal. Though Ali's response kept Pakistani options open and undermined Dixon's plan, it was not the reason it died. Instead, the plan foundered over recognition of the Abdullah government. Dixon was adamant that any plebiscite would have to be held under a 'neutral administration'. Indeed, he called Abdullah's administration a 'police state'.[13]

Having supported Abdullah for close to two decades, Indian leaders could not agree to his dismissal. Their case at the UN was based on a twofold argument—that Jammu and Kashmir's maharaja had legally acceded to India, and that this accession was backed by the state's people, proven by their leader Abdullah's support. Nehru's personal loyalty to Abdullah, which formed the Indian response, was a third factor. Dixon had reached the end of his road and resigned.

Continuing his criticism of the UN's handling of the Kashmir issue, Abdullah argued, '[W]as the Maharajah's accession to India legally valid or not? The legality of the accession has not been seriously questioned by any responsible or independent person or authority.' If the UN demanded that Pakistan fulfil the obligation to vacate, he concluded, then 'India herself, anxious to give the people of the State a chance to express their will freely, would willingly cooperate with any sound plan of demilitarization'. His government, he added, would then 'be happy to have the assistance of international observers to ensure fair play and the requisite conditions for a free choice by the people'.[14] This was a compromise formula that the Indian cabinet too had inched towards.

In the meantime, while the state's constituent assembly continued to debate various clauses of the future constitution of Jammu and Kashmir, Abdullah and Nehru negotiated the Delhi Agreement in 1952 to flesh out areas in which the state would have autonomy. 'In view of the uniform and consistent stand taken by the Jammu and Kashmir constituent assembly that sovereignty in all matters other than those specified in the Instrument of Accession continues to reside in the State',[15] the agreement stated, the two governments had decided that the people of the state would have Indian citizenship under Article 35 of the Indian Constitution, but the state legislature could confer 'special rights and privileges' on state subjects (codified as Article 35A in 1954). They could also make laws for state subjects 'who had gone to Pakistan on account of the communal disturbances of 1947, in the event of their return to Kashmir'.

The state would have its own flag, the agreement added, provided it 'would not be a rival of the Union flag'. The constitutional head of the state, to be called sadr-i-riyasat, would be elected by the state legislature instead of being nominated by the union government, though the President of India would have to formally appoint him, as he did other state governors.

On fundamental rights, the Delhi Agreement was peculiarly ambiguous. Given that the state had internal autonomy, 'the whole chapter relating to Fundamental Rights of the Indian Constitution could not be made applicable to the State'. Thus 'the question which remained to be determined was whether the chapter on fundamental rights should form a part of the state constitution or the Constitution of India as applicable to the State', meaning Article 370. The Indian Supreme Court, meanwhile, would have only appellate jurisdiction in Jammu and Kashmir.

Whether and what 'emergency powers' could reside with the union government were hotly contested. The Government of India insisted on the application of Article 352 of the Indian Constitution, empowering the Indian president to proclaim a general emergency in the state. The Abdullah administration argued that they were prepared to accept that the Government of India would have full authority to proclaim an emergency when it came to war or external aggression, but when it came to internal conflict, the decision must be made by the state government, not the President of India. Eventually, Indian negotiators agreed to modify Article 352 to say that as far as internal disturbance in Jammu and Kashmir was concerned, the union government would intervene only 'at the request or with the concurrence of the Government of the State'.

Article 370 was amended in November 1952 to incorporate the changes made by the Delhi Agreement. The Praja Parishad responded with an agitation in Jammu, under the slogan 'Ek vidhan, ek pradhan, ek nishan (one constitution, one head of state, and one flag)'. The demand was based on how other princely states had been handled post-independence: after their leaders had acceded to India, Patel negotiated their merger into the Indian union. Merger bound the princely states to follow the Indian Constitution; accession did not. Failing merger of Jammu and Kashmir into the Indian Union, the Parishad threatened, it would seek separation of Jammu from Kashmir.

Karan Singh was elected sadr-i-riyasat in November 1951 by the state's constituent assembly. When he arrived in Jammu, he was greeted with black flags and, in the months to follow, there were Parishad-led demonstrations across Jammu, supported by the RSS and a newly formed Hindu right-wing party called the Jan Sangh. Founded in 1951 by Syama Prasad Mookerjee, who had resigned from Nehru's cabinet to protest the Delhi Pact, the Jan Sangh had few cadres in Jammu but sent volunteers from bordering states to swell Parishad demonstrations, as did the RSS. Intelligence reports of a brewing revolt in Jammu began to surface as early as 1949. In April, Nehru wrote to Patel, citing an intelligence report that referred to 'a growing Hindu agitation in Jammu province for what is called a zonal plebiscite... It is carried on by what is known as the Jammu Praja Parishad.' The idea of a zonal plebiscite, Nehru added, was based on the assumption that if a vote on accession was held, the valley would go to Pakistan. Such an assumption, he said, was 'most harmful' to India.[16]

Actually, the Parishad's zonal plebiscite idea built on Dixon's proposal on behalf of the UN Commission. It was accompanied by the demand for Jammu and Kashmir, or what of it remained with India, to be divided into three states, with Jammu and Ladakh integrated into India and the valley given special status.

The Jan Sangh did not originally support the demand for a

three-way division of the state. At its first annual session at Kanpur in December 1952, delegates resolved to campaign for the full integration of Jammu and Kashmir into India, rather than the autonomy offered by Article 370. After the session Mookerjee wrote to Nehru asking that he get the state's constituent assembly to pass a resolution ratifying its accession to India. At the same time, he asserted that the people of Jammu had 'the inherent right to demand that they should be governed by the same Constitution as has been made applicable to the rest of India. If the people of Kashmir Valley think otherwise, must Jammu also suffer because of such unwillingness to merge completely with India?' Moreover, he said, the 'Kashmir Valley, Jammu and Ladakh represent different types of people; their languages, their outlook, their environments, their habits and modes of life, their occupation differ from one another in many vital respects'.

Nehru and Abdullah both remonstrated with Mookerjee, arguing that his support for the Praja Parishad's agitation had had a disastrous impact on the valley and was leading many to question the wisdom of acceding to India. 'You are not perhaps unaware of the attempts that are being made by Pakistan and other interested quarters to force a decision by disrupting the unity of the State,' Abdullah wrote to Mookerjee in early February 1953. If a fair plebiscite was held, he said, the decision was 'bound to be' in favour of India. But the Parishad's demands played into Pakistan's hands and ran the risk of turning Kashmiris against India. 'If the agitation grows, unforeseen forces may be released which would seriously threaten the foundations of the State.' Pointing out that Patel had negotiated Article 306A, which was the precursor to Article 370, not Nehru—since Mookerjee admired the former but despised the latter—Abdullah concluded that Kashmiris had 'voluntarily offered to associate ourselves with India' and if the basic principles of Article 370 were not compromised, they would 'like this association to be abiding'.

Unfortunately, Patel was now gone: he had died in December 1950. Mookerjee heeded neither Nehru nor Abdullah's warnings. Instead, he set up a committee to mobilize support for the

Parishad's agitation across India. In March 1953, the Jan Sangh and Parishad launched a non-violent satyagraha to push for their twin demands to retain the monarchy and revoke the state's autonomy. The satyagraha rapidly degenerated into violent street protests; apparently the Parishad had started stockpiling arms some months earlier. Mookerjee went himself to the valley in May, against advice to stay away lest his appearance inflame sentiments on both sides of the accession issue. He was arrested there by Abdullah's police and died in detention a month later, on 23 June, of a heart attack.

If the impact of the Praja Parishad's agitation on the valley was grave, the impact of the news of Mookerjee's death on Jammu was even graver, leading the demand for separation from the valley to spiral. Watching this, a depressed Nehru wrote to B. C. Roy, the then chief minister of West Bengal, 'It is difficult to speak openly about the injurious results of this movement. It has made the Kashmir problem far more difficult than it ever was. Before this movement was started, I had little doubt in my mind that the final decision about Kashmir would be in our favour, however long it might take. But this movement has upset all my calculations and weakened our position in Kashmir terribly.' The 90 per cent Muslim population of the valley, Nehru said, had 'become frightened of the communal elements in Jammu and in India and their previous wish to be attached to India has weakened'. Indeed, he continued, 'at the moment, all the hostile forces against us are dominant in Kashmir... During the past few months, I have had no greater trouble or burden than this feeling of our losing grip in Kashmir.'[17]

Karan Singh had a different take. Though he did decide to accept his election as sadr-i-riyasat against the urging of the Praja Parishad, after an internal struggle and under considerable pressure from Nehru and his father on opposite sides, he believed that the Dogras of Jammu needed to be reassured and asked Nehru and Abdullah to meet Parishad leaders. Both refused. In the end, he was the only government representative to meet them. In his view, an important opportunity for reconciliation was lost and he may have been right. He had himself persuaded the Parishad president, Prem Nath Dogra, to issue a statement saying that it was 'premature' to 'give a definite opinion' on whether or not Karan Singh should accept the position of sadr-i-riyasat. On the other hand, when he arrived as sadr-i-riyasat in late 1951, Karan Singh was greeted by black flags in Jammu despite Dogra's statement, and there is little to show whether the agitation could have been prevented if Nehru or Abdullah had sought talks with Parishad leaders.

Why were Nehru and Abdullah so opposed to engaging with the Parishad? Common sense suggests that if they had met Parishad leaders, some if not all of the sting might have been taken out of the growing anger in Jammu. Each, however, had his predicament. For Nehru, the Jan Sangh-RSS-Parishad tie-up was part of a larger game plan of the Hindu right to assert a Hindu majoritarian India and undermine the Congress's attempt to keep church out of state. It was one of the RSS's supporters who had assassinated Gandhi.[18] For Abdullah, the Parishad were enemies of his agenda for Jammu and Kashmir to abolish the monarchy, redistribute land and bring democracy to the valley. The Jan Sangh's support for the Parishad weakened his case for Kashmir to remain with India.

Clearly there was little room for compromise. Nevertheless, by refusing to engage in dialogue, both leaders lost the middle ground in Jammu, where the situation continued to deteriorate with its inevitably negative fallout on the valley. Under pressure, Abdullah began to posit 'Muslim secularism' against 'Hindu communalism' in a string of speeches that eroded his relationship with both the sadr-i-riyasat and New Delhi. Though he was pro-accession, he was against merger. The special status of Jammu and Kashmir, he believed, was essential to keeping Kashmir with India as the only Muslim-majority state in the federation.

In the summer of 1953, when US Governor of Illinois, Adlai Stevenson, visited, Abdullah sounded him out on the option of independence for the valley. He had apparently discussed the idea earlier, with Warren Austin, the US representative at the UN, and with the US Ambassador to India, Loy Henderson, telling him that the leaders of Pakistan-administered Kashmir were likely to support such a proposal.[19] In his autobiography, Abdullah referred to a conversation he had with Ghulam Abbas before sending him to Pakistan at his request in 1948. Abbas and he, Abdullah said, 'concluded that a plebiscite, if it was held, would only lead to further bloodshed.[20] Of course, the situation might improve if India and Pakistan guaranteed the state's independence.' The two agreed, Abdullah added, that Abbas would sound out Pakistani leaders for support on independence and he would sound out Indian leaders. Jinnah's response to Abbas was a firm no. Abdullah did not go into Nehru's response but, according to Abdullah's biographer, Ajit Bhattacharjea, Nehru did not brush the idea aside.

That Pakistan opposed independence for Jammu and Kashmir, as did India, was no secret. When Dulles, then US President Eisenhower's Secretary of State, raised the issue of Kashmir's independence with Pakistani leaders on a 1953 visit to the Indian subcontinent, Foreign Minister Zafrullah Khan 'dismissed the idea... But, he added sardonically, "If the people of the Valley wished to commit suicide, Pakistan would not stand in the way."'[21]

In India, Dulles sounded Nehru out on the possibility of formally partitioning Jammu and Kashmir. Nehru was cautiously receptive, but Dulles soon found that Nehru saw partition of the state as ratifying the territorial status quo, which would leave the bulk of the valley with India. This, Dulles believed, Pakistan would never accept, and by now Pakistan's participation in the anti-communist alliance in Korea was vital for the US. War had raged in Korea since 1950, threatening the Cold War division of the world into Atlantic and Soviet spheres of influence. The country had been partitioned on ideological lines in 1948, following its liberation from imperial Japan in 1945, with North Korea in the communist bloc and South Korea in the democratic bloc. China took over Soviet power in North Korea in 1951 with Soviet assent, when Mao's government entered the war. The war ended in summer 1953 with an armistice under which the two Koreas returned to their original partition line; its impact was to throw greater momentum into the Cold War division of power. Pakistan bordered communist China, and it became imperative for the US and Britain, the two chief drivers of the Atlantic alliance, to bring the country into their fold.

Dulles's own attitude towards India changed between 1948 and 1953. The Truman administration began to reverse its position on accession as early as 1950, under British influence, when the State Department's legal adviser concurred with Britain's Attorney General, Sir Hartley Shawcross, that accession was conditional.[22] After meeting Nehru in 1953 to canvass him on Korea as well as Kashmir, he believed Nehru was 'wildly impractical' on international affairs though a realist on Kashmir. Nehru had already started toying with the concepts of non-alignment and Asian unity; the former was to isolate him from the US and the latter to bring deep disappointment.

The US, instead, began to work more closely with Britain on a security alliance to include Pakistan. In July 1953, there were US–British talks on creating a 'Northern tier' alliance of countries from Turkey to Pakistan to defend the Middle East against communism. In October, the US agreed to provide Pakistan $25 million in military aid. Indian government representatives loudly protested, telling their US and British counterparts that the Pakistan Army would use the aid against India in Kashmir. Their protests fell on deaf ears, and Nehru took fright.

By this point, the Jammu and Kashmir constituent assembly had debated the state constitution for over eighteen months. While it had passed two resolutions—for land redistribution and the election of a sadr-i-riyasat—little else had been decided, including adoption of the amended Article 370 on accession to India. Under pressure from his Congress colleagues, many of whom were beginning to share the openly expressed view of the Parishad and Jan Sangh that Abdullah did not intend to affirm accession, Nehru began to doubt Abdullah. Abdullah himself vacillated, telling Nehru in May 1953 that there was no point in the assembly's passing a resolution to support accession to India, given India's commitments to the UN—'If we decided the accession through the Assembly, how could we face the world?'[23] When the National Conference set up a committee in May 1953,[24] to explore the option of a plebiscite that would include the choice of independence and 'evolve a solution that Pakistan could accept',[25] Nehru's faith in Abdullah frayed.

The National Conference leaders too were divided on what sort of relationship Jammu and Kashmir should have with India. According to Karan Singh, three out of the five ministers in Abdullah's cabinet—Bakshi Ghulam Mohammad, Shyam Lal Saraf and Girdhari Lal Dogra—favoured 'a more comprehensive relationship covering the judiciary [and] financial arrangements',[26] while one, Mirza Afzal Beg, stood firm with Abdullah that it should comprise only the three areas in the Instrument of Accession. In fact, the issue had already been settled by the Delhi Agreement and amended Article 370, both reflecting Abdullah's view. If Abdullah had pushed the state's constituent assembly to adopt these two agreements, his colleagues would have had no grounds to seek a broader relationship and could not have proceeded with their successful effort to depose him.

Abdullah himself appears to have been conflicted over whether to make Article 370 permanent or keep it temporary, as it was described in the Indian Constitution's margins. India's constituent assembly had kept the Article temporary until the state's constituent assembly ratified it and had, moreover, hoped that the state would gradually come to merger. But when the state's constituent assembly came to debate ratification, concerns over guarantees of autonomy as well as changing circumstances came to the fore, including for Abdullah himself.

As he stated repeatedly in his autobiography and correspondence with Nehru, Abdullah suspected the union government had little intention of making the state's autonomy a permanent feature of the Indian federation. He had also come to the conclusion that lasting peace could only be achieved if India and Pakistan both agreed to special status. 'The accession of Kashmir to India, otherwise complete in all other respects, possesses one essential disqualification. It is an accession accepted provisionally being subject to subsequent ratification by the people and, therefore, lacking finality and, as such, a major contribution to the uncertainty itself,' he wrote in a speech he planned to give on Eid in August 1953. 'It is also true that Pakistan has come to occupy the position of a party directly and vitally concerned with this issue. It is important to bear this fact in mind when we propose, in our eagerness to end the uncertainty, to settle the issue of accession quickly.'[27]

Defending his reluctance to adopt Article 370, he added: 'Then there is the suggestion that the accession should be finalized by a vote of the constituent assembly. The question is, are decisions of the constituent assembly binding on India, Pakistan, and the United Nations?'

Within the state, Abdullah had begun to emerge as a popular leader but a poor politician. Impulsive and hot-headed, he would often act without considering the possible consequences, including the feelings of his cabinet colleagues. He described at length in his autobiography how he found out Saraf was corrupt, nepotistic and negligent and tried various means to oust him, including putting together a list of charges to place before the National Conference cadre. But he did not touch upon the question of why he, as prime minister, failed to convince his cabinet or his government of the need for Saraf to depart quietly.

In late July 1953, the three cabinet ministers that Karan Singh was most closely in touch with, Bakshi, Saraf and Dogra, presented the sadr-i-riyasat with a letter saying they had lost confidence in Abdullah as prime minister. Karan Singh was just twenty-two at the time. He called Abdullah to discuss the letter and urged him to meet with his cabinet that evening to resolve the problem, but Abdullah had already made plans to go to Gulmarg and departed promising, according to his autobiography, that he would call a cabinet meeting as soon as he returned. Karan Singh's own account does not refer to this promise, indeed it implies that Abdullah brushed his suggestion aside.

Events moved at high speed from that point on. The union government, together with Karan Singh, treated the Bakshi, Saraf and Dogra letter as akin to a vote of no confidence in the state government. Abdullah was dismissed and arrested at the dead of night in Gulmarg.

That Abdullah was dismissed without due process is now well established. Critics pointed out that his cabinet colleagues should have sought discussion with him and amongst party leaders instead of turning to New Delhi. As New Delhi's representative, the sadr-i-riyasat, too, could have considered a more consensual procedure to determine whether or not Abdullah should be dismissed. But the state was still emerging from conflict and its economy and polity were in shambles. Karan Singh was, as he said, an Indian first; he was too torn between his ancestral loyalties to the Dogras and his role as constitutional head of state. What comes through in his autobiography is that he and several members of the union cabinet came early to the conclusion that Abdullah sought to leverage the dispute at the UN to weaken Jammu and Kashmir's accession to India, and therefore he must go. They were prepared to use dissidents from amongst the National Conference for the purpose.

Nehru concurred, but weakly. He was at that point engaged in negotiations over the plebiscite issue with the new Prime Minister of Pakistan, Mohammad Ali Bogra, and visited Karachi on 25 July, receiving a tumultuous welcome. Photographs of the time show hundreds of thousands of Pakistanis lining the streets to the airport to catch a glimpse of the Indian prime minister. A predictably evasive and hostile Pakistani government may have seemed a better bet than an unpredictably evasive and periodically hostile Abdullah.

The man who had already been identified to take over from Abdullah was his close colleague and deputy prime minister as well as home minister, Bakshi Ghulam Mohammad. A school dropout from a poor family, Bakshi had worked as Abdullah's 'lieutenant' since 1927. He was a skilled organizer who built the National Conference and affiliated student and labour organizations. Known for his efficiency in the valley, he had also developed close relations with leaders in Jammu. Abdullah's trust in him was so great that he appointed him deputy prime minister when the maharaja devolved power in 1947. When Abdullah was away for UN negotiations, it was Bakshi whom he deputed as acting chief administrator.

Abdullah's arrest was laid squarely at the doors of Bakshi, who said he would only take over as prime minister once the former was removed from the state. Delhi's decision-makers agreed Bakshi was no match for a free Abdullah, who would have mobilized the National Conference against him in no time. Both Karan Singh and Abdullah's accounts reveal the strong hand of Indian intelligence in the dismissal and arrest. B. N. Mullick, then director of Indian intelligence, and Nehru's protégé, Brigadier B. M. Kaul, played a key role in assembling the information that led to Abdullah's downfall. Mullick seems to have been the one person who briefed all the Indian decision-makers, from the prime minister and his cabinet, especially the home minister, to the sadr-i-riyasat. Kaul was the liaison between Srinagar and New Delhi.

The murky months of July and August brought another figure to the fore: the left-wing Kashmiri Pandit, D. P. Dhar, who had been a close adviser of Abdullah but now veered towards the Bakshi faction. Dhar brought Abdullah's dissident ministers to Karan Singh as well as to union cabinet ministers in Delhi. Bakshi, he said, was more likely to promote the accession to India and work for the merger of the state into the union. He was also more likely to provide a stable administration.

Abdullah's dismissal and arrest caused immediate furore in the valley. Protest spread like wildfire and spilled over the border into Pakistan-administered Jammu and Kashmir as well as Pakistan proper. Alarmed, Prime Minister Bogra rushed to New Delhi for talks with Nehru on 16 August. Lasting four days, the talks concluded with a joint communiqué that stated the two prime ministers had discussed 'the Kashmir dispute...at some length', and had decided that 'certain preliminary issues' would have to be settled before a new plebiscite administrator could be appointed. They set the deadline for appointment at April 1954. In January, however, Pakistan signed a defence pact with Turkey to set up the Northern Tier alliance envisaged by Dulles in the summer of 1953, and in September, Pakistan joined seven other countries to sign the Manila Pact, establishing a security alliance to fight communism in Southeast Asia.

The Southeast Asia Treaty Organization (SEATO) was intended to be an Asian version of NATO that did not include troop contributions or inter-operability, and soon mutated into a US-led alliance. But Pakistan's membership of it, along with its earlier pact with Turkey, further estranged the country from India. Pakistan had arrayed itself with the Atlantic allies in the Cold War while Nehru was in pursuit of non-alignment. Though he would have preferred good relations with the US and Europe and was wary of the USSR and its communist allies in India, he was not prepared to make a choice between Cold War opponents, and that choice was all that was on offer.

There was little follow-up to the Nehru–Bogra talks and, in 1955, Bogra was forced to resign by Pakistan's governor general, Major General Iskandar Mirza. A Bengali from East Pakistan, Bogra had suggested a federal structure for Pakistan while attempting to forge West Pakistan into 'One Unit'. At the time, Pakistan's constituent assembly was still discussing the framing of a constitution. A federal structure was advocated by many political parties, but implacably opposed by the military and Pakistan's dominant Punjabi leadership. Though Bogra's defence and interior ministers were both military, Governor General Mirza clearly doubted his allegiance. Within two years, the military had again intervened in the civilian administration.

In Jammu and Kashmir, Bakshi proved to be a far better administrator than Abdullah, and the state managed to achieve some degree of calm under him. In his eleven-year tenure, he instituted free education from the primary to the graduate level, built housing for the homeless, abolished the levy on foodgrain, introduced free rations for the poor, expanded healthcare, developed the valley as a tourist as well as official conference destination and entered into a customs and tax agreement with the union government, under which duties on goods entering the state would be abolished and the union government would provide the state an annual grant of ₹2 crore. His council of ministers included the Ladakhi lama Kushak Bakula, and so, for the first time, Ladakh was politically represented in the state government.

But Bakshi also ran a tight ship through his police and private semi-militia, risibly named the Peace Brigade, which rapidly became infamous for suppressing dissent by force. His administration was simultaneously accused of being corrupt.[28] In the late 1950s, partly to palliate a restive Delhi that was now aware of his growing unpopularity, he brought the state administrative service into the Indian administrative service and the state's Franchise Commission under the Election Commission of India. Both measures were widely seen as undermining the underlying principles of the Delhi Agreement and Article 370.

Abdullah was imprisoned for close to five years in Jammu, though Nehru and Bakshi began discussing his release in 1955. One reason for the delay was that the state's constitution still had not been passed. It was introduced in draft in October 1956, and a fierce debate ensued, led by Mirza Afzal Beg. Beg had been detained with Abdullah and released in 1954, after which he formed the Plebiscite Front in 1955. Apparently, he was released to allow some representation of Abdullah's views in the constitutional debates; if so, the initiative was unsuccessful. While Beg attacked accession to India in the assembly, Abdullah wrote a lengthy denunciation of assembly proceedings to the then president of the assembly, G. M. Sadiq. For its part, the Praja Parishad, which had by now formally affiliated to the Jan Sangh, condemned the draft constitution for stopping short at accession instead of going to merger.

Despite these criticisms, the constitution was adopted in November 1956 and signed by 68 of the 75 members of the assembly (the remaining seven including Abdullah and Beg, who had been rearrested, were in detention). It came into force on 26 January 1957. Stating in its preamble that it would 'further define the existing relationship of the State with the Union of India', the constitution laid down that the 'State of Jammu and Kashmir is and shall be an integral part of the Union of India', and its territory would 'comprise all the territories which on the fifteenth day of August, 1947, were under the sovereignty or suzerainty of the Ruler of the State' (Part II, Articles 3 and 4). To mark the desire for reunification, the constitution reserved 25 seats in the 100-member legislature for representatives from the Pakistan-held territories of the former princely state, to be kept vacant until the Kashmir dispute was resolved.

Pakistan turned to the UN and, in January 1957, the UN Security Council issued a fresh resolution reiterating that the dispute could only be settled through a plebiscite. The Pakistan delegate to the UN then produced a letter repudiating the constitution, that he claimed was from Sheikh Abdullah, which Abdullah later denied. The Soviet Union, now under Khrushchev, vetoed the resolution, in a first for the Security Council on Kashmir. With Pakistan in the Anglo-American bloc, the Soviet Union, which had displayed contempt for India under Stalin, moved to court India. Khrushchev and Bulganin visited Kashmir in December 1955 and declared they supported the state's accession to India. They repeated their statements at the Security Council.

Abdullah was finally released at Nehru's intercession in 1958 and lost no time in whipping up opposition to both Bakshi's administration and the state's new constitution. Joining Beg's Plebiscite Front, he also began to question the validity of the state's accession to India. He was rearrested within months, this time on charges of conspiring with 'imperialists' to wrest Kashmir. Meanwhile, the Pakistani government began a small-scale and covert war in Kashmir by infiltrating groups of three to five guerrillas who conducted a series of low-grade bomb attacks in Jammu and the valley. The strategy was suggested by Akbar Khan, who had led the Pakistani guerrillas in the 1947–48 war.

Alleging that the Plebiscite Front was in league with Pakistani intelligence, Mullick and Kaul collected reams of ambiguous evidence indicating that the Front received large funds from Pakistan.[29] The charge was corroborated by Bhutto decades later in his autobiography. But the intelligence that was used to charge the Front was difficult to prove; much of it was coded and there were no witnesses to swear to the false names used. There was only one document suggesting Abdullah's own involvement and it could have been fabricated by anyone including rival intelligence services.[30] The case dragged on in the lower courts until Nehru intervened in 1959 to halt the prosecution, on the grounds that it would further roil India's case at the UN. He was, however, unable to have Abdullah released until 1964, so strong was cabinet and intelligence opposition.

◆

While the Indian and state governments were preoccupied with politics inside the valley, external pressures led Jammu and Kashmir to attack on another front. In 1950, at the same time as it expanded its influence to the southeast in Korea, Maoist China announced its intention of integrating Tibet to its southwest, invading in 1951. Nehru opened negotiations over Tibet with Mao and Zhou Enlai that spanned the best part of the 1950s. In 1954, the two countries signed a seventeen-point agreement under which India recognized China's 'historical sovereignty' over Tibet and China agreed to negotiations for Tibetan autonomy. But the northwestern and eastern boundaries between India and Chinese-held Tibet remained undemarcated. In 1959, the Dalai Lama fled to India, provoking Mao's ire. There were skirmishes between Indian and Chinese troops in Ladakh.

The vast plateau of Aksai Chin acquired new strategic importance with the Chinese push to annex Tibet. Formally a part of the British empire under an agreement with the Tibetan government in 1865 (the Johnson Line), the plateau offered the most viable route between Tibet and the western Chinese province of Xinjiang. Nehru considered allowing China transit access through Aksai Chin following talks with Mao's prime minister, Zhou Enlai, but met with fierce opposition from within his government and party as well as from opposition parties such as the Jan Sangh and the newly formed Swatantra Party. China's People's Liberation Army (PLA) built the road anyway, and moved farther to set up posts in the Aksai Chin region. Combined with the flight of the Dalai Lama, these moves set alarm bells ringing in Ladakh, which echoed in New Delhi. When the Indian media revealed that the Indian government had known of the PLA-built road for two years but suppressed the information fearing public outcry, criticism of the government's seeming passivity rose to a crescendo.

Advised by his disastrously non-military Defence Minister V. K. Krishna Menon, who had defended India's case on Kashmir at the UN in 1957 with the longest speech ever made at that body, Nehru adopted a 'Forward Policy' to establish Indian military posts in Aksai Chin. The posts were thinly manned and armed, and the Defence Ministry made few arrangements to stockpile the arms and supplies that would be required in the event of conflict. Krishna Menon, Mullick and Kaul, who was now chief of general staff of the Indian Army, were convinced that China would not attack India and assured Nehru of it. They ignored General Thimayya, who warned that China could well respond militarily over a much less threatening issue, such as the Indian decision to bring the North Eastern Frontier Areas (that later became Arunachal Pradesh) under the Indian Army instead of border guards.

Thimayya, who retired in 1961, came closer to predicting the Chinese reaction than Krishna Menon or Kaul. In October 1962, China responded to the Forward Policy by attacking India on both the northern and eastern fronts and won the war within four weeks, despite the US airlift of military equipment to India (made in the hope of winning Indian support for the Atlantic alliance). The PLA seized Aksai Chin and China was henceforth on the border of Ladakh. Jammu and Kashmir lost another part of the state, one that had been an invaluable security bulwark.

◆

The China debacle brought Kashmir back into international focus. Having supported India with military aid during the war, in its aftermath, the US helped India embark on a rearmament programme. At the same time, US and British envoys visited India to urge renewed talks on Kashmir with Pakistan. According to J. N. Dixit, who was to become India's National Security Adviser

(NSA) forty years later, both Averell Harriman for the US and Duncan Sandys for Britain advised Nehru to consider ceding territory.[31] Harriman was anxious to assure Nehru that the US did not seek Indian concessions to Pakistan as a quid pro quo for US aid. Both he and Sandys were equally anxious that India–Pakistan tensions should not drive Pakistan into a Chinese embrace. Pakistan's military leaders had moved to strengthen ties with China after India's defeat in the 1962 war. A Pakistan–China alliance was also deeply feared in India, since the country could then face attack on multiple fronts.

Pakistan had suffered the first of its many military coups in 1958, when General Ayub Khan took over after Governor General Mirza dismissed Feroze Khan Noon's administration. This was the third civilian administration that Mirza dismissed in the short span of two years before he was himself ousted by Ayub Khan. Noon had, in talks with Nehru, suggested that the two countries rationalize the Radcliffe Line dividing East Pakistan and West Bengal that left princely enclaves stranded on either side. This goal was eventually achieved almost sixty years later, when Bangladesh and India signed a historic land boundary agreement in 2015. An earlier agreement had been signed in 1974 but not ratified by India.

Under US and British pressure, Ayub Khan offered India a joint defence agreement in 1959, after Indian and Chinese troops clashed in Ladakh following the Dalai Lama's flight to India. Famously retorting 'Against whom?', Nehru responded in 1960 by repeating his 1949 suggestion of a no-war pact. In the same year, the two leaders signed an agreement accepting international arbitration over water sharing from common rivers, in Punjab and Kashmir (the Indus Waters Treaty). The World Bank stood guarantor to the treaty, which has held firm to this day.

Nehru's no-war pact proposal foundered on Khan's insistence that the two countries should first settle their differences over Kashmir. It was briefly revived in 1963 after US pressure led India and Pakistan to agree to talks, which began at the foreign minister level in December 1962. Indian foreign minister Swaran Singh and Pakistani foreign minister Zulfikar Ali Bhutto were tasked with defining an international border in Jammu and Kashmir and deciding next steps to the 1949 ceasefire, comprising troop dispositions.

Two days before the talks commenced, the Pakistani government announced it would soon ink an agreement with China to demarcate the border between China and Pakistan-administered Gilgit and Baltistan, which India claimed as part of disputed Kashmir. Nehru had raised the border issue with Ayub in 1960, having heard rumours of Pakistan–China negotiations. He appears to have dismissed the possibility of the two countries reaching an agreement, saying in parliament that Ayub knew next to nothing about where the border should lie. For the Indian delegation, Pakistan's announcement cast a pall over the talks, though both countries persisted with them for the next five months. Bhutto rehashed the arguments that Zafrullah Khan had advanced at the UN fifteen years earlier. According to Dixit, Swaran Singh tied him up in legal technicalities, leading an exasperated Bhutto to exclaim, 'the objective of the Sardarji was not to negotiate but to exhaust'.[32] After six months of circling debate, the talks ended in May 1963.

The Pakistani diplomat Shamshad Ahmad, who was to become foreign secretary in 1997, had a more charitable description of the 1962–63 talks. They 'were the only high level India–Pakistan negotiations', he said, 'dedicated to exploring a political solution' of the Kashmir dispute, which, as both sides agreed, was to be 'honourable, equitable and final'. Pakistan, he continued, was prepared to accept the partition of the state but 'urged that territorial division should take into account the composition of the population of the State, control of rivers, requirements of defence and other considerations'. The Indian delegation accepted partition, too, but argued that it 'should take into account geographic, administrative and other considerations, and that the settlement should involve the least disturbance to the life and welfare of the people'.[33]

In other words, talks stuck on the same point that had bedevilled them since 1947: Pakistan's adherence to the ethnic principle of Muslim majority, and India's pragmatic insistence that a settlement should codify the situation on the ground.

Swaran Singh also floated the idea of softening the ceasefire line to allow Kashmiris to trade and travel with each other. According to Rajeshwar Dayal, then Indian high commissioner to Pakistan, Nehru and he had discussed the idea earlier when Dayal briefed the prime minister on talks with Ayub. Ayub, said Dayal, felt that continuing talks between him and Nehru would, over time, smooth tensions and make a settlement more possible. 'With the easing of the Kashmir situation, trade could have opened up, helping to ease the financial burden on India while creating a new and profitable market in Pakistan for Kashmiri goods.' Pakistani tourism in Kashmir, Dayal added, would also help; to prevent misuse, the government could regulate visas and keep 'the activities of visitors closely monitored'.[34] Though Nehru listened carefully, Dayal's proposals did not surface in his talks with Ayub. Forty-five years later they were to become the core of a Kashmir peace process.

♦

Back in the valley, there was more political change to come. The same month that the Swaran Singh–Bhutto talks ended, the Congress, disturbed at losing three important parliamentary by-elections, decided that half a dozen union ministers and state chief ministers should resign to devote themselves to party work. Though Bakshi was not a member of the Congress, Nehru had become increasingly concerned at the corruption of his administration. He accepted Bakshi's resignation, offered in a fit of bravado along with other chief ministers. The announcement caused consternation in the valley, where by now Bakshi commanded the loyalty of a large number of National Conference members. Delhi was constrained to accept his nominee and loyalist Khwaja Shamsuddin as chief minister.

Within months of the lacklustre Shamsuddin's takeover from Bakshi, he was embroiled in a serious crisis. In December 1963, the Mo-i-Muqaddas relic, believed to be a hair of the Prophet kept the Hazratbal shrine, was reported stolen. There was uproar in the valley, where demonstrations were held daily. Women in black came out to wail in the downtown Maisuma area of Srinagar, and cars that did not fly black flags were not allowed to ply. A citizens' group was formed to recover the relic. Called the Action Committee, it was the first time that descendants of the pro-India Abdullah and the pro-Pakistan Mirwaiz Yusuf worked together: both Abdullah's son Farooq and Yusuf Shah's nephew, Mirwaiz Mohammad Farooq, were members. Mirwaiz Farooq split the Action Committee soon after to form the Awami Action Committee. The committee played an important role in preventing religious anger from becoming a political onslaught on the state government. But uproar in the valley quieted only a month later, when the relic was recovered by Indian intelligence and local clerics certified that it was the original Mo-i-Muqaddas.

In the wake of the Mo-i-Muqaddas crisis, Khwaja Shamsuddin stepped down and G. M. Sadiq, a socialist who had headed the constituent assembly under Bakshi but fell out with him, took over. After Bakshi's administration began to fall into disrepute, Sadiq had founded a splinter party called the Democratic National Conference in 1957, along with fellow socialists D. P. Dhar and Mir Qasim. In fact, according to Qasim, Nehru flew to Srinagar to try to patch up things between Bakshi and the trio, but they foiled him by announcing their new party a day before he arrived.[35] When the three met Maulana Azad to plead their case, he told them that in Nehru's opinion, Sadiq was a poor replacement for Bakshi, who still carried the support of a large proportion of Kashmiris, despite his many faults. As Abdullah said, Bakshi 'had a thorough understanding of the people's psychology despite his lack of a proper education, and was peerless in his public dealings'.[36]

Though Sadiq, Dhar and Qasim failed in their bid for power in 1957, they succeeded six years later, when Sadiq, with assiduous lobbying by Dhar, got Delhi to accept him as chief minister. A defiant Bakshi, reportedly with the support of a majority of state legislators, almost succeeded in toppling Sadiq through a no-confidence vote, but the sadr-i-riyasat prorogued the assembly and Bakshi was arrested under the Defence of India Rules, to be released a few months later. He made a brief foray into state politics in 1967, and was elected to the Indian parliament as a National Conference candidate in the general election that year.

Sadiq began well, restoring civil liberties, cracking down on corruption and bolstering the civil administration to act against police high-handedness. While he consolidated power, however, an ailing Nehru, cast down by yet another failure of talks with Pakistan, returned to his view that the only man who could negotiate lasting peace for the state was Sheikh Abdullah. In April 1964, with Sadiq's nod, Nehru succeeded in having Abdullah released and the two agreed that Abdullah would go to Pakistan on a peace mission, carrying an invitation from Nehru to Ayub Khan to visit Delhi for talks. By this point, Abdullah had come to the view that the most feasible solution for Kashmir was a confederation with India and Pakistan. 'It is already well known that while agreeing to go to Pakistan to explore the possibility of finding a solution, the Sheikh argued that a confederation of India, Pakistan and Kashmir was the best way to cut the Gordian knot,' commented the veteran Indian journalist Inder Malhotra who accompanied Abdullah on his visit to Pakistan in May. 'This was unacceptable to Nehru, who said that a federation was the maximum he could agree to.'[37]

Nevertheless, Malhotra added, Abdullah did raise the confederation idea with Ayub Khan, who characterized the proposal as 'absurd' in his memoir *Friends, Not Masters*. 'I told him plainly that we would have nothing to do with it. It is curious that whereas we were seeking the salvation of Kashmiris, they had been forced to mention an idea which, if pursued, would lead to our enslavement. It was clear that this was what Mr. Nehru had told them to say to us,' Ayub wrote.[38] According to Abdullah, it was Khan who raised the confederation issue, asking Abdullah what that idea was.

Nehru died on 27 May while Abdullah was in Muzaffarabad where he was greeted with rapture. Though he met all the leaders, the only one with whom he held a private conversation was

Mirwaiz Yusuf, who told Abdullah that he was now 'disappointed' with Pakistan and would support Abdullah in a struggle for independence. He may have been the only person in a semi-official position to express this view. At no point, Ibrahim averred in his autobiography, did the government of Pakistan-administered Kashmir contemplate or support the option of independence though it was mooted. Independence was not economically feasible, said Ibrahim, since the statelet would always be dependent on Pakistan.

After addressing a mammoth public demonstration in Muzaffarabad, Abdullah flew back for Nehru's last rites, accompanied by Bhutto. Returning to the valley after Nehru's funeral and now with the Plebiscite Front, he focused on building his new party.

In early 1965, Sadiq agreed to extend Articles 356 and 357 of the Indian Constitution to Jammu and Kashmir. The two articles allowed the Indian president to proclaim an emergency in any state on account of a breakdown of the constitutional machinery. Sadiq also introduced a bill in the state assembly to change the title of prime minister of Jammu and Kashmir to chief minister, and of sadr-i-riyasat to governor, as in other Indian states, allowing the governor to be appointed by the Indian president rather than elected by the state assembly. Both changes altered the status of Jammu and Kashmir as agreed in the Delhi Agreement and Article 370.

At the same time, the Congress formally opened a branch in Jammu and Kashmir with the backdoor support of Sadiq, Dhar and Qasim, who announced that the National Conference stood dissolved and merged into the Congress. Abdullah immediately denounced the extension of further articles of the Indian Constitution as undermining the state's autonomy in his Friday speech at Hazratbal and called for a social boycott of anyone joining the Congress. Bakshi refused to accept the dissolution of the National Conference and headed its rebel wing.

Soon after, Abdullah and Beg decided to go on Haj with their wives, and from there on a tour of Arab and European countries. There was considerable debate in Delhi over whether he should be allowed to go. Intelligence sources warned he might use the opportunity to canvass independence, but India's new prime minister, Lal Bahadur Shastri, who had worked with Abdullah as Nehru's interlocutor, overruled them. Though Abdullah's tour was private, he was received as a state guest in Arab capitals and held extensive discussions with President Gamal Abdel Nasser of Egypt and other heads of Arab states on Kashmir's future. The climax came in Algeria, where he met Zhou Enlai. According to Abdullah, he and Beg asked Zhou about the border agreement with Pakistan under which Pakistan ceded the Shaksgam valley of Jammu and Kashmir to China. Zhou clarified that the agreement stipulated that when an India–Pakistan settlement was achieved, the agreement would be renegotiated with whichever power headed the state. He also invited Abdullah to visit China.

But in the aftermath of war with China, and the Indian experience of Zhou during talks on Tibet, his invitation to Abdullah raised hackles in Delhi. When Abdullah went on to hold public meetings across Britain on the plebiscite issue, most of them with diaspora Kashmiris from Poonch and Mirpur, the union and state governments responded aggressively, imprisoning hundreds of Plebiscite Front cadre. On his return, Abdullah was arrested and interned, first in Ootacamund and then in Kodaikanal.

Chapter V

BETWEEN WARS: 1965–1971

The third arrest of Sheikh Abdullah galvanized the Plebiscite Front. Incendiary posters appeared across Kashmir and the demand for self-determination, used by some as a euphemism for independence and by others as the cry for a referendum, gathered steam. As unrest threatened to engulf the valley once again, the Pakistani government concluded the time was ripe to foment an uprising. Bhutto was still smarting from the failure of the 1963 talks and sore that Indian leaders did not take the opportunity of his presence at Nehru's funeral to discuss restarting them. Together with Pakistan's foreign secretary Aziz Ahmed, he pushed Ayub Khan to massively expand the small-scale guerrilla infiltration that Akbar Khan had initiated in the mid-1950s. Ayub, they said, must direct the Pakistan Army to send raiders into Kashmir.

Ayub was initially reluctant. He believed an uprising might well lead to a military confrontation between India and Pakistan and was not convinced that Pakistan would win. His financial advisers told him a war would strain the economy that he had built to a 6.8 per cent growth over the past five years with US and British aid. He had just won the January 1965 presidential election against Jinnah's sister, Fatima, by the skin of his teeth and the aid of Pakistan's second constitution, which he promulgated in 1962. The 1962 constitution established a presidential system in Pakistan, with the president to be elected by 80,000 'Basic Democrats', members of local bodies that would in turn be elected by groups of 800–1,000 citizens. As quasi-government employees, the Basic Democrats owed allegiance to Ayub Khan and could be influenced to vote in his favour. The election was widely seen as rigged by Ayub; it was alleged that Fatima Jinnah won the popular vote. Her nomination as the rival presidential candidate had come as an unpleasant shock to Ayub. The public outcry that greeted the election results shook him further.

Yet, Ayub Khan had also regained confidence with a successful visit to China in March. When the US cancelled his scheduled meeting with President John F. Kennedy in retaliation for his China visit, he turned to Premier Aleksey Kosygin, signing trade and oil exploration treaties with the Soviet Union. Bhutto had negotiated both foreign policy gains, and an indebted Ayub was inclined to trust Bhutto's assurance that India would not counter by crossing the border into Pakistan; after all, India had desisted from doing so in 1947–48.

Ayub Khan was in any case annoyed with Nehru, who, he said, treated him with contempt. At his 1960 meeting with Nehru, he had suggested that Pakistan could seek a settlement based on partition rather than a plebiscite and asked Nehru to suggest possible partition lines. In 1963, Bhutto and Swaran Singh discussed rationalizing the ceasefire line to make it more defensible. Nehru, Ayub felt, should have done more to follow up on these openings. In parallel, however, Ayub's administration seized on the Moi-Muqaddas crisis to implement Akbar Khan's earlier proposal to bring Kashmiris across the ceasefire line and train them as guerrillas. The plan failed: few Kashmiris were willing to take up the offer. Ayub decided to implement Bhutto's far more ambitious proposal, in which the Pakistan Army would play the lead role rather than Kashmiris.

Asked to come up with an operational plan, Pakistan's chief of army staff, General Muhammad Musa, and Major General Akhtar Hussain Malik, commander of the Pakistan Army's 12th Division into which the 'Azad Army' had been absorbed, dusted off an earlier proposal titled Operation Gibraltar. The proposal outlined a three-stage operation in which infiltrators would conceal themselves amongst villagers to sabotage military targets and disrupt communications; meanwhile they would distribute arms to local recruits and spark a guerrilla movement that would eventually lead to a public uprising.

Operation Gibraltar was basically a rehash of the 1947 invasion, this time with a far greater number of fighters. Nine separate forces of combined army troops and volunteers were created under Malik's command, named after famed and feared Arab, Mongol and Ottoman generals such as Ghaznavi, Tariq and Salahuddin. Estimates of the total guerrilla force vary. India later put the figure at 30,000–40,000, Pakistan claimed it was no more than 5,000–7,000, and independent sources, including local ones, suggested it was around 15,000 (8,000 regular troops and 7,000 volunteers).

The nine forces were assigned to nine strategic regions of the state: Srinagar–valley, Mendhar–Rajouri, Kargil–Drass, Nowshera–Sundarbani, Bandipura–Sonarwain, Qazinag–Naugam, Tithwal–Tangdhar, Gurez and Kel-Minimarg. Crossing the thinly manned border, they were to entrench themselves in these regions until 9 August, the date of Abdullah's arrest in 1953, which the Plebiscite Front planned to mark with a strike demanding his release. Pakistani troops would cash in on the strike, seize government installations and proclaim a liberation government of Jammu and Kashmir.

As in 1947, infiltration first began into Jammu province. The guerrillas came in July 1965, led by men that survivors called 'Razakaars', an Urdu word for volunteers that was to become infamous in the 1972 East Pakistan war. The Razakaars were mostly Poonchis and Mirpuris from across the Line of Control who spoke the same language and wore the same dress as their counterparts in the Poonch and Rajouri districts of Jammu province. Some were volunteers but many were former and some current soldiers. With a relatively soft border between divided Poonch, they came in the thousands. Overnight, said journalist Zafar Choudhary, who conducted interviews about the 1965 war forty years later, they were able to take over local government and police offices and establish a parallel administration.

Interviewees told Choudhary that there was little local protest because the Razakaars were able to convince the residents of Poonch and Rajouri that their districts would soon go to Pakistan. Persuasion was not difficult: the districts were barely governed and there was no one to defend against an armed force numbering several thousand. Rumours of an impending partition were rife. Poonch had been partitioned once already, by the ceasefire line of 1949, and the abortive Bhutto–Swaran Singh talks had discussed the partition of Jammu in 1964, only a year before the Razakaar invasion. The UN Commission, too, raised the question of whether a solution might be found by further partitioning Jammu to cede its Muslim-majority districts to Pakistan. For many, the Razakaars ended the painful uncertainty in which the Muslims of these border districts lived.[1]

A napping Indian Army and a clueless state government did not discover the intrusion until weeks later. On 5 August, a shepherd boy in Tanmarg reported the presence of outsiders to the local police, telling them that strangers had suddenly arrived and were offering bribes for information. By this time, as the Jammu interviews revealed, thousands of Pakistan Army troops and guerrillas had infiltrated across the ceasefire line.

Though the Pakistani troops and guerrillas conducted stray acts of sabotage of roads and bridges, the state and union governments did not suspect their origin at first. Their attention was directed elsewhere. The Indian and Pakistani navies had just drawn down a conflict over the waters of the Rann of Kutch between Balochistan and Gujarat, which the two governments finally decided to refer to an international tribunal at British prime minister Harold Wilson's intercession. Kashmir was still in ferment following Abdullah's arrest. Preoccupied with the Kutch dispute and the internal politics of the valley, Delhi and Srinagar did not initially realize that the infiltrators were Pakistani; they thought the stray acts of sabotage were by disgruntled Kashmiris. The UN's military observers too did not report the infiltration; indeed, they appear not to have noticed it. Eventually, it was a shepherd boy who tipped the union and state governments to the fact that they faced a large-scale invasion akin to 1947.

Once discovered, the Indian Army began with a counter-insurgency campaign within the state, as Bhutto had predicted. His further prediction that Kashmiris would rise in revolt proved, however, to be misplaced. Though some Plebiscite Front cadre joined the invaders, the party kept its distance and the general public of the valley did not rise in revolt. On the contrary, many in the valley caught and handed over Pakistani guerrillas to local police or Indian security forces.

India's counter-insurgency gains led Pakistani commanders to move to their backup plan, Operation Grand Slam. The operation involved crossing the international border to Akhnoor from where they had direct access to Jammu city, while deploying air power against Indian troops and bases. As Ayub had feared, the two countries went to war again. Now India crossed the border to Lahore and deployed its air power in turn and, by September, both armies had won some territory and lost some. India's gains were greater than Pakistan's—the Indian Army controlled around 1,140 kilometres of Pakistan-held territories including parts of Poonch and the vicinity of Sialkot, Sindh and Lahore, as against the Pakistan Army's gain of around 330 kilometres in the vital Chhamb area of Jammu and Punjab.

Military analysts argue that India's position in mid-September was such that the Indian Army could have won a decisive victory. But China's entry into the conflict, with an accusation that India was building forward posts in the disputed territory to its northeast, opened the threat of conflict on another front, this time by a larger and better equipped force than had defeated the Indian Army less than three years earlier. Under UN pressure to agree a ceasefire, and a US and British arms embargo on both countries, India's prime minister Shastri asked his chief of army staff if India could win the war with Pakistan. He was told the air force was close to exhausting its ammunition, though it was later discovered that only 15–20 per cent had been used. Under this advice, he agreed to negotiate a ceasefire with Pakistan.

On the other side, Ayub Khan, facing possible defeat and having exhausted over 80 per cent of the Pakistan air force's ammunition, was willing to comply. According to his biographer, Altaf Gauhar, Ayub secretly visited China to seek military support on 19 September and was assured of it by Zhou Enlai, with the proviso that Pakistan would have to be prepared for a long war in which the country might lose some of its territories, including Lahore.² Zhou's proviso made a mockery of his pledge of support and might have been added at Soviet intercession. Apparently, Kosygin had sent Mao a message that China should stay out of the war. The threat to Lahore was a price that no Pakistani leader would pay. Ayub had already replaced Malik with General Yahya Khan when Indian troops were getting close to Lahore.

Premier Kosygin now adopted a two-pronged policy to edge the Soviet Union into the role of an honest broker. At the UN Security Council, the Soviet delegate vetoed a resolution reiterating the call for a political settlement on Kashmir, to placate India. The UN's focus, he said, had to be on a ceasefire. At the same time, to rescue Pakistan from its quagmire, Soviet interlocutors pushed Shastri to agree to a return to the status quo ante. Shastri and Ayub Khan agreed to a ceasefire on 22 September. Four months later, at a meeting in Tashkent hosted by Kosygin in January 1966, they declared that troops would withdraw within a month to the positions they had held before 5 August 1965. Tanmarg's shepherd boy could have little imagined that the date of his warning would become the official date of the war's commencement. The Jammu intrusions of a month earlier were brushed under the carpet.

Declaring that the Indian prime minister and the Pakistani president had both agreed to 'discourage any propaganda directed against the other country' and 'encourage propaganda which promotes the development of friendly relations', the Tashkent Declaration bound India and Pakistan to resolve their disputes through peaceful negotiation, to work together for the return of refugees and refugee property, set up joint bodies to oversee these commitments, and continue talks.³ Few of its clauses, except for withdrawal, were implemented.

The 1965 war lasted six weeks and both countries lost. Pakistan's war aims were defeated, and India had to return its war gains, including the strategic Haji Pir pass that connected Poonch to Uri and was used by Pakistani invaders in 1947–48. India's control of Haji Pir would have made future Pakistani attack on the valley near impossible, but an India dependent on US food aid was in no position to bargain. Shastri died of a heart attack the day the Tashkent Agreement was announced and Indian criticism of the agreement was drowned in the public wave of sympathy for the government that followed. His death came within eight months of Nehru's; the country had lost the last of its founding fathers.

In Pakistan, public outcry mounted to the point that Ayub Khan was forced to step down in 1969, to be replaced by General Yahya Khan. Throughout the short war, Ayub's administration had fed the media stories of glorious victories—mosques, markets and tea shops resounded with patriotic songs. The war's ignominious end came as a shock to Pakistanis fired with war fervour. There were protest demonstrations in all the country's major cities, many orchestrated by Bhutto. Reading the writing on the wall, Bhutto resigned from Ayub's cabinet and founded the Pakistan People's Party (PPP) in 1967 on an anti-Tashkent plank. The army leadership, he alleged, had betrayed the country to its 'archenemy India', a phrase popularly used by US and British strategists. Ayub later remarked it had been an 'unnecessary' conflict.

◆

What impact did the six-week war have on Kashmir? One immediate and overall effect was to tighten the borders on both sides. Up until 1965, the international border between the two countries and along the ceasefire line was relatively loosely manned; indeed, a free trade market flourished in its interstices. After the war, both India and Pakistan stationed a large number of troops along their borders, and ease of movement as well as communication ceased. On the Pakistani side of the border and ceasefire line, a new communal element crept in. Suddenly, large signs in Urdu appeared welcoming all Muslims to 'the land of Islam'. I saw the signs on the Poonch ceasefire line in 2010; they are still there today.

The greatest impact of the war was on Jammu. Pakistani forces had thrust 160 kilometres into the province. Their conquests in the Chhamb sector left over a quarter of a million internally displaced in Jammu against 20,000 in the valley. The state government struggled to house and feed them. According to contemporary accounts, local residents stepped into the breach, opening their homes to the displaced.

While the state government struggled to cope, there was a second flight of refugees from and into Jammu. Muslims, mostly from Poonch and Rajouri, fled to Pakistan-held territories of the former princely state, and Pakistani Hindus and Sikhs, under communal backlash from Pakistan's perceived defeat, fled to Jammu. Most of the latter were resettled in mainland India and over time gained citizenship rights, but some, mostly Sikh, families remained in Jammu as refugees. Of the estimated 100,000 Muslims from Poonch and Rajouri who crossed over to Pakistan-administered Kashmir during the war, over 60,000 returned after the Tashkent Agreement; they accused the Pakistani government of leaving them stranded without aid.[4] Returnees often found neighbours in possession of their lands. Several had been proclaimed collaborators with the Razakaars and were wanted by the state police and the Indian Army. It took years for these problems to gradually dissipate.

Politically, the impact of the war was negative in the valley and across the Line of Control. Kashmiris on both sides of the divided state began to feel India and Pakistan had dragged them into yet another inconclusive war. But it had a counter-intuitive effect in Jammu, where the Muslims who remained began to seek greater integration into the regional politics of Jammu as well as directly with India. There was already considerable resentment at valley domination in the province. Since Abdullah's days, there had never been more than one Jammu minister in the state's cabinet, though the province's population was almost as large as Kashmir's. Abdullah himself had been accused of exacerbating a communal divide in the province in 1948, when he divided Udhampur to create the Muslim-majority district of Doda. It was the only new district to be established in the state. Employment, too, was a sore point. Kashmiri Muslims now filled the bulk of government jobs in the valley, but in Jammu most government jobs were still held by Hindu Dogras.

Neglected by Kashmir's political leaders and unsure of their position in Jammu, Jammu Muslims began to look to Indian national political parties for support and to regional political participation as a means of security. They found common cause with Jammu's liberal and socialist Hindus who had advanced the demand for regional autonomy since the early 1950s, arguing that Article 370 must be a part of Jammu and Kashmir's constitution, but autonomy for the state should be accompanied by devolution to its three regions.

A key leader of the Jammu autonomy movement, the prolific political writer and activist Balraj Puri first discussed regional aspirations with Nehru and Abdullah in 1949. Telling the two leaders that regional autonomy was the best way to integrate Jammu with Kashmir and would take the wind out of the Parishad's sails, he received a sympathetic hearing. Both Nehru and Abdullah referred to regional devolution in 1953, Nehru announcing on 2 July that the state government 'was considering [giving] autonomy to its regions', and Bakshi saying the next day that 'Sheikh Abdullah has consented to the proposed scheme of autonomy for the constituent units of the state'.[5] Despite these statements, no action was taken, partly because Abdullah was arrested a month later but chiefly because valley politicians did not wish to share power, as their continuing inaction through the decades was to show.

On being elected Abdullah's successor by the National Conference, Bakshi, too, declared his support for regional autonomy. Soon after, the state's constituent assembly created a subcommittee on the issue, composed of Dhar, Qasim and Dogra. They recommended, in Puri's words, 'a substantial measure of autonomy for each region', including the powers to tax and legislate. But when the state's constitution was adopted in 1956, these recommendations found no place.

By this point, Puri had left the National Conference. Most of the party's Jammu members quit along with him to express their disappointment at its failure to recognize Jammu's aspirations. Puri joined the newly-founded Praja Socialist Party, whose mentors were Jayaprakash Narayan and Asoke Mehta. He contested the

1962 assembly election on the plank of autonomy for Jammu, but lost. Despite its growing corruption, the National Conference under Bakshi—who had developed ties in the province when he set up the party's Jammu branch—still promised a more equal security for Hindus, Sikhs and Muslims. Small or new parties, however secular or communal, could not promise the same. In the 1962 election, the National Conference won 27 of the 30 seats allocated to Jammu, and the Praja Parishad won the remaining 3.

The demand for regional autonomy increased after the 1965 war, this time with support from Muslims. Puri hoped that Sadiq, who had recently displaced Bakshi and had been a member of the assembly's subcommittee on autonomy for the state's three regions, would push constitutional change. His hope gained ground when Sadiq 'frankly admitted' in 1967, 'the tensions existing between the two regions of Jammu and Kashmir and stressed the need to find a way to resolve them.'[6] Yet, when Sadiq returned to power after winning the 1967 assembly election on a Congress platform, he turned against the demand. In the months to follow, Sadiq, the Congress party, the Plebiscite Front and the Jan Sangh each separately vilified Puri for seeking self-rule for Jammu and Ladakh within the broader framework of the state's autonomy.

As Puri commented, they made strange bedfellows given that their goals were so different, but each had a reason. The Congress, led by Indira Gandhi, had just made its debut in Kashmir and adhered to Nehru's 1948 dictum that the 'prize we are fighting for is the valley'. With Sadiq's support, they hoped to turn the valley in favour of merger. The Plebiscite Front rejected the state constitution entirely and would not support a demand for constitutional amendment. The Jan Sangh was full steam ahead on merger and saw regional autonomy as at best a distraction and at worst a way of reinforcing the state's autonomy.

Watching the situation, a troubled Jayaprakash Narayan wrote to Indira Gandhi in 1966, urging Abdullah's release. Indira had taken over as prime minister following Shastri's death and turned her attention to Kashmir within months, but Narayan was not among the people she consulted. Saying, 'We profess democracy but rule by force in Kashmir', Narayan added, 'Kashmir has distorted India's image for the world as nothing else has done... No matter how loud and how long we shout that Kashmir is an inalienable part of India and that therefore there was no Kashmir problem, the fact remains that a very serious and urgent problem faces and will continue to face us in that part of the country.'[7]

Only Abdullah could now make peace, he asserted. 'Could the Kashmiri people be enthused over autonomy within the Union? I think they could, with Sheikh Saheb frankly telling them that that was the only way they could save their territory becoming a battleground for India and Pakistan.' Abdullah had indeed flirted with independence, Narayan conceded, but 'I believe he is realist enough to realize that (a) no solution of Kashmir could ever be accepted by India, after the last war with Pakistan, that involved de-accession of the State, or any part of it, from the Union, and (b) an independent state in that part of the world could have little chance of survival in the face of Pakistan's consuming hunger for the Valley of Kashmir and the emergence of the Chinese power in the region—a power that cannot be expected to exercise self-denial in relation to its weak neighbours.' Prophetically, Narayan concluded: 'To think that we will eventually wear down the people and force them to accept at least passively the Union is to delude ourselves. That might conceivably have happened had Kashmir not been geographically located where it is. In its present location and with seething discontent among the people, it would never be left in peace by Pakistan.'

Within the valley, resentment at Abdullah's rearrest and Sadiq's extension of various articles of the Indian Constitution remained strong. The state already faced a problem of the educated unemployed. As Sadiq reproachfully pointed out to Indira Gandhi, industrial investment in the province was near zero. Bakshi's free education had created a class of young Kashmiris who aspired to urban and professional jobs but there were very few to be had. Industry was not prepared to invest in a conflict area, said a rueful Inder Kumar Gujral, deputed by Indira Gandhi to mobilize financing for the state's economic development. Gujral could only get two factories for Jammu and Kashmir, and that too by a reluctant public sector. Restive youth turned to the Plebiscite Front and it inspired two armed offshoots, one in the valley and the other across the ceasefire line.

In late 1965, members of the Young Men's League, founded by Beg as a youth branch of the Plebiscite Front, formed an armed group that called itself Al Fatah, after the Palestinian militia of the same name. Mobilized by a Front activist from Srinagar, Ghulam Rasool Zahgeer, Al Fatah claimed that Pakistani intelligence had offered them large funds and training to support Kashmir's accession to Pakistan—an offer they rejected because they stood for independence. But they did receive funding from Pakistan via Pakistan-administered Kashmir, and many of their members spent time there training. Al Fatah was implicated in a series of botched attacks from 1967–70, mostly in Srinagar. In 1967, Zahgeer and a small team of chosen guerrillas attempted to murder a Central Reserve Police Force (CRPF) jawan in the Nawakadal locality of the city, and in 1968 they mounted an unsuccessful raid on the armoury of the National Cadet Corps in Srinagar's Islamia College. In January 1971, when the group robbed the Jammu and Kashmir Bank's university branch in Hazratbal, twenty-two of them were arrested, including Fazal Haq Qureshi. Beg led the defence team and Qureshi went on to negotiate a Government of India–militia ceasefire in 2000.

Abdullah was released in 1968. Soon after, he convened a States People's Conference to which all the Jammu and Kashmir and national political groups were invited. Puri, who founded a Jammu Autonomy Forum in 1967, bargained hard with the conference conveners to put regional aspirations on the conference agenda. Supported by Prem Nath Bazaz, he had his way, and the second conference convention in 1970 issued a resolution in favour of regional devolution. The Union government's Gajendragadkar Commission, formed to consider the issue, ended in a whimper and, in November 1968, its members recommended statutory regional development boards instead of the political devolution that Puri's Autonomy Forum sought. The state government accepted the commission's relatively innocuous recommendations, but did little to implement them.

The conference's discussion of autonomy was immediately overtaken by references to India and Pakistan. Addressing the conference, Narayan repeated the argument he had made to Indira Gandhi in 1966—that a resolution could be found within the framework of accession to India. He was met with boos and jeers from some in his audience. When he added that Pakistan had ceased to be a party to the Kashmir dispute, the Young Men's League issued a fierce denunciation: 'We are at loss to understand as to how and on what grounds Mr. Narain [sic] has made this statement which is absolutely incorrect and far from the reality,' their statement said. 'India signed [the] Tashkent Declaration... UN Military Observers are still posted in this state after 1965 as they were from [the] 1948 ceasefire agreement. The Kashmir problem is as usual on [the] UN agenda. One-third of Jammu and Kashmir's territory is as usual under the control of Pakistan.'[8] No solution would be lasting without Pakistan's involvement.

◆

In the same years, there was political change in Pakistan-administered Kashmir, too, but of a different order. By this point, the statelet was no longer the place that Sardar Ibrahim had ruled, where no one questioned accession to Pakistan. But the starting point for change was a polity that had essentially remained frozen since the days of the maharaja.

The first set of changes came after Ayub Khan's takeover. Khan dismissed Ibrahim's government in November 1959, appointing K. H. Khurshid, a Kashmiri, in his stead. In 1960, Ayub extended the Basic Democracies Act to the statelet, under which local bodies would be elected. Prefiguring the 1962 Pakistan constitution, the Basic Democracies Act for the statelet laid down that local body members would elect a council which in turn would elect the president. Apart from its power to elect the president, the twenty-four-member council was primarily an advisory body.

Basic Democrats would be divided into two groups of equal

numbers. One, numbering 1,200 people, would be elected by residents of the statelet. The other, also numbering 1,200 people, would be elected by Kashmiri refugees, most of whom lived in Pakistan. Through these refugee representatives, Rawalpindi—then the capital of Pakistan as well as its military headquarters—would have another and, in many ways, more powerful string to influence developments in the statelet, in addition to the Ministry of Kashmir Affairs. Pakistani bureaucrats may be resented in Pakistan-administered Kashmir, but who could naysay Kashmiri refugees? There was an ancillary advantage too. As voters in the statelet, Kashmiri refugees were dispossessed of the right to vote for local bodies in the Pakistani towns where they lived and so could not influence Pakistani politics.

Despite these restrictions, the ruling authorities in the statelet and Pakistan's Ministry of Kashmir Affairs seem not to have been certain of the outcome. Both Abbas and Ibrahim were disqualified from contesting the 1961 election on charges of corruption.

K. H. Khurshid, who was the first president elected under Ayub's 1960 system, soon fell out with the Ministry of Kashmir Affairs, whose officials resented his direct access to Ayub Khan. Ghulam Abbas, who had faced much of the same resentment from ministry officials for his access to Jinnah, made common cause with them when it came to undermining Khurshid. Eventually, Khurshid was compelled to resign without completing his term in August 1965, but not before new rules were introduced that no legislation could be passed or implemented in the statelet without the approval of a chief adviser appointed by Rawalpindi.

Following his resignation, Khurshid allied with Ibrahim and Qayyum Khan to demand a 'responsible government', an elected president and a legislature with powers to enact laws and approve the state's yearly budget. These were demands that had been made of the maharaja forty years earlier.

There was a wave of support for elected government across Poonch, Mirpur and Muzaffarabad, some of which spilt over to Karachi where a significant number of Kashmiri refugees lived. Coinciding with political protests in Pakistan for comprehensive adult franchise to replace Ayub's Basic Democracy, the 'responsible government' demands garnered considerable backing in Pakistan too. In 1969, when General Yahya Khan took over as chief martial law administrator, he pushed the then president of the statelet, Hameed Khan, to resign and appointed retired Brigadier Rahman Khan as interim president. Rahman was to prepare a new constitution and hold fresh elections based on adult franchise. Known as a moderate, he met with Khurshid, Ibrahim and Qayyum to assure them of a more democratic dispensation.

Meanwhile, there were other forces at work. In the same year that Al Fatah was born and similarly inspired by the Plebiscite Front, a small group of diaspora Kashmiris led by an ex-Pakistan Army major, Amanullah Khan, set up a counterpart across the Line of Control. The Amanullah-led Plebiscite Front was to be a political wing. An armed wing, established simultaneously, was called the Jammu and Kashmir National Liberation Front (JKNLF). According to the Muslim Conference leader, Muhammad Saraf, Amanullah's group sought his support but would not agree that the goal should be accession to Pakistan.[9] For the first time, there was an organization in Pakistan-administered Kashmir espousing independence, an idea hitherto whispered only behind closed doors.

Though it was seeded in the statelet, the JKNLF's focus was on the valley. Maqbool Butt, a key founder, had migrated to Pakistan-administered Kashmir in 1958 after Bakshi expanded police powers to arrest and detain for five years without filing charges. Butt claimed that the JKNLF was set up to mount 'an Algerian type struggle to free Kashmiris from Indian occupation'.[10] Given Hindu refugee property by the Pakistani government in Peshawar, where he settled, Butt returned to the valley in June 1966 on a mission to create and train local guerrillas. He was able to cross the ceasefire line despite the strong presence of Indian and Pakistani troops there. In September, he murdered a local policeman in his hometown Handwara, and was arrested. Two years later, he and an associate were sentenced to death for the Handwara murder, but they succeeded in escaping and crossed the

Line of Control again in January 1969. Several of the guerrillas Butt had trained were arrested and imprisoned at the same time.

Soon after his escape, Butt met two young Kashmiris from Srinagar who were in Peshawar on a business trip. The two, Hashim and Ashraf Qureshi, were from a political family. Hashim's father was a member of the pro-Pakistan Political Conference that was founded by breakaway National Conference activist Mohiuddin Karra, but he and his cousin were pro-independence. They had seen the corruption in the Political Conference and other Kashmiri political parties, Hashim wrote later; and Butt's daring escape from prison fired their zeal. Together with Butt, the two cousins hatched a plan to hijack an Indian airliner, demanding the release of JKNLF members from Kashmiri prisons. They returned to Srinagar to put the plan into action in 1970.

Hashim was not as successful as Butt at crossing the ceasefire line undetected, but when he was caught by the Indian Border Security Force (BSF), he talked his way out by offering to act as an agent for them. Released, he and Ashraf proceeded to work on the hijack plan, and in January 1971 they boarded a flight from Jammu to Srinagar with a toy gun and a wooden replica of a grenade. A panicked crew agreed to divert the flight to Lahore, where the Qureshis originally met a rapturous reception, being felicitated by Bhutto and other senior members of his party.[11] Twenty years after, both Hashim and former finance minister turned peace activist, Mubashir Hasan, described to me how the PPP feted the two cousins.

The adulation soured within days. Prime Minister Indira Gandhi refused to release the thirty-six JKNLF guerrillas that the hijackers demanded. She also cancelled Pakistan's overflight rights between its western and eastern wings—the East Pakistani agitation for independence had begun. Pakistan released the passengers of the hijacked plane at US intercession and they returned to India. The plane itself was destroyed when a Pakistani policeman, who arrived with fuel for the arson, told Hashim that Butt had ordered it burned. Soon after, Pakistani authorities arrested the Qureshis and several other JKNLF and Plebiscite Front members on charges of treason. They were accused of conspiring with India's external intelligence organization, the Research and Analysis Wing (R&AW), to put Pakistan in the dock.

Pakistan was already in the worst turmoil it had experienced since partition. There were mounting demands in West Pakistan, led by Bhutto, for Ayub Khan to resign. Across the country, provincial leaders began to demand devolution, led by the Awami League in East Pakistan. In spring 1969, after forcing Ayub to step down, General Yahya Khan became chief martial law administrator and pledged to hold national assembly elections within two years. Held in 1970, the election returned a divided verdict. Bhutto's PPP won close to two-thirds of the seats in West Pakistan and Mujibur Rahman's Awami League swept East Pakistan, winning 160 of its 162 seats. The election results were entirely predictable—the Awami League represented Bengali aspirations and was wildly popular in East Pakistan, whereas West Pakistani political parties were divided between local constituencies—but they threw the Pakistani military into crisis.

West Pakistan dominated East Pakistan politically, economically and militarily from the start. East Pakistani leaders asked repeatedly for this imbalance to be redressed, either through provincial autonomy or through proportional federal representation. But frequent and regular attempts to find a compromise successively failed. West Pakistan's military and civilian leaders were inimical to the idea of provincial autonomy—or even a federation—fearing either might lead to the break-up of Pakistan. The Pakistan Army staged its first coup in 1958, largely because Pakistani politicians had failed to resolve the key problem of how to integrate Pakistan's fractious provinces and, in particular, how to integrate Pakistan's Eastern and Western wings. Suspicion of Bengali aspirations for power-sharing led to the downfall of the country's two Bengali prime ministers, Hussein Suhrawardy and Mohammad Ali Bogra. Suhrawardy had suggested Pakistan be reformed into a federation of two units—East and West Pakistan—and Bogra had revisited Suhrawardy's two-unit proposal (while implementing the 'one unit' policy to integrate West Pakistan's provinces). Both leaders indirectly challenged Punjab's dominance as the richest agricultural and largest troops-contributing province in the country.

Geographic separation and economic and demographic differences ensured that the task of integration was always going to be problematic. The two wings of Pakistan were separated by 1,500 kilometres of Indian territory, which in itself made integration extremely difficult, if not impossible. Then, there were demographic differences. East Pakistan's population was greater than West Pakistan's, and it was predominantly Bengali. By contrast, West Pakistan was formed of four ethnically distinct provinces—Punjab, Sindh, Balochistan, the NWFP and the Federally Administered Tribal Areas (FATA). The population of each was a minority in relation to the Bengalis. In other words, a political system based on 'one man one vote' might lead to Bengali dominance.

Ayub's 1962 constitution made few concessions to East Pakistan. All decisions were concentrated in the hands of the president, and Ayub's first interest was to consolidate West Pakistan. Federal spending brought about a Green Revolution in Punjab and boosted West Pakistan's textile industry. Similar resources were not spent on developing East Pakistan's agricultural base or economic potential. Admittedly, this would have been a much harder task. Rural Bengal had long been much poorer than Punjab and international demand for jute, East Pakistan's principal export, had begun to decline by 1960.

When Suhrawardy's death brought Mujibur Rahman to the helm of the Awami League in 1963, the stage was set for confrontation. It began to build in 1965 with Ayub's declaration of a state of emergency, to which Rahman responded in 1966 by unveiling six points for a federal Pakistan based on provincial autonomy. Rahman's definition of autonomy came perilously close to confederation. His six points stipulated that Pakistan have a new constitution under which the federal government would be responsible only for foreign affairs and defence. East and West Pakistan would have their own currency and separate fiscal accounts. Each federal unit would levy its own taxes, with a constitutionally guaranteed contribution to the federal government. Each unit would control their own foreign exchange earnings. Each would also be entitled to raise its own militia or paramilitary forces.

Ayub interpreted Rahman's demands as tantamount to secession and arrested him in January 1968 on charges of conspiring with India to secede. But Rahman was not the only leader to protest against Ayub's controls. Ayub feared that growing calls for devolution across the country would strengthen Rahman's hand. He tried to mend fences by calling a conference of opposition leaders on the issue and cancelled the state of emergency. His attempts were too little too late for East Pakistani leaders, while they fed West Pakistani fears of being overwhelmed.

After year-long protests across East Pakistan, Rahman was released in 1969. He muted his six points, but his victory in the 1970 election brought earlier suspicions flooding back. Under pressure from Bhutto, Yahya did not convene the national assembly. Rahman, whose party held a majority in the assembly, might have abandoned the idea of a confederation, but he was still wedded to the promise of a federal government. Bhutto convinced Yahya that Rahman's demands were not only anathema for East and West Pakistani unity but that they might be the thin end of the wedge for West Pakistan's internal unity too.

From December 1970 to March 1971, there were hectic negotiations for a compromise between Yahya and Bhutto on one side, and Rahman on the other. They came close to a power-sharing agreement, but Rahman was adamant that a new federal constitution be the starting point for the national assembly's deliberations. While Yahya explored political options, he also prepared for a military solution. By February, opinion in the military had reached a consensus that East Pakistanis should be 'taught a lesson', sufficiently forceful to deter future aspirations to federation. A troops build-up in the East followed.

On 2 March 1971, Rahman announced his intent to 'outline a program for achieving the right of self-determination for the people of Bengal'.[12] There were sporadic clashes between Awami activists and the Pakistan Army, and between Awami activists and

Bihari Muslims who had resettled in East Pakistan after the 1947 partition of India. The Bihari minority looked to the West Pakistani government and army for protection, and volunteered in the thousands for unofficial militias to defend the country against East Pakistani irredentists. Called Razakaars, they engaged in the most brutal massacres of the conflict that followed.

On 6 March, Yahya did a turnabout and announced that the national assembly would meet on 25 March. Last-ditch negotiations followed in which both sides softened their positions considerably. On 15 March, Yahya flew to the East Pakistani capital Dacca (today's Dhaka), and by 20 March a rough compromise had been chalked out. Pakistan would have an interim constitution under which Yahya would continue as the president and head of state until the national assembly drew up a new constitution. The powers of the central legislature would be as provided in the 1962 constitution except for 'certain limitations and modifications to be agreed upon with respect to the Province of East Pakistan'. There would be a central cabinet of ministers and provincial cabinets, selected from the members of the provincial or national assemblies and representatives of the political parties of East and West Pakistan. Martial law would be revoked on the day the provincial cabinets took office, but the president would be able to impose central rule if either provincial government was no longer able to govern.[13]

It looked as if the two sides might yet pull compromise from the jaws of confrontation, and Yahya called Bhutto to Dacca. But Bhutto saw a number of alarming possibilities in the rough agreement between Yahya and Rahman. Specifically, he warned that the Awami League would exercise its 'brute majority' in the national assembly to break up Pakistan. Instead, he said, martial law should be prolonged and the future constitution must be subject to a presidential veto. Negotiations broke down again, and Rahman issued a 'declaration of emancipation' in which he called for mass civil disobedience. A new 'Bangladesh' flag was hoisted over hundreds of public and private buildings all over the country.

Yahya flew back to Islamabad on the evening of 25 March.

The military crackdown in East Pakistan began that same night.

The Qureshis, with their hijack, stepped right into the middle of this high-wire situation. Indira Gandhi's decision to snap overflight rights posed a major obstacle to military supplies for the crackdown in East Pakistan, and Bhutto now accused India of having orchestrated the hijack in order to have a pretext for preventing Pakistani planes from reaching Dacca. Hashim and Ashraf were arrested and charged, along with Maqbool Butt and four others, on charges of conspiring against Pakistan. In his statement, Butt confirmed that he had plotted the hijack along with the Qureshis and that their purpose had been to free JKNLF guerrillas held in prison in Jammu and Kashmir. K. H. Khurshid, who had been president of Pakistan-administered Kashmir, went to the airport to meet the Qureshis, and also testified in their defence, but to no avail.[14] Hashim, who was only seventeen at the time, was imprisoned for nine years, and the others for much shorter sentences.

In the aftermath of the hijack, hundreds of JKNLF members were arrested and imprisoned in Pakistan. Amanullah Khan had already been arrested in 1970 on charges of being an Indian agent, and jailed in Gilgit. Riots broke out in Gilgit against his prolonged imprisonment and he was released in 1972.

◆

The Pakistani military crackdown on East Pakistani protesters soon assumed the proportion of genocide. Within a matter of weeks, East Pakistan lost a quarter of its middle class and intelligentsia as well as large numbers of poor Hindus. East Pakistanis fleeing the conflict flowed into India. By the end of the summer, eastern India hosted over 8 million refugees, 75 per cent of them Hindu.

The domestic reaction in India was already fierce. On 24 May, during a Lok Sabha debate on the crisis, Prime Minister Indira Gandhi warned, 'This suppression of human rights, the uprooting of people, and the continued homelessness of vast numbers of human beings will threaten peace.'[15] One week later, both houses of India's parliament unanimously adopted a resolution calling upon the Indian government to defend human rights in East Pakistan.

From April through July, India tried to get various UN bodies, from the Security Council to the Economic and Social Committee and the Human Rights Council, to act against the atrocities in East Pakistan under Chapter VII of the UN Charter. A year earlier, at Indian prodding, the UN had adopted sanctions on Rhodesia against apartheid. Indian diplomats were hopeful of getting some action against Pakistan on similar grounds of immense human rights abuse.[16] They failed. Apart from a Soviet statement on restoration of human rights in East Pakistan, other members of the Security Council either blocked Indian efforts or were indifferent to them. Britain and several European countries did offer immediate humanitarian assistance, and the US later contributed heavily to refugee aid, but that was the limit of support. The UN's overall position, pushed by the US, China and Saudi Arabia, was that any action would constitute interference in the internal affairs of a sovereign state.

For the US and China, involved in delicate negotiations towards a rapprochement mediated by the Yahya administration, national interest outweighed human rights. Archer Blood, the US consul general in Dacca, sent daily, sometimes hourly, telegrams to the State Department describing the atrocities in East Pakistan and calling for the US administration to act, but President Nixon and Secretary of State Kissinger ignored Blood's appeals. Indeed, in his account of the period, Kissinger is quite frank about how the opening to China far outweighed what was happening in East Pakistan. In any case, he added, 'An independent Bengali state was certain to emerge, even without Indian intervention. The only question was how the change would come about. We wanted to stay aloof from this if we could.'[17]

The US and China condemned India's efforts as aggressive violations of sovereignty. Declassified tapes of the Nixon–Kissinger conversations on the issue, liberally peppered with expletive abuse of India and Indira Gandhi, show that from June onwards, the Nixon administration was bent on putting India in the dock.

Transcripts of the Kissinger–Zhou Enlai conversations further show convergence between the two influential allies, with Zhou feeding the Nixon–Kissinger paranoia about 'deceitful' Indians. Blood, who with nineteen members of the US consulate in Dacca, sent a formal protest to the State Department that was signed on arrival by another nine members of the State Department's South Asia staff, was recalled. In late April 1971, Kissinger thanked Yahya for his 'delicacy and tact' in the China negotiations.[18]

At the same time, Kissinger also reached out to the Soviet Union. Seeking Soviet support in the Arab–Israeli conflict and believing Sino–US rapprochement would pressure the Soviet Union, he told Soviet ambassador to the US, Anatoly Dobrynin, that he was leaving for India to warn Indira Gandhi against military aid or support for East Pakistani rebels. The US, he said, would welcome a continuing backchannel with the Soviet Union on events in Bangladesh; after all, both countries had a common interest in containing another India–Pakistan conflict.[19] In July 1971, Nixon announced rapprochement with China and Kissinger went there on a path-breaking visit. The Soviet Union and India reacted by signing a Treaty of Peace, Friendship and Cooperation on 9 August. The treaty, negotiated by D. P. Dhar, who was then India's ambassador to the Soviet Union, bound both countries to defend each other if either was attacked. Neither thought the clause would be invoked. In September, Soviet foreign minister Andrei Gromyko informed Kissinger that he had told Indira Gandhi that the Soviet Union was concerned that there should be no India–Pakistan conflict.

Persuaded that India would have to go it alone—a phrase that subsequently became the underpinning for Indian policy in relation to Pakistan—the Indian government began to covertly train and arm the Mukti Bahini, a liberation militia formed by rebel Bengali contingents of the Pakistan Army and its volunteers, using the cover of refugee camps along the border. Cross-border skirmishes began and by late November Indian troops and armour supported the Mukti Bahini, which had vast public backing in East Pakistan. The Pakistan Army began to mass troops on East Pakistan's external borders, and the Razakaars massacred Awami League members and supporters, as well as Hindus, in the interior.

On 3 December, a panicked Yahya launched ground operations in Kashmir, Punjab and Rajasthan, mounting air attacks on Indian airfields in Punjab and Udhampur in Jammu and Kashmir. The next day, Indira Gandhi sent the Indian Army into East Pakistan, with close air support that soon put the Dacca airfield out of commission. In the meantime, the Indian Navy effectively blockaded East Pakistan and mounted two successful attacks on Karachi's port in West Pakistan. Nixon, who had promised to come to Pakistan's defence, ordered the US 7th Fleet's USS *Enterprise* to the Bay of Bengal, only to find Soviet submarines already there. India had intercepted the secret telegram from the US ordering the *Enterprise* to action and alerted the Soviets, invoking the Treaty of Peace, Friendship and Cooperation.

In Kashmir, the ground war replayed 1965. Pakistani troops again attacked through Poonch and Chhamb and again made gains in Chhamb, forcing Indian troops to withdraw from their positions. Indian troops counter-attacked in Sialkot–Shakargarh, taking the war to the edge of Lahore and, within a fortnight, it was all over. Dacca fell to combined Indian and Mukti Bahini forces on 16 December, and India declared a ceasefire in West Pakistan. East Pakistan became an independent country, Bangladesh, and India was in possession of over 8,000 kilometres of West Pakistan's territory and 93,000 Pakistani soldiers. Over half a million East Pakistani lives were lost.

In the aftermath of the war, when Bhutto became Pakistan's prime minister, he appointed a judicial commission led by retired judge Hamoodur Rahman to examine the events of 1971. The Hamoodur Commission's report was never released, nor tabled in Pakistan's parliament. By the time it was completed, Bhutto was already in trouble with the army, though he had courted them assiduously. He was arrested and hanged soon after, in 1979. Decades later, in 2000, the weekly *India Today* managed to lay hands on a copy of the supplementary report that the commission had issued. It is now available on a number of sites on the Internet, a simple search brings it up.

That was the first time that Pakistanis had an inkling of what was in the report, which was pretty much a damp squib as far as assessing atrocities went. Most of it focused on 'misdemeanours', such as illicit sex between army officers and civilians, and the misuse of military position to take bribes or demand protection money. Nevertheless, its conclusions were explosive. They indicted the Pakistan Army for a war badly and stupidly fought, and recommended that the army be barred from interfering in political disputes, especially when they were domestic.

In Pakistan, the 1971 war grew to be regarded as proof that India always wanted Pakistan to disintegrate, and seized her opportunity when the East Pakistanis rebelled. Within India, by contrast, there was a debate between Indian policymakers, mostly hard-nosed realists, on how far to take Indian support for the East Pakistani uprising.

Both sides agreed that India needed a proactive containment policy towards Pakistan in order to protect the country from future attack, but they disagreed on whether breaking up Pakistan was the best strategy. There were influential policymakers who argued that any disintegration of Pakistan would harden Pakistani enmity towards India, might even turn it implacable. Instead, they argued, the East Pakistani conflict should be allowed to simmer because it would tie Pakistan down in internal battles and make it difficult for the Pakistan Army to focus on attacking India in Kashmir. Neither approach was actually proactive. Both were defensive, sometimes even bordering on the puerile. Unsurprisingly, the debate was overtaken by the rapid escalation of conflict in East Pakistan and the flow of refugees into India.

The fourteen-day war was followed by an India–Pakistan summit in Simla in June 1972. Though there was strong domestic pressure on Indira Gandhi's administration to use Indian military gains to force Pakistan to settle Kashmir on Indian terms—turning the ceasefire line into an international border—she decided to withdraw from Pakistani territory and repatriate the soldiers in return for two agreements. First, that henceforth India and Pakistan would settle their disputes peacefully through bilateral negotiations in issue-based working groups (the 'composite dialogue'); and second, that the ceasefire line would be converted into a 'Line of Control'. This latter was viewed as a step towards formalizing the de facto border. The language of the agreement certainly indicated a change in status. 'In Jammu and Kashmir, the Line of Control resulting from the ceasefire of December 17, 1971 shall be respected,' it said. 'Neither side shall seek to alter it unilaterally, irrespective of mutual differences and legal interpretations. Both sides further undertake to refrain from the threat or the use of force in violation of this Line.'[20]

Indian negotiators who were at the Simla talks also believed that Bhutto agreed privately with Indira Gandhi to turn the Line of Control into an international border, but begged her to let him bring the Pakistani people and army around before doing so. This was what she told P. N. Dhar, who was at the talks as a senior adviser.[21] If so, Bhutto broke his word almost immediately. Returning to Pakistan after the Simla talks, he announced triumphantly that he had got India to return what Pakistan had lost without conceding anything in return.

True, the Simla Agreement had been hard won. After three days of talks, both between the two countries' leaders and between their delegations, it looked as if no agreement was possible. Bhutto then made a last-ditch effort, visiting Indira Gandhi at 10 p.m. It was then that the private conversation that Dhar referred to took place.

Bhutto was both right and wrong in saying he had conceded nothing. The Simla Agreement did not result in progress towards a Kashmir settlement and the Line of Control was not turned into an international border. Yet, forty years later, there is a general international consensus that India and Pakistan have to resolve their dispute bilaterally, and that a Kashmir settlement will have to be based on the Line of Control.

After the war, the Pakistan Army embarked on restructuring and launched a nuclear programme to counter India's own unannounced nuclear weapons programme. Pakistanis would eat grass, Bhutto declared, but they would never let the defeat of 1971 occur again.

◆

Once again, the UN had failed an India–Pakistan conflict. The UN Secretary-General did warn the Security Council of a looming crisis that could embroil South Asia in war, but rather late, in July 1971. However, two members of the Permanent Five (the US and China) were in Pakistan's corner, and one (the Soviet Union) was in India's. The UN had another chance to help end the conflict when Yahya proposed, in late November 1971, that Indian and Pakistani troops withdraw from the border and UN troops be stationed there instead. The proposal would have cut Mukti Bahini support and supply lines from India and left them helpless against the Pakistan Army. India rejected the proposal.

The UN finally dealt with the issue only after the two countries went to war in December, calling for an immediate ceasefire and the withdrawal of troops. But it failed to suggest a resolution to the political problem between East and West Pakistan, or propose a mechanism for its resolution. India resisted the UN's calls for a ceasefire, and the UN's efforts were pre-empted when India won the war twelve days later. After India won the war, the UN amended its call for immediate withdrawal of troops, asking that Indian troops withdraw as soon as practicable. The amendment was partly because troops were needed to fill the security vacuum in Bangladesh that would inevitably ensue, and partly to help with refugee returns and reconstruction.

The 1971 war marked India's turn away from the UN on Kashmir. Following the 1972 Simla Agreement, the Indian government pressed for the termination of the UNMOGIP mandate. Since Pakistan refused to agree, the Indian government was forced to announce that it would no longer report ceasefire violations to UNMOGIP. Going by the experience of 1947,

1965 and 1972, Indian policymakers concluded that the UN was determined to ignore—or even worse, legitimize—Pakistan's repeated acts of aggression. UNMOGIP has been in semi-limbo since 1972, when India stopped referring complaints on cross-border firing to them while Pakistan continues to do so.

Chapter VI

TWO DECADES OF RELATIVE QUIET?

There was a lull in India–Pakistan hostilities following the 1972 war. Both countries had to focus on gathering storms at home, and this time the Pakistani government lacked the resources to offset internal turmoil with war fever.

Jammu and Kashmir held its fourth assembly election in January 1972. The Congress, now under Mir Qasim, won 58 seats, the state's Jamaat-e-Islami won 6 and the Jan Sangh 3. The Plebiscite Front, that had planned to contest the election on Abdullah's advice, was banned.

A young civil servant on his first posting, Wajahat Habibullah, described the situation in the valley on the eve of the election as gloomy. There was already a culture of electoral brokers. The local strongman instructed villagers which party and candidate to vote for. Party stalwarts knew pliant officers who would look the other way when voter identities were stolen and even allow ballot boxes to be stuffed before certifying them. The civil administration had little authority; the police and army wielded power on the ground, often with contempt for citizens. Habibullah, who was deputed to oversee the election in Anantnag, quoted his Kashmiri poll officer as saying, 'Four days of moonlight, five years of darkness.'[1] Yet, the election in Anantnag, which Habibullah oversaw, was free and fair. Mufti Mohammad Sayeed, minister for public works in the Qasim administration, had ordered so.

India's success in the 1972 war had a limited but significant impact on the valley. While Abdullah declared that the creation of Bangladesh had exploded the two-nation theory that the Muslims of India were entitled to a separate state, others were shocked at the Pakistan Army's humiliating 'surrender'.[2] Hostility towards Indira Gandhi for her 1970 speech in Srinagar had not died down,

Habibullah said. She had asserted in ringing tones, 'We will build a new Kashmir, quickly if you help, slowly if you don't, but build it we will!'[3] Her authoritarian streak was beginning to emerge, but was not full-blown as yet.

In Jammu, the impact of the war was unambiguous. When she went to campaign in the city during the 1972 election, Indira was hailed as the ten-armed goddess Durga who defeated the enemy. The real impact of her trip to Jammu, however, was to open another unanticipated window for peace between Delhi and Srinagar. According to Balraj Puri, he told her in Jammu that an agreement with Abdullah was possible; he had been to see Abdullah and the latter was interested.[4] Getting his message to Indira was not easy. Puri was turned away when he first tried to meet her and left a note with little hope that she would see it. He was surprised to receive a summons at night, but the prime minister was curious and, as it turns out, cautiously hopeful. Chief Minister Sadiq had died the year before, and though Mir Qasim had taken over, the absence of Abdullah remained an open wound.

What Puri proposed was basically a deal in which Indira Gandhi would agree to roll back most of the encroachments on Article 370 and Abdullah would agree to retain the titles of chief minister and governor instead of prime minister and sadr-i-riyasat. It seems both Indira Gandhi and Abdullah were willing to explore the option. Abdullah, who had been interned in Delhi by the union government during the war, was released in June 1972. The Plebiscite Front was still banned, but Abdullah and Beg revitalized the National Conference, and Indira initiated negotiations with Abdullah on the lines that Puri had proposed. Formal talks began in August 1974 between G. Parthasarathy, on behalf of Indira Gandhi, and Beg, on behalf of Abdullah. Parthasarathy, who was the son of former Jammu and Kashmir prime minister, Gopalaswami Ayyangar, and a notable diplomat and journalist, proved to be as tough a bargainer as Beg. After months of hard back and forth, the two negotiators drafted their 'Agreed Conclusions' on 13 November.

The core issue was the status of Jammu and Kashmir. Abdullah and Beg wanted a return to the constitutional position before the former's arrest in 1953. In fact, he wrote to Parthasarathy that he would, according to lawyer and indefatigable analyst of events in the state, A. G. Noorani, 'assume office "only on the basis of the position as it existed on 8th August, 1953"'.[5] Under the pre-1953 position, a prime minister ran the state, not a chief minister, and the constitutional head, known as sadr-i-riyasat, not governor, was elected by the assembly. The state had its own election commission and administrative service and did not fall under the Supreme Court's jurisdiction. The union government had gradually usurped these functions and many more, including budgetary controls, over the late 1950s to 60s.

In other words, though the accession and Article 370 could not be withdrawn, some encroachments on both were accepted and others would be examined to see if they could be rolled back. Key features of the document, announced as a Kashmir accord in February 1975, were that Article 370 would continue to govern relations between the Indian union and Jammu and Kashmir. The state would retain its residuary powers of legislation but India's parliament would have the power to make laws 'relating to the prevention of activities directed towards disclaiming, questioning or disrupting the sovereignty and territorial integrity of India or bringing about...secession of a part of the territory of India from the Union or causing insult to the Indian National Flag, the Indian National Anthem and the Constitution'.[6]

The extension of articles of the Indian Constitution that encroached upon the state's autonomy could be rolled back, though the accession itself and Article 370 could not. The governor would continue to be appointed by the Indian president, not elected, and the Indian Election Commission would continue to organize and supervise state elections. The document concluded, 'No agreement was possible on the question of nomenclature of the Governor and the Chief Minister and the matter is therefore remitted to the Principals.'[7]

When Abdullah wrote to Indira ten days later to suggest

follow-up talks on the document, she replied after a fortnight to say that there was no point in reopening issues already settled by Beg and Parthasarathy. Abdullah still wanted to 'start from the point...left off in August 1953'.[8] The union government, on the other hand, was prepared only for a slow incremental rollback. Indira Gandhi and he met in Pahalgam in early 1975 for talks, and on 11 February, Abdullah accepted the Agreed Conclusions. The Kashmir Accord was signed by Beg on behalf of Abdullah and by Parthasarathy on behalf of the union government, on 24 February in New Delhi. In both the valley and the rest of the country, Abdullah was seen as having been compromised. 'The accord,' Noorani said, 'put a seal on the erosion of Article 370 and the destruction of Kashmir's autonomy.'[9] He was proved right. Perhaps if an incremental rollback had been implemented as envisaged in the accord, autonomy might have been restored over time. Unfortunately, it was not.

There was already disquiet in the valley as leaks of the Beg–Parthasarathy negotiations surfaced in 1974. Two months after the talks started, members of Al Fatah who were out on bail formed a political party, the Jammu and Kashmir People's League, with Fazal Haq Qureshi as its chairman. Founders of the People's League included many who were to become leaders of the insurgency of the 1990s: Sheikh Abdul Aziz, Musaddiq Adil, Bashir Ahmed Tota, Azam Inquilabi, Abdul Hamid Wani, and Shabir Shah, its general secretary.

Abdullah and Indira Gandhi attempted to spin the accord as primarily between political leaders, Abdullah saying it was 'a good basis for my cooperation at the political level' and Indira that it represented a 'new political understanding'.[10] But there were demonstrations against it in Pakistan—Bhutto called a national strike on 28 February 1975—and two bomb attacks in Kashmir, one in late February and the other in mid-March. The Jan Sangh, like the People's League, called the accord a surrender, but by Indira Gandhi.

Abdullah was back in power after twenty-two years. Opposition by the People's League could not dent his triumphal return; though he became chief minister with the support of the Congress, his popularity was unquestioned in the valley—and unquestionable. The People's League underwent a series of splits shortly after its founding. Azam Inquilabi left to set up the Islamic Students and Youth Organization, later renamed the Jamiatul Tulaba, a wing of the state Jamaat-e-Islami. On becoming chief minister, Abdullah dropped the cases against Al Fatah and rehabilitated many of the accused, a policy that the state government had used successfully under Sadiq and Qasim. While some former Al Fatah members became businessmen or joined political parties, Qureshi himself accepted a job in the state government's education department. With two young children and no family wealth, he needed a salary.[11]

Meanwhile, there was turmoil in the rest of India. The drain of the 1971 war had resulted in a fall in gross domestic product (GDP), compounded by drought, high rates of unemployment and an oil crisis in 1973. The 1974 railway strike, to which Indira Gandhi responded with mass arrests, gave a fillip to public disaffection. Abdullah's old friend, Jayaprakash Narayan, came out of retirement to lead mass protests against what he called Indira Gandhi's corrupt and autocratic administration. In June 1975, the Allahabad High Court ruled that the 1971 election, in which she had come to power, was marred by electoral malpractice and therefore illegal. Under pressure of rising political and economic unrest and with her own prime ministership threatened, Indira Gandhi declared a state of emergency in the country.

Jammu and Kashmir remained relatively unaffected by the Emergency. Indeed, it relieved Congress pressure on Abdullah for a time, since the party was embroiled in crises. Internally, however, disaffection grew. Abdullah governed with only Beg and members of his family—his wife, two sons and son-in-law—at his side. Rumours of corruption sprouted and spread rapidly.

Two years after declaring the Emergency, Indira Gandhi lifted it and announced general elections in March 1977. An angry Indian public voted the Congress out—for the first time in independent India—and the newly-founded Janata Party came to power, led by former Congress veteran Morarji Desai. At the same time, the Congress withdrew support from Abdullah. Desai dissolved the Jammu and Kashmir assembly and called for fresh elections.

The Kashmir Accord collapsed with the departure of the Congress. In the June 1977 assembly elections, the National Conference and Congress contested separately. The National Conference won 47 of the 76 assembly seats, sweeping the valley with 40 of its 42 seats but winning only 7 out of Jammu's 32. The Congress won 11 seats in Jammu but none in Kashmir. The Janata Party (which the Praja Parishad now joined) also won 11 seats in Jammu and 2 in the valley. The Jamaat-e-Islami fell from 5 to 1 seat.

The 1977 Jammu and Kashmir election was widely seen as having been the first free and fair election in the state. It was certainly the first to take place in a situation of relative peace, and also the first in which leading political figures were not in jail. Habibullah, however, recounted how he was pressed by the president of the Janata Party's Kashmir branch, Hameed Karra, as well as senior officers of the state administration, to put pliant electoral officers in charge of the polling in Srinagar, where Habibullah now served, and arrest National Conference volunteers. Fortunately, he was able to resist. According to his own account, Prime Minister Morarji Desai inadvertently aided him. On a visit to Srinagar during the election, Desai was asked by a zealous civil servant whether he favoured any of the candidates. The famously suspicious Desai replied, 'It was difficult to know whom to trust.'[12] That put paid to the game of currying favour by influencing the vote.

◆

Abdullah had redeemed himself, but only briefly and partially. He was back in power without the burden of the Congress, and with a new government in Delhi to deal with. One of his first steps was to try and end the subsidies that Jammu and Kashmir had come to depend on under Bakshi and Sadiq, but the task proved too difficult to execute. A compliant union government did not ask for strict accounts of the grants the state received. Politicians and industry, including traders, had long misappropriated the funds. This group constituted a powerful constituency that Abdullah could not afford to alienate. Though he tried to protect the rare civil servant who challenged them, he more frequently gave way. Habibullah, for example, recounts how Abdullah backed an honest agriculture secretary for several years but eventually transferred him.[13]

A year into Abdullah's second stint in power, the demand of autonomy for Jammu again gained salience. When he became chief minister in 1975, Abdullah had promised regional devolution, including the restoration of the District Development Boards that Sadiq set up at the Gajendragadkar Commission's recommendation, and that Qasim wound up. Initially it looked as if he meant to honour his commitment. In March, while introducing a parliamentary debate on the Kashmir Accord, Indira Gandhi mentioned that the state government was going to work on regional autonomy. In his address to the assembly in the same month, Governor L. K. Jha repeated the statement, saying the state government planned to devolve power 'from the state to a region, and further afield to the district and Panchayat levels'.[14] In January 1976, the National Conference issued a pamphlet declaring the party was committed to autonomy for the state's three regions. In August, Puri, back with the National Conference, was felicitated in Srinagar for his work on regional autonomy. After winning the 1977 election, however, Abdullah concentrated on the state's autonomy within the Indian union rather than regional devolution within the state. Soon after, Puri was expelled from the National Conference.

By this point, Abdullah had lost most of his closest colleagues. In spring 1977, Maulana Masoodi, who had been speaker of the constituent assembly, established the state Janata Party branch. A year later, Abdullah's most loyal friend and colleague, Beg, was marginalized, reportedly by the former's son-in-law, Ghulam Mohammad Shah, who was an influential party member and hoped to be appointed Abdullah's successor. Without Beg's restraining hand, Abdullah was persuaded to issue the state's most draconian law in October 1977, the Public Safety Ordinance (enacted in 1978), which allowed unfettered powers of arrest and detention without charges.

Abdullah now discovered what Indira Gandhi should have recognized, that leaving an issue to fester generally backfires. In 1978, Poonch erupted over the question of regional autonomy. The district was one of the most neglected in the Jammu, with high rates of unemployment and a stunted agrarian economy. Government jobs were the only employment to be had for educated youth in Poonch town, and they were allotted through a system that gave weightage to interviews rather than grades, which basically translated to nepotism. When their demand for a 'merit versus interview' process of appointment was rejected, students took to the streets in massive public demonstrations that resulted in police firing on 2 December, killing one and injuring several others. There were violent clashes between armed police and students in the days that followed, and for two weeks the administration disappeared, leaving a student 'commander' in charge of the town.

According to local historian K. D. Maini, the state government initially responded with counter-demonstrations, mobilizing students in the neighbouring towns of Mandi, Surankote and Mendhar to allege that the Poonch protests were anti-Muslim. Actually, Muslims, Hindus and Sikhs led the protests together.[15] The ruling National Conference's counter was seen as an attempt to communalize regional aspirations and protest spread across Jammu province, crystallizing in the demand for Jammu's autonomy. Abdullah's Agrarian Reforms (Amendment) Act of 1978, dispossessing absentee landlords, added further fuel to Jammu's resentment.

When Puri met Desai to ask for central intercession, he found the prime minister unsympathetic. Had the protests remained non-violent, Desai said, the union government might have pushed the state government to consider Jammu's aspirations. Returning to Jammu, Puri and his cohort were able to persuade the bulk, if not all, of the protesters to use the Gandhian satyagraha as their preferred means of protest. Meanwhile, the state government convened a meeting of Poonch representatives at which the demand for reform in the government appointments process—which included teachers, doctors and engineers—was accepted. A new district commissioner was appointed who proved to be more honest and efficient than his predecessor, and gradually Poonch returned to normal. After the union government appointed a second commission to look into regional devolution for the state, Jammu's protests too died down.

Indira Gandhi returned to power soon after, in 1980, with an openly expressed antipathy to Abdullah. When he piloted a Jammu and Kashmir Resettlement Bill in the assembly, the union government sought various methods of delay. Introduced in March 1980, the bill was passed by the assembly and legislative council after considerable debate in April 1982. Five months later, Governor B. K. Nehru returned the bill, seeking reconsideration. The assembly and council passed it again without change in October and this time B. K. Nehru, a strict constitutionalist, gave his assent. Its provisions were never implemented and remain unimplemented today.

Why was the act so controversial? In itself there should have been no problem. It permitted the return of state subjects who had fled to Pakistan-controlled Kashmir or Pakistan, something that had been agreed in 1966 at Tashkent. Upon return they were to swear an oath of allegiance to both the Indian and the state constitutions. But there was no corresponding legislation in Pakistan-held territories of the former princely state, which meant that Muslim refugees from Jammu would be able to return to Jammu, but Hindu and Sikh refugees from Poonch, Mirpur, Gilgit and Baltistan would not be able to return to their homelands. Refugee return became a communal issue.

Abdullah died in September 1982, a few weeks before the bill passed into law. His son Farooq became the next chief minister, following elections in 1983.

◆

Abdullah's death set off a wave of mass mourning in Kashmir. His funeral cortège was attended by almost as many as Nehru's. He had dominated Kashmiri politics for fifty years, starting in 1931. He inspired political aspirations in the valley that remain central thirty-five years after his death. Moreover, political mobilization after Friday prayers was his invention, as was a political philosophy that tied Muslim rights with Muslim social transformation. His economic reforms were far-reaching; though 'land to the tiller' drew ire from some, it transformed the mountain state's economy and allowed a far greater number of Muslims to become middle class, especially when combined with education. His vision of a self-sufficient Kashmir, one that was not dependent on subsidies from the Indian union, was not implemented. But if it had been, it might have provided an effective motor for the state's integration with India. Most important of all, he took an everyday culture of coexistence between Hindus, Muslims, Sikhs and Buddhists and turned it into a Kashmiri political identity—which began to erode in his later life, with tragic consequences in the valley after his death.

What about Abdullah the man? His biographer Ajit Bhattacharjea called him a tragic hero, but he was the most popular leader Kashmir has ever had. In an era of great visionaries—Gandhi, Nehru, Azad, Ambedkar, Patel, Ghaffar Khan, to mention but a few—he held his own. Though the whole of India was gripped by a sense of foreboding after Gandhi's assassination, he was one of the rare few to see what a far-reaching blow to the fabric of a pluralist India the assassin Nathuram Godse had dealt. Gandhi's assassination by 'Hindu communalists', he said 'had shaken the foundation of Indo-Kashmir relations.'[16]

His faith was now pinned entirely on Nehru. From a valley point of view, he was right. Nehru was the last prime minister to understand Kashmiri sentiments and have the political legitimacy to push a settlement through, until Vajpayee came in the late 1990s. Despite his profound understanding of Kashmiri sentiments, however, Vajpayee was not able to fulfil his policy, unlike Nehru who was able to negotiate the 1952 Delhi

Agreement and enshrine it through an amended Article 370 of the Indian Constitution. The problem was that Abdullah did not make common cause with Nehru while he could. Patel had already died when the Jammu and Kashmir constituent assembly was elected, but if Abdullah had embedded Article 370 in the draft constitution and had the assembly pass it, as they would have, many of the problems of later years could have been avoided, including his arrest in 1953.

Instead, he argued that since the Nehru administration continued to abide by its stand in the UN that a plebiscite should be held after Pakistani troops and irregulars withdrew, it followed that Article 370 could only be temporary and a Kashmiri constitution would have questionable validity. To this extent, he ignored the hoary truth that facts on the ground count more than legal rights on paper. Here, it was Nehru who was at fault—the Indian government could have done far more to persuade UN member-states that the Delhi Agreement and Article 370 reaffirmed the accession to India. But the Jammu and Kashmir constituent assembly's adoption of Article 370 would have strengthened Nehru's hand immeasurably, certainly with his cabinet. Abdullah might never have been arrested and the state's political evolution might have been far less contested.

Critics allege that Abdullah vacillated about tying the state to India. His actions, however, do not necessarily bear out the allegation. That he flirted with the hope of independence—or at least limited sovereignty—is undeniable. But, as he himself suggested, independence was not feasible given Kashmir's geopolitical situation, in which the state would inevitably be dependent on either India or Pakistan. In those circumstances, he chose India, not once but repeatedly, because he believed that Kashmir's pluralism would be best protected by an alliance with India. Though he always returned to this belief, it was repeatedly questioned. What comes through in his speeches and autobiography is a profound feeling that India was not willing to fight for Kashmir beyond a point, whether on the battlefield or at the UN.

Abdullah's last act—the 1975 Kashmir Accord—was often

dismissed as surrender, with many suggesting he did it for power. But when he did become chief minister, his first priority was to complete his 'Naya Kashmir' agenda, not to consolidate power. He seemed to know his days were numbered; he had had a heart attack shortly before he was sworn in, and received felicitations from his hospital bed. In his second and last stint as the head of the state, he ruled with only his family and a tiny number of friends.

Perhaps his greatest failing was his inability to become a leader for Jammu and Ladakh as well as the valley. In his heyday, he had colleagues who were Jammu leaders but the same valley focus that led him to become so popular in Kashmir alienated both Jammu and Ladakh. He could have consolidated power by devolving to colleagues and through them to regions, but he chose not to.

At the end, he died a tired man, horribly saddened by his experiences with his closest colleagues as well as successive Indian leaders. In his autobiography, which was a torrent of sorrow, bitterness and self-defence, he put the greatest personal blame on his colleagues, Bakshi, Sadiq and Qasim, and the greatest political blame on Indian leaders, including Patel and Gulzarilal Nanda, both home ministers whom he saw as exerting undue influence on their prime ministers. His only remaining hero was Gandhi.

◆

The 1970s were years of change for Pakistan-administered Kashmir too. In 1970, the Pakistani government passed an 'Azad Kashmir' Act (I of 1970), under which the statelet acquired the same autonomy as offered by Article 370, with the portfolios under the Pakistani government restricted to defence, foreign affairs and currency. The Act, however, made it mandatory for the statelet's office-bearers to take an oath of allegiance to the Pakistani government and Kashmir's accession to Pakistan. At the same time, the Pakistani cabinet issued instructions to all government ministries and departments that the statelet should be treated like other provinces, 'as if it were another administrative unit of the country'.[17] Sardar Qayyum later criticized the Act as a 'deception of independence' that prevented the statelet from uniting with Pakistan.

Nevertheless, the elections held under the 1970 Act were, according to one of the few scholars of Pakistan-administered Kashmir, Christopher Snedden, perhaps the freest and fairest elections ever held there. People voted for the first time on the basis of universal suffrage. For the first time, too, they elected their president. Four political parties contested—the Muslim Conference, the Azad Muslim Conference, the Liberation League and the Plebiscite Front. Sardar Qayyum's Muslim Conference won.

In 1973, after Bhutto became prime minister, a new Pakistani constitution was promulgated which defined the country as extending to all territories that were or might be included in Pakistan, by accession or any other means. The 1970 'Azad Kashmir' Act was repealed, and replaced by an Interim Constitution Act of 1974 that introduced a parliamentary system, with the proviso that all members had to swear that they 'remain loyal to the country and the cause of accession of the State of Jammu and Kashmir to Pakistan'.[18] Indeed, it went further: political parties and individuals were forbidden to take part in activities 'detrimental to the ideology of the State's accession to Pakistan'.[19] The interim constitution created a legislative assembly based on adult franchise, and—like the Jammu and Kashmir constitution—an upper house or legislative council. Unlike the Jammu and Kashmir Council, whose members had to be state subjects, Pakistani politicians could be members of the statelet's legislative council and the Pakistani prime minister chaired it.

In a strange reversal of the common bicameral procedure in which the lower house has the chief legislative power, and again unlike the Jammu and Kashmir constitution, the legislative council of Pakistan-administered Kashmir had the sole power to legislate on major issues affecting the statelet, including foreign affairs, finance, transport, communications, police, electricity, and nuclear energy. The legislative assembly could only legislate on subjects that were not covered by the legislative council, which essentially amounted to municipal administration.

The May 1975 election under the interim constitution was widely criticized as rigged by Bhutto's political adviser, Hayat Mohammad Khan Tamman, an accusation that Bhutto indirectly validated in 1977, when he told a closed group that the forthcoming Pakistani election would not be like 'the Tammani elections'.[20]

When the 1977 general election took place, however, having been advanced to March 1977 by Bhutto, the results did suggest rigging, or so the opposition Pakistan National Alliance alleged. Led by Ghaffar Khan's Awami National Party and his son Wali Khan, whose governments in the NWFP and Balochistan had been twice dismissed by Bhutto, the Alliance launched a massive agitation against the election result, in which the PPP won by a landslide. Bhutto called all-party talks and it seemed as if a compromise might be possible, but on 5 July General Zia-ul-Haq, whom Bhutto had appointed, staged Pakistan's second military coup. In the same year Amanullah Khan, released from prison, moved to Britain and set up the JKLF in Birmingham in 1978.

Bhutto was arrested and hanged in 1979. The statelet was put under military rule and its government dismissed on the day of Zia's military coup. Zia appointed retired Major General Rahman chief executive instead and allowed Ibrahim to remain as president until October 1978, when Brigadier Hayat Khan replaced both Rahman and Ibrahim as chief executive and president. In 1983, following public protest against his autocratic regime, Hayat Khan resigned and Major General Rahman came back. The two had been the Pakistan Army's preferred local leaders from the 1960s.

♦

The early 1980s seemed like a time of hope in Jammu and Kashmir. The valley turned away from Pakistan following Bhutto's death; the news of his hanging had been received with massive protests. Pakistan's attention, under President Zia-ul-Haq, was focused on mobilizing a pan-Islamic jihad against the Soviet invasion of Afghanistan, and Pakistan-administered Kashmir was quiet. Unlike Kashmir's previous leaders, who had kept the fiction of Kashmir's special status alive by staying away from Indian politics, Farooq Abdullah made common cause with chief ministers from the west and south of India who were pressing for federal devolution. The campaign offered a significant opportunity for India to integrate Kashmir by devolving power across the country.

This surface calm was belied by political conditions in India and Pakistan. Both countries were grappling with domestic insurgencies that had been ongoing since the mid-1970s. Bhutto had sent the army into Balochistan to crush rising insurrection. He had also created a Federal Security Force that acted as his political hatchet men. Writing in 1974, the Pakistani analyst Eqbal Ahmad warned that Pakistan's stage was being set for another military coup.[21] Two mutually reinforcing trends of fascism and separatism were in motion under Bhutto, he said. The Pakistan Army, with a new class of petty bourgeois officers drawn from the recently Green Revolution-rich agrarian belt of Rawalpindi, would increasingly turn to the Jamaat-e-Islami for an ideology of the Muslim state. Already smarting from their humiliating defeat in 1971, these officers blamed civilian politicians for every military defeat they had suffered from 1948 on.

As Ahmad predicted, there was a military coup in Pakistan, supported by the new class of officers he described. Again, as he predicted, Zia-ul-Haq's first actions were Islamization of the army, along with a crackdown on the judiciary in which hundreds of lawyers were jailed. The 1973 constitution was abrogated and an Afghan jihad was launched against the Soviet invasion of Afghanistan.

Soon after Zia took over, Indira Gandhi suggested to him that their two countries devise a 'regional strategy' to deal with the Soviet Union's invasion of Afghanistan, but he considered her suggestion 'hegemonistic' and instead approached US president Ronald Reagan with the proposal to organize an Afghan jihad if the US would provide military aid and funds.

As a palliative, Zia offered a non-aggression pact between India and Pakistan to which Indira Gandhi responded by suggesting a treaty of peace, friendship and cooperation. Each leader regarded the other's offer as made in bad faith. Zia thought the treaty offer was an effort to undercut his negotiations with the Reagan administration for a $3.2 billion grant of military aid for the Afghan jihad. The Indian government had campaigned against the grant on the grounds that the weapons would be used against India. For her part, Indira Gandhi considered Zia's offer of a non-aggression pact as cover for the Pakistan Army and intelligence programme to arm and train insurgents in Indian Punjab, which India had just uncovered. The Punjabi Sikh demand for establishment of a separate state of Khalistan was not the only insurgency India faced, nor the only one that had external support. Chinese arms flowed to insurgents from Nagaland in the northeast of India to Andhra Pradesh in the southeast.

At the same time as they discovered the Pakistani government's involvement in arming and training Khalistani insurgents, the Indian government found that Pakistan had started mountaineering expeditions to the Siachen Glacier, and US government maps showed the glacier as part of Pakistan. Lying north of the Line of Control between India and Pakistan, the seventy-five-kilometre-long Siachen Glacier is located in the eastern Karakoram Range of the Himalayas that separate Pakistan's Khyber–Pakhtunkhwa and Gilgit–Baltistan, and India's Ladakh, from China. Its strategic value is chiefly as a watching post. Whoever controls the glacier can monitor troops deployment and movement in the other two countries. For India, however, there is a further concern. If either Pakistan or China were to acquire the glacier, the two allies could mount a pincer attack on India through Ladakh. The fear is mostly presumptive: China did not provide military support to Pakistan in 1972 or in the India–Pakistan conflicts that followed, though it did enable the Pakistani military with arms and weapons technology, including nuclear technology, in peacetime.

The Siachen problem was rooted in the 1949 ceasefire agreement, under which the ceasefire line was demarcated up to Khor in the foothills of the glacier but not northwards of it. Neither the Indian and Pakistani militaries nor the UN negotiators thought further demarcation was important in 1949. After all, what army could fight a war at heights of 5,400 metres?

In 1983, however, when Indian intelligence learned that the Pakistan Army was in the process of acquiring high-altitude mountaineering gear, Indian strategists thought it prudent to pre-empt what might be a Pakistani tactic to seize the glacier. In April 1984, the Indian Army landed two platoons of soldiers on key passes of the Saltoro Ridge abutting the glacier to its west. The passes, Bilafond La and Sia La, not only blocked Pakistan's access to the Siachen Glacier but also gave India control over Siachen's tributary glaciers as well as the Saltoro Ridge. The Pakistan Army riposted but was unable to dislodge Indian troops from the two passes. It was, however, able to establish its presence on an outcrop overlooking Bilafond La, which the Indian Army went on to capture in 1987.

◆

The move to federalize India, launched by the chief ministers of Bengal, Andhra, Karnataka and Tamil Nadu, plopped into this volatile situation. When Farooq joined the four eastern and southern chief ministers, Indira Gandhi saw it as a threat to her authority and treated Farooq's part in it as a personal betrayal. The two had already fallen out when Farooq refused to ally with the Congress for the October 1983 assembly election, arguing that the state needed its own party, the National Conference. Though the two discussed an unofficial seat-sharing arrangement, Farooq rejected the idea, turning instead to Mirwaiz Farooq with whom he made a tacit agreement that the latter's supporters would campaign for the National Conference. The party won 47 of the 75 assembly seats, the bulk of them in the valley. The Congress won 23 seats in Jammu and one each in the valley and Leh. Neither the Jan Sangh nor the Jamaat won any.

Farooq won the 1983 election partly on a sympathy wave and partly because, as 'the lion's cub', he was seen in the valley as defending the state's autonomy. Despite Indira Gandhi's dissatisfaction with him, he was feted in Delhi as the first Kashmiri chief minister to assert he was Indian. His popularity did not endear him to Indira; rather, it increased her distrust. When Farooq hosted a three-day conference for opposition leaders from seventeen different Indian state parties, the die was cast.

Like his father and other chief ministers before him, Farooq was soon caught in a cleft stick. While his assertion of being Indian relieved many in Delhi, it aroused hostility amongst the pro-Pakistan and pro-independence groups in the valley. Though these still had relatively small constituencies, some of them had turned to overt rather than covert political activities. The Jamaat-e-Islami and People's League were not the only parties to represent pro-Pakistan constituencies. The People's Conference, led by Abdul Ghani Lone, was another. Lone was elected to the assembly in 1983. One of the leaders of the time who rose again to prominence during the 2010 and 2016 youth uprisings, Syed Ali Shah Geelani was the Jamaat-e-Islami candidate elected from Sopore in 1972 and 1977, who lost in 1983. He was to contest again and win in 1987; that was his last election.

Sporadic armed attacks began soon after Farooq was elected. In August 1983, a guerrilla attempted to blow up the transmission tower on Srinagar's Hari Parbat, and in October guerrillas attacked a one-day cricket match between India and the West Indies, breaking through the stadium fence to pelt Indian players with stones and dig up the wicket. When, in January 1984, a crude bomb went off while Farooq was taking the Republic Day salute, Indira Gandhi summoned him to Delhi.

A wave of arrests followed. 'Virtually the entire top leadership of the Jamaat-i-Islami, the Jamiatul Tulaba, the Mahaz-e-Azadi and the People's League were swept up by the police dragnet,'[22] reported the weekly *India Today*. Geelani was amongst those arrested, as was Hashim Qureshi's brother and nephew. 'The pattern of the arrests revealed a blend of half-heartedness and overkill,' *India Today* commented. The majority of those held were from the Jamaat-e-Islami 'though their participation in recent militant activities was nil'. Others who went underground, however, could not be traced. They included Shabir Shah of the People's League, who was on bail for cricket vandalism, Bashir Ahmed Butt, chief organizer of the Mahaz-e-Azadi, and Tajamul Islam, head of the Jamiatul Tulaba.

There was immediate outcry in the state assembly, then in session. 'The Centre and Farooq Abdullah are together defaming the Muslims of Kashmir,' Lone accused. Farooq replied, 'I have full confidence in myself and my own people.'[23]

He was right when it came to Kashmir. In Delhi, however, the arrests uncovered how many former and rehabilitated guerrillas remained active; indeed, their families followed them into militancy. Government fears were strengthened when, in early February 1984, the assistant commissioner of the Indian consulate in Birmingham, Ravinder Mhatre, was kidnapped. The kidnappers demanded a ransom of £1 million and the release of Maqbool Butt along with nine other Kashmiris, giving a deadline of less than twenty-four hours and appointing Amanullah Khan's JKLF as their negotiator. By the time the Birmingham police reacted, half of the time allotted by the kidnappers had been spent. Mhatre was assassinated before the Indian government could formulate a response. In retaliation, the Indira administration hanged Butt.

The reaction in Kashmir was immediate. In Butt's home village, Trehgam in Kupwara district, shopkeepers downed shutters for a fortnight. In Anantnag, 'a group of youngsters, tears welling from their eyes, went round schools, banks and government offices, requesting the authorities to close down', said *India Today*. Downtown Srinagar was deserted. 'The convoluted phraseology of the years of the plebiscite movement was back again in the tea-shops, the coffeehouses and the street squares.' The Indian government and Farooq, said Lone, had made Butt 'the first martyr on the question of Kashmir's accession'. Overnight, a police officer told *India Today*, guerrillas who were 'not even known to their neighbours' became household names in the valley.[24]

The Congress was already gearing up to oust Farooq. Union ministers Ghulam Nabi Azad and Arif Mohammad Khan had led a deputation to President Zail Singh requesting him to dismiss Farooq at the end of 1983, and after the Mhatre assassination, Congressmen began a campaign of innuendo against him. He had associated with terrorists, they said, pointing to a 1974 meeting with Amanullah Khan in Srinagar; he had met Butt, too, at the same time. The Butt meeting occurred in Poonch, where he went after attending a Plebiscite Front event in Mirpur, and there was no indication that he had discussed independence, let alone militancy with Khan or Butt. In fact, according to Farooq, he was told in 1974 by 'the entire bureaucracy of Pakistan and Bhutto's secretary himself' that India and Pakistan had agreed on a settlement based on the existing division of Jammu and Kashmir.[25]

The Congress was disingenuous in more ways than one. Congressman Shafi Qureshi had at one time supported the state's accession to Pakistan, founding a Pakistan Students' Federation in Kashmir in 1947 and joined Mohiuddin Karra's Political Conference, which advocated accession to Pakistan in the early 1950s, becoming its vice president. The leader of the Congress's Legislature Party in the state, Moulana Iftikhar Hussain Ansari, had founded the Shia Youth Federation to support the Plebiscite Front. In joining the Congress, they stood as successful examples of political reconciliation under Sadiq, and Farooq's election actually showed how much further Kashmiris were willing to reconcile.

Indira Gandhi, who had encouraged Sadiq's reconciliation programme, must surely have seen Farooq's potential. Why then did she take the steps that she did in spring-summer 1984? One reason might be that she was confronted by multiple crises. There were growing insurgencies across the country—in Punjab, Assam, Mizoram, Bodo and Gurkha territories—that she had not succeeded in tackling either politically or through force. Farooq allowed the Khalistanis to hold 'educational' camps in Jammu and Kashmir, at a time when they were being armed and trained by the Pakistani military and intelligences forces.[26] It is not surprising that she struck where she could. In April, she shifted Governor B. K. Nehru to Gujarat because he advised against dismissing the Farooq administration. B. K. Nehru later wrote in his autobiography, *Nice Guys Finish Second*, that she was determined to undercut Farooq even before the 1983 election. In late June, at a meeting of newspaper editors, 'she made no secret of her belief that the continuance of Farooq Abdullah was bad for the state and the country. That shook most of us,' added Inder Malhotra.[27]

Governor Nehru was replaced by Jagmohan,[28] notorious for his eviction of illegal dwellers from Old Delhi during the 1975–77 Emergency, when he served as vice chairman of the Delhi Development Authority. Jagmohan's appointment, Congress members told *India Today*, indicated 'a significant hardening of the party's attitude towards the National Conference Government'. Two weeks earlier, Ghulam Nabi Azad and Indian Youth Congress president Tariq Anwar had reported that the state police were 'not taking stern action against extremists'.[29]

In June 1984, Indira Gandhi ordered the Indian Army into Amritsar's Golden temple, which had been occupied by Khalistani insurgents. On 2 July, Jagmohan dismissed Farooq's administration. Farooq's brother-in-law, G. M. Shah, whom he had expelled from the National Conference after winning the succession battle, had in pique founded his own party, the Awami National Conference. Shah succeeded in winning over a dozen National Conference legislators by promising them ministerial positions. Farooq now had the support of only 34 out of 75 legislators and, with Congress support, Shah staked claim to the majority. He was sworn in by Jagmohan without seeking a floor test. Farooq's dismissal, said journalist Tavleen Singh, set Kashmir back thirty years. 'Kashmir has been reminded that no matter how much it belongs to the mainstream of India, no matter how often its chief minister asserts he is Indian, it will always be special, always be suspect.'[30]

The entire opposition, from the Bharatiya Janata Party (BJP, successor of the Jan Sangh) to the Communist Party of India (Marxist) (CPI-M), came out in support of Farooq. BJP president Atal Bihari Vajpayee demanded Jagmohan's recall at the Home Ministry's parliamentary consultative committee meeting, and the CPI-M-led West Bengal cabinet denounced him for installing a government of 'stooges and defectors'. The recently formed United Front of centrist and communist parties sent a six-member delegation to Srinagar that included such political stalwarts as West Bengal finance minister Ashok Mitra and Janata Party leader I. K. Gujral—the former Congressman whom Indira Gandhi assigned to boost Kashmir's economy under Sadiq—to express their support for

Farooq. Andhra Pradesh Chief Minister N.T. Rama Rao castigated the 'patently indefensible action' of Governor Jagmohan, as 'an affront to the dignity and self-respect of any popular government', adding grandiloquently that 'history will not forgive us if we fail to fight and overcome the forces behind such an act'.[31]

Never before had Indian political parties so forcefully criticized the government's finagling in Jammu and Kashmir. Had they done so when Farooq's father was dismissed in 1953, or even when he was repeatedly arrested, the course of the state might have been different—Nehru was reluctant to have Abdullah arrested and opposition support might have turned the decision. The opposition would not be united again on Jammu and Kashmir for the next thirty years.

Indira Gandhi's Sikh guards assassinated her in October 1984 as revenge for sending the army into the Golden Temple, the most sacred of Sikh shrines. Her son, Rajiv, who was elected prime minister in 1985, moved his focus to peacemaking. In July 1985, he signed an accord with Punjab's Akali Dal leader Harcharan Singh Longowal. In August, he agreed peace with the armed All Assam Students' Union and the All Assam Gana Sangram Parishad (who demanded an end to illegal migration from Bangladesh), and the next year with insurgent leader Laldenga in Mizoram. Now he sought to patch up with Farooq.

While Rajiv and Farooq negotiated through a backchannel, the valley remained turbulent. In early 1986, communal riots in Anantnag district and neighbouring tehsils shook the Shah administration. What started the 1986 riots is unclear, but a string of events led up to them. On 15 February, police in Srinagar opened fire on crowds protesting the opening of the disputed Babri Masjid in Uttar Pradesh.[32] Around the same time, there were Hindu–Muslim clashes in Jammu, sparked by Shah's decision to allot two rooms for Muslim prayer in the Jammu civil secretariat, abutting a temple. Indefinite curfew was clamped on several towns in the state, earning Shah the dubious sobriquet 'Gul-e-Curfew' or 'curfew blossom'. On 20 February, mobs attacked Pandits in villages across Anantnag. Shah, said analyst Praveen Swami, had been forced to turn to Islamists in the absence of a popular mandate. Others alleged that the riots were orchestrated by then Congress leader Mufti Mohammad Sayeed because Anantnag was his constituency.[33]

Though no lives were lost in the riots, over twenty-three villages were affected. Quoting the district commissioner, the Calcutta *Telegraph* reported that 129 Pandit houses were looted, burnt or damaged, along with 16 temples, 9 shops, 2 paddy stores and 2 cowsheds. The Vijeshwari temple built by Ashoka was one of the sixteen destroyed. Villagers said that mobs of 2,000 to 5,000, armed with sticks and iron rods, came to attack them. It was only their Muslim neighbours' intervention that saved them, said one group of villagers. Others added that the local police did not come; they had to plead with nearby army units to save them. The Pandits, who had slowly but steadily migrated out of Jammu and Kashmir over the decades since 1947, were 'feeling bitter, frustrated and bewildered', journalist H. K. Dua wrote. 'The recent violence has shattered their confidence.'[34]

In July 1986, Jagmohan extended Article 249 of the Indian Constitution—under which state legislatures could not enact laws that contravened laws passed by parliament—to Jammu and Kashmir. Partly in reaction, Muslim political entities such as the Jamaat-e-Islami, People's Conference, Ummat-e-Islamia and Ittehad-ul-Muslimeen formed an electoral alliance named the Muslim United Front in August.

In September, Shah's administration was dismissed and the state was put under President's Rule. Jagmohan was efficient; he mobilized central resources to deliver an economic dividend and cracked down on corruption. But there were protests at Farooq's dismissal across the valley, which Jagmohan quelled with widespread arrests.

In any case, Governor's Rule was the last resort. Rajiv Gandhi wanted Farooq back. With only seven years between them—Rajiv was forty-two and Farooq forty-nine—the two got on well and trusted each other. In November 1986, they agreed that they would form an interim Congress–National Conference coalition administration and would contest the next elections together. According to Jagmohan, they also informally agreed to share power in the ratio of 60 per cent seats for the Conference and 40 for the Congress.[35] Farooq was sworn in as chief minister. Governor Jagmohan, who had first dismissed him and then had sworn him in under duress, remained.

As had happened with his father, Farooq was roundly criticized in Kashmir for his agreement with Rajiv Gandhi. He was seen as 'crawling' to Delhi and the Gandhi family, said Tavleen Singh.[36] Unlike his father, Farooq did not have the popular legitimacy to ride the wave of criticism that hit him. The National Conference was again a house divided, this time between Farooq's supporters and Shah's. When it was announced that there would be an assembly election in early 1987, Muslim political parties, led by the Shia cleric Maulvi Abbas Ansari, decided to band together and contest under the banner of the Muslim United Front.

In March 1987, when the election was held, it witnessed the largest turnout the state had seen. Over 80 per cent voted in the valley and 75 per cent in the state overall. The Congress–National Conference alliance won 66 of the 75 assembly seats. The Muslim United Front won 4 and the BJP 2.

Not all Muslim parties had joined the Muslim United Front. Influential parties like the People's Conference and the Awami Action Committee disagreed with the coalition's agenda, though they had earlier been a part of it. The Front's election manifesto stated it would work for a Kashmir settlement under the Simla Agreement. It added that the coalition's goal was Islamic unity and non-interference by the union government in the internal affairs of the state. Their election slogans, however, focused more on the rule of Sharia. The coalition's largest component, the Jamaat-e-Islami, was known to be pro-Pakistan. 'The Jamaat's accent was on secession,' said People's Conference founder Abdul Ghani Lone, 'we are looking for economic justice and a better deal from India.'[37] Riven by internal dissension, the Front split in June 1988, with the expulsion of the Jamaat and four Front members of the legislative assembly (MLAs).

In Delhi, the election result was hailed as a fresh start for the troubled state. In Srinagar, there were loud allegations of rigging by the Congress–National Conference alliance. Journalist Inderjit Badhwar reported that allegations of rigging poured in from all over the valley. 'The fact that details of the election results remained unannounced almost a week after the polling had ended gave credence to opposition charges that there was rigging and electoral bungling.' There would be a backlash in the form of 'a flight to obscurantist or secessionist causes', as in the past; its signs were already visible. 'Farooq faces a formidable challenge,' concluded Badhwar. 'If he fails, increasing numbers of young voters—there will be 24 percent new ones in the next elections—will be drawn into anti-national causes as a protest.'[38]

What made the allegations curious was that there seemed to be little reason for rigging. The Front had expected to win 10 seats instead of the 4 they did, and posed no serious electoral challenge to the alliance. But the threat of Islamic radicalism in the valley, which Indira Gandhi had pointed to in the early 1980s, was still fresh for a Congress whose leader had been assassinated by Sikh radicals. Governor Jagmohan continued to play up the Islamic threat, as he had when dismissing Farooq's administration in 1984.[39] Campaign stories were murky too. Intelligence sources claimed that Sayeed, still the state Congress head but angry with both Farooq and Rajiv for denying him a seat in the state cabinet, covertly supported the Front when campaigning in Anantnag. While telling voters they knew who to vote for, intelligence sources said, Sayeed brought out a pen—the Front's election symbol—and caressed an imaginary beard.[40] Sayeed was dogged by accusations: he had been accused of having a role in the anti-Hindu riots of 1986 too.[41]

With splits in their own leadership, the Congress–National Conference alliance took fright when early results showed the Front leading in 15 to 20 seats. Just prior to voting, and even as the results trickled in, a large number of Front activists were arrested. Many of the coalition's polling agents were thrown out of polling stations during the counting of votes. One of the

Front candidates who lost through alleged rigging was Muhammad Yusuf Shah, who later emerged as a leader of the Pakistan-based jihad against India. According to contemporary accounts, Shah's opponent had conceded defeat but was 'summoned back—to be declared the winner by presiding officials'.[42] Years later, Farooq Abdullah told journalist Harinder Baweja, 'I am not saying the elections weren't rigged. But I didn't rig them.' Senior Congressman Taj Mohiuddin, who was then in the Muslim United Front, concurred: 'The elections weren't rigged by the NC [National Conference] but by the Government of India.'[43] Habibullah's opinion was that rigging was likely to have occurred in some booths, but was not as widespread as claimed. 'Clear indications of malpractice' had been found in only ten constituencies, he said, mainly in Srinagar.[44] They were all constituencies that the National Conference then won.

Numerically small though the instances of rigging might have been, the fact that they were concentrated in Srinagar gave them great weight. Srinagar had been the political heart of the valley since the 1930s, from where the movement for an end to monarchy began. The city steadily gained in clout after it became the seat of political power in the 1950s. Decades of misrule, combined with Delhi's unseating of successive chief ministers, led to mounting anger in Srinagar, which now began to smoulder. The election of 1987 proved a turning point. Farooq, who was acclaimed as 'the lion's cub' in the early 1980s, especially after his dismissal by Governor Jagmohan, was covered with contumely when he returned as chief minister. There were mass demonstrations protesting the rigged election and affirming 'Kashmiriyat', a syncretic combination of elements of Sufi, Buddhist and Hindu traditions with Sunni Islam, as the cohesive force of a multi-ethnic Kashmiri nation that aspired to self-determination. A new Kashmiri movement began. Unlike prior movements, it was armed.

According to Kashmiri nationalist Arif Shahid, who was assassinated in Rawalpindi in 2013, the JKLF was approached by Pakistan's Inter-Services Intelligence (ISI) after the loss of Siachen in 1984 and the rise of the anti-Zia 'Movement for the

Restoration of Democracy'. The ISI asked the JKLF to train and arm insurgents to fight in Jammu and Kashmir, said Shahid, and they agreed on the condition that Kashmir would be granted independence after it was wrested from India.[45]

The group was initially more successful at recruiting Punjabi insurgents angered by Indira Gandhi's attack on the Golden Temple in Amritsar. Amanullah Khan, who had been deported from Britain to Pakistan in 1986 after serving a year in prison for possession of explosives, set up arms training camps along the Line of Control, many in Mirpur, with support from the Pakistan Army. But he was unable to recruit many from the valley until the controversial 1987 election, which offered a new opportunity to build a Kashmir jihad. Making a series of visits to the Kashmir border in the months following the election, President Zia announced on a visit to Muzaffarabad in July 1987, 'I can say with confidence that the sacrifices of [the] Mujahideen and their blood would not go in vain and the people of Pakistan and Kashmir would achieve success',[46] underlining that the defence of Pakistan rested on the defence of the statelet in his talk to troops in the forward areas.

This time, the Pakistani calculation that the valley was ripe for an uprising proved right. Infiltrating guerrillas were welcomed by many Kashmiris, as Nayeema Mahjoor's haunting account, *Lost in Terror*, attests. Gradually, young Kashmiris, too, began to cross the Line of Control to be trained and armed for guerrilla warfare in the valley. In mid-September 1988, the security forces arrested a number of young Kashmiri guerrillas who had returned from training in Pakistan-administered Kashmir. A few days later, a Pakistan-trained Kashmiri insurgent, Aijaz Dar, was killed in a security operation.

◆

The withdrawal of the Soviet Union from Afghanistan in 1988 helped bring the brewing crisis in Kashmir to a head. Pakistan's ISI, already giddy with the success of its decade-long Afghan policy that created the Taliban, and bloated by the power it had gained through it,[47] hastened to make hay and had the means to do so. The Pakistani media was rife with rumour of military planning for a quick Taliban victory in Afghanistan, which would release '30,000-40,000' Afghan Taliban fighters for 'what was being calculated by a Pakistani general as a decisive phase in Kashmir'.[48]

Through the 1980s, Pakistan used US and Saudi aid for the jihad against Soviet intervention to bolster the military, and in 1986, the US agreed a fifteen-year grant of $4.02 billion to be disbursed from October 1987 to September 1993. A considerable portion of the aid was to be spent on the purchase of US-manufactured military equipment such as the F-16 fighter aircraft. Pakistan's further request, for sale of the Airborne Warning and Control Systems to counter a perceived threat from the Soviet Union, added in turn to Indian threat perception. Reports of a Pakistani nuclear test in the third week of September 1986 further fuelled India–Pakistan tensions, already exacerbated by Pakistan signing a nuclear energy cooperation agreement with China on 15 September.

The end of US support for the Afghan jihad after the Soviet withdrawal meant the ISI no longer had to account for what it did with the arms that had been provided for the Afghan resistance. With plenty of stockpiled arms and no one to account to, Pakistan could easily divert consignments to Kashmir—and now at last there were takers. Beginning as a trickle in 1988 and growing into a flood by 1990, thousands of young men, many no more than boys, crossed over the Line of Control to train in hastily set up camps in Pakistan-administered Kashmir and the NWFP. Some were to make it as far as the Bin Laden complex at Khost.

The earliest recruits were candidates who had been kept out of the 1987 elections and their polling agents, chiefly from the Muslim United Front. They had been arrested and kept without bail under the draconian Public Safety Act (PSA). While in jail, they had been subjected to abuse as well as countless humiliations. Front candidate Yusuf Shah, for example, was arrested and imprisoned after the 1987 election. When he was released in 1989, he crossed over to Pakistan, where he was given aid and support to form a militia titled Hizbul Mujahideen, himself adopting the name

Salahuddin after the twelfth-century Kurdish general who fought the Crusaders. Shah's polling agent Yasin Malik, also arrested and imprisoned, founded a valley wing of JKLF, and was initially the leader of the uprising in the valley.

Though the first recruits to Islamic militias were members of the Muslim United Front, the bulk of recruits in the ensuing years were young graduates without jobs. Educational reforms in the 1950s and 1960s had created a new middle class and the Indian government poured development aid into the state under every five-year plan. Successive corrupt regimes siphoned off the money, and the economy did not keep pace with the growing middle class. As Kashmir stagnated and unemployment became a pressing problem, students with few prospects blamed their condition on Indian rule. Denied a hearing, they resorted to violence.

◆

As happened over and over again in the history of Indian and Pakistani peacemaking, Pakistani leaders, both civilian and military, put out feelers for peace while simultaneously pursuing a Kashmir jihad. A key actor in one of the India–Pakistan negotiations, A. K. Verma revealed that in early 1988, Pakistani President Zia, who was under US and European pressure following alleged nuclear tests in 1986, 'was particularly concerned about the expenditure on the operations in Siachen and was convinced that an agreement with India was possible to cut down on these expenses'.[49] Verma, then secretary of India's external intelligence organization, the R&AW, went on to describe how Zia approached Crown Prince Hassan of Jordan to speak to Indian prime minister Rajiv Gandhi. Hassan, Zia requested, should advocate 'a meeting between the Intelligence Chiefs of the two countries', who were at the time Verma and Hamid Gul, the architect of both the Afghan and Kashmir jihads.

When Prince Hassan broached the offer, Rajiv Gandhi agreed immediately, and Verma was deputed to hold backchannel talks with Gul. The two met twice in secret, first at Amman and then in Geneva. According to Verma, they succeeded in mapping out an agreement under which Pakistani forces would withdraw in the west to the ground level of the Saltoro Mountains. Pakistan would renounce claims to territory from NJ 9842 to the Karakoram Pass. The Line of Control would run north from NJ 9842 along the western ground level of Saltoro to the Chinese border. Pakistani troops would reduce by two divisions with corresponding adjustments on the Indian side.

The two countries went far in negotiation, by Verma's description. 'In confirmation of this understanding, General Hamid Gul sent a GHQ [general headquarters] Survey of Pakistan map where the new line of LOC [Line of Control] north of NJ 9842 and the western foot of Saltoro was clearly demarcated,' he said, convincing the Indian authorities that Zia was serious. While Verma did not clarify who took over the task of piloting the proposal through the various echelons of Indian decision-making, he described a process that began with the director general of military intelligence (DGMI), who was sceptical that Pakistan would agree—neither the DGMI, nor any but a handful, were told of the Verma–Gul meetings—but was willing to go along. The Ministry of Defence agreed next, and a meeting of the defence secretaries of the two countries was scheduled. 'It was decided that India would put forth the proposal for demilitarization of Siachen from its side and await Pakistani reactions.' On the day of the meeting, 17 August 1988, President Zia was killed in an air crash. A civilian government, headed by Benazir Bhutto, took office soon after. Hamid Gul was removed as ISI head after a botched plan for the Taliban to capture Afghanistan's Jalalabad, which was a crucial hub on the road to Kabul. 'When the Indian authorities made efforts to pick up the threads of the covert operation, they were told that no such operation was ever carried out and there was not a single paper in the Pakistani records which would testify to its existence,' Verma concluded. Gul did not speak; perhaps he was advised to remain silent. Only Niaz Naik, the then Pakistan High Commissioner to India, knew of the Verma–Gul negotiations. He was to play a key role in attempted peace talks in the next decade.

The one positive to come out of the talks was a small confidence-building measure (CBM): four Sikh soldiers, who had defected to Pakistan in protest at the attack on the Golden Temple, were handed back to India during the course of the Verma–Gul negotiations.

Chapter VII

BENAZIR, RAJIV AND THEIR SUCCESSORS

As young prime ministers, much was expected of Rajiv Gandhi and Benazir Bhutto. Both were good-looking, had charisma and glamour, though Rajiv's was understated and Benazir's cultivated. Both had parents who were assassinated while serving as prime minister, though Zulfikar was killed by his chief of army staff and Indira by her bodyguards. Both had studied at Britain's premier universities: Rajiv at Cambridge and Benazir at Oxford, where she shone as president of the Oxford Union while Rajiv retreated into the Cambridge shire. Both were welcomed to power by Indian and Pakistani voters, who turned out en masse to elect them.

Best of all, the two had political chemistry. Photographs at summit meetings show them smiling and relaxed, with an air of achievement. In a world of ageing right-wing leaders such as the US's Ronald Reagan and Britain's Margaret Thatcher, Rajiv and Benazir were not only young, they were liberal and even socialist in some of their policies. Each was grappling to transform his or her country—modernization in India and civilianization in Pakistan—and each brought new blood into their administrations, including young professionals from various fields. No wonder the media gushed over the golden boy and girl of South Asian politics, and analysts predicted they would usher in a new decade of India–Pakistan peacemaking.

Rajiv and Benazir began well, reviving Siachen talks and negotiating a trade agreement. In December 1988, Rajiv visited Pakistan for the fourth South Asian Association for Regional Cooperation (SAARC) summit. No Indian prime minister had visited Pakistan in the previous twenty-four years; indeed, the last visit was made by his grandfather Jawaharlal Nehru in 1964. Benazir expressed the hope that their meeting would 'herald the dawn of a new era',[1] and the two leaders signed a historic agreement pledging that their two countries would not attack each other's nuclear installations.

Though the Verma–Gul intelligence conversation was not renewed, Rajiv Gandhi and Benazir Bhutto did agree that their two countries' security agencies would adopt measures to curb terrorism, smuggling and illicit border crossing under the Simla Agreement, and revived backchannel and formal negotiations on Siachen. On 17 June 1989, the Indian and Pakistani defence secretaries issued a joint India–Pakistan statement declaring that they would work towards 'a comprehensive settlement based on redeployment of forces' that would limit the potential for conflict as well as 'avoidance of the use of force' should a conflict appear. Indian and Pakistani military officers would work towards 'determination of future positions on the ground so as to conform with the Simla Agreement and to ensure durable peace in the Siachen area'.[2]

The two countries' armies did not come to a determination of the pullback positions. Finding that Pakistani intelligence officers were arming and training insurgents in Punjab and Kashmir, 'India conveyed in unequivocal terms to Pakistan that the latter's continued support to terrorism directed against India was not only in contravention of the Simla Agreement and of universally accepted norms of inter-State conduct, but also adversely affected any confidence-building in [the] bilateral relationship.'[3]

Despite the hopes of Benazir and Rajiv, little was achieved. Rajiv lost the 1989 election and a weak coalition government led by the Janata Dal took power. Tensions remained high between India and Pakistan through 1989, compounded by events in Afghanistan where, post peace treaty, warlords fought for control over the land and people, some such as Gulbuddin Hekmatyar with backing from Pakistan. Hekmatyar was a privileged guest of the ISI, at whose request he also trained and armed Kashmiri guerrillas.

Talks resumed in 1990 when India's then external affairs minister I. K. Gujral met with Pakistani foreign minister Sahabzada

Yaqub Khan in New York on 25 April. The two agreed that the directors general of military operations (DGMOs) of India and Pakistan would be in regular communication in order to reduce tension and avoid confrontation. A month later, Indian representatives proposed a set of both military and non-military CBMs to Pakistan, and three rounds of foreign secretary-level talks were held, in July (Islamabad), August (New Delhi) and December (Islamabad).

Before the talks could gather steam, Benazir's administration was dismissed in late 1990, and Nawaz Sharif became prime minister of Pakistan. In November, Sharif and Indian prime minister Chandra Shekhar met at the SAARC summit in the Maldives and agreed to set up a hotline. In January 1991, the two governments exchanged Instruments of Ratification of the 1988 Agreement on Prohibition of Attack against Nuclear Installations and Facilities. The agreement came into effect three years after it had been signed. In March, the Surveyors General of India and Pakistan met to discuss demarcation of the land boundary in Sir Creek, which led, the Ministry of External Affairs reported laconically, to 'a better understanding of each other's perception'.[4]

In India's parliament, opposition members were sceptical, asking whether the Pakistani government was using talks as a cover to pursue its clandestine nuclear weapons programme. Chandra Shekhar replied with some bravado that 'India had the capability to meet the challenge, in whatever form it may arise'.[5]

◆

In Jammu and Kashmir, the 1990s were years of high conflict, in which insurgency multiplied, as did security forces. The 1987 election provided a proximate cause of the armed uprising, in the sense that widespread protests against its outcome reflected generations of frustration with Kashmir's illiberal democracy and repeated interventions by Delhi. But the immediate triggers for the spread of insurgency—without which the armed groups might not have gained in strength and public support—were the kidnapping of union Home Minister Mufti Mohammad Sayeed's daughter, the assassination of Mirwaiz Mohammad Farooq, and the reappointment of Jagmohan as governor, leading to Farooq Abdullah's resignation in protest. The state went under President's Rule again, after two short years.

Rubaiya Sayeed was kidnapped by the JKLF on 8 December 1989. The new Janata Dal-led government had just been sworn in at the centre, with Mufti Mohammad Sayeed as home minister. His first security meeting was on his daughter's kidnapping. Sayeed ensured that the state government met the kidnappers' demand for the exchange of five guerrillas in return for his daughter's release, overriding Chief Minister Farooq Abdullah's strenuous objections. There had been public revulsion at the kidnapping of a young woman—indeed, Mirwaiz Farooq had condemned it as un-Islamic—but the exchange gave an enormous fillip to armed groups. Kashmir's public saw the releases as denoting a weak government that was unable to protect them and, indeed, which caved to terrorism. Sayeed later confessed to Baweja, 'That is a guilt I will carry to my grave.'[6]

He attempted to compensate by adopting a counter-insurgency policy in which President's Rule was proclaimed in Jammu and Kashmir. Jagmohan was reappointed governor, Kashmir was declared a 'troubled area' and the army given special powers to quell armed rebels. The policy had mixed results. Over the years, it led to growing human rights abuses, and in the immediate term, militancy grew, as did public acceptance of it. Twenty years later, a spate of novels by young Kashmiris described how the decade set Kashmiri against Kashmiri. Basharat Peer's compelling account of suffering and dilemma in *Curfewed Night* (2010) serves as a reminder of the troubled 1990s, as does Siddhartha Gigoo's dirge to the pain and longing of exiled Kashmiri Pandits in *The Garden of Solitude* (2011).

Governor Jagmohan's assumption of office on 19 January 1990 coincided with a large-scale exodus of Kashmiri Pandits from the valley. He was accused of having 'facilitated the migration', said Mohammad Yusuf Taing, a contemporary political commentator, even of encouraging Pandits to leave so as to give him a free hand against unrest.[7] Irrespective of the truth or falsity of the allegation, which Jagmohan denied, it is highly unlikely that people would have left their homes, livelihoods and property unless they were threatened, as thousands of Pandit accounts of those dark days attest.

The guerrillas burnt buses and destroyed bridges. In Srinagar, they bombed the headquarters of the National Conference and shot a National Conference leader, as well as the vice president of the state unit of the BJP and the Pandit head of the state's Doordarshan television channel. The newly formed militia, Hizbul Mujahideen, which overtook the JKLF within a year, issued a call for Pandits to leave the valley, and mosques blared messages reiterating the call. Hindus began to be and feel threatened. Jagmohan, said Habibullah, added to the sense of threat when he, in response, set up 'refugee camps' for Pandits and ensured their safe passage out of the valley.[8] Habibullah had returned to the valley in 1990 as special commissioner of Anantnag, a post created by Jagmohan to oversee all civil works in south Kashmir. He negotiated an assurance from eminent citizens in Anantnag that they would protect Pandits in south Kashmir and wanted Jagmohan to endorse the offer, a plea that Jagmohan brushed aside. Whether the offer would have stood firm in the face of mounting insurgency is debatable. In any case, it was not put to the test. What started as a trickle of Pandits out of the Kashmir valley soon became an exodus. Of the roughly 300,000 Pandits in the valley in 1989, more than two-thirds left in 1990.

The counter-insurgency crackdown began immediately after Jagmohan assumed office. On the night of 19 January, security forces conducted house-to-house searches in Srinagar to find hidden guerrillas and weapons. Hundreds were arrested. The next day, paramilitary troops opened fire on protesters at Srinagar's Gawkadal Bridge. Twenty people were killed in what is now called the Gawkadal Massacre. Another opportunity for Pakistan was presented and, in February, large processions from Pakistani Punjab and Pakistan-administered Kashmir attempted to cross into Jammu and Kashmir, first through the Jammu border and then through the Line of Control. In the valley, tension further exacerbated when Jagmohan dissolved the state assembly on 19 February, and dissident leaders such as Geelani, Lone, Abdul Ghani Bhat (who was a founder of the reconstituted Muslim Conference in 1990), Abbas Ansari and Qazi Nissar were arrested. Shabir Shah, whose People's League was supported by the armed group Al Jehad, was already in prison, having been arrested in 1989.

Three months later, Mirwaiz Farooq was assassinated. Intelligence on the threat to him had trickled in for months. As early as April 1990, the analyst G. N. Khayal noted a flurry of criticism by 'a section of the Pakistani press pursuing a particular political ideology', who branded the Mirwaiz a 'stooge of India and the paid agent of New Delhi'.[9] The Mirwaiz's meeting with union Minister for Kashmir Affairs George Fernandes had rankled, and his statement that Rubaiya Sayeed's kidnapping was un-Islamic hardened Pakistani suspicion into hostility. His Islam threatened the interpretation that the ISI developed for guerrillas.

Returning from his visit to Pakistan, Khayal went to caution the Mirwaiz and found that he was being pressed by the state and union governments to accept security. A reluctant Mirwaiz told Khayal, 'How can I accept police guards? Tell me, tell me, am I not the Mirwaiz of Jammu and Kashmir? Scores of men and women throng my house day in and day out for paying their regards and for receiving my blessings. How can I tolerate their being frisked before their entrance into my premises? Can I, tell me?'

Khayal left Mirwaiz Farooq 'with a heavy heart', fearing he might never see him again. On the morning of 21 May, a senior officer of the state police rang him to say that the Mirwaiz had been shot at point-blank range by three gunmen in the same room where Khayal had met him.

Though it was widely known that the Mirwaiz was assassinated by the Hizbul Mujahideen, public ire turned on Delhi when security forces fired at the Mirwaiz's funeral procession. Ironically, mourners had defied the Islamic militias' edict that there should be a three-day curfew following the assassination, doubtless to ensure his funeral be low-key. But as the procession swelled, some began to shout pro-independence and anti-India slogans. According to one of the mourners who was injured, 'Security forces deployed on roads did not shoot',[10] but when the procession reached Islamia College, security men camped inside the college compound began to fire at the crowd. According to the police, the firing started when gunmen were seen mingling with mourners. Close to fifty people were killed and the Mirwaiz's coffin was riddled with bullets.

In a final irony, one of Mirwaiz Mohammad Farooq's killers, Abdullah Bangroo, was buried in the same Martyrs' Graveyard as he was, the Eidgah ground adjoining his Jamia Masjid in Srinagar.

The Mirwaiz's murder took place in the context of a guerrilla campaign for Islamization when armed groups ordered the closure of all liquor shops and cinema halls in the Kashmir valley from 1 January 1990. The Hizbul Mujahideen and the newly formed all-women's Islamic political organization, the Dukhtaran-e-Millat, called on Muslim women in the valley to observe strict purdah, backing the call with attacks on unveiled women, including girls.[11]

The situation was compounded by Jagmohan's 'counter-insurgency alone' policy. His dissolution of the state assembly in February 1990 ripped the last figment of democracy off the valley.[12] Disaffection grew when he proceeded to ignore the civil administration and police, whose loyalty he suspected, relying instead on a small group of military and intelligence officers.[13] Jagmohan later justified his actions as the only way to crush an externally driven and internally supported terrorist movement, saying in his characteristically overblown and often bizarre prose: 'Obviously, I could not walk barefoot in the valley full of scorpions. Wherein inner and outer forces of terrorism had conspired to subvert the Union and to seize power... I must equip myself to face all eventualities. I could leave nothing to chance. A slight slip or error would have meant a Tiananmen Square or a Blue Star or a formal declaration of a new theocratic state with all its international embarrassment.'[14]

The combination of Pakistan's Salafization strategy and India's harsh counter-insurgency response crippled the fledgling Kashmir democracy movement. Met by Indian military force—with Indian troops shooting to kill—Kashmiri enthusiasm for armed struggle began to wane by late 1991. If India had offered a political outlet for Kashmiri grievances, the uprising might have died a natural death. But India's weak coalition governments, that rose and fell from the end of the 1980s through the 1990s, lacked the courage for political reform. Pakistan's ISI began to fill the vacuum with Islamic militias of its own creation.

Alarmed by the exponential and rapid rise of militancy in Kashmir and the rising criticism of Jagmohan's handling of it, the Janata Dal government began to reconsider his appointment. When he refused to attend the Mirwaiz's funeral, his fate was sealed. Five days after the Mirwaiz's assassination, he was replaced by Governor Girish Saxena, the former head of India's external intelligence agency, R&AW.

Governor Saxena was appointed to calm the anger that Jagmohan had provoked, but he found a situation in which he had few assets. Governor Jagmohan's response, of arbitrary arrests and detentions, and the subordination of civil and human rights to an extent that had not been seen since the days of Maharaja Hari Singh, had led to an increase in armed attacks. As is common in civil conflicts, administration had been the first casualty. The Islamic guerrillas enforced bandhs and hartals, attacked government offices, convoys and infrastructure and murdered police and intelligence officers. They targeted both government and independent media, killing or wounding more than two dozen prominent journalists, including editors, and destroying their offices and presses. As the previous chapters show, administration and the media were regarded as soft but prime targets by Pakistani strategists since the 1948–49 war.[15]

Saxena's first challenge was to reconcile the state's administrative officers and the police, who were in open rebellion against Jagmohan. A day after the latter resigned, 137 senior state officers sent a memorandum to the UN Secretary-General, pleading for intervention in Kashmir. Immediately after, a separate and much smaller group of civil servants presented a memorandum to Saxena criticizing the union government's handling of dissent in the state. Their resentment multiplied when the state was again put under President's Rule in July 1990. The announcement was followed by a three-day strike of Muslim state government employees, allegedly sponsored by Islamic militias. In August 1990, Yasin Malik of the JKLF and other top JKLF armed insurgents were arrested at Srinagar. In September, following Saxena's transfer of several of the protesting civil servants, state government employees again went on strike. This time the strike lasted for close to two and a half months and it looked as if India was on the verge of losing the valley.

In January 1991, Prime Minister Chandra Shekhar offered talks with the armed groups, and in February, the Hizbul Mujahideen and the Jamaat-e-Islami accepted his offer, but with preconditions. The Chandra Shekhar administration fell soon after, but backchannel negotiations with armed groups continued.

◆

The Janata Dal coalition collapsed in 1991 and fresh elections were called, during which Rajiv Gandhi was assassinated by a cadre of Sri Lanka's Liberation Tigers of Tamil Eelam (LTTE). He was campaigning in South India, where fellow feeling for the beleaguered Tamil minority in neighbouring Sri Lanka had morphed into support for the insurgent LTTE. The Congress came back to power on a sympathy wave, and the stalwart Congressman P. V. Narasimha Rao became prime minister.

Rao was a backroom politician but an able administrator. His first priority was to rescue India from a debt crisis induced by its stagnating economy, which he achieved through a programme of economic liberalization that paved the way for India to achieve a 7–9 per cent rate of growth in the next decade.

He was less successful in his efforts to make peace with Kashmiris or Pakistan. Though India and Pakistan agreed to ban the use of chemical weapons in August 1992, Pakistan avoided further negotiation on Siachen. In his first stint as prime minister, Sharif had won the 1991 election as head of a conservative political and religious alliance created by Hamid Gul, the Islami Jamhoori Ittehad. His father's religious mentor was a fiery preacher of one of Punjab's largest Islamic seminaries, and he—like most of Pakistan's military and religious leadership—believed Pakistan was on the verge of winning the valley through the Kashmir insurgency.

Sharif did put out feelers for a Kashmir peace process. He sent his foreign secretary to Delhi on 17 August to propose bilateral discussions on Jammu and Kashmir under Article 6 of the Simla Agreement. At the same time, pressured by the military and religious leadership, Sharif's administration sought international intervention on Kashmir at the tenth summit of the Non-Aligned Movement and the UN General Assembly, a ploy that successive Pakistani governments had used since 1948 and which continued to rile Indian leaders. In continuation of its jihad policy, again in play since 1948, the ISI expanded infiltration of Islamic militias into Jammu and Kashmir along with arms training for Kashmiri insurgents. Rao had to find ways to limit Pakistan's covert intervention.

Pakistani aid to armed militia groups was increasingly evident. Estimated at over $3 million per month in 1993, it was briefly suspended under US pressure but resumed on a smaller scale in 1994. In February of that year, India's parliament passed a resolution noting 'with deep concern Pakistan's role in imparting training to the terrorists in camps located in Pakistan and Pakistan Occupied Kashmir, the supply of weapons and funds, assistance in infiltration of trained militants, including foreign mercenaries into Jammu and Kashmir with the avowed purpose of creating disorder, disharmony and subversion'.[16] The resolution called on Pakistan to 'stop forthwith its support to terrorism, which is in violation of the Simla Agreement and the internationally accepted norms of inter-State conduct', but met with little response.

Pakistani aid now began to be diverted from the more secular militias to radical protégés of the Pakistani religious party, Jamaat-e-Islami.[17] According to Arif Shaheed,* the ISI paid its agents in

---

*Arif Shaheed's name is spelled differently—Shahid, Shahed, Shaheed—in different articles.

Jammu and Kashmir between ₹50,000-100,000 a month and hosted them lavishly in Rawalpindi (while interrogating them). When insurgency spread, the ISI reneged on its pledge to independence for Kashmir, engineering a split in the JKLF and pitting the Jamaat-sponsored Hizbul against it. The ISI, said Shaheed, preferred to boost Islamic militias that were pro-accession to Pakistan.[18] Yusuf Shah of the Hizbul, who remained in Pakistan, was pliable, whereas the JKLF's Srinagar-based Malik, like Amanullah Khan, was not. He favoured independence over accession to Pakistan.

The Pakistani tactic of using religious parties as a conduit for insurgency had been tried fifty years earlier through the Jamaat-e-Islami in the run-up to partition, but without success. It led the Jamaat to split. The Kashmiri branch of the organization was closer to the Pakistani branch than the Indian one, but relatively small in the decades following partition. Abdullah's Sufi-influenced Islam held greater popular sway in the valley.

Counter to its India experience, Pakistan's adaptation of the strategy in its Afghan policy was relatively successful, and it renewed the ISI's interest in its potential efficacy in Kashmir. Some alleged that the Jamaat also received a fillip when Farooq Abdullah resigned in 1990 over Jagmohan's appointment. Farooq, they said, made common cause with the Jamaat to oppose the governor. If true, the alliance did not last long, since National Conference leaders and cadre were amongst the armed groups' prime targets.

By the early 1990s, Islamic militias and the Indian Army dominated life in the valley, with an estimated 10,000 to 15,000 fighters and 'several hundred thousand' security forces (combining army, paramilitary and police).[19] Guerrilla clashes with government security forces jumped from 390 in 1988 to 2,154 in 1989, and doubled to 4,971 by 1992. The number remained in the high 4,000s till 1996. Schools in rural areas were occupied by security forces, some of whom were also installed at university campuses. According to official figures, schools functioned for only 93 days in 1993–94, and 140 days in 1994–95. Kashmir's capital, Srinagar, was under a double curfew. One imposed by the security forces, who controlled Srinagar's city centre, the Lal Chowk, and the government residential areas; the other by armed guerrillas, mostly from the JKLF, who ruled the surrounding streets and suburbs of Srinagar as well as the villages of south Kashmir. Increasing numbers of civilians died in terrorist attacks or crossfire; the numbers jumped from 29 in 1988 to 862 in 1991 and over 1,000 per year in the years immediately after.[20]

Though Saxena did succeed in restoring some confidence in the police and civil administration, rising communal tension in India and the army's counter-insurgency methods in Kashmir provided ongoing triggers for the further spread of insurgency.

Military cordon and search operations—in which the army would cordon off a village on receiving intelligence that there might be guerrillas sheltering there, to conduct house-to-house searches, generally under cover of darkness—caused growing public resentment. The soldiers did not speak Kashmiri, they were more often rough than polite, and they did not have any women officers with them. Reports of enforced disappearances and human rights abuse began to pour in.[21] In February 1991, there were allegations of mass rape during an army cordon and search by the 4th Rajputana Rifles in the northern Kashmiri villages of Kunan and Poshpora (in Kupwara district, bordering the Line of Control).[22] The army held that the accusations were 'a hoax orchestrated by militant groups' as 'part of [a]cleverly contrived strategy of psychological warfare'.[23] Human rights and women's groups accused the army of a cover-up.[24] Three separate enquiries concluded that the evidence was inconsistent but, as the reports indicated, neither the state nor the union governments conducted a methodical investigation into the incident. It is not even known how many alleged rapes there were. Estimates range from 23 to 150.

Irrespective of the evidence, the women who made allegations of rape paid with ruined lives. They were ostracized in their villages and their children were taunted by classmates at school. None were able to resume lives free from stigma. An enquiry into the incident was reopened in 2015 with few results so far.

Habibullah was himself a casualty of the incident. Sent by Saxena to enquire into the allegations of rape, his report concluded that the evidence was inconclusive but recommended further investigation. When the report was published, the latter recommendation was deleted and Habibullah was seen as engaging in a whitewash. Soon after, he was shot while visiting Hazratbal. He survived but several of the officers accompanying him were killed.[25]

The Janata Dal coalition, then in power, was already under pressure from rising Hindu chauvinism. The BJP had gained Hindu acceptability as a partner in the coalition. For the first time, the party moved beyond its single digit performance to win 85 seats in the 1989 Lok Sabha. In 1990, however, the BJP fell out with the Janata Dal. The first fallout was over the administration's attempt to expand reservations in government institutions to include other backward classes (OBCs) as recommended by a government commission headed by B. P. Mandal, which aroused upper-caste Hindu ire. Following hard on the heels of the 'Mandal agitation', as the protests were dubbed, BJP leader L. K. Advani announced he would lead a campaign to demand construction of a new temple at the disputed Babri Masjid in Ayodhya. The fifteenth-century masjid was said to have been built on the ruins of an ancient Hindu temple commemorating the birthplace of the god Ram. When the government prevented Advani from entering Ayodhya, the BJP withdrew support for the Janata Dal administration and it fell.

In the 1991 general election, the BJP improved its seat count to 120, largely on the election plank of uniting a Hindu nation. Pursuing its promise, the BJP announced in January 1992 that party leaders would hoist the Indian flag at Srinagar's Lal Chowk on India's Republic Day, in culmination of the party's month-long 'one nation' or Ekta Yatra campaign that started from the southern tip of India in Kanyakumari. The announcement caused immediate alarm in Srinagar, where guerrillas set off a bomb in the police headquarters, critically injuring the director general of police and killing several police officers, including the BSF Inspector General Ashok Patel, who was credited with having broken the back of the JKLF.

Then BJP president Murli Manohar Joshi, who planned to lead the march from Jammu to Srinagar to hoist the flag at Lal Chowk, was warned that armed guerrillas could attack their route. He changed his plan to demand an airlift to Srinagar, a demand the Janata Dal complied with, imposing an indefinite curfew on the city and issuing shoot on sight orders to the security forces.

Srinagar turned into a battle zone. The army erected sandbag bunkers and temporary checkposts around Lal Chowk; they took its rooftops and stood at the door of each building lining its streets. 'On Jan 26, 1992, we heard only firing,' said a resident of the area. 'There were explosions...from all directions of the city neighbourhood. It was like a war.'[26] Around twenty people died in army–guerrilla shoot-outs that day. Bathetically, when Joshi raised the flag, its rod broke and the flag fell on his forehead.

By late 1992, the number of armed groups had spiralled, though the JKLF and Hizbul remained the largest. The Pakistani military, contemporary analysts noted, felt it was safer to invest in a number of armed militias than in one or two large ones that might make peace with India. As the number of guerrillas grew, they also aligned with individual religious and political leaders. The young Mirwaiz of Kashmir, for example, who had succeeded to the post after his father's assassination, was linked to the Al-Umar Mujahideen through his Awami Action Committee, while Shabir Shah's People's League and Democratic Freedom Party was supported by Al Jehad and Al Fatah, and Lone's People's Conference was associated with Al Barq. These and affiliated groups were ensconced in the hub cities of Anantnag, Baramulla and Sopore, as well as Srinagar.

Pakistani influence had, for the first time in close to fifty years of conflict, spread through a dozen armed groups and their civilian leaders. The ISI judged that a united front of anti-India militias would give their political message weight while allowing the militias to keep a check on each other. The policy intensified internecine violence. Beginning in 1991, incidences of inter-militia clashes mounted from 80 in 1991 to 139 in 1992. The loss of guerrilla lives began to become a high cost for their sponsors.

An early effort to create a united front, the Tehreek-i-Hurriyat Kashmir, forged by the pro-Pakistan advocate, Mian Abdul Qayoom, was unsuccessful. The Tehreek comprised ten groups: the Jamaat-e-Islami, JKLF, Muslim Conference, Islamic Students League, Mahaz-e-Azadi, Muslim Khawateen Markaz, Kashmir Bar Association, Ittehad-ul-Muslimeen, Dukhtaran-e-Millat and Jamiat Ahle Hadees. Lacking heavyweights such as the Mirwaiz, Shabir Shah and Abdul Ghani Lone, the group was seen as essentially a rework of the Muslim United Front.

A second stab, this time by the nineteen-year-old Mirwaiz, proved more lasting. In December 1992, Mirwaiz Umar called a meeting of religious, social and political organizations at Mirwaiz Manzil, to form a broad alliance of parties opposed to 'Indian rule'. Seven months later, the All Parties Hurriyat Conference was announced in July 1993, with Umar as its first chairman. The coalition brought together the Jamaat-e-Islami, Awami Action Committee, People's League, Ittehad-ul-Muslimeen, Muslim Conference, JKLF, and People's Conference. The heavyweights were all present.

Armed insurgency continued to grow. Attacks on security forces increased from below 50 in 1989 to over 3,000 in 1992. The numbers of security forces killed in these attacks rose by over 200—from 13 in 1989 to 216 in 1993. By this point, the number of guerrillas killed had also shot up, from 0 in 1989 to 873 in 1992 to 1,328 in 1993.[27] In January 1993, a group of 7 or 8 JKLF fighters attacked a BSF patrol in the Sopore market, killing one trooper. In retaliation, the BSF opened indiscriminate fire, killing more than 50 civilians. Hundreds of shops were gutted in a fire that was alleged to have been set by the BSF, though the BSF said it was caused by a guerrilla cache of explosives catching fire which spread through the market.

There was uproar in the Indian parliament, already rocked by the demolition of the Babri Masjid by Hindu fundamentalist groups in December 1992. The demolition was followed by Hindu–Muslim riots across north and central India. In a surcharged communal condition, Narasimha Rao announced compensation of

₹100,000 each for the families of civilians killed in Sopore, and Saxena ordered an enquiry into the incident. Though the enquiry report was not made public, several BSF troops were suspended.

These actions were viewed as too little in the valley. When prominent Muslim leaders and left-wing MPs demanded that Saxena be sacked and a parliamentary delegation visit Kashmir, he was replaced by General Krishna Rao in March 1993. In the same month, a series of synchronized terrorist attacks took place in Bombay, killing close to 200 people. The attacks were funded by a crime lord named Dawood Ibrahim, who ran a coercion and protection racket in the city. Ibrahim fled to Pakistan soon after, involving himself there in the ISI-engineered Kashmir and India jihads. In April 1993, Sharif assured Rao, when they met at Bangladesh's capital Dhaka, that his administration would extradite Ibrahim to India. The promise was soon forgotten. Ibrahim continued to live between Karachi and Dubai and remained under ISI protection.

Chapter VIII

THE SIEGE OF HAZRATBAL

In April 1993, the same month Prime Minister Sharif promised Prime Minister Rao that Yakub Memon would be extradited to India, the valley was rocked by a JKLF occupation of Hazratbal, a delicately beautiful shrine built in white marble, rising from the banks that separate the majestic Dal and dreamy Nigeen Lakes.[1] Hazratbal was the most popular shrine in Kashmir, a place that Shias and Sunnis worshipped at and that Sheikh Abdullah had made a centre of his political mobilization.

The JKLF controlled the streets and outlying areas of the Hazratbal area and occupied the shrine and adjoining buildings in the Hazratbal complex before they were detected. The Indian Army cordoned off the mosque and, after negotiations led by Rajesh Pilot, then minister of state for Home Affairs, the guerrillas accepted safe passage in return for vacating Hazratbal.

The Indian Army protested the offer of safe passage. A siege of the mosque, they argued, would force the guerrillas to surrender and be arrested. But the Rao administration, through Pilot, was committed to restart backchannel talks with the JKLF that started under Governor Saxena and continued under his successor. Rao had just taken office when the April occupation took place.

On the JKLF side, Hamid Sheikh, who was imprisoned with Yasin Malik, was principal messenger in the backchannel. Released in 1992 in the hope that he would persuade the JKLF to enter a peace process, he ended up rejoining one of its militias and was shot by the BSF in November, along with a group of guerrillas who were trying to cross the Jhelum to flee across the Line of Control. The Hizbul Mujahideen, security sources added, set up death squads after Sheikh's release to ensure peace negotiations would fail. In April 1993, the Hizbul guerrilla Zulqarnain murdered

Abdul Ahad Guru, a doctor and JKLF mentor, who negotiated the releases of Congress leader Saifuddin Soz's daughter, Naheed, and Indian Oil executive director, K. Doraiswamy, in 1991. Though it was a Hizbul guerrilla who killed Guru, the police colluded in his killing, according to Habibullah. Guru presented 'a reasonable face of separatism'[2] and was widely respected, so he was a counter-insurgency target. Zulqarnain was killed in a security operation soon after.

Frustration in the security forces grew in the months to follow. In Sopore, the aftermath of the market firing saw growing support for insurgency. Reports of guerrillas massing in the town began to flow from May 1993, but the state and union governments did not react. 'Intelligence and others urged decisive and early action', wrote Arun Shourie, editor of the *Indian Express*. 'Nothing was done. By September, about 600 [of the guerrillas] were reported not only to be there, they were reported to have entrenched themselves in bunkers dug out in some houses at various points in the town. Minimal action in May–June would have seen the end of them. By September, a Blue Star-type operation alone would have sufficed. And intelligence was warning that if that sort of action was not launched immediately, and the snow were allowed to set in, the mercenaries would get another four to five months to fortify their presence. What sort of an operation would be necessary then?'[3]

The challenge came in October 1993. A month earlier, intelligence agencies began to report that guerrillas, both Kashmiri and Pakistani, were using the Hazratbal mosque and its adjoining buildings to stockpile arms and interrogate informers whom they took prisoner. The JKLF, they said, planned a show of power against their arch-rival, the Hizbul. Though security agencies repeatedly requested permission for an operation to rid the mosque of armed militias, they were told not to enter Hazratbal or the university and college campuses in Srinagar. As a result, guerrillas were able to entrench themselves. According to Shourie, the intelligence agencies urged, 'Even if the shrine is out of bounds, at least raid and clean up the barracks',[4] but the proposal was vetoed. Still committed to negotiation with the JKLF, though Sheikh was dead, the Rao administration feared to take any steps that might prejudice talks even if those were in limbo.

The union government finally took action when rumours floated that guerrillas planned to steal the Mo-i-Muqaddas, whose theft once before had almost led the state administration to fall in 1963. The army and BSF were asked to surround the Hazratbal complex as they had done in April, but not to shoot or even train guns on the shrine. The area was cordoned off on 15 October, the day after guerrillas 'held what was virtually an exhibition of arms and ammunition they had piled up inside the shrine', commented Shourie. Along with the JKLF, the Al-Umar Mujahideen had staged armed parades inside the shrine for some weeks already. The guerrillas held 170 civilian hostages, who had been in the shrine to worship when the security cordon was laid.

Within days of the siege, the newly formed Hurriyat Conference called for an end to it, and there were youth protests in Srinagar, Sopore and Bijbehara that ended in violence, with around forty civilians shot by the BSF in Bijbehara. Eyewitness accounts recount how the demonstration of around 300 youth passed peacefully on the streets of Bijbehara, the ancient town of Vijeshwari held in myth to have been built by the god Shiva. The violence started when they went on to the highway, where demonstrations were banned since guerrillas regularly attacked military convoys using the highways.[5] A government enquiry indicted the BSF and recommended thirteen troops be charged with murder, but a subsequent security review in 1996 exonerated them.

The siege dragged on. Habibullah, who had returned to Kashmir as divisional commissioner just a few weeks ago, was appointed chief negotiator with the guerrillas inside the mosque, along with the Additional Chief Secretary (Home), Mehmood-ur-Rahman. The two held round after round of talks with the JKLF's Idris. The talks centred on safe passage for the guerrillas to exit Hazratbal, but stalemated on the details of exit. On 17 October, guerrillas threatened to blow up the shrine if any attempt was made to storm it. The union government, with the looming spectre of the Golden Temple, whose storming in 1984 led to the expansion of insurgency in Punjab, was loath to use force. Both Prime Minister and Governor Rao stated publicly that there would be no military action.

The next sticking point was the release of hostages and surrender of arms. The government agreed to safe passage provided these two conditions were met, but the guerrillas refused. In the meantime, there was the problem of providing food for the hostages. The guerrillas initially refused to accept food packages and the army was in favour of cutting off water and electric supplies. After hectic parley, the guerrillas allowed food to be sent in for the hostages. Governor Rao had already given orders to cut off water and electricity, only to rescind them after being urged to do so by the negotiators.

Negotiations were further complicated by dissonance amongst various government actors and the entry of additional actors. The army held to its argument that the guerrillas should be forced to surrender, whereas civilian negotiators pushed for a government–guerrilla agreement. Their publicly aired disagreements were exploited by guerrilla negotiators to wrest concessions. Surprised by how well-informed the guerrillas were, indicating they 'were in touch with the outside world', Habibullah found that the Intelligence Bureau had secretly installed a phone with an unlisted number in the mosque so that they could eavesdrop on guerrilla conversations. The line was not cut when the siege started, and though Habibullah requested it be disconnected, the Bureau ensured it remained open. It continued to be used by the guerrillas to broadcast statements to the international media, who were all agog.[6]

Eventually, the siege was lifted when the guerrillas were allowed to exit with their arms after freeing their hostages. Exit with arms had been a guerrilla demand from the start of the siege, but the Rao administration had not been prepared to concede it initially. Government negotiators started by insisting that safe passage would only be offered if combined with the surrender of arms and arrest for interrogation, but they lowered the bar as negotiations continued and the siege protracted. Habibullah's opinion had been, from the start, that safe passage and not surrender would be the guerrillas' bottom line. Though he had shared this opinion with Governor Rao, he had been overruled, with the union and state governments saying that surrender was non-negotiable. They soon backed down.

The end of the Hazratbal crisis was greeted with both a sigh of relief and a storm of protest. The crisis had been handled ineptly, said critics. There was already dissension between intelligence and security forces on the one hand and the Rao administration and its negotiators on the other. Key decisions were taken without consultation between political leaders and the army, for example, on whether or not to cut water and electricity. The security coordination group that had been set up under Governor Saxena was marginalized during the crisis, said Shourie, with Governor Rao relying on his own advisers.

Nor were the union and state governments in sync. According to Shourie, by late September–early October, 'communication between Srinagar and the home ministry had broken down completely'.[7] The Home Ministry was itself a house divided: Home Minister S. B. Chavan washed his hands off the issue, and Minister of State Pilot and Governor Rao no longer spoke to each other. Prime Minister Rao 'saw how dear the "personality clashes" were proving for the country. But habits ingrained deep by a lifetime of lying low had left him little inclination to intervene.'

Some of the criticism was just plain wrong. According to Habibullah, Governor Rao set up a Unified Command to handle the crisis, comprising the chief and home secretaries of Jammu and Kashmir, the director general of the state police, the divisional commissioner (Habibullah), the corps commander of the army's 15 Corps or his representative, the inspectors general of the BSF and CRPF and the head of the Kashmir police division. Day-to-day decisions on handling the crisis were taken by the governor after discussion in the Unified Command. That there were often disagreements amongst the group, with the governor overruling some, was not surprising; indeed, it indicated consultation rather than high-handedness.

To be fair, there was little consensus on how to deal with the crisis outside of government as well as within it. Six days into the siege, Prime Minister Rao convened a meeting of the standing committee of the National Integration Council, which included opposition and state leaders, on Hazratbal and the Kashmir insurgency. He received widely differing views, from storming Hazratbal to sending 'the fellows packing to Pakistan',[8] to leaving the decision about how to handle the crisis to the state government.

Rao already faced severe challenges both at home and abroad. His liberalization policy was contested by rivals within the party as well as in opposition-ruled states. There were insurgencies in northwestern and northeastern India. Politically incited communalism swept much of northern and central India. There were tensions with Sri Lanka over the Tamil issue and with Pakistan over support for insurgency in Punjab and Kashmir. And the US and Europe had begun to back Pakistani claims on Kashmir.

Most immediate of all, there were ongoing elections in four states, including the most populous and influential state, Uttar Pradesh, and the BJP was using the Hazratbal crisis to paint the Congress government as weak. Rao was in a no-win situation. Had he allowed the mosque to be stormed, he might have come across as strong, but that would have alienated Muslims and risked a further boost to the Kashmir insurgency. That is what had happened after Indira Gandhi sent the army into Punjab's Golden Temple in 1984. Though she was feted as a strong leader, the insurgency in Punjab had spread like wildfire and Sikh nationalists turned to Pakistan.

More importantly, the security versus political approach posed a structural dilemma, not merely a functional one. The criticism over Hazratbal's handling, unfortunately, clouded this question. In the plethora of articles questioning the government's approach and belittling negotiations, none looked closely at what had been achieved. Though the siege was prolonged beyond need, not a single life was lost. The guerrillas lost a sanctuary and their claim to be 'liberators of Hazratbal', if not their arms. Local residents, according to Habibullah, appealed to the guerrillas to vacate the shrine. For the first time too, the Hurriyat acted as intermediaries in an initiative marshalled by the chief secretary to the Government of Jammu and Kashmir, Sheikh Ghulam Rasool. He persuaded Abdul Ghani Bhat of the Muslim Conference and the Shia cleric Maulvi Abbas Ansari of the Ittehad-ul-Muslimeen, both members of the Hurriyat executive, to urge the guerrillas to accept the government's offer of a safe passage along with surrender of arms.

At the same time, the intelligence agencies were able get leaders from the JKLF, Operation Balakote and Al Jehad militias to jointly address a letter to the Hazratbal guerrilla urging them to surrender: 'We have already gained as much as we could. You all have become heroes and so your lives are very valuable to us.' According to news reports, the intelligence agencies had been cleared by Governor Rao to assure the signatories to the letter that the guerrillas would not be handed over to the army or the BSF, but 'would be bailed out through the judicial process'.[9]

The two initiatives should have been complementary but were seen as undermining each other in a turf war. The Hurriyat leaders, critics said, had 'gained legitimacy by the Government repeatedly seeking their help'. They had gained so much in the month-long siege that they could now set 'a civil curfew'.[10] Though the government curfew had been lifted in most areas of Srinagar, the shutdowns called by the Hurriyat had continued.

Once again, the critics obscured a key point. It is true that the Hurriyat had little authority over the militias at that point, or even later. But if a civil coalition, however unpalatable their ideology, gained ground over armed groups with the same ideology, the net result would be to make peace negotiations more feasible, not less so. True, the Hurriyat were sponsored by Pakistan, but so were the guerrillas.

This dichotomy, of the union government finding it easier to talk to armed actors than their civilian-political counterparts, persisted through the 1990s and early 2000s. Partly, it was created by facts on the ground. Not only did the Hurriyat have little influence on the guerrillas, the latter often proved to be more independent of Pakistan, engaging in peace negotiations with the union government when the Hurriyat bowed to Pakistani opposition. Perhaps the gun gave them some autonomy, just as the threat of the gun cowed the Hurriyat.

◆

The Hazratbal siege was the first time that excerpts of the negotiation between the guerrillas and government representatives were leaked to the media. Though they will be ruefully familiar to most peace negotiators around the world, their humdrum nature comes as a surprise to those unfamiliar with other government-guerrilla negotiations.

Three weeks into the siege, government negotiator Habibullah and the JKLF's Idris agreed that the guerrillas would free hostages and be given safe passage out of the mosque. The surrender was set for 8 a.m. on 3 November. Idris had reluctantly accepted that the guerrillas would be 'screened' as they filed out, by former guerrillas who now worked with the government. At 7.30 a.m., however, Idris demanded a change in the place of exit. He had noticed that the official television channel, Doordarshan, was waiting at the agreed exit and suspected that they would present the surrender as what it was rather than as a mutual evacuation in which both the guerrillas and the government would win, which was what he had agreed with Habibullah.

> Idris: 'We will not come out from the Dhobi Mohalla side (northern part of the shrine). The army has fitted cameras there and we know that a Doordarshan team is there. We are not surrendering.'
>
> Habibullah: 'OK, you can come from the Halwai Mohalla side. Doordarshan will tape everything but I promise it will not be televised.'
>
> Idris: 'Screen us on the lawns facing the dargah.'

Habibullah consults the army and they agree to bring them to the Green House (a house that falls within the army cordon).

Idris then upped the ante. The guerrillas would not give up their arms at the time of exit, he said, but only later, away from Hazratbal.

Idris: 'We won't give up our arms. Give us two police vehicles. We'll leave them on the way and disappear.'

It's 5 p.m. by now. The deal is off.

Two days later, the government tried again. Habibullah was grievously injured when a military truck accidentally rammed the vehicle he was travelling in.[11] The state government negotiator, Mehmood-ur-Rahman, took over. Negotiations stalemated once again, this time over the guerrillas' demand that they be allowed to come out bearing arms. The Rao administration, in the knowledge that the BJP would make hay of this debacle, could not agree. Idris, however, had another fear, that the security forces might not abide by Habibullah's word. He wanted insurance.

November 5, 1.30 p.m. Rahman goes in.

Idris: 'Why have you come? We told you we will only come out with our arms. Have you brought the vehicles?'

Rahman: 'Why don't you come out unarmed?'

Idris: 'What are we without our arms?'

Rahman: 'Don't give them to us. You can dump them in the well.'

Idris: 'Give us two hostages (Rasool and Suri). I will send the others out and then see.'

The deal's off again.[12]

Eventually the guerrillas were allowed to come out with their arms. The Congress did badly in state elections, but it is doubtful how much impact the Hazratbal incident had on the election results. As political commentators pointed out, the state elections of 1993–94 showed the emergence of a multi-party system with a number of regional as well as national parties sharing the vote.[13]

Chapter IX

'THE SKY IS THE LIMIT'

Despite criticism of their handling of the Hazratbal siege, the Rao administration continued backchannel negotiations with the JKLF. In May 1994, JKLF leader Yasin Malik was released from prison as part of an unofficial agreement with Rao's emissaries that he would announce a shift to non-violence and peace talks. In return, the government would negotiate a settlement with him based on autonomy for the state. In October, People's League head Shabir Shah was released, on similar terms. Named Amnesty International's 'prisoner of conscience', he had been cultivated by the Intelligence Bureau's A. S. Dulat since 1989–90, when he was in prison. According to Dulat, they met sometimes in Shah's prison cell and sometimes in a nursing home where Shabir was sent for medical check-ups. The two began by 'talking about talks', and from there moved to discussions of the futility of the gun, and then about peace with honour. 'I began to call him the Nelson Mandela of Kashmir, and he liked to be known that way. We spoke of a settlement with India and that he could become chief minister—or even prime minister—of Kashmir in the way that Sheikh Saheb was in the period 1947–53,' Dulat wrote in his memoir *Kashmir: The Vajpayee Years*.[1]

On their release, Malik and Shah received rapturous receptions. Though the JKLF had not organized an official rally, Malik was showered with petals and sweets by crowds at the Srinagar airport, who led him in a procession through the streets to his home. Officially, he had been released on bail because of his deteriorating health. The official reason was also a fig leaf for secret talks. Malik had offered to hold unconditional talks and Minister of State Pilot had responded that the government was open to meeting. Habibullah visited Malik in jail after he was granted bail, and returned with the message that Malik favoured a political dialogue.

The move was a 'calculated gamble', said journalist Harinder Baweja. 'Malik can scale down the demand for independence only at grave risk to his life or at the least, of being branded an Indian agent. Nor can he at this stage openly take on the Hizbul or the Kul Jamaat Hurriyat Conference, led by Mirwaiz Omar Farooq, a respected religious head.' Malik's aides, she continued, said he wanted to carve an independent position, but would have to tread cautiously lest he make open enemies of the Hurriyat and Hizbul. 'Few in Kashmir missed the fact that Malik's procession went way past the Mirwaiz's residence and he turned back to visit [U]mar Farooq at home, only after the Mirwaiz personally sent for him.'[2]

Home Ministry officials were themselves divided. Prime Minister Rao had just concluded a successful visit to the US, where President Clinton supported India–Pakistan talks under the Simla Agreement, though the Clinton administration had earlier been sympathetic to the Pakistani position. Just six months before, in the autumn of 1993 (around the time of the Hazratbal siege), US Assistant Secretary of State for South Asia Robin Raphel had set off a diplomatic war of words when she asserted that the Clinton administration viewed 'Kashmir as a disputed territory', and added 'We do not recognize the instrument of accession as meaning that Kashmir is forever more an integral part of India.'[3] In 1991, as a counsellor at the US embassy in India, she met Javed Mir, the second in command of the JKLF, and promised him US support if the JKLF eschewed the gun. The promise was not fulfilled when, three years later, Yasin Malik announced a unilateral JKLF ceasefire. Following the Rao–Clinton summit, US attention turned to India–Pakistan peacemaking and away from the India–Kashmir conflict.

Raphel muted her words subsequently. Two decades later, she was investigated under US law for smuggling strategic information to Pakistan. She had worked in Pakistan for USAID (United States Agency for International Development) and after her retirement, joined a lobbying firm, Cassidy and Sons, which represented the

Pakistani government. In 2009, Raphel was appointed Senior Adviser to the Envoy for Afghanistan and Pakistan, Richard Holbrooke. In November 2014, the FBI found she had classified documents in her house. It was reported that they had also intercepted a conversation with a Pakistani official, suggesting 'his government was receiving American secrets from Ms. Raphel'. Indian diplomats were both triumphant and smug that the US had found what they had said all along, that Raphel was a Pakistani agent.[4] But in March 2016, the US Justice Department closed the investigation without filing charges. Though it was a crime to keep classified documents at home, many US officials had done so without prosecution.

◆

Rao's success in turning Clinton to support the Simla Agreement was widely viewed as a diplomatic coup. The turnaround was influenced by US industry that saw immense opportunity in Rao's liberalization programme and formed an India Interest Group, a lobby which included heavy hitters such as AT&T, Coca Cola, IBM, General Electric, General Motors and other corporate giants.[5]

In the same month as the Rao–Clinton summit, the Indian government successfully rebuffed the Pakistani government's attempt to have the UN indict India on human rights abuses, at both New York and Geneva. Pakistani representatives pointed to the 1992 demolition of the Babri Masjid and the Hindu–Muslim riots that followed, along with the insurgency and counter-insurgency in Kashmir, to argue that India was committing violence against Muslims. The Indian delegation that countered Islamabad's allegations in New York comprised four Indian Muslims: India's representative to the UN, Hamid Ansari, former Chief Minister of Jammu and Kashmir Farooq Abdullah, Indian Union Muslim League MP, E. Ahamed, and Congress party leader, Salman Khurshid. The delegation to Geneva was headed by opposition leader Atal Bihari Vajpayee of the BJP, and again included Khurshid.

Rao's masterstroke, said commentator K. P. Nayar, 'was to permit a Hurriyat delegation to travel to Geneva and campaign against India in favour of Pakistan's human rights resolution on Kashmir'.[6] Noting this move, and informed by their embassies that the Indian government was attempting peace talks, UN member-states reserved judgment. The only forum in which Pakistani lobbying had an impact was the Organization of Islamic Countries.

Within Kashmir, the mood was hopeful. The Hazratbal occupation and siege had caused consternation, and Pakistani and Afghan guerrillas were increasingly seen to inflict abuses such as rape, extortion and forced shelter at gunpoint. Alarmed by rising Kashmiri Shia anger against Sunni attacks on Shias in Pakistan, Iran asked Pakistan not to put the human rights resolution against India to the vote at Geneva. Benazir Bhutto, back at the helm after the Nawaz Sharif government fell in 1993, announced that her country did not favour a plebiscite 'as they could lose if the option of independence was given to the people of Kashmir'. Her statement 'only confirmed what the people suspected all along—that Pakistan was using them and may not, when the crunch comes, support the *azaadi* movement', commented Baweja.[7]

Having just succeeded in some measure of damage control, Home Ministry officials wondered if Malik's release might be counterproductive. His rapturous reception, some feared, would give a fillip to calls for independence. Others argued that, on the contrary, it would fuel a peace process. The Kashmiris, a senior Home Ministry official told Baweja, 'would not turn to India but they may settle for an honourable way out. It's better than living under the fear of the gun.'[8] When Malik announced a unilateral ceasefire pending talks, the pro-talks constituency had the upper hand.

Shah, too, was greeted by crowds wherever he went, somewhat to Dulat's puzzlement, who understood Shah's popularity only when a Kashmiri friend told him, 'Look, there is a feeling that he has done a deal with Delhi and therefore he gives us a lot of hope. That is the reason so many people are backing him or following him.'[9] Dulat concluded that Kashmiris wanted relief from five years of armed conflict, but alongside they wanted peace with honour.

Initially, the prospects were promising. Shah came to Delhi, where every senior politician from the government to the opposition held meetings with him. The Rao administration allowed him to set up a Kashmir Awareness Bureau in south Delhi's Malviya Nagar, which was inaugurated by former foreign minister I. K. Gujral. Beginning to believe that Delhi meant business, Shah asked to go to Kathmandu to meet with a senior People's League member, Mehmood Sagar, who had crossed over to Pakistan-administered Kashmir. Though Dulat sought clearance for the visit, it was denied. Feeling that Delhi was unwilling to trust him, Shah began to backtrack.

Meantime, the guerrillas associated with Shah began to lose patience. Their leaders had approved Shah's dialogue with Dulat in the hope of an agreement that would allow them to lay down arms and reintegrate to local civilian life. As Shah dithered, Dulat suggested he depute a team to continue negotiations, but the suggestion was dismissed. Guerrilla leaders decided to take matters into their own hands and, instead of a negotiated agreement that would allow 'peace with honour', they made individual agreements that would allow beleaguered fighters to give up arms on the assurance they would no longer be targeted by security forces. The guerrillas, said Dulat, were in a more precarious position than their civilian leaders 'because the lifespan of a militant was two to two-and-a-half years before they would get bumped off by the army or the police or somebody else'.[10]

In 1996, Firdous Sayeed's Muslim Janbaz Force concluded one such agreement, paving the way for others to follow. 'This was also a setback to Shabir because he believed he had a monopoly with New Delhi,' Dulat commented. 'When Firdous and other militants began a dialogue then Shabir began to think that Delhi was double-dealing with him.'[11] Once again, the union government found it easier to negotiate with armed guerrillas than dissident political leaders.

Shah, too, was extremely vulnerable, albeit in a different way. Unlike Malik, he had not broken from the Hurriyat to conduct his own negotiations; rather, his fellow Hurriyat members took a cautious interest in his talks with the government. However, Shah's talks were parallel to Malik's, not jointly with him. Both Shah and Malik were under the Pakistani scanner for initiating peace talks with the Indian government and were threatened by Pakistan-backed militias. On the ground, army–militia battles had seen a brief lull. But the lull was to regroup, not the beginning of an end to violence, as what happened at Charar-e-Sharif showed.

The town of Charar-e-Sharif is located on the road to Srinagar, in the Budgam district where a large number of the valley's Shias live. Sandwiched between Srinagar and the border district of Poonch, Charar-e-Sharif was a traditional stop for infiltrating guerrilla who came across through Poonch. It was also a sanctuary for guerrillas fleeing the army in Srinagar. From late December 1994, it was reported, guerrillas had begun trickling into Charar-e-Sharif to escape the winter. By the first week of March 1995, around seventy-five guerrillas had congregated in the town. They built bunkers and mined the area around the town's central shrine, a delicate and intricately carved wooden building dedicated to Sheikh Nooruddin, the fourteenth-century Sufi preacher of pluralism and transformation. On 8 March, the army cordoned off the town in a counter-insurgency operation. The cordon led the residents of Charar-e-Sharif to vacate; at end-April, barely a thousand of the town's 20,000 population remained. Though the guerrillas were more exposed, they also had a less impeded playing field. With Hazratbal in mind, the government ruled out any storming of guerrilla boltholes, since they were concentrated in and around the shrine.

This time the government did not deploy civilian negotiators nor, said Habibullah, did they attempt to coordinate with town representatives or involve the local community in negotiations, as had been done at Hazratbal. Army negotiators used loudspeakers to offer safe passage to the guerrillas and Governor Rao publicly offered that they could be transported to the Suchetgarh border post in Jammu and handed over to Pakistani authorities. Led by a Pakistani called Mast Gul, the guerrillas refused the offer, presumably under ISI instruction. Accepting a guerrilla handover would have blown Pakistan's plausible deniability in the covert cross-border war, in the Pakistani government view. Five years later, the same consideration led the ISI to ensure that the terrorists released during an airplane hijack were handed over to the Taliban in Afghanistan while the ISI watched.

By the first week of May, there was continuous small-arms fire between troops and guerrillas, with army snipers stationed at all the town's vantage points. The guerrillas began to explore means of escape, using arson to obscure their exit. On the evening of 8 May, they set fire to deserted houses around the shrine where they had sought sanctuary; caught by a strong wind, the fire spread to engulf two-thirds of the town. The shrine survived, but on 11 May, it, too, was set on fire. Though Mast Gul escaped with a large number of guerrillas, twenty-seven of them were subsequently killed. Abu Jindal, the self-styled chief of the Pakistani militia trained by Hekmatyar, Harkat-ul-Ansar, was arrested. According to the media, he 'later helped the army in the detection of IEDs [improvised explosive devices] and hideouts of the surviving militants'.[12]

When the battle ended, it had taken over two months and the army had failed to protect either the shrine or peoples' houses. Most of the town was in ruins. Though the Rao administration declared that the damaged buildings would be rebuilt and residents compensated, anger rose high in the valley. As one news outlet commented: 'At a time when people had begun to denounce the culture of the gun, the destruction of the shrine has whipped up emotions that threaten to overwhelm reason.'[13]

Charar-e-Sharif was a shock to the union government's security analysts and a setback to peace negotiations. The Rao administration had come to believe it had broken the back of the insurgency by 1994. The militias were fragmented and fighting each other as well as the security forces. The time was ripe, they thought, for peace talks. Yet, the Charar-e-Sharif battle showed that the Rao administration had been optimistic to the point of complacency. The insurgency still had capacity to inflict loss. Even so, Rao's advisers were right to think that Hurriyat leaders and Kashmiri militias were open to peace talks. Using the Nagaland, Mizoram and Assam peacemaking models, intelligence officers encouraged leaders like Malik and Shah to participate in elections and received a positive hearing. With these inputs, Rao and his ministers decided it was time to hold assembly elections in Jammu and Kashmir, which had been delayed for five years due to the insurgency. But before announcing elections, they wished to ensure that parties such as the National Conference would participate.

Now Farooq Abdullah leapt into the fray. Sensing an opportunity to regain legitimacy, Farooq insisted that his party would participate only if the union government agreed to roll back all the encroachments on Article 370 and, indeed, return to the pre-1953 position when Kashmir had a prime minister. At the beginning of November, he had three days of discussions with the Rao administration, including a two-hour meeting with the prime minister on 2 November. Two days later, Rao made a special broadcast from Burkina Faso, where he was on an official visit, in which he stated that 'the sky is the limit' when it came to autonomy for Jammu and Kashmir, adding that the Indian government was willing to consider returning to the pre-1953 position when Kashmir had a head of state and a prime minister (sadr-i-riyasat and wazir-e-azam). On the same day in Delhi, the union cabinet announced that the state's legislative elections would be held in 1996. Though Dulat told Shabir Shah that Rao 'was signalling to Shabir that he was ready to give Kashmiris peace with honour', Shah thought Rao's offer 'was for Farooq and the National Conference to draw them in and thereby legitimize elections'. His own position, which was a non-starter as far as Delhi was concerned, was 'We are only interested in elections held under UN supervision.'[14]

Shah showed more flexibility in other interviews. Talking to former foreign secretary J. N. Dixit, who took to political journalism after he retired and before he was appointed NSA in 2004, Shah said Rao should have discussed whether or not to hold elections with the Hurriyat and not just with Farooq. 'The Centre's insistence that any reconciliation should be strictly within the framework of the Indian Constitution is too rigid a precondition,' Shah added, telling Dixit the Hurriyat was ready to talk without preconditions. His own roadmap for negotiation was that there should first be talks between the union government and the Hurriyat, then the union government should involve representatives from Pakistan-administered Kashmir, and then 'at some stage, Pakistan will also have to be brought into the discussions so that it does not sabotage the process'. At the end of the article, Dixit concludes: 'Shah leaves me with an impression of idealism and reasonableness facing the elemental forces of India's volatile politics. I hope his voice will be heard and there is a response.'[15]

Rao's Burkina Faso broadcast did not have the desired impact. He had referred to the 1975 Indira–Abdullah accord, which had been widely reviled, and his formula of autonomy plus elections was greeted with scepticism. In Srinagar, Farooq announced that the National Conference would not contest the election unless the union government spelt out an acceptable package for the state's autonomy. Rao had not agreed to his demand for a rollback to the pre-1953 status before the polls. Farooq suddenly became more powerful than the Hurriyat, said Kashmiri journalist Zafar Meraj. Though the Hurriyat called a strike against elections and the JKLF-led demonstrations called for a poll boycott, leaders such as 'Shabir Shah, A. G. Lone and Syed Ali Shah Geelani, even while expressing their strong opposition to the polls, pleaded helplessness in stopping the elections, saying that the Centre could manage it with the help of guns'.[16] Under Farooq's influence, even the state government employees' association announced they would not vote.

The ground situation worsened again. Incidents of terrorist attack decreased slightly, but the number of civilians and security forces killed went up. While a little over a thousand civilians were killed in 1994, by 1996 the figure was over 1,300. The number of security forces killed similarly rose from 236 in 1994 to 387 in 1996. Most alarming, said journalist Baweja, 1995 saw the highest number of trained guerrillas coming into the valley from across the border: 'even conservative estimates put the figure at 1,000 a month'.[17]

The Indian government tried once more to negotiate a ceasefire in 1995, this time seeking to insure ceasefire negotiations with militia leaders by getting the ISI's backing for a meeting in Casablanca. But the ISI placed three conditions on a ceasefire—formal Indian recognition of Kashmir as a territorial dispute involving Pakistan, trilateral talks between India, Pakistan and Pakistan-appointed Kashmiri representatives, and international engagement for a solution. Each of these conditions spelt anathema to Indian policymakers, and Pakistani–Kashmiri politicians themselves saw the ISI position as unrealistic. Commenting on the Casablanca meeting, the veteran leader of Pakistan-administered Kashmir, Sardar Qayyum Khan, later remarked ruefully, 'Our side bungled it. They made the talks a matter of success or failure [of Pakistan's Kashmir Policy].'[18] Another opportunity was lost, as so many had been before.

At end-November 1995, India's Election Commission decided that elections could not be held, and President's Rule was extended for another six months.

Eventually, the Jammu and Kashmir legislative election was held in late 1996. Having gained legitimacy with his 1995 stand, Farooq Abdullah began to be seen as strong again when guerrilla groups such as the Janbaz Force made their separate peace, laying down arms. Though the Indian government did not roll back to pre-1953, the National Conference participated in the 1996 state election and won. Talks with the JKLF and Hurriyat receded into the background.

Chapter X

GUJRAL'S SHORT FORAY

The late 1990s were an uncertain time for both countries. In Pakistan, Benazir Bhutto's government was dismissed in 1996—the second time this happened to her—and Nawaz Sharif won the February 1997 election on a thumping mandate to make peace with India. In India, the 1996 election led to a hung parliament. With the largest number of seats, the BJP was invited to form a government that fell after two weeks in the absence of support from other parties, and the United Front coalition came to power with Congress backing. Under Prime Minister H. D. Deve Gowda and External Affairs Minister I. K. Gujral, who took over as prime minister in April 1997, a new peace process began.

Gujral assumed office with a 'neighbourhood first' policy that was later named the Gujral Doctrine by his adviser and senior journalist, Bhabani Sen Gupta. At a September 1996 speech in Chatham House, Gujral spelt out the five principles of his neighbourhood policy:

> First, with the neighbours like Nepal, Bangladesh, Bhutan, Maldives and Sri Lanka, India does not ask for reciprocity but gives all that it can in good faith and trust. Secondly, no South Asian country will allow its territory to be used against the interest of another country of the region. Thirdly, none will interfere in the internal affairs of another. Fourthly, all South Asian countries must respect each other's territorial integrity and sovereignty. And finally, they will settle all their disputes through peaceful bilateral negotiations. These five principles, scrupulously observed, will, I am sure, recast South Asia's regional relationship, including the tormented relationship between India and Pakistan, in a friendly, cooperative mould.[1]

Contemporary commentators noted the sting in the tail. Gujral had bluntly distinguished between Pakistan and the remaining five of India's neighbours. To the latter, he offered unilateral concessions because he believed real progress could be achieved. To Pakistan, his four relatively tough principles applied with peculiar salience, given that the past eight years had been marked by cross-border violence and high tension, especially in Jammu and Kashmir. Against this backdrop, Gujral's speech was a major step forward. It signalled his intent to reverse the 'tormented relationship' between India and Pakistan.

A Punjabi born in the city of Jhelum, now in Pakistan, Gujral had first met Sharif while on a Track II visit in 1994, when he lunched with the latter in Lahore. Sharif and his brother, Shahbaz, had already emerged as leading politicians of Pakistani Punjab. Sharing a common, if violently divided, cultural heritage, Gujral and Sharif talked for hours about the vicissitudes of India and Pakistan and the potential for change. 'Our relationship deepened in 1996 when I became the foreign minister. He sent Gohar Ayub with a message of cooperation. This inaugurated a new phase,' Gujral later remarked in an interview to the *Hindustan Times*.[2]

The opportunity came when Sharif was elected in February 1997 and made Gohar Ayub his foreign minister. According to Sartaj Aziz, the then finance minister, when Sharif received the usual congratulations from Prime Minister Deve Gowda, he sought Aziz's advice on whether to send the usual formal reply drafted by the Foreign Office. 'I asked, "Why don't you add a few sentences..."' The sentences added were: 'I share your desire for improved relations but that requires serious negotiations and I suggest that we begin negotiations at the Foreign Secretaries' level if possible before the end of March 1997.'

'The reply came: "We are ready."'[3]

A month later, in March 1997, it was agreed that the two prime ministers would meet on the sidelines of the SAARC summit at Male. The foreign secretaries of India and Pakistan, Salman Haidar and Shamshad Ahmad, held four days of talks in Delhi to prepare for the meeting, tentatively identifying eight issues to resolve—

peace and security, Jammu and Kashmir, Siachen, Sir Creek, Wullar Barrage, terrorism and organized crime, economic cooperation and promoting 'friendly exchanges'.[4] They also tentatively agreed that the first two issues would be discussed at the foreign secretary level, while the latter six would be discussed in specialist working groups. The eight tracks would run in parallel but would not be tied, so that disagreement in one would not impede progress on another. The formula was later to be called the 'composite dialogue'.

In April, Deve Gowda resigned and Gujral became prime minister. Though Gujral and Sharif were briefed on the foreign secretaries' proposals, both agreed that they would first test the waters with a broad-brush statement at Male that India and Pakistan would resolve all issues through talks. Kashmir was not specifically mentioned in the short joint statement, but at their press conference, Sharif announced that the issue would feature in talks and Gujral did not contradict him.

The announcement was the first time in twenty-five years that the two countries had agreed to discuss Jammu and Kashmir. The last time had been 1972, when the Simla Agreement stated that India and Pakistan would settle their disputes bilaterally, including on Kashmir. Instead of talks, what followed the Simla Agreement was nuclear armament. Now, fifteen years later, the two countries were going to discuss Kashmir, at a time when cross-border insurgency was still present in the state. In both India and Pakistan, commentators wondered, hoped and feared: what would talks achieve?

Fissures soon became evident at Male. Gujral and Sharif's joint address to the media was cordial, but the foreign secretaries followed with separate press conferences. Ahmad went first, announcing that there would be India–Pakistan working groups on eight issues, the most important of which was Jammu and Kashmir. He had jumped the gun—the working groups were to be announced a month later in June 1997, when the two countries' delegations were scheduled to meet in Islamabad. Moreover, peace and security and Jammu and Kashmir were to be discussed only between the foreign secretaries. The distinction was primarily a procedural one;

the working groups would comprise officials from all the relevant ministries and line departments, on the presumption that the six issues that they covered were ones on which decisions could be feasibly reached, in real time. The foreign secretaries' talks, on the other hand, would be on the two politically challenging issues—Jammu and Kashmir and terrorism—and would therefore work towards finding mutually acceptable approaches.

Rational as it sounds, the distinction sparked discord immediately. Pakistani representatives suspected that it was a cover for India to downplay talks on Kashmir, and Indian representatives feared Pakistan would seek to focus solely on Kashmir. A visibly ruffled Haidar was forced to hastily organize his own press conference after watching Ahmad's. When Haider was asked about Ahmad's 'assertion that a joint working group on Kashmir would soon be a reality', according to journalist K. P. Nayar, 'flashing his famous temper, the Indian foreign secretary snapped: "It is his preoccupation".'[5]

Haidar was right. Pakistan had clearly changed the terms under which there would be a gradual progression through talks. Reporting the day before, the *New York Times* quoted Ayub as saying that 'the two leaders would probably establish working groups to review possible breakthroughs in different areas, and then we will see how it is, because Kashmir naturally will take a long time'.[6]

What happened in the twenty-four hours since the *Times* report? Retrospectively the inescapable conclusion is, the Pakistan Army. If the two prime ministers had agreed, as Ayub indicated, to tackle low-hanging fruit first and accept slow progress on Kashmir, then this was a step too far. Kashmir had to be acknowledged as 'the core issue' for the Pakistan Army to allow even the smallest step towards détente, as successive Indian governments were to discover in the years to follow. Gujral had been given an inkling of this at Male, where he and Sharif also discussed an immediate CBM, the purchase of power by India from Pakistan, which produced a surplus in the late 1990s. 'We were sitting with our respective delegations when Sharif remarked, "Why don't you purchase power from us?" I said I was keen and suggested that our commerce ministers, who were also with us, should explore the possibility. His foreign secretary piped in: "Let us first solve the Kashmir problem before you talk of cooperation." Sharif and I ignored the discordant note, but later, in private, I asked him how his officer could dare to speak like that in front of him. Nodding his head, he said, "Do you think I didn't see it".[7]

The lesson that Gujral derived from this episode was that 'Sharif was interested in improving relations with India, but faced impediments from the hard-liners'. It was an assessment that was shared by Vajpayee, who was consulted by Gujral along with other opposition leaders and concurred with him on his Pakistan approach, discovering that the truth was even more ambiguous two years later. Oddly enough, another eighteen years would pass before India's prime minister Modi would make the same journey from optimism to disenchantment with Sharif and come to the same conclusion.

The impact of the separate Ahmad–Haidar press conferences was immediate and negative in both countries. The cardinal rule of diplomacy in peacemaking, that both sets of leaders would coordinate their public responses, had been violated by the Pakistani government, and would continue to be violated over the next decades, with both countries' leaders using the media to score points against each other.

According to Haidar, the understanding was to have only one press conference at which Gujral and Sharif would make a joint statement. The Pakistani government then decided that Ahmad would address his own press conference after Gujral and Sharif, in which he would highlight Kashmir as the most important issue, but neglected to mention this to their Indian counterparts, who were taken by surprise.

Already weak, the Gujral government could justify the eight-issue formula for talks with Pakistan, but not if Kashmir was the priority issue. The Indian government had just held elections in Jammu and Kashmir, after a long hiatus caused by the insurgency. The 1996 election was marked by armed attacks on candidates and campaign workers. Seventy-five political activists died, the bulk of them members of the National Conference. Despite this toll, the National Conference won the election with a two-thirds majority of assembly seats.

Farooq Abdullah was once again elected chief minister and was deeply sceptical of talks with Pakistan. Understandably so, given the number of his party workers who were killed by Pakistan-backed guerrillas. Amongst both politicians and the Indian public, anger at Pakistan's involvement in the Kashmir insurgency was high. The Indian parliament's 1994 resolution was still fresh in political memory, denouncing 'Pakistan's role in imparting training to the terrorists in camps located in Pakistan and Pakistan Occupied Kashmir, the supply of weapons and funds, assistance in infiltration of trained militants, including foreign mercenaries into Jammu and Kashmir with the avowed purpose of creating disorder, disharmony and subversion', and asserting that Pakistani-controlled territories of the former princely state belonged to India.[8]

Though the ground situation had improved slightly, armed attacks were still frequent, killing over 4,000 people in 1996 and around 3,000 in 1997. With an opposition that was already stringently scrutinizing the government for any giveaway on Kashmir, and a difficult restoration process in a state roiled by violence, talks with Pakistan on Kashmir, always difficult, were going to be infinitely more complex—as they would have been for Sharif too. Pakistan had ridden high on the insurgency and would have to backtrack if talks on Kashmir were to be substantive instead of mileage-driven. Unusually, Sharif was actually in a position to alter the course for substantive talks with India. Although Pakistan-administered Kashmir had gone to the polls in 1996 and elected Sharif's rival the PPP, the statelet's new prime minister, Barrister Sultan Mahmood, was prepared to focus on development and leave policy to Sharif and the army without supporting one against the other.

At this point, neither Gujral nor Sharif had explored the options for a mutually acceptable Kashmir solution. The Indian government suspected that the Pakistani government would use the opportunity of talks to grandstand. Indeed, while engaging in negotiations with Indian representatives, Gohar Ayub asked India to 'clarify' that Jammu and Kashmir was a disputed territory. Sharif asserted at an extraordinary summit of the Economic Cooperation Organization on 14 May that his country sought a peaceful resolution of the Kashmir conflict based on UN resolutions, and a week later, Gohar Ayub asked UN Secretary-General Kofi Annan to mediate. Both were demands that India had vehemently opposed for decades.

Tempers were clearly rising, and were further exacerbated when the *Washington Post* reported in early June that India was 'deploying' its Prithvi missiles to Jalandhar, 110 kilometres from the Pakistan border. In fact, the missiles had been sent there for storage, not deployment, but the report set alarm bells ringing in Pakistan, and Gohar Ayub threatened 'counter-measures'.[9] It looked as if the second round of foreign secretaries' talks, scheduled for mid-June, might have to be cancelled, but a statement by Gujral clarifying that the missiles were not being deployed and would not be saved the day.

The June meeting in Islamabad between Ahmad and Haidar returned to script and the two formally announced the eight working groups. They also drafted a Memorandum of Understanding for the power purchase agreement discussed at Male. This time, Ahmad and Haidar addressed the media jointly—indeed, in another first, they agreed to appoint the spokesman of Pakistan's Ministry of Foreign Affairs as joint spokesman for the meeting—and after the joint statement was read, the two foreign secretaries made short prepared comments. The next round of talks, they said, would be held in September.

But cross-border firing and infiltration through Uri in Jammu and Kashmir rose in July. In the same month, Pakistan test-fired the HATF-III missile, widely suspected to use Chinese technology. In August 1997, the Pakistan Senate's Kashmir Committee shot off a letter to Kofi Annan, demanding that the UN resume a mediating role in Kashmir. When the two foreign secretaries met for the third round of talks in mid-September, Indian mistrust generated by these Pakistani actions was so high that the talks were inconclusive. The Pakistani government, however, saw the change as personality-driven. 'Unfortunately, I must say that the Indian side headed by Mr. Raghunath, who had by that time become Foreign Secretary, reneged on the June 23, 1997, agreement. The whole idea of Working Groups was again challenged by Mr. Raghunath and his team, which was a big setback and disappointment for me and for everybody,'[10] Ahmad remarked later, a trifle disingenuously. It was the proposal for a working group on Kashmir that was contentious, not the other agreed six. It did not help that the power purchase agreement backed by Gujral and Sharif was also abandoned, by Pakistan.[11]

The two leaders tried again five days later, this time with a Gujral–Sharif meeting on the sidelines of the UN General Assembly in late September. The meeting was almost cancelled when Sharif again demanded UN mediation in his UN General Assembly speech. Gujral, who had already set up bilateral meetings with Sharif as well as US President Clinton, was enormously embarrassed but persisted in his meeting with Sharif.

In India, the fact that Clinton also had bilateral talks with Sharif set off speculation that the US was reinserting itself into India–Pakistan negotiations and Sharif had won the long-standing Pakistani goal to 'internationalize' the Kashmir conflict. Actually, the US's heightened interest in India–Pakistan peace initiatives was due to reports that India was considering testing its newly developed Agni missile. The US, too, had recently tested a subcritical nuclear weapon, and though such tests were allowed to signatories to the Comprehensive Nuclear Test Ban Treaty, India was not a signatory. The US test fuelled pressure on Gujral to state that India would not abjure further tests.[12] He later remarked that he was relieved that 'the word Kashmir was not uttered once' in his meeting with Clinton.[13] Sharif was less pleased when Clinton told him that the US supported bilateral talks between India and Pakistan.

Sharif and Gujral made a last set of attempts in October, when they met at the Commonwealth Summit at Edinburgh and the SAARC Summit at Dhaka. By this time, there was little hope. From August 1997, heavy and frequent firing across the Line of

Control had become a new normal, with rising infiltration across the border. Stung by reports of corruption, the Gujral government was increasingly criticized for the weakness of his Pakistan policy, and the Congress began to consider withdrawing support to his administration.

The United Front government collapsed in November 1997 and fresh elections followed. A BJP-led coalition, the National Democratic Alliance (NDA), came to power in 1998, with Atal Bihari Vajpayee as prime minister. The Vajpayee government's first act was to conduct nuclear tests, as promised in the BJP's election manifesto. After two weeks of agonizing indecision, Pakistan followed suit.

Gujral's six-month foray did not result in any breakthroughs. But it provided a structure for talks that lasted well into the next century, and a series of lessons yet to be fully learned.

Chapter XI

SADA-E-SARHAD

The May 1998 Indian and Pakistani nuclear tests invited widespread condemnation. The US slapped sanctions on the two countries and, under international pressure, Prime Ministers Sharif and Vajpayee began peace negotiations. The first breakthrough came in August. At the Non-Aligned Movement's Durban summit, Sartaj Aziz, who had moved from finance to foreign minister, paid a 'courtesy call' on Vajpayee. According to Aziz, the Indian and Pakistani foreign secretaries agreed in principle that they would seek to revive the eight working groups set up by Sharif and Gujral in 1997.

The formal announcement was made soon after, when Vajpayee and Sharif met on the sidelines of the UN General Assembly in September. While chatting over lunch, Sharif mentioned that he had driven from Lahore to Delhi to watch the Asian Games, since no other transport was available. The two prime ministers brainstormed about starting a bus service, which was to be poetically named Sada-e-Sarhad (the call of the frontier). After their meeting, they issued a joint statement reaffirming 'their common belief that a durable environment of peace and security was in the supreme interest of both India and Pakistan' and that 'the peaceful settlement of all outstanding issues, including Jammu and Kashmir, was essential for this purpose'.[1]

Two rounds of foreign ministers' talks were held in Islamabad and Delhi in October–November, which included meetings of the working groups agreed under the Gujral–Sharif composite dialogue. The core issue for India remained cross-border terrorism; for Pakistan, it remained Kashmir. But at this initial stage Vajpayee and Sharif agreed mainly to talk about talks on these two issues while beginning with low-hanging fruit such as opening the borders for a Delhi–Lahore bus, restarting sports matches, liberalizing the grant of visas and exchanging information to prevent accidental or unauthorized use of nuclear weapons. The travel and sports CBMs were agreed immediately, the others were announced in the Lahore Declaration that followed in February 1999.

Repeating the 'common belief' outlined by the Gujral–Sharif joint statement in New York, the Lahore Declaration also committed the two governments to 'refrain from intervention and interference in each other's internal affairs' and 'condemned terrorism in all its forms'.[2]

Though the declaration was internationally important for the commitment to nuclear risk reduction, within India and Pakistan it was the summit and its optics that had a lasting impact. On its eve, Sharif invited Vajpayee to take the inaugural trip of the bus to Lahore. Vajpayee promptly accepted, bringing with him a delegation that included film stars and cricketers as well as the usual political leaders, journalists and officials.

The visit was carefully scripted and the journey itself was decked in pomp and panoply. Vajpayee boarded the bus at the Sikh city of Amritsar in Indian Punjab. As it 'arrived at Wagah, the BSF and the Rangers pulled opened the heavy iron gates of the check-posts. Then a group of Punjabi bhangra dancers performed in front of the bus as the vehicle drove slowly into no-man's land.' For the first time in thirty years, the Pakistan Rangers played the Indian national anthem when Vajpayee dismounted the bus to meet Sharif, who too had crossed over into the no-man's land between the Indian checkpost at Attari and the Pakistani checkpost at Wagah. Wagah was draped in Indian and Pakistani flags. 'This is a defining moment in South Asian history,' Vajpayee said, 'It is with a sense of elation that I find myself on Pakistani soil after a gap of 21 years.'[3]

Arriving a day early, Vajpayee visited Lahore's many Muslim, Sikh and Hindu shrines and monuments, culminating in an address from the Minar-e-Pakistan, where Jinnah had first called for a Muslim homeland. Indians, Vajpayee said, believed that a stable, secure and prosperous Pakistan was in India's best interest. 'Let no-one be in doubt,' he proclaimed.[4] That afternoon, he repeated his point at a civic reception by Lahore's mayor, Khwaja Ahmed Hassan, receiving a standing ovation. Vajpayee had reversed the Pakistani perception that India never came to terms with partition. It was especially significant that he represented the Hindu-nationalist right-wing, thus far seen as reflexively anti-Pakistan.

In a sign of the euphoria that Vajpayee's words generated, the normally matter-of-fact newspaper *The Hindu* gushed poet-lyricist Sardar Jafri, 'Tum aao gulshan-i-Lahore se chaman bardosh, Ham aayen subh-i-Banaras ki roshni le kar: Phir uskay baad yeh poocchein ki kon dushman hai (You come bearing the fragrance of Lahore, I come carrying the light of Banaras at dawn: Only then ask, who is the enemy?)'.[5]

Yet the euphoria masked danger signs. Indian officials later noted that a group of army officers led by General Musharraf, who was appointed chief of army staff in October 1998, did not respond when Vajpayee took the army salute along with Sharif. Pakistan's Jamaat-e-Islami, traditionally close to the army, held demonstrations stoning Vajpayee's cavalcade. They were joined by the JKLF's Pakistan wing. Accusing Sharif of selling out the guerrillas, they demanded independence for Kashmir.

At the time, these seemed like small blots in the generally positive. Though Indian analysts had noted the upheaval in the Pakistani military following the nuclear tests, they may not have drawn its grim conclusions. Despite winning a two-thirds majority twelve months earlier, Sharif's position had rapidly grown precarious. He began his term by seeking a constitutional amendment to limit the powers of the president—an office that the military had used to strengthen its hold over the civilian administration—and to appoint loyalists to the judiciary, which had also been used to dismiss elected prime ministers. By the time of the nuclear tests in May–June 1998, he had already alienated these powerful institutions. The sanctions and flight of capital that followed the tests weakened him even further. When then Chief of Army Staff and Chairman of the Joint Chiefs General Jahangir Karamat proposed that the Cabinet Defence Committee be replaced with a National Security Council, an angry Sharif sacked him and appointed General Musharraf in his stead.

As Sharif's appointee, it was expected that Musharraf would be loyal to Sharif. But Musharraf had fought in the 1965 and 1971 wars and, in the early 1980s, he was tasked by Zia-ul-Haq to train mujahideen for the Afghan jihad—that is when he first met Osama bin Laden. In the late 1980s, he participated in Zia's plan for a combined overt and covert operation in Kashmir named Tupac. As brigade commander of the Special Services Group of commandos in Siachen, he led a failed operation to retake the routes to the glacier in 1987. Indeed, the Indian high commissioner to Pakistan in 1998, Satish Chandra, red-lit Musharraf in a telegram to the foreign secretary in October 1998 as an 'ambitious and scheming individual'. He further called him a 'hard-liner on India' and warned that 'his elevation as Chief of the Army Staff does not bode well for Indo-Pak relations. And he will not toe Sharif's line over a longer period.'[6] Musharraf's refusal to salute Vajpayee, therefore, should have alerted the Indian leadership to a possibly negative reaction after the Lahore summit, but appears not to have done so.

When later asked what was the main achievement of the Lahore summit, Sartaj Aziz answered: the backchannel. Aside from the official talks and declaration, the two prime ministers had decided at Lahore to open a backchannel with R. K. Mishra, chairman of *The Observer* newspaper group, nominated as the Indian representative, and Niaz Naik, former foreign secretary under Zia-ul-Haq, as the Pakistani one. Naik had previously been involved in Zia's peace initiatives in the 1980s.

Between March and June 1999, Mishra and Naik held over a dozen meetings, mostly focused on Kashmir. The meetings were free and frank, Mishra later told me, because both he and Naik accepted them as exploratory, and because both prime ministers had agreed that each would settle for less than his country's stated positions, which were in any case maximalist. What progress they made in substance is ambiguous. Mishra neither wrote nor gave interviews about the backchannel, so Naik's account is the only one available.

According to Naik, he brought up the Dixon proposal of district-wise communal referenda, which Mishra said would be untenable in India given the history of partition. Mishra countered with a proposal to make the Line of Control an international border, which Naik said would be untenable in Pakistan since it would be seen as caving to India. Naik then suggested division on the basis of a 'Chenab formula', with lands to the east of the Chenab River in Jammu and Kashmir going to Pakistan, and lands to the west going to India. He had to buy a map to explain the proposal to Mishra.[7] What his explanation was remains a mystery: the Chenab originates in Himachal Pradesh and flows from west to east bisecting Jammu and Kashmir into north and south, not east and west. If he meant giving all the lands on the left bank of the Chenab to Pakistan, this would have meant handing over the predominantly Muslim Kashmir valley and all of Jammu's Muslim districts, something no Indian negotiator would contemplate. India's Ministry of External Affairs understandably rubbished Naik's assertion, but that does not mean Naik did not raise the proposal.[8] As Mishra said, both he and Naik accepted that neither government was bound by anything they discussed.

Mishra and Naik also looked at other examples of peace settlements, for example in Northern Ireland where the Belfast Agreement had been signed the year before, as well as the recently developed 'Livingston Proposal' of 1998, issued by a Kashmir Study Group founded by expatriate Kashmiri and head of Ethan Allen, Farooq Kathwari. Basically, the Kashmir Study Group suggested creating a sovereign entity 'without an international personality' from 'a portion of the state...to be decided by an internationally supervised ascertainment of the wishes of the Kashmiri people on either side of the Line of Control.'[9] In other words, a plebiscite on independence for the valley. There would be freedom of movement between India, Pakistan and this entity, and its security would be guaranteed by both by India and Pakistan.

Sartaj Aziz later repeated Naik's account of the talks, but with an important addition. When he met External Affairs Minister

Jaswant Singh in Colombo in March 1999—a month after Vajpayee's famous Lahore trip—the two reviewed the backchannel discussions and agreed that the overall focus should be to 'narrow down the problem to the Kashmir valley and adjoining areas'. The components of the solution, said Aziz, included the integration of Poonch, Mirpur and Muzaffarabad and the Northern Areas of Gilgit–Baltistan into Pakistan. Similarly, India would integrate the Jammu and Ladakh regions, leaving the Kashmir valley and 'some adjoining areas' for further discussion. 'We had discussed giving the Kashmir valley maximum possible autonomy, and also set a timeframe of four-to-five years for the implementation of the solution,' Aziz added.[10]

Variations of this formula had been discussed since the early 1950s, both at the UN and between Indian and Pakistani leaders. Yet the time was never ripe to agree it. As it transpired, nor was the time ripe now.

Clearly, the Mishra–Naik discussions were preliminary, and before they could move towards further exploration, they were pre-empted by the Kargil conflict that erupted in May. Yet, they made a significant contribution to the peace process that eventually broke through in 2003. They set the precedent for backchannel talks to be a preferred method for discussion on Kashmir, though only after a considerable lag on the Indian government's part. Naik's revelations about the talks sowed distrust of officially sanctioned backchannels in India that took years to overcome and recurs periodically.

In fact, both Mishra and Naik had been involved in unofficial talks for some months before they were officially nominated. Each had given his input to the Lahore summit. In its run-up, each got his respective prime minister to agree that he would abjure references to 'atoot ang' (literally: indivisible limb) or 'integral part' (terms used by India) and 'jugular vein' or UN resolutions (terms used by Pakistan). Like Gujral, Vajpayee tied progress in talks with an end to cross-border violence, sending a message through Naik to Sharif on 1 April that Pakistani shelling and infiltration must cease if talks were to be sustained.[11]

The most important legacy of the Lahore Process was the Sada-e-Sarhad bus. It was the first step towards softening the international border between the two for travel and trade, and was followed by the revival of the Samjhauta (Conciliation) Express in 2000. The train service had started in 1976 but was allowed to lapse in the 1980s after Zia's coup. In 2006, two other services were launched: an Amritsar–Lahore–Nankana Sahib bus and a Jodhpur–Karachi train (the Thar Express). Though both countries built on the Sada-e-Sarhad opening, it was only in the interstices of conflict. Indeed, these 'people-to-people' initiatives themselves became targets of armed attack. In February 2007, the Samjhauta Express was bombed, killing 68 people, and in 2014 the Pakistani post at Wagah underwent a suicide attack in which 55 people died and 120 were injured. Subsequent investigations confusingly showed both a Lashkar-e-Taiba and a Hindu extremist hand in the Samjhauta bombing.[12] Similarly, Jundullah and the Tehrik-e-Taliban Pakistan, not known to have collaborated earlier, both claimed responsibility for the Wagah attack. In 2009, when there was a terrorist attack on the Sri Lankan cricket team in Lahore, Pakistan restricted the bus services to terminate at the Wagah border, and again in January 2015, following terror threats.

◆

What impact did the Lahore Process have on Jammu and Kashmir? Initially not much; in fact, it divided Kashmiri dissidents. The All Parties Hurriyat Conference (APHC), then under the chairmanship of Syed Ali Shah Geelani, called for a hartal or shutdown on 20 February to protest the summit, fearing that Pakistan might arrive at a solution without them. Other dissidents did not agree. Shabir Shah, Chairman of the People's League, facing a decline of his popularity, opposed the call and appealed to 'the people of Jammu and Kashmir to send a clear message to India, Pakistan, and the world community that they want India and Pakistan to...start discussing real solutions', adding that India–Pakistan rapprochement was 'as important for peace as is the inclusion of the people of Jammu and Kashmir at the negotiating table'. Criticizing Geelani, he said that it was 'unreasonable of the APHC to insist that one ingredient must come before the other'.[13]

Shah was one of the few dissidents to argue that the Lahore Process represented a ripe moment, but he may have been seeking to reinsert himself as a peacemaker, having been the first to make a breakthrough with the Indian government in 1995.

Violence continued to rise in the Pir Panjal region of Jammu and the valley, continuing the communal trend noticed earlier. There was a series of terrorist attacks on Hindus through 1998. Notably, three of the four attacks took place in Jammu province and one in Ganderbal district in the valley (adjoining Srinagar), the traditional seat of the Abdullahs.[14] On 26 January 1998, twenty-three Pandits were killed in Wandhama village of Ganderbal, on 18 April, twenty-six Hindus were shot dead in Parankote village of Udhampur district, on 19 June, a Hindu wedding party was attacked in Chapnari village in the multi-ethnic Doda district leaving twenty-six dead (allegedly by a Lashkar-e-Taiba operative who was killed in September), and on 28 July, twenty-eight Hindus were killed in Hama and Saranwar villages of Kishtwar. Hindu deaths as a result of the conflict more than doubled from 64 in 1997 to 159 in 1998. Muslim deaths, which were ten times higher, declined marginally from 717 in 1997 to 678 in 1998.[15]

In a new departure, Kashmiri political parties and their members began to be targeted. The 1996 assembly election campaign in the state was the first time political activists were systematically targeted by guerrillas. Given that the insurgency began when the 1988 election was manipulated, and 1996 was the next election to be held after a long hiatus, the attacks were not really surprising. However, the trend continued till 2009 and was not limited to election periods alone. Anyone who had participated in elections at whatever level, or was about to, began to be considered a 'legitimate' target. Attacks on political activists—relatively few up to now—jumped from sixteen in 1995 to fifty-two in 1997 and forty-five in 1998.[16]

Both armed groups and government security forces gained experience of each other's vulnerabilities. Though overall civilian casualties declined between 1997 and 1998, the numbers of government forces and guerrilla deaths rose. Significantly, armed encounters between foreign fighters and Indian troops increased while armed encounters between local guerrillas and Indian troops decreased. As compared to seventy-two state and ancillary police killed by armed groups in 1997, eighty-two were killed in 1998, including fifty police officers, twenty-two Special Police Officers (counter-insurgency) and ten members of Village Defence Committees.[17] The number of foreign fighters killed also shot up between 1997 and 1998, from 197 to 319, while the number of local guerrillas killed fell from 878 to 680.[18] Kashmiri militias began to stage attacks in neighbouring states too. In August 1998, the Hizbul Mujahideen killed thirty-five Hindus in Chamba district of bordering Himachal Pradesh.

This environment of violence prompted Vajpayee's message to Sharif that cross-border guerrilla warfare must be curtailed. In fact, attacks by armed groups had declined in the months before the Lahore summit, from over 250 in December 1998 to below 200 in January and February 1999, but began to rise again in March. Incidents of infiltration by Pakistan-backed foreign fighters shot up following the Lahore summit, from 7 in January–February 1999 to 85 in March, and hit a peak of 425 in August.[19] Similarly, more than two-thirds of the total deaths in guerrilla violence for 1998 occurred after the nuclear tests (1,567 of 2,175 deaths were between June and December 1998).[20] A new Pakistani tactic emerged, of escalating or de-escalating cross-border attacks according to whether the civil–military establishment was dissatisfied or satisfied with the state of play between the two countries.

Chapter XII

KARGIL: PAKISTAN'S IMPLAUSIBLE DENIABILITY

To the Vajpayee government's shock, though not perhaps entirely to its surprise, the small improvements announced in the Lahore Declaration proved a step too far for the Pakistani military, who responded with a covert operation in the Kargil region of Jammu and Kashmir. Ostensibly, the goal was to capture Indian checkposts guarding the strategic national highway connecting Srinagar to Leh through Drass and Kargil on the Himalayan border, thus cutting off the supply line between the two. Control in this sector would allow the Pakistan Army to supply its occupying troops, giving them military access both to Siachen and the Kashmir valley. But the operation had a second or ulterior prong—to smuggle a mass of arms and guerrillas into Kashmir while Indian troops were focused on Siachen. Together, the two operations formed a pincer movement on Jammu and Kashmir.

The Kargil offensive began in early 1999 but was discovered by the Indian government only at the beginning of May, when local shepherds reported the presence of intruders. By this time, wrote A. S. Dulat, then incumbent director of the R&AW, between 1,500–2,400 troops of the Pakistan Army's 10th Corps, the Northern Light Infantry, had established themselves in the Mushkoh valley in the northwest of the Line of Control to Batalik in the east, along with an unidentified number of non-state militia.[1] There was consternation in India at this costly and prolonged intelligence lapse. But the military response, when it came, was forceful. According to Jaswant Singh, at the time external affairs minister in a caretaker NDA government, the first task was to limit Pakistani penetration and then to drive their troops out.

Yet, newspaper reports suggest that India came close to launching air strikes on targets within Pakistan, and decided only at the last moment to focus instead on recapturing the Indian checkposts in combined land and air operations. In other words, the Indian Army would restrict itself to a defensive response on the Indian side of the Line of Control.

The decision earned India brownie points internationally and translated into pressure on Pakistan. But it demanded Herculean effort from the Indian military. Given the heights at which operations would take place—from 16,000–18,000 feet—Indian military forces were required to undertake a painstaking peak-by-peak effort requiring immense fortitude from troops scaling the Himalayas, as well as immense skill from pilots flying through its narrow ravines. India's first victory came only after three weeks, when troops retook the Tololing peak, one of three strategic checkposts between the Mushkoh valley and Drass. After an overnight hand-to-hand battle, the Indian Army's 2nd Rajputana Rifles recaptured Tololing on 13 June, at the high cost of twenty-three men, and in the next six days, four more posts were recaptured: Point 4590, Rocky Knob, Hump and Point 5140.

It took another three weeks and 2,200 troops—200 forward and 2,000 rear, drawn from the 18th Grenadiers, 2nd Naga, and 8th Sikh Regiments, with support from the Indian Artillery—to recapture the most strategic of the posts, on Tiger Hill (Point 4660). Though hundreds of Pakistani intruders remained to be expelled, the war was all but won.

The Tiger Hill defeat of 3 July convinced the Pakistan Army that they were not going to achieve their military goals, and a crestfallen Nawaz Sharif flew to Washington to see if he could retrieve some leverage diplomatically. He met a frosty President Clinton, who had just received intelligence that Pakistan was preparing to deploy nuclear weapons.[2] According to then Deputy Secretary of State Strobe Talbott, Sharif first pled ignorance and then fear for his own survival, to seek US mediation on Kashmir. Clinton's condition was that the Pakistan Army would have to immediately withdraw its troops and militias from Kargil, after which the US would support resumption of the bilateral Lahore Process, but no more. If Sharif refused these terms, the US would release a statement accusing Pakistan not only of an unwarranted intrusion in Kargil but also of supporting Al Qaeda. With much expostulation, Sharif agreed. The two premiers then read out a US-drafted joint statement listing Sharif's pledges—which, apparently, the US was only able to get after keeping Sharif advisers Sartaj Aziz and Shamshad Ahmad, whom the Clinton administration now judged as hawks, out of the talks. Clinton pre-cleared the statement with Vajpayee, who remained non-committal, prompting Talbott to compare him to the US's Missourians, famous for wanting proof before they venture.[3]

One week later, on 11 July, the Indian and Pakistani DGMOs met at Attari to work out the details of Pakistani withdrawal, including sector-by-sector plans for routes the Pakistani forces would use to withdraw, accompanied by cessation of Indian air and ground operations to allow safe passage. The war officially ended, six weeks after it began.

Over 4,000 Indian and Pakistani troops died in the Kargil War. Nawaz Sharif was vilified by Islamist groups following the Pakistani defeat and ousted by a military coup in October, the Pakistan–US relationship suffered the first of many blows, and the fledgling India–Pakistan peace process was mortally wounded. Why did Pakistan embark on the Kargil operation?

From available information, it would seem that the Pakistan Army had prepared plans for such an operation as far back as the late 1980s, to reverse the 1984 status quo established by India in Siachen. But Zia-ul-Haq died, and subsequent civilian governments refrained from putting the plans into action. In 2003, Benazir Bhutto revealed that Musharraf had suggested a Kargil operation to her in the mid-1990s, claiming it would provide a secure route into Kashmir—'he said he would put the flag of Pakistan on the Srinagar Assembly'—but she rejected it.[4] For fifteen years, the Indian and Pakistani armies had followed the procedure of withdrawing from high-altitude checkpoints during the harsh winter and returning in the spring, neither side attempting to occupy vacant posts in the interim. With Kargil, Pakistan violated this tacit agreement.

Sharif denied knowledge of the Kargil operation and BJP leaders at the time appear to have believed him. Vajpayee called Sharif when the infiltration was discovered; according to Khurshid Kasuri, who was to become Pakistan's foreign minister under Musharraf, Sharif promised to check and call back. Three weeks of hectic if unofficial negotiations to end the conflict followed. The Mishra–Naik backchannel, established to anchor the Lahore Process and bring it substance, met several times between late May and the third week of June. They worked out a formula combining Pakistani withdrawal across the Line of Control with an Indian ceasefire to enable safe passage for departing troops and a resumption of dialogue.

Mishra and Naik also came close to a four-point agreement, said Pakistani analyst Nasim Zehra. First, each country would take appropriate steps to mutually respect the Line of Control under the 1972 Simla Agreement. Second, India and Pakistan would immediately restart the composite dialogue that had been initiated under the Lahore Process. Third, Islamabad would use its influence with the guerrillas to request them to disengage. And fourth, the two countries would seek a solution to the Kashmir dispute within a specified timeframe. It was also agreed that the India–Pakistan dialogue would resume at the level of foreign ministers, and the two countries' DGMOs would meet for immediate de-escalation.[5]

According to Niaz Naik, the two leaders went so far as to work out how this agreement would be presented. On 26 June, Sharif would send greetings to the Indian prime minister while flying through Indian airspace on a visit to China, and together, the two leaders would announce an end to the Kargil War.

The plan, if it really existed, was bizarre. Hundreds of Indian and Pakistani troops had died and Sharif was on his way to China to muster support for a Pakistani cover-up that would project the offensive as a small-scale effort by non-state actors without official Pakistani backing and support. In these conditions, any 'greetings' from Sharif to Vajpayee would surely be perceived as outrageous in both Delhi and Islamabad, and any invitation by Vajpayee would surely have met widespread condemnation in India. Indeed, then foreign minister Sartaj Aziz had been sent to Delhi in mid-June to seek just such a formula, but his mission foundered when he insisted that the Pakistan Army was not involved and the Line of Control had never been properly demarcated (presumably he was referring to Siachen, but the invasion had happened in Kargil, in sectors that had been fully demarcated in 1949).[6]

Sharif's pleas of ignorance now fell on deaf ears. Evidence had begun to trickle out that he did have knowledge—not to mention forewarning—of the operation. He and Sartaj Aziz clearly obfuscated when they denied it was state-initiated. In the run-up to the Lahore summit, Sharif is alleged to have asked the Pakistan Army to provide him cover to pacify radical Islamist groups while he pursued peace with India. General Musharraf dusted off the Kargil plan and presented it to Sharif. According to Dulat, Musharraf had determined to put the Kargil plan into operation much earlier, upon appointment as army chief. He had visited the Force Command Northern Areas in late October 1998 to explore opportunities. In late May 1999, the Indian government released taped intercepts of conversations between Musharraf and then Chief of General Staff General Mohammad Aziz Khan, asking whether the 'politicians' were now trying to retreat from the Kargil operation.

India's government-appointed Kargil Committee's Report of February 2000, authored by security guru K. Subrahmanyam, former Lieutenant General K. K. Hazari, journalist B. G. Verghese and then Deputy NSA Satish Chandra (the man who had red-lit Musharraf in October 1998), concluded that Sharif did know and had approved the Kargil operation though he may not have grasped its ramifications. Moreover, the plan had started to be put into operation even as the Indian and Pakistani governments negotiated key points for the Lahore Declaration. A Pakistan Army reconnaissance team had visited the region in January 1999, four additional battalions of the Pakistan Army had been moved to forward posts on the Kargil border, there had been increased shelling in the Kargil sector and reports had been received of intensified training of Islamic guerrillas.

In his autobiography, Musharraf insisted that Sharif was given a full briefing on the operation two weeks before the Lahore summit.[7] Sharif himself visited Skardu twice in January–February 1999, visiting the Line of Control in the Neelam valley on his second trip. The 10th Corps commander, Lieutenant General Mahmud Ahmed, later told interviewers that he personally briefed Sharif on the planned Kargil operation at this time.[8] Ahmed was to join the group of generals who engineered Musharraf's coup in October 1999.

Asking why the Pakistan Army undertook Kargil without anticipating a forceful Indian response, the Kargil Committee answered that the Pakistani calculation was that even if India did respond militarily, the international community would push for a ceasefire, leaving some part at least of the strategic heights in Pakistan's possession (though this would overturn the UN-negotiated ceasefire line of 1949). Pakistan would gain leverage in subsequent negotiations on Jammu and Kashmir and, moreover, it would bring the US into a mediating role.

Sharif did attempt international intervention between June and July, lobbying for pressure on India to agree to cease fire, but by this time the Indian government had released the taped intercepts showing that Kargil was a Pakistan Army offensive. There was broad support for the Indian position that Pakistani forces must withdraw, including statements by the outgoing German and incoming Finnish EU presidents as well as by the European Council and G8. Clinton and Blair were in regular touch on Kargil. According to Bruce Riedel, then in charge of South Asia at the US National Security Council, Clinton also spoke to his counterpart in Beijing to enlist Chinese pressure on Pakistan.[9] The only commitment Sharif received from the US was to support resumption of the Lahore Process that he had crafted with Vajpayee, after Pakistani withdrawal.

Yet, it was Sharif who dragged his feet on follow-up to this commitment. From mid-July onwards Clinton and Talbott and his team pressed Sharif to appoint an envoy for talks with India since by this time the Mishra–Naik talks had run their course, but he procrastinated for two months on the grounds that he did not trust anyone. Eventually, he sent his brother Shahbaz to Washington in September with a proposal that Sharif would pledge to prevent cross-border infiltration and open a direct line to Vajpayee. The offer came with the precondition that no 'legitimization of the status quo'—that is, turning the Line of Control into an international border—would be accepted. Talbott took the message to Jaswant Singh, who warned that India expected a military coup against Sharif. In these conditions, Jaswant said, it was unwise for either India or the US to get involved.

The anticipated military coup followed a month later, in October. In an attempt to stave it off, Sharif precipitated it. He dismissed General Musharraf while the latter was on a military mission to Sri Lanka and tried to prevent him from returning to Pakistan. The army rebelled and arrested Sharif. Musharraf took over as president of Pakistan. Sharif had promoted Musharraf out of turn and green-lit Musharraf on Kargil; for these sins he was deposed, arrested and finally—after US and Saudi intercession— exiled. The parallels with Bhutto and Zia were inescapable, but Sharif did at least escape with his life, unlike Bhutto. Ironically, Sharif was a Zia protégé, discovered in 1980, and Musharraf, too, was a Zia promotee.

What were the lessons of Kargil? For India, there were several. The most immediate concern was the intelligence failure, followed by questions of whether the army could have lowered the cost to our troops. The Kargil Committee pointed to the lack of interagency cooperation as one reason for failure, resulting in shoddy analysis of what information there was. The committee's extensive interviews showed that the government's various intelligence departments possessed different snippets of information that were not put together; had they been, warning signals would have emerged. Dulat clearly considered this judgment unfair. As early as June 1998, he said, the Intelligence Bureau had flagged reports of troops' build-up and construction of new infrastructure on the Pakistani side of the Line of Control, but there had been no follow-up investigation or action. The Kargil Committee, however, found fault with the Bureau for not sending the information to the intelligence services that *were* in a position to act: R&AW and the Joint Intelligence Committee.

The military issues were not publicly discussed, but most analysts noted that it took a full three weeks after the first reports were received for the air force to deploy. B. G. Verghese, one of the members of the Review Committee, argued in his memoir *First Draft* that the delay in aerial bombardment was because of the decision to limit operations to the Indian side of the Line of Control, which required complicated logistics. But the committee's report also tellingly remarks that a level of complacency had crept in—the Indian Army had grown so used to thinking that the arduous Himalayan terrain permitted only localized skirmishes that they did not take reports of a large-scale Pakistani intrusion seriously. The same complacence had left them ill-equipped for high-altitude warfare.

The Kargil Committee suggested a series of measures to upgrade and modernize defence, some of which were later adopted, such as investment in aerial surveillance and improved management of the Line of Control, including beefing up troops along the Kargil–Batalik sector, which was relatively poorly manned, and setting up the Defence Intelligence Agency to coordinate military intelligence. While the Kargil gap was plugged, India's multifarious other gaps in defence were to be penetrated by Pakistan time and again in the years that followed.

Though the Indian government had long experience of Pakistani civil–military duplicity, the picture of the Pakistani state that emerged during and after Kargil was salutary. It underlined the powerlessness of Pakistan's civilian administration relative to the military—Sharif was at best occasionally briefed and did not oversee the Kargil offensive. It also drew a warning picture of Sharif as both lightweight and duplicitous, ever fearful, and worst of all, unable to comprehend the consequences of his actions.

Was Sharif any different from previous Pakistani prime ministers in these failings or had they been endemic to Pakistani civil–military relations from partition on? Broadly speaking, the military dominated civilian policymaking from the start; indeed, Pakistan had yet to see a peaceful transfer of power from one civilian administration to another.

Yet Sharif's relationship to the Pakistani military was more tormented than Benazir Bhutto's before and after him, or Asif Ali Zardari's in his first and possibly only term, combining a mix of fear and defiance that led him to repeat the same mistakes over and over again. Having emerged as a politician because of the Pakistan Army, Sharif expected old loyalties to continue but did not recognize the boundaries the army set. He was first identified as a promising candidate by retired ISI director Ghulam Jilani Khan in 1980, then appointed chief minister of Punjab in 1985 by Zia, and contested the December 1988 general election as part of the Islami Jamhoori Ittehad, an alliance of nine conservative Muslim parties that was put together by then ISI chief, Hamid Gul. The alliance lost the 1988 election but won the next one in 1990, with Sharif as prime minister. Sharif's troubles with the Pakistan Army started now. As chief minister, he had focused on economic development and religious education in Punjab. As prime minister, he attempted to restrict the powers of the president to dismiss elected governments, a step too far for the army that had successfully used presidents to sack prime ministers. Though Sharif thwarted then president Ghulam Ishaq Khan's attempt to dismiss him in retaliation, his government collapsed in 1993 when army chief Abdul Waheed Kakar persuaded him to step down.

The lesson was clear if unpalatable, but Sharif appears to have believed—and continued to believe—that he could both work with the army and seek to limit its influence. For the next two decades, he continued to look for loyalists in the army, though his punishment for doing so grew increasingly severe. He appointed Musharraf against Karamat in 1998, superseding more senior candidates for chief of army staff, and suffered a military coup. Fifteen years later, he appointed General Raheel Sharif, once again superseding more senior candidates, thinking that Raheel would be the most likely to refrain from asserting military–political muscle. Instead, Raheel took full control over Afghan and India policy and allowed the army to back Imran Khan's Pakistan Tehreek-e-Insaf against Sharif, almost toppling him in 2015. As Pakistani columnist Cyril Almeida commented on Sharif's appointment of Raheel, 'Look where that got Nawaz.'[10] Ayesha Siddiqa, an expert on the Pakistan Army, added, 'It seems the prime minister hasn't gotten rid of the habit of owning sins committed by the army—and then getting punished for it.'[11]

We are running ahead. In 1999, Sharif's strident bluster, his obeisance to the Pakistan Army and its upping the ante with India, the ease with which he had deceived the Vajpayee government, were a new low reminiscent of Bhutto in the 1970s.

The lessons for Pakistan were of another order. The Pakistani government had, once again, misread India, thinking that the caretaker NDA government would be too weak and preoccupied with marshalling its coalition to act with determination. The Pakistan Army was as complacent as the Indian Army, believing they would have a walkover. At a military briefing for the Pakistani Air Force in mid-May 1999, Lieutenant General Ahmed, the 10th Corps commander with whom Musharraf had planned the Kargil offensive, laid out the intrusion plan as a combined ground and artillery offensive to occupy vacant Indian Army posts and use them as observation points for the Pakistani artillery to cut off the Drass–Kargil link road that supplied the Indian Army in Siachen. Supplemented by the monsoon whose onset would preclude Indian airlifts, this would effectively starve Indian troops. 'Come October, we shall walk into Siachen—to mop up the dead bodies of hundreds of Indians left hungry, out in the cold.'[12] After Musharraf's coup, Ahmed was made director general of the ISI.

Worse still was the domestic impact. The civilian government and Pakistan Army projected the offensive as a guerrilla initiative and disavowed their own troops, refusing to take back the bodies of the dead. The then director of the Analysis Wing at the ISI, Lieutenant General Shahid Aziz, expressed the rage born of humiliation that some in the Pakistani military felt, in a passionate denunciation of the Kargil operation. 'There were no mujahedeen, only taped wireless messages, which fooled no one. Our soldiers were made to occupy barren ridges, with hand-held weapons and ammunition. There was no way to dig in, so they were told to make parapets with loose stones and sit behind them, with no overhead protection. The boys were comforted by their commander's assessment that no serious response would come. But it did—wave after wave, supported by massive air bursting artillery and repeated air attacks. The enemy still couldn't manage to capture the peaks, and instead filled in the valleys. Cut off and forsaken, our posts started collapsing one after the other, though the General [Musharraf] publicly denied it.'[13]

The unkindest cut of all was that the Pakistan Army's Northern Light Infantry was composed mostly of recruits from Gilgit, another part of the disputed Jammu and Kashmir state under Pakistani control, bordering China in what were then called the Northern Areas. Till the end, Pakistani leaders denied these troops were part of Pakistan's security forces. Describing the terms of withdrawal in a press statement on 12 July, Sartaj Aziz claimed, 'Following the mujahedeen's positive response to our appeal to de-escalate in Kargil, the Government of Pakistan and the Government of India have been in contact on the question of restoration of the LOC.'[14]

Pakistan's disavowal of their stranded troops drew on sickening sophistry. At the time, the Northern Light Infantry had the status of a paramilitary run by Pakistan's Interior Ministry. It was only after the Kargil War ended that the Northern Light Infantry was incorporated into the regular army; by this time, hundreds of Gilgiti families had encountered first denial and then return of their dead in the middle of the night, shrouded in body bags. Whether this memory played a role or not, thirteen years later, following the 2012 Gilgit avalanche in which 129 troops lost their lives, the Gilgitis refused to raise a replacement battalion.

Seventeen years after the Kargil War, Sharif acknowledged its perfidy. 'Vajpayee told me that he was stabbed in the back because of Pakistan's misadventure in Kargil, especially during the process of [the] Lahore Declaration. Vajpayee was right. I would have said the same thing—he was certainly backstabbed.'[15] Curiously, Sharif made this statement while addressing a rally in Muzaffarabad in 2016.

Chapter XIII

THE NDA'S ANNUS HORRIBILIS

The NDA government's Pakistan travails did not end with Kargil. While the Pakistan Army was defeated at Kargil, it succeeded with the other prong of its offensive, an uptick in cross-border attacks on Jammu and Kashmir. During and immediately after the Kargil War, the Indian government withdrew troops from parts of the Pir Panjal region and northern Kashmir in order to plug gaps in the Kargil sector, not anticipating that the Pakistan Army would make use of the new gaps thus created while they were fighting a losing battle in Kargil.

The Pakistan Army, however, seized the opportunity. As the Kargil Committee later reported, armed groups had also begun preparations for large infiltration in early 1999. Militia commanders such as Muhammad Saleem Wani, 'chief organizer' of the Tehreek-e-Jihad, and ideologues such as Hafiz Muhammad Saeed, head of the Lashkar-e-Taiba, described the Kargil operation as part of a deliberate shift in their long-term strategy. Improvements in India's counter-insurgency operations had led armed groups to alter their tactics, said Saeed. 'The Indians have now sent five brigades to Kargil and sustained heavy losses, and that has made our movement much easier in other areas of Kashmir. The struggle in the valley is not separate from Kargil, it will intensify because of Kargil.'[1]

Attempts to forcibly impose a religious dress code on women, even girls, were revived along with a ban on 'obscene programmes'. Two girls were shot in Srinagar in February for 'wearing tight jeans' and a cable operator attacked for allegedly carrying graphic shows.[2] In the same month, Pakistani newspapers, both English language and Urdu, carried the following advertisement by the Lashkar: 'Jihad is the divine order and the Kashmir issue will only be resolved by it. To express solidarity with the oppressed Kashmiri

Muslims and the Mujahideen who have been waging a war against the Indian forces, donate your one-day income to them.'[3] The advertisement included contact numbers and bank details.

In April, newspapers published what they claimed were leaked interrogation reports[4] in which two arrested Pakistani guerrillas—a Shams ul-Haq from Balochistan and another 'code-named Sikander'—said that the training camps along the Line of Control, at Gadi Habib, Nowshera, Nowsada, Kotla and Bhimber in the Mirpur district of Pakistan-administered Kashmir, had been turned into staging grounds or what the Indian Army calls 'launch-pads' for guerrillas who were now being trained in Pakistan's NWFP by Afghans. 'Buoyed with huge profits,' from poppy cultivation on the Pakistan-Afghan border, ul-Haq and Sikander said, 'the ISI was ready to pump in several crores to revive the dying militancy'.[5] Lashkar militants, they added, had been asked to move into the higher reaches of Jammu and Himachal Pradesh. Afghans were increasingly being recruited, but many of them 'prefer to surrender at the border'.

The Lashkar's funding network had already expanded beyond Pakistan. In April, Pakistani national Shafiq-ur-Rehman was deported from Britain for the 'recruitment of British Muslims to undergo training and in fund-raising for the Mujahideen in Kashmir'.[6] Rehman had ties to the Markaz ud Dawa'ah wal Irshad (Centre for and Invitation to the Spread of Islam), the Islamic seminary headed by Hafiz Saeed whose armed wing was the Lashkar-e-Taiba. He raised funds for the Lashkar and helped publish Markaz literature. In November, the British government found that an IT executive of Railtrack, Mohammed Sohail, had been using the company's computers to enlist recruits and raise funds for the Lashkar, Harkat-ul-Ansar and other groups operating in Kashmir, Kosovo and Chechnya. Sohail was affiliated to the Global Jihad Fund, which 'aims to facilitate the growth of various jihad movements around the world by supplying them with sufficient funds to purchase weapons and train their individuals', and had set up an Internet site called the 'Islamic Gateway' with a sister site in Pakistan.[7] According to an intercepted e-mail sent by Sohail to a potential recruit, 'Currently jihad training is being done in Muzaffarabad in Pakistan. It is on for 21 days and is of beginners' level. It is organized by Lashkar-e-Toiba [sic]... Then there are special courses. If anyone wants to go to Afghanistan I can also do this by arrangement.' Apparently, he met would-be recruits and donors at a London Underground station.

Sohail himself was unfazed by the allegations. 'It is true that I am connected with both the Global Jihad Fund and the Islamic Gateway,' he told *The Telegraph*. 'We are involved only with struggles abroad. We see it as a form of self-defence. We have a duty to help brothers who are fighting oppression overseas.'

In late May, villagers fleeing the border areas in the Jammu districts of Rajouri and Poonch reported a fresh influx of foreign fighters from across the Line of Control. The situation had become intolerable they said; even banks were refusing to issue or encash money drafts as they feared cash transactions might invite trouble. According to Kashmir police reports, the number of Pakistani-backed fighters who infiltrated was 13 in January 1999 but shot up to 240 in April and hit a peak of 520 in June—of whom 425 were foreigners (and the remaining 95 were Kashmiris).[8] Attacks on security forces rose sharply with casualties going from 258 in 1998 to 407 in 1999.[9] In September, guerrillas succeeded in storming the battalion headquarters of the BSF at Bandipora, killing a deputy inspector general, a deputy commandant and two others. A few days later, they attacked a Rashtriya Rifles barracks in Kupwara, killing five troops.

The communal trend noted in 1997–98, with armed groups seeking to divide Muslims from Hindus and Sikhs in the Pir Panjal region, also continued. There were six mass murders of Hindus in 1999, in Poonch, Doda, Rajouri, Udhampur and Anantnag, with fifty-two killed.[10] In Anantnag, the BJP candidate's seven-year-old son was kidnapped and released after the family paid a ₹250,000 ransom.[11]

From the Pir Panjal districts, infiltration spread to northern Kashmir, resettling in the old guerrilla strongholds of Kupwara and Baramulla. Quoting official and unofficial sources, newspaper reports put the number of foreign fighters in the two districts at anything between one and three thousand. Over 90 per cent of them, said *The Excelsior*, were Pakistani and Afghan cadres of five armed groups: the Harkatul Jihad-e-Islami, Al-Badr, Lashkar-e-Taiba, Harkatul· Mujahideen and Hizbul Mujahideen. 'Unlike in the past, they have a "unified command"',[12] the newspaper commented. There had not been 'a single incident of group clash... since May this year'. The reference was to the Muttahida (United) Jihad Council, an umbrella organization for Islamic militias fighting jihad in Kashmir, formed in summer 1994 at the prodding of the ISI with thirteen affiliated militias.

The newspaper report might have indicated a brief moment when Pakistani-backed armed groups worked together, but otherwise the council was little more than a useful cover. The Lashkar-e-Taiba was already Pakistan's preferred group. In September, a 'coded diary' captured by the Rashtriya Rifles during a shootout revealed 'one of the slain militants identified as Babood…was having specific instruction of his appointment as "chief controller" of Thatri tehsil. He had been directed by the ISI to take over from the current "tehsil commander" Jehangir belonging to the Hizbul Mujahideen outfit.'[13]

By September 1999, when the general election took place in India, it was reported that parts of Kupwara had been turned into 'liberated zones': 'Everybody here says that thick groups of heavily-armed foreigners have been making daytime movement, conducting identification parades, checking identity cards of passengers, raising concrete bunkers in dense forests and taking essential commodities from the main markets to their hideouts.'[14] The militants, local residents said, were fearsome but at least they paid for food and shelter. By contrast, security forces had 'adopted foolish strategies to stave off an attack'.[15] 'The camps of security forces have reduced ten-fold since Kargil. At all formations, local people are made to maintain nocturnal vigil with kerosene oil lanterns. At several places, people are taken forcibly for felling trees and transportation of timber to sawmills.'[16] Both activities exposed villagers to attack by armed groups.

In fact, the Indian Army had begun to move to plug the gaps left by redeployment to Kargil, setting up three additional counter-terrorism units comprising a military corps in Ladakh, two divisions in north and south Kashmir and one in the Pir Panjal region of Jammu (named Kilo, Victor and Romeo forces respectively).[17] But it took some weeks to get the divisions in place and, in the interim, there were widespread violations of villagers' rights.

Like the state election of 1996, the general election of September 1999 was marked by violence in the Kashmir valley. The Hurriyat called for an election boycott, led by Yasin Malik of the JKLF, who went to mosques across the valley to campaign. The Farooq government had arrested most of the Hurriyat leaders in the run-up to polling, but released them when Election Commissioner G. V. G. Krishnamurty observed that canvassing for a poll boycott is a democratic right.

Covering one Malik campaign visit, the Kashmiri journalist, Muzamil Jaleel, reported: 'The [APHC] leaders head for Jamia Masjid, the main mosque of the town, the day being Friday. By the time they are offering prayers, the news of their arrival spreads like wildfire among the villagers who have come from the adjoining areas to offer the Friday namaaz. The prayers over, a makeshift stage is erected and the leaders begin their speeches. "The elections are a farce. After sacrificing thousands of lives, nobody can participate in this sell-out. We do not want to be a part of India and we should show that by boycotting the polls," says Yasin. He asks those present "to resist all pressures and keep themselves away from this futile exercise".'[18]

The Hurriyat's focus, added Jaleel, had shifted from the National Conference to the newly formed People's Democratic Party of Mufti Mohammad Sayeed, because it is 'seeking [a] mandate on issues like human rights abuses allegedly committed by the security forces, unconditional dialogue with militants and most importantly, the demand for resolution of the Kashmir "dispute"—issues that resemble to a greater extent the main planks of the APHC.'

◆

The horrors of 1999 peaked with two attacks on Christmas Eve: a Lashkar-e-Taiba suicide attack on the headquarters of the Jammu and Kashmir police's Special Operations Group (SOG), and the hijack of the IC-814 flight from Kathmandu to New Delhi, carrying 178 passengers and 11 crew. Eleven police personnel were killed in the Srinagar attack, along with the terrorists, in an encounter that lasted a day. Though the SOG was hated for using extra-judicial methods in counter-insurgency, there was little support in the Kashmir valley for the Lashkar attack. The valley tide had turned against militancy, as the Vajpayee government was to discover in 2000.

Only one passenger was killed in the airplane hijack, but its outcome once again underlined India's stark security gaps at the political and administrative levels. At 5 p.m. on 24 December, a group of five armed Pakistanis boarded Air India flight IC-814 at Kathmandu, threatening to bomb the plane, and directed the pilot to fly to Lahore instead of Delhi. The Pakistani authorities refused to let the plane land and at risk of running out of fuel, the pilot flew to Amritsar. The Indian government had the opportunity to defuse the crisis at this point—the Punjab security forces had successfully pre-empted a similar hijack in 1993, of an Indian Airlines flight from Delhi to Srinagar—but that was a different director general of police under a different administration. Though the Vajpayee administration was alerted to the Amritsar landing before IC-814 arrived, and the plane was grounded for 45-50 minutes, the police on the ground did not receive clear instructions from New Delhi. By the time Home Minister L. K. Advani flew to Amritsar to direct operations, the plane had taken off, without refuelling. The Punjab director general of police was to say later, astoundingly, 'I was not told to stop the plane.'[19]

A sorry saga of ineptitude emerged. BJP MP Kanchan Gupta, who was Vajpayee's aide in 1999, recounted in 2008 how Vajpayee was on an official trip outside New Delhi when the hijack took place and could not be informed of it until he landed an hour after, because his aircraft was not equipped with satellite phone technology.[20] The Cabinet Committee on Security meeting that followed appears to have been in shambles. According to Gupta, 'Desperate calls were made to the officials at Raja Sansi Airport (Amritsar) to somehow stall the refuelling and prevent the plane from taking off. The officials just failed to respond with alacrity. At one point, an exasperated Jaswant Singh, if memory serves me right, grabbed the phone and pleaded with an official, "Just drive a heavy vehicle, a fuel truck or a road roller or whatever you have, onto the runway and park it there."' The appearance of the truck tipped off the hijackers, who forced IC-814's pilot to take off immediately.

IC-814 flew next to Lahore, where the Pakistani government allowed it to land only when External Affairs Minister Jaswant Singh once again asked them to let the plane refuel since its supplies were running dangerously low. A further request, to allow Indian commandos to try and rescue the passengers in a joint operation with domestic forces, was refused by Pakistan and also by the United Arab Emirates (UAE), where the aircraft flew after refuelling at Lahore. It took US intercession for Dubai to even agree to allow a handful of mothers and children to disembark as a result of pressure on the hijackers.

The next stop was Kandahar in Taliban-ruled Afghanistan. This was where the serious negotiations began. By this time the Indian government, under pressure from relatives of the 178 passengers on IC-814, had more or less decided to seek a negotiated end to the crisis. In any case, they were by now powerless to influence the situation. Pakistan had all the levers. Mullah Wakil Ahmed Muttawakil, then the Taliban's foreign affairs minister in Kabul, later confessed 'the hijackers were taking instructions from Pakistani officials present at the airport'.[21]

After several days of bargaining—with the Taliban acting as go-betweens for the Indian team, the hijackers and their Pakistani handlers—it was agreed that all the passengers would be released in return for the Indian government handing over three terrorists held in Indian jails. With a little help from the Taliban, the hijackers' original list of twenty-five was whittled down to three. Intriguingly, one of the Taliban that helped India in the gruelling negotiations was Mullah Mansour, who led peace negotiations with the Afghan government in Murree in 2015, but was assassinated soon after.

The three terrorists who were released had been amongst India's most wanted and their arrests had been feathers in the Indian police's cap. Masood Azhar, then a member of the Harkatul Mujahideen (a faction of the Harkat-ul-Ansar), was a fiery Pakistani preacher from Bahawalpur whose speeches motivated acts of jihad. Umar Sheikh, also a member of the Harkatul Mujahideen, was a British citizen of Pakistani origin who had been implicated in the kidnapping of Europeans in the Kashmir valley. Mushtaq Ahmed Zargar, of the Al-Umar Mujahideen, was a Kashmiri from Nowhatta in Srinagar who had killed over twenty army officers, policemen and political activists, and been involved in the 1989 kidnapping of the then Indian home minister's daughter, Rubaiya Sayeed.

Chief Minister Farooq Abdullah vehemently opposed Zargar's release until told that the exchange had already been agreed and he had to back off. By this time, Indian investigators had learned that the hijackers too were members of the Harkatul Mujahideen, had started planning the hijack in August with Azhar's brother and brother-in-law in Dhaka, visited Afghanistan several times to make arrangements with the Taliban and had finalized their plans on 13 December at, of all places, the Kathmandu zoo. A few small bribes had enabled them to get through security at the lax Kathmandu airport.[22]

All three freed terrorists were welcomed in Pakistan, with Azhar leading victory processions. Within days of his return he founded the Bahawalpur-based Jaish-e-Mohammad, which would be responsible for the Indian parliament attack of 2001. Umar Sheikh—now bumped up by his jihadi colleagues to 'Sheikh Umar'—went on to kill the US journalist Daniel Pearl in 2002. Zargar was housed in Muzaffarabad, the capital of Pakistan-administered Kashmir, and encouraged to resume training for cross-border attacks on India.

Jaswant Singh was to describe 1999 as one of the worst years for India in relation to Pakistan: 'troubled neighbour, turbulent times'.[23] It certainly provided a case study in humiliation. Worse still, the NDA government had proved bumbling. Kanchan Gupta remarked bitterly that the relatives of passengers shouted at Jaswant Singh when he went to explain what the government was doing to free the IC-814 hostages to 'ditch national security, give them Kashmir but bring our relatives back'. But the government had remained silent for days before this, having only failure to relay, and the relatives' frustration was palpable.

The only person to emerge with some credit was Jaswant Singh. As during Kargil, he had to be the public face of the Indian government during the hijack. He not only shouldered the burden but also insisted he would lead the team to Kandahar, where he underwent the ignominy of handing terrorists over to the ISI-driven Taliban. He was the only cabinet minister who was prepared to talk to the relatives of the IC-814 hostages.

For Pakistan, the hijack and its aftermath, following soon after Kargil and the military coup, reinforced the dawning international recognition that the country was gradually becoming one of the most dangerous places on earth. 1999 was almost as bad a year for Pakistan as for India. Its leadership, both civil and military, had embroiled the country in three conflicts, one domestic. The economy plummeted and even international allies such as China and the US drew away. The unkindest cut of all was that some of the Kashmiri dissidents turned severely critical. In a pamphlet titled 'Kargil: A Short Review', Hurriyat Chairman Geelani castigated Sharif's Washington visit as 'nothing but blatant unfaithfulness to the fifty-one-year-old freedom struggle and the ten-year-old bloody and self-sacrificing movement'.[24] The 'ad nauseam repetition of the Lahore declaration and bilateral talks', he added, was damaging the movement even further.

With General Musharraf at Pakistan's helm, it looked as if 2000 might repeat 1999, with no guarantee that the Indian government would show as much restraint as with Kargil and the IC-814 hijack. But Clinton was now personally involved and the US began to actively seek opportunities for India–Pakistan peacemaking. First, however, the Clinton administration had to rejig the US approach to armed guerrillas operating in Jammu and Kashmir, an issue on which the State Department had been ambiguous at best.

Chapter XIV

THE RISE OF JIHAD

Though the Kashmir insurgency began in 1988–89 and had strands of Muslim chauvinism from the start, it took close to ten years for it to morph into an Islamist jihad against India. By the time Gujral became prime minister, it had been taken over by Pakistani militias such as the Lashkar-e-Taiba—'Army of the Pure', a reference to the Persian and Pashto translation of Pak-i-stan as 'Land of the Pure'—and Jaish-e-Mohammad or 'Mohammad's Army'. Based in the south and central districts of Pakistani Punjab bordering India, both militias were spawned by Salafist ideologues: the Lashkar by Ahle Hadees member and religious studies teacher Hafiz Muhammad Saeed, and the Jaish by Jamia Uloom preacher and former Harkat-ul-Ansar 'motivator' Maulana Masood Azhar. The Lashkar provided foot soldiers for the Kargil War and went on to commit a number of major terrorist acts in Kashmir as well as the rest of India. The Jaish was implicated in a string of terrorist acts in India, beginning with the 2001 Parliament attack in Delhi.

Together, the two militias are responsible for over 90 per cent of cross-border attacks on India. A genealogy of each shows common points. First, the Afghan and Kashmir jihads are inextricably intertwined. Both the Lashkar and Jaish were founded to support General Zia's Afghan jihad against the Soviet Union, launched in 1980 with US and Saudi support. Both expanded their focus to India and a Kashmir jihad after the withdrawal of the Soviet Union, in many cases merging the three jihads against Afghanistan, India and Kashmir. Both militias were born of the nexus between the Pakistan Army, religious political leaders and criminals that was spurred by the Afghan jihad. The Lashkar and Jaish's support structure and ideological and funding base is

Martand Sun Temple, built in eighth century BCE

Dogra monarch Maharaja Gulab Singh of Jammu and Kashmir, circa 1846

Hari Singh (r. 1925–1961), the last ruling monarch of the princely state of Jammu and Kashmir

Hindustan Times, 28 October 1947

The Indian Army, on road patrol along the Baramula-Uri road, 1948

Yuvraj Karan Singh at the Jammu and Kashmir University convocation on 24 September 1949. Jawaharlal Nehru is sitting behind him

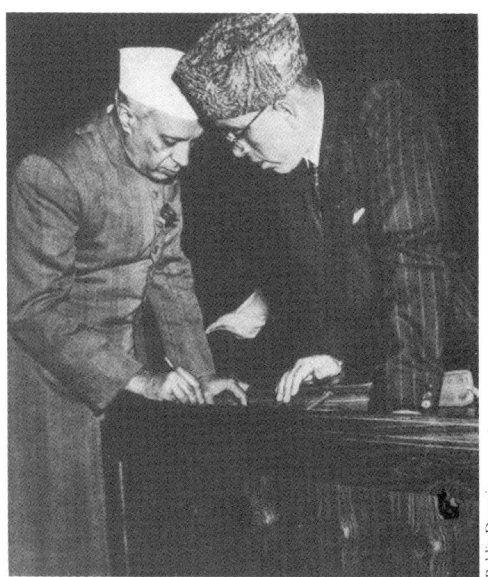

Nehru in conversation with Sheikh Abdullah in the constituent assembly, circa 1950

Zulfikar Ali Bhutto, fourth president and ninth prime minister of Pakistan, during the Bangladesh war in December 1971

Indira Gandhi addressing a crowd in Srinagar

Hazratbal Shrine

Kargil War Memorial

Prime Minister Atal Bihari Vajpayee with President Pervez Musharraf at the 12th SAARC summit, Islamabad, 5 January 2003 (when Musharraf made his famous pledge to crack down on terrorism against India)

Hurriyat (M) meeting with Prime Minister Vajpayee, 23 January 2003. L to R: Bilal Lone, People's Conference; Abdul Ghani Bhat, Muslim Conference; Maulvi Abbas Ansari, Ittehadul Muslimeen; Prime Minister Vajpayee; Mirwaiz Umar Farooq, Awami Action Committee; Fazal Haq Qureshi, People's League

Flagging off the Srinagar-Muzaffarabad Bus in Srinagar, 7 April 2005. L to R: Minister for Parliamentary Affairs and Urban Development Ghulam Nabi Azad, INC President Sonia Gandhi, Prime Minister Manmohan Singh, Chief Minister of Jammu & Kashmir Mufti Mohammad Sayeed, National Conference leader Omar Abdullah and External Affairs Minister Natwar Singh

Prime Minister Manmohan Singh attending the Second Round Table Conference in Srinagar, 24 May 2006. Participants included Home Minister Shivraj Singh, Chief Minister Ghulam Nabi Azad, former Chief Minister Mufti Mohammad Sayeed, leaders of the National Conference Farooq and Omar Abdullah, head of the Communist Party of India (Marxist) Yusuf Tarigami

Stone-throwing protest in Srinagar, 2010

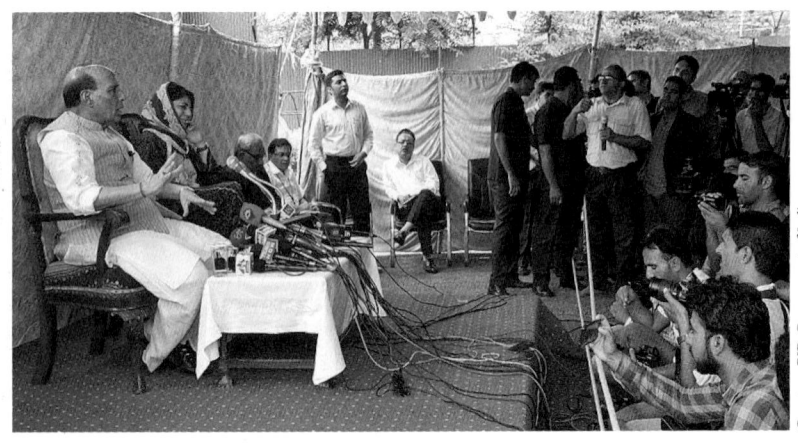

Union Home Minister Rajnath Singh and Chief Minister of Jammu and Kashmir Mehbooba Mufti addressing a press conference in Srinagar during the summer agitation, 25 August 2016

Pakistani Punjab, with some help in arms, training and recruits from the NWFP, which was renamed Khyber–Pakhtunkhwa in 2009. Each militia revolves around a single figure—Hafiz Saeed for the Lashkar and Masood Azhar for the Jaish—and this single figure is a preacher, not a fighter. While such a leadership structure could be seen as separating the political–ideological and armed wings of the militias—in the same way as the Sinn Fein and Irish Republican Army (IRA) in Northern Ireland were distinct—in fact, it was Saeed and Azhar who provided the inspiration and set the goals and targets of the militias, not their armed commanders.

Born in Pakistani Punjab during the turbulent partition of India in 1947, Saeed is said to have lost thirty-six members of his family in the horrific riots that followed. His parents were refugees from Indian Punjab who made the long journey to Lahore, settling in Sargodha in Pakistani Punjab, a district known for its high number of conservative madaris or religious schools. Saeed's family was devout and he became an Islamic scholar, gaining the title of hafiz for being able to recite the Quran at fourteen. While studying in Saudi Arabia under the then grand mufti, Abdul Aziz Ibn-e-Baz, he was deeply influenced by the writings of Palestinian scholar and radical, Abdullah Azzam, whose slogan was 'Jihad and the rifle alone; no negotiations, no conferences, no dialogues.'[1] Azzam moved to Islamabad in 1981 to teach the Quran and Arabic at Pakistan's International Islamic University, and soon became involved in the Afghan jihad.

With Azzam and colleague Zafar Iqbal, Saeed founded the Lashkar in 1987. According to counter-terrorism expert, Bruce Riedel, Saeed took the 'lead role' in the Lashkar, which originally trained its guns on Afghanistan but expanded to Kashmir in the early 1990s after insurgency broke out. Saeed and Azzam were 'close partners' of Osama bin Laden in the late 1980s, a time when bin Laden also envisaged Kashmir as a potential theatre for Al Qaeda operations (though Azzam's focus remained on Afghanistan). After Azzam's death in 1989, Saeed founded an Islamic seminary called the Markaz ud Dawa'ah wal Irshad in 1990. The Markaz became a preaching, recruiting and training ground as well as an umbrella for the Lashkar. Al Qaeda's interest in Kashmir dwindled by the mid-1990s, but bin Laden and Saeed remained in close touch until the former's assassination,[2] and the Lashkar continued to support Al Qaeda. Senior Al Qaeda member Abu Zubaydah was captured at a Lashkar safe house in Faisalabad in Pakistan in 2002.

Saeed had networked with successive Pakistani governments from the 1980s when Zia appointed him to the government's Council of Islamic Ideology. He was a frequent guest at Pakistan Army functions, perhaps still is. When he founded the Markaz, bin Laden provided seed money of $200,000, and Pakistan's Punjab government, under the leadership of the Sharif brothers, gifted him 200 acres at Muridke near Lahore, for a heavily guarded complex that houses a seminary, dormitories, training grounds, a hospital, market, fish farm and agricultural tracts. His Markaz is close to high-security ISI offices, and the Pakistan Army enabled the Lashkar to set up training camps in Pakistan-controlled Jammu in the 1990s, mostly in the Neelam valley of Mirpur district along the Line of Control.[3]

Though the Lashkar's stated enemies are Christians, Jews and Hindus, especially in the US, India and Israel, India is a key focus of its jihad, spurred by a longing to recapture lost Muslim glory and, according to Riedel quoting a Lashkar newspaper, 'bring back the era of Mughal rule. We can once again subjugate the Hindus like our forefathers'. Following the Kargil defeat, Saeed announced his goal: 'The break-up of India, Inshallah [God willing]. We will not rest until the whole of India is dissolved into Pakistan.' On the opening page of its website in 2002, the Markaz ran a poll on whether the US's post-9/11 war was against Islam or terrorists. The poll was pre-programmed to vote Islam, and another section of the site quoted a prominent Islamic cleric's claim that the war in Afghanistan is a clash of civilizations. 'This battle will take [the] shape of the religious war of Hind in which the Muslims stood victorious,' he added.[4]

The guerrillas of the Lashkar were and are mostly Pakistani Punjabis, and until 2001 it drew heavily on the radical fringe of Britain's Pakistani diaspora, also mostly Punjabis, who provided it with handsome funds and fewer foot soldiers. The Lashkar website was set up and run by a group of teenagers in Birmingham and it advertised a Birmingham bank account for donations. After an attack on Delhi's historic Red Fort in December 2000 that the Lashkar boasted of on its website, Britain banned the group in February 2001 and the supply of British foot soldiers trailed off, though the flow of funds continued, as much as $3 million per year.[5]

Other major Markaz–Lashkar funding sources included Saudi Arabia, the UAE (which too has a sizable Pakistani diaspora) and Kuwait. Domestically, the Lashkar raised millions by selling hides collected from Eid sacrifices, and for many years had collection boxes in shops across Pakistan. The group runs 16 Islamic institutions, 135 secondary schools, an ambulance service, mobile clinics, blood banks and several seminaries across Pakistan. It publishes an Urdu-language monthly journal, *Al Dawa*, an Urdu weekly, *Gazwa*, and an English-language monthly, *Voice of Islam*. Its publications are periodically banned but reappear under different names after a short lull.

In January 2002, following the attack on India's Parliament, the US State Department added the Lashkar to its list of banned terrorist organizations. The Markaz renamed itself the Jamaat-ud-Dawa and split from the Lashkar, turning the latter into an autonomous militia headed by its former commander of armed operations, Zakiur Rahman Lakhvi, instead of Saeed, who was proclaimed ameer of the Jamaat-ud-Dawa alone. The Jamaat website went underground briefly but reappeared within weeks and was relaunched in 2003 and again in 2012.

The Jaish was founded in 2000 after Azhar was released in the IC-814 prisoner-hostage exchange of December 1999. Reportedly, he first went to Kandahar to seek bin Laden's approval for his madarsa-cum-militia and secured both approval and funding. The son of a government schoolteacher of the Quran in Bahawalpur, who ran an Islamic charity called the Al-Rahmat Trust, Azhar was educated at the Haqqani-run Jamia Uloom ul Islamia at Banuri Town in Karachi, a school infamous for the number of

Harkat-ul-Jihad-e-Islami, Harkatul Mujahideen and Taliban it recruited. He was introduced to the Taliban by the then principal of the Jamia Uloom, Nizamuddin Shamzai, and was invited to accompany Shamzai to Afghanistan. At Shamzai's suggestion, while in Afghanistan, he took a forty-day course in guerrilla warfare, or jihad, as he called it, but failed because he was physically unfit. Like Saeed, he was no fighter, but proved to be an inspired motivator. His brother, Ibrahim, fought in the Afghan jihad and his sister worked for the Taliban. His other brother, Abdul Rauf, headed the military wing of the Jaish. The family had a jihad lineage. Azhar's ancestors were members of the al-Ahrar militant group in undivided India, which was based in Punjab and periodically active in Kashmir.

The Jaish is the grandchild of the Harkat-ul-Jihad-e-Islami, headed at one time by Rasool Sayyaf of Afghanistan. Created in the early 1980s to fight in the anti-Soviet Afghan jihad, the Harkat-ul-Jihad soon split, and in 1985, Azhar co-founded the Harkatul Mujahideen with Fazlur Rahman Khalil of the Jamiat Ulema-i-Islam. He had been introduced to Fazlur by his patron Shamzai, also a member of the Jamiat shura or consultative council. Initially focused on Afghanistan, the Harkat shifted targets to Kashmir after the Soviet withdrawal in 1989. In 1994, the militia sent Azhar to the Kashmir valley to negotiate a merger with the Harkatul Mujahideen. At the time, the Harkat was strong in the Pir Panjal region of Jammu and the Harkatul was in the process of establishing itself in north Kashmir. Azhar succeeded in persuading the two to merge under the name of Harkat-ul-Ansar (literally 'helpers', the Ansar were tribes that fought alongside the Prophet Muhammad). Azhar was appointed the Harkat's lead recruiter and fundraiser, rising to the top of its hierarchy when he was twenty-five, but arrested in India soon after and imprisoned in Jammu's Kot Balwal jail.[6] The Harkatul Ansar was placed on the US's terrorism watch list in October 1997, and separated back into its original constituents, the Harkat-ul-Jihad and Harkatul Mujahideen, the latter headed by Fazlur Rahman Khalil.

Khalil and Azhar appear to have fallen out during this period, since Azhar's first act upon release was to found the Jaish-e-Mohammad, dividing the Harkatul Mujahideen. In a last-ditch attempt to prevent Azhar's split, Khalil apparently offered to resign as commander and let Azhar take over, an offer that Azhar summarily rejected. Two-thirds of the Harkatul fighters followed Azhar into the Jaish, and the two militias fought pitched battles for control of Harkatul assets in Pakistan, most of which the Jaish won.

The Jaish also has ties to the sectarian Pakistani militias Sipah-e-Sahaba and Lashkar-e-Jhangvi, which were involved in a spate of anti-Shia attacks in Gilgit–Baltistan. Its ranks include foreign fighters from Central Asia, North Africa and the Middle East as well as the Pakistani diaspora in Europe and the Gulf countries. Its base was in Karachi, where Azhar had studied, but by 2013 shifted to his home, Bahawalpur, where it is now headquartered and owns considerable lands, including a seminary and training grounds in the ruins of Fort Maujgarh in the adjoining Cholistan desert. According to journalist Praveen Swami, the slogan at Azhar's seminary gate read: 'Delhi, Delhi ya hanood, Jaish-e-Muhammad sauf yauood (To Delhi, O Hindus, the army of the Prophet will soon return)'.[7]

Like Sargodha, Bahawalpur houses a very large number of radical madaris. In 2008, a Pakistani Intelligence Bureau report cited by analyst Ayesha Siddiqa stated that there were 1,383 madarsas in the Bahawalpur division that housed 84,000 students, more than any other region of Pakistan. In 2001–02, Bahawalpur provided the biggest share of armed and trained guerrillas of any district in Pakistan, as many as 15,000–20,000.[8]

Bordering Bahawalpur, Rahim Yar Khan district nurtures the largest number of Maududi's Deobandi and Salafi madaris (559 in 2008) and its Makhzan-ul-Uloom madarsa was a centre of anti-Shia propaganda in the 1990s. Rahim Yar Khan was home to the late Lashkar-e-Jhangvi commander, Malik Ishaq, and Azhar's ties to the Lashkar-e-Jhangvi allow the Jaish's influence to span both districts. Poverty, poor governance and lack of development in these two districts, along with neighbouring Dera Ghazi Khan and Rajanpur, from where the Lal Masjid clerics originated, made their people natural candidates for recruitment to jihad. The madaris were the only readily available schools and they provided free board and lodging for students. The armed groups also gave pensions to the families of slain guerrillas.

While the Lashkar and Jaish recruit from these districts, along with the Lashkar-e-Jhangvi and Sipah-e-Sahaba, their constituencies are different. The Lashkar is stronger amongst Punjabi- and Urdu-speaking Mujahirs (Muslims who migrated from India after partition) and the Jaish amongst Seraiki-speakers and desert tribes. Siddiqa pointed out that that all four groups grew as the syncretic Punjabi culture and Barelvi and Sufi Islam weakened in face of Zia's Islamization programme in the 1980s. Their growth may also be linked to semi-urbanization and the unplanned development of small towns with no institutional, health and education infrastructure. 'Socially and politically,' she commented, 'there is a gap that is filled by these militant outfits or related ideological institutions.' These distinctions apart, the Punjabi middle class contributed funds to all four groups and the two collaborated whenever they saw fit.

Both Punjabis, Saeed and Azhar had a Salafist education in common though their points of departure were different, and Saeed had a very personal hatred for India, born of his partition history. Saeed's Jamaat-ud-Dawa and Lashkar have a longer, deeper and more consistent focus on Kashmir than the Jaish, although both seek to destroy India and both support calls for a caliphate which would ideally unite 'all Muslim majority regions in countries that surround Pakistan'.[9] The Jaish also attracts more foreign (non-Pakistani) fighters than the Lashkar does, including educated youth such as Omar Sheikh, the British terrorist of Pakistani origin who was freed by India in 1999 and followed Azhar from the Harkatul Mujahideen to the Jaish.

Unlike Saeed and Azhar, Sheikh was no Islamic scholar, even of the Salafi or Wahhabi variety. His education was secular. While he was an immigrant like Saeed, his parents were economic migrants to Britain, not refugees driven by ethnic violence as Saeed's family was. He had no personal animosity against India. But as a second-generation migrant and member of the Muslim minority in Britain, he may well have felt discriminated against. Bosnia was his first choice for jihad. His handlers sent him to India instead.

In many ways, Sheikh prefigured the thousands of Britons who joined the Islamic State (ISIS) fighting in Iraq, Libya and Syria in the 2010s. Born in London and a dropout from the London School of Economics, Sheikh was first radicalized by a 1993 Hizbut Tahrir video on Bosnia. He tried to go to Bosnia to join the guerrillas fighting Serbia but got no further than Croatia, where he was directed to change track for Pakistan. In Pakistan, he trained with the Harkatul Mujahideen, becoming an instructor himself, and was sent to India in 1994 with instructions to kidnap foreigners, especially US, British and French nationals. His account of the kidnappings, lodged in Delhi's Patiala House Court records, described how he arrived in Delhi and frequented tourist spots to strike up an acquaintance with foreigners whom he, along with two accomplices who were his handlers, took hostage. Though he insisted that there were no plans to kill the young men he befriended and kidnapped, his account was notably absent any pity for them or remorse for their suffering. According to one of his hostages, Rhys Partridge, Sheikh relished his role as potential killer. 'He became very excited, and he was—the whole thing really turned him on, I believe... He was very pleased with himself. He was sort of on the verge of giggling.'[10] Apparently, Sheikh also handed his hostages Islamic pamphlets of a crude and 'childish' nature, and believed his acts of cruelty would send him to heaven. When Partridge tried to reason that Islam did not sanction brutal acts against random civilians, Sheikh became angry and shut down the conversation.

Fortunately, Sheikh and his accomplices inadvertently aroused the suspicions of the local police. The hostages were freed in an Indian Army operation, though, sadly, two policemen were shot. Sheikh was arrested along with one of his accomplices. His commander, however, escaped. Indian police later discovered he was Ilyas Kashmiri, one of India's most wanted. While in prison,

Sheikh met Uttar Pradesh gangster, Aftab Ansari, then a local boss of organized crime. Sheikh and Ansari were both released in late 1999; the latter, having served his sentence, migrated to Dubai. They teamed up to organize a series of kidnappings of Indian businessmen for ransom. Some of their proceeds were funnelled into jihad; allegedly, Sheikh also sent $100,000 to Mohammad Atta for the 9/11 attacks.[11]

The last word on Sheikh came from a BBC journalist who interviewed him while he was recovering from wounds sustained during the gunfight that led to his arrest. Sheikh, he said, begged him to speak to consular officers to secure his release and/or repatriation. He had been misled by the Islamists who brought him to India, he said, this was not a war he wanted to fight. Yet, on his release he went to Pakistan, started calling himself 'Sheikh' Omar, married and had a child, and continued to kidnap, ransom and murder. After his arrest in Pakistan for beheading US journalist Daniel Pearl, he confessed to having helped organize the Jammu and Kashmir assembly bombing in October 2000, the raid on India's Parliament in December 2001 and the United States Information Service (USIS) shootings in Calcutta in January 2002.[12]

◆

Do these brief bios allow us to limn a profile, or even a portrait, of the jihadi? A profile maybe, revealing what have now become platitudes—all three believed Islam would reward them for killing or having killed those they identified as enemies, and relished the deaths they were responsible for. All three shared a global worldview that there was an ongoing clash of civilizations in which Muslims in particular and Islam in general were persecuted and the only remedy was for Islam to regain its past glory through recreating its fifteenth-century empires. All three listed the same specific targets: Hindus, Christians and Jews, India, the US and Israel.

The occasional Sheikh aside, the bulk of the new Kashmir guerrillas were bred in Pakistan's radical Islamic schools and trained in hit-and-run warfare in both Pakistan and Afghanistan.[13]

They had their own hagiography of liberation, an Islamic and militarist rather than political history, which went against Kashmiri norms of coexistence and fractured Kashmiri aspirations. Kashmiri opposition groups, even in their brief armed incarnation, traced their roots to a failed political process culminating in the rigged 1987 elections. But Islamic militias like the Lashkar traced their origins in Kashmir to the 1990 assassination of 'one squadron leader and three pilots of the same Indian Air Force whose 704 sorties from 27 October to 17 November 1947 landed [the] Indian Army at Srinagar airport'. The 1990 murders were, in fact, committed by JKLF head, Yasin Malik, who sought independence for the former princely state.

Borrowing from Azzam's Arab recruitment campaign for the Afghan jihad, the Lashkar's tale of liberation is a litany of the dead and martyred. Following the assassination of the Indian airmen, they said, volunteers 'started pouring into Ma'skar Taiba of Afghanistan to train for Jihad-e-Kashmir. Then, for their special training, Ma'skar Aqsa was founded in the nearby hills. And then, Baitul Mujahedeen was established in Muzaffarabad in Azad Kashmir to organize Mujahideen and to facilitate jihad in Kashmir.

'Finally, the day came which was eagerly awaited. In August 1992, a group of Mujahedeen which received training at Ma'skar Aqsa made its way to the occupied Kashmir through towering mountains. It was the morning of August 26, 1992 when Mujahedeen clashed with Indian Army in Rashi Ghund, district Kupwara. Abu Khalid Aftab fired a rocket from his RPG-7. In that encounter one captain, two JCOs, five NCOs and eleven soldiers were killed. Indian government admitted these casualties. The Mujahedeen and the people of Kashmir heaved a sigh of relief and said Allah's help has arrived.'[14]

Between 1992 and 2002, the Lashkar claimed, their militia killed over 14,000 Indian soldiers, and 1,500 of its own men were martyred (the official Indian figure of overall losses of security personnel in the Kashmir conflict from 1989–2002 was just over 4,000). These deaths, the Lashkar concluded, spelt the guerrillas' determination to fight 'until Allah's Deen (writ) prevails on the earth, this is our Manhaj (spiritual journey), this is our Jihad, this is the Central point of our Da'wah and this is our goal.'

By the end of the 1990s, there were more Pakistanis than Kashmiris amongst the guerrillas. The Lashkar's list of 'martyred commanders', for example, named men from districts all over Punjab and northwestern Pakistan, including Swat, Faisalabad, Gujranwala, Bahawalnagar, Khanewal and Sheikhupura.[15] Guerrilla attacks were no longer restricted to Kashmir, though most occurred there. The guerrillas had more sophisticated arms, communications and planning, and they inflicted much greater damage in raids on army and police posts, convoys and barracks, government buildings, and civilians. Outside Kashmir, they targeted India's capital city, Delhi, and linked into the mafia-type network developed by the criminal Bombay financier Dawood Ibrahim, who fled India for Pakistan in the mid-1990s.

The Indian government adopted increasingly draconian measures in response, applying the Disturbed Areas Act and the Armed Forces Special Protections Act to the state (district by district).[16] The army's 'area domination' strategy—a component of its counter-insurgency policy—under which troops patrolled every town and village, meant civilians were frequently trapped in the battle between Indian troops and Islamic militias. India's army, once welcomed as providing security against Pakistani invasions, building roads and bringing medicines to remote areas, began to become a hated symbol of military occupation and human rights abuse. Its tactic of using erstwhile guerrillas to fight present ones worsened an already fragile law and order infrastructure, letting in revenge killings.[17] In 1994, when the state government created the counter-insurgent SOG as a wing of the state police, Kashmir's losses began to pit Muslim against Muslim at an even more intimate level. Over 80 per cent of the complaints received by the state Human Rights Commission in 1997 were against the SOG, reported the *Economic Times*.[18] In 2002, Chief Minister Mufti Muhammad Sayeed dissolved the group. It was revived after 2014.

By the end of the decade, more than 35,000 people had been killed,[19] the vast majority Muslim, and families who had lost one member at the hands of Islamic militias and another at the hands of the security forces were more a norm than exceptions in the Kashmir valley.[20] The border village of Dardpora (which also translates to 'village of pain' though it must have originally been named after the Dard tribes) in Kupwara district lost almost all its 200 men to guerrilla–army conflict. When interviewed, one of the Dardpora widows, Mamta Lone, said troops killed her husband because he had joined the Al-Badr militia. 'He was forced to become a jihadi,' she said. 'Men here had no choice. If they didn't toe the terrorists' line, they would be finished.'[21]

But the place where Pakistan's Kashmir policy had the most far-reaching impact was within Pakistan itself. The free rein that the ISI had to mobilize the Afghan and Kashmir jihads led to the rapid spread of militant Islamic schools across the country, from the NWFP frontier through Sindh, Balochistan and Punjab.[22] Afghanistan-focused groups were headquartered in the northwest frontier and tribal areas as well as Sindh and Balochistan, and India-focused groups were headquartered in Pakistani Punjab. Jihad rallies began to attract crowds of 200,000 and recruit upwards of 50,000 volunteers at a single rally (to sign-up, not necessarily to be called up). By summer 2000, Islamic militias collected funds for jihad in every shop in Lahore, Islamabad, Rawalpindi, Karachi and Peshawar. Dismayed Pakistanis saw that the precarious lines of separation that had existed between the Afghan jihad, sectarian groups in Pakistan, and the Kashmir guerrillas had been erased. The same men fought in Afghanistan, Pakistan and Kashmir.[23]

Rabid as the Islamic militias were, the Lashkar's website also shed light on a softer side to some of them. For a brief period, from early to mid-2000, it carried a chat room that must surely have been run by the Lashkar's British volunteers. Leading the chat was a mock academic discussion of the sexual preferences of ancient Romans, Greeks and Carthaginians that could only have been written by the products of a British classroom. And its overall irreverence—for instance it carried an ongoing correspondence on the animal antics of bin Laden—raised more questions than the rest of the site answered, on whether it was at all possible to develop a profile of the jihadi.[24] In 2001, while searching the site, I found nestled among grandiose pronouncements on holy war the startling announcement that Wrigley's chewing gum was no longer halal (kosher).

It would take an Orwell to write how these ambiguities of identity coexisted with the certainties of jihad as preached by the ISI's favoured clerics. What does emerge, however, is a tangled skein of distinct and separate motives that combined by force of circumstance and led to the death of thousands. Most of the young volunteers for jihad in Kashmir were little more than cannon fodder in a war they had only book or hearsay knowledge of.

Chapter XV

SUDDENLY IN 2000

Though 1999 was one of the worst years of cross-border violence for India and in particular Jammu and Kashmir, local criticism of Pakistani and Afghan guerrillas had already started when the Kargil intrusion occurred. It gathered momentum after the intrusion's inglorious end. In February 1999, Maulana Mohammad Khan Shirani, a leading cleric of Pakistan's powerful Islamic party, the Jamiat Ulema-i-Islam, 'asked the people of Kashmir to remain within the Indian Union but with greater autonomy'.[1] Shirani was a Baloch member of the Pakistani government's Council of Islamic Ideology. The Jamiat had its largest support base in the NWFP and was headed by Fazlur Rahman, who had earlier mentored Islamic militias fighting in Kashmir.

Shirani's statement was directed as much at the Jamaat-e-Islami as at Kashmiri dissidents. There had been an ongoing rivalry between the Jamaat and Jamiat since the former became the ISI's preferred conduit for a Kashmir jihad. But all was not well with the Jamaat's handling of the Kashmir jihad either, where Pakistani guerrillas had taken an upper hand over their Kashmiri counterparts. In March 1999, while Vajpayee visited Lahore, the Hizbul Mujahideen's 'district administrator' for Anantnag who had surrendered to the Indian Army, Khurshid Ahmad Reshi, said: 'We local militants clashed often with the foreigners over the ruthless killings of civilians, including those enrolled in the BSF, Army, CRPF... A suspected security force informer was interrogated so brutally by an Afghan militant, Abdul, that he died in our custody.'[2]

In April, the MLA from Gurez raised 'the deplorable plight of people' in Pakistan-administered Gilgit–Baltistan, close to Gurez in northern Kashmir with a shared population of Dachin speakers, appealing to international human rights organizations to highlight the denial of civil rights there.[3] Ten days later, dissidents from Gilgit–Baltistan deposed in a civil society meeting at the 55th session of the UN Human Rights Commission in Geneva that Pakistan had 'changed the demographic composition of Pak-occupied-Kashmir (PoK) by systematically settling outsiders there'.[4] What's more, they said, though Gilgit–Baltistan was free of 'insurgency or terrorism, there are intelligence agencies and the army all over. This is one region where people have no civil or constitutional rights… [P]rotests against this state of affairs are crushed by security forces and through sectarian clashes.' The ISI had encouraged training of sectarian as well as anti-India militias in the forests of Gilgit–Baltistan and there were frequent Shia–Sunni clashes in the predominantly Shia region which had once been part of the princely state of Jammu and Kashmir.

In May, when the Kargil War was at its height, Farooq Siddique, a diaspora Kashmiri and founder of the Council for Independent Kashmir, announced at the Hague Appeal for Peace conference that 'guns and violence in Kashmir should be replaced with dialogue', accusing the Hurriyat of glossing over crimes by foreign fighters.[5] The Hurriyat, he said, were silent over 'widespread atrocities committed by the ISI-controlled groups in Jammu and Kashmir'. In September, just before General Musharraf's military coup, Hurriyat executive member Mirwaiz Umar lamented, 'We were better off without the Kargil conflict. It did not result in a movement forward.'[6] In the same breath, he argued that the conflict proved the guerrillas' fervour was unabated.

Musharraf's October coup disrupted this potential turnaround. At his first press conference, in November 1999, he announced that 'Kashmir cannot be sidelined' and defended the Kargil offensive as within 'the "framework" of Kashmir.'[7] He added that 'with due regard' to international concerns—the US and European administrations had begun to push Pakistan on its nuclear programme and sanctuary for radical Islamic groups, and the Commonwealth suspended Pakistan's membership after the coup—he would go according to the 'needs and requirements' of

Pakistan. 'These will be supreme in my mind and not international demands,' he maintained. Following the coup, violence in Jammu and Kashmir increased. It had already risen sharply after the Kargil conflict. A review of newspaper reports for the period indicates that between the autumn of 1999 and the summer of 2000, on average seven people died each day in army–guerrilla battles.

Pakistan Army support for this escalation was evident. Immediately after his press conference, the Musharraf administration gave permission to the Lashkar-e-Taiba to hold a three-day convention, to which President Tarar and 'chief executive officer' Musharraf were invited along with the Poonch and Muzaffarabad leaders, Sardar Ibrahim Khan and Sultan Mahmood, who had already accepted the invitation.[8] At the Lashkar convention, Hafiz Saeed called on guerrillas to ratchet up attacks in Jammu and Kashmir. In the following days, there was intense firing by Pakistani forces across the Line of Control along a sixty-kilometre stretch from Yusmarg to Tangdhar. Four Indian troops were killed at a forward post in the Gulmarg sector. Another four were killed at a border post in the Tangdhar sector, and twelve were injured in the two attacks. Musharraf's military regime, Indian intelligence sources said, had a new plan '"of basing hit-and-run" commando groups of 15–20 guerrillas at military posts along the Line of Control'.[9] The groups were later named Border Action Teams and became official units of Pakistan Army offensives on and across the Line of Control.

When the Kashmir attacks were followed by attacks in Pakistan's capital Islamabad, on the US embassy, the American Cultural Centre and the offices of the UN, international concern, already heightened by the coup, rose further. With an economy that had plunged from crisis to crisis since the 1998 nuclear tests, and the country in hock to international lending agencies that urged his government to roll back the Kashmir jihad, Musharraf began to look for ways to engage India as well as to contain the internal threat of blowback. The years 2000 and 2001 were marked by a series of initiatives, most of which ended in failure. A 'de-weaponization scheme', aimed at collecting illicit arms, was abandoned after Pakistani religious and militia leaders made a show of resistance. So too were attempts to curtail the great arms bazaars in the tribal agencies of the NWFP and to tax the great smugglers' bazaars around Peshawar. A decision to close down operations to collect funds for jihad ended when the government agreed to leave Islamic parties and militias alone if they refrained from fomenting sectarian conflict within the country.

◆

Pakistan's disruption of a nascent peace process in Kashmir was, however, temporary. Unknown to most observers, the Vajpayee government had put out feelers to Kashmiri dissidents and armed groups from late 1998 on. Independently of the Lahore Process, Vajpayee encouraged Mishra to set up a parallel track of quiet talks with the Hurriyat, the JKLF and affiliated organizations. Between late 1998 and mid-2002, Mishra told me, he established a rapport with each one of the azaadi leaders; several of them confirmed this later when I asked.

What did Mishra discuss with the azaadi leaders? Once again, accounts are sparse but his talks with the Hurriyat, JKLF and affiliated groups were based on the principle of being confidential, exploratory and deniable, and therefore free and frank, as had been his talks with Naik. The issues ranged from the role that the Hurriyat could play in a peace process to what a lasting political solution could comprise, including possible participation in elections, and the agenda for India–Pakistan talks on Kashmir. While the key interlocutors for Mishra were Kashmiri dissidents in the valley, the union government also revived connections to the Kashmiri diaspora and Pakistani-controlled parts of Jammu, Gilgit and Baltistan.[10]

Scattered reports in 1999 suggest that the Mishra-azaadi groups' discussions came close to a breakthrough at several points. According to some reports, 'Hurriyat members Shabir Ahmed Dar and Ghulam Rasool...mooted the idea of joining the electoral process under the Farooq Abdullah government.' The Hurriyat, others said, was prepared to participate in elections if international monitors were allowed, a point that Shabir Shah had earlier made during his talks with Prime Minister Narasimha Rao's emissaries.[11] Contradicting these reports, the Hurriyat spokesman Abdul Majid Bandey clarified: 'We will only participate in an election which is held to choose representatives of Kashmir for negotiations on the future of the state but that too if conducted under the observation of any impartial international organization like the United Nations.'[12]

The idea of electing representatives in Jammu and Kashmir for negotiations was borrowed from the Northern Ireland peace process, where a 110-member all-party forum was elected in May 1996 to participate in talks with the British and Irish governments, yielding a lasting peace agreement in 1997. The forum did not include armed groups and a majority of its members were from electoral parties. The Sinn Fein, which called for Northern Ireland's independence from Britain and did not participate in elections for the Northern Ireland administration, did participate in the forum election and gained 17 per cent of the vote.

Up to this point, the Hurriyat had refused talks with members of the state legislature or representatives of the state government. It was not willing to even be in the same room with them. It was unclear, therefore, whether it had shifted its position to accept an inclusive forum along the Northern Ireland lines or wished only to borrow its broad contours. It was even unclear whether the Bandey statement was an offer by the Hurriyat executive, though the JKLF's Malik was known to be campaigning for it. The union government did not respond to the offer, made through the media. No such process had taken place in India in previous peace processes, whether with the Mizos, Nagas or Akalis.

Indian negotiators were familiar with backchannel negotiation through a range of agencies, from intelligence to military to political, but not to a public negotiation process. Their focus remained the backchannel. Admittedly the Northern Irish peace process too was heavily dependent on backchannels, without which no breakthrough would have been possible. But the British and Irish governments moved to a frontchannel of inter-government talks, which in turn set the stage for an intra-Irish frontchannel, the forum for negotiation. The real importance of the forum was to allay local suspicion that Britain and Ireland might sell their interests short; in this sense, it was a key confidence-building mechanism. This point was taken on board by the Indian government only several years later, in 2003. Perhaps the idea was ahead of its time in 1999, given that India and Pakistan were still dealing with the remnants of the Kargil War, and cross-border attacks from Pakistan had increased after Musharraf's coup. There were no India–Pakistan peace talks in sight, despite continuing efforts in backchannels and growing international pressure.

Though the Hurriyat decided to campaign for a boycott of the 1999 general election in India, its leaders also held out hopes for a 'new initiative' after the election, which the BJP won. The Hurriyat, said its Chairman Mirwaiz Umar, was 'not averse to a "bilateral dialogue"' with Delhi. 'All we are saying is let us take the initial step to resolve Kashmir politically, we need phased confidence-building measures,' he added. 'We had offered to talk to the militants for a ceasefire to facilitate a political solution to the problem... Autonomy, self-determination, independence are all issues that can be negotiated and talked about.'[13] Similar and stronger comments were made by Abdul Ghani Lone, Chairman of the People's Conference and member of the Hurriyat executive: 'If we are sure that the government of India will make the Hurriyat party to the talks, we will be in [the] field to stop the violence... Whatever is the agreed solution will be acceptable to the Hurriyat, even if it is to stay with India.'[14]

The two statements by prominent independence leaders brought a bright ray of light to what had been a dark decade of violence. They were clearly the result of prolonged backchannel discussion despite frequent disruption, on the one hand by Pakistan and its sponsorship of Islamic guerrillas, and on the other by domestic politics, including within the state. Opposed to talks with the Hurriyat, Deputy Prime Minister and Home Minister L. K. Advani imprisoned dissident leaders Geelani and Malik in September 1999, announcing that they would be in jail for two years. They had been in touch with the ISI, the Home Ministry said, and supported

Islamic armed groups.[15] The arrests were a major setback to the Mishra–Hurriyat channel, though it stayed open. Lone and Mirwaiz Umar also sought India–Pakistan talks, but were told by Pakistan's then high commissioner to Delhi, Ashraf Jehangir Qazi, that there was little likelihood of talks in the near future.

Whether deliberately or unintentionally, Chief Minister Farooq Abdullah almost closed the Hurriyat window when he placed his State Autonomy Commission's report before the assembly and introduced a resolution calling for restoration of autonomy under the original Article 370. The resolution was passed by the assembly on 26 June 2000, but rejected by the union cabinet on 4 July.

Why did the union cabinet reject the autonomy resolution? Both Prime Minister Vajpayee and Deputy Prime Minister Advani were initially cautious, the former acknowledging that the resolution was 'well within the domain of constitutional validity', and the latter saying it would be placed before parliament for discussion.[16] But the RSS attacked autonomy for Kashmir as tantamount to secession and the BJP ally Shiv Sena argued similarly. The cabinet was due to discuss the resolution on 8 July. Under attack, the Vajpayee administration moved the cabinet meeting up to 4 July, when it declared the resolution 'unacceptable'.

In Kashmir, the cabinet rejection was seen as yet another instance of Delhi's high-handedness. Yet, had the cabinet accepted the assembly resolution, it would have precluded discussion on autonomy with the Hurriyat. Indeed, it might instead have forced the Hurriyat to dismiss autonomy as too little, returning to the independence or Pakistan options of the early 1990s.

Farooq's National Conference was then in coalition with the BJP at the centre. In the days following the cabinet rejection, the National Conference discussed whether to withdraw from the coalition and Farooq upped pressure on the union government with statements of support for autonomy from opposition leaders. The Vajpayee administration made haste to defuse mounting tension with Farooq. Vajpayee, Advani and Defence Minister George Fernandes attended the funeral of Farooq's mother, Akbar Jehan, and Law Minister Ram Jethmalani said that his government would be willing to consider repeal of specific laws that 'had hampered the interests of Jammu and Kashmir in their application' if the state government would provide examples. The State Autonomy Report and assembly resolution, he added, were 'too general in their scope'.[17]

Farooq too had reasons to backtrack. The State Autonomy Commission report had been dogged by dissension, resignations and ousters. Its first chairman, Balraj Puri, was replaced by National Conference member Mohammad Shafi of Uri, who soft-pedalled the recommendations for internal devolution within the state. Puri had suggested devolution to the existing provinces and districts; Shafi suggested redefining the state as a collection of Muslim, Hindu and Buddhist-majority regions. In Jammu and Ladakh, Shafi's proposals were seen as threatening their unity by creating communal enclaves.

Ladakh had been in a state of simmering tension since the early 1990s, when Ladakhi grievance at decades of development neglect by the state government took the form of a demand for union territory status—in other words, to separate from Jammu and Kashmir and come under direct rule from Delhi. The demand led to a growing communal rift between Ladakh's Buddhists and Muslims. The latter preferred to remain within the state. In the hope that partial devolution might obviate the union territory demand, the union and state governments set up the Ladakh Autonomous Hill Development Council in 1995. The measure met with initial resistance. Indeed, the communal divide strengthened when representatives of the Muslim-majority Kargil district of Ladakh refused to bring their district under the council. Following the assembly resolution, the council passed its own resolution, rejecting autonomy and renewing the union territory demand. In protest, there was a bandh in the Kashmir valley and Doda district of Jammu, and Buddhist Leh in Ladakh was placed under a blanket curfew.

With a possible ethnic conflict in the state confronting him, Farooq put the autonomy report on a back burner. Vajpayee's administration, under pressure from its own party and allies, and with a larger goal of involving the Hurriyat in autonomy talks, was happy to let the issue rest.

◆

The year 2000 also marked India's most sustained effort at a Kashmir peace process. Three tracks were put in place: ceasefire negotiations with militia leaders, political negotiations with the Hurriyat, and peace negotiations with Pakistan. The effort failed because the three tracks did not progress in parallel but in succession, and so undermined each other. Each track ended sadly in an escalation of violence. Yet, the year also witnessed the largest breakthroughs for a Kashmir peace process since 1994.

On 24 July 2000, quiet negotiations between the Indian Army and the Hizbul Mujahideen led the valley's Hizbul commander, Majid Dar, to announce a unilateral ceasefire, calling for unconditional talks, inclusion of Pakistan in the peace process, and an end to reprisals. Dar gave the union government three months to begin implementing measures. Talks with the army were initiated by Dar. Based in Pakistan, he crossed over to India with the proposal of a ceasefire and talks, after discussing it with his ISI handlers. Through third party routes, he made contact with Indian intelligence and through them, with Indian Army commanders based in the valley.

In Delhi, Vajpayee welcomed Dar's announcement and Indian Army troops in the valley were given orders to curtail counter-insurgency operations against the Hizbul, which, in practice, also entailed a curb on all army–guerrilla encounters. Meanwhile, the government took over talks with the Hizbul to work on details of the ceasefire, and Dar appointed Fazal Haq Qureshi as negotiator on the Hizbul's behalf.

Negotiations appeared to be going quite well when two developments stymied them. Pakistan's ISI, which had appeared to be on board, grew cold feet at the rapid progress in negotiations, which were already well on the way to agreeing steps for disarming and disbanding the militia in return for an end to reprisals and human rights violation. Then the Hurriyat, which had not been consulted on the Dar initiative, took umbrage. Qureshi was a member of the Hurriyat, but not in its seven-member executive. When I asked him why he had not discussed Dar's initiative with the Hurriyat, he told me that Dar had sworn him to secrecy, fearing that any leaks could lead to disruption by other armed groups.[18] Neither the Hurriyat nor the Hizbul were a house united.

Dar was proved right. The Hurriyat, now under the chairmanship of Abdul Ghani Bhat, wrote to Jamaat-e-Islami head Hussain Ahmed, protesting Dar's unilateral initiative. Ahmed contacted the ISI and the Hizbul's Yusuf Shah, who was head of the United Jihad Council. On 1 August, within a week of Dar's announcement, the Lashkar-e-Taiba attacked a pilgrim base camp in Pahalgam, killing thirty people including pilgrims, shopkeepers and porters. It was the first of a string of attacks. On 2 August, seven residents and nineteen migrant labourers from Bihar and Madhya Pradesh were massacred in Anantnag. In Kupwara, five members of an alleged 'informer' family were killed.

The attacks were not limited to the valley. In Jammu's Doda district, the guerrillas shot twenty-two people and in Kishtwar eight members of a village defence committee. Over eighty people were killed on what came to be known as 'Bloody Tuesday' (though in fact the killings started on Monday and continued through Tuesday).

Discussing the Hizbul ceasefire in his autobiography *Wular Kinaray* (On the Banks of the Wular), Jamaat-e-Islami leader Geelani described it as 'a serious matter for the leadership and people of Kashmir'. It raised 'doubts and questions in the minds of the people' as to Dar's motives, Geelani said, dismissing Dar's explanation that the guerrillas wanted to prove that they were not extremist. He was especially critical of 'the drama' that followed the ceasefire announcement. '[S]uch an atmosphere of friendship was created in Kashmir that Hizb militants and the Army played a friendly match at a playground in Handwara (north Kashmir), which was witnessed by thousands of people.'[19]

In Pakistan, Shah announced that he was taking over ceasefire negotiations. Eight days of televised brinkmanship followed, with a visibly shaky Shah, surrounded by ISI agents, upping the ante every hour. Dar and Qureshi had agreed with their Indian counterparts that there would be a staggered process, beginning with a mutual ceasefire and graduating to political talks in which, at some later date, Pakistan would be involved. Shah abruptly reverted to the 1995 Casablanca formula, demanding international recognition of Kashmir's disputed status and tripartite talks involving the governments of India, Pakistan and the Hurriyat. Even while the union government was formulating a response, he called off Dar's ceasefire—which had in any case been shattered by Bloody Tuesday—and expelled him from the Hizbul.

Despite the carnage and the Hizbul split, the union government and the Dar faction persisted with their talks. On 3 August, Home Secretary Kamal Pande announced that a Home Ministry team headed by Special Secretary (internal security) M. B. Kaushal, would meet with the Hizbul's former chief commander, Khalid Saifullah, to draft ground rules for a mutual ceasefire. 'We're keen to take the peace process to its logical conclusion. The modalities for restoration of peace will be pursued seriously,' Pande told *Outlook* magazine.[20]

To further underline the government's commitment to peace, Vajpayee led an all-party delegation to Pahalgam, with George Fernandes and Congress president Sonia Gandhi. The purpose of the visit, commented *Outlook*, 'was to demonstrate that the Centre was not going to be cowed down by the killings and was keen on capitalizing on the Hizbul's olive branch'. Intelligence sources added, 'Once the modalities for the ceasefire are worked out, we hope to extend it. Maybe for six months... If the government can win the confidence of the Hizbul, wonders can be worked.'[21]

Yet, hopes for a peace process had already weakened. The Hizbul split marginalized Dar and his faction. The Pakistan-based Islamic militias had already made their opposition clear. Virtually shunned by the Hurriyat and the Jamaat-e-Islami, Dar was no longer in position to lead a ceasefire initiative. Though the Clinton administration backed the government–Hizbul negotiations, their influence on the Pakistani government was limited. During his

March 2000 visit to South Asia, when he was rapturously received in India, Clinton refused to visit Pakistan and bypassed Musharraf's administration to address the Pakistani people by video. Pakistani military resentment against the US was high.

The ISI and Islamic militias were not the only spoilers of the government–Dar negotiations. India's parliament, deeply polarized by the BJP's election victory in 1999, went into a frenzy over the Bloody Tuesday massacres in Kashmir, asking why the government was persisting with a meaningless ceasefire, and Farooq Abdullah's autonomy initiative spiced the mix still further. Autonomy within the Indian union was an option the Hizbul and many Kashmiri separatists were beginning to consider once again as the way out of a gridlock that had caused so much suffering, but they could not support autonomy if it was seen as the plank of 'pro-India' Kashmiri parties. When the Hizbul–Home Ministry meeting venue was leaked and photographs of the Hizbul negotiating team hit the newsstands, it was the last straw. Kashmiri observers believed the leak was deliberate, either by intelligence officers opposed to the Dar–government initiative or by Farooq Abdullah, or by both.

Under the weight of so much opposition, the Hizbul talks collapsed. In the aftermath of the failed ceasefire, two of the Hizbul's negotiators were killed by the ISI and two others died in army–guerrilla shoot-outs. There was open war between the Dar and Yusuf Shah factions of the Hizbul, in which hundreds died. Dar himself was assassinated by ISI-backed guerrillas two years later, during a visit to his mother. 'The Indian Government did show sincerity during the talks', Qureshi acknowledged, 'but why did they kill two of the Hizbul negotiators later?'

Speaking in parliament, an angry Home Minister Advani accused Shah and the Hurriyat of dancing to the ISI tune, but declared, 'In the days and months to come India will not deviate from its chosen course of talks with all those in Kashmir who eschew the path of terror and violence and our simultaneous battle against all those who continue to stick to that path. We shall persist with our policy of firmness and flexibility.'[22]

Indian attention now turned to the Hurriyat. According to Dulat, a thaw in the government–Hurriyat ice was at least partly Dar's doing. Following Shah's abrupt cancellation of his ceasefire offer, Dar had spent the next six months visiting Hurriyat leaders to canvass support. As a result, renewed backchannel efforts yielded a new plan to get a peace process going in Kashmir. The Hurriyat would call for, and get, a unilateral ceasefire by the Indian Army. Hurriyat members would then visit Pakistan to seek a reciprocal ceasefire from the United Jihad Council that Shah headed.

At the suggestion of the valley's Communist Party leader Yusuf Tarigami, Vajpayee announced a three-month army ceasefire for Ramzan on 19 November 2000, which was extended for another three months. The army's ceasefire was wildly popular—there were fireworks and dancing in the streets in Jammu, and a more muted, but also more powerful, expression of hope in the valley—and it reduced the abuse of human rights in Kashmir, but only partially. The ceasefire was limited to the army and did not cover police counter-insurgency operations. Human rights organizations reported four instances of police firing in February 2001, and the alleged custodial death of a JKLF activist, Jalil Ahmed Shah, adding that the BSF assaulted journalists covering a suicide bomb attack against a BSF camp.[23] At the same time, violence against security forces actually increased because a reciprocal ceasefire by militias did not materialize.

The Hurriyat was divided. Its December 2000 statement welcomed the ceasefire extension as 'praiseworthy', saying, 'This is a positive development which will finally lead to the resolution of the Kashmir dispute.' The Hurriyat, chairman Ghani Bhat said, would visit Pakistan in January 2001, to 'plead our case' with the guerrillas, 'in the interest of peace and resolution of [the] Kashmir problem permanently'. In an indirect reference to the need for a guerrilla ceasefire, he added, 'We will try to convince them about solving the problem politically.'[24] But Geelani, now the Jamaat-e-Islami representative on the Hurriyat executive, opposed the call for a reciprocal ceasefire by the militias, repudiating the Hurriyat's support for it.

Alarmed, the Jamaat-e-Islami and Hizbul insisted that Geelani be included in the Hurriyat delegation to Pakistan, though the initial plan was for those involved in backchannel negotiations with both the Indian and Pakistani governments to go. The Hurriyat executive split and the visit to Pakistan fell through. Instead, guerrillas used the army's halt in counter-insurgency operations to rearm and regroup, and the ceasefire was called off after three months.

Once again, the focus shifted, this time to negotiations with Pakistan. Musharraf had called for talks with India for some months—'any time, any place' is what he said—but the Indian policy consensus was against talks with 'the architect of Kargil'. Vajpayee, however, gained the support of his powerful deputy, Advani, and the two gave their tacit support to Track II as well as semi-official backchannel negotiations to see if common ground could be found.

The backchannel negotiators found enough common ground to convince Vajpayee and Advani, and the governments of India and Pakistan announced a summit at Agra in July 2001. The summit was to find a via media towards a Kashmir settlement, and it showed how far Vajpayee had moved the Indian position. At Lahore, Kashmir was put on the back burner. In Agra, it was up front—only for the two countries to discover once again that they could not agree, or even agree to disagree.

Pakistan wanted a declaration in which Kashmir was recognized as the central issue of conflict between the two countries, which India had long refused. India was finally ready to grant that recognition, but in return wanted Pakistan to eschew violence, or support for violence, in Kashmir and the rest of India. For Pakistan, this was too high a price to pay. A tight-lipped Musharraf departed for Islamabad. Once there, he gave a press conference accusing Indian 'hawks' in the government of sabotaging the summit. He and Vajpayee had agreed a joint declaration, he said, and the Indian and Pakistani foreign ministers had drafted one. But before the two premiers could sign it, members of the Indian cabinet, alarmed by the primacy given to Kashmir, wrecked the declaration. He had been 'humiliated' at Agra, Musharraf said.

Why was Agra such a debacle? Were Vajpayee and Advani misled into believing there was common ground, which in India meant an agreement to end the violence? Or was Musharraf misled into believing that India would not seek a formal commitment to ending support for Pakistani-backed guerrillas, and would be satisfied by a verbal pledge? Speaking in Indian parliament, Foreign Minister Jaswant Singh clarified. The summit was 'a retreat', he said, where the two premiers could address 'complex and intricate issues' without the glare of publicity. There had been hitches in preparation for the summit, he continued. Indian officials had presented their Pakistani counterparts with four agendas for the Agra talks, each of which followed on from the Lahore summit and the Simla Agreement. Pakistani officials were not prepared to finalize any of these agendas or a combination of them. 'The Pakistan establishment until the last was not clear itself because the establishment had not been taken into full confidence by the President of Pakistan himself.'[25] The idea of a joint declaration only came up during Vajpayee's talks with Musharraf on 15 July. Jaswant and his counterpart, Abdul Sattar, were tasked with preparing a text. Their juniors drafted a text studded with 'square brackets' or sentences that the two sets of officials could not agree on.

Vajpayee, also speaking in parliament, elaborated further. 'We did not succeed to make the Pakistani delegation agree that cross-border terrorism should find a mention in the declaration. They went a step forward and termed it as the freedom struggle. This was totally unexpected of them and this is where the atmosphere of negotiations got sullied.' Musharraf, he added, also wanted to ensure that the Simla and Lahore agreements did not find a mention in the final declaration. 'We did not accept this.'[26]

Relations between the two countries plummeted still further when the Agra summit ended in disarray. Once again, there were massacres in both the valley and Jammu. On 21 July, thirteen Hindus were killed on the Amarnath pilgrimage, and the next day fifteen Hindu villagers were killed in Doda. On 1 October, at least thirty-eight people, mostly Muslim, were killed when a suicide attacker drove a hijacked government jeep to the main entrance of the state assembly in Srinagar and detonated explosives loaded in the car. The Pakistan-based Jaish-e-Mohammad claimed responsibility for the attack but retracted the following day, most likely under ISI pressure to maintain deniability.

The Indian government declared both Jammu and the Kashmir valley 'disturbed areas' where the security forces could make preventive arrests, shoot on sight, or cordon and search entire villages. In December 2001, India's Parliament was attacked by Lashkar and Jaish guerrillas. It looked as if India and Pakistan were locked in implacable hostility, and Kashmir was locked in an endless cycle of violence and siege.

◆

The Agra summit was the first time I was offered the opportunity to work for an India–Pakistan peace process, though only in a small way. In 1997, R. K. Mishra, on a Track II mission to explore options with Pakistan, asked me for names of people to meet in Lahore and Islamabad. After that, he kept me peripherally in the loop. At the time, I was based in the US, doing comparative research on partitions and peace processes. While I did engage with civil society movements such as the Pakistan–India Peoples' Forum for Peace and Democracy, my work was primarily academic. In 1999, when working at the US think tank, the Council on Foreign Relations, I drew on my research to prepare a roadmap for a Kashmir peace process, which I sent to Mishra, who continued as an unofficial backchannel negotiator for both Kashmiri dissidents and Pakistani interlocutors.

Soon after, Michael Krepon of the Stimson Center, a US think tank, asked me whether I would help prepare a roadmap for Kashmir to send to the Bush administration. Krepon was an expert on India–Pakistan nuclear negotiations who was more acceptable than many to the Indian government. I shared my roadmap with him and he reworked it and sent it to Richard Haass, the then head of the White House's Policy Planning division. Haass read the roadmap but I do not know whether he pushed it, or indeed, what Mishra did with the earlier version I had sent him. I saw several elements of it in the peace initiatives that unfolded from 2000 on, but that does not mean policymakers drew from my roadmap since they must have read several similar.

In 2001, Mishra asked me to help with preparations for the Agra summit. My task was small: he asked me to write two scenarios of the summit, one based on Indian expectations, the other on Pakistani expectations. Though it was not clear to me why he wanted these, I did as he asked. A week later, he called. 'Your scenarios have been read by the foreign minister (Jaswant Singh),' he said. 'They will be in the documents discussed at the preparatory meeting for the summit.' When I checked years later with the then Joint Secretary of the External Affairs Ministry, Vivek Katju, who had prepared the documents for the summit, he had no recollection of the two scenarios. Nor had Pakistani High Commissioner to India, Ashraf Qazi, present at the summit. Jaswant Singh later told me that he had read them.

Soon after, Musharraf landed in Delhi. He was given a press reception like no Pakistani leader before or after him, and I watched with increasing alarm as he let the flattery go to his head. In the Hindi phrase, 'phule nahin samaye (he swelled up with gratification)' well before the summit, and risked going into talks with unrealistic expectations. In the meantime, as he flew from meeting to meeting making statements that were guaranteed to arouse Indian ire, I watched Indian officials swell in their turn, this time with red-faced and tight-lipped anger. The day before Musharraf flew to Agra for the meeting, I was invited by Ashraf Qazi to a small gathering for him. I asked Mishra if I could share the scenarios I had written with Qazi and Musharraf, in the hope that my rather grim sketch might add to the former's efforts to sober the latter. Unfortunately, by the time the permission came—and remarkably, it did come—the meeting had concluded, and I was on my way home. With tight security around the Pakistan High Commission, I could not return to deliver the papers.

The next day, Mishra invited me to monitor the Agra summit along with him. He had broken his leg, and was going to input the proceedings from his study in Vasant Vihar. Both sides were working on a draft joint declaration, and Mishra was anxious that it should have wording that would resonate with Kashmiris. He asked me to ring up Farooq Kathwari, the CEO of Ethan Allen, a Kashmiri himself, who had founded the Kashmir Study Group in Washington in the mid-1990s and whom I had met through former Indian foreign secretary Salman Haidar. Kathwari stressed that any peace agreement must be 'honourable', and Mishra included the term in his draft for the joint declaration.

It looked as if the Agra summit might actually result in a breakthrough, but a disagreement soon developed over the wording of the joint declaration. Surprisingly, it was not over Kashmir—I was told that our paragraph had been accepted, including the stress on an honourable settlement—but over terrorism. Indian negotiators wanted cross-border terrorism mentioned in the opening paragraph along with the commitment to resolve the Jammu and Kashmir conflict whereas Pakistani negotiators wanted it down in the fourth paragraph, clubbed with crime. In the end, neither was willing to compromise, and the summit ended in a whimper, followed by recrimination.

That evening, before the Agra failure went public, I was with a Pakistani journalist who had come to cover the summit. Pakistan's then deputy high commissioner to India burst into her room. 'The Indian Government are refusing to let President Musharraf hold a press conference,' he exclaimed angrily. 'You must tell your friends in the international media that Indian hawks have wrecked the summit.' After he left, I tried to persuade her to ignore his request. It was rare for a host government to allow a visiting premier to hold his own press conference when talks had failed. Surely it would be better not to engage in recrimination. I failed to persuade my friend and the next day the international media all carried the same story—that hawks within the Indian government had wrecked the summit.

◆

Then the September 11 attacks in New York and Washington occurred, and they altered the dynamic sharply. Pakistan became a key US ally in the war against terrorism and its government officially severed links to the Taliban (the extent to which the army, ISI and political and religious parties actually severed links is debated by Pakistani as well as international analysts). A decline in the Kashmir conflict might have ensued naturally, but Indian analysts worried that Pakistan would adopt a revolving door policy.

When India's Parliament was attacked on 13 December 2001, the Indian government cancelled air, rail and road links with Pakistan, recalled its high commissioner to Islamabad and sent half a million troops to the border. With US troops in Afghanistan and Pakistan, and the renewed threat of a war that was gruelling even in more distant times, the Bush administration pushed Pakistan to break with the Kashmir jihad.[27] On 11 January 2002, Musharraf delivered a path-breaking address to the Pakistani nation. He said that Pakistan would no longer allow its soil to be used for terrorism. Soon after, he arrested close to 2,000 members of Islamic militias and closed over 300 of their offices.

The international community hoped Musharraf's arrests would revive talks between the two countries, while Pakistan hoped India would respond by withdrawing troops from the border. But Indian analysts feared the arrests were more symbolic than substantial; the arrested guerrillas were mostly foot soldiers and messengers, and key militia leaders were either left free or confined to a loose house arrest. The Vajpayee administration also feared that if talks opened with Pakistan, there would be no progress in demilitarizing or decommissioning the militias. India decided to keep its troops on the border until the snow melted, when it would be possible to assess whether the rate of cross-border movement had fallen. That was too long a wait for Pakistan and, at the end of March, the Pakistani government released the guerrillas who had been arrested, most of their offices reopened, and violence rose again in Kashmir.

Tensions remained high between the two countries throughout 2002 and much of 2003, but were contained by active international diplomacy, led by the US and UK. Their pressure on Pakistan to close down the Islamic militias did not garner effective Pakistani action or even a ceasefire in Kashmir.

India's coercive diplomacy was seen by many analysts as having yielded nothing. But it gave the Indian government and the Kashmiri independence groups another opportunity to seek peace, this time through political change on the ground. Farooq Abdullah would step down; there would be a fresh election in Jammu and Kashmir. The Hurriyat would not oppose the election, nor would it prevent any of its members from contesting it. Privately, many backchannel actors told me that there was a tacit agreement between the Indian government and the Hurriyat that each would call a two-year 'time out' from the battle over Kashmir, in order to restore peace and some measure of governance in the state. In the meantime, there would be formal talks between the Government of India and the Hurriyat, and between the Indian and Pakistani governments.

The formula provided a via media for the three sets of leaders, Indian, Pakistani and the Hurriyat. The latter two could claim that their demand for tripartite talks had been met; the former could claim it had not. There would be three separate bilateral tracks— Indian government–Hurriyat, India–Pakistan, and Hurriyat–Pakistani government, in that order. This structure, actually strategy, had first been outlined during the union government–Hurriyat talks in late 2000. 'With India not at all keen on tripartite talks among the Kashmiri groups, New Delhi and Islamabad, one suggestion was that the Hurriyat leadership could talk to India and also to Islamabad separately,' *The Hindu* commented. 'After this groundwork, a dialogue between New Delhi and Islamabad could begin, provided Pakistan stopped abetting cross-border terrorism.'[28]

The strategy was brilliant. It allowed the Hurriyat to seize the initiative and put Pakistan on the back foot. Pakistani representatives could no longer claim to speak on behalf of the Hurriyat. Indian negotiators had noted that a significant number of the Hurriyat's constituent members felt 'the urgency of seriously following up on India's peace initiative',[29] and had continued to talk to them quietly. Dulat was now in the Prime Minister's Office (PMO) to monitor Kashmir developments and ensure follow-up with guerrilla contacts. Mishra had retreated from the backchannel role he had played earlier, but was still closely consulted by Hurriyat members.

According to Dulat, the People's Conference leader, Abdul Ghani Lone, was one of his chief interlocutors. Lone, a lawyer from Kupwara, had joined the Congress party in the 1960s, contested elections and served as a minister in Sadiq's government. He had some knowledge of the workings of the Indian government as well as the major national parties. Though he was close to Farooq Abdullah in the 1980s, he was horrified by the botched 1987 election and the Indian government's counter-insurgency response that followed. He sheltered guerrillas, including the young Yasin Malik, and was instrumental in forming the Hurriyat Conference. Lone's relationship with the ISI, however, was combative and had grown increasingly so. In 2000, when in Pakistan-administered Kashmir for his son Sajad's wedding to Amanullah Khan's daughter, Asma—regarded on both sides of the Line of Control as a grand alliance of two leading Kashmiri nationalist families—he spoke openly of the need for peace talks and an end to cross-border violence. At the same time, he turned down ISI Director General Mahmud Ahmed's invitation to dinner.

Despite these efforts, the Hurriyat track proved elusive once again. Farooq Abdullah's arrest of Yasin Malik on charges of receiving smuggled goods might have followed the rule of law but was, in context, disruptive. Farooq's act paled when Lone was assassinated in June 2002. Lone had continued to publicly campaign for an end to armed conflict and the withdrawal of Pakistani fighters, whom he called 'guest mujahideen'. He fell out with Pakistani government representatives at a conference in Dubai shortly before he was assassinated, telling them that their government should 'project yourself as our supporters and not "owners" of Kashmir'. Five hours before his death, he told the magazine *India Today*, 'It's time the foreign militants left us alone and the forces of dialogue take over.' After the 9/11 attacks on the US, he added, 'Nobody at the global level is now going to support extremism and violence, however genuine may be the cause. At the same time, Kashmir has got into international focus and brought about an awareness that peace has a chance here if the issue is resolved through dialogue.'[30]

Lone was killed by Pakistan-backed local guerrillas while paying his respects at the annual commemoration of Mirwaiz Farooq's assassination. It took the Hurriyat a decade to publicly acknowledge this fact, though Lone's son, Sajad, had said as much in an outburst of grief at Lone's funeral when he barred Geelani from offering condolences on the grounds that he supported Lone's killers. Geelani later commented that he had disagreed politically with Lone 'but it does not mean that we bayed for each other's blood'.[31] In fact, he added, he had not been invited to the 21 May 2002 function at the Eidgah at which Lone was assassinated.

Lone's assassination drove a wedge between the Hurriyat and the Pakistani government, leading the former to alter their position on the forthcoming state legislative election. Lone had said that though Kashmiris were aggrieved by their history of 'fake and fraudulent' elections, 'as a political worker, I am not averse to elections provided Delhi comes up with legitimate and trustworthy guarantees that the elections would be fair and free. If the Government gives this commitment, it can motivate the Hurriyat to take part in the polls.' Though the Hurriyat leaders decided not to allow members to participate directly in the 2002 state legislative election, they did not oppose it. In a bow to the Hurriyat's long-standing demand, the Indian government allowed international monitors to evaluate the election. Though guerrillas targeted candidates and party workers prior to the election, and attempted to intimidate voters through IED blasts, voter turnout was 45 per cent.[32] For the first time since the 1970s, free and fair elections were held in Jammu and Kashmir in October 2002.

Chapter XVI

NEW BEGINNINGS

The largely free and fair 2002 election put in place a coalition led by a relatively new political party, the People's Democratic Party (PDP). The PDP announced a 'healing touch policy' which combined human rights, such as the release of political prisoners, with efforts to jump-start the economy through reviving tourism. It came to power in coalition with the Congress party. With the Vajpayee-led BJP at the centre, this was the first time the two national parties cooperated on Kashmir. And the Indian government appointed a respected former cabinet and home secretary, N. N. Vohra, as interlocutor for talks with Kashmiri dissidents. The stage appeared to be set for a new peace process to begin within the troubled state, but Pakistan remained sceptical and it took close on another year to achieve a breakthrough.

In April 2003, Vajpayee called again for peace with Pakistan (his third and last try, he said), from Kashmir's capital Srinagar. When asked by a reporter whether his call for talks with the Hurriyat, made in the same breath, would be within 'the ambit of the Indian Constitution', he famously dismissed the question, saying talks would be within the ambit of humanity ('insaniyat ke daire mein'). Five days later, he told members of the Lok Sabha, 'I assured the people of Jammu and Kashmir that we wish to resolve all issues, both domestic and external, through talks. I stressed that the gun can solve no problem, brotherhood can. Issues can be resolved if we move forward guided by the three principles of insaniyat, jamhooriyat aur Kashmiriyat (humanity, democracy and Kashmiri oneness)'.[1]

The lyrical phrase 'insaniyat ke daire mein' electrified Kashmir. It avoided the sour and contentious issue of the constitution which had divided the valley with electoral parties seeking autonomy within the Indian Constitution and independence groups arguing that Article 370, which bound Kashmir to the Indian union, was invalid. The divide was artificial and politically constructed; the Indian Constitution had been amended over a hundred times and any peace settlement would inevitably have required its amendment, even if it were to only change Article 370 from temporary to permanent. But the issue had caused conflict for five decades. By avoiding it, Vajpayee allowed for a sour history to be put aside. He also allowed a cover for the Hurriyat to enter talks.

Vajpayee's offer was made possible, at least in part, by quiet feelers from Pakistan over the first three months of the year. A delegation of Pakistani MPs in March 2003 bore a message from Musharraf that his government would no longer aid cross-border infiltration, and would not attempt to prevent or impede Indian counter-insurgency efforts, including border fencing and surveillance. 'The Indian Government can complete its border fencing,' the Pakistani MPs assured a small group of Indian diplomats and analysts that I was part of, at a closed-door meeting. 'We will look the other way.'

In late April, following Vajpayee's statement in Srinagar, Pakistani prime minister Mir Zafarullah Khan Jamali called Vajpayee to discuss reopening talks. In July, R&AW director C. D. Sahay went to Pakistan on an under-the-radar mission to discuss Musharraf's offer of a ceasefire. In November, Pakistan announced a ceasefire on the Line of Control, which India reciprocated, following which there was a decline in cross-border movement of guerrillas.

As before, the Pakistani government was subsequently ambiguous about its pledge. The Pakistan Army did not attempt to disrupt India's border fencing militarily, but the Pakistani government protested it at the UN and tried unsuccessfully to draw a parallel between India's fencing and the Israeli wall that was being constructed in the West Bank.

Yet, the ceasefire held and paved the way for dramatic breakthroughs at the SAARC summit at Islamabad in early January 2004. These included a pledge by the seven member-states to implement a South Asian Free Trade Agreement by January 2006, alongside a Social Charter to share expertise on development goals. All seven leaders also pledged to work together to end support for terrorist groups and/or activities.

Meeting at the same time, Vajpayee and Musharraf issued a joint statement in Islamabad, saying that the two countries would revive a composite dialogue on all contentious issues, including Kashmir, and would begin on an ambitious series of CBMs. The statement included a personal pledge by Musharraf to prevent the 'use of Pakistani (and Pakistani-held) soil' for terrorist acts against India.

The attempt to place India–Pakistan peacemaking within the larger context of regional cooperation was not new. SAARC had been founded in 1985, partly at the initiative of Rajiv Gandhi, with the hope that it would encourage regional trade, improve the daily lives of South Asian citizens, and strengthen the political will to solve disputes amongst SAARC member-states. Despite these noble intentions, the India–Pakistan standoff in Kashmir had kept SAARC largely ineffective. So had petty disputes between India and her neighbours over resources, migration and diaspora support for internal civil conflicts. Some of the latter disputes were resolved by careful diplomacy, beginning in the late 1990s under Prime Minister Gujral, which laid a foundation of goodwill for SAARC to move forward. At the January 2004 summit, SAARC leaders were remarkably frank in confessing that they had lacked the political will to resolve or set aside their disputes in order to tackle their people's needs jointly—and pledged that they would now do so.

These achievements would not have been possible without a dawning India–Pakistan peace process. SAARC provided the framework for Pakistan to agree to put intra-regional trade on a fast track, and Pakistan played a constructive role in ironing out last-minute creases in the South Asian Free Trade Agreement. But the Musharraf administration needed the assurance of formal talks on Kashmir in order to move forward on trade, which India provided at Islamabad. In other words, the relationship between SAARC and an India–Pakistan peace process proved to be symbiotic—each needed the other in order to further its separate goals.

Out of the public glare, there was considerable behind-the-scenes work to achieve the results in Islamabad. Starting in spring 2003, around the same time as Pakistani MPs brought the ceasefire offer to India, Brajesh Mishra, then India's NSA and Principal Secretary to the Prime Minister, and Pakistan's special secretary to the president, Tariq Aziz, opened backchannel talks, both face-to-face and on a hotline. The two countries began to move simultaneously on a number of CBMs some months before the SAARC summit. On Kashmir, Musharraf declared his willingness to 'leave the UN resolutions [on a plebiscite] behind' if India agreed to talks. His formula for talks was to (a) consider the range of solutions on offer; (b) weed through the ones that were unacceptable to India or Pakistan or the Kashmiris (though who would represent the people of Jammu and Kashmir was left ambiguous); and (c) begin to work on solutions that might be acceptable.

On the economic track, the two governments' representatives worked to get the free trade agreement in place and renewed proposals for gas pipelines from Iran and Central Asia through Pakistan to India. Combining economic and social tracks, they set up negotiations to reopen trade and travel routes between Rajasthan and Sindh, Mumbai and Karachi, and the different parts of divided Jammu, Kashmir and Ladakh. On 'people-to-people' issues, they restored travel links, encouraged cultural and civil society exchanges, and began talking about freer access to each other's media.

These steps forward were backed by a public constituency for peace that put pressure on government and guerrillas alike. Encouraged by Vajpayee, and to a certain extent by Musharraf, the constituency grew between 1999 and 2004 despite the many setbacks to Indian and Pakistani attempts to get talks underway.

Civil society groups began to develop the public constituency for peace in the mid-1990s, forming cross-border networks such as the Pakistan–India People's Forum mentioned above, which brought together women's, environmental, media and human rights groups in the two countries. By 2000, there were a large number of human rights and women's networks in both countries rallying for peace. The key issues that were raised at this point were people-to-people contacts, denuclearization and, more warily, Kashmir. By 2003, non-governmental groups and an occasional think tank had started Kashmir programmes. The think tank for which I now worked, the Delhi Policy Group, started a civil society dialogue jointly with the Centre for Dialogue and Reconciliation, between activists in Jammu, Kashmir and Ladakh and representatives across the Line of Control, from Muzaffarabad, Mirpur, Gilgit and Baltistan.

There were more powerful backers in the public constituency for peace. The enormous Jang group of publications in Pakistan started an India–Pakistan parliamentary dialogue and helped found the South Asian Free Media Association. Business groups in both countries argued that peace between India and Pakistan would boost trade as well as consumption and savings, and stimulate overall economic growth in industry and agriculture. They pointed out that while the official trade between the two countries was worth around $200 million, unofficial trade was over $1 billion. If trade relations were normalized between the two countries, Indian industrial and commercial associations estimated, official trade could rise to $5 billion per annum relatively quickly. There was talk of 'pipeline diplomacy' to bring gas from Central Asia through Afghanistan and Pakistan to India. As it became clear that Afghanistan's civil war was not nearing an end any time soon, this proposal was replaced with one to pipe gas from Iran through Pakistan to India.

In India, a newly confident middle class, basking in the glow of Indian software success and a ready-to-migrate pool of hi-tech labour, was more receptive to ideas of a 'peace dividend' than it had hitherto been. This new constituency allowed Vajpayee to stare down opponents in his own party and its affiliates, and gave India the confidence to pursue a risky peace process even in the face of rising violence.

Most important of all, influential members of the Kashmiri diaspora in Europe and the US, whose energies had been revived by the abortive Lahore peace process, reconsidered the unconditional support they had offered to armed struggle, and many now swung into the fray for a peace process. Where diaspora leaders had earlier asked, 'If there can be international (military) intervention in Bosnia, East Timor and Kosovo, then why not in Kashmir?', many now backed the ceasefire negotiations of 2000–01 as well as the attempted peace process of 2001 onwards.

Neither India nor Pakistan made full use of the opportunity diaspora leaders offered, although their change of heart could be crucial to ending violence in Kashmir. Diaspora funds traditionally kept armed groups afloat long after their local sources of support dried up. It was, in fact, the Irish-American diaspora's decision to stop supporting sectarian groups fighting in Northern Ireland that paved the way for a Northern Ireland ceasefire, and its active promotion of peaceful and inclusive negotiations helped open the door to the Belfast Agreement.

◆

Following the 2003 India–Pakistan ceasefire, the union government–Hurriyat track slowly fructified and in early 2004, the Hurriyat held two rounds of talks with Deputy Prime Minister Advani, who also held the Home Ministry portfolio. The first meeting, on 22 January, lasted for two and a half hours and agreed a step-by-step process through which, said Ghani Bhat, 'guns should be replaced by political talks'. The Hurriyat asked that political prisoners be released as a CBM. Advani responded favourably, requesting a list of suggested releases which could be discussed at their next meeting.

A summary of key points of the meeting, drafted by the Home Ministry's interlocutor, N. N. Vohra, and jointly approved by Advani and the Hurriyat, said that they 'agreed that today's meeting was the first significant step in the dialogue process initiated by the Government of India'. The Hurriyat delegation 'stressed that an honourable and durable solution should be found through dialogue', and committed itself to 'the enlargement of the dialogue process to cover all regions of Jammu and Kashmir and the concerns of all communities'. For his part, Advani 'observed it was the government's foremost concern to safeguard the security of all people and ensure against the violation of their rights', agreeing that the Home Ministry would undertake a rapid review of political prisoners' cases 'except those accused of heinous crimes'.[2]

The five-member Hurriyat delegation was led by Maulvi Abbas Ansari, head of the Shia Ittehad-ul-Muslimeen and then chairman of the Hurriyat. Its members were Mirwaiz Umar, who had won his congregation's support for peace talks when he asked for endorsement during Friday prayers at the Jamia Masjid, former Hurriyat chairman Ghani Bhat, Ghani Lone's eldest son, Bilal Lone, and Qureshi, Dar's negotiator during the 2000 Hizbul ceasefire initiative.

Discussing the two rounds of talks in his book *My Country, My Life*, Advani commented, the 'Hurriyat leaders laid stress on two points: human rights violations by the security forces and political prisoners... Assuring them that the government would take steps to curb alleged human rights abuses, I told them: "We have given orders that security forces must have a human face while discharging their duties." This assurance was swiftly acted upon.' Between the January and March meetings, he added, the government released 'sixty-nine prisoners, and was actively processing more than five hundred other cases'. Frankly stating that he was surprised at the headway in talks, Advani concluded, 'I found the Hurriyat leaders to be genuine, earnest and, to some extent, open-minded in their interactions with me.'[3]

The Advani–Hurriyat talks were approved by the Cabinet Committee on Security in October 2003. They followed a split within the Hurriyat. Geelani left the group because he opposed dialogue with the union government. Advani and Vajpayee judged the right moment had come in January 2004, when Musharraf committed that the Pakistani government 'would not allow any part of its territory, or territory under its control, to be used for terrorist activities against India'. Though Advani did not say so, the real significance of Musharraf's statement was that it was made in Islamabad. Statements made anywhere else were deniable, but those made in Pakistan were heard across the country. Musharraf was shocked when radical Pakistani Islamic guerrillas attempted to assassinate him in December 2003 and his January declaration was a reflection of new but limited intent against groups that threatened Pakistan internally.

Unlike previous Indian government initiatives with pro-independence or pro-Pakistan Kashmiri groups, this time talks with the Hurriyat had tacit Pakistani, regional and international backing, as well as support from the PDP-led state government and opposition parties. Pakistani and international backing provided a cushion for the Hurriyat, while national and state political backing provided a cushion for the BJP. A critical new element was the recognition that progress depended on maintaining two separate but parallel and connected tracks. 'Our strategy had two dimensions—external in relation to Pakistan and internal in relation to Jammu and Kashmir—and our government had achieved significant progress on both counts,' Advani stated.

Nevertheless, there was dissension within the BJP administration, led by Advani himself. He disagreed with NSA Brajesh Mishra, who backed Dulat, adviser in the PMO on Jammu and Kashmir affairs. 'I learnt that Dulat, who was in regular contact with the leaders of various groups in Kashmir, had given some Hurriyat leaders the impression that the government was prepared to look at solutions to the Kashmir issue outside the ambit of the Indian Constitution. I was very upset at this and, in my very first meeting with the APHC delegation, I made it clear that there was no question of the government entertaining any proposal outside the Indian Constitution.' As mentioned earlier, this was a non sequitur and the Hurriyat appear to have treated it as such. Advani simultaneously held out a loophole. 'At the same time, I said that the government was willing to consider realistic ideas about certain special powers for the state, which would help the political process to move towards the goal of permanent peace.'

Advani's explanation of why he agreed to the Hurriyat talks was also revealing. 'Why did I decide to hold talks with the Hurriyat Conference, whose pro-Pakistan leanings were well-known, which had boycotted the 2002 assembly elections and some of whose leaders had links with militant organizations?' he asked, taking some pleasure in the fact that 'these Hurriyat leaders had insisted on having a dialogue with me, despite my image as a "Hindu hard-liner" and a "hawk".' Their demand for talks with him offered a way out—though the Vajpayee administration had created the office of an interlocutor with all shades of the 'socio-political spectrum' in Jammu and Kashmir, the Hurriyat had refused to talk with them officially on the grounds that they were not decision-makers. Two interlocutors had come and gone: K. C. Pant, Deputy Chairman of the Planning Commission and then Law Minister Arun Jaitley. Vohra had gone further than the previous two, having met Hurriyat members many times informally, but he had not got them to agree to formal talks. The Hurriyat's request for Advani acknowledged him as a decision-maker and was encouraged by Vajpayee and Brajesh Mishra. The hawk had been brought into the dovecote, albeit as a limited advocate.

Chapter XVII

THE PEACE PROCESS, 2004–2008

The third round of Advani–Hurriyat talks was scheduled for June 2004, on the assumption that the BJP would win the general election in May. The BJP lost the election, however. The Vajpayee government fell and the Congress-led United Progressive Alliance (UPA) came to power. The alliance continued with the peace process that began in 2003–04, and built on it. Indeed, Prime Minister Manmohan Singh, on assuming office, asked Vajpayee if he would act as the Indian government's special envoy to head an India–Pakistan–Kashmir peace process. Had Vajpayee accepted the offer, it would have been a tremendous boost for Indian peacemaking. He had invested considerable political and personal assets in his Kashmir policy and had acquired large credibility in the valley with his 2000–01 talks initiative and the famous phrase 'insaniyat ke daire mein'. He had won Musharraf's respect despite a difficult transition. He had silenced critics from within his party, the BJP, and its mentor RSS, as well as alliance partner the Shiv Sena. Unfortunately, Vajpayee refused. The next years belonged to Singh and Musharraf.

Their first meeting was in September 2004, on the sidelines of the UN General Assembly. Though Vajpayee had refused his offer, Singh held a one-hour briefing with him in preparation for the September meeting, at which Foreign Minister Natwar Singh and former foreign minister Yashwant Sinha were also present. Natwar Singh also met with Advani to canvass his support for the Singh administration to take forward the process that he and Vajpayee had begun. By this point, Singh, a former professor of economics who took policy research seriously, had enormously expanded the Vajpayee administration's support for civil society. I was one among a few dozen Kashmir watchers whom he consulted while developing his Kashmir policy in the months after he assumed office. We had first talked Kashmir when I went to him in the summer of 2000 to ask that he get the Congress to support the Vajpayee peace process instead of so severely attacking it. True to his word, Singh succeeded in persuading Congress leaders that the peace process was in the national interest and should be supported. He asked me to let Brajesh Mishra know that the Congress would mute its criticism, which I did. Upon becoming prime minister, Singh asked me if I could explore whether Vajpayee would consider carrying forward the peace process as a special envoy. I took the offer to Brajesh Mishra, who thought Vajpayee would be interested. Some days later, he told me regretfully that the BJP was not in favour and Vajpayee would have to decline.

Following their September meeting, Singh and Musharraf issued a joint statement reiterating their commitment to peace, and the two countries increased institutional contacts between their border security forces, coast guards and foreign offices. Visiting Kashmir in November, Singh appealed for Kashmiri support and advice in a peace process, and promised immediate economic and human rights relief.

The Hurriyat track proved more difficult. Though Singh called for talks, the Hurriyat took umbrage at Home Minister Shivraj Patil's statement that talks would only be held 'within the ambit of the Indian Constitution' and refused Singh's invitation.[1] The Congress party was 'not sincere', Mirwaiz Umar said. The initiative shifted to India–Pakistan breakthroughs, though still with a Kashmir focus.

The first major breakthrough came in February 2005, when the Indian and Pakistani foreign ministers announced at Islamabad that the two countries would start a Srinagar–Muzaffarabad bus service, reopening a route that had been closed since the war of 1948–49.

In both symbolic and actual terms, the reopening of the route was a landmark achievement of the nascent peace process. The idea of a Srinagar–Muzaffarabad bus service had been first bruited during the Sharif–Vajpayee talks of 1999–2000 and had been revived by Chief Minister Sayeed and Vajpayee in 2002, again without gaining much purchase from Pakistan. As a coalition partner in the state, the Congress was already on board and Sayeed suggested to Singh the proposal be refreshed. The move was supported by civil society groups such as the Centre for Dialogue and Reconciliation–Delhi Policy Group initiative, which had already taken up the proposal. In the late summer of 2004 we sent a note to Foreign Secretary Shyam Saran suggesting a Srinagar–Muzaffarabad bus service be the priority CBM on an India–Pakistan talks agenda. Saran was unusually open to civil society interaction: he told me he was putting the proposal on the agenda of his talks with Pakistani foreign secretary Riaz Khokhar, which started in September 2004.

When the two countries' foreign ministers announced the bus service, Sayeed seized the opportunity to claim it as his own and, overnight, billboards sprang up every few metres along the Srinagar–Muzaffarabad road advertising its reopening. This was the first step in peace for Kashmir, the PDP trumpeted, and it had been achieved by the state and union governments working together and with Pakistan. Sayeed's publicity blitz helped build large support in the valley for the bus as the harbinger of a new peace process. The bus's inaugural journey on 7 April was flagged off by Prime Minister Singh, Congress president Sonia Gandhi and Chief Minister Sayeed. Guerrillas tried to disrupt the launch by setting fire to Srinagar's Tourist Reception Centre on 6 April but the government decided to go ahead. PDP president Mehbooba Mufti, in fact, boarded the first bus as far as its last stop in Jammu and Kashmir, the Kaman Post. 'The opening of the road can be considered the biggest Kashmir-centric confidence-building measure,' an observer commented.[2]

Though the Hurriyat, JKLF and other dissident leaders had been invited to the bus's inaugural journey, they refused the invitation. The Hurriyat had not been involved in negotiations to reopen the road. In fact, there had been discussion in the PMO on whether and how to involve it; I was one of what I presume were many, who suggested that—in continuance of the Vajpayee policy to let the Hurriyat be bridge-builders with Pakistan on Kashmir—the Hurriyat be encouraged to claim the Srinagar–Muzaffarabad reopening as their achievement. Whether the offer was made or not is unclear. Years later, I asked Mirwaiz Umar if the Hurriyat had been asked, and he said no. Had they been asked, he said, they would have accepted.³

Within ten days of the launch of the bus, Musharraf visited Delhi to watch a cricket match (shades of Zia's cricket diplomacy), and he and Singh issued a joint statement pledging to enhance trade and intensify transport links between two parts of divided Kashmir. Both also agreed to set up a joint business council to improve trade, launch a rail link between the two countries, raise the frequency of the bus service crossing Kashmir and open new bus links between the two countries. Soon after, they opened the Line of Control to cross-Kashmiri trade, another major CBM that was intended to boost local economies.

Following a devastating earthquake that ravaged the statelet in November 2005, Pakistan allowed another route to be opened, this time in the Jammu sector of the Line of Control. Pakistani agreement had been difficult to get. Opening the route would make Poonch, Mirpur and Muzaffarabad vulnerable to Indian influence, the Pakistan military feared. But the shortest route for aid to the region was through Indian Jammu, and international aid agencies pressed the Pakistani government to open the route; some even made aid contingent on its opening. The Indian government made its own offers of aid, and calls mounted from within the region too. Reluctantly, the Pakistani government allowed five 'meeting points' to be opened along the Muzaffarabad–Jammu and Kashmir border, where earthquake victims could come to receive medical treatment and other relief. When the first point was opened, at Mirpur–Jammu, the throng to cross over from Mirpur was so large that Pakistani soldiers fired tear gas at them. Pakistan finally accepted Indian aid only after India agreed to remove all the labels that identified goods as Indian.

Grim as they were, these events paved the way for another bus service to unite divided families. In June 2006, the Poonch–

Rawalakot bus was launched. This time it was Ghulam Nabi Azad, who took over as Chief Minister of Jammu and Kashmir in November 2005, who flagged it off.

The Hurriyat also began to thaw. When the Singh administration revived the three-track formula that had been developed under the Vajpayee administration and allowed a Hurriyat delegation to visit Muzaffarabad for peace talks, hopes revived. In early June 2005, a seven-member Hurriyat delegation left for a two-week visit to Pakistan-administered Kashmir—Poonch, Mirpur and Muzaffarabad—along with the JKLF's Yasin Malik, who, however, travelled separately from the Hurriyat.

In Muzaffarabad, the Hurriyat and JKLF leaders appealed for an end to violence, accompanied by talks, a step that had been planned in 2002–04 and initiated by Abdul Ghani Lone. Their appeal met with mixed reactions in both Muzaffarabad and Islamabad, where they went next. Groups such as the Lashkar and Jaish opposed the proposal and Malik had a public spat with Pakistani Information Minister Sheikh Rashid at his press conference. Rashid, said Malik, had himself been involved in training and sheltering guerrillas for the Kashmir jihad. Malik later clarified that he had spoken of shelter not training. Musharraf also met the Hurriyat delegation. Returning from the visit, Ghani Bhat declared, 'We did the talking with the Pakistani leadership and now we will be talking to India... this has lent credibility to the ongoing dialogue process as Kashmiris are being involved for the first time.'[4]

Though Singh's administration had made efforts to mobilize all-party support for the peace process, focusing especially on the opposition BJP, the party went on an offensive against Singh for allowing the Hurriyat to visit Islamabad. 'The Pakistani government should have ensured that they did not enter Pakistan without Indian passports. Our apprehension that the bus to Muzaffarabad would facilitate separatist elements to enter Pakistan without Indian passports has been proved true,' BJP parliamentary party spokesman V. K. Malhotra was reported as saying.[5] The BJP demanded that the Singh administration 'explain what action it contemplated against Hurriyat leaders'. Reportedly, the BJP's broadside followed an editorial exhortation in the RSS journal *Organiser*, 'Giving political cover to Manmohan Singh's Pakistan mission—if there is one—is not [the] BJP's role.'

Singh's own willingness to accept civil society support was as great if not greater than Vajpayee's. He not only consulted a very large group of Kashmir experts and activists but also encouraged Track II endeavours. With his approval, I went to Brajesh Mishra again—Singh had persuaded the Congress to support Vajpayee's peace initiatives, I reminded Mishra, should not the BJP now reciprocate, especially since Singh was expanding the framework that the BJP-led previous government had put in place? Mishra heard me out and did try to persuade BJP leaders, he later told me, but to no avail. Vajpayee was by now sidelined in the party's decision-making.

Singh held his first round of talks with the Hurriyat—and separately with Malik—on 5 September 2005, eighteen months after the last round of Advani–Hurriyat talks. The 2005 meetings were prepared by Dulat, who used his Hurriyat backchannel, and Habibullah, who had known Malik since the 1990s. Talks with the Hurriyat were held ten days before Singh was due to meet Musharraf in New York, where both would attend the UN General Assembly. Talks with the JKLF took place after Singh's return from New York; Malik had said he would prefer the Hurriyat to go first.

According to Vohra, the talks focused on CBMs that would impact on the ground. Singh told Hurriyat leaders that 'his government would consider troops' reduction, among other measures, to boost the peace process in Jammu and Kashmir'.[6] Hurriyat leaders wanted to pick up where the Advani talks had left off, the release of political prisoners. 'The Home Ministry has advised the Government of Jammu and Kashmir to examine the cases and make their recommendations at the earliest for the consideration of the joint screening committee' that had been set up under Advani, media were told. Union Home Secretary V. K. Duggal said the review would 'be completed in a time-bound manner, as desired by the Prime Minister'.

After a second round of talks, Singh announced that 40,000

troops would be redeployed out of civilian areas in the valley, and spoke of a 'meeting of minds' with the Hurriyat.[7] Mirwaiz Umar told reporters that 'we have undertaken to evolve very shortly a mechanism to carry out a continuous dialogue'. For the first time since the 1989 uprising, guerrilla violence fell to below its 1990 levels. Total fatalities declined from the high of 4,507 in 2001 to 1,810 in 2004 and further to 1,116 in 2006. Civilians killed in crossfire fell from over a thousand in 2001 to around 350 in 2006.[8]

The Singh–Hurriyat talks were anchored by an India–Pakistan backchannel. In August 2005, S. K. Lambah, a former high commissioner to Pakistan, was appointed Special Envoy in the PMO, to conduct confidential talks with Tariq Aziz, Musharraf's trusted aide. Aziz had previously held a backchannel with the Vajpayee administration's NSA, Brajesh Mishra. The mechanism was not a decision-making forum but a means by which all possible solutions to the disputes between India and Pakistan could be explored and differences narrowed. Notably, its confidentiality, which permitted frank discussion, was maintained, showing that when government appointees wished to prevent leaks they could do so despite India and Pakistan's leak-prone polities.

The Aziz–Lambah backchannel was perhaps the most successful confidence-building exercise of all between the two governments. Towards the close of 2005, Musharraf began to say that elected political representatives would also need to be involved in talks, reversing a Pakistani position held since the 1960s, that elections in Jammu and Kashmir were illegal, though elections in Pakistan-administered Kashmir were not.

Following Musharraf's lead, Mirwaiz Umar, now Hurriyat chairman for the second time, praised the Indian government for 'talking to the Hurriyat as a party', and added: 'The Kashmiris must be masters of their own fate. Self-rule and autonomy are two different things. Autonomy is within the framework of the Indian Constitution. Self-rule is not.'[9]

These and similar statements repeated through 2006–07, showed how far the Hurriyat had moved towards a solution that both the Indian and Pakistani governments could accept. Despite opposition from Pakistan-based Islamic militias, including several armed attacks on the Mirwaiz's home, fortunately unsuccessful, the Mirwaiz Hurriyat stood firm.

It looked as if the struggling peace process that started in 2000 was finally beginning to stabilize, but there were other disruptions to come. The PDP–Congress coalition that came to power in Jammu and Kashmir in 2002 had agreed to divide the chief ministerial term into two, with the first three years led by a PDP nominee and the last three by a Congress one. As the day neared for the transfer of power, many—including Chief Minister Sayeed—began to think that the state would do better if Sayeed continued. He had shown a masterly grasp of peacemaking, and the combination of his focus on restoring administration with his daughter Mehbooba's emphasis on a 'healing touch' had an important impact on the ground. The state had had a bumper tourist season, with close to a million visitors over the summer of 2005. Jammu and Kashmir had always been ruled by state political parties, not national ones, analysts argued; Congress rule would be construed as another attempt by the central government to disempower Kashmiris. Moreover, the chief minister had always been a valley Muslim. Switching to a Jammu politician, as was the Congress's nominee for Chief Minister Ghulam Nabi Azad, could upset the reconciliation process that the Muftis had begun, just when it was beginning to restore shattered confidence in the valley.

But the Congress was not willing to forego or subordinate its share of power, and Azad took over as chief minister in late 2005. There were a series of armed attacks following Azad's swearing-in, in which the National Conference's former Minister of State for Education, Ghulam Nabi Lone, was killed and PDP leader, Ghulam Hassan Mir, was critically injured.

Azad's chief ministership soon stabilized. The fact that he was a Jammu politician actually worked in his favour—he was able to build bridges between the estranged provinces of Jammu and Kashmir. He made administration his focus and proved to be a relatively able administrator. Continuing progress in CBMs for divided Kashmir, as well as between India and Pakistan, helped. India and Pakistan agreed on a gas pipeline from Iran, and possibly others from Central Asia. Several rounds of trade talks took place, and Indian and Pakistani businessmen were given new promotion opportunities in each other's countries. Journalists from both countries, including some Kashmiris, were allowed to visit two parts of the divided state, Jammu and Kashmir and Pakistan-administered Kashmir, but not the third, Gilgit–Baltistan. Though Azad lacked Sayeed's skill at promoting a peace process by picking up nuance, the lack offered the state a breather from the high decibel India–Pakistan focus that Sayeed had brought.

These rapid strides occurred because there was a rare confluence of political and civil society inputs on the Indian side, and a rare confluence of military, political and Kashmiri inputs on the Pakistani side. The years 2004–06 saw a flurry of Track II meetings and conferences that brought together Kashmiri leaders from the two sides of the Line of Control, in which international organizations such as Pugwash, founded to combat the use of nuclear weapons, were also involved. To have Farooq Abdullah, Abdul Ghani Bhat and Sajad Lone at the same table with leaders like Sardar Qayyum from across the Line of Control, discussing a peace process proactively instead of combatively, was in itself a huge confidence-booster. It freed the Hurriyat leaders to speak openly and in their own right about the next steps they would like to see.

Sardar Qayyum, who was now in his seventies, was a much-changed man. The youth who had mobilized guerrillas for a Pakistani conquest of Kashmir in 1948–49, and had worked closely with the ISI for the next six decades, committed to the Vajpayee–Musharraf peace process in 2000–01 and the Singh–Musharraf 'four-point formula' that followed. He remained committed to it for the next decade. I met him in New York in 2002, soon after Lone had been assassinated. He suggested we set up an intra-Kashmiri Track II to develop ideas for a Kashmir solution. When I consulted R. K. Mishra on the offer, he replied angrily,

'Ask him, does he feel he has blood on his hands?' I did. Tears came into Qayyum's eyes when I asked, and he looked silently at the ceiling of the Roosevelt Hotel, which was owned by the Pakistani government. I later learned it was a Pakistani intelligence practice to put hidden microphones in the ceilings of rooms they wanted to listen in on, including the high commissioner's office at the Pakistan High Commission in India.

The Hurriyat's statements of September 2005—in favour of a dialogue mechanism—eased the way for the Singh administration to involve a range of Kashmiri representatives. In February 2006, Singh set up a round table conference with Kashmiri political, regional and civil society leaders, to discuss ideas for a settlement and how to build peace on the ground.

The Hurriyat and other independence groups did not attend the round table, but it was far too early for them to do so. Most of them had had only two or three rounds of discussion with the prime minister. This should not have mattered. The Hurriyat had continuous backchannel contacts with a number of government-appointed interlocutors who reported to the prime minister. Their task was to develop implementable ideas for a Kashmir peace process jointly with dissident groups, which the prime minister would approve or refine. The purpose of the prime minister–Hurriyat meetings should have been to announce agreements that had already been fleshed out through the interlocutors. For some unfathomable reason—the Pakistan hand?—the Hurriyat refused to grasp this principle. According to them, the sheer number of separate interlocutors, each with his different style, cast doubt on the extent to which any one would influence—let alone make—policy. Hence, the Hurriyat measured their dialogue with New Delhi by meetings with the prime minister. Their stance made the New Delhi–Hurriyat track logistically impossible, given the demands on Singh's time as prime minister to over a billion people.

Read in this context, the Mirwaiz's statement that elected political leaders and civil society must be involved in talks, suggested that the Hurriyat would join the round table conferences once there had been new movement on the Delhi–Hurriyat track. In fact, there were hectic backchannel efforts to bring the Hurriyat and other dissident leaders to the second round table in Srinagar in May 2006, including a last-ditch meeting between Singh and the Hurriyat leaders. But—as some analysts had anticipated—there was an escalation of terrorist attacks in the run-up to the Srinagar round table. Mirwaiz Umar's uncle was killed, in what was clearly a message to the Hurriyat to stay away. Speaking to reporters in late April, Mirwaiz Umar said the Singh–Hurriyat talks should not be linked to the round table meeting in Srinagar. 'We are not against the round table but we will not be part of a crowd,' he added.[10] According to Singh, the Hurriyat reneged on their promises. 'The round table conference process was developed to enable all segments of Kashmir's political groups the opportunity to join hands with the Centre to look at the problem. It is my regret that the Hurriyat, despite promises, did not come for talks.'[11]

The Srinagar round table took place in an atmosphere of violence. I was one of the people that pleaded against holding all-party round tables, arguing in a private meeting with Singh that they might pre-empt a peace process with the Hurriyat. I lost the argument and gradually faded from the prime minister's consultative circles.

While the round tables did not succeed in consolidating the constituency for peace in the valley because the Hurriyat ostracized them, the Srinagar round table did set up five working groups to recommend concrete steps the government could take, on:

- strengthening relations across the Line of Control;
- centre–state relations;
- good governance;
- infrastructure and economic development; and
- CBMs within Jammu and Kashmir, especially for widows and orphans of violence, return of displaced persons, and return of people who crossed over during the insurgency.

The composition of the working groups was intended to include representatives of Kashmiri political parties, regional and civil society leaders, and pro-independence groups. As the latter continued to stay away, the round tables that eventually met from October 2006 were composed of the former three.

Meantime, the Aziz–Lambah backchannel made rapid progress on a set of ideas based on devolution and self-governance.[12] There were by-elections in the Doda district of Jammu province in which over 70 per cent of the electorate came out to vote, and the state government announced the formation of eight new districts, which was welcomed across the state. In late 2006, Musharraf began to lay increasing stress on his four-point formula for self-governance and demilitarization as a solution.

His four points, which he also listed in order of progression, were:

1. Demilitarization or phased withdrawal of troops;
2. No change of borders of Kashmir. However, the people of Jammu and Kashmir would be allowed to move freely across the Line of Control;
3. All parts of the divided state would have self-governance without independence; and
4. The two countries would set up a joint supervision mechanism involving India, Pakistan, and Jammu and Kashmir.

By 2007, it was widely rumoured that the Aziz–Lambah backchannel was discussing whether self-governance should be offered by India and Pakistan simultaneously, and whether it should be 'harmonized'. In other words, should the same structure of constitutional relations be applied on both sides of the Line of Control, albeit with different countries? It was also rumoured that the Musharraf administration continued to be reluctant to include the Northern Areas or Gilgit–Baltistan in any settlement.

Self-governance was a form of 'autonomy plus', insofar as it offered relations between divided Kashmir and would be jointly monitored by India, Pakistan and the elected state governments. The set of ideas that the Indian government presented in the backchannel in late 2005 detailed the elements that could go into the four-point formula and was drawn from various civil society proposals. In his autobiography, B. G. Verghese mentioned that he had outlined a plan for self-governance in Jammu and Kashmir as member of the US–India Track II Neemrana Dialogue some years earlier, which contributed to the Indian set of ideas. Similarly, I had prepared a draft framework for a Kashmir settlement for Prime Minister Singh in early 2005—at my own initiative, though it was kindly received by him—which Ambassador Lambah later told me provided a basis for the set of ideas in the backchannel. Along with Ambassador G. Parthasarathy, I later expanded the framework and, in 2006, it was published as a booklet by the Delhi Policy Group.[13] Parthasarathy, who wrote the CBMs section of the booklet, disseminated it in policy forums across India and the world, helping to build a policy consensus for the set of ideas that had been developed in the Aziz–Lambah backchannel, but were for obvious reasons kept confidential.

Many of us who were peripherally involved in India–Pakistan and Kashmiri peacemaking now began to wonder if confidentiality had run its span. In 2006, I was one of many, I presume again, who urged the Singh administration to push Musharraf to go public with the Aziz–Lambah set of ideas and get political backing for them. Aziz and Lambah had arrived at a framework and it was now time to move to the next level: mobilizing support for a formal agreement to be negotiated between the two governments. At the very least, I felt, by pushing to go public, the Indian government would learn to what extent Musharraf was committed to the framework that had been agreed in the backchannel.

♦

On the security side, too, there was some hope in the air. The India–Pakistan ceasefire continued to hold, and the Indian government was able to complete fencing the Line of Control. Violence had steadily though slowly declined, and with its reduction, human rights abuses declined too. The Indian government had begun gradual security reforms from 2003, when the practice of using surrendered militants for counter-insurgency was put on a tight leash by Sayeed. From 2005, the security duties that the army had conducted in urban areas, such as manning check points, began to be transferred to the Jammu and Kashmir police and the CRPF. By 2006, the Singh administration was pressing the security forces to take stringent steps to curb human rights violations, a pressure that was resisted by troops on the ground and which took over a year to show effect. That it did do so by 2007, however, indicated that the Singh administration was determined to pursue peace in Kashmir.

There was, too, considerable international support for these peace initiatives, both quiet and in public. Though the Bush administration spoke in two different voices in India and Pakistan, largely due to dependence on Pakistani routes for supplies to the US-led NATO mission in Afghanistan, they treated cross-border attacks in both Afghanistan and Jammu and Kashmir as terrorism. For the first time, in 2006, the European parliament's foreign affairs committee released a report indicting Pakistan for its role in armed conflict in Jammu and Kashmir and denial of democracy in Pakistan-administered Kashmir and Gilgit–Baltistan, while urging the Indian government to curb human rights violations by security forces.[14]

The report was roundly condemned by the Pakistani government, Pakistan-based militias and pro-Pakistan and pro-independence groups. At Vohra's suggestion, I had accompanied the author of the report, Baroness Emma Nicholson, to Jammu and Kashmir and was blamed for her conclusions in jihadi chatter. The accusation was absurd: Baroness Nicholson was a woman of strong and unshakeable opinions. She had already been alienated by the machinations of the Kashmir Centre in Brussels that was set up with ISI funding and had successfully lobbied members of the European parliament up to this point. Her observations on Pakistan-held territories of the former princely state were based on her visit there and meetings with diaspora leaders. Nevertheless, the Indian government offered me security, which I declined.

The promising developments of 2004–07 were marred by continuing violence in the valley. The transfer of security duties to the Jammu and Kashmir police and the CRPF did not bring great relief; instead, they became targets of armed attacks.

The bus service was smothered by restrictions (it was open only to members of divided families) and cumbersome procedures. Permits to use the bus had to be cleared by a host of security agencies, including intelligence, given that the armed groups were no nearer to offering a ceasefire than they had been three years ago.

The years 2004–07 were also marked by terrorist attacks in Delhi, Mumbai, Bangalore, Coimbatore, and finally on the Samjhauta Express. In July 2006, just as the backchannel appeared to be getting concrete and the prime minister's working groups were being formed, blasts in Mumbai killed close to 200 people on commuter trains. India demanded that Pakistan fulfil its 2004 pledge to act against militant groups and, in September 2006, the two countries agreed to set up a Joint Counter-Terrorism Mechanism.

Though three meetings took place under the mechanism, they yielded no visible progress. Then came the blasts on the Samjhauta Express in February 2007, and they underlined once again how significant and yet how frail the nascent peace process was. Indian investigators found contradictory evidence—while the US proclaimed the attacks had been carried out by the Lashkar-e-Taiba, Indian investigators found ties to the Students Islamic Movement of India as well as the Lashkar. They also found evidence linking a former Indian Army lieutenant colonel and two fiery Hindu preachers, one of whom confessed to involvement and had been charged in an earlier bomb blast in Ajmer. He was exonerated in the Ajmer case in 2017 on the grounds that the evidence was inconclusive.[15]

Singh and Musharraf spoke in the same voice, condemning the Samjhauta blasts as an attack on the peace process. Hopes rose once again for more rapid progress on containing violence and establishing a roadmap for its end. But it was too late. In early March 2007, Musharraf suspended the Chief Justice of Pakistan, and a series of terrorist acts ensued within Pakistan. When clerics in the Lal Masjid mosque and madarsa in Rawalpindi attempted an attack on the capital, Musharraf put the Kashmir peace process on the back-burner.

It appears that the BJP too attempted to play the spoiler role in reaching an India–Pakistan peace settlement. While the BJP accused the Singh administration of being a 'sell-out' to Musharraf, Advani advised visiting Pakistani foreign minister Khurshid Kasuri against 'any haste' in the peace process in February 2007, and Vajpayee repeated the warning the next day. 'Sotto voce Kasuri was told, "wait till we return to power"—implying, "you will get better terms from us",' Noorani commented.[16] More likely, the message was that the BJP would oppose any peace initiative that was not led by them.

◆

In April 2007, four of the five working groups set up by Singh presented their recommendations to the prime minister's third round table, held in Delhi. The most significant recommendations were made by the Working Group on Strengthening Relations across the Line of Control and the Working Group on Confidence-Building Measures within Jammu and Kashmir. The former recommended:

- Opening the Kargil–Skardu, Jammu–Sialkot, Turtuk–Khaplu, Chhamb–Jorian, Gurez–Astore–Gilgit, Tithwal–Chilhan and Jhanger–Mirpur routes across the Line of Control;
- Lifting restrictions on travel to include pilgrims, patients and tourists, if necessary, unilaterally by India; and
- Creating a free trade area between Jammu and Kashmir and Pakistan-administered Kashmir.

And the Working Group on Confidence-Building Measures within Jammu and Kashmir recommended:

- Reviewing the Armed Forces (Special Powers) Act (AFSPA) and the Disturbed Areas Act (DDA) and if possible, in light of the improved situation, revoking them;

- Starting an unconditional dialogue with armed groups to find a sustainable solution to militancy in the state;
- Making the return of Kashmiri Pandits a part of state policy;
- Providing better relief and rehabilitation for widows and orphans of violence in the state, including widows and orphans of guerrillas; and
- Facilitating the return of Kashmiris stranded across the Line of Control, many of whom had crossed over for arms training but now wished to return peacefully.

Agreeing on recommendations had not been easy for any of the working groups' members. Several of the recommendations of the group on internal CBMs aroused ire at the discussion stage, in particular, on AFSPA, dialogue with armed groups and return of former guerrillas. The BJP and Panun Kashmir leaders walked out of the group while these recommendations were being discussed. The latter was an organization of Pandits displaced from the valley who demanded a separate territory.

Nevertheless, the chairmen of four of the five groups managed to produce their reports by April 2007. Not so the fifth.

The Working Group on Centre–State Relations met first in December 2006 and then twice in early 2007. The other four working groups had already met several times, but this one had been plagued by difficulties in finding a chairperson; the first two people approached refused. Finally, Justice Saghir Ahmed, who had retired from the Supreme Court in 2002 and had spent a brief stint in the Jammu and Kashmir High Court in 1994, agreed.

This was not the end of the working group's troubles. Its first meeting, in December 2006, was boycotted by the National Conference to protest continued human rights violations despite the prime minister's promise of 'zero tolerance' in May. In the second and third meetings in February and March 2007, debate was so heated that they ended without agreement even on issues for further discussion. The BJP and Panun Kashmir were vehemently in favour of integration with India and vehemently opposed talks with pro-independence, pro-Pakistan and armed groups. But the former had a limited base in Jammu, and the latter was the voice of some Kashmiri Pandits, again mainly in Jammu and Delhi. The Jammu and Kashmir National Panthers' Party (JKNPP), which had 4 seats in the legislature, and the CPM, with 2, favoured the status quo, but both supported talks with the Hurriyat and armed groups. The Ladakh Union Territory Front was, as its name stated, in favour of integration with India, and there were simmering tensions between them and the Kargil Hill Council, which favoured the Jammu and Kashmir union. Both, however, supported regional and district-level devolution, and neither was opposed to talks with the Hurriyat and armed groups. Among the major Kashmiri parties, the National Conference was in favour of autonomy, the PDP was in favour of 'self-rule', and both supported talks with the Hurriyat and armed groups.

There was a long hiatus after the third meeting, until the chair called a fourth meeting for September 2007, partly under pressure from the centre to wrap up and produce a report. The report that was eventually produced had to be put together by interlocutor Vohra's office.

The issue of centre–state relations was in any case one that perhaps a working group could not address. It touched on the crux of the problem, irrespective of differences in what analysts saw as the roots of conflict. If the roots were competing India–Pakistan claims, then centre–state relations would have to be discussed by both countries, along with the leaders of Jammu and Kashmir and Pakistan-administered Kashmir and Gilgit-Baltistan (Chinese control of the Aksai Chin territory of Ladakh was an issue that was yet to be addressed). If it was an issue of Kashmiri independence, it would still have to be discussed by the same actors.

Only if it was an issue of democracy could it be addressed internally by each country, but there was little consensus on this in Jammu and Kashmir. Many in India believed that democratizing the state would dissolve what they considered to be old and outpaced grievances over autonomy and independence. What they failed to recognize was that substantive democracy might only be possible when the latter two issues were resolved. Even then it could be a long haul, given that Jammu and Kashmir went straight from feudal, imperial and monarchical rule to conflict and thus had little time to build democratic institutions.

◆

Within the state, 2007 opened optimistically with the settlement of another long-standing dispute over the Baglihar Dam on the Chenab River in Doda. India had begun building the dam thirty years earlier, but had put it on hold when Pakistan objected. Pakistan feared that the dam might allow India to shut off shared river waters from Kashmir, an issue that was easily resolvable under the 1960 Indus Waters Treaty. After being hounded by the Kissinger administration at the UN over the Bangladesh War, however, India was loath to risk its chances at the then US-dominated World Bank. When the international strategic calculus began to shift with the end of the Cold War, these fears gradually dissipated. By the early 2000s, power shortages in Jammu and Kashmir had made the development of the state's hydel power an urgent necessity. In 2005, India and Pakistan agreed to refer the Baglihar dispute to a World Bank appointed arbitrator under the dispute resolution mechanism of the Indus Waters Treaty. Two years later, the World Bank arbitrator ruled in India's favour.

But 2007 was also the year in which Pakistan itself was subjected to a number of terrorist attacks by radical Islamists, as well as a regrouping of Taliban and Taliban supporters in FATA and a surge in cross-border attacks on coalition forces in Afghanistan. Pakistan's attention turned west and inwards.

Ironically, Pakistan's westward and inward turn offered Jammu and Kashmir a brief respite. Azad's administration put governance and development on a fast track, and initiated security reforms—army back in barracks, checkpoints much reduced, Kashmiri and Indian armed police forces replacing the army—that presaged a state on its way to post-conflict reconstruction.

Then, in the summer of 2008, the handover of a parcel of land to a Hindu trust to manage the centuries-old Amarnath

Yatra sparked renewed protest in the Kashmir valley. The yatra, a Hindu pilgrimage to a holy cave housing an ice stalagmite held to represent Shiva, contributed in large measure to the local economy, with surrounding villagers providing tents, ponies and guides to as many as 200,000 pilgrims. Local residents feared that the trust was going to usurp their livelihood, and their fears soon translated into a cry of Hindu encroachment on Kashmir's autonomy, accompanied by strikes and demonstrations. The unrest sparked a counter-reaction in Jammu, where protesters enforced a blockade on the valley for a few stark days. The Jammu–Srinagar highway was the only route for supplies to Kashmir and, as supplies began to run short, the state government imposed a curfew. The army was back on the streets again. It looked as if the bad old days might return, but the curfew was relaxed and then lifted.

Azad's government was, however, a fatality. Though the land issue was provoked by retiring governor General S. K. Sinha, who headed the Amarnath trust, the PDP, Azad's coalition partner, withdrew and his government fell. Newly appointed as governor, N. N. Vohra had to step in to face a high-stakes Jammu-valley crisis. Despite the curfew being lifted and the highway cleared within days, animosity between Jammu and the valley remained high. There were scattered incidents of violence and continuing shortages of supplies to the valley as the result of a more limited blockade by transporters and suppliers. It took Governor Vohra several weeks to negotiate an end to hostility, with aid from a number of local civil society groups.

Had all other matters been equal, India and Pakistan might have renewed the Kashmir peace process in 2009. But the Mumbai attacks of 26 November 2008, targeting the iconic Taj Hotel at the Gateway of India, the Chhatrapati Shivaji Terminus station and the Jewish Chabad House, put an end to that. Close to 200 people were massacred, including nationals of a dozen countries. At the Taj, attackers killed Hindus, Christians and Jews whereas Muslims were spared.

US and Indian intelligence intercepts indicated that the attacks had been planned by the Lashkar-e-Taiba with strategic and logistical support from some among the ISI. Faced with the choice of a military or diplomatic response, an enraged Indian government made the difficult decision to seek rule of law diplomacy to bring the perpetrators to justice. In Pakistan, the recently elected PPP government's initial response was cooperative. Benazir Bhutto had been assassinated during the 2008 election campaign, many believed by the ISI, and the PPP had won on a sympathy wave prompted by revulsion against Pakistan's home-grown terrorists.

In fact, Pakistan's foreign minister Shah Mehmood Qureshi was in India on the day the attacks took place. Qureshi was on a mission to revive the India–Pakistan peace process. When news of the attack broke, he sought urgently to meet with Indian foreign minister Salman Khurshid but was refused. Congress MP Mani Shankar Aiyar, who tried to set up the meeting, later called the Indian refusal a costly mistake. But the Mumbai attacks, which were telecast as they unfolded for five agonizing days, left most Indians with a searing sense of humiliation and anger, and calls for a military response mounted. Qureshi's offer was made while the attack on the Taj was still ongoing and the Singh administration was in a fix about how to deal with the attack. Singh concluded there could be no joint statement or photo op at such a time.

The Indian and Pakistani media's calls to war put pressure on each government to up the ante. Though President Zardari promised, in a phone call to Singh, that director general of the ISI, Shuja Pasha, would be sent to India to discuss investigation and prosecution of the attackers, the visit did not materialize. When Pakistani journalists tracked one of the attackers to a village in Pakistani Punjab, the Pakistani government turned hostile, and the Indian government began to talk of exploring all its options. Eventually, concerted international diplomacy ensured that the Zardari administration took a series of steps: first they arrested Lashkar suspects and closed down their offices (as Musharraf had done in 2002), then they received Indian evidence on leads and, finally, Pakistan's federal police conducted a substantive investigation and began prosecution of those involved in the direction, planning, funding and logistics of the Mumbai attacks. In February 2009,

Pakistan announced its findings and registered a case against nine people, including two high-level Lashkar functionaries and their aides.

Expectedly, the Zardari administration's seeming determination to follow through on the Mumbai prosecution, taken together with other efforts to limit the military's political interference, met with threats from the Pakistan Army, including on corruption. Confrontation was averted through an unofficial understanding that Zardari would go slow on Mumbai and the army might allow his administration to complete its full term. The prosecution now proceeded at snail's pace, with hearings still in the initial stage one year later.

In July 2009, soon after court hearings finally began, Singh and Pakistani prime minister Gilani met at Sharm el Sheikh in Egypt and announced that they would work towards resuming the peace process. A second terrorist attack on the Indian embassy in Kabul in October 2009 derailed the effort. In February 2010, India and Pakistan made another effort, with the two countries' foreign secretaries meeting in New Delhi, but there were bomb blasts in Pune; in Muzaffarabad, Lashkar commander Abdul Makki had threatened to bomb India only a few days earlier. The issue of terrorism dominated the foreign secretaries' talks, which ended without a joint statement. Another series of attacks in Kabul followed, in which Indians were the chief target. The Mumbai case dragged on. After one prosecutor was killed, the case was further vitiated, and ten years after the attacks, the chief accused were freed.

By 2008, the theatre of India–Pakistan conflict had widened to Afghanistan. There were two attacks on the Indian embassy in Kabul in July 2008, which US intelligence tied to the Haqqani group and Pakistan's ISI. Alarmed by India's growing presence in Afghanistan as one of the largest aid donors, Pakistan Army-backed guerrillas had expanded operations against India to include Indian installations in Afghanistan. The army's strategic depth doctrine, which dictated that Afghanistan must be within the Pakistani sphere of influence because it provided a rear guard against India, returned to dominate the Pakistani government's India policy. When US president Obama came to power in the 2008 election, announcing he would gradually withdraw US troops from Afghanistan, it put the focus back on Pakistan as the most likely broker of a peace deal with the Taliban. Indian analysts feared India's vulnerability in Kashmir might increase.

◆

Despite the Amarnath conflict and the Mumbai terrorist attack—or perhaps because of them—Kashmiris turned out in record numbers to vote in the December 2008 legislative election. Once again, the vote was divided. The National Conference won the largest number of seats in the valley and the Congress in Jammu and Ladakh. A Congress–National Conference administration took office, headed by Omar Abdullah, the son of Farooq and grandson of Sheikh Abdullah, as chief minister.

Initially Omar was received with enthusiasm, especially in the valley. Armed conflict, which had steadily declined since 2001, was at an all-time low. Fatalities had fallen to 541 deaths in 2008 and 375 each in 2009 and 2010. The number of civilians killed in crossfire was, for the first time, well below 100, at 69 in 2008 and 55 in 2009.[17] The state was ready for peacebuilding and Omar was young and handsome, with the legendary Abdullah charm. He had worked in the corporate sector as well as the Vajpayee administration, where his duties as minister of state for external affairs included dealing with Europe and the US. His political vision was global, not inward looking; indeed, he had spent his working life outside the state. Perhaps he could overcome the baggage of history—or set it aside—many Kashmiris told me when I visited the state six months later. At the least, he might bring a nepotism-free administration.

Omar Abdullah began with a focus on reviving India–Pakistan and union government–Kashmir talks, as Sayeed had done before him. I was one of a dozen or so people whom he asked to consult for a peace process; A. G. Noorani was another. The invitations were not followed up. Perhaps he was advised that it was unwise to be seen consulting with mainland Indians. Both Noorani and I had been critics of the National Conference's actions during their stints in government during the 1990s, as had most Kashmir watchers.

Omar's other feelers were better received. The Hurriyat and JKLF welcomed his call for a peace process. It looked as if, for the first time in two decades of conflict, the two dissident organizations might enter talks with the state government. Their earlier position had been that the state government had no role to play in what was a dispute between the union government and pro-independence or pro-Pakistan groups. Before Omar–Hurriyat or JKLF talks could materialize, however, the state was again rocked by protests, this time against an alleged rape and murder of two young women by security forces in the Shopian district of south Kashmir. Though Omar ordered an enquiry, in which a medical examiner confessed she had fudged the medical samples, its findings were dismissed as eyewash, just as the Kunan–Poshpora enquiries had been.

Army pickets were again stoned by disgruntled youth following the Shopian murders, mostly in rural areas where the troops were fewer and strung out. Twelve people were killed and over 1,000 injured. Though protests gradually died down, the summer of 2009 was turbulent in Shopian. Gujjars and alleged 'informants' began to be targeted. On 4 April, guerrillas shot sixty-year-old Reshma Begum; on 30 May, a young man named Sahibuddin was killed; three days later, twenty-six-year old Nageena Akhtar was shot. In July, another young woman, Parveena, was killed. Later that month, Mohammad Aslam Awan and his three-year-old son were shot. In December, twenty-one-year old Sheeraza Akhtar was killed on the eve of her wedding.[18]

Omar Abdullah had other problems too. He had inherited a state that had begun to gradually limp back to normalcy after the Amarnath contretemps only to have it erupt again over murder, and possibly rape, in Shopian. His allies within the state were few and the PDP mustered a powerful opposition. Though he had been a union minister, he had never dealt with the state or local administration. The fact that he had spent his working life outside the state was actually to his disadvantage. He knew little of the intricate familial relations that dominated politics and governance in Jammu and Kashmir. With constant obstacles to efforts to improve services, and lack of interaction with local elites, his government rapidly lost its promised sheen.

In early 2009, the Singh administration renewed talks with the Hurriyat and the JKLF, and it looked as if their efforts might yet yield a breakthrough. In September, Home Minister P. Chidambaram announced during a visit to the valley that his government was ready to hold 'quiet talks, quiet diplomacy' for an honourable solution to the Kashmir conflict. In October, while at the 15th ASEAN Summit in Thailand, Singh again repeated his offer of talks, 'I have always maintained that it is our sincere desire to engage all sections of political opinion in Jammu and Kashmir to find practical and pragmatic solutions to the problems facing the State.'[19] The next day, Ghani Bhat, now acting chairman of the Hurriyat, welcomed Singh's offer, saying, 'We want purposeful dialogue with a view to finding a permanent solution to the Kashmir problem.' There would be no preconditions, he added, since 'dialogue and conditionalities don't go together'. In November, Mirwaiz Umar called for the withdrawal of troops from the valley and, a few days later, Chidambaram announced there would be a troops' cut. In December, Defence Minister A. K. Antony stated that two army divisions, comprising around 30,000 troops, had been moved out of the valley.

By this point, the Mirwaiz Hurriyat and Geelani's Tehreek-e-Hurriyat, founded after his break with the original Hurriyat in 2003, were in open confrontation. Warning that 'any exclusive bilateral engagement between any Kashmiri group and the Centre' would be a 'violation of the Hurriyat constitution', the Tehreek spokesman said that on 19 June 2008, the two Hurriyat factions had agreed that 'the basic demand for freedom would be confined to the right of self-determination'.[20] The Tehreek's demands overlapped with the issues being discussed by the Singh administration and Hurriyat. The difference was that the Tehreek demanded troops' withdrawal, repeal of draconian laws and prisoner releases before a dialogue could start, while the Hurriyat treated the three issues as CBMs to be negotiated.

There was dissension within the Hurriyat too. In November, following criticism of the backchannel talks with Chidambaram by some members of its general council, the Hurriyat's executive 'disbanded all its posts and issued a gag order'. In December, Hurriyat leaders expelled Mohammad Yousuf Naqash, president of the Islamic Political Party (IPP), a member of the Hurriyat's General Council.[21]

The Chidambaram–Hurriyat backchannel, meanwhile, had progressed to discussing the core elements of a permanent peace settlement, building on the set of ideas that the Singh administration had developed through Aziz and Lambah in 2006–07. On the Hurriyat side, talks were chiefly conducted by Fazal Haq Qureshi, whom the Hurriyat had nominated their representative. Qureshi had led the 2000 Hizbul ceasefire talks and was growing to be recognized as one of the dissidents' most credible negotiators. Though the Chidambaram–Hurriyat and parallel Chidambaram–Malik talks were secret, in November, news of them was leaked to the media, possibly by sceptical intelligence agents.[22] Deliberate or not, the leak was a spoiler act. Qureshi was shot by a local guerrilla in December while on his way home from the mosque.

Such targeted shootings had derailed previous attempts at dialogue in 2000, 2004 and 2006, and they were once again successful, though initially it seemed they might not be. Within days of Qureshi's shooting, Mirwaiz Umar stated that there was 'no other option' but to 'carry on talks with New Delhi and Pakistan'.[23] A senior leader of Qureshi's own party, the People's Political Front, Musadiq Adil announced his party would not be 'overawed and unnerved by the inhuman physical assault...Those looking upon dialogue as a sell-out are, in fact, demonstrating their intellectual bankruptcy and lack of confidence and vision.'

Despite these brave words, the New Delhi–Hurriyat track lapsed for the third time, amidst signs that the Pakistani government was turning back on the tacit agreement reached in the Aziz–

Lambah backchannel. In Islamabad, Foreign Minister Qureshi and a number of Pakistani politicians said that the agreements reached during President Musharraf's rule were inconsequential since he had seized power in a coup. The Pakistani Foreign Office denied any knowledge of the Aziz–Lambah talks, let alone the draft framework developed in them. In New York, President Zardari called for US mediation.[24] In Muzaffarabad, Yusuf Shah, who continued to head the United Jihad Council, said in November that 'quiet diplomacy' was a sham and in December that the time was wrong for talks because they would be 'useless'.[25] The Srinagar–Muzaffarabad bus, the Kashmir police discovered, was being used by the ISI to smuggle agents in.[26] One had actually married a woman called Sobia from Surankote, the wife of a local Lashkar commander who was in prison, in order to ensure frequent permits to visit. Infiltration in Kashmir, which had continuously decreased from 2004–08, began to rise again.

The Singh and Zardari administrations continued to talk in 2010. At the Thimpu SAARC summit that April, Singh and Gilani agreed to continue formal talks, and in June, Chidambaram visited Pakistan. Reportedly, his talks with Interior Minister Malik went well, with cooperation against terrorism as the focus. 'We will wait for the outcome,' said Chidambaram. One positive step was Pakistan's announcement of a Task Force to combat terrorist groups, including the Lashkar and its parent organization, Jamaat-ud-Dawa. The announcement came as a run-up to the Indian and Pakistani foreign ministers' meeting on 15 July. The Hurriyat again indicated willingness for talks in spring-summer 2010, but by this point, a new wave of protests had broken out, led by Geelani's Tehreek-e-Hurriyat.

The decade closed with two major setbacks: the targeting of Indians in Afghanistan, and a question mark over the achievements of the peace process.

Chapter XVIII

INTIFADA, 2010

At end-April 2010, Rashtriya Rifles troops stationed at Machil, on the Line of Control in north Kashmir, announced that they had killed three Pakistani infiltrators.[1] It was soon found that the three were not Pakistani but local residents of Nadihal village in neighbouring Rafiabad tehsil. Villagers claimed that the young men, who were daily wage earners, had been lured with the promise of army jobs by a counter-insurgent and former special police officer of Baramulla district, Bashir Ahmad Lone. Lone, it was alleged, had conspired with army officials to stage an 'encounter' in order to win cash awards[2] (in the early 2000s, the Indian Army instituted a one-time cash grant to personnel who received gallantry awards for counter-terrorism achievements, a practice that was curtailed in the late 2000s but was revived ten years later).[3] A police investigation ordered by Chief Minister Omar Abdullah confirmed the Machil villagers' claim prima facie.

As news of the killings filtered out, public protests began in Baramulla and Kupwara and spread to Srinagar. The army announced its own investigation led by a Brigadier Mehra, attached the commanding officer of 4th Rajputana Rifles, Colonel Pathania, and removed the main accused in the police complaint, Major Upinder, from active duty. Despite these steps, the issue dominated Singh's visit to Kashmir in early June. The National Conference called for the repeal of AFSPA and resumption of dialogue with the Hurriyat, while the CPI-M stressed an early trial and sentencing of the accused. In an attempt at damage control, Singh underlined that 'the government policy is to protect the human rights of the people even when dealing with terrorism. The security forces in Jammu and Kashmir have been strictly instructed to respect the rights of civilians. We will act to remove any deficiency in the implementation of these instructions.'[4]

Singh's assurance had little impact. Three days after his visit, the two Hurriyats came together to call for a strike against the killings. The strike led to clashes in Srinagar, in which a seventeen-year-old passer-by, Tufail Mattoo, was killed on 11 June. He was hit by an unexploded tear gas shell. As protests mounted, they spiralled into demands for troops to 'quit Kashmir'. In late June, the Geelani-led Tehreek-e-Hurriyat launched a 'protest calendar', asking residents of the valley to stock essentials in order 'to prepare for a long-drawn protest programme against Indian rule', and supporters to 'draw anti-India graffiti on Kashmir streets and paste provocative slogans on social networking websites, extending street protests to the virtual world'.[5]

The campaign was announced by Tehreek leader Masrat Alam at a secret location in downtown Srinagar to a select group of journalists. Campaigners were asked to organize a 'social boycott' of policemen who obeyed instructions to quell protests, he added. A sample of his weekly protest calendar read: '25 June: Kashmir shutdown, 26 June: Koneet Nazila (special prayers), 27 June: writing 'Go India Go' on walls and social networking sites, 28 June: boy students' protest, 29 June: girl students' protest, 30 June: protests after Friday sundown prayers, 1 July: march to Pather Masjid, 2–3 July: complete shutdown.'

Alam's programme was a typical form of student campaigning, as most student activists will recognize. The Indian government was seasoned in dealing with student campaigns and should have been able to apply tried and tested means of doing so without violence. But this was Jammu and Kashmir and the situation was complicated in innumerable ways. Alam's discussion with journalists indicated that protests would be mobilized around stoning; risibly, stoning was described as non-violent. His protest calendars were enforced by youth armed with wooden rods as well as stones who threatened anyone who violated instructions. 'In one bizarre incident, a group of women travelling for a wedding in north Kashmir were lashed with stinging-nettle,' reported Praveen Swami.[6]

Indian intelligence had already warned that cross-border guerrillas would step up attacks. In mid-January, the United Jihad Council called for 'reinvigorated jihad until Kashmir was free of "Indian occupation"', at a meeting in Muzaffarabad chaired by former ISI director Hamid Gul. In Srinagar, a police station and a hotel were attacked by guerrillas. It was reported that the Lashkar had bought 200 kanals of land (around 40 acres) in Muzaffarabad district to set up guerrilla recruitment and training centres. 'This land transaction could only be done with the help of the Pakistani establishment, as legally no Pakistani individual or organization could purchase land in any part of the State,' wrote Shabir Choudhry, director of the Institute for Kashmir Affairs in Britain.[7] In March 2010, the Jihad Council's member militias stepped up recruitment in Pakistani Punjab. In May, guerrilla build-up was reported across the Line of Control in the Neelam valley of Mirpur; local residents reported that the guerrillas 'did not appear to be Kashmiri'. In Srinagar, Defence Minister Antony was warned by military intelligence, 'Pakistan is up to something big' and 'we need to know what it is'.[8] Home Ministry figures indicated a 30 per cent increase in infiltration along the international border and the Line of Control in Jammu and Kashmir, from 342 recorded incidents in 2008 to 499 in 2009. The Multi-Agency Centre, set up to streamline anti-terrorism action by coordinating over a dozen federal and state intelligence agencies, cautioned the union government that there would be a more 'violent' summer ahead.[9]

Neither military nor civil intelligence anticipated that the 'something big' was going to be a sustained summer of stoning, though there had been a slow build-up of security–youth clashes in preceding months. The state and union governments' response was inept at best and lethal at worst. The police were unable to arrest Alam, but they put Geelani and Mirwaiz Umar under house arrest. At the same time, the Omar administration continued to call for talks with the Hurriyat.

Nor could the chief minister make up his mind about whether the police or the CRPF should handle the protests. Worst of all, the two forces did not work well with each other. In late June, following the deaths of several young men in clashes with the police, Omar Abdullah ordered a major reshuffle in the police department. Simultaneously, over a hundred youth were arrested in a crackdown on protesters in Srinagar, Baramulla and Sopore; they had been recorded on camera while stoning the police. When more young men died after clashes with the CRPF, Omar asked for the army to replace the police and paramilitary dealing with stoning mobs.

A union government that had at considerable cost arranged the transfer of policing from the army, was not pleased. Though the army conducted flag marches through Srinagar, the chief minister was told to use police and paramilitary forces to deal with protesters. The army would not be employed for crowd control, a senior Home Ministry official told *The Telegraph*: 'The essential task of restoring public order is of the state police and paramilitary, they will have to do the job.'[10] Referring to the blame game between state police and the CRPF, he added, 'There is some security disarray and the state government appears to be in the grip of unnecessary panic, it needs to assert its authority in a determined way.' But when Omar announced he was setting up a commission to look into the deaths of youth in clashes with security forces, he added fuel to the blame game. The commission would be authorized to look into the seventeen deaths that occurred in June–July 2010, he ordered. This was when internal security was led by the CRPF. The commission would not enquire into the hundred or so deaths that occurred after the state police was given charge, in July. No wonder the commission was never set up.

The state and union governments made an effort to control escalation by imposing curfew in Srinagar and other major towns in the valley in August, but Kashmir's young defied it. As the curfew stretched on, first over one month and then two, residents in the valley began to suffer shortages of essential supplies. 'People are running out of milk, vegetables and baby food,' the *Hindustan Times* wrote, calling the curfew a 'collective punishment' for the valley.[11] From mid-September, the curfew began to be partially relaxed in parts of Srinagar and other towns for a few hours each day to allow people to buy supplies.

In the same month, street protests morphed further into an 'Islam and Muslims in danger' issue when an American cleric burnt a copy of the Quran on the ninth anniversary of 9/11.[12] Protesters attacked Christian schools and churches, burning down a missionary school and its outhouses. They also attacked government buildings, including in Jammu province. In Poonch, the offices of the sub-divisional magistrate, the Forest Department, the Block Development Office and police vehicles were set on fire when police prevented the burning of a Christian school. In Mendhar, dozens of government offices, a police station, and eight vehicles were burned when the police again prevented mobs from setting fire to a Christian school. In Srinagar, Samajwadi Party leader Fayaz Ahmad Bhat was attacked; so were police stations and even policemen's homes. In south Kashmir's Awantipora, a young Sikh who worked for the Border Roads Organisation was beaten and his beard—religiously ordained under the Sikh faith—was cut off.

The form of the protests—stoning army and police pickets or patrols and destroying public property—was not new to the valley. Protesters had stoned the maharaja's army in 1931. But stoning had not taken place daily, nor were protesters led by a seemingly inexhaustible pool of youth, some in their early teens. Though stoning of army and police had started in Kashmir's rural areas in 2008–09, first in the context of the Amarnath land transfer order and then the Shopian alleged rape and murders, it had been under-reported, partly because troops were told not to react. Stoning revived in February 2010 when a young man named Wamiq Farooq died in Srinagar upon being hit by an unexploded tear gas shell, but it did not spread. What happened in the summer of 2010, therefore, came as a shock.

Perhaps it should not have. In late 2005, Pakistani Senator M. P. Bhandara told me in Srinagar that he had delivered a letter from Musharraf to pro-Pakistan and pro-independence leaders advising them that it was time for cross-border armed conflict to end. Instead, Musharraf suggested, Kashmiri dissidents could choose between the Gandhian form of non-violent protest through civil disobedience or the Palestinian intifada.

Bhandara was cock-a-hoop and clearly regarded Musharraf's letter as an important indicator of Pakistan's changed view. He was quite taken aback when I berated him on how Pakistan would do better to stay away and let the Hurriyat and Indian government pursue a peace process along the lines outlined in their talks. For Pakistan to stay away was an unreasonable demand, as he saw it.

The Indian government knew of the Bhandara delivery, as did the state government, but they may have concluded Musharraf's letter was a non-starter. The peace process was going quite well at the time, and the fact that neither civil disobedience nor an intifada started in the months after the Musharraf letter might have led to such a conclusion. In the event, the stoning movement started only two and a half years later and there is no way of knowing whether Musharraf's letter had any influence.

Alam's use of social media proved to be resoundingly successful. Seeing videos of mobs stoning security forces on YouTube and exhorted to join them by cell phone messages and Facebook groups, Kashmir's young responded enthusiastically. They were in many ways the 'lost generation' that Mandela spoke about in apartheid-era South Africa, born and bred in two decades of armed conflict, when blocked streets, curfews, frisking and school shutdowns were frequent, cinema halls were closed and there was little to do other than pick up the gun or attend the mosque where, most often, they were exhorted to arms. By now, Wahhabi mosques and madaris had mushroomed across the valley, from less than two dozen in 1990 to over 700 in 2009. Most of them were led by non-Kashmiri preachers. For example, when the Assam government cracked down on illegal Bangladeshi migrants in the 1990s, Islamist preachers from Assam were given sanctuary in Kashmir's new Wahhabi mosques.

Some of the youth who responded to Alam's call were middle class and educated while others were peasants who had turned to education in the two decades of armed conflict, when they were unable to work their orchards. According to Omar Abdullah, a government survey of around 200 stone-throwers revealed that over 60 per cent came from families in which both parents were uneducated, and had themselves dropped out at the middle-school level. With frequent school shutdowns, the young received more propaganda than education. 'There are no opportunities for children with such educational backgrounds,' he said.[13]

Frustration amongst the valley's young was exacerbated by lack of change on the ground. As militancy trickled to a low with a new young chief minister and peace talks, both educated and lumpen youth expected the promised peace dividend. Before it could materialize, they were out on the streets. 'I have taken to stone-throwing to show my anger, my hatred at the present state of affairs,' the son of a government employee told reporters.[14] A British psychiatrist who worked in Kashmir, Justine Hardy, wrote that the young men she treated were in despair at seeing no future. Their anger, she said, sought a physical outlet or, as a young man put it to her, 'It will explode inside me, it will really kill me.'[15]

Employment was one of many long overdue reforms that the Omar administration grappled with. Unlike any other state in India, the bulk of jobs in Jammu and Kashmir were with the government. Private enterprise had not found roots in the valley, partly due to its traditional economy but mostly due to the decades of conflict. Speaking to the *Indian Express* in December 2009, Omar lamented, 'Unfortunately in Jammu and Kashmir, due to the circumstances, particularly in the Kashmir valley, the only employment one has talked about is government employment. The only way youngsters feel they are employed productively is if they have a government job. They will happily turn down private sector jobs paying them ₹10,000–12,000 a month for an uncertain salary in a government job. We need to change that because there isn't much scope in the government for employment. The number of unemployed youths, according to our latest tabulation, has crossed 5 lakhs [500,000].'[16]

Job creation through private enterprise was doing better than during the Sadiq administration thirty years earlier, but was still limited. Attempts to replicate the Haryana model of offering cheap back office services for international sales operators did result in one such office being set up on the outskirts of Srinagar, but did not multiply. Similarly, a cell phone company did set up its Uttar Pradesh (UP) operations centre in Srinagar, but again, one back office did not lead to more. Kashmir-focused entrepreneurial initiatives promised better, but were pitifully small. Usman Ahmed of the US-based NGO Mercy Corps, for example, set up a training programme focused on information technology, agriculture, green business and food processing. The goal was 'to find young entrepreneurs "angel" investors, connect them with business development services such as banks, chartered accountants and lawyers and, importantly, a peer network that would provide both inspiration and mentoring'.[17] Their target was to encourage 200 young entrepreneurs, but even that target was not met. Kashmir's violent conflict had long discouraged Indian industry. Though violence had declined by the late 2000s, the constant strikes called by the Tehreek and other dissident groups continued to discourage. When industry responded to Prime Minister Singh's appeal to invest in Kashmiri youth during the 2010 disturbances, they provided training and employment outside the state.

Alam himself was no student, but then nor were the leaders of most of the students' unions in India. Thirty-eight years old and a college graduate, he was one of the Srinagar youth who joined guerrilla ranks after the botched 1987 election. In 1989, he founded the pro-Pakistan Muslim League, with the objective of 'fighting Indian aggression…propagating Islamic teachings to fight out socialism and secularism, removing *taghut* [false leaders; traitors] rule and uprooting western ideology'.[18] Arrested in 1990, Alam spent the next seventeen years in and out of jail. In 2003, when the Hurriyat split, he joined the Geelani faction and rose to prominence in the 2008 Amarnath agitation, during which he was said to have made inroads into Mirwaiz Umar's stronghold in Srinagar. In the summer of 2010, when his protest programme was at its height, Alam issued a leaflet addressing security troops in Jammu and Kashmir, resent by Geelani in 2016. 'You will be tired of killing us,' the leaflet said, 'some day you might be horrified at what you have done to humanity. We will never tire of struggling for our history, for our future, our freedom. We will not forgive.'[19]

In December 2010, according to the Kashmir police, Alam confessed that he had received ₹4 million through the Tehreek to fuel stoning protests, and in February 2011, the state police arrested a Tehreek-e-Hurriyat fundraiser who collected door to door in areas of Jamaat-e-Islami and Tehreek influence.[20] Locally sourced funding was small in comparison to Pakistani funding, which, according to Director General of Police Kuldeep Khoda, came through multiple channels. Some Tehreek agents collected cash when visiting other Indian states, some received funds through net banking. The Srinagar–Muzaffarabad cross-Line of Control trade route provided a means of smuggling funds overland. So did drug-smugglers and 'hawala' or illegal transfers. The means of transaction, he added, were becoming more and more complex, and therefore difficult to track. Had the Pakistani funding mechanism been 'simple', he said, the authorities 'would have choked it'.[21]

◆

When mobs of youth, some masked, appeared on television screens hurling stones—some as large as small rocks—at poorly defended CRPF and police pickets in 2010, both an unsuspecting public and the union and state governments were caught unawares. The CRPF and state police responded first with tear gas and then with guns. As daily reports of deaths due to firing poured in, a hapless government watched. According to government figures, 110 young Kashmiris lost their lives in stoning conflicts from June to September; 537 civilians were injured, along with 1,274 CRPF troops and 2,747 state police personnel.[22]

Ironically, the 2010 protests came at a time when the union government had begun far-reaching security reforms in the state. In October 2009, speaking to reporters in Srinagar, Chidambaram announced that the union government was working towards sending the army to the borders and transferring internal security to the state police, with paramilitary such as the CRPF as backup.

'I myself have confidence in the Jammu and Kashmir police, but I want people to express their faith in the police so that we can assign them a lead role and keep the paramilitary forces on a second line of defence and send the Army to the borders,' he said.[23] In November, Omar Abdullah revealed that the army was soon to transfer internal security duties to the state police, who were being trained by the army's 15 Corps in Srinagar 'with a view to preparing them for more responsibilities on the internal security front'.[24] In January 2010, Antony confirmed that the union government's long-term aim was to have the army protect the borders and the state police handle internal security. Though the government was aware of the heightened threat of infiltration, he said, 'on the whole, the situation in Kashmir is improving'[25] when compared to the previous decade. As the first step in redeployment, he added, the army had completed vacation of government buildings, including schools.

Security reform was one of three pillars of the union and state governments' peacemaking policy. The other two pillars were talks with dissident groups and improved administration. In late June 2010, even as stoning clashes intensified, then army chief V. K. Singh said that 'bold and far-sighted political steps' were urgently needed to control the situation in Jammu and Kashmir. 'I feel there is a great requirement for political initiatives that take all people together.'[26]

By this point, resentment against misgovernance had become painfully acute. In an initiative to restore confidence, the Omar administration made overtures to civil society leaders through a series of meetings. At the same time that V. K. Singh called for political initiatives, Omar announced the formation of three ministerial teams for Baramulla, Anantnag and Pulwama districts, who would 'work with citizen groups for speedy restoration of peace and monitor the day-to-day situation'.[27] In Srinagar, a group of eminent citizens, comprising retired government officials, educationists and health care professionals, wrote to him seeking revival of talks, release of innocents and separate homes for juvenile stone-throwers, along with protection of the livelihoods of the poor, who had been severely affected by the Tehreek's shutdown calendars.[28]

Despite Omar's efforts, however, his administration was beset by non-performance. In October 2009, Chidambaram confessed his dismay that not a single project under the Prime Minister's Reconstruction Plan (PMRP) had been completed. The reconstruction plan was developed as a complement to security reforms and was an essential pillar of the Singh administration's peacebuilding programme. His government intended to invest in power and other sectors to generate employment, Chidambaram said, 'it will help to boost confidence in the youth'.[29] Indeed, he added, 'I will personally monitor the PMRP every week and will try to visit the State every month.'

The problem of policing had by now become formidable. Omar's overhaul of the state police in June, under which police officers would be posted to their home districts, met with great resentment. Policemen felt, justifiably, that it would expose their families to harassment and even mob fury, and several refused to serve where their families lived. They were also infuriated by orders to display restraint when facing young stone-throwers—already, over 1,000 policemen had been injured, some with broken jaws and limbs. 'I don't want a posting in the present environment where authorities stop us from using force against the protesters who can even lynch us,' a police officer told the *Times of India*.[30] The Omar administration and union Home Ministry overcame what might have become a police revolt by leaving it to the director general of police to decide arrest and response policies. While this abnegation did nip a potential revolt in the bud, complaints of police excesses abounded.

I visited Srinagar in July on a civil society mission with Jawaharlal Nehru University Professor Amitabh Mattoo and retired Vice Admiral K. K. Nayyar. We were startled by the seeming lack of response from Delhi as clashes mounted and, inexorably, more and more young men died. The many civil society engagements between Delhi and Kashmir that had been so evident during the early 2000s appeared to have faded away by 2009–10 and we hoped there might be some scope to bridge the ensuing gulf. While in Srinagar, we met Geelani, who had been placed under arrest at the VIP Chashmashi detention house. In a room decorated with red plush sofas, Geelani repeated his discomfort with stoning and we asked him whether he would make a public appeal to youth to desist when released. He said yes.

Geelani had distanced himself from the Shopian stoning agitation of 2009 and was criticized by Asiya Andrabi, the firebrand Islamist leader of the Dukhtaran-e-Millat (the women's organization that had sought imposition of the burkha in the 1990s). 'I don't think that he did what he was supposed to do as a leader,' she said in 2009. In February 2010, stone-throwers protesting the death of Wamiq Farooq 'lashed out' at Geelani and Mirwaiz Umar for 'leading a lavish lifestyle at the expense of the people'. In June, Geelani remonstrated that 'stones were being hurled "on ambulances, local transport and common people". Even if stone-throwing was legitimate "when used for self-defence against the police and Indian occupation forces",' he said, it had 'no justification if it is done for the sake of fun (sic)'.[31]

Geelani was true to his word; he did appeal for an end to stoning when he was released soon after our meeting. His appeal had a limited impact, mostly on his own supporters within the Tehreek, but it was important at a time when the state's chief opposition party, the PDP, was unwilling to speak out against stoning. PDP president Mehbooba Mufti was vocal in condemning arrests, but not so much on the methods of the protesters. 'The incompetence and ineptitude of the coalition government has resulted in the squeeze of political space and reversal of the democratization process in the state,' she said.[32] When Omar called an all-party meeting in early July to discuss how to handle stoning protests, Mehbooba refused to attend, though both Singh and Chidambaram phoned her to urge participation. Instead, she held a press conference to announce, 'I thank the Prime Minister and Home Minister for having called me. But I expressed my inability to take part.'[33] Clearly, she aimed to derive political advantage by showing she could resist the powerful union government, though boycotting a crisis meeting was a debatable means of conveying the message.

Yet, Mehbooba's criticism of the Omar administration did have a point. Her father, Mufti Sayeed, had made engagement with civil society and local leaders a key plank of his peacemaking strategy and she herself had authored the policy of a 'healing touch' in which she visited the families of guerrillas who were killed in battle with the army. The Omar administration did not engage with civil society or local leaders in the same way as had Mufti, nor did they continue Mehbooba's healing touch. Nevertheless, she and her party leaders could certainly have helped them to calm the situation, even if only to a limited extent. The most intense stoning was in the PDP-dominated areas of south Kashmir.

By end-August, spiralling violence had drawn a mounting volume of public criticism, as well as fear that the valley was lost to India. Intellectuals such as the policy analyst Pratap Bhanu Mehta and journalist Vir Sanghvi called for the government to agree to independence for the valley since India had lost all moral credibility in Kashmir. Visiting Srinagar in early September, the Hindu reformer and civil society activist, Swami Agnivesh, observed that 'the alienation of people had touched new heights. People were not for Pakistan, but they surely talk about "Azaadi".' He added that 'the situation immediately needs a human touch though the problem is of a political nature. But the wounds inflicted on the people here are deep and need healing.'[34]

In mid-September, Singh called an all-party meeting to discuss ways to end the standoff in the valley, and a few days later, Chidambaram led a thirty-nine-member all-party delegation to Kashmir. Though the Hurriyat refused the delegation's invitation to meet with them, they sent a memorandum to its members. Quoting Nehru's 1952 speech to the Indian parliament that his government would not keep the people of Kashmir 'against their will, however painful it may be to us', the memorandum restated the four issues on which the Hurriyat had begun dialogue with the union government in 2002—revocation of draconian laws, release of political prisoners, withdrawal of troops and zero tolerance for human rights violations—and said that 'these suggestions were not taken seriously'.[35] The delegation, said the Hurriyat, should 'establish and empower an official body, a Kashmir Committee, consisting of senior representatives of all major Indian political parties, to develop and enter into a process of engagement with the representatives of the people of Jammu and Kashmir'. For their part, the Hurriyat would persuade the Pakistani government to set up a similar committee of Pakistani parliamentarians to engage with their Indian counterparts and Kashmiri representatives.

Despite the Hurriyat's refusal to meet the delegation, a group of five MPs, which included CPI-M's Sitaram Yechury, T. R. Baalu of the DMK (Dravida Munnetra Kazhagam) and Asaduddin Owaisi of the All India Majlis-e-Ittehadul Muslimeen, went to meet Geelani, Mirwaiz Umar and Yasin Malik at their residences.

In late September, a week after the all-party delegation's visit, Chidambaram unveiled an eight-point programme to restore some degree of confidence in the valley, repeating his 2009 remark that 'Jammu and Kashmir has a unique geographical identity and a unique history'[36] and hence required a unique solution. The Singh administration would, he said:

1. Appoint a group of interlocutors to begin sustained dialogue with political parties and dissident groups, youth and student organizations, civil society organizations and other stakeholders.
2. Advise the state government to immediately release all students and youth detained or arrested for stone-pelting or similar violations of law and withdraw charges against them.
3. Advise the state government to immediately review the cases of all PSA detainees and withdraw detention orders where appropriate.
4. Request the state government to dismantle bunkers and checkposts that were no longer necessary in Srinagar and other towns—a process that began under Azad in 2006 but had barely progressed since—as well as to consider

whether the 'disturbed areas' ordinance could be lifted from selected areas of the state.
5. Grant ex gratia 'relief' to the families of those killed in the clashes since 11 June 2010 at ₹5 lakh [500,000] each.
6. Appoint two Special Task Forces, one each for Jammu and Ladakh regions, to examine their developmental needs and make suitable recommendations.
7. Request the state government to reopen all schools, colleges, universities and other educational institutions; hold special classes, if necessary; and ensure examinations for the academic year 2010–11 were conducted.
8. Provide the state government ₹100 crore [1 billion] as additional central assistance for schools and colleges to augment their infrastructure.

At the same time, the JKLF issued a press statement criticizing Pakistani guerrillas, especially those belonging to the Jamaat-ud-Dawa, for 'hijacking' the Kashmiri cause and seeking to subvert 'the indigenous movement'. The Jamaat-ud-Dawa had just launched a three-day 'mass contact drive' across Pakistan-administered Kashmir to 'raise awareness about the latest agitation in Indian-administered Kashmir'.[37] According to the organization's spokesman, 3,500 people had joined their campaign. Observers said they were mostly non-Kashmiri.

Chapter XIX

'TALKING TO THE PEOPLE'

Whether likely or unlikely, you have been made part of history by assigning you the role of an interlocutor to Kashmir. I don't have any brave offers to offer but I would like to know from you that in between the competing expectations of the Indian state on one hand and to some extent of the people of Kashmir on the other where do you place yourself as an interlocutor, as an Indian and as a human. Because sometimes at the end of day one realizes that I could have served the purpose in a better way had I done this and that thing?

Facebook message, November 2010

In October 2010, Dileep Padgaonkar, M. M. Ansari and I were appointed to the Government of India's Group of Interlocutors for Jammu and Kashmir. Our appointment came as a surprise to us as well as others. It was the first time the Indian government had appointed a group of people rather than a single interlocutor. It was also the first time that non-government people were appointed to such a mission. Previous interlocutors had been retired government officers or politicians.

At first it seemed as if the Indian government may also appoint a senior politician to lead our team, perhaps one of the members of the all-party delegation. In Srinagar, the immediate reaction to our appointment was one of dismay. Mehbooba Mufti called the appointment a dampener. 'It is more or less a useless exercise,' she said. Geelani predictably called the appointment of interlocutors an 'exercise in futility'.[1] People's Conference chief Sajad Gani Lone said our appointment was 'insulting' to the people of Kashmir. More soberly, Mirwaiz Umar commented that 'a Parliamentary panel, representing all shades of opinion, would have been a [more] appropriate forum for reaching out to [the] people of Kashmir'.[2] To the Hurriyat's long-standing position of refusing to have talks with interlocutors was added another grievance: they had suggested a group of parliamentarians and we were not. The only one of the pro-independence leaders to reserve comment was Yasin Malik.

Noting these reactions, Chief Minister Omar Abdullah flew to Delhi to urge Chidambaram to appoint a senior parliamentarian to lead our team.[3] I was in favour of his proposal; the inclusion would bring parliament to a more regular and direct role, something that had been missing in previous missions. I also hoped that Wajahat Habibullah, who had unofficially facilitated backchannel talks between the Omar administration and the JKLF in 2009–10, might join our team. The union Home Ministry, however, decided to keep the team to us three, with Dileep Padgaonkar, who had been editor of the *Times of India*, as chairman. It seems the Congress leadership was divided on whether or not to appoint a senior political leader. The team would report to Home Minister Chidambaram and they doubted whether a seasoned parliamentarian, including from within their own ranks, would be happy reporting to anyone but the prime minister.[4]

The Kashmir reactions were certainly a dampener for us, to use Mehbooba Mufti's term. Yet our brief was political and it was wide. According to the Home Ministry's official announcement of our appointment, we were 'entrusted with the responsibility of undertaking a sustained dialogue with the people of Jammu and Kashmir to understand their problems and chart a course for the future'.[5] Our terms of reference were to 'hold talks with all shades of opinion including…separatists and other stakeholders in all the three regions—Jammu, Ladakh and Kashmir'. Chidambaram further clarified that there were 'no red lines' on whom we talked to and our 'main brief' was 'to chart a course towards a political solution. All the rest is in aid of a political solution,' he added, referring to CBMs we might recommend.[6]

Unofficially, we also sought and got Prime Minister Singh and

Congress president Sonia Gandhi's approval to engage Pakistani opinion-makers and cross-border representatives of Pakistan-administered Kashmir and Gilgit-Baltistan. Additionally, we sought appointments with the BJP leadership but only got these after six months. When Padgaonkar announced that we would be talking to Pakistanis and cross-border representatives, the BJP's hackles rose, both nationally and in Jammu. We were giving Pakistan a role in Jammu and Kashmir, they said. 'What was the Pakistan dimension?' BJP General Secretary Nirmala Sitharaman asked.[7] Were we interlocutors exceeding our brief?

The argument was puzzling. The Indian parliament's 1994 resolution asserted that the Pakistan-administered portions of the former princely state belonged to India. Our talking to them was an extension of that resolution. As for talking to Pakistanis, their officials did not recognize our mission and civil society appeared largely unaware, except for the representatives of Pakistan-administered Kashmir, Gilgit and Baltistan, many of whom did engage with us quietly. Successive Indian governments had talked to their Pakistani counterparts about Jammu and Kashmir from 1948 on, including the BJP-led Vajpayee administration. In fact, the Singh administration also sought to revive official talks with Pakistan, including on Jammu and Kashmir, while our mission was underway. Three rounds of quiet talks were held between Indian envoy Satinder Lambah and Pakistani envoy Riaz Khan, a former foreign secretary.[8] In other words, our group would talk to cross-border Kashmiris, whom our Parliament saw as part of India, Indian officials would talk to their Pakistani counterparts. The BJP's opposition, however, ruled out our even requesting visas to visit Pakistan-administered Kashmir, Gilgit and Baltistan. Though the request would have been denied, it would have at least put some pressure on the Pakistani government to recognize India's peace initiative.

For its part, the Singh administration hoped to revive the three-pronged talks framework that had been developed by Vajpayee and Sayeed—with one difference. There would be talks between the governments of India and Pakistan, matched by Kashmir-specific

CBMs, but instead of a government–Hurriyat track, there would be a wider set of discussions with representatives of the state, including the Hurriyat, by a group of interlocutors.

The strategy was intended to protect the Hurriyat, not undercut it. After the attempted assassination of Fazal Haq Qureshi, restarting the Chidambaram–Hurriyat quiet dialogue was too dangerous. Equally, public Indian government–Hurriyat talks were too politically risky in the wake of the 2010 clashes and Singh's faltering second term, in which the opposition appeared to have an upper hand. Both sides would be pressured to draw red lines by the prevailing fragility of the situation in the state as well as at the centre. Our mission was, therefore, to establish conditions under which it would be relatively safe for the Hurriyat to engage in substantive talks with the union government.

Before making our first visit to the state, we had extensive discussions on how we would approach the mission amongst ourselves as well as with Home Minister Chidambaram, Home Secretary Gopal Pillai and our Home Ministry point person K. Skandan. Our work would be step by step: we would visit the state every month and give the ministry monthly reports with recommendations that would be both for CBMs and towards a political resolution. The ministry would act in real time on some if not all of the CBMs we recommended, so that at the end of a year, when we presented the Home Ministry with a final report, the ground would have been set for next steps towards a political resolution.

We agreed with Mirwaiz Umar's statement that '[s]tep one is that the ground realities should change first'.[9] Indeed, Chidambaram's eight-point programme and Omar had already mentioned some of the steps to be immediately taken. Geelani's 'five points' also overlapped to some extent; the release of political prisoners had been discussed between the Vajpayee administration and the Hurriyat and was an issue to be taken forward, as was an end to human rights violations. While there was no question of withdrawal of armed forces from the state, redeployment out of thickly populated areas and troops' reduction following a security assessment were already sought by the state government.

Within the army, too, a 'hearts-and-minds' approach had gained salience. Speaking to journalists in December, the new GOC (general officer commanding) of the army's 15 Corps, which oversaw security in the valley, Lieutenant General S. A. Hasnain, said he was 'looking at a long-term perspective where [the] Army can assist the State administration and the Government in reaching out to the people by putting a balm on [their] wounds', a phrase that Mehbooba Mufti had used during the Sayeed administration. 'Our main weapon is our heart,' Hasnain added.[10]

The Machil investigation also indicated that the army was following up on punishment for the killing of civilians. This time, Hasnain told us, the evidence appeared to clearly indict the four accused troops. In fact, over 100 troops had already been courtmartialled in the twenty years of conflict in Kashmir, with varying sentences.[11] This information was not publicized because the army feared it could lead to a loss of morale. But because punishment for violations was kept quiet, it allowed the conclusion that the army covered up violations by its own, which certainly occurred, especially in the insurgent decade of the 1990s. The most infamous example was that of Major Avtar Singh, who was accused in the murder of human rights activist Jalil Andrabi and implicated in at least four unsolved 'disappearances' in 1996–97.[12] He fled to the US and committed suicide in California in 2012, after killing his wife and daughter.

As to Kashmir's 'being accepted as a dispute', Padgaonkar had already used the term in interviews with the press, though Geelani probably meant it as a code for acting on the 1949 UN plebiscite resolution that was non-binding, which Padgaonkar did not. A week earlier, Ghani Bhat's Muslim Conference, a member of the Hurriyat's Executive Council, had stated that 'the UN resolution testifies that Kashmir is a dispute. Unfortunately, its implementation has been made conditional and seems unlikely at this stage. Therefore, the issue should be resolved through negotiations.'[13] No Hurriyat member had previously clarified that the UN's plebiscite resolution was conditional. Though Bhat did not elucidate—it was Pakistan that rejected the UN's conditions—his statement recognized that the UN resolutions were no longer the basis for a peace agreement.

We decided that priority CBMs—release of stone-throwers and political prisoners, along with human rights improvement—would be high on our agenda. Despite this messaging, we knew pro-Pakistan and pro-independence groups were unlikely to send us a delegation or receive us in their homes or offices. Though Padgaonkar and I knew most of the dissident leaders through our previous Track II engagements, this did not work in our favour once we had become official. As Yasin Malik of the JKLF said later, 'One of them was my friend, but I could not meet the group.' For the dissident leaders, we would have to find a different strategy.

On our first visit, therefore, we visited the Srinagar Central Jail and Shopian, as well as following the established schedule of meeting political parties and sectoral groups. Our Shopian visit was intensely painful. The town was silent and brooding, with only a few people to be seen. The husband of one and father of both murdered girls accepted our condolences with a single message for us: troops should be withdrawn from Shopian. They believed that two army men had raped and killed the girls; we heard from others that the murders were organized by an errant policeman and there was no medical evidence of rape. Whatever the truth, it was not an issue to debate with the bereaved, and Padgaonkar promised to raise their demand with the chief minister as well as with the union Home Ministry.

As we left Shopian, we noticed that the junction roundabout had army encampments on three sides. Clearly, it was unnecessary to have three where one would have sufficed—their presence was obtrusive. Equally clearly, there were three only because the army was working on poor resources, erecting basic structures that required large tracts of land rather than modern and fortified structures that would economize on space. In our report for that month we suggested that security experts examine the potential to reduce army encampments from three to one at Shopian. We later expanded this recommendation in our final report.

Our visit to the Srinagar jail was more substantive. After we had discussed the release of stone-throwers with the jail superintendent, it was suggested we talk to the Hizbul and other guerrillas who were in the prison to probe whether there was scope to renew the 2001 ceasefire. It was taken for granted that they still exerted influence, even from inside the jail. A meeting was fixed for the next day. Ushered into a large cell, we were surprised to find around seventy prisoners waiting for us. To our even greater surprise, most of them—even those who were imprisoned as Hizbul—told us that they belonged to the Lashkar-e-Taiba. The earlier, bitterly violent, rivalry between the two militias appeared to have ended, at least in prison. Or perhaps their announcement, made somewhat defiantly, was intended to provoke us. If true, the former was a warning development for the Indian and state governments, indicating that the line between foreign (aka Pakistani, with a sprinkling of Afghan) and local guerrillas had been erased.

When we began our discussion, it became clear that the guerrillas had already prepared for the meeting. Their spokesmen came quickly to the point. If they were able to convince their militias in the field to cease fire, would their releases be a quid pro quo, they asked. We were obviously not in a position to say yes or no, but we could certainly convey their proposal, Padgaonkar said, adding that they should firm it up and present us with a plan.

Leaving the cell after a two-hour-long discussion, we decided to keep the talks confidential, just in case the guerrillas' proposal did materialize. But when we exited the prison gates, we found a group of local journalists waiting for us. They had already received a statement from the prisoners that they would be submitting a 'peace plan' to us. I had heard how porous the Srinagar jail was, but the ease and speed with which prisoners could communicate with the media—and presumably anyone else with a cell phone, including guerrillas in hiding and maybe even cross-border agents in Pakistan—was still astonishing. Perhaps it was a continuation of the counter-insurgency 'listen in' policy during the Hazratbal siege that Habibullah had described.

There was an immediate uproar at the news of our jail discussion. Why were the interlocutors talking to terrorists, the BJP clamoured, and television channels echoed their accusations.[14] In Jammu, there were demonstrations denouncing us. In fact, the Home Ministry and state government had cleared our meeting, and state intelligence officials accompanied us. And the terrorists were behind bars.

Within days of the BJP's clamour, the Pakistan-backed United Jihad Council followed suit. 'Having failed to garner support and endorsement from Kashmiris, New Delhi's interlocutors have taken undue advantage of the helplessness of detained militants in an unsuccessful bid to prop up their falling credibility,'[15] the council's spokesman, Sadaqat Hussain, said. 'The detained militants are at the mercy of the usurping enemy, and have been condemned to a struggle of life and death. The peace plan claim has been thrust on the heads of these helpless people under a planned conspiracy.' In Srinagar, Geelani called for a boycott of us.[16]

The Jihad Council's statement indicated that the prisoners' ceasefire proposal was local in origin, not cross-border. It might have reflected exhaustion from the field, just as Majid Dar's offer had ten years earlier. Terrorist attacks in the state had continued to decline and the army's counter-insurgency had grown far more successful at targeting terrorists and keeping civilians out of crossfire. There was little overall support for guerrillas, whose sources of local shelter and sustenance had shrunk enormously from 2008 on. Total casualties had fallen to 375 in 2009 and remained at that figure in 2010, declining to 183 in 2011. Civilian casualties were below 50, but did not include those who died in stoning protests. When added, civilian deaths due to the conflict were 170 in 2010–11.[17]

Despite these signs of diminishing violence, the clamour in Jammu and Delhi made it impossible for us to probe the prisoners' offer further. In any case, as I argued and my colleagues reluctantly agreed, we were not the right people to do any further probing. The Indian and state governments had seasoned ceasefire negotiators; we had no experience. Besides, the guerrillas' press release and resultant publicity made any follow-up by us impossible.

Though our Srinagar jail discussion proved stillborn, its impact in the valley was considerable. The home minister, people began to feel, may have been serious when he said there were no red lines on whom we could talk to. It helped too that we defended the decision to hold a discussion with guerrilla prisoners without either claiming it as a victory or disclaiming it as never having taken the shape it did. Slowly, the tide against us in the valley began to turn.

Despite this small and struggling shoot of opportunity, the hostility towards us in Jammu and Delhi continued to remain high. When Padgaonkar, a former newsman, organized a closed-door and off-the-record session with the national and state media in Srinagar, excerpts of our discussion were leaked by the correspondent of a leading English daily. I had, he insinuated, advocated amendment of the Indian Constitution to accommodate pro-independence views.[18] My remarks were actually in answer to a question about whether our talks would be 'within the framework of the Constitution', a statement I considered fatuous, since Indian peace agreements—on Nagaland or on Jammu and Kashmir—had been ratified by the insertion of new articles in our Constitution. If and when a permanent peace agreement was reached on Jammu and Kashmir, it would have to be included in our Constitution, whether by upholding Article 370, or amending it.

Padgaonkar, meanwhile, was castigated for inviting students of Kashmir University, with whom we had held a round table as part of our outreach to youth, to flesh out their demand for azaadi in terms of what it should comprise and its feasibility. It was again an innocuous invitation; though he said we would be prepared to discuss any idea that was developed and argued across a table, it was also obvious that we were not going to spend a great deal of time discussing student essays. The headlines, however, thundered: 'Interlocutors now talk of azaadi',[19] as if a professorial call for papers would alter government decision-making.

These onslaughts forced us to change our strategy. Our initial focus had been to woo the alienated. The jail discussion was only one element of this strategy. The most important task was to secure the release of stone-throwers, beginning with first-time offenders, and those political prisoners who were not accused of heinous crimes such as murder. Alongside, there was the issue of unresolved human rights abuses, such as whether and which youth disappearances were forced and which were voluntary (those who had crossed to the Pakistan-held territories of the former princely state for guerrilla training).

◆

To:
Srimati Radha Kumar
Interlocutor

24.11.2010

Respected Radha Kumar ji,

My son, Mushtaq Ahmed [name changed], was picked up by the police on October 29 for stone-pelting. He is being held at the [name deleted] police station. My family and I visit the police station every day but we are not allowed to meet him. The SHO [station house officer] is demanding we pay ₹5,000 to see him and also ₹15,000 to get him released on bail. They do not give any date for his court appearance.

My son is only 15 years of age. He is our only son. He is innocent. We are sure he is being put in a false case. He was just picked up by the police on his way home from the market.

I request you to see into his case. We are in great mental anguish. My wife has not slept since his arrest, she keeps on crying and fearing he is being tortured. We do not know what to do or whom to go. I am a poor man, there is nobody to help us. You please try what you can—please speak to the Honourable Home Minister.

Waiting anxiously for your reply,

Yours sincerely,
Bashir Ahmed [name changed]
Anantnag [town changed]

I received dozens of such letters between October and December 2010. My colleagues had asked me to deal with human rights issues, perhaps knowing what a complex and thankless task it would be. Though I requested a list of youth detained by the state government during the recent unrest and those who were still under detention, I did not receive one. Instead, parents began to write to me with individual complaints. Follow-up entailed endless file-pushing, not to mention liaising, with the police and families at various levels to ensure that action was taken. By the end of November, I had only succeeded in ensuring thirty releases, and we turned to the union Home Ministry to push for overall releases of first-time offenders rather than case-by-case recommendations from us. Eventually, we were informed in late December that all but 50 of the 3,000 arrested stone-throwers had been released,[20] and in February 2011 Omar announced that thirty-nine security bunkers had been removed from crowded urban areas in valley towns.[21] Though it seemed like a long time then, it is to the credit of the state and central police that so many releases and removal of bunkers were achieved in three months. By contrast, the removal of fortified police stations took years in Northern Ireland.

Arrests, however, continued. Though stoning protests were by now much reduced, they were still frequent in areas such as Baramulla, Pattan and Shopian. The state police, who had begun to video protests to identify the ringleaders, also continued to arrest as their recordings were processed. A general amnesty was finally declared on Eid 2011, but only after our mission had ended.

Among the political prisoners that the union and state governments agreed to release were Naeem Khan, Shabir Shah and Abdul Qayoom, then president of the Kashmir Bar Association. We had met Shah in Jammu's Kot Balwal prison, but not the other two. Though we had recommended the three names, the terms of their release were negotiated by the state government, not us.

Some of the steps we took were clearly going too far for our critics, while others saw them as too small. Our visit to the office of the Association of Parents of Disappeared Persons

(APDP), for example, ended up counterproductive. Just as our jail discussion aroused the ire of the Jihad Council, so did this visit. The impressive head of the parents' group, Parveena Ahangar, showed us painstaking work tracing close to 130 disappearances that the state government had not followed up on. She mentioned there were over 8,000 complaints of disappearances that her group had not been able to verify in detail. This disclosure was treated as if she had cast doubt on the complaints, which she had not. There were articles in the local media decrying her meeting with us and she subsequently disclaimed our discussion.

A year later, while submitting their research to the state Human Rights Commission, the association's spokesman Yasin-ul-Hassan Malik announced that 'according to the documented findings, out of 132 disappearance cases, 21 have been perpetrated by the Army, 24 by different militant groups and one by the personnel of Jammu and Kashmir Police'. In 43 cases, he added, 'perpetrators were unidentified gunmen', and in the remaining 43 cases, victims 'disappeared under unknown circumstances'. Reporting the association's submission, *The Hindu*'s correspondent commented, 'for the first time in the two-decades-long turmoil in Jammu and Kashmir, a valley-based human rights group has admitted that militants were responsible for more enforced disappearances than security forces'.[22]

Despite our setback with the association, the Hurriyat began to come under pressure from local media who asked them as assiduously as they asked us, why we were not meeting. Partly under this pressure, the Hurriyat, JKLF and Tehreek leaders said they would engage with Indian civil society groups and parliamentarians, but not with government representatives or appointees. Their efforts to engage with civil society met with attack. In October 2010, while we were on our first visit to the state, Geelani was manhandled while addressing a seminar in Delhi provocatively titled 'Azaadi—the Only Way'. He was later charged with sedition, but the case was not prosecuted.[23] In November, Mirwaiz Umar was similarly manhandled at a seminar in Chandigarh.[24] In February 2011, Yasin Malik was attacked by members of the BJP youth wing, Bharatiya Janata Yuva Morcha, at Ajmer, where he had gone to worship at the Chishti shrine.

In view of Jammu and Delhi's hostility, as well as lack of response from the Hurriyat and JKLF, we decided to focus on the second prong of our strategy, to hold consultations in each district of the state. We did not want to sit in a government office and receive Kashmiri delegations, we told the Home Ministry and the state government. Rather, we would hold district and public meetings with local leaders and civil society.

Our visits were arranged by the state government, but I was also able to draw on my civil society friends from previous Track II work to ensure that we met local leaders. We went to the higher altitude districts first, before the onset of winter made visiting difficult if not impossible. By end-November, we had visited Anantnag, Baramulla, Bandipora, Uri, Leh, Kargil and Jammu as well as Srinagar (the latter two cities several times). Though each revealed differing priorities, common strands emerged. In Jammu province and Ladakh, the chief issues were economic development and political devolution within the state. In the valley, the chief issues were human rights, an end to violence, political status vis-à-vis India and economic development. With some give and take, these priorities could be incorporated into an overarching structure.

Our dilemma in the valley was how to balance immediate needs that would calm the situation with longer-term solutions. Everyone we met expressed a burning desire for us to recognize the suffering of people, and each of our meetings started with an explosion of anger by participants, as did the phone calls I received from Kashmiris across the valley, as many as forty a day, starting at 7 a.m. and ending at midnight. I often felt that we were sponges to absorb hate—a necessary but gruelling task. At the same time, it became clear that most of the valley supported four priority CBMs: release of young stone-throwers, easing restrictions on movement, addressing the aspirations of youth, and putting in place a responsive and effective public grievance redressal machinery. Most of our interlocutors stressed that implementation of these four CBMs would act as game changers.

While some of these points overlapped with our early priorities, others did not. The release of political prisoners (from the Hurriyat, Tehreek and other dissident groups), for example, was not high on the majority agenda. It was not regarded as an immediate CBM, though most people we met in the valley agreed that the dissident groups would have to be on board any lasting settlement. Talks with the Hurriyat, therefore, would have to be a part of any dialogue framework. Engagement with youth, by contrast, was an essential element of both CBMs and a sustainable peace process.

In the same months, I opened a Facebook page to interact with Kashmiris on social media. Within a week, over 5,000 people signed up to the page, mostly youth. Initially, our discussions worked well. Beginning with questions about the Indian government's sincerity in solving the Kashmir problem, one Facebook post commented: 'Peace is to be brought by way of peace only and no economic package or change of political dispensation is ever going to make up for the same.'[25] Another said that peace was an 'assiduous exercise, rather, a process'. Several agreed that peacemaking was a hard, slow and painful task, in which they would willingly join. Sadly, the conversation soon degenerated into abusive exchanges between pro- and anti-independence supporters, most of whom I suspect were trolls.

Our visits were coordinated by the state government and we met with Chief Minister Omar Abdullah every month and Governor Vohra when he was available (he toured the state frequently). The Omar administration was also deeply committed to reviving earlier peacebuilding strategies that had been poorly implemented or allowed to lapse, such as the rehabilitation of surrendered guerrillas under the policy of disarmament, disbanding and reintegration (DDR) of non-state militias. Classically, DDR is an arm of security reforms, whose other arm is military de-escalation, troops' reduction and, ultimately, demilitarization. Normally, DDR either precedes troops' reduction and allied security reforms or goes hand in hand with it, but in Jammu and Kashmir, the two strategies have rarely been coordinated.

In December 2010, as a confidence-booster to keep former guerrillas from rejoining their militias, Omar announced what the media called a 'new package for surrendered militants'.[26] Under the package, if a former guerrilla was killed by another guerrilla—as several thousand had been—his kin would be entitled to an ex gratia payment by the government and also to government employment. Previously, such compensation was offered only to the families of civilians who had been killed by guerrillas. As I discovered some months later, former guerrillas who had surrendered under a government reintegration programme had begun to complain that they were being threatened by radical youth.

Surrender and rehabilitation policies were first introduced in the 1990s, when Dulat was posted in the state. A number of guerrillas had made individual agreements under Dulat's policy. Several of them, in fact, set up newspapers with government aid as part of their rehabilitation. These newspapers went on to form the core of the valley's independent media.

Former guerrillas who had successfully reintegrated were, however, the minority. In spring 2011, a group of ex-guerrillas sought a closed-door and unrecorded meeting with us. None of the state government's rehabilitation policies were being implemented, they complained, whether previous or current. Sayeed had said they 'would be able to lead a normal life', their spokesman pointed out.[27] 'Three regimes, since then, changed, but our plight has only added to further dimensions.' When they applied for jobs, they 'were asked to get No Objection Certificates from [the] police department', he explained. But the police said such certificates could only be supplied after pending cases against them had been adjudicated. Yet, they had surrendered under the government's pledge that charges against them would be quietly dropped.

They wanted to form a 'union' for former guerrillas, the spokesman added; this too the government refused to register.

The Dulat surrender and rehabilitation policy of the early 1990s was imaginative and did help to phase down insurgency. But the fact that it was not part of an overall peace settlement meant its application tended to be ad hoc. The policy may have contained conflict but it did not become a building block towards the larger goal of resolving conflict. More often than not, surrendering guerrillas were seen as being rewarded rather than rehabilitated, both in the state and the rest of India. When the new wave of protests started in 2008–09, they became obvious targets. Some had already returned to militancy, this time as hired guns who were willing 'to settle personal scores' for as little as ₹25,000 per kill.[28]

Omar's pursuit of a related CBM, the surrender and return of guerrillas who had crossed over to Pakistan to train, involved more complicated issues of national security. The policy had first been mooted in 2004 by the Sayeed administration, and the union and state governments had facilitated several dozen returns under conditions of strictly civilian rehabilitation. As a CBM, the policy foundered on the ISI's efforts to keep former guerrillas under their control and the state and Indian intelligence agencies' inability to plug the ISI's reach.

Omar proposed to revive the CBM by creating a legal framework for the return of former guerrillas. 'Several Kashmiri youth are coming back from PoK via Nepal or other routes, illegally crossing the border into Indian territory and landing up in police custody,' he said. 'We want to make the return of all such youth, who want to lead a normal life giving up violence, legal through the recently announced rehabilitation policy.'[29]

Under Omar's policy, former guerrillas who went to Pakistan-administered Kashmir or Pakistan between 1989 and 2009 would be eligible to return with their dependents. Their applications would first be cross-checked by district superintendents of police and then forwarded to the Central Intelligence Division, which would vet the applications for final clearance by the union Home Ministry. There would be three return routes: via the Wagah checkpost on the international border in Punjab, and the Salamabad and Chakan-Da-Bagh crossing points on the Line of Control. Returning guerrillas would spend three months at special counselling centres, and would not be entitled to benefits under the surrender and rehabilitation policy.[30]

The union Home Ministry was initially sympathetic to Omar's policy, urging the state government to expedite verification of applications since 'militants ready to join the mainstream should be given a chance on priority to return'.[31] Returns, the Omar administration hoped, would also clarify the issue of disappearances. Around 10,000 youth were reported to have disappeared, Omar said in 2011: 'Many of them may actually be living across the LoC.'[32] If they returned under his policy, it would 'address the grievance that all the disappeared people...vanished in the security forces custody'. A 2005 survey by the Sayeed administration had found that of 2,000 youth reported as having disappeared, 1,950 had crossed the Line of Control to Pakistan-administered Kashmir. What action was taken in the fifty cases that might have been custodial deaths was not reported by the Sayeed survey,[33] but in April 2011, the Jammu and Kashmir High Court ordered the Defence Ministry to pay compensation of ₹10 lakh (1 million) to the family of Mushtaq Dar, who had been taken into custody by the army's 20th Grenadiers in April 1997 and subsequently disappeared.

Six months into Omar's return policy, the rigorous process of screening applications had resulted in only a couple of dozen being cleared out of 600. Though the Singh administration was sympathetic, his own Congress party, under attack from the BJP for considering such an 'anti-national' policy, was lukewarm.[34]

The return of former guerrillas was always going to be fraught. While they had gone across voluntarily to wage war against India, Pandits who had been pushed out of the state were yet to return. Singh created a fund for Pandit returns under his Reconstruction Plan, but the Omar administration did not prepare a substantive policy for its application. By contrast, the Sayeed administration had announced Pandit returns as a priority and constructed transit accommodation for them (though Pandit returns were sluggish at best, comprising no more than two or three dozen). We also found that the issue of returns from across the Line of Control was not confined to guerrillas alone: displaced from Keran, Tithwal and Poonch during the wars, many Jammu residents had ended up in Poonch, Mirpur and Muzaffarabad, where they eked out their lives in camps. This forgotten issue, we said in our report, should be put front and centre in a returns policy.[35]

Justice was an issue too. The guerrillas had brutally murdered political activists and civilians whom they accused of being informers, not to mention bystanders who were caught in the crossfire, families who refused to provide shelter and food at gunpoint, girls who rejected their advances. They had targeted minorities such as Pandits and Sikhs. If justice was demanded against security forces' abuses, what about the non-state actors?

Justice has long been a casualty in insurgency and counter-insurgency the world over. The few efforts to reconcile demands for justice with the need for an end to conflict have had mixed results. In South Africa, the nobly intentioned Truth and Reconciliation Commission did help the transition out of apartheid, but put aside the issue of justice for all but the most heinous apartheid crimes. In Bosnia, the International War Crimes Tribunal focused on justice but put the issue of reconciliation aside, and the country continued to suffer from a de facto partition decades after the war ended.

In both South Africa and Bosnia, these initiatives took place after the end of conflict, not during it. Though Omar called for a Jammu and Kashmir Truth and Reconciliation Commission in 2011, his proposal was made during an ongoing conflict, not after it had ended. As a result, it remained a proposal with few takers.

Properly speaking, returns have the best chance of succeeding after a peace settlement, not before, whether they are of displaced people, refugees or former guerrillas. But in the endless stalemate of political resolution in Jammu and Kashmir, returns began to be seen as a peacebuilding step towards resolution. They continue to be a pending issue.

◆

Meantime, the old adage that too many cooks spoil the broth was proving to be true once again. Picking up on the Hurriyat's refusal to engage with us, a group of politicians who had been members of the all-party delegation announced that 'there was no forward movement on [the] Kashmir issue'.[36] Given the disappointing appointment of 'non-political interlocutors', they said, they would lead another delegation to Kashmir and perhaps form a separate panel. The delegation was drawn from communist and socialist parties and organized by an NGO, the Centre for Policy Analysis. It was led by Ram Vilas Paswan of the Janata Dal (United), a faction that had broken away from the Janata Dal of the 1990s. On their visit to Srinagar, the delegation met Geelani, Mirwaiz Umar and Malik.[37] Following these meetings, they suggested revocation of the PSA and selective withdrawal of the AFSPA. The latter was also sought by the state government while the former was not, though it was within the purview of the state legislature and had been widely used to arrest during the summer 2010 clashes.

We also continued to offend, adding new estrangements to old. In December, our monthly press release reported a trust deficit between the state government and valley residents, and urged serious effort to reduce it through transparent and accountable governance and due process of law. The release alienated many in the coalition government. The interlocutors were 'trying to divert attention', admonished senior National Conference leader and MP from south Kashmir, Mehboob Beg. 'Their efforts should have been directed at addressing the alienation instead of using the word trust deficit,' he added. 'Their mandate is to suggest ways for permanent political settlement—engaging Pakistan or initiating a meaningful dialogue. Criticizing the government, which faced [its] worst-ever five months, doesn't make any sense.'[38] Beg's irrepressible party colleague, Mustafa Kamal, Farooq Abdullah's younger brother, went a step further. '[The] Interlocutors are only creating confusion,' he accused.[39] 'Instead of meeting with representatives of [the] public, they are directly talking to the people.' Though the state Congress president, Saifuddin Soz, was guarded, journalists reported a senior Congress minister as saying we 'should deliver' on our mandate 'rather than raising [a] finger on the coalition's functioning'.[40] People's Democratic Front president, Hakeem Muhammad Yasin, added, 'accountability, transparency, building trust are things that can be taken care of once the bigger issue' of Jammu and Kashmir's political status was settled.

Common as Yasin's perception was, it misconstrued the situation. Trust-building through governance is widely understood today as paving the way for a durable peace settlement, one that can take hold on the ground. Institutional development is also now widely seen as critical to a successful transition to stability. In country after country, where destroyed institutions were not revived prior to a peace agreement, warlords and/or hardliners gained the upper hand in negotiations and grew to dominate public institutions. As a result, post-conflict stabilization failed.

In our meetings, the vast majority of delegations had expressed anger at administration—governance was universally seen to be a crying need even when they disagreed on political solutions. My Facebook page revealed the same conclusion. Of the thousands who wrote, all agreed that a more receptive and accountable administration was key. Protection of human rights followed a close second.

Since 2008, armed conflict had trickled to a near end and the state was well placed to embark on institutional reconstruction. It didn't happen, not because the Omar administration was ill-intentioned but because the union and state governments, along with their respective opposition parties, were unable to forge a collective approach. Within the state, political leaders feared for their lives. Close to 700 representatives and cadre of the National Conference and PDP had been killed by guerrillas between 1989 and 2010, with the National Conference bearing the brunt. One hundred had been killed in the run-up to the 2002 elections alone.[41]

Despite cross-purposes, the situation did improve on the ground. By late November, dissatisfaction with the Tehreek's 'protest calendar' started to be publicly expressed. Their strike calls began to be ignored by educational and government institutions as well as markets. Resentment against the calendar was openly voiced by shopkeepers, student groups and NGOs, and incidents of coercion began to surface. In December 2011, when a twenty-five-year old shopkeeper refused to shut down in a protest against the police's use of pepper spray, he was beaten to death by a mob of stone-throwers wielding cricket bats. Srinagar shut down against the murder.[42]

According to state estimates, Jammu and Kashmir's economy had suffered losses amounting to ₹27,000 crore (270 billion) due to the five months of protest in 2010. Industry groups put the figure at ₹40,000 crore (400 billion). Over 60,000 people, mostly youth, lost their jobs due to the fall in tourism, and around 200,000 labourers from UP, West Bengal, Punjab, Bihar and Orissa fled the valley fearing attack after stoning protests began.[43]

Seeing the public turning against the 'protest calendar', the United Jihad Council's titular head, Yusuf Shah, disclosed that he had opposed the frequent calls for shutdown as 'wrong policy and emotionalism' since 'no nation can remain dependent on constant strikes', which had 'diluted' the stoning agitation.[44] Instead, he urged, the Tehreek, Hurriyat, JKLF and allied dissident groups should jointly campaign for separation from India.

Yusuf Shah, I was told by various members of the state government, wanted to return to the valley and would be willing to aid peace negotiations if he were allowed back. The Omar administration raised the issue with the union Home Ministry, but then dropped it. We were not involved and I was not in favour, in any case. Shah's influence on the Hizbul or Jihad Council was debatable. His authority derived from the ISI, for whom he was a figurehead. The ISI's previous pretence of negotiation with Indian counterparts had resulted in Lone's assassination. There was no indication of a change in their approach.

♦

Our big breakthrough came in late December, two days before Christmas. Independent MLA Mohammad Rashid, who had formerly been a member of Sajad Lone's People's Conference, organized a large public meeting with us at Langate in Kupwara, at which over 500 participants took a pledge to refrain from stone-throwing if 'there was an assurance that the Indian government would move for a peaceful resolution of the Kashmir issue and protect human rights'. Asserting that they wanted to 'live a dignified and honourable life', speakers called for political space for non-violent protest. 'The men with guns in their hands should also be included in dialogue' for a lasting solution, Rashid urged.[45]

News of the pledge made headlines across Jammu and Kashmir. 'This is the biggest breakthrough since Vajpayee,' a Facebook user wrote to me. Even the BJP, which had revived its campaign to hoist the Indian flag in Lal Chowk, welcomed the pledge and flooded Rashid with congratulations on his initiative.

Though I urged that the prime minister or home minister respond to the pledge with a formal statement of welcome, repeating the government's commitment to protection of human rights, the response was lukewarm. I was puzzled, and remain so. Both had stated these commitments innumerable times. Was it that they did not want to be seen welcoming a pledge against what was in any case illegal? Or were they cautious about the maverick MLA Rashid, who had himself been pro-independence and may still be?

Slogans for independence resounded during the Kupwara meeting. Padgaonkar, who attended with me (Ansari had remained in Srinagar), was visibly uncomfortable. Though we both saw the significance of the meeting and indeed how subtly it redefined the azaadi or independence slogan, he was worried about the optics. He had been attacked for hearing students on azaadi at a closed-door meeting; how would the BJP react when we were televised listening to azaadi slogans? We were already so controversial that Chidambaram had been constrained to remark there should not be 'a ball by ball commentary' on our every doing.[46]

In fact, BJP leaders such as Sushma Swaraj, who had been a member of the all-party delegation, welcomed the pledge; indeed when we went to consult with the three BJP leaders, Swaraj, Advani and Jaitley, they all congratulated us on the Rashid initiative and advised us to focus on human rights in our report. The BJP might have been the only party to see how important the meeting was, both symbolically and in its potential ground impact. Since neither the prime minister nor the home minister responded with a statement along the lines that the meeting's participants sought, its impact fizzled out.

We continued to emphasize human rights and security reforms, but the fact that reforms were not tied to a specific peace initiative, such as talks with the Hurriyat or Rashid's public meeting, diluted their effect on the ground. Though we approached reforms as a basket of issues that would each strengthen the other, in practice they were undertaken in separate steps. For example, we recommended simultaneous action on two interconnected sets of issues, change in the security forces–citizen interface, and reforms in the justice system. On the first, we recommended minimizing security barriers and checkposts, use of least damaging methods of crowd control, including provision of non-lethal weapons, human rights training for police and paramilitary forces, and redeployment of troops out of heavily populated areas. These measures should be matched, we said, by better work conditions for security forces, such as troops' rotation every six or nine months instead of the prevailing eighteen months, more frequent leave periods and fortified barracks and vehicles. Recent reports showed that the paramilitary who were responsible for crowd control suffered such high stress that 215 troops killed themselves between 2007 and 2011. The paramilitary suicide rate in Kashmir was higher than in any other part of India.[47]

On reforms in the justice system, we suggested incorporating the Supreme Court guidelines for standard operating procedures into the AFSPA, setting up public grievance redressal cells in army encampments, amending the state's PSA to remove its sweeping powers of arrest and detention, and designating special areas for public protest, as in Delhi (which used to be Jantar Mantar but are now the Red Fort grounds). The state's Human Rights and Accountability Commissions, we said, should be empowered to take suo moto cognizance of human rights abuses, as happened in other Indian states.

In January 2011, Home Ministry officials told journalists that they had 'already initiated action on many of these recommendations'. A new set of standard operating procedures for non-lethal methods of crowd control had been drafted by a high-level committee, and the state government was working on 'a mechanism to check the harassment of civilians due to security curbs'.[48] In February, the union Home Ministry announced it was withdrawing another 10,000 paramilitary troops from Kashmir. Home Secretary Gopal Pillai said that 'proposals for amendments in the AFSPA were before the Cabinet Committee on Security',[49] but the state government could in any case decide on removal of the 'disturbed areas' designation from certain areas of Jammu and Kashmir. 'I think you can move forward and say some parts of Kashmir need not be declared disturbed.' Since AFSPA kicked in only when an area was pronounced disturbed by a state government in concurrence with the governor, removal of the designation would automatically revoke the application of AFSPA. In parallel, union minister Farooq Abdullah asked forgiveness for the ethnic cleansing of Kashmiri Pandits under his chief ministership during the 1990s, calling it 'the darkest chapter in the history of Jammu and Kashmir'.[50]

Both the army and state police launched recruitment drives at which record numbers of youth turned up—10,000 for the army recruitment and several hundred for the police drive in Srinagar, which was the first to be held in over a decade. In March, the army announced it had set up human rights cells, and gave out personal mobile numbers, asking residents 'to call any time of the day or night to register their complaint'.[51] The cells' officers, an army spokesman promised, would 'take instant action on the complaints'.[52] In August, three policemen accused of custodial death were suspended in Sopore.[53] Though sadly late in the day, the Delhi courts freed several wrongfully imprisoned Kashmiris, chastising the Delhi police for producing insufficient evidence for terrorism charges. One of the men who had been wrongly implicated was a local Youth Congress leader and historian, who fought his case without a lawyer.[54]

We had discovered that Kashmiri students who studied in other states were asked to register with the police and report at regular intervals to their local police station. This might have been convenient for the police but led to all sorts of harassment, including from landlords. In Mumbai, an unsigned notice had been issued to all police stations asking them to 'keep a close watch on Kashmiri people'. We asked that this requirement be withdrawn—it violated fundamental rights—and that police be asked instead to help Kashmiri students who might be harassed. We also asked Chidambaram to write to universities and colleges requesting them to ensure that Kashmiri students were not harassed on campus. In February, the Home Ministry issued an advisory to all states and union territories 'to issue appropriate instructions to all police stations that they (Kashmiris) should not be singled out unnecessarily for police reporting merely on grounds of their being original Kashmiri residents', and asked states and union territories to report back on action taken. 'The Indian Constitution and the law of the land does not permit discrimination on account of race, religion, caste and creed,' the advisory said.[55]

Some states did follow through on the Home Ministry's advisory—my Kashmiri former students in Delhi, for example, told me they were no longer required to report to the police—but others did not.

Other related issues came up too. In July 2011, at the request of the RSS's students' union, the Akhil Bharatiya Vidyarthi Parishad, the BJP-headed Madhya Pradesh state government altered rules of admission to allow only Kashmiri Pandits to take advantage of the quota for displaced students, though the union government had recommended priority admission for all displaced students from the state following the 2010 agitation. The issue was taken up by Omar, and the union government sought to compensate with scholarships.[56]

◆

The BJP leaders' praise for our breakthrough in Langate did not translate into support of our mission or even muting of the BJP's criticism of us. The interlocutors were 'working on an agenda of autonomy and self-rule', the BJP's state spokesman, Ramesh

Arora, accused, instead of considering 'the viewpoint of nationalist forces'.[57] He was certainly right insofar as we saw both the National Conference's autonomy report and the PDP's self-rule document as important responses under Article 370. But he was wrong to juxtapose the two documents to nationalism. As far as I was concerned, both supported constitutional provisions and by extension the principles on which independent India was founded, whereas the BJP's campaign to remove Article 370 and forcibly integrate Jammu and Kashmir violated the accession agreement, the Indian Constitution, and the Jammu and Kashmir constitution.

At the turn of the year, the party's announcement that it would repeat Advani's Ekta Yatra to hoist the Indian flag at Lal Chowk on 26 January, India's Republic Day, brought it to loggerheads with the state government. Fearing that the yatra could provoke renewed violence, the state and union governments pled with BJP leaders to attend the official flag hoisting in Srinagar instead. When the BJP refused, the Omar administration prohibited demonstrations in Srinagar on Republic Day and arrested half a dozen BJP cadres. An angry Advani denounced the Omar administration, saying the yatris were 'challenging the separatists' whereas 'the State [was] surrendering to them'.[58] When the BJP persisted with the yatra, the state government sealed the state borders and arrested BJP leaders Sushma Swaraj and Arun Jaitley at Jammu airport, taking them back over the border to Punjab. Though the JKLF's Yasin Malik and the Hurriyat's Shahidul Islam were also arrested when they tried to 'sneak in' to Lal Chowk to prevent the BJP's attempt at flag hoisting, political opinion against the BJP's yatra was united in the valley. The PDP too offered rare support to the Omar administration.[59]

For the first time, the BJP turned its attention to quieter work in the valley, setting up a Jammu Kashmir Study Centre under joint RSS–BJP patronage, headed by senior BJP leader Rajnath Singh. Singh visited the valley, and the study centre organized a conference in Srinagar that was small and low-key. Deplorably, we were not invited.

◆

Our district-by-district visits were organized as round table or town hall meetings. The tactic was deliberate. Previous interlocutors had received delegations one by one, in the routine pattern of government appointments. Unintentionally, in a conflict situation, this routine scheduling led to sectoral divisions and, more importantly, meant that groups with differing or antagonistic viewpoints did not have to share a table or hear each other. As a result, political discourse in the state was a cacophony of voices talking over each other but never to each other. We tried to break through this deadlock, and in some areas the approach worked. Commenting on our meeting in Bandipora, organized by PDP MLA Nizamuddin Bhatt with around fifty political leaders and intelligentsia, the newspaper *Rising Kashmir* said, 'Unlike past precedence, there was no one-to-one or secret conversation with any group as representatives of political parties, academicians, lawyers and senior citizens of the town talked in open air and called for resolution of the Kashmir issue.' Bhatt himself stressed that Kashmir was disputed, and 'the policy of PDP is obvious and the party wants the issue to be resolved politically and amicably'.[60]

In other areas, our tactic was less successful. At our town hall meeting in Uri, participants were divided between pro-dissident and pro-India groups and they almost came to blows. The meeting only settled after repeated calls for calm, and our insistence that all voices should be heard. In Baramulla, there was no public meeting at all. Stoning continued in the town and when we arrived there was an ongoing guerrilla–army shootout on the Baramulla Bridge. The district commissioner, who headed the Baramulla administration, was unwilling to organize any meetings for us. He could not guarantee our security, he said. That evening, the administrative officer who accompanied us to Baramulla quizzed me for several hours on what—if anything—the Indian government would 'give the Kashmiris'. Eventually he said, 'Well, if the Indian government ensures full and free cross-border trade and travel, I will be satisfied.' The next day we received half a dozen delegations, but had to meet them one by one.

My strongest memory of Baramulla is of the rats in the guesthouse. They were huge and so scary that I did not sleep all night but remained huddled on the bed with lights blazing and my boots and winter coat on. Months later, I saw equally large rats in the Anantnag guesthouse. They ran around the floor while the district collector briefed me; to my astonishment, he was not a whit disturbed. Ironically, both guesthouses had been newly renovated with plush furniture and coverings. They smelled of new paint with whiffs of rotting food.

While district hearings and consultations with political leaders formed the core of our mission, we identified three communities whose views were of special interest because they were critical for both peacemaking and peacebuilding: women, cultural groups and the intelligentsia. We held one- to two-day round tables with each of these communities. The round table with cultural groups provided a string of recommendations that would have gone a long way towards peacebuilding had they been implemented, which they were not. We had two purposes in organizing the women's round table: by and large, the issues that concerned women as victims of conflict had not been highlighted in government policies, either at the centre or the state administration; equally significantly, women had not been involved in any of the peace processes, though they were active in both politics and civil society.

I was surprised to discover that this was the first time that women legislators, members of government institutions and civil society activists had sat around a table. At one point, it looked as if the meeting might end in a walkout—some of the women activists said they could not sit at the same table as women legislators whom they accused of being complicit in the deaths of 120 youth during the stoning protests. Barely had I persuaded them that this was an opportunity to seek accountability and change, when the state Minister for Social Welfare, Sakina Itoo, who gave the keynote address, took exception to being questioned by one of the Islamists who attended the round table. Itoo, who was from Kulgam, had twice been attacked by armed Islamist guerrillas in attempts to assassinate her.

Despite such agonizing moments, the round table did engage in substantive discussion. Given the two decades of conflict, human rights were obviously a priority. Most Kashmiri participants demanded fresh enquiries into the alleged rapes in Kunan–Poshpora and Shopian. Some from Jammu raised the issue of rape by guerrillas. The bulk demanded that the Indian government set up a commission to look into disappearances. Though jobs were a secondary issue, it was also clear that the impact of conflict had put the onus on thousands of women to become sole breadwinners. Government employment programmes, such as sewing, provided only a bare income and there were few training programmes for women at higher levels of skill development.

A couple of participants criticized the round table for not including families who had lost their sons during the summer protests. We met them separately. Four women MPs who came from Delhi for the round table—three belonging to the ruling Congress party and one from the CPM—accompanied us to this meeting. It was heart-rending. What can you say to people who have lost their children in conflict? In Langate I could offer an apology as an Indian citizen: but an apology for the death of a child—of 120 children, in fact—was too little and surely would ring hollow. We could not even offer justice, since that was not within our power to ensure. I still feel shame when I think of that meeting.

The diminishing sex ratio in Jammu and Kashmir was a critical issue. Recently released census data revealed that the overall sex ratio in the valley had declined from 892 in 2001 to 889 in 2011. The child sex ratio had fallen from 941 per 1,000 boys in 2001 to 862 in 2011. The state's female literacy rate was also much lower than the rest of India, at 56.4 per cent.[61] The sex ratio figures were especially puzzling since prolonged conflict generally leaves more women than men. How had the reverse occurred in Kashmir? My own suspicion was that data collection in the state was severely flawed, but that suspicion will only be tested when the next census is done.

Though we flagged this concern at the round table, political issues took precedence. The Omar administration was more receptive. In May 2011, two months after our round table, he and his cabinet sought civil society support to campaign against female foeticide, which they saw as the chief cause of the declining sex ratio, probably erroneously, since neglect is a more frequent reason. Both the JKLF's Malik and the Hurriyat's Mirwaiz Umar joined the campaign. 'We will have to rise against this crime or else be ready not to be counted among civilized nations,' said Malik. 'Our religion has given respect to the girl child and our ulemas and religious heads must start a campaign for mass awareness against this evil [female foeticide],' added Mirwaiz Umar.[62]

◆

Despite the intimidating rats, most of our district meetings were productive. Across the valley, participants hammered a number of common points, some repeated over decades but imperfectly grasped, others continuously ignored.

Broadly, all the Muslim-majority areas of the state opposed any further division of Jammu and Kashmir. In other words, they were against the union territory status demanded by Buddhist-majority Leh and the Hindu-majority districts of Jammu province. In effect, one of two districts in Ladakh opposed the political aspirations of the other, as did seven of Jammu's ten districts. Any attempt to grant union territory demands would, thus, lead to communal conflict, especially in Jammu's mixed districts such as Doda (54 per cent Muslim and 46 per cent Hindu), Reasi (50 per cent Muslim and 49 per cent Hindu), Kishtwar (58 per cent Muslim and 41 per cent Hindu) and Ramban (71 per cent Muslim and 29 per cent Hindu).[63] Ladakh, with a culture of peaceful political resolution, might not suffer communal conflict since its two districts were high-majority and low-minority. But it might suffer division since Kargil was unlikely to opt for union territory status, which most in Leh demanded.

Despite the Muslim consensus against division, there were differing views on the state's political constitution. While there was support for pro-independence groups in several parts of the valley, there was broad agreement amongst the Muslims of Jammu and Kargil that neither independence nor further division was acceptable. In Poonch and Rajouri, for example, the delegations we met told us that they 'strongly rejected the concept of either "azaadi" or trifurcation of the state... [T]he accession of the state with India [was] final and [could not] be challenged.'[64] But then, Poonch had been divided between Indian Jammu and Kashmir and Pakistan-administered Kashmir since 1947, and bordering Rajouri had also suffered the fallout.

At the same time, we found that administrative devolution—self-governing institutions at the district level—was a cross-cutting issue for Muslims, Hindus and Sikhs throughout the state. Srinagar's track record of poor governance was resented by all, irrespective of religion. In several districts, in fact, delegations demanded that the Union Planning Commission should mark district-wise funds instead of leaving it to the state government to make budgetary allocations for the regions. Ladakh did receive direct funds from the union government as well as through the state budget, but the union funds were for border infrastructure. In Poonch and Rajouri, also border districts, most of the people we met looked to Ladakh as an example; not only did they want direct funding from the centre, they also wanted Hill Councils as had been set up in Leh and Kargil under the Sayeed administration.

Administrative devolution, many told us, offered a way out of conflicting aspirations. In Kargil, for example, it would avoid a tussle over union territory status. 'We also demanded creation of Ladakh division for better development in Leh and Kargil districts,' Asghar Karbalai, then head of Kargil's Imam Khomeini Trust, told journalists after meeting us. 'At the moment, there are only two provinces as per the State Constitution—Kashmir and Jammu.'[65] It would also help, he added, if one of the two parliamentarian seats allotted to Ladakh—in the Lok Sabha and the Rajya Sabha—was reserved for Leh and the other for Kargil.

By contrast in Jammu, the JKNPP, which had won three seats in the 2008 legislative assembly election, took devolution perilously close to division. Demanding reorganization of the state into three units, Jammu, Ladakh and Kashmir, with separate legislatures, budgets, administration and finances, JKNPP leader Bansi Lal Sharma called it 'a win-win situation for the stakeholders' of the state. 'Ladakh, Jammu and Kashmir have nothing in common in terms of culture, lifestyle, language, geographical area and historic identity.' JKNPP's 'new formula,' he added, 'will ensure end of inter-regional discrimination, equal development and will also strengthen communal harmony and regional cooperation'.[66]

Actually, geographic proximity, which was indeed a major influence, created different priorities at the district level. In all the Muslim-majority districts bordering Pakistan-administered Kashmir, residents supported cross-border trade and travel and sought further and upgraded facilities. At our town hall meeting in Uri, a representative of the traders' association suggested that 'instead of having a restricted number of items on the exchange list, trade should be free and all items should be allowed to be exported and imported'.[67] Similarly, in the Buddhist-majority district of Leh, former MP Pinto Norbu told us, there was considerable interest in opening up to Chinese Xinjiang as a trade route to Central Asia.

On the other hand, the residents of Hindu-majority districts and those bordering Pakistani Punjab sought security against cross-border shelling rather than porous borders. In their effort to communalize Jammu and Kashmir, Pakistan's army targeted the Hindu areas of Jammu across the international border and Line of Control, restricting their shelling of Muslim areas to a minimum. Predictably, the Pakistani government also sought to block Shia connectivity. Though they agreed to open the Srinagar–Muzaffarabad road as a peace process CBM, and grudgingly allowed the Poonch–Rawlakot road to be opened after the 2005 earthquake, they steadfastly refused to open the Kargil–Skardu route, though a large number of Balti-speaking Shia families had been divided by the 1949 war and division. 'We are not able to talk to our relatives in Gilgit and Baltistan,' said Karbalai, 'because the Pakistan government jammed their telecommunications.'[68]

Sadly, the experience of cross-border trade, which was a hallmark CBM of 2003–06, was mixed. When we visited the

Kaman Post on the Uri–Muzaffarabad border, we found an impressive infrastructure for travellers—with ID counters, ATMs, a waiting room and toilets—but not for goods. Trucks had to be checked manually, and the goods that were being traded, we were told, included chillies from Kerala and mangoes from Pakistani Punjab. The spirit of the CBM, which was to stimulate the state's economy by trading locally made products, stood in tatters. Instead, the CBM was used to evade customs and taxes, since inter-Kashmiri cross-border trade was exempted.

The misuse of the CBM did benefit local traders and by extension might have had a trickle-down effect on some sectors of the regional economy, albeit restricted to a very few. In 2017, the state government reported that trade across the Line of Control for the three years 2014-17 had reached the whopping figure of ₹2,800 crore (28 billion).[69] Yet its major impact was to fuel corruption, already rampant in the state. Added ills were that it was used to smuggle drugs and, in some cases, weapons. As trade based on barter and cash payments, a sizable portion of earnings was also funnelled into stoning protests, intelligence investigations found later.

In spring 2011, when an India–Pakistan dialogue resumed, the issue of upgraded infrastructure and regulation of trade across the Line of Control was top of the agenda. In August, the foreign secretaries of India and Pakistan agreed to improve facilities, including banking, and the Government of India proposed multi-entry permits for traders to travel across the Line of Control.

The obvious way to deter tax evasion on goods produced outside Kashmir was to regularize trade across the Line of Control. The issue became a priority but negotiations with Pakistan did not lead anywhere. Traders on both sides, always a powerful lobby, were implacably opposed to regularization. It would entail paying customs and tax duties. In 2017, the Modi administration suspended trade across the Line of Control, on discovering it had become a route for illegal fund transfers, including to guerrillas and stoning protests. Trade was resumed in a few months.

◆

Difficult as these political issues were, the most painful and complex issue for us was the return of Kashmiri Pandits. Pushed out in the 1990s, the community lived in a kind of permanent limbo in Jammu. In their government-provided housing blocks, the dominant sentiment was anger and loss, sustained by memory of their homes, culture and place in the valley. As the conflict dragged on, their return became more and more difficult. They feared repeated communal attack if they did go back, and over time, an ugly narrative grew in the valley—that Pandits had fled at Jagmohan's command, that they did not want to share the suffering of Muslims in the valley, that they benefited from allowances given by the union government. This narrative, and the communal sentiments it bred, diminished the chances of Pandits ever returning.

We met a number of Kashmiri Pandit groups, some in Delhi, others in Jammu and the valley, and yet others who had migrated to the US and Europe (by Skype). Depending on the group, their demands ranged from seeking a separate Pandit homeland in the valley to hiking the allowance they got as internally displaced, to ensuring safe returns and employment and to protecting their places of worship. Unsurprisingly, it was the far-flung Pandit diaspora—in the US, Europe, New Zealand, Australia—who most vehemently demanded a separate homeland.[70] The history of ethnic conflicts shows that it is generally the far-flung diaspora that has the most radical demands.

In 2006, the Singh administration adopted a policy of encouraging graduated and quiet Pandit returns under the PMRP. The core of the policy was to bring Pandit teachers back to the valley. It was an imaginative idea, given that Kashmiris, whether Muslim or Hindu, valued education and their role as teachers would give Pandits a productive space in valley communities. But the state government had not reckoned with how communalism had embedded itself over two decades of conflict. In 2010, four years after the PMRP was launched, we were told that the state government had sought to recruit 3,000 displaced Pandit teachers from Jammu and 1,179 had joined their posts, many of whom were young women. They were housed in transit accommodation—one-bedroom flats—located in Budgam and Anantnag districts and constructed under the Sayeed administration. When we visited the flats, we found that they had been built on the outskirts of the two towns, in relatively isolated areas. The Budgam accommodation was slightly less vulnerable than the Anantnag accommodation. It was closer to town and consisted of three blocks of flats in a gated enclosure. The Anantnag flats were in two rows set amidst fields several kilometres out of town. Though they were in the process of being fenced when I visited, they were impossible to protect.

To our shock, we found that returning Pandits had to sign an agreement when allotted a transit flat. The agreement pledged that their families would not accompany them to stay in government-provided transit accommodation. Given that the policy was to encourage Pandits to return permanently to the valley, this seemed both self-defeating and illegal. A large number of the teachers we met in the Budgam and Anantnag flats were young women in their early twenties, some with infant children whom they had been forced to leave behind with their husbands and/or in-laws. When we asked why the state government had sought such a punishing agreement, the relief commissioner told us that the government was afraid residents of the transit accommodation might never leave if they brought their families with them. Transit flats were allotted for only a six-month period, he said, after which returning Pandits were expected to find their own accommodation. An understandable bureaucratic reservation had been turned into a cruel second separation for people who were refugees in their own land.

The biggest obstacle to Pandit returns, we grew to believe, was the lack of a serious state government policy to reintegrate them into local communities. In Budgam, we were told by the Pandit teachers we met that individuals from the town had come to welcome them, but no collective efforts had been made. My colleagues were not with me on the Anantnag visit. When I reached there, accompanied by Motilal Bhatt, one of the Pandits who had stayed in the valley and worked for the local community,

I found an activist of the Vishwa Hindu Parishad sitting with the women I had come to meet. Yasin Malik had visited once to welcome them, they said, but nothing had been organized with or by Anantnag community leaders. Given their insecurity, asked the Parishad lady, could Pandit teachers return to Jammu but continue drawing their salary? Her question took my breath away, but also led me to wonder just how many people in Jammu and Kashmir drew a salary without doing the job.

The best practice for the return of ethnic refugees or internally displaced, as history shows, includes not only jobs but, even more importantly, sustained community and government policies to reintegrate them. This was a gap we underlined to the state as well as union governments, both privately and in our report.

To pave the way for Pandit return and reintegration, we felt, the state government could begin by aiding those Pandits who remained in the valley. Though the community had suffered a large exodus in 1990–93, Pandits continued to migrate steadily in the years that followed and the community continues to shrink to this day. If more were done to help the Pandits who remained to preserve their property, culture and employment, it would be a confidence-booster for Pandits who had left to come back. In a society where symbolism and metaphor held a high place, it would also help if the state government repaired heritage Pandit properties, such as we had seen in Pulwama, a cluster of ruined but once beautiful brick and carved wood houses. In an area of pro-independence militancy, none had occupied this Pandit land, a sign that returnees might be more welcome if they returned to their original homes.

While the return of Pandits was a priority issue that was mishandled by the sluggish state administration, communities that had been internally displaced in Jammu due to constant cross-border shelling received little to no attention from both the state and the union governments. We discovered that even the compensation paid to victims of guerrilla attack was different in the valley and Jammu. In the valley, compensation ranged from ₹2 to 2.5 lakh (200,000-250,000) whereas in Jammu it was between

₹1 to 1.5 lakh (100,000–150,000).

West Pakistani refugees who could not return also had a problem in the state. Mostly Sikh or Hindu, some had come during the 1948–49 India–Pakistan War and others during the 1965 and 1971 ones. The bulk of them had crossed through the state to other parts of India, but a small proportion remained in the state. Some had lived there for over sixty years but had neither property nor voting rights. Their children were not eligible for government jobs or scholarships in universities, nor were there reserved seats for them as for most communities in Jammu and Kashmir. In effect, they were stateless.

The issue was tricky since it impinged on the State Subjects Act and its incorporation in the Indian Constitution under Article 35A. Though the Act, passed by Maharaja Hari Singh, laid down conditions and rights for the residents of the state, it also allowed the state government the flexibility to use its own discretion in exceptional cases, which West Pakistani refugees clearly were. Sheikh Abdullah had refused to allow refugees state subject status in the hope that they would be able to return to Pakistan, though by 1971 it was obvious that Pakistan would not accept them. Pakistani authorities did not encourage even the return of Muslims who had crossed over during the wars.

Demography became a key concern, with many arguing that the demand of West Pakistani refugees for residency rights would alter the composition of the state by swelling the non-Muslim population. The argument drew from Jammu's painful communal history and had little to do with demography. Communal conflict during the 1948–49 war had driven over 100,000 Muslims out of Jammu, and refugees had participated in it, leaving the province with a slightly larger Hindu majority than it already had. The West Pakistani refugees were relatively small in number—just under 20,000 households in 2010—and settled mostly in Hindu-majority Jammu district. Granting them voting and property rights would not alter the state's demography. In 2016, the state government gave them domicile certificates, which enabled them to apply for government jobs. Minor as it was, this sop sparked protest in the valley, but it died down after a few months.

♦

Unlike communal, regional and district-level issues, sectoral demands— primarily of Gujjars and Paharis—were cross-cutting. The Muslim Gujjars and Paharis of the state were concentrated in the border areas of Jammu and some parts of the valley. While Gujjars were designated a tribe in Jammu and Kashmir and some other states, in yet others they were classified as a caste. Paharis were not designated as either in any part of India, because they were primarily a linguistic community. Since they lived in the same border areas as Gujjars and shared a similar economic and social profile, Paharis sought the same tribal status as Gujjars— who had reserved seats in the state's legislature and a 10 per cent quota in government jobs and student enrolment—from 1992 on. The Pahari demand was opposed by Gujjars who feared they would have to share their quota. As it was, according to the state's Tribal Research and Cultural Foundation, Gujjars were not able to access the economic, social or cultural benefits that they were entitled to as a tribe and a minority. While acknowledging that both Gujjars and Paharis had grievances, the foundation's secretary, Javaid Rahi, argued that the solution lay in giving special benefits to Paharis, who were also Muslim, without disturbing the tribal status issue.[71] In fact, there were already some benefits available through the state's Pahari Advisory Board.

As I saw it, the economic aspect had less to do with questions of tribal status and benefits and more to do with the neglect of peripheries. Tribes were not discriminated against in the state as they were in several other parts of India, but Jammu and Kashmir's border areas tended to be poorer than other parts of the state. This was puzzling, given that independent India had poured resources into developing the neighbouring border state of Punjab, both for immediate security imperatives and the longer-term strategy of ensuring its people knit to India. Why had a similar policy not been adopted in Jammu and Kashmir, whose border areas had suffered repeated invasions from Pakistan since 1948, and indeed saw weekly incursions from both Pakistan and China?

This point was taken on board by the union government's Task Force for Ladakh, set up at the same time as our Group of Interlocutors. The Task Force recommended direct funding for development in the border regions of Ladakh. Though Ladakh was part of Kashmir province, the state government was not averse to direct funding for Ladakh, despite opposing it for other parts of the state. The state's political leaders worried about fissiparous trends if Jammu or any part of the valley received direct funding from the union. Like their counterparts elsewhere, they also preferred to keep control over funds. When former prime minister Rajiv Gandhi introduced district-level devolution through the Panchayati Raj Act in 1988, with central funding for municipal and village councils, chief ministers across India accused him of trying to undermine the powers of state governments and erode Indian federalism. Ladakh was an exception for the state government, because Srinagar's reach had traditionally been thin in the region, which had been ruled by different monarchs and empires.

Why did the state government not seek earmarked funds for the border districts of Jammu and Kashmir, as had the Punjab government? There is no clear answer. Perhaps the simplest answer is the most rational one—regional political leaders and electorates were mostly in the hinterland of the state, whereas people in border districts tended to look at national parties and/or Delhi for support. Whatever the reason, poor border development was as much of a loss to the state's security as it was to its residents.

As far as Gujjars were concerned, they had an active and well-networked political leadership. There had been Gujjars in the state council of ministers since the days of Sheikh Abdullah. Though Gujjar associations sought electoral reservation, their problem was not lack of representation but indifferent or venal leaders, another common problem in the state and India at large. Paharis were less networked, and the small nomadic shepherd community of Bakerwals was not networked at all.

What united Gujjars and Paharis were their cultural grievances.

Both the Gojri and Pahari languages had rich literary and folk traditions. Decades of neglect had withered them. Neither was taught in schools and there was pitiful state support for institutions that kept these languages and literature alive.

◆

Meantime, another peacemaking strand began to fall in place. In January 2011, Musharraf's former foreign minister, Khurshid Kasuri, revealed that India and Pakistan had come close to a Kashmir peace agreement in 2006–07. The two governments had 'almost signed off on a draft agreement', he said, which 'included self-governance on both sides of the Line of Control and a joint mechanism to oversee governance'.[72] Pakistan's then ISI head, General Ashfaq Parvez Kayani (who became army chief in 2009), was 'actively involved in the backchannel talks', Kasuri added.

Soon after, the Hurriyat called for dialogue, stating, 'We have reached a stage where we need to rise above political affiliations and show statesmanship in starting a political process... After all, it is Kashmiris who are getting killed and therefore, Kashmiris, through mutual consultation, will have to come forward to find a solution to the vexed problem.'[73] The statement raised hopes that we might be able to open talks with the Hurriyat, but that did not happen, despite our renewed invitation.

Though the Hurriyat and JKLF did not meet us, they began internal reforms that helped a larger peace process. In early January 2011, at a seminar to commemorate the 1993 assassination of JKLF mentor Abdul Ahad Wani, Ghani Bhat exploded the long-entrenched canard that Wani and other pro-independence or pro-Pakistan leaders had been killed by 'unidentified gunmen'. 'Let me speak the truth today,' Bhat said, 'It was not the army or the police who killed Farooq or Prof Wani or Lone sahib. It was our own people.' Had the Hurriyat 'chosen to say the truth in the 1990s, our movement would have gone in a better direction', he added.[74]

Bhat's disclosure came as a rude shock to many pro-Pakistan groups, and he was widely criticized in the local media where dissidence was strongest. Three weeks later, Sajad Lone followed with an impassioned appeal. 'For all those cynics and sermonizers who are questioning (Bhat's) timing, his intentions, I—a son who lost his father to bullets—would want to put my appreciation on record. Truth, however bitter, has to prevail... The culture of unaccountability, impunity, cultivated and nourished by a select group of intellectuals, thinkers, has only emboldened the killers to indulge in more heinous acts, aimed at disempowering the Kashmiri voice and coercing it into submission.'[75]

Bhat and Sajad appeared to have read the changing local pulse. In February 2011, when two sisters were shot by alleged Lashkar guerrillas, Sopore erupted in protest. A relative of the girls, Mukhtar Ahmed, called upon dissident leaders for 'a solution to such killings'.[76]

While holding his stand that there could be no talks with the union government until they accepted Kashmir 'as a disputed territory', Geelani also sought reform of the stoning movement. Speaking at a seminar in early January, this one on the UN resolution for a plebiscite, he urged, 'our struggle has to be peaceful as a matter of policy, despite grave provocations... I stress upon the youth not to be emotional and to adopt peaceful demonstrations as their weapon. Even provocative slogans should be avoided.'[77] Five months later, when Osama bin Laden was killed by US commandos in a house reported to be owned by the Hizbul Mujahideen, Geelani offered fateha (prayers) for his soul.[78]

The Tehreek-e-Hurriyat was also under pressure from Pakistan. The three rounds of Lambah–Khan talks had raised fears that 'Islamabad might return to the framework of the former Pakistani president Musharraf's four-point proposals on the state', which Geelani bitterly opposed. The Zardari administration initially gave Geelani more weight than Musharraf had, but 'now, there are indications that this phase is ending. Though Pakistan continues to maintain a public posture of pursuing its traditional Kashmir policy which stresses implementation of UN resolutions, behind the scene[s] they are picking up the threads where Musharraf left [off],' a Tehreek leader told the newspaper *Greater Kashmir*.[79] Geelani, said another Tehreek representative, had refused to go to Pakistan to visit his ailing son because he feared the Pakistani government might push him to support their effort to revive talks along previous lines.

In this more propitious atmosphere of reform, some dissidents did meet us. In January 2011, Sajad Lone spent an hour with us going over his 'Achievable Nationhood' proposal (elaborated in a 100-page volume). He had moved away from pro-independence and pro-Pakistan groups, but his People's Conference was still loosely linked to pro-independence sentiments. In late March, Maulvi Abbas Ansari, the Shia leader who had headed the Hurriyat and was an Executive Council member, also held a lengthy discussion with us at his home, on how the Hurriyat could be brought on board a new peace process.

I had arrived late at the meeting and was startled when my colleagues told me they were declaring it in our weekly press release. They had discussed a public announcement of the meeting with Ansari, and he had agreed. It was certainly a major breakthrough for us to have had a substantive discussion with a Hurriyat leader. But a public announcement would equally certainly put the Hurriyat on the back foot and curtail Ansari's ability to act as a channel. In the event, the news was leaked and came up in our press conference. I sought to downplay it by saying the meeting was simply a courtesy call, to my colleagues' displeasure. They believed the announcement might pave the way for Hurriyat talks. Perhaps they were right, though the idea went against my received wisdom.

Any such possibility was pre-empted when, a few days later, Maulana Showkat Ahmed Shah of the Jamiat Ahle Hadees sect was killed by a bicycle bomb placed at the rear entrance to his mosque in downtown Srinagar. Virtually non-existent in Kashmir during the 1990s, the Ahle Hadees had multiplied to 600 mosques in the valley with close to a million followers, according to its general secretary Ghulam Rasool Malik, who came to see me carrying a heavy pile of membership logs to show how influential the organization was. Shah had spoken out against stoning, calling it un-Islamic. In his last post on Facebook, on 30 March, he wrote,

'With great shock and pain...I have to say that some youth in our society are turning into self-styled judges, who are passing *fatwas* and judgments. It is these few misguided men who are ruining society. May God show all of us the right path.'[80] Shah's predecessor, Mohammad Ramazan, had also been murdered by guerrillas, and he had himself escaped an attempted assassination in 2006.

Dissident groups and electoral parties alike condemned Shah's assassination. The valley shut down in silent protest. Together with the Ahle Hadees, the Hurriyat and JKLF set up an all-party inquiry committee into the assassination. 'The black sheep who are out to kill prominent social and political leaders in the Valley have to be identified,' said Mirwaiz Umar.[81] Within two weeks, the state police and intelligence arrested three guerrillas from the Lashkar-e-Taiba and a little-known new militia group, Sautul Haq (the Voice of Truth). The assassination, said Inspector General of Police S. M. Sahai, was planned by Qasim Fakhtoo, husband of Dukhtaran-e-Millat's Asiya Andrabi, from his cell in the Srinagar Central Jail.[82]

In a first, the Lashkar-e-Taiba announced its own investigation into Shah's assassination. In August, it submitted a report to the all-party inquiry committee. The report supported the police findings, concluding, 'We initially thought that the murder was the handiwork of Indian forces to weaken the freedom struggle and to create confusion in the pro-freedom camp. We never thought that the killers will be our own people... [T]he death of Moulana Showkat was planned by the traitors from within our own ranks.'[83]

The JKLF's Yasin Malik was to be the next target, the report warned. Malik was close to Shah and supported his reform efforts. Dissident leaders already saw a threat in the assassination to the peacemakers amongst them. 'It's a message for us. Don't you dare deviate from the script, we will get you no matter where you are, politician or preacher, you will be silenced,' one of them told the *Times of India*.[84]

Shah had met us in Delhi to canvass support for an Ahle Hadees university in Srinagar. The organization had applied for clearance to set up a university several years earlier but had been denied because of their Wahhabi teaching and ties to pro-independence groups. He supported peace talks, Shah told us; the university trust would invite the governor of the state to be chancellor and have other government members on their board to monitor courses and curricula. Shah was clearly sincere and his assurance sounded reasonable to me, but others warned me not to take it at face value. An Ahle Hadees university could be the thin end of the wedge, they said. My colleagues, too, inclined to this view.

Curiously, the BJP joined in condemnation of Shah's assassination, and a group of its leaders, including Rajnath Singh, Ravi Shankar Prasad and Shahnawaz Hussain, visited Shah's family in Srinagar's Lal Bazaar. 'This is the first time that senior BJP leaders have visited the family of any slain separatist leader in Kashmir,' commented *Rising Kashmir*.[85]

Soon after Shah's assassination, the Hurriyat suspended Ansari for meeting us. 'We are not against talks [with New Delhi] but want our conditions to be met first. That was the reason we had decided not to meet the interlocutors,' said Mirwaiz Umar.[86] Whether under pressure of the gun, as some suspected, or under pressure from the ground, Mirwaiz Umar's statement showed that the Hurriyat had reversed its earlier position in favour of unconditional talks. Fear of the gun, reportedly, also closed any option of us opening a backchannel through Ansari. 'They meet Maulvi Showkat and he gets assassinated,' the *Times of India* cited 'a top Hurriyat source' as saying. 'That's the ground reality. This is what we are facing. Who would take a chance talking to them for a few paragraphs in their report? A piece of paper that will sit in a file in the home ministry!'[87]

Ansari was only reinstated six months later. Another hopeful opening closed before it could achieve results.

◆

By end-July 2011, when we began writing our final report, the ground situation had improved considerably. Stoning protests had dwindled and over a million tourists and pilgrims visited the valley that summer. Despite the Tehreek's call to boycott the panchayat polls, supported by the Hizbul Mujahideen and the Lashkar-e-Taiba, who put up warning posters at mosques,[88] there was a 78 per cent voter turnout. Held between April and June 2011, the panchayat polls were the first local body elections in eleven years; the previous panchayat polls were in 2000. A relieved Omar Abdullah declared, 'In reality this is the first panchayat election after 33 years because the poll in 2000 was only on paper. More than half the seats remained empty.'[89] By contrast, 32,335 local council officials were elected in 2011. Journalists covering the poll commented on how 'relaxed' voters were. 'It feels strange to cover an election [in Kashmir] without the words "militant", "rockets" and "killed" once entering my mind,' said one.[90]

Under the panchayat system, elections were non-political insofar as political parties were not permitted to contest. Nevertheless, most of the candidates did have political affiliations. While the majority supported the National Conference and PDP, in Handwara—near where MLA Rashid had hosted our public meeting—the People's Conference won a third of the seats they contested. It was the first time that the Lone brothers cooperated. Though Bilal Lone was in the Hurriyat, he supported Sajad's decision to field candidates in the panchayat election.[91] Unlike Geelani's Tehreek, the Mirwaiz Hurriyat had not opposed the panchayat polls. They had not opposed the 2008 assembly election either.

The panchayat elections were widely welcomed on the ground, in the anticipation that panchayats might plug the governance gap. As one villager, Aftab Ahmad of Wusan, put it, villagers usually took local problems to their MLA, who was not reachable sometimes: 'Now we will have locals who represent us and they will deliver,' he hoped.[92] We met several of the panch associations, holding half a dozen consultations with them. The vast majority of panches were young—in their twenties and thirties—and had been elected for the first time. They included engineers, business studies graduates and teachers. All of them took their tasks seriously and were enthusiastic about bringing infrastructure and accountability to their villages. They were also enthusiastic about peacemaking. 'The desire for a peace process is very strong on the ground,' Shafi Mir, convenor of the Jammu and Kashmir Panchayat Conference, told us at a round table meeting. 'If we were empowered, we could bring inputs from our villages and anchor the work of your mission.'

We thought the proposal was revolutionary, and took it to the union Home Ministry. If panches at the village level were involved in a peace process, the groundswell that would ensue in favour of an end to conflict and a negotiated settlement would undermine the power of spoilers and radically alter the face of the conflict. We did not factor in that opposition to the proposal would be as strong as the ray of light it shone.

Our hopes were soon disappointed. There were no takers for Mir's proposal in either the Singh or Omar administrations. The panchayat system was tiered and, to fully function, the panchayats needed to work with the Block and District Development Boards that were constituted by the state government. Though India's Panchayati Raj Act of 1993 (the 73rd and 74th Amendments to the Constitution of India) laid down that block- and district-level councils too would be elected, in their case by panches, the Jammu and Kashmir Panchayat Act of 1989 laid down that members of the block and district boards would be nominated by the state government. Since powers to authorize and fund development plans vested in the district boards, the state Act left panchayats with virtually no powers other than to submit proposals.

In July 2011, a state government committee on devolution of powers to the panchayats recommended a series of amendments to the state Act. Remarking that 'the great enthusiasm shown by the voters in the recently concluded elections' prompted the committee to consider 'a substantive and considerable devolution of functions', the committee's report stated that the role of the panchayats should 'extend to active supervision and oversight of the activities currently being performed by a number of departments at the local level'.[93] These activities included agriculture, animal and sheep husbandry, consumer affairs, school education, fisheries, forestry, health and family welfare, horticulture, public works, rural development and social welfare.

Noting that the state government had not been able to fully access the grants available from central funds for panchayats because the state budget preceded the panchayat election, the committee recommended that a state finance commission be appointed to decide what proportion of state taxes, duties, tolls and fees should be allocated to panchayats and the newly constituted District Planning and Development Board 'should be mandated to transfer funds' to them. Though it would 'not be at all desirable at this stage to consider any amendment that may lend uncertainty to the constitution' of panchayats, block- and district-level bodies, Section 45 of the state Panchayat Act could be amended to allow for election of the chairman of the District Planning and Development Board by an electoral college of panches, sarpanches and the chairman of the Block Development Council.

Further, the committee said, the state Act could be amended to incorporate reservation for women and scheduled castes and tribes. The performance of panchayat bodies, they added, could be brought under the state's Ombudsman Act.

The committee's recommendations ran into an immediate roadblock by legislators, both within the government and from the state assembly, who feared that financial empowerment of panchayats would create alternate authorities in their constituencies.[94] The Block Development Council elections, scheduled to be held later in 2011, were postponed to 2012. In October 2012, they were again postponed at an emergency cabinet meeting.

As the promise of the panchayats slowly dissipated, elected panches and sarpanches began to be targeted. Ten panches were killed and, under threat from guerrillas, close to another 150 resigned. Many announced their resignations in newspaper advertisements and notices on mosque walls.[95] Though the panchayat associations demanded government security, there was no way that the state police could provide security for 32,000 people. Significantly, the bulk of resignations were in districts with entrenched guerilla: Budgam, Baramulla, Pulwama, Kupwara, Shopian, Anantnag, Kulgam, Srinagar and Bandipora. Ganderbal,

Chief Minister Omar Abdullah's constituency, was also high on the list. Of the ten panches who were murdered, seven were killed in Baramulla and three in Shopian.[96]

◆

Our conversations in Jammu and Kashmir taught us that conflict narrative was at least as important as peacebuilding on the ground. Indeed, the former most often overshadowed the latter, especially as far as the young were concerned. With frequent curfews and shutdowns, their chief access to information was social and local media, where facts counted less than emotion. It is difficult to measure the damage that abusive exchanges between young Kashmiri and mainland Indian nationalists inflicted on the potential for peace, but I saw how every fruitful beginning on my Facebook page rapidly ended in hate-filled abuse. The high-casualty and widely broadcast terrorist attacks of 2006–08 had taken their toll. Indian public opinion, which previously supported an India–Pakistan–Kashmir peace process, slowly turned against talks and in favour of military response. The Indian electronic media played into this narrative with its constant reporting of terrorism in Kashmir and little else, an approach that the local Kashmiri electronic media countered with cries of Hindu state repression. Identified as terrorists by one and as persecuted by the other, young Kashmiris turned to support for violence.

Kashmiri, and to some extent national, print journalism was more reliable, but the former often carried contradictory news reports. As one editor confessed to me, the state's newspapers were under threat from both guerrillas and the government to publish 'their' news items as supplied. Government advertisements were a favoured lever. National print media, on the other hand, while less jingoistic than electronic media, tended to report Kashmir on the basis of Home Ministry briefings.

With the new technologies that enable individuals to produce and circulate their own multimedia reports, documentaries and even movies at low cost, the valley and Jammu were hotbeds of real, selective and fake news jostling each other. At Sri Pratap College, an institution known for having produced both Kashmiri chief ministers and pro-independence leaders, I accidentally discovered that the valley had a thriving local film industry whose products were broadcast by local cable operators without clearance. In a closed-door interaction with the college's students and faculty, a row of five schoolboys sat silent until one got up and asked me 'Madamji, have you seen *Sholay*?' Did I not think, he continued, that the state's ministers and senior advisers were like various villains in the film?

Sholay was India's first spaghetti western. It had been released in 1975, when I was a student, and I was surprised that a fourteen-year old had seen it. The hall rocked with laughter at the boy's analogy. That evening, I went to a friend's house for dinner. Their children were watching television in an adjoining room. Hearing gales of laughter I went in, and found there had been a local remake of *Sholay* with Kashmiri actors. This is what my schoolboy questioner had seen.

Staying to watch the remainder of the film, I was struck by how innocent it was. Even the villains were appealingly weak. The only message I got was sexist: women appeared chiefly in dance sequences, portrayed as corrupted by Bollywood or maybe 'Indian' culture in general. Geelani had already suggested that only boys should be allowed cell phones because the devices made 'Kashmiri girls dishonourable'.[97]

The *Sholay* analogy was not the only point the schoolboy made. He popped up each time with another question, mostly on the evils of the Indian government. After the third question, I noticed that someone from outside the hall was sending him notes, presumably with questions to ask. On exiting, I found a small group of four or five local journalists waiting for me. While two engaged me in conversation, the rest disappeared midway. My guess is that they were the ones who sent notes to my schoolboy questioner and now went to assemble a small group of schoolboys—the same ones in the hall?—who gathered at a distance and began shouting 'Go India! Go Back!' When I started to walk over, their voices quavered and they retreated. Since I did not want to frighten children, I stopped, waved at them and left. Soon after, a Kashmiri friend called. 'How could you let yourself be filmed leaving while boys shouted "Go back India!"?' he scolded. Image was far more important to the narrative than speech, I learnt.

The incidence of prompting came up for a second time at a round table in Sopore with a group of youth, consisting of only boys. Again, there was one who asked the most persistent questions, always with eyes fixed on his cell phone. When I asked him a question, he paused to type into his phone. He answered only after his phone pinged a reply.

Incidents like these seemed like light relief in our otherwise grim conversations, but they could not detract from the battle for hearts and minds that was being fought. While we had focused on ending the violence in which youth, guerrillas and security forces were killed or grievously hurt, the psychological wounds, inflicted by contesting Kashmir, Jammu and Delhi narratives that brutalized and, indeed, vulgarized one another, deepened by the hour. Their gravity was underscored by repeated resistance to any form of cultural activity in the valley. In July 2011, the protest rapper M. C. Kash was forced to call off a concert at Kashmir University because a section of students called music haraam or sacrilegious.[98] In August, the organizers of the prestigious Jaipur Literary Festival were forced to call off a planned event in Srinagar, which was to showcase young writers in the state. 'The idea came from people in Srinagar who want to create a platform for dialogue in the valley, focusing on poetry, the written word and the writers of Jammu and Kashmir and Ladakh,' said Sanjoy Roy, one of the organizers.[99]

A backlash kicked in immediately. Opponents of the planned festival set up a Facebook page to call for its cancellation. 'Holding such a festival would dovetail with the state's concerted attempt to portray that all is normal in Kashmir,' a group of Kashmiri intelligentsia wrote in an open letter, whose signatories included acclaimed Kashmiri novelists Basharat Peer and Mirza Waheed, filmmaker Sanjay Kak and journalist Muzamil Jaleel.[100] The festival organizers were warned that there could be violence—calls for protests at the venue were already circulating on social media. In a public statement announcing cancellation, Roy and his colleagues remarked bitterly, 'We neither have the desire to be responsible for yet more unrest in the valley nor to propagate mindless violence in the name of free speech... It is a sad day for us and a victory for a vocal minority who feel that they alone are the doorkeepers to people's minds and hearts.'

Sports were a casualty too. Argentinian coach Juan Marcos Troia, who had set up a football academy in Srinagar in 2007 with a grant from the Brazilian government, was forced to leave after he received a series of anonymous threats and his dogs were killed. He had trained former stone-throwers and sons of former guerrillas. Though the union Sports Ministry tried to help him, the state equivalent did not.[101] Bishan Singh Bedi, one of Indian cricket's most famous bowlers, had a similar experience—this time at the hands of the famously corrupt state cricket administration. When I asked him whether he would consider training young Kashmiri cricketers, he agreed immediately and spent close to a year with the Kashmir cricket academy. Though he fought the obstacles local cricket officials put in his way, they finally became too numerous and he returned to Delhi. Sports training and tournaments continued, but they were organized by the army and police.

It seemed as if Kashmir's young could explore their potential only under security protection. M. C. Kash could not play at Kashmir University, but he did play at a youth summit organized by Kashmiri NGO One Kashmir, held at the well-guarded government convention centre. The summit, which brought together 2,000 young people from across the state, pledged to 'build a better Kashmir'.[102] Contrary to the doubts expressed in the open letter against the Srinagar literary festival, the One Kashmir summit was far from apolitical. Its closing session called for an end to conflict and talks between representatives of India, Pakistan and Kashmir. 'The Kashmir issue must be resolved with due respect to the aspirations of the people,' said a One Kashmir organizer, while reading his summary of key points at the conference.

In this contested environment, it is no surprise that the biggest peacebuilding initiative of the Singh administration—the 2011 Rangarajan Committee's proposal for employment of Kashmiri youth—did not have its intended effect. Outlining 'placement-linked and market-driven' skills training, the committee recommended a targeted industry initiative in Jammu and Kashmir that could create as many as 400,000 jobs in three to five years. Companies such as Infosys, Tata Consultancy Services, Crompton Greaves, Bajaj Auto, Tata Motors, Godrej & Boyce and Apollo Hospitals responded to Singh's call for participation, and tens of thousands of the state's young were hired through government programmes.[103]

But the initiative met with limited success. Jammu and Kashmir's legislators decided that non-Kashmiri companies could only acquire thirty-year leases to set up shop in the state, a clear disincentive to investment and industrial development since there were few Kashmiri companies. The educated young whom industry trained and hired under the Singh initiative got jobs outside the valley, leaving it more not less vulnerable to lumpenization.

◆

Writing our final report was not easy. We had to examine possible solutions to the conflict and also suggest the roadmap to consensus. In order to do either, we had to draw lessons from past experience and factor in the changing ground situation as well as new actors, with their new demands, in both the state and the country at large.

Being very different individuals with very different backgrounds was both a plus and a minus. Padgaonkar was a seasoned journalist who knew the leaders of all the major parties, a large bonus when it came to considering what could be politically acceptable. Ansari was an economist who had worked with the government and could cover development issues. I had a background of policy work on Kashmir and with Kashmiri civil society, and had devised a roadmap towards peace in the state. In theory we complemented each other, though in practice we sometimes competed, to our own loss. It also became clear that we had different ideas of what constituted a solution. Our differences were even greater when it came to what the Indian government should do.

On two major points, we agreed. Article 370 and Kashmir's autonomy within the Indian union had to be taken as the baseline for a solution, we believed—as had most of our predecessors. To mitigate reservations in Jammu and Ladakh, any strengthening of the state's autonomy should be accompanied by regional and local devolution, as Sheikh Abdullah had recognized over thirty years earlier.

It was an anomaly that Article 370 remained 'temporary' in the Indian Constitution seventy years after its inclusion. It should, we argued, be made permanent after a constitutional committee was set up to review its provisions and the changes made through a series of presidential orders. Once the committee decided which elements of Article 370 needed to be strengthened or altered, and which changes rolled back, the union and state legislatures could amend Article 370, if required. For example, the term 'autonomy' could be replaced by 'special status'. This would keep Article 370 in the general basket of states with different relations to the union, all of which have special status under Articles 371A to I of the Indian Constitution. Special status is synonymous with autonomy in, for example, Nagaland, which has very similar powers to Jammu and Kashmir, arguably even greater. Eleven out of twenty-nine Indian states have special status under Article 371: Maharashtra and Gujarat (371), Nagaland (371A), Assam (371B), Manipur (371C), Andhra Pradesh and Telangana (371D and E), Sikkim (371F), Mizoram (371G), Arunachal Pradesh (371H) and Goa (371I). Significantly, several BJP-ruled states were in the list.

On a third associated point, we disagreed: the question of Pakistan. That Pakistan played a role was indisputable, as was the fact that it was a spoiler role. Whether Pakistani spoilers could or would transform to being part of the solution was debatable, but again we agreed there was no option but to try. Where we disagreed was whether our report should have a chapter on

Pakistan-administered Kashmir and Gilgit–Baltistan. My colleagues argued that we had only been appointed to canvass opinion in Jammu and Kashmir. I argued that if we went by the 1995 parliament resolution, then the Pakistan-held parts of the former princely state became part of our brief, even if in practice we were restricted to long-distance communication. We compromised when Padgaonkar decided that a section on cross-border CBMs was necessary—if we talked about trade relations between divided parts of Kashmir, then why omit discussion of issues of concern for Pakistan-administered Kashmir, Gilgit and Baltistan, such as human rights and political control?

Our biggest debates were on security issues and the tension between immediate, median and long-term steps. On some security issues, my colleagues were initially more in sync with Kashmiri views than I was. They argued that the Disturbed Areas Ordinance could be applied selectively, to specific districts, and lifted selectively. I was doubtful. The ordinance had been applied to the valley first, and then extended to Jammu when insurgency spread from the valley to Jammu's neighbouring Chenab valley districts, and then extended to cover all of Jammu province.

Our argument was limited to the valley. The Omar administration continued to lobby for lifting the ordinance from districts that the security agencies had declared 'terrorism-free', and my colleagues suggested we should support the state government on this issue. On the ground, however, this meant that guerrillas could seek refuge in districts where the ordinance did not apply. If the army needed to pursue fleeing guerrillas to these districts, they would only be able to do so under highly restricted and as yet unspecified terms. This would impose costs on the security forces that were likely to prolong conflict rather than telescope it, and lead to a severe loss of morale. It was a halfway step of doubtful cosmetic gain for politicians but not for peacebuilders. Eventually, my colleagues agreed to allow my doubts to be stated in the report.

On AFSPA, on the other hand, my colleagues were more conservative than I. They argued that we should focus on the Disturbed Areas Ordinance, under which AFSPA applied, rather than deal with AFSPA itself. My view was that AFSPA should be repealed and the Indian parliament should incorporate safeguards into the Indian Army Act. The Army Act as it stood was chiefly technical, dealing with promotions, conditions of work and so on. While the principle on which it rested, that the army's task is defence of our external borders, was essential to democracy, it was also true that the use of the army in internal security required regulation. In 2007, the Prime Minister's Working Group on CBMs for the state recommended reviewing the Disturbed Areas Ordinance and AFSPA and, if possible, lifting the former and revoking the latter. As a follow-up, Prime Minister Singh appointed the Jeevan Reddy Commission to look into AFSPA wherever it was in force in the country. The commission proposed the Act's repeal and the incorporation of some of its provisions into a new national law, to be called the Unlawful Activities (Prevention) Act.

The Ministry of Home Affairs recommended several amendments to AFSPA, which would bring it into line with the Indian Criminal Procedure Code while allowing for the protections for armed forces that exist in every democratic country. The government's Second Administrative Reforms Committee also suggested replacing AFSPA with an amended Army Act. Finally, the Supreme Court issued guidelines in 2009 qualifying the army's powers under AFSPA, but these had not been legislated in parliament. Was it not time that the court's guidelines be enacted as law? Once again, we compromised, listing these points and recommending that the Ministry of Defence take an early decision on reforms to AFSPA.

Our most difficult decisions were on how to frame the political solution, whether we should go into its details, and if so, which? There had already been several official reports examining the political issues and recommending solutions, from the 1960s on. We could either refer to each report and highlight its salient points, or we could present a comprehensive set of ideas on autonomy and internal devolution, drawing on what past reports had recommended. There was also the question of whether we should put the political solution front and centre, or whether the roadmap should have pride of place. We had already received several inputs from political parties. The BJP leaders whom we met—Advani, Jaitley and Swaraj—advised us to concentrate on human rights. The National Conference wanted us to adhere to their autonomy report and refer to internal devolution only in passing, if at all. The PDP wanted us to emphasize their 'self-rule' document and Sajad Lone his 'Achievable Nationhood' proposals.

Though the BJP leaders had implicitly warned us that their party was likely to oppose our report if it dealt with political solutions and took autonomy as a baseline, there was no way we could omit that discussion. Nor did we wish to leave it ambiguous as the Saghir Ahmed report of the Working Group on Centre–State Relations had done. Ahmed's report had focused on the unbridgeable differences between parties of different strengths and popular support. We, on the other hand, found that there were large overlaps between proposals for a solution, especially between Kashmiri political parties. We sought to build on these, but at the same time also had to consider how to reconcile the regional devolution issue, which was a source of tension between Jammu and the valley.

In Jammu, regional devolution provided a way around the union territory demand which would have divided the state. In the valley, it was seen as a way of further undercutting Srinagar's powers and paving the way towards another division. Many in the valley advised us not to recommend regional devolution as part of a political solution. Instead, experienced Kashmir administrators advised that we would achieve the same impact in terms of improved governance if we recommended district-level devolution.

The problem was that regional devolution was as much about political power as it was about improved governance. Jammu and Ladakh were unlikely to accept a rollback of encroachments on Article 370 without some degree of power-sharing as regional units. To devolve to the districts without devolving to the regions would also run the risk of giving primacy to religious identities, since most of the state's districts were either Muslim- or Hindu-majority. It could lead to further fracturing residents instead of enabling them to integrate.

The way we chose to address the problem was through a three-tiered system of devolution of powers, from the union to the state, from the state to its provinces (renamed regions with the additional creation of Ladakh as a region), and from the provinces to the districts. The legislature would, however, remain as one, and the powers of regional councils would be largely limited to budgetary allocations and development administration.

We had quite a heated debate on the powers that regional councils should have. My own view was that their powers should be strictly limited to oversight of administration. My colleagues argued that since regional councils would be elected bodies, they should have 'limited legislative powers to pass 'enabling' orders for enactments by the state assembly. I feared that this inclusion could allow regional councils to act as separate legislatures, de facto dividing the executive powers of the state government, as had happened in Bosnia. In an unhappy compromise, we finally agreed to leave the clause in our report but to specify the regional councils' jurisdiction as being over administrative decisions on agriculture, fisheries, charitable endowments and the like.

Though we were aware that our solution would be unpalatable to start with, we also believed that once it began to be seriously discussed, it would gain a wide degree of acceptance. Most of its elements had been proposed earlier and accepted by the chief political parties in the state; they had also begun to be accepted by Pakistan's Musharraf regime as the core of a solution. Pakistani acceptance was new. India and Pakistan had discussed Kashmir and its status for over half a century, but the idea that both Jammu and Kashmir and the Pakistan-administered portions of the state should have the same relations with their respective powers—India and Pakistan—gained currency only during the 2004–07 peace process.

•

While national and international attention was fixed on the stoning protests in the valley, Pakistan-administered Kashmir, Gilgit and Baltistan underwent their own change. The civilian

Zardari administration that came to power in 2008 gave the Northern Areas, as Gilgit and Baltistan were then called in Pakistan, a political and economic package through the Empowerment and Self-Governance Order for Gilgit–Baltistan of September 2009. Under the package, the Northern Areas were renamed Gilgit–Baltistan, as demanded by local nationalists, and granted their own assembly, governor, chief minister, election commission and other key state bodies. To reduce the role of the Pakistani government's Ministry of Kashmir Affairs, a Gilgit–Baltistan Council was formed with equal representation from the region and the national assembly of Pakistan. In its structure and powers, the Gilgit–Baltistan Council was modelled on the council of Pakistan-administered Kashmir and was headed by the prime minister of Pakistan.

Limited though it was, the package did offer some degree of reform for Gilgit–Baltistan, which had been ruled directly by the Ministry of Kashmir Affairs until then. Yet, the reforms it offered were severely restricted. Like the council of its counterpart, the Gilgit–Baltistan Council's composition left substantive central and federal authority with Islamabad, whose appointees would dominate. The powers that were devolved were chiefly for local administration.

Intriguingly, the nomenclature used in the package resembled that used in Article 370. In form, Gilgit–Baltistan acquired a political and administrative structure that was closer to that of Jammu and Kashmir than that of Pakistan-administered Kashmir, whose administration began as a War Council. In substance, however, the powers it devolved remained minor in comparison to Article 370—similar to Schedules II and III of Article 370 and not Schedule I—and were closer to those offered to the panchayats in Jammu and Kashmir. To this extent, the reforms could not be considered a step towards autonomy. Rather, they constituted a step towards representation.

Nevertheless, the use of language similar to Article 370, which was incorporated into the framework agreed in the Aziz–Lambah backchannel, raised hope for a return to the peace process of

2004–07. Was the Zardari administration preparing the ground for revival of the Aziz–Lambah framework? Though the PPP and Pakistan Foreign Office disclaimed all knowledge of it, it seems likely that the Zardari administration was moving in that direction. In September 2010, a former prime minister of Pakistan-administered Kashmir, Sultan Mehmood, visited the valley while I was there, ostensibly to attend a wedding. His main purpose was, however, to explore the possibility of a new inter-Kashmiri dialogue to settle the conflict.

A friend from Mirpur who had participated in Track II meetings with me rang me a few days before Mehmood visited. He asked whether we interlocutors could meet Mehmood and if I could help plan his meetings. Mehmood, he said, was anxious not to be left in the hands of dissidents alone. I relayed the request to the Home Ministry and the NSA, but failed to get a go-ahead. Mehmood did end up being piloted by pro-Pakistan and pro-independence groups, but spent more time with the JKLF than with the Tehreek. His visit was facilitated by the state government and he was allowed to pay his respects at the Martyrs' Graveyard and make a speech at Lal Chowk, where he called for 'making the LOC irrelevant', a phrase that Musharraf and Singh had both used.[104] Meeting Geelani, Mehmood was rebuked for saying that though the UN resolutions of 1949 were a base for settlement, 'we are ready to move beyond [them]'. Kashmiris, said a statement by the Tehreek, 'had not sacrificed for self-rule, autonomy, joint control, soft borders'.[105]

Though we did not meet Mehmood formally, I did meet him at the wedding, to which I was invited through intermediaries. Knowing that Chief Minister Omar Abdullah would be there, I went.

Mehmood and I had an hour-long conversation.[106] He had come with a proposal for talks between Jammu and Kashmir legislators and their counterparts in Pakistan-administered Kashmir and Gilgit-Baltistan, to be paralleled by talks between Indian and Pakistani parliamentarians.

I was enthusiastic. The Pakistani government had refused to

recognize the elected leaders of Jammu and Kashmir after 1964. It was only in 2006 that there was a small thaw and both Omar Abdullah and Mehbooba Mufti were invited to a Musharraf-sponsored conference in Islamabad. They had not been invited again. A dialogue between legislators from both sides of the Line of Control could be just the breakthrough we needed. It would also enable the Hurriyat to come back on board a peace process. Again, I relayed Mehmood's proposal to the Home Ministry and NSA, and again received no answer. The proposal did not materialize.

When I asked former Home Minister Chidambaram about it years later, in 2017, he was impatient. He did not remember Mehmood's offer, he said and, in any case, it was irrelevant. Our concern was with Jammu and Kashmir and no intervention from across the Line of Control was required. Clearly, we were on different pages. I believed that no solution would hold unless representatives of Pakistan-administered Kashmir and Gilgit-Baltistan were on board, because they could push the Pakistani authorities.

Meanwhile, pressure on the Pakistani government rose in both regions. Despite the reforms package, there were widespread complaints about the conduct of the 2009 legislative assembly elections in Gilgit–Baltistan, while further human rights violations were protested in Muzaffarabad. Political parties that refused to take the oath of allegiance to Pakistan were banned from contesting, and dissidents were rounded up and imprisoned to prevent them from campaigning in the elections. They included members of the All Parties National Alliance, the Gilgit–Baltistan Democratic Alliance, the Gilgit–Baltistan Thinkers' Forum, the JKLF and the Karakorum National Movement. In November–December 2009, there were a series of protests in Muzaffarabad against the 'clandestine activities' of the ISI, which was accused of kidnapping four Kashmiri students from the city. 'One of the four was released after many days of torture and inhuman treatment,' wrote Shabir Choudhury, 'but the remaining three are still kept in a secret location by the ISI.'[107] In January 2010, newspapers reported a rising number of suicide bombings in the statelet, conducted by a new coalition of Islamic guerrillas, the Lashkar-e-Zil, which brought together Al Qaeda, Tehrik-e-Taliban Pakistan, the Harkat-ul-Jihad-e-Islami, the Lashkar-e-Jhangvi, the Afghan Taliban, the Hizb-e-Islami Afghanistan and the Haqqani network. The Lashkar-e-Zil's operational commander, said the *News International*, was Ilyas Kashmiri.[108]

Visiting Poonch, Mirpur and Muzaffarabad a few days later, members of the Pakistan parliament's Kashmir Committee heard a host of grievance. The statelet's government should have been consulted before the Gilgit–Baltistan package was announced, its ministers complained. Moreover, the package should have rolled back amendments to the interim constitution of 1974, which had further reduced government powers. The $2.1 billion Neelam–Jhelum Hydel Project, considered to be critical for Pakistan, would reduce the water flow to Muzaffarabad. Under the dam contract, the statelet would not receive a share of profits, a problem that the Gilgit–Baltistan administration had also highlighted in reference to the Diamir–Basha dam being constructed in Gilgit. Worst of all, the committee was told by civil society, the Council was a white elephant, 'answerable to no one'.[109]

In March 2010, the pro-independence activist Shafqat Inquilabi filed a petition in Pakistan's Supreme Court against the Gilgit–Baltistan package, claiming it was an act of 'illegal hegemony'. He began to be pressured to withdraw his petition by the ISI and Pakistan's Intelligence Bureau. Memorably, when a phone call 'from one of these clandestine agencies' came during a press conference that he was holding in Muzaffarabad, Inquilabi put the phone on loudspeaker 'so that the media could sample a taste of the harassment he was undergoing'.[110]

I began to receive appeals from dissidents, including Amanullah Khan and the Balawaristan National Front (a Balti nationalist group), whose members were regularly imprisoned. In his submission to the UN Human Rights Council's 15th session on 23 September 2010, the Chairman of the Front alleged that seven political prisoners had been sentenced to execution and another five to life imprisonment. In 2011, it was reported that hundreds of pro-independence activists and former guerrillas were missing and were presumed to be held by the ISI. The BBC reported Atique Khan, the then prime minister of Pakistan-administered Kashmir, as saying, 'The authorities in Muzaffarabad do not dispute this claim, but justify such action on the grounds that local laws do not allow pro-independence politics. "There may be some innocent people among [those arrested]...there may be mistakes made [by the intelligence operatives]...but the imperatives of national defence sometimes necessitate such arrests..."'.[111] Under Pakistani law, the Pakistan Army, intelligence and paramilitary had immunity from prosecution for human rights violations.

Even if the Singh and Zardari administrations did pick up from the Aziz–Lambah framework negotiations, we noted, the changes made over decades by the Pakistani government in the status of Pakistan-administered Kashmir and Gilgit–Baltistan added complications, in particular, the de facto separation of the Northern Areas from Poonch, Mirpur and Muzaffarabad from 1949 on. This separation began to be challenged in the 1990s. In 1993, the Muzaffarabad High Court laid down that the Northern Areas were under the jurisdiction of Pakistan-administered Kashmir.[112] But in 1994, the statelet's Supreme Court overturned this decision, stating that the Northern Areas were part of Jammu and Kashmir but not of Poonch, Mirpur and Muzaffarabad. In 1999, the Supreme Court of Pakistan affirmed this decision, adding that the people of the Northern Areas were citizens of Pakistan, a decision that made it even more difficult to find a solution for the former princely state. Effectively, the Pakistani position meant that any peace process would have to deal with three divided territories and peoples, not two.

Further, from 1974 onwards, when Bhutto abolished the state subject provisions that applied in the former princely state, outsiders, especially from Pakistan's Khyber–Pakhtunkhwa and Punjab, were encouraged to settle in Gilgit–Baltistan, altering the demographic balance and leading to sectarian conflict between Shia and Sunni militias, especially in Gilgit. The issue of the future of these settlers and their rights within Gilgit–Baltistan would have to be discussed, as persons from outside Jammu and Kashmir were not regarded as state citizens.

Similarly, while the property of those who fled Jammu and Kashmir during 1948–49 had been protected by the Jammu and Kashmir government, no such system existed in Pakistan-administered Kashmir or Gilgit-Baltistan, where the property of those who fled to Jammu and Kashmir was assigned to migrants and displaced persons. Thus, while migrants and displaced persons in Pakistan-administered Kashmir could claim their original properties in Jammu and Kashmir, migrants and displaced persons in Jammu and Kashmir could not claim their original properties in the Pakistan-held territories of the former princely state. Clearly this issue needs to be on a talks agenda.

Further issues have accrued since we wrote our report. In 2016, China's $45 billion investment in the China–Pakistan Economic Corridor (CPEC), which would run through a part of Gilgit–Baltistan, was contested by the Indian government on grounds that the area was disputed. In 2017, while China hosted its Belt and Road Initiative summit, protests broke out in Gilgit, Hunza, Skardu and Ghizer. Pro-independence student and political organizations such as the Karakoram Students' Organization, the Balawaristan National Students Organization, the Gilgit–Baltistan United Movement and the Balawaristan National Front demonstrated, describing CPEC as 'an illegal attempt' and naming it 'a Road of Gulami or Slavery for Gilgit–Baltistan'.[113]

In other words, a large number of legal and constitutional reforms and changes on the ground would be required if the same political, economic and cultural freedoms were to be offered on both sides of the Line of Control.

◆

We submitted our report to Home Minister Chidambaram in October 2011. Some weeks later, he briefed the union cabinet on our report, and four months later, the Cabinet Committee on Security. Though the report was then supposed to be placed before the members of the 2010 parliamentary delegation, no meeting was held with them. When we contacted some of them later to ask whether the meeting was going to happen, we received evasive replies. By this point, corruption scandals had rocked the winter session of parliament, with Chidambaram himself accused of fiddling with spectrum allocations. The only members of parliament to table questions on our report were Karan Singh, the prince who ended the monarchy, and Shashi Tharoor—both represented the Congress party.

The Singh administration did not act on any of the political recommendations made in our report, nor on the major human rights and security reforms we suggested. Eventually, it was put in the public domain as a link on the Home Ministry's website in spring 2012, with a disclaimer that it represented our opinions alone. Its release was greeted by loud criticism from the BJP, whose Jammu unit burned copies of it. The Congress, CPI-M and other political parties ignored it. In the valley, the PDP was the only party to say that they were glad to see some of their proposals incorporated. The state cabinet, comprising National Conference and Congress ministers, did not discuss the report either; but then, they were yet to discuss the Ahmed report of 2008. In December 2011, the state's cabinet subcommittee on the Ahmed report 'sought yet another extension of three months…as it failed to evolve a consensus on the recommendations' of the report.[114]

Chapter XX

2016 AND AFTER: LOSING KASHMIR?

In the summer of 2016, the Kashmir valley was again engulfed in an agonizing period of turmoil. Angry mobs attacked police stations and security installations. Masked youth paraded the streets, some as young as eight, forcing shopkeepers to down shutters, stoning army and police forces, painting anti-India graffiti on every available wall. The police retaliated by firing pellet guns and inflicting gross injuries. In four weeks, close to fifty people died and over 6,000 were injured. Around twenty people were fully or partially blinded and 4,000 policemen were wounded.

What led to this horrible and tragic situation?

The immediate trigger was the death of a twenty-two-year-old Kashmiri guerrilla named Burhan Wani, killed in an encounter with security forces. Wani had become a social media icon for young Kashmiris, who saw him as a symbol for the struggle for freedom. Born into a Jamaat-e-Islami family in the guerrilla stronghold of Tral in south Kashmir, Wani dropped out of school to join the Hizbul Mujahideen when he was fifteen. According to his family and friends, he made his decision following the humiliation of his older brother at a security checkpost. His father said he wanted to join the Indian Army when he was ten. He was the Hizbul's commander for south Kashmir when he died.

The organization he belonged to had withered by the mid-2000s, but Wani infused new life into it. He was not particularly notable as an armed guerrilla; according to the Jammu and Kashmir police force, he had been implicated in the murders of two sarpanches and three troops over the course of six years. But he was adept at social media, posting selfies in army fatigues complete with gun, and recording speeches calling for azaadi and the establishment of a caliphate. Fair and brown-eyed, with the slightly chubby cheeks of an adolescent, his social media campaign was a hit amongst the valley's unemployed and partially educated youth, who were, as in the rest of India, a sizable demographic.

Pulwama district, where Wani grew up, had recently emerged as a hub of Hizbul guerrillas driven out of Srinagar and Budgam. But it had been a dissident centre for much longer. Lying between Budgam and Shopian, it was a prosperous area of orchards clustered around a merchant town, frequently visited for funds by the guerrillas. The deep and thick forests of Tral had provided hiding and training grounds for cross-border guerrillas since 1948.

The valley erupted over Wani's death. Reports of attendance at his funeral varied from 30,000 to 150,000; armed guerrillas who were present vowed revenge. Protesters set fire to police stations and attacked security installations. The police were not in a position to deter them with effective barricades, tear gas or water cannon. Lacking supplies of tear gas or water cannon, the police fell back on the pellet guns as non-lethal weapons. The guns proved lethal when fired in proximity. Close to thirty people died in the three days following Wani's killing.

Kashmir was back on the boil, and the union and state governments appeared as unprepared as they had been in 2010. Though essential supplies were rushed to the valley, and union Home Minister Rajnath Singh called back-to-back emergency meetings—indeed, Prime Minister Modi and NSA Ajit Doval were said to monitor the situation hour by hour—violence continued to mount over subsequent months. It was exacerbated by the full glare of social and electronic media, the former spouting visceral hate and the latter an inhuman callousness to the intense suffering of the bereaved. Anchors chorused on national television channels that Kashmiris were seditious, anti-national and traitors, and the refrain was taken up by the ruling BJP's spokesmen.

Chief Minister Mehbooba Mufti's weak response played into the rapidly increasing rift between Delhi and the valley. Her statement that she would have stopped the police operation had she known Wani was the target infuriated the police, who had tried to persuade him to surrender when he was surrounded.

Her appeals to civil society groups, religious organizations and dissidents to help end the violence had little effect. Though she directed PDP MLAs to visit their constituencies and help calm the situation, they continued to huddle in their homes, afraid of reprisal. By the end of the year, over 100 youths had died in clashes between stone-throwers and security forces in the valley.

♦

If Wani's death was an immediate trigger of the 2016 violence, the warning signs had mounted since we ended our mission in October 2011.

Though the Singh administration did not act on our recommendations, 2012 seemed like a year of peace. In February, the valley celebrated when a young Kashmiri called Shah Faesal topped the all-India Civil Services Examination. A 'face of hope reflects calm in Kashmir', wrote the *New York Times* correspondent describing the young administrator's first public meeting.[1] The state government achieved a record tax collection of ₹4,800 crore (48 billion).[2] Tourists continued to pour in. Municipal elections were planned and the state government announced sixteen new councils.

Yet, counter-trends continued. There were sporadic incidents of stoning. A re-emboldened Dukhtaran-e-Millat, led by Asiya Andrabi, sent groups of burqa-clad activists to raid city restaurants and public parks to 'prevent young couples from celebrating Valentine's Day'.[3] In Pakistan, the Lashkar and Jaish launched new drives to mobilize guerrillas to 'support the freedom struggle' in Kashmir. India–Pakistan initiatives to pick up on peacemaking withered as Pakistan entered a pre-election phase with elections scheduled in spring 2013. Sadly, the state government's attempt to hold municipal elections widened the Jammu–valley gulf. Twelve of the sixteen new municipal councils were in the valley and only four in Jammu. Jammu commentators called it 'a glaring act of discrimination'.[4] These signs of continuing volatility apart, 2012 was still a year of calm compared to the five preceding years.

The tenuous peace of 2012 came to an abrupt halt in February 2013 when the Singh administration decided to hang Afzal Guru, who had been sentenced to death a decade earlier for his role in the parliament attack of 2001. He was secretly hanged without being given the chance to meet his family, and his body was buried in the compound of Tihar jail, where he had been on death row since 2002. Thirty-six people were injured in protests in his hometown Sopore, Baramulla and Pulwama. Twenty-three were policemen. In Delhi, there were clashes between BJP and Kashmiri student activists.

Terrorist attacks rose in the aftermath of Guru's hanging. In late February, a series of blasts in Hyderabad killed sixteen; in March, a guerrilla attack in Srinagar left seven dead; in April, there was a blast in Bengaluru in which, fortunately, no one died; and in June, there was another guerrilla attack in Srinagar in which eight were killed.

Guru's hanging elicited more protest than his sentence had. He had been a double agent, working for Pakistani as well as Indian intelligence services. Most Kashmiris accepted his complicity but asked that his sentence be commuted to life imprisonment. There had been presidential clemency before, notably in the case of Rajiv Gandhi's assassins. Moreover, Guru's execution was bumped up over others still pending on death row, some of them with earlier sentences than Guru. Many in the state concluded that the decision to hang him was a message to Kashmiris. The BJP had begun a campaign for his execution in 2012; it was part of their strategy to portray the Singh administration as weak and corrupt, with an eye to the 2014 polls.

Why did the Congress cave to the BJP campaign? Omar Abdullah said the decision was taken for political reasons, and the general consensus was that Guru's hanging silenced BJP critics. The families of the victims of the Parliament attack—mostly paramilitary guarding the complex—had returned their posthumous medals during the BJP campaign. After Guru's hanging, they took the medals back.

Seeing anger in the valley, the Singh administration tried to scramble back by renewing peace initiatives with Nawaz Sharif, newly elected Pakistan's prime minister for the third time. The efforts were fruitless. At first, it looked as if the Indian offer to provide electricity to Pakistani Punjab might be accepted. Discussion went as far as negotiations between the two countries' power ministries, but then a call upon Sharif by Chief of Army Staff General Parvez Kayani brought negotiations to a halt.

Whatever the Congress's reasons, Guru's execution did not help them electorally. In May 2014, the Congress lost the national election to the BJP, who came in with a thumping majority. In December, they lost the Kashmir state election. The BJP won the majority of seats in Jammu and the PDP and National Conference divided seats in the valley, with the PDP gaining more than the National Conference.

The BJP and PDP had fought a vitriolic campaign against each other, which became a Jammu *vs.* valley contest. In the valley, the National Conference, PDP and Congress all campaigned on a 'keep the BJP out' plank. In Jammu, the BJP campaigned on a 'keep the PDP and National Conference out' plank. For the National Conference and PDP, the BJP were Hindu communalists who wanted to roll back the state's special status and alter the valley's demography. For the BJP, the National Conference and PDP were 'soft separatists'. When the election results came out they showed how far Jammu and the valley had grown apart. Of the 87-member assembly, the PDP won 28 seats, mostly in the valley; the BJP won 25 seats, all in Jammu; the National Conference won 17 seats and the Congress 12. The only party which had a coalition choice was the PDP. The BJP and National Conference were not in the position to form a government without support from at least two other MLAs. The PDP could enter into a coalition with the Congress and with support from the National Conference, as Omar suggested, but if they did so, they would be seen as ostracizing Jammu.

After hectic negotiations, the PDP and BJP announced they were forming the government. Their coalition, they said, was based on an 'Agenda for Alliance', drafted by the BJP's general secretary Ram Madhav and the PDP's senior leader Haseeb Drabu, who became the state's finance minister. Announcing that the purpose of the alliance was to 'catalyse reconciliation and confidence-building within and across the Line of Control in Jammu and Kashmir, thereby ensuring peace in the state',[5] the agenda said the coalition would maintain 'the present position…on all the constitutional provisions pertaining to Jammu and Kashmir, including special status in the Constitution of India'. There would be talks with dissident groups; following Vajpayee's policy of 'insaniyat, jamhooriyat aur Kashmiriyat', the coalition government would 'help initiate a sustained and meaningful dialogue with all internal stakeholders, which will include all political groups irrespective of their ideological views and predilections'. Externally too, the coalition would support Modi's efforts to 'normalize relations with Pakistan'. Modi had invited Pakistan's prime minister Sharif to his swearing-in and Sharif had come.

On human rights and security, the agenda continued the policy adopted by the previous Congress–National Conference coalition. 'While both parties have historically held a different view on the Armed Forces (Special Powers) Act (AFSPA) and the need for it in the State at present,' it stated, 'the coalition government will examine the need for de-notifying "disturbed areas". This, as a consequence, would enable the union government to take a final view on the continuation of AFSPA in these areas.'

The agenda represented a major shift for the BJP. On the first day that Modi had assumed office, Minister of State in the PMO, Jitendra Singh, announced that the new government would abolish Article 370.[6] Now, they said, they would maintain the constitutional status of Jammu and Kashmir. Indeed, they went further and described Article 370 as special status, a term we had suggested in our report. Most importantly, a BJP–PDP coalition offered hope of reconciliation between Jammu and the valley.

These signs of hope rapidly dissipated. Sharif's attendance at Modi's swearing-in had led to the revival of peace talks, but they were accompanied by an exponential rise in cross-border firing by the Pakistan Army. According to Home Ministry figures, there were 583 ceasefire violations in 2014 as against 347 in 2013 and 114 in 2012. Between 2012 and 2015, 215,110 families were affected by cross-border shelling—including those who had to flee the border districts—and 193 houses were fully or partially damaged.[7]

The Modi administration responded with what they called 'massive retaliation', but the escalation did not yield deterrent results. In a thoughtful analysis of the relative thresholds of India and Pakistan, a group of scholars at the Takshashila Institution, a small Indian think tank, pointed out that Pakistan responded to escalation with further escalation since it had a much higher threshold than India, thus calibration was both difficult and risky.[8] As the Modi administration's attempts to 'give a befitting response' to Pakistan's cross-border firing showed, the human cost was too high to persist to the point that the damage inflicted on Pakistani forces would deter them from cross-border infiltration and firing.

The end result of escalation was that the directors general of both countries' border forces met in September 2015 and resolved to better implement CBMs agreed a decade ago, which were intended to limit or defuse incidents of cross-border firing. The agreement was violated immediately, but cross-border firing reduced to some extent. Meanwhile, the Pakistani military focused on building up their arsenal, arming themselves with tactical nuclear weapons and upgrading their air force. In 2015, Pakistan declared a doctrine of 'full-spectrum deterrence', in other words, that they would deploy weapons of mass destruction if considered necessary.

By mid-2015, it became clear that the Sharif administration and the Pakistan Army were at loggerheads over the country's India policy. In July, Modi and Sharif pledged counter-terrorism cooperation on the sidelines of the Shanghai Cooperation Organisation and BRICS (Brazil, Russia, India, China and South Africa) summits at Ufa in Russia. Their teams also decided on a sequence of talks divided into a two-stage process. The first stage, detailed in the joint statement issued at Ufa,[9] would be to create conducive conditions for dialogue through cooperation against terrorism and de-escalation on the Line of Control and international border. The second stage would comprise talks to resolve conflicts over Kashmir, Sir Creek and Siachen. Hence, the first set of talks would be between the Indian and Pakistani NSAs, directors general of the Indian BSF and Pakistan Rangers, and DGMOs of the Indian and Pakistani armies. The next set of talks would be between the foreign secretaries.

Faced with an outcry in Pakistan against the joint statement at Ufa, the Pakistani government sought to telescope the two stages into one. The then Pakistani NSA, Sartaj Aziz, they proposed, would engage in parallel talks when he visited New Delhi in August: on terrorism with the Indian NSA, Ajit Doval, and on Jammu and Kashmir with India's foreign secretary, S. Jaishankar. At the same time, Aziz also invited the Hurriyat, Tehreek and allied dissidents to meet with him. The Modi administration objected and Pakistan called off the talks, but only after a petty game of brinkmanship was played out in the media by both sides.[10]

Did the Modi administration's stance on 'no talks with the Hurriyat' signify a departure from previous policy? That depends. The Singh administration had ignored frequent meetings between Pakistani representatives and various dissident leaders from the Kashmir valley even whilst there were few meetings between the latter and the union government. But that itself was a departure from the Vajpayee administration's policy for the Hurriyat to play a bridging role by talking to Pakistani representatives on one track and the union government on another track.

Whether the Modi administration would accept the Hurriyat in a mediating role was moot. Many in the BJP and its affiliates had already started asking whether the Hurriyat and other dissident groups could be considered stakeholders. They brushed aside the PDP–BJP coalition's pledge to talks in its Agenda of Alliance.

For Mufti Sayeed, his second stint as chief minister, this time heading the PDP–BJP coalition, was painful in the extreme. He had made a peace process with Pakistan his core policy, with some success between 2004 and 2006. The Agenda of Alliance put his policy at the forefront too, but little follow-up was allowed by the Modi administration. Despite Sayeed's efforts, there were no talks with the Hurriyat or other dissident groups. To the contrary, he had to deal with the fallout of the BJP's campaign to enforce a ban on beef sale and consumption across India, which soon morphed into mobs of self-appointed 'gau rakshaks' (cow protectors) lynching anyone they suspected of eating or selling beef, including in Jammu. In most cases the gau rakshaks' suspicions were found to be misplaced. In September 2015, Jammu and Kashmir legislators came to blows over the issue. The Islamist campaigner Asiya Andrabi slaughtered a cow as an act of defiance, and MLA Rashid similarly hosted a 'beef dinner'.[11] It seems absurd to talk about the politics of cow protection, yet this single issue alienated Kashmiris and Muslims in the rest of India, in a way that few other issues had. Though not in Kashmir, it also led to the loss of hundreds of thousands of jobs in the rest of India.

Natural disasters added to the state's woes. Devastating floods in September 2014 left over 450 dead and 300,000 stranded. Though the Modi administration released funds for flood relief, they were a first instalment, to be followed by further funds when the state and union governments approved post-flood reconstruction plans. The plans took over a year to clear. When Modi visited Srinagar in November 2015, he announced a government grant of ₹80,000 crore (800 billion), which would include flood relief, connectivity and infrastructure development.

Sayeed had used the weeks preceding Modi's visit to promote a political initiative to complement the aid initiative. The coalition would make 'a new beginning', he said.[12] It was widely expected that Modi would announce political measures, including talks with Pakistan and the Hurriyat, during his November visit. Instead, when Sayeed referred to a peace process during Modi's address at the Sher-e-Kashmir stadium, Modi retorted that he did not 'need any advice on Kashmir'.

Sayeed died in early January 2016, days before his eightieth birthday. Soon after his death, a Jaish-e-Mohammad attack on an Indian Army base at Pathankot in Punjab caused outrage in India. The Sharif administration acknowledged that the Jaish was responsible for the attack and promised action. The Indian government gave Pakistan's Federal Investigation Agency (FIA) access to Indian witnesses and the Pathankot airbase, but the FIA investigation came to a dead end in Pakistan, as previous Pakistani investigations had. Any hopes of rapprochement were buried.

Jammu and Kashmir suffered a constitutional vacuum after Sayeed's death. Deeply hurt by the rebuffs to Sayeed during his year as chief minister, Mehbooba Mufti insisted she would not take his place until the Modi administration committed to a timeline for implementing the Agenda of Alliance. After three months of hectic backchannel negotiation, she finally agreed to assume office days before the governor was to call for fresh elections. Her party had suffered enormous loss of public support when the agenda was turned into a meaningless piece of paper. They would be decimated if fresh elections were held.

The coalition had just resumed office when Wani was killed. In an effort to contain the fallout, the Rajya Sabha passed a resolution on 10 August appealing 'to all sections of society in Jammu and Kashmir to work for the early restoration of normalcy and harmony' and unanimously resolved to restore confidence 'among the people in general and youth in particular'.[13] The resolution had no impact. Turmoil continued through 2016 and into 2017.

On 7 September 2016, an all-party delegation marshalled by the union Home Ministry asked the Modi administration to start talks with the Hurriyat, Tehreek and allied groups, and Mehbooba called for an 'institutionalized mechanism for dialogue', a call she was to repeat the next year.[14] Dissident leader Ghani Bhat responded promisingly on 8 September: 'Given the political environment and economic developments around, we cannot afford to assume a harder attitude. We have to be flexible.'[15] Soon after, an influential group of retired civil servants from Jammu and Kashmir wrote to the President of India to 'implore and beseech Your Excellency, to impress upon the Government of India to initiate and announce direct, immediate, purposeful and result oriented dialogue with all the stakeholders especially those with whom such dialogue has been held in 2004 and 2007 for a lasting solution of [the] "Kashmir Dispute" within a reasonable time frame.'[16] BJP president Amit Shah said his party was considering Mehbooba's call, but talks did not transpire.

Disturbing new trends emerged. In 2015, the Jammu and Kashmir police force warned that though guerrilla numbers were down overall, local guerrillas outnumbered foreign terrorists for the first time in ten years, making up 62 per cent of the total. The conclusion they drew was that local support for armed attacks was on the increase, and the events of 2016 bore them out. Guerrilla funerals became spots for public protest against the state and union governments, with increasing numbers of Kashmiris attending. Women were seen leading protests. Slowly, armed attacks returned to the valley. According to state government figures, the number of young men taking to arms rose from 66 in 2015 to 88 in 2016 and 126 in 2017.[17] In the first six months of 2018 alone, 82 young men joined armed groups.[18]

For the first time in the history of the Kashmir conflict, civilians attacked security forces from the rear when they conducted cordon and search operations, to allow guerrillas to escape. Stone-throwers who were interviewed said they were fighting for Islam; several said they supported the Islamic State. Worst of all, insurgents set fire to government schools that refused to obey shutdown calls. Over twenty-four schools were burnt in seven weeks. Despite the arson, the Tehreek refused to lift their shutdown edict from educational institutions. Geelani issued a statement that the government's push to reopen schools was 'nothing but mockery and imperialistic designs to strengthen this unwanted occupation'.[19] A year later, Hizbul commander Zakir Musa threatened that any dissident who called the 'Kashmir movement' political instead of an Islamic uprising would be killed.[20] When criticized by Hizbul head Yusuf Shah, he left the militia, vowing to continue his battle.

In early 2017, the Modi administration adopted a hard-line policy aimed at cracking down on armed groups and their supporters. Civilians who impeded security operations, the new army chief General Bipin Rawat announced, would be treated as 'overground workers' of terrorist groups. In April, by-elections in Srinagar and Anantnag saw the lowest turnout ever in Jammu and Kashmir, of between 3 and 10 per cent. An army major who had tied a Kashmiri to the bonnet of a jeep to ensure safe passage for election officers was hailed as a hero by the union government; even though he had violated the law, he was awarded a medal some months later. In July, an Armed Forces Tribunal overturned the 2013 conviction of five soldiers for the Machil 'fake encounter', though they had been convicted by army court martial and sentenced to life imprisonment in 2015. At the same time, seven second-rung Hurriyat, Tehreek and other dissident leaders were arrested by the National Investigation Agency, on charges of criminal conspiracy and waging war against India. They had, it was alleged, taken funds from Pakistan for stoning protests. By this point, shoot-outs between security forces and guerrillas had become daily occurrences, mostly in the districts of south Kashmir that had been PDP strongholds. Stoning protests rose and fell but not below two or three a day. There were 201 incidents in May 2017, 92 in June and 113 in July.[21] Talks with dissidents receded into the far distance, as did the peace process.

◆

The worsening situation in the valley did prompt a partial rethink in the Modi administration. In his August 2017 Independence Day speech, the prime minister exhorted his countrymen to 'embrace' Kashmiris instead of fighting or demonizing them, adding 'na goli se na gali se, baat banegi boli se (the solution will come through talks, not bullets or abuse)'.[22] In October, Dineshwar Sharma, a former head of India's Intelligence Bureau, was appointed Special Representative for Jammu and Kashmir.

Sharma's mandate was similar to the mandate we had had, insofar as he was empowered to hold talks with dissidents such as the Hurriyat. But it also appeared to be more restricted than ours, since his appointment letter specified he would discuss only the 'legitimate aspirations' of Kashmiris.[23] What the Modi administration defined as legitimate was unclear. At the same time as his administration appointed an interlocutor, the prime minister likened the autonomy demand to the independence demand in his October 2017 Gujarat election campaign speeches, implying that even autonomy was off the table.

The Tehreek, Hurriyat and JKLF—who had recently banded together under the rubric of a 'Joint Resistance Leadership'—immediately denounced Sharma's appointment, announcing that they would not participate in talks with him. But their statement was par for the course. They had made similar statements on our appointment as well as those of previous interlocutors, but unofficially encouraged us to develop conditions on the ground that would permit a dialogue between them and the prime minister or home minister.

Sharma's mission appeared to follow a similar structure and trajectory to ours. He began visiting districts and met the breakaway peacenik Ghani Bhatt. Just before his second visit to Jammu and Kashmir, the Home Ministry supported the state government in announcing an amnesty for first-time stone-throwers on 23 November 2017. The Mehbooba administration began to implement this policy more speedily than the Omar administration had, though the amnesty failed to give Sharma's mission the boost it was intended to, since the army's counter-insurgency campaign continued full tilt.

Though we too were dogged by the AFSPA debate, which reopened in January 2018 following the deaths of three youths in army firing in Shopian during a stoning protest, Sharma had a harder task in relation to the army than we did. The chief of army staff during our mission, General V. K. Singh, was also sceptical of a peace process, but he was advised to allow his commanders on the ground to do more talking about Kashmir than he did, and they espoused a hearts-and-minds policy. Towards the end of his tenure, however, General Singh embroiled himself in ugly spats with the Singh administration, including over Kashmir. The chief of army staff since 2016, General Bipin Rawat, did far more talking on Kashmir than the commanders on the ground, and his often-unguarded remarks were negatively received. In early 2018, his criticism of the valley's educational practice sparked a row with the state education minister, adding to valley hostility towards security forces.[24]

As of late 2017, the Modi administration appeared to be

pursuing a two-pronged strategy in the valley, reconciliation on one prong and counter-insurgency on the other. The two prongs sat uneasily together. While Sharma's mission was reconciliation, the security forces' counter-insurgency operations ratcheted up and widened to a crackdown on illegal funding for dissidence. Targeting the black economy was necessary for peacebuilding, but would carry more weight if all illegal financial transactions were targeted, including corruption and nepotism, not just dissident funds. There were also hard considerations to factor in—how could Sharma expect to talk to dissidents if they and their colleagues were arrested for illegal funding (which they also periodically received from Indian government agencies, mostly through slush funds)?

This was a dilemma that previous administrations faced and dealt with in different ways. The Vajpayee administration countenanced pay-offs, especially to surrendering militants and their mentors. Singh's administration gradually terminated grants to former militants but did allow occasional pay-offs, for example, to wean away stone-throwers in 2010–11. Both administrations attempted to curb the flow of funds for militancy from Pakistan, the Middle East, Southeast Asia and the Pakistani or Kashmiri diaspora in Europe and the US. But they did so quietly, without linking Kashmiri grievances to funding or implying that Kashmiri protests occurred only because they were paid, both of which erroneous assumptions seemed to have become axioms for the Modi administration.

The space for peacemaking shrank so rapidly between 2014 and 2018 that it was difficult to imagine how, if at all, talks with Kashmiri dissidents would resume. The same conditions applied to talks with Pakistan.

◆

Unsurprisingly, the Pakistani government began to ramp up its Kashmir campaign from 2015 on, across the border and in international forums. They had already signalled their intention, with the last but one salvo being fired by the then Turkey-dominated Organisation of Islamic Cooperation (OIC). The OIC invited pro-Al Qaeda Asiya Andrabi and pro-Pakistan Geelani to speak at a discussion on Kashmir during its summit meeting on the sidelines of the UN General Assembly in New York in September 2015, but did not invite the chief minister or leaders of electoral parties. It was standard practice for the OIC to exclude elected representatives from Jammu and Kashmir and invite only radical dissidents. Conversely, they invited only government-approved representatives from Pakistani-administered Kashmir and no dissidents. But then, the OIC was itself an anomaly. In a world where religious inter-governmental institutions had been phased out, it was the one remaining bastion of official communalism.

As the NATO-led International Security Assistance Force withdrawal from Afghanistan proceeded through 2014–15, and the pressure for a deal between the Afghan government and the Taliban intensified, Pakistan's India policy underwent a shift back to the 'strategic depth in Afghanistan-unrest in Kashmir' dyad, which had long been on the hard-line Pakistanis' wish list. The Pakistani civil and military establishment had sought to turn Kashmir into a 'Muslim issue' since partition and independence. They had failed, thanks in part to India's anti-colonial credentials in the Arab world, which led a large number of Muslim-majority countries to remain politely indifferent to Pakistani lobbying. But Afghanistan—first under the Taliban and then post 9/11—offered a new opportunity. Pakistan's importance to the US-led coalition grew as the Afghan war dragged on with no end in sight. The Pakistani government and military took advantage of their new leverage to tie a Kashmir settlement, on their terms, to the use of their good offices with the Taliban, with varying results. When Mullah Omar's death was announced and the Taliban fragmented, Pakistan's role in an Afghan settlement and its influence in that country grew further, but so did the pressure on Pakistan.

That the Pakistani government would attempt to use their leverage against India was inevitable. Indian analysts had forecast that conflict over Jammu and Kashmir would rise in parallel to Pakistan's importance in and for Afghanistan—and were proved right. It was less accurately noted, however, that Pakistan's efforts to up the ante on Kashmir would meet with pressure to negotiate with India, thus offering some leverage to the Indian government. Russia and China, for example, were likely to have played an important role in facilitating the July 2015 Ufa statement by Modi and Sharif.

Both India and Pakistan overplayed their hands. Having seen the outcry in Pakistan against the Ufa statement, the Modi administration could have planned to announce jointly with Sharif that talks on Jammu and Kashmir would follow. Instead, it blamed the Hurriyat for calling off talks, which had a negative impact in the valley and upped Pakistan's profile in Kashmir, hurting India domestically. The Sharif administration, on the other hand, hurt itself internationally by calling off talks because of the Hurriyat tangle. What relevance do the Hurriyat leaders have to Saeed, Azhar and Lakhvi's prosecution or to CBMs between the border security forces?

Though Modi and Sharif tried backchannels to restart the India–Pakistan peace process, leading to a surprise visit by Modi to Sharif on his birthday in December 2015, Sharif had already become a lame-duck prime minister. The military-backed agitation against the Sharif administration in 2014, led by cleric Tahir ul Qadri and political leader Imran Khan, shut down the government and left the Sharif administration tottering. Sharif's Ufa statement was, at least in part, an attempt to defy the Pakistan Army's opposition to peacemaking with India. He lost this battle, as he did all others with the military, whether over their domestic political finagling or over their proxy war in Afghanistan. Finally, in mid-2017, he was given his congé by the Pakistani courts who sentenced him for corruption on surprisingly flimsy grounds and deposed him. The PML leader who succeeded him in August 2017, Shahid Khaqan Abbasi, followed the Pakistan Army's continuing hostilities with India and Afghanistan.

In other words, the Pakistan Army had once again consolidated its dominance over Pakistan's foreign relations as well as domestic politics.

The year 2017 was one of the worst for ceasefire violations across the Line of Control. There were 241 incidents of cross-border firing, up from 105 in 2016. From 2009–12, the corresponding yearly figures were below 100; they were as low as 35 in 2009, but rose after Afzal Guru's hanging to 116 in 2013 and continued to mount in 2015, 2016 and 2017.[25] According to press reports, there were over 160 ceasefire violations in January 2018 alone.[26] Interestingly, in the last year that Modi and Sharif attempted peace initiatives, 2015, the greatest number of cross-border firings were at the international border, not Line of Control. At 131, the figures were ten times higher than in the preceding decade.

By end-2017, it seemed the Pakistani government had again veered to open support for an anti-India jihad by non-state actors. All those implicated in the 26/11 attacks were freed; indeed, Hafiz Saeed sought protection from the courts against arrest when the UN Security Council's sanctions monitoring team arrived in Pakistan in January 2018 to assess government curbs on over thirty organizations, including the Lashkar-e-Taiba, Jamaat-ud-Dawa and Falah-i-Insaniyat. Ahead of the visit, the Pakistani government took no steps against Saeed. Instead, they launched 'an advertisement campaign cautioning [the] public against making donations to banned organizations' and issued a directive 'barring media houses from publishing statements and advertisements of Hafiz Saeed, LeT, JuD and Falah-i-Insaaniyat'.[27] Pakistan's Securities and Exchange Commission also issued a notification asking companies not to do business with banned organizations.

In early February 2018, Pakistan's ambassador to the UN, Maleeha Lodhi, asked the UN Security Council to 'review', or rather, revive the 1948 plebiscite resolution. While the request was not agreed, it reinforced the conclusion that the Abbasi administration sought to escalate conflict over Kashmir.

At the same time, PPP leader former President Zardari issued a press statement saying he possessed a copy of Musharraf's 'secret plan', which Musharraf's army peers had refused to accept. The reference was to the Aziz–Lambah framework, which the Zardari administration had claimed to have neither knowledge nor record of. So when had Zardari come into possession of it?

Sharif, Zardari added, deserved to be deposed, because he was 'a friend of Modi' and had 'betrayed' the Kashmir cause.[28]

♦

Finally, in March 2018, there was a small breakthrough. The gruesome rape and murder of an eight-year old girl in the Kathua district of Jammu precipitated a crisis followed by outcry that forced two BJP ministers in the state government to resign. They had defended the accused and marched in a rally demanding their release, organized by the Hindu Ekta Manch.[29] Alongside, the Jammu Bar Association tried to prevent the police from filing reports of their investigation before the court.[30] The Supreme Court called both the union government and the Jammu Bar Association to book.

Public outcry across India, led by the media, courts and civil society, prompted the BJP—which had originally defended the ministers—to seek their resignation. Kashmiri Muslims, who had begun to feel increasingly threatened and isolated from the rest of India, noted Indian civil society support with relief. The Mehbooba administration, too, regained some legitimacy for having pushed the Modi administration to seek the ministers' resignations.

In Pakistan, Chief of Army Staff General Bajwa, and in India Chief of Army Staff General Rawat, both called for dialogue rather than the gun, prompting the newspaper *Greater Kashmir* to ask in an editorial whether their statements harbingered a 'new beginning'. It was too early, the editorial concluded, to assume their statements were part of a coordinated India–Pakistan approach, but they should be.[31]

The editorial's call was partially answered in May 2018, when the Modi administration announced a unilateral cessation of hostilities against guerrillas for Ramzan. The ceasefire was widely welcomed, though violence rose in its aftermath, both by Pakistan Army firing across the Line of Control and increased attacks on security forces in south Kashmir. Armed groups began by announcing that they would not reciprocate but that was par for the course. It took almost a year before the Vajpayee ceasefire yielded results, and those came as a result of talks. Pakistan's General Bajwa reiterated a cautious willingness for talks at end-May 2018, and Indian home minister Rajnath Singh responded positively, with the proviso that Pakistan restore the 2003 ceasefire.

These small steps forward came to an abrupt halt when the editor of *Rising Kashmir*, Shujaat Bukhari, was assassinated the day before Eid. The state police said he was shot by three men on a motorcycle, one of whom was a Lashkar-e-Taiba guerrilla from Pakistan, but did not succeed in arresting any of them. Media was rife with rumour that he was killed because he had called for a reciprocal ceasefire at an India–Pakistan civil society meeting in Dubai in August 2017.[32] Apart from being one of Kashmir's best-regarded editors, Bukhari was an influential civil society activist with a reach to policymaking circles in India and abroad and an ardent restorer of Kashmir's literary heritage, which he saw as essential to the Kashmiri nationalist project. He had campaigned for peace talks for over a decade and was an active monitor of CBMs across the Line of Control. Whoever killed him dealt a grave setback to prospects for a peace process, but they were not alone in that endeavour. In both New Delhi and Srinagar, the prevalent attitude was one of confrontation not conciliation.[33]

On the same day that Bukhari was killed, an army rifleman from Rajouri who was posted in Shopian, Aurangzeb, was kidnapped by guerrillas. His bullet-ridden body was found in Pulwama, with clear marks of torture.[34] His death was one of a series of murders of Kashmiris in the army and police, a practice that had risen and fallen since the 1990s and was on the rise again from 2016.[35] One again, Kashmiri was pitted against Kashmiri.

Saying that the two killings revealed it was futile to persist, the Modi administration announced that the Ramzan ceasefire would not be extended beyond Eid. Almost immediately after, the BJP withdrew from their coalition with the PDP, causing the state government to fall. The state went under Governor's Rule and a war of words ensued between the former coalition partners.[36]

Coming in rapid succession, Shujaat Bukhari's assassination, the withdrawal of the Ramzan ceasefire and the BJP's toppling of the coalition government plunged the political and security situation in Kashmir to a low such as the state had not seen since the 1990s. Commentators warned that fear gripped the valley, with a deep and abiding sense that the Modi administration and, by extension, the people of mainland India, cared little for Kashmiri lives.[37]

Most Kashmiris, according to a contemporary report, believed the Modi administration and BJP acted with an eye to the 2019 general election, in which they would again play the communal card, suggesting that they alone could provide India with a strong response to the Islamic threat. Within the state too, the BJP was losing support in Jammu for non-performance on development programmes.[38] In any case, the Modi administration had agreed to a ceasefire only at the urging of Chief Minister Mehbooba Mufti and Home Minister Rajnath Singh, both of whom had limited influence on policy as the brief history in preceding chapters indicates.

It did not help that a few days before Eid, the Office of the UN High Commissioner for Human Rights (UNHCHR) published a scathing report on human rights abuses in Jammu and Kashmir.[39] Though the report indicted Pakistan and Pakistan-backed guerrillas, the bulk of it concentrated on actions by Indian security forces and laws such as the AFSPA and PSA. There were, too, surprising omissions indicating weak research—for example, little was said about dissidents imprisoned or murdered in Pakistan-administered Kashmir and Gilgit-Baltistan or Pakistani laws of impunity. Most importantly, it did not factor in the ugly action–reaction problem of guerrilla conflict. Nevertheless, it touched on critical issues for Indian policymakers to consider, many of which had been discussed by the 2007 Working Group on human rights, headed by Hamid Ansari, and our 2011 interlocutor's report. India's own constitutional principles should have dictated amendment if not repeal of AFSPA. Kashmir's legislators—who spoke a great deal about AFSPA but relatively little about the PSA—were even more puzzlingly inactive. They were surely aware of how the PSA was misused.

Despite its many valid points, the UNHCHR report could not have been worse timed. The Modi administration's ceasefire was already under attack since casualties rose under it (as they had done in 2000-01). It had not received the international attention it should have, which might have bolstered resolve to persist. With the BJP reconsidering an already lukewarm support for the ceasefire, the Modi administration lashed out at the UNHCHR report as 'fallacious, tendentious and motivated'.[40]

On the other side, Pakistan, too, was in a quandary. At end-June 2018, the country was put back on the 'grey list' of the UN Financial Action Task Force because of 'its strategic counter-terrorist financing-related deficiencies'.[41] Pakistan's election commission removed a number of Islamic radicals from the list of those banned from contesting. Following conviction for corruption, Sharif and his daughter were imprisoned on their return to Pakistan on 14 July. As Pakistan prepared for elections on 25 July 2018, Indian commentators concluded that the only winners would be the Pakistani military.[42]

As the decade moved to a close, the prognosis for Kashmir remained alarming.

Chapter XXI

A DOOM ONLY PARTIALLY FORESEEN

The worst fears of the Kashmiris materialized in the spring and summer of 2019. Between January and August, 237 people were killed in terrorist and/or counter-insurgency operations.[1] On 14 February, a suicide attack on a CRPF convoy in Pulwama, held to have been organized by the Jaish-e-Muhammad, led to the death of forty-one troops. Reportedly, the forces had asked the union Home Ministry for an airlift for their contingent following intelligence alerts that an attack was imminent, but received no reply. Though the union Home Ministry clarified that it did provide the CRPF air transport on occasion, it did not explain why that had not been done this time.[2]

India retaliated with air strikes on a Jaish training camp in Pakistan's Balakot, allegedly killing dozens. Pakistan countered by sending its jets to the Line of Control (LoC), the Indian Air Force pushed back, losing a pilot to Pakistani custody. He was later released under combined Indian and international pressure.[3]

During these operations and for weeks after, the main highway from Jammu to Kashmir was closed to public traffic, causing large food and medicine shortages. Kashmiri students were attacked in Delhi, Haryana, Karnataka, Punjab and Uttar Pradesh. The Jamaat-e-Islami Kashmir and JKLF were banned. The properties of dissident political leaders began to be attached. State employees such as civil administrators and teachers began to be investigated for ties to guerilla, including distant family connections, irrespective of whether they had been involved in or supported illegal acts.[4]

By the end of July, around 38,000 additional troops were rushed to the valley. Government departments were asked to stockpile rations. With rumours rife that the union administration might abrogate Article 370, Kashmiri political leaders met Prime

Minister Modi on 1 August and were given the impression that the troops build-up was solely for security.[5] Within a day, however, the hammer struck.

On 2 August, the annual Amarnath Yatra was abruptly cancelled due to an unspecified security threat of which nothing further was heard. On 3 August, when Kashmiri political leaders met Governor Satya Pal Malik, they were assured that no political change was contemplated.[6] But between 4 and 17 August, over 4,000 Kashmiri politicians, activists and journalists were preventively arrested and/or detained; the figure swelled to over 5,000 by November.[7] Section 144 banning gatherings of more than four people was imposed, all telecommunications were snapped, and the state was effectively blacked out. An estimated 8.8 million mobile telephones were blocked in the Kashmir valley alone.[8] Section 144 remained in force for the next eight months, after which a national lockdown was declared due to the COVID-19 pandemic. The Internet shutdown continued for the same length of time—it was 'the longest ever in a democracy'[9]—and when restored was restricted to slow 2G services.[10]

On 5 August, President Ramnath Kovind issued constitutional orders 272 and 273, removing Jammu and Kashmir's special status under Article 370 and replacing the state's constitution with the Indian constitution. Four days later, on 9 August, parliament enacted the Jammu and Kashmir Reorganization Act, 2019, which divided the state into two union territories, Jammu and Kashmir, and Ladakh.[11]

Statutory state bodies to which citizens could go to seek redress—for human, child and women's rights, against corruption, and for information—were automatically terminated following the loss of statehood and were not reinstated, though union territories too were entitled to statutory oversight bodies.[12]

Less than a quarter of those arrested had been released by March 2020, including close to 400 held under the state's public safety act (PSA), which allowed for detention without trial for up to two years. The act's repeal had been repeatedly recommended (see chapter 19); curiously, this particularly draconian state legislation was retained under the Reorganization Act though it contravened Indian law on preventive detention.[13]

Following initial denial, the union and Jammu and Kashmir administrations finally admitted that 144 children had been detained in August-September 2019, 75 of them under the PSA. The youngest was nine years old. Though police detention of children was barred by both the state and national juvenile justice legislations,[14] the court remarked in December 2019 that there was no cause for alarm if children were detained for a few hours or for a day, because in certain situations it was 'for their own good'.[15]

The justifications provided for political detention were as alarming. The dossier against Ali Mohammad Sagar, the NC general secretary, read: 'Your capacity can be gauged from this fact that you were able to convince your electorates to come out and vote in huge numbers even during the peak of the militancy and poll boycotts... You reportedly impressed upon your party workers... to be ready for mass agitation in case Article 370 was revoked.' Yet, Sagar's detention in August 2019 was quashed only in June 2020.[16] Others were released after they signed bonds that they would not protest the administration's actions.[17]

Crackdowns on the media included arresting journalists under the stringent Unlawful Activities (Prevention) Act (UAPA).[18] Originally intended to target organizations supporting terrorist activities, the act was amended around the same time that Kashmir's special status was abolished, to include prosecution of individuals.[19] Seven of the 16 Indian journalists arrested or charged under the UAPA between 2017 and 2022 were Kashmiri.[20] Even Muharram processionists were not spared—over 200 were detained and seven charged under the UAPA by end August 2020.[21] The office of the Association of Parents of Disappeared Persons, a widely-respected NGO, was raided by the National Investigative Agency, the Crime Investigation Department and the Jammu-Kashmir police, who seized confidential files of survivors of security forces' firings, arrests and alleged torture.[22] In July 2021, the Pegasus spyware's leaked database revealed that over 25 Kashmiri journalists, politicians, businessmen, and human rights activists were potential targets of surveillance (along with almost 300 counterparts across India).[23]

The union administration claimed these actions would bring peace and prosperity to the beleaguered former state. 'The Paradise on Earth will be restored to its glory', prime minister Modi said in a televised address on 8 August 2019. True, 'some precautionary measures' had to be taken to prevent protest, but terrorism would end and there would be elections soon. Investment would flow.[24]

The one certainty in the prime minister's speech was that 'Kashmiris would bear the brunt' of his measures. By end December 2019, the economy of the valley was in dire straits. According to the Kashmir Chamber of Commerce and Industry, its members suffered a loss of ₹17,878 crores (roughly US$ 2.4 billion), while job losses in the valley were just under half a million (497,000).[25] The Niti Aayog ranked the former state's export preparedness at the bottom of all states and union territories.[26]

Other changes came hard and fast. In May 2020, Article 35A, which restricted voting and property rights to permanent state residents, was replaced by new domicile rules that expanded the category of residents to people who had lived in Jammu and Kashmir for fifteen years or had studied there for seven years or whose parents were government officials who had served there for ten years. People registered as migrants, such as refugees from Pakistan-held parts of the former princely state, were also eligible.[27]

In October 2020, Jammu and Kashmir's land laws were brought under the union's 2016 Real Estate Act, opening the sale of land, including government-owned, to promoters from across the country.[28] The Jammu and Kashmir administration set up a land bank to encourage national investment. Nomadic tribes were evicted from forest lands they had traditionally held the right to use.[29] Once again, protesters were arrested.[30] In December 2022, the administration announced that existing land leases would not be renewed, instead they would be put to auction. In the tourist centre Gulmarg, hoteliers said applications for lease renewal had been pending for years. Auctions would benefit national hospitality chains over local tourism providers, who did not have the capital to compete.[31]

Similar fears were expressed in Jammu. Led by the Jammu Chamber of Commerce and Industry and the Traders Federation, scores protested when corporate retailer Reliance opened a store in the city. They had repeatedly appealed to the administration to protect small traders, but 'no plea is being heard', said Federation president Deepak Gupta.[32]

The Internet's restriction to 2G affected almost every sector, from education and health to horticulture, handicrafts, tourism, information technology, start-ups, and financial services. The fruit industry, which supplied apples across India, lost around 1.35 lakh metric tonnes of its crop due to restricted transport facilities.[33] For the first time, mining rights were granted to non-local companies.[34] Urban unemployment rose from 10.1 percent in 2018-19 to 15.6 percent in the first quarter of 2022; rural unemployment rose from 39 percent in 2018-19 to 43 percent in 2020-21.[35]

The incidence of child wasting rose from 12.2 to 19 percent between 2015-16 and 2019-21; the proportion of underweight children under five rose from 16.6 to 21 percent. Jammu and Kashmir ranked sixth out of nine union territories on the Niti Aayog's sustainable development goals India index, falling from a score of 54 for quality education in 2019 to 49 in 2020, from 53 to 46 on gender equality, and from 49 to 42 on industry, innovation, and infrastructure. Though the 2023 budget presentation forecast a NSDP growth rate of 14.9 percent in 2022, the economic survey said figures for per capita NSDP in Jammu and Kashmir were not available from 2019 onwards, as did the 2022 Reserve Bank handbook of statistics.[36]

It soon became clear that Modi's promise of elections was limited to municipal and panchayat polls. 'Corrupt' and 'dynastic' parties such as the NC and PDP had to be replaced, Home Minister Amit Shah said repeatedly; new leaders would rise from the panchayats.[37] Efforts to replace the NC and PDP included filing cases against their leaders[38] and encouraging breakaway parties (several were birthed, such as former PDP leader Altaf

Bukhari's Apni Party and former Congressman Ghulam Nabi Azad's Democratic Progressive Azad Party), but with little impact. The valley's main regional parties banded together as 'The People's Alliance for the Gupkar Declaration' (PAGD), committed to regaining special status and statehood.

Reportedly, Lieutenant Governor Manoj Sinha's administration also attempted to bias local elections in favour of the BJP and union-supported parties. According to the PAGD and independent candidates in the district development council polls of November to December 2020, they were moved to hostels for 'security reasons' and hobbled from campaigning. They were banned from using their own vehicles to visit constituencies and were provided six vehicles to be shared in turn by dozens of candidates.[39] After the elections, another seventy-five political leaders were taken into detention.[40]

In May 2022, the Delimitation Commission constituted under the Reorganization Act submitted its report. It granted six additional assembly seats to Jammu and only one to the valley, brushing the disparity under general remarks on methodology with no explanation of how that methodology was applied. For example, it claimed to have taken +10 percent of the average population at the patwari or ward level as a measure for redrawing constituencies in flat areas and -10 percent in hill areas. But that did not explain why Jammu province had more seats relative to its population than the valley, with a differential of as much as 20,000 people per seat. Neither did it explain why Jammu's Muslim-majority seats now comprised less than a quarter of the province's total seats, though Muslims comprised over a third of its population. Nor why the majority of Jammu's six new constituencies were Hindu-majority. One had a population of just over 50,000, but shared the same physical features as a Muslim-majority constituency of close to four times its population.[41]

In February 2021, parliament amended the Reorganization Act to dissolve the former state's administrative service.[42] In a policy of purge, Lieutenant Governor Sinha constituted a special task force in April 2021 to investigate government employees who may have been involved in 'anti-national activities' for dismissal.[43] In October 2022, it was reported that forty-four such had been dismissed, and in February 2023, three more were added to that number.[44] The dismissed included teachers, engineers, and hospital and panchayat staff.

Inevitably, security worsened. 1,034 people were killed in terrorist attacks and/or counter-insurgency operations between August 2019 and December 2023, compared to 896 in the last four and a half years of the Singh administration (2010 to May 2014). Official figures showed that ceasefire violations in 2020 were the highest in twenty years; overall too, they were twenty times higher between 2014-20 than between 2004-13.[45] Attacks on the CRPF doubled, from 25 between 2010-2014, with 18 deaths, to 51 between August 2019-October 2022, with 30 deaths. The number of policemen killed remained roughly the same (57 and 59).[46] Alarmingly the Poonch-Rajouri region, which had been peaceful since the Vajpayee-Manmohan Singh peace process took hold, re-emerged as a locus for cross-border militancy and army excess in 2023. Analysts suspected that the union administration's addition of Pahari Bakarwals and other smaller communities to the reserved tribal quota, resisted by the Gujjar tribes, might have contributed to alienation in the region, which has a large Gujjar population.[47]

Targeted civilian killings of Kashmiri Pandits, Hindu and Sikh teachers and shopkeepers, migrant workers and elected representatives, even a young Muslim actress, which had ended by 2013, resurged. In 2021, ten panches resigned from their posts in Budgam after receiving phone calls from militant groups threatening to behead them. Rajputs, who had not been targeted earlier, reported receiving similar calls.[48] In May 2022, following the killing of a Pandit schoolteacher and a bank manager, 350 Pandits who had returned under the prime minister's rehabilitation scheme resigned when their demand for relocation to safer areas was rejected.[49] In June, hundreds fled back to Jammu.[50] In October, Pandit families that had remained in the valley through decades of conflict joined the exodus.[51] In December, the Resistance Front posted a list of 56 Kashmiri Pandit teachers on their blog 'Kashmir Fight', claiming they would turn their transit accommodation into graveyards.[52]

Though the constitution of Ladakh as a separate union territory was initially welcomed in Leh, it caused heartburn in Kargil, whose majority Shias wished to retain ties to the Muslim valley. The Leh Buddhists' welcome soured too, when Ladakh's Lieutenant Governor R. K. Mathur undermined the authority of the elected hill councils and the union administration continued to stall on the demand that Ladakh be included in the sixth schedule, under which tribal-majority states had developmental benefits and a large degree of self-rule.[53]

China's response to the August 2019 actions added further insecurity. While the Xi administration failed in its attempt to get the UN security council to censure India's August 2019 actions, thwarted by the US and French administrations, PLA incursions across the Ladakh border succeeded in wresting Indian patrolling posts in the Galwan valley and Pangong Tso region bordering Ladakh.[54]

By end 2023, Jammu and Kashmir and parts of Ladakh faced political and economic dispossession on the one hand and the threat of renewed cross-border conflict on the other.

AFTERWORD

In December 2023, the Supreme Court of India upheld the constitutionality of the 2019 presidential orders and Reorganization Act and by default all the administrative actions that followed.[1] In doing so, the judgment not only vindicated the draconian measures used by the union administration to vitiate Jammu and Kashmir's rights, it set an alarming precedent in which Indian states and their people could be over-ridden at will. In contravention of an earlier ruling by the court that Article 370 had acquired permanence through the passage of time,[2] a five-judge bench ruled that since it had been included under the heading of 'temporary and special provisions' it had been temporary for too long and should go. Curiously too, while its judgment cited the proviso to Article 3 of the Indian constitution, that legislation altering a state's area or boundary must be referred to the state's legislature 'for expressing its views', it did not discuss the failure to refer the Reorganization Bill to the state's political representatives (since the assembly had been dissolved, an alternative consultation could have been with the state's political parties), or the Ladakh Hill Councils (which had not been dissolved). On the issue of whether parliament could demote a state to a union territory under Article 3—something that had never been done—it refused to rule at all, on the grounds that Solicitor-General Tushar Mehta had assured the court that the union administration planned to restore statehood at an undefined time.[3] Whether states could exercise their federal rights appeared to depend on the whim of the union administration instead of the writ of the constitution.

The fact that over 5,000 political leaders, their cadre and members of the intelligentsia had been arrested and the state was locked down in order to prevent protest—against the removal of special status, permanent residency rights and the division and demotion of the state—was not considered by the bench at all. It found no mention in its 352-page majority judgment.

Given that it had been whittled down to a mainly symbolic rather than substantive set of rights over the decades, why was Article 370 so important? There were two primary reasons. First, it offered a baseline for reconciliation with the large number of Kashmiris, not just dissidents, who felt that successive Indian administrations had betrayed the promise made to Sheikh Abdullah in the Delhi Agreement and Article 370. Second, it offered a baseline for a peace agreement between India and Pakistan, and by extension with armed groups.

The Aziz–Lambah framework of 2006, which guaranteed wide-ranging autonomy or self-rule for all three parts of the former princely state, was the outcome of negotiations first between the Vajpayee and Musharraf administrations and then the Singh and Musharraf administrations from 2002. Elements of it had been discussed since the early 1990s, some drawn from civil society inputs, and by 2006 it was worked out in detail. Under it, Pakistan-held Kashmir and Gilgit–Baltistan, and Indian Jammu and Kashmir, would have the same autonomies. While the former two would remain under formal Pakistani control, and the latter would remain with India, the three units would be able to jointly develop their resources. A soft border would erase the lines of division, and could be jointly managed by India and Pakistan. Internal reconciliation between the people of the state would be central, and they would have access to both Indian and Pakistani markets, as well as a wider South Asian market through SAARC.[4]

Not everyone was on board the framework. Negotiations on it and after were repeatedly stalled by terrorist attacks in India. A post-Vajpayee BJP opposed it in India, and the Zardari and Sharif administrations in Pakistan did not pick up where the Aziz–Lambah talks had left off.[5] But it remains the only framework that had been agreed by the majority of stakeholders. It is likely, therefore, to be a reference point in any future peace process between India, Pakistan, and the people of divided Jammu and Kashmir.

ACKNOWLEDGEMENTS

This book would not have been written had it not been for encouragement by friends and family. In particular, I must thank my Kashmiri friends for their careful reading of the manuscript even where they disagreed with my conclusions, and my daughter Sushila for her tolerance of my preoccupation. Grateful thanks also to Emma Nicholson, Khurshid Kasuri, Robert Blackwill and Shyam Saran for reading the ms and sending quotes. An especial thanks to the late Shujaat Bukhari, who also read the manuscript and sent me a quote. I did not realize the danger that he was in, and deeply regret having troubled him at such a time. His quote is the more dear as the last communication I had with him.

I owe a deep debt to Aruna Rajkumar whose painstaking help with the footnotes spurred me to complete the book. Finally, thanks to David Davidar and the Aleph team for their constant support through the arduous process of writing.

NOTES

EPIGRAPH
1. *Nilamata Purana*, Ved Kumari (trans.), *Kashmir Pandits Network*, verses 12–13, 17, 19–21 <http://ikashmir.net/nilmatapurana/verses1-100.html>, Translation edited.
2. Baba Daud Khaki, quoted by Chitralekha Zutshi, *Kashmir's Contested Pasts: Narratives of Sacred Geographies and the Historical Imagination*, New Delhi: Oxford University Press, 2014, p. 42, Translation edited.

PREFACE
1. Of course, the British were implicated in three out of these four partitions, an issue I have discussed in *Divide and Fall? Bosnia in the Annals of Partition*, London: Verso Books, 1997.

CHAPTER I: A WONDER THAT WAS KAS'MIRA
1. A Mahatmya was a text that extolled the claims of a particular area to a high spot in the list of sacred places. For a discussion of the distinction, see Khalid Bashir, 'Aborigines', *Kashmir: Exposing the Myth Behind the Narrative*, New Delhi: Sage Publications, 2017.
2. A sacred syllable in Hinduism.
3. *Nilamata Purana*, verse 227.
4. Ibid., verse 302.
5. Ibid., verses 14–16.
6. Ibid., verse 401.
7. Ibid., verses 904–06.
8. Ibid., verses 12–13.
9. Kalhana, *Rajatarangini*, Marc Aurel Stein (trans.), Vol. 1, Stein's Introduction and Books I–VII, New Delhi: Motilal Banarsidass, 1900.
10. Quoted in 'About the Silk Road', UNESCO, <http://en.unesco.org/silkroad/about-silk-road>.
11. Kalhana, Introduction, *Rajatarangini*, p. 91. U-li-to was the name given to the envoy in the Chinese annals of the Tang dynasty, where this episode is mentioned.
12. Andre Wink, *Al-Hind: the Making of the Indo-Islamic World*, Vol. 1, New Delhi: Oxford University Press, 1990, p. 243.
13. al-Biruni, *India*, Qeyumuddin Ahmad (ed.), New Delhi: National Book Trust, 2005, p. 99.
14. Kalhana, Introduction, *Rajatarangini*, p. 8.
15. Parvez Dewan, *A History of Kashmir*, New Delhi: Manas Publications, 2011, p. 17.
16. Kalhana, Introduction, *Rajatarangini*, p. 98.
17. Ibid., Book V, verse 118.
18. Ibid., Introduction, p. 18.
19. Dewan, *A History of Kashmir*, p. 25.
20. Ibid., p. 105.

21 G. M. D. Sufi, *Kashir: Being a History of Kashmir from the Earliest Times to Our Own*, Srinagar: Gulshan Books, 2015, p. 86.
22 Bashir, 'Malice', *Kashmir*.
23 Dewan, *A History of Kashmir*, p. 110.
24 Translations carried in *Saints and Sages of Kashmir: Ancient and Modern Ascetics in Kashmir*, Kashmir News Network, 2007 <https://selfdefinition.org/tantra/Saints-and-Sages-of-Kashmir-koausa.org.pdf>.
25 Yusuf Shah was accused of such persecution of Sunnis that they appealed to the Mughal emperor Akbar to take over. See G.M.D. Sufi, op cit, p. 223; Census of India 1941, Vol. 22, Part 2, Essays and Tables, Captain R. G. Wreford, Census Commissioner, p. 9.
26 Ajit Bhattacharjea, *Sheikh Mohammad Abdullah: Tragic Hero of Kashmir*, New Delhi: Roli Books, 2008, p. 44.
27 Treaty of Amritsar, Article 10, 16 March 1846, <http://jklaw.nic.in/treaty_of_amritsar.pdf>.
28 Governor-General to Gulab Singh, 4 January 1848 in Mohan Krishen Teng, Ram Krishen Kaul Bhatt and Santosh Kaul, (eds.), *Kashmir: Constitutional History and Documents*, New Delhi: Light & Life Publishers, 1977; Report of the Constitutional Reforms Commission, 1932.
29 Ibid., 26 September 1873.
30 Victoria Schofield, *Kashmir in Conflict*, London: I. B. Tauris and Co., 2000, pp. 11–13.
31 Teng, Bhatt and Kaul, The Secretary to State for India to the Government of India, 23 May 1884.
32 Ibid., From Pratap Singh to the Viceroy, 18 September 1885.
33 Ibid., Report on the affairs of the State of Jammu & Kashmir by the Resident of Kashmir, 5 March 1888.
34 Ibid., New Arrangements for the Administration of Kashmir by the Resident in Kashmir, May 1906.

CHAPTER II: THE RISE OF POLITICS

1 Sufi, *Kashir*, pp. 797–98, 812–14, 841–12; Mridu Rai, *Hindu Ruler, Muslim Subjects*, New Delhi: Orient BlackSwan, 2007.
2 Parvez Dewan, *A History of Jammu*, Jammu: Manas Publications, 2014, p. 45.
3 Census of India 1941, Table XIII (II), 'Distribution of Main Communities by Districts', pp. 346–47.
4 John Strachey, *India*, London: K. Paul, Trench, 1888, p. 225.
5 Teng, Bhatt and Kaul, The Secretary to State for India to the Government of India, 23 May 1884.
6 Ibid., Lord Curzon's Speech on Restoration of powers to Maharaja Pratap Singh, 1905.
7 Ibid., Durbar Proclamation, 25 September 1885.
8 M. K. Kaw, (ed.), *Kashmir and Its People: Studies in the Evolution of Kashmiri Society*, New Delhi: A. P. H. Publishing, 2004, pp. 161–62.
9 Zafar Choudhary, *Kashmir Conflict and Muslims of Jammu*, Srinagar: Gulshan Books, 2015, p. 50.
10 Teng, Bhatt and Kaul, Letter from Chief Minister Jammu and Kashmir State to Maharaja Pratap Singh, 2 July 1919.
11 Ibid., Sri Pratap Reforms Regulation No. IV of 1922.
12 State Subject Definition Notification dated 20 April 1927, Legal Document No 44, *South Asia Terrorism Portal* <http://www.satp.org/satporgtp/countries/india/states/

jandk/documents/actsandordinances/State_Subject_Rules.htm>.
13 Bhattacharjea, *Sheikh Mohammad Abdullah,* pp. 62–63.
14 K. B. Jandial, 'More than Hari Singh's birthday, Accession Day merits holiday', *Rising Kashmir,* 7 February 2017 <http://www.risingkashmir.com/article/straight-talkmore-than-hari-singhs-birthday-accession-day-merits-holiday>.
15 Quoted by Hasnat Sheikh, 'Homage' <http://unveilkashmir.com/homage/>, Retrieved 30 October 2017. The account has since been suspended.
16 Sheikh Abdullah, *The Blazing Chinar,* translated by Muhammad Amin, Srinagar: Gulshan Books, 2016.
17 Sir Muhammad Iqbal's 1930 'Presidential Address to the 25th Session of the All-India Muslim League', Allahabad, 29 December 1930, Columbia University <http://www.columbia.edu/itc/mealac/pritchett/00islamlinks/txt_iqbal_1930.html>.
18 Bhattacharjea, *Sheikh Mohammad Abdullah,* p. 33.
19 Prem Nath Bazaz, *Kashmir in Crucible,* New Delhi: Pamposh Publications, 1967, p. 81.
20 Teng, Bhatt and Kaul, Report of the Constitutional Reforms Commission, 1932.
21 Ibid., Report of the Franchise Committee, 1933.
22 Bhattacharjea, *Sheikh Mohammad Abdullah,* p. 53.
23 *All India States Peoples Conference Papers,* National Archives of India, File No. 14, Part II, Resolution No. 13, p. 195.
24 Ibid., p. 83.
25 *Martand,* Srinagar, 28 June 1939, cited by Santosh Kaul, 'Freedom Movement in Kashmir 1939-1947', PhD thesis, University of Kashmir, 1982, Chapter II, accessed from Shodhganga Library and Information Network, Gandhinagar, p. 88.
26 Ibid, p. 94.
27 There is some confusion about the date of Jinnah's visit: it may have been in 1939 or in 1944, when he visited to persuade Hari Singh to opt for Pakistan.
28 Mohammad Ishaq, *Pakistan aur Musalmani Kashmir,* Maulana Sayeed Masoodi Interview, Pamphlet, Jammu, April 1940, p. 8. These meetings are not referred to by historians of the period, which casts some doubt on Ishaq and/or Masoodi's account.
29 Chitralekha Zutshi, *Languages of Belonging: Islam, Regional Identity, and the Making of Kashmir,* New Delhi: Permanent Black, 2003, p. 301.
30 Mir Qasim, *My Life and Times,* New Delhi: Allied Publishers, 1992, p. 31.

CHAPTER III: TWIN PARTITIONS

1 Jeff Kingston, 'The unfinished business of Indian Partition', *The Japan Times,* 12 August 2017; 'Kashmir is the "unfinished business of Partition"', says Pakistan Army chief', *Scroll.in,* 8 September 2015 <https://scroll.in/article/754127/kashmir-is-the-unfinished-business-of-partition-says-pakistan-army-chief>; Ishtiaq Ahmed, 'The Unfinished Partition', *The Friday Times,* 23 October 2015 <http://www.thefridaytimes.com/tft/the-unfinished-partition/>; Banyan, 'The unfinished Partition of India and Pakistan', *The Economist,* 17 August 2017.
2 Lord Wavell to Lord Pethick-Lawrence, 7 February 1946, from Great Britain, Foreign and Commonwealth Office, *The Transfer of Power in India, 1942–47,* Vol. 6, Document 406, London: Stationery Office Books, 1976, p. 912.
3 'A History's Witness', *KASHMIR LIFE,* 24 May 2012 <http://Kashmirlife.Net/A-Historys-Witness-3736/>.
4 Sardar M. Ibrahim Khan, *The Kashmir Saga,* Revised and enlarged Edition, Mirpur: Verinag Publishers, 1990, p. 57.

5   Devin T. Hagerty and Herbert G. Hagerty, 'India's Foreign Relations' in Devin T. Hagerty (ed.), *South Asia in World Politics*, Oxford: Rowman & Littlefield, 2005, p. 19.
6   Christopher Snedden, 'The forgotten Poonch uprising of 1947', No. 643 of March 2013: Eye On Kashmir, *Seminar* <http://www.india-seminar.com/2013/643/643_christopher_snedden.htm>.
7   Karan Singh, *Autobiography*, New Delhi: Oxford University Press, 1994, p. 54.
8   Term first used by M. A. Jinnah in a speech opposing the partition of Bengal and the Punjab, on 4 May 1947 (FO 371/63533), accessed from <http://www.nationalarchives.gov.uk/wp-content/uploads/2014/03/fo371-635331.jpg>.
9   For a discussion of the level and nature of their collusion see Schofield, *Kashmir in Conflict*, Chapter 3.
10 Ibid., quoting George Cunningham's diary entry on 26 October 1947.
11 Balraj Madhok, *Kashmir: The Storm Center of the World*, Houston: A. Ghosh Publishers, 1992, accessed on archive.org <https://archive.org/stream/MergedF681b8be4cc54471BfcfD2d477673ef0/merged_f681b8be-4cc5-4471-bfcf-d2d477673ef0_djvu.txt>.
12 Sarvepalli Gopal, *Selected Works of Jawaharlal Nehru*, New Delhi: Navrang Publishers, 1994, pp. 263–65.
13 Mohammad Hafizullah, *Towards Azad Kashmir*, Lahore: Bazam-i-Froghi-i-Adab, 1948, p. 93, cited by Snedden, Chapter 4:1, e-book edition.
14 Manekshaw interview with Prem Shankar Jha, *Kashmir 1947: Rival Versions of History*, New Delhi: Oxford University Press, 1996. The interview became controversial when L. K. Advani quoted it; PTI, 'Nehru was not reluctant to send troops to Kashmir as alleged by Advani: Jha', *Hindu Business Line*, 8 November 2013.
15 S. S. Chib, 'The Valiant Dogra Who Saved the "Paradise on Earth"', *The Tribune*, 8 December 2001.
16 For a complete and anguished account of what happened in Baramulla, see Andrew Whitehead, *A Mission in Kashmir*, New Delhi: Penguin Books India, 2007.
17 Agha Humayun Amin, 'The 1947–48 Kashmir War: The War of Lost Opportunities', accessed on archive.org, <https://archive.org/stream/The1947-48KashmirWarTheWarOfLostOpportunities/49202996-The-1947-48-Kashmir-War-Revised_djvu.txt>.
18 Aman M. Hingorani, *Unravelling the Kashmir Knot*, New Delhi: Sage Publications, 2016, p. 167.
19 Sisir Kumar Gupta, *Kashmir: A Study in India–Pakistan Relations*, Mumbai: Asia Publishing House, 1966, p. 106.
20 C. Bilqees Taseer, *The Kashmir of Sheikh Muhammad Abdullah*, Lahore: Ferozsons Books, 1986.
21 Khalid Bashir, 'Circa 1947: A Long Story', *Kashmir Life*, 5 November 2014 <http://kashmirlife.net/circa-1947-a-long-story-67652/#_edn27>. Also cited by Sheikh Abdullah in his autobiography, *The Blazing Chinar*, p. 301. Also see Madhok, *Kashmir: The Storm Center*; Choudhary, *Kashmir Conflict*, pp. 83–84; Saeed Naqvi, 'The Killing Fields of Jammu: How Muslims Became a Minority in the Region', *Scroll.in*, 10 July 2016, accessed on 2 July 2018.
22 Ibid.
23 Bashir, *Kashmir*.
24 Census of India 1941, Vol. 22: Jammu and Kashmir, Part I and II: Essay and Tables, Captain R G. Wreford, Officer of the Commissioner of Census; Census of India 1961, Vol. 6, Jammu and Kashmir, Part I-A (i), General Report, M.H. Kamili, Superintendent of Census Operations Jammu and Kashmir, Srinagar.

25 For a full discussion of how Jammu lost its Muslim leaders, see Choudhary, *Kashmir Conflict*, pp. 106–110.
26 William Alexander Brown, 'Return to Gilgit (June–September 1947)', *Gilgit Rebellion: The Major who Mutinied Over Partition of India*, Barnsley: Pen & Sword Books, 2014. For a full account of his 'Operation Datta Khel' see 'The Gathering Storm (September–October 1947)'.
27 This and other extracts from Kachru's letters to Nehru cited by Sandeep Bamzai, 'Nehru's Pacifism and the Failed Recapture of Kashmir', Observer Research Foundation Special Report, 13 August 2016.
28 Rakesh Ankit, *The Kashmir Conflict: From Empire to the Cold War, 1945-66*, Abingdon: Routledge, 2016, p. 48. For an in-depth analysis of the British role in the India–Pakistan conflict over Kashmir, see Chandrashekhar Dasgupta, *War and Diplomacy in Kashmir, 1947-8*, New Delhi: Sage Publications, 2004.
29 *Collected Works of Mahatma Gandhi*, Vol. 90, New Delhi: Publications Division, Government of India, 1999, pp. 356–58.
30 Ankit, *The Kashmir Conflict*, p. 49.
31 Ibid., p. 50.
32 Ibid.
33 Ibid., p. 52.
34 Ibid., p. 53.
35 Josef Korbel, *Danger in Kashmir*, Princeton Legacy Library, Princeton: Princeton University Press, 1954, p. 136.
36 United Nations Commission for India and Pakistan, Resolution of 13 August 1948 <https://www.mtholyoke.edu/acad/intrel/uncom1.htm>.
37 Ibid., Resolution of 5 January 1949.
38 In 1949, the UN set up a monitoring group for India and Pakistan (UNMOGIP) to report on observance of the ceasefire line. After the 1972 Simla agreement, India took the position that now that the dispute was to be resolved bilaterally, UNMOGIP was no longer necessary. Though UNMOGIP continues to occupy office space in Delhi and a mansion in Srinagar, it has since monitored the ceasefire line only on the Pakistani side of the border.
39 It has been argued that this division of Kashmir sharpened the distinction between the syncretic Islam of Kashmiriyat and the Sunni Islam of the Muslim districts of Jammu, which now formed 'Azad Kashmir'. See Balraj Puri, *Kashmir: Towards Insurgency*, Tracts for the Times, New Delhi: Sangam Books, 1993, p. 17.

CHAPTER IV: A LION IN WINTER
1 Snedden, Chapter 4:2, e-book edition.
2 Muhammad Ibrahim Khan and Sardar Ibrahim Khan, *The Kashmir Saga*, Mirpur: Verinag Publishers, 1990, Chapter 10, pp. 102–114.
3 Ibid., Chapter 11, pp. 115–32.
4 Ibid., p. 206.
5 The Karachi Agreement 1949, *United Nations Peacemaker* <https://peacemaker.un.org/sites/peacemaker.un.org/files/IN%20PK_490729_%20Karachi%20Agreement.pdf>.
6 Ershad Mahmud, 'Status of AJK in Political Milieu', *Policy Perspectives*, Vol. 3, No. 2 (July–December 2006), pp. 105–23.
7 Ibid.
8 Christopher Sneddon, *Kashmir: The Unwritten History*, New Delhi: Harper Collins, 2013, Chapter 4:2, e-book edition.

9   Karan Singh, *Autobiography*, pp. 93–104.
10 Ibid., p. 120.
11 Speech of Sheikh Mohammad Abdullah in the Constituent Assembly, Kashmiri Pundit Network, April 1951 <http://www.ikashmir.net/historicaldocuments/sheikhspeech.html>.
12 A. G. Noorani, 'The Dixon Plan', *Frontline*, Vol. 19, No. 21, 12–25 October 2002.
13 Ibid.
14 Ibid.
15 The Delhi Agreement, 1952, https://www.satp.org/satporgtp/countries/india/states/jandk/documents/papers/delhi_agreement_1952.htm.
16 Mookerjee–Nehru–Abdullah correspondence published in Verinder Grover and Ranjana Arora, *50 Years of Indo–Pak Relations: Chronology of All Important Events and Documents from 1947–1997*, New Delhi: Deep and Deep Publications, 1990, pp. 314–24.
17 H. Y. Sharada Prasad and Mushirul Hasan, (eds.), *Selected Works of Jawaharlal Nehru*, Vol. 22, New Delhi: Jawaharlal Nehru Memorial Fund, 2005, pp. 203–05.
18 A. G. Noorani, 'The RSS and Gandhi: a necessary backstory', *The Wire*, 24 July 2016.
19 Howard B. Schaffer, *The Limits of Influence: America's Role in Kashmir*, Washington D. C.: Brookings Institution Press, 2009, p. 40.
20 Abdullah, *Blazing Chinar*, p. 313.
21 Ibid.
22 Noorani, 'The Dixon Plan', *Frontline*.
23 Abdullah, *Blazing Chinar*, p. 370.
24 Wajahat Habibullah, *My Kashmir: The Dying of the Light*, New Delhi: Penguin Viking, 2001, p. 25.
25 A. G. Noorani, 'Roots of the Kashmir dispute', *Frontline*, 27 May 2016.
26 Karan Singh, *Autobiography*, pp. 158–64.
27 Nyla Ali Khan, 'Sheikh Abdullah's speech before his arrest in August 1953', *Rising Kashmir*, 24 January 2017.
28 Praveen Swami, *India, Pakistan and the Secret Jihad: The Covert War in Kashmir, 1947–2004*, Kiribati: Routledge, 2007, pp. 32–33.
29 Ibid., pp. 35–41.
30 Ibid.
31 J. N. Dixit, *India-Pakistan in War and Peace*, London: Routledge, 2002, pp. 133–34.
32 Ibid.
33 Shamshad Ahmad, 'Reversing the tide of history: Kashmir policy—an overview-II', *Dawn*, 6 August 2004.
34 Rajeshwar Dayal, *A Life of Our Times*, Hyderabad: Orient Longman, 1998, p. 291.
35 Qasim, *My Life and Times*, p. 83.
36 Abdullah, *Blazing Chinar*, p. 439.
37 Inder Malhotra, 'The Sheikh's last stab', *Indian Express*, 25 March 2012.
38 Mohammad Ayub Khan, *Friends Not Masters: A Political Autobiography*, New York: Oxford University Press, 1967.

CHAPTER V: BETWEEN WARS: 1965–1971

1   Choudhary, *Kashmir Conflict*, pp. 144–155.
2   Shruti Pandalai, 'Recounting 1965: War, Diplomacy and Great Games in the Subcontinent', *Journal of Defence Studies*, Vol. 9, No. 3 July–September 2015, pp. 7–32; Sajjad Haider, 'Straight Shooting on the 1965 War', *Dawn*, 6 September 2017.
3   Tashkent Declaration signed by Prime Minister of India and President of Pakistan,

        Ministry of External Affairs, Government of India <http://mea.gov.in/bilateral-documents.htm?dtl/5993/Tashkent+Declaration>.
4   Choudhary, *Kashmir Conflict*, pp.171–72.
5   Balraj Puri, *Simmering Volcano: A Study of Jammu's Relations with Kashmir*, New Delhi: Sterling Publishers, 1983, p. 40.
6   Ibid.
7   'Kashmir: letter written by late Jayaprakash Narayan to the then Prime Minister of India, Smt. Indira Gandhi, on 23 June 1966', *Mainstream*, Vol. 54, No. 38, 10 September 2016.
8   Rao Farman Ali, *History of Armed Struggles in Kashmir*, Srinagar: J. K. Books, 2017, pp. 94–95.
9   Schofield, *Kashmir in Conflict*, p. 114.
10   Ibid.
11   For a full account of the hijacking, see Hashim Qureshi, *Kashmir: The Unveiling of Truth*, Lahore: Jeddojuhd Publications, 1999.
12   The International Commission of Jurists, 'The Events in East Pakistan, 1971: A Legal Study', Geneva: The International Commission of Jurists, 1972, p. 16.
13   Government of Pakistan White Paper, 'The Crisis in East Pakistan', 5 August 1971.
14   Butt and Khurshid's statements in Qureshi, *Kashmir*, Appendices.
15   Prime Minister Indira Gandhi, Statement in Lok Sabha, 24 May 1971, transcript available in New Delhi: Nehru Memorial Museum and Library, Haksar Papers, Subject File 166.
16   Gary J. Bass, 'The Indian Way of Humanitarian Intervention', *Yale Journal of International Law*, Vol. 40, No. 2, 2015, pp. 228–297.
17   Henry Kissinger, *White House Years*, London: Simon and Schuster, 1979, pp. 842–864.
18   Christopher Hitchens, *The Trial of Henry Kissinger*, London: Verso Books, 2001, p. 44.
19   US Department of State, *Soviet-American Relations: The Détente Years, 1969–1972*, Washington D. C.: G. P. O., 1972, Introductions by Henry A. Kissinger and Anatoly Dobrynin, pp. 224–25.
20   Simla Agreement, 2 July 1971, Article 4, Ministry of External Affairs, Government of India <http://mea.gov.in/in-focus-article.htm?19005/Simla+Agreement+July+2+1972>.
21   Bhattacharjea, *Sheikh Mohammad Abdullah*, pp. 214–15.

CHAPTER VI: TWO DECADES OF RELATIVE QUIET?

1   Habibullah, *My Kashmir*, p. 40.
2   Ibid., p. 37.
3   Ibid., p. 35.
4   Balraj Puri, 'How the Indira-Abdullah Accord was signed in 1974', *Mainstream*, Vol. 50, No. 17, 14 April 2012.
5   A. G. Noorani, 'Accord & Discord', *Frontline*, Vol. 27, No. 6, 13–26 March 2010.
6   Beg-Parthasarathi, 'Agreed Conclusions', later known as the Indira Gandhi–Sheikh Abdullah Kashmir Accord, November 13 1974, <http://www.jammu-kashmir.com/documents/kashmiraccord.html.>
7   Noorani, 'Accord & Discord', *Frontline*.
8   Habibullah, *My Kashmir*, pp. 44–5
9   Noorani, 'Accord & Discord', *Frontline*.
10   Ibid.
11   Qureshi interview with author, 21 July 2000.

12 Habibullah, *My Kashmir*, p. 48.
13 Ibid., pp. 66–67.
14 Puri, *Simmering Volcano*, p. 62.
15 K. D. Maini, *Poonch: The Battlefield of Kashmir*, Srinagar: Gulshan Books, 2012, pp. 260–64.
16 Hafizur Rehman Khan, 'Abdullah's Release and Re-Arrest', *Pakistan Horizon* (journal of the Pakistan Institute of International Affairs), Vol. 11, No. 2, June 1958, p. 104.
17 Cabinet Division, D.O. No. 8/9/70-Coord. I, Government of Pakistan, Rawalpindi, 11 May 1971, cited by Snedden, Chapter 4:4, e-book edition.
18 The Azad Jammu and Kashmir Interim Constitution Act 1974, Schedule I <http://1-to-n.com/clients/ajkcourt/wp-content/uploads/2014/04/Azad-Jammu-and-Kashmir-Interim-Constitution-Act-1974.pdf>.
19 Ibid., Paragraph 7, item 2.
20 Ibid.
21 Eqbal Ahmad, 'Signposts to a police state', *Journal of Contemporary Asia*, Vol. 4, No. 4, 1974, pp. 423–440.
22 Sumit Mitra, 'Jammu & Kashmir: Tremors of Tension', *India Today*, 29 February 1984.
23 Ibid.
24 Ibid.
25 Schofield, *Kashmir in Conflict*, p. 214.
26 Swami, *India, Pakistan and Secret Jihad*, p. 157.
27 Inder Malhotra, *Indira Gandhi: A Personal and Political Biography*, London: Hodder and Stoughton, 1989, p. 297.
28 In fact, the Shah Commission of Inquiry, Third and Final Report, 6 August 1978, pp. 250–253, censured Jagmohan for having 'grossly misused his position and… became a law unto himself', p. 252.
29 Prabhu Chawla, 'Governors: Calculated Moves', *India Today*, 15 April 1984.
30 Tavleen Singh, *Kashmir: A Tragedy of Errors*, New Delhi: Penguin Books India, 2000, p. 74, citing her article in *The Telegraph*, 11 July 1984.
31 Ibid.
32 Sumit Ganguly, *The Crisis in Kashmir: Portents of War, Hopes of Peace*, Cambridge University Press, 1999, p. 94.
33 Praveen Donthi, 'How Mufti Mohammad Sayeed shaped the 1987 elections in Kashmir', *Caravan*, 23 March 2016.
34 Anil Maheshwari, *Crescent over Kashmir*, Chapter 4, *Kashmiri Pandit Network*, citing H. K. Dua, *Indian Express*, 3 March 1986. <http://ikashmir.net/COPYRIGHTED/crescent/chapter4.html>.
35 Jagmohan, *My Frozen Turbulence in Kashmir*, New Delhi: Allied Publishers, 1991, p. 163.
36 Tavleen Singh, *Kashmir*, p. 98.
37 Schofield, *Kashmir in Conflict*, p. 138.
38 Inderjit Badhwar, *India Today*, 5 April 1987, pp. 76–78.
39 Swami, *India, Pakistan and Secret Jihad*, p.158.
40 Donthi, 'How Mufti Mohammad Sayeed'.
41 Habibullah, *My Kashmir*.
42 Sumantra Bose, *Kashmir: Roots of Conflict, Paths to Peace*, Cambridge: Harvard University Press, 2005, p. 49.
43 Donthi, 'How Mufti Mohammad Sayeed'.

44   Habibullah, *My Kashmir*, p. 73.
45   UNI, '90 per cent of PoK people want to end Islamabad's Control', *Rediff.com*, 3 May 1999, citing Arif Shaheed's book *Kaun Azad Kaun Ghulam?* <http://www.rediff.com/news/1999/may/03pak.htm>.
46   *The Muslim* (Pakistan), 21 July 1987.
47   The ISI is generally held to have become a state within a state during the Afghan war, when it dealt directly with the CIA, Saudi Arabia and other supporters of the Afghan jihad, but it had already acquired some of its powers during Bhutto's rule, when he used it to suppress political opposition.
48   'Alien mercenaries "control J&K militants"', *The Tribune* quoting the *London Times* and *Jane's Defence Weekly*, 17 September 1998, <https://www.tribuneindia.com/1998/98sep17/world.htm>.
49   A. K. Verma, 'When Hamid Gul offered India peace', *Times of India*, 28 August 2015.

CHAPTER VII: BENAZIR, RAJIV AND THEIR SUCCESSORS

1   Shaikh Aziz, 'The "dawn of a new era" that remained a dream', *Dawn*, 21 August 2016.
2   Baqir Sajjad Syed, 'India asked to honour 1989 accord on Siachen', *Dawn*, 14 April 2012.
3   Ministry of External Affairs, Government of India, Annual Report 1990–91, 'India's neighbours', pp. 1–13, New Delhi: Ministry of External Affairs Library.
4   Ibid.
5   Ibid.
6   Harinder Baweja, 'Mufti Sayeed's dark hour: militants released for abducted daughter', *Hindustan Times*, 9 January 2016.
7   Sumegha Gulati, 'Why Kashmiris are using the hashtag #JagmohanTheMurderer after the Padma award announcement', *Scroll.in*, 12 July 2018.
8   Habibullah, *My Kashmir*, p. 86.
9   Ghulam Nabi Khayal, 'Who killed Mirwaiz?', *Greater Kashmir*, 24 February 2008.
10   'When Kashmir Road was painted with blood', *Kashmir Watch*, 20 May 2016 <http://kashmirwatch.com/may-21-1990-when-kashmir-road-was-painted-with-blood/>.
11   Law Kumar Mishra, 'Jammu and Kashmir militants target jeans, cable TV', *Times of India*, 25 February 1999.
12   P. R. Chari, Pervaiz Iqbal Cheema, Stephen P. Cohen, *Perception, Politics and Security in South Asia: The Compound Crisis of 1990*, London and New York: Routledge Curzon, 2003, p. 60.
13   Habibullah, *My Kashmir*, p. 87.
14   Jagmohan, *My Frozen Turbulence*, p. 21.
15   Chari, Cheema, Cohen, *Perception, Politics*, pp. 59-60; Human Rights Watch, '"Everyone Lives in Fear": Patterns of Impunity in Jammu and Kashmir', 11 September 2006, <http://www.hrw.org/report/2006/09/11/everyone-lives-fear/patterns-impunity-jammu-and-kashmir>; Praveen Donthi, 'Under Jagmohan, Jammu And Kashmir Entered A Period Of Unfettered Repression', *Caravan*, 25 January 2016.
16   'Parliament resolution on Jammu and Kashmir', *South Asia Terrorism Portal*, 22 February 1994, <http://www.satp.org/satporgtp/countries/india/document/papers/parliament_resolution_on_Jammu_and_Kashmir.htm>.
17   Human Rights Watch Arms Project, *India: Arms and Abuses in Indian Punjab and Kashmir*, September 1994, Vol. 6, No. 10, p. 20; R. A. Davis, 'Kashmir in the balance',

International Defense Review, Vol. 24, No. 4, April 1991, p. 301; Radha Kumar, 'Untying the Kashmir Knot', *World Policy Journal* Vol. 19, No. 1 (Spring, 2002), pp. 11–24.
18   Shaheed, *Kaun Azad Kaun Ghulam?*
19   These numbers rise and fall according to the intensity of conflict, but have not fallen below 150,000 since the rise of the armed conflict, or risen above 400,000. Kenneth J. Cooper, 'Indian Forces Repress Kashmir Insurgency—And Citizens', *Washington Post*, 6 July 1996.
20   'Fatalities in terrorist violence 1988–2017', *South Asia Terrorism Portal* <http://www.satp.org/satporgtp/countries/india/states/jandk/data_sheets/annual_casualties.htm>.
21   'India's Secret Army in Kashmir: New Patterns of Abuse Emerge in the Conflict', 'A Human Rights Watch Report, Vol. 8, No. 4 (C), May 1996, <http://www.hrw.org/campaigns/kashmir/1996>.
22   Habibullah, *My Kashmir*, p. 91.
23   'Army Files Petition To Shut Kunan Poshpora Mass Rape Case', *Kashmir Observer*, 7 July 2018; Prashant Jha, 'Unravelling a "mass rape"', *The Hindu*, 8 July 2013.
24   Mohammad Umar, '26 Years After Kunan Poshpora, Army Still Enjoys Immunity For Sexual Violence', *The Wire*, 23 February 2017; Essar Batool, Ifrah Butt, Munaza Rashid, Natasha Rather, and Samreen Mushtaq, *Do You Remember Kunan Poshpora?*, Delhi: Zubaan Books, 2016. In 2013, survivors filed a writ petition in the Jammu and Kashmir High Court. The court directed that the state government pay the vicitims compensation. In December 2017, the state government appealed against the High Court's order in the Supreme Court, 'Kashmir "mass rape" survivors fight for justice', BBC.com, 7 October 2017; '1991 Kunan Poshpora mass rape incident: Supreme Court admits Jammu and Kashmir's plea', *New Indian Express*, 4 December 2017.
25   Habibullah, *My Kashmir*, p. 92.
26   Wasim Khalid, 'When Joshi hoisted flag in Lal Chowk', *Greater Kashmir*, 23 January 2011.
27   'Fatalities in terrorist violence 1988–2017', *South Asia Terrorism Portal*.

CHAPTER VIII: THE SIEGE OF HAZRATBAL
1   Shekhar Gupta, '1993 Bombay serial blasts: search on for Bombay's 12-member Memon family', *India Today*, 15 April 1993.
2   Habibullah, *My Kashmir*, p. 96.
3   Arun Shourie, 'Hazratbal mosque crisis: how and why it happened?' *The Observer*, 27 October 1993.
4   Ibid.
5   Ajaz ul Haque, 'October 22: When bullets rained like hell and Bijbehara was bathed in blood', *Greater Kashmir*, 21 October 2017.
6   Iftikhar Gilani, 'Hazratbal shrine siege: Indian chief negotiator reveals secret manoeuvring during crisis', *Daily Times*, 28 October 2006 <http://www.jammu-kashmir.com/archives/archives2006/kashmir20061028b.html>.
7   Shourie, 'Hazratbal mosque crisis'.
8   Ibid.
9   Harinder Baweja, 'Dancing to the militants' tune', *India Today*, 30 November 1993.
10   Baweja, 'Hazratbal siege: Militants gain upper hand while govt fumbles around for face-saving device', *India Today*, 30 November 1993.
11   Habibullah, *My Kashmir*, pp. 106–07.

12 Baweja, 'Hazratbal siege', *India Today*.
13 Yogendra Yadav, 'Reconfiguration in Indian politics: state assembly elections, 1993–95', *Economic and Political Weekly*, 13–20 January 1996.

CHAPTER IX: 'THE SKY IS THE LIMIT'

1   A. S. Dulat with Aditya Sinha, *Kashmir: the Vajpayee Years*, New Delhi: Harper Collins, 2015, pp. 72–73.
2   Harinder Baweja, 'Government releases JKLF chief Yasin Malik in the hope of reviving political dialogue', *India Today*, 15 June 1994.
3   Bilal Handoo, 'The Diplomatic Secret', *Kashmir Life*, 26 January 2015.
4   Matt Apuzzo, 'U. S. ends spying case against former envoy', *New York Times*, 21 March 2016; Suhasini Haider, 'MEA feels vindicated', *The Hindu*, 8 November 2014; Chidanand Rajghatta, 'Pakistan lobbyist Robin Raphel under lens for alleged spying', *Times of India*, 8 November 2014.
5   For a prescient analysis of the changing US–Pakistan relationship prior to 9/11, see Dennis Kux, *The United States and Pakistan, 1947–2000: Disenchanted Allies*, Baltimore: John Hopkins University Press, 2001; Dilip Bobb, 'PM Narasimha Rao meets President Bill Clinton, talks business, plays down Kashmir' *India Today*, 15 June 1994.
6   K. P. Nayar, 'The good old days—Delegations from India and Pakistan, then and now', *The Telegraph*, 26 August 2015.
7   Baweja, 'Government releases JKLF chief Yasin Malik', *India Today*.
8   Ibid.
9   Dulat, *Kashmir: Vajpayee Years*, p. 74.
10 Ibid., p. 75.
11 Ibid., p. 77.
12 Ramesh Vinayak, 'A shocking setback', *India Today*, 3 May 1995.
13 Ibid.
14 Harinder Baweja, 'J&K elections: Resounding rebuff', *India Today*, 30 November 1995.
15 J. N. Dixit, '"Farooq has no credibility": A face to face with Shabir Shah, leader of the People's League', *Outlook*, 22 November 1995.
16 Zafar Meraj, Bhavdeep Kang, Padmanand Jha, 'A failed gambit', *Outlook*, 22 November 1995.
17 Harinder Baweja, 'With evidence to indicate worsening situation in Kashmir Valley, EC decides against polls', *India Today*, 30 November 1990 <https://www.indiatoday.in/magazine/cover-story/story/19951130-with-evidence-to-indicate-worsening-situation-in-kashmir-valley-ec-decides-against-polls-808017-1995-11-30>.
18 Qayoom Khan interview with Aasha Khosa, *Indian Express*, 26 November 2000.

CHAPTER X: GUJRAL'S SHORT FORAY

1   Gujral speech carried on Institute of Defense Studies and Analysis website <http://idsa.in/askanexpert/GujralDoctrine%3F>.
2   'Gujral says Nawaz provided details about terrorists with Stingers', reprinted by *Jang*, 28 October 1999.
3   A. G. Noorani, 'The truth about the Lahore summit', *Frontline*, Vol. 19, No. 4, 16 February–1 March 2002.
4   Salman Haidar, speech at Institute for Peace and Conflict Studies, 16 May 2016 <http://www.ipcs.org/event-details/india-pakistan-under-prime-ministers-gujral-

sharif-a-retrospective-1146.html>.
5   K. P. Nayar, 'Gujral finds himself at odds with the IFS over talks with Pakistan', *Rediff.com*, 21 May 1997.
6   John Burns, 'India and Pakistan to hold talks on reducing tensions', *New York Times*, 12 May 1997.
7   'Gujral says Nawaz provided details about terrorists with Stingers'. Gujral seemed to think this conversation took place at Edinburgh in October, but in fact the power purchase proposal was made in May and was dead by September.
8   'Parliament resolution on Jammu and Kashmir', *South Asia Terrorism Portal*, 22 February 1994, <http://www.satp.org/satporgtp/countries/india/document/papers/parliament_resolution_on_Jammu_and_Kashmir.htm>.
9   Kenneth J. Cooper, 'India denies it has deployed missiles', *Washington Post*, 12 June 1997.
10 Shamshad Ahmad interview with A. G. Noorani, 'An insider's view', *Frontline*, Vol. 24, No. 8, 21 April–4 May 2007.
11 George Iype, 'LOC firing, Kashmir push Indo-Pak power deal into the cold', *Rediff.com*, 4 September 1997.
12 George Perkovich, *India's Nuclear Bomb: The Impact on Global Proliferation*, Oakland: University of California Press, 2001, pp. 400–03.
13 N. Ram, 'Impressive foreign policy foray', *Frontine*, Vol. 14, No. 20, 4 October–17 October 1997.

CHAPTER XI: SADA-E-SARHAD

1   Oliver Meier, 'Involving India and Pakistan: nuclear arms control and non-proliferation after the nuclear tests', *BITS Research Report No. 99:2*, Berlin Information Center for Trans-Atlantic Security.
2   Lahore Declaration, February 1999, New Delhi: Ministry of External Affairs Library.
3   George Iype, 'Vajpayee drives across the border into Pakistan and history', *Rediff. com*, 20 February 1999.
4   Dulat, *Kashmir: Vajpayee Years*, p. 17.
5   Cited by Eqbal Ahmad, 'The bus can bring a Nobel prize', *Dawn*, 21 February1999. Originally in *The Hindu*, 20 February 1999.
6   Sheela Bhatt, 'The US has not fully delivered': Interview with Satish Chandra, *Rediff. com*, 11 August 2005.
7   Kushanava Choudhury, 'After the Lahore summit: the real story', *Rediff.com*, 23 November 2000.
8   'Back channel: the promise and peril', New Delhi: Media Center, Ministry of External Affairs, Government of India, 20 May 2003.
9   Kashmir Study Group, 'Livingston Proposal' of 1998 <http://kashmirstudygroup.com/>.
10 Iftikhar Gilani, 'Mechanism to settle Kashmir dispute was ready: Sartaj Aziz', *Daily Times*, 25 November 2009.
11 A. G. Noorani, *The Kashmir Dispute: 1947–2012*, New Delhi: Tulika Books, 2003, p. 283.
12 Praveen Swami, 'Samjhauta blast: UNSC still blames Lashkar-e-Taiba operative Arif Qasmani', *Indian Express*, 26 July 2017.
13 Press Release, 'Shabir Shah asks Ind–Pak meet to adopt CBM's with the people of J&K', *Jammu & Kashmir*, 18 February 1999 <http://www.jammu-kashmir.com/archives/archives1999/99february18.html>.
14 'Jammu and Kashmir timeline, 1931–1999', *South Asia Terrorism Portal* < http://

www.satp.org/satporgtp/countries/india/states/jandk/data_sheets/attack_hindu.htm >.
15   'Civilians killed in militancy', *South Asia Terrorism Portal* <http://www.satp.org/satporgtp/countries/india/states/jandk/data_sheets/religious_identity_civilians_killed_in_militancy.htm>.
16   'Political activists killed by terrorists in Jammu and Kashmir, 1989–2010', *South Asia Terrorism Portal*, <http://www.satp.org/satporgtp/countries/india/states/jandk/data_sheets/political_assination.htm>.
17   'Casualties during militancy (Jan. 1990 to Nov. 30, 2007) in Jammu and Kashmir', *South Asia Terrorism Portal*, <http://www.satp.org/satporgtp/countries/india/states/jandk/data_sheets/casualtiesmilitency.htm>.
18   'Local and foreign terrorists killed in Jammu and Kashmir', *South Asia Terrorism Portal* <http://www.satp.org/satporgtp/countries/india/states/jandk/data_sheets/local_and_foreign_terrorists_killed.htm>.
19   'Estimated infiltration in J&K', *South Asia Terrorism Portal* <http://www.satp.org/satporgtp/countries/india/states/jandk/data_sheets/infiltration.htm>.
20   'Monthwise killing, 1998–2000', *South Asia Terrorism Portal*, <http://www.satp.org/satporgtp/countries/india/states/jandk/data_sheets/monthwise_killing_199,8_00.htm>.

CHAPTER XII: KARGIL: PAKISTAN'S IMPLAUSIBLE DENIABILITY

1   Dulat, *Kashmir: Vajpayee Years*, p. 25.
2   Emma Henderson, 'Kargil war: Pakistan planned to drop nuclear bomb on India during conflict, former CIA officer claims', *The Independent*, 3 December 2015.
3   For a full description of US mediation during the Kargil conflict, see Strobe Talbott, *Engaging India: Diplomacy, Democracy and the Bomb*, Chapters 8–9, Washington D. C.: Brookings Institution Press, 2004.
4   'Musharraf had brought Kargil plan to me: Benazir', *Rediff.com*, 25 June 2003. US analysts say there is no evidence of a 'Kargil Plan' having been presented to her, or even having existed prior to 1999. See Peter R. Lavoy, ed., *Asymmetric Warfare in South Asia: The Causes and Consequences of the Kargil Conflict*, Cambridge: Cambridge University Press, 2009, Chapter 3.
5   Nasim Zehra, 'Covert contacts', *The News*, 2 July 1999.
6   George Iype, 'Talks collapse amidst accusations, bitterness', *Rediff.com*, 12 June 1999; M. L. Kotru, 'Pakistan's cunning loss of memory', *The Tribune*, 12 June 1999.
7   For a wonderfully self-serving account of Kargil as well as the 2004–07 peace process, see Pervez Musharraf, *In the Line of Fire: A Memoir*, New York: Free Press Books, 2006.
8   Lavoy, *Asymmetry Warfare*.
9   Bruce Reidel, 'American diplomacy and the 1999 Kargil Summit at Blair House', in Lavoy, *Asymmetric Warfare*, pp. 130–43.
10 Cyril Almeida, 'Wresting back space', *Dawn*, 18 September 2016.
11 Ayesha Siddiqa, 'Pakistan: the siege within', *Kashmir Monitor*, 24 October 2016.
12 B. G. Verghese, *First Draft: Witness to the Making of Modern India*, New Delhi: Tranquebar Press, 2010.
13 Shahid Aziz, 'Putting our children in the line of fire', *The Nation*, 6 January 2013.
14 For a blow by blow account, see Noorani, *The Kashmir Dispute*, Chapter 25.
15 'Nawaz Sharif accepts Kargil intrusion was stab in back-for Atal Bihari Vajpayee', *India Today*, 16 February 2016.

CHAPTER XIII: THE NDA'S ANNUS HORRIBILIS

1. Pamela Constable, 'As peace hopes arise, "martyrs" train for Kashmir', *Reuters*, 11 July 1999.
2. Mishra, 'Jammu and Kashmir Militants target jeans, cable TV'.
3. Seema Mustafa, 'Jammu and Kashmir rebels advertise in Pakistan papers', *Asian Age*, 8 February 1999.
4. Constable, 'As peace hopes arise' *Reuters*.
5. 'ISI pumps several crores to revive militancy in J&K', *Daily Excelsior*, 4 April 1999.
6. Aasha Khosa, 'UK authorities order deportation of Pak ultra involved in Kashmir insurgency', *Indian Express*, 27 April 1999.
7. 'Briton sends email to launch jihad in Kashmir', *Asian Age*, 1 November 1999.
8. 'Estimates of infiltration', *South Asia Terrorism Portal*, <http://www.satp.org/satporgtp/countries/india/states/jandk/data_sheets/infiltration.htm>.
9. 'Casualties during militancy (January 1990 to November 30, 2007) in Jammu and Kashmir', *South Asia Terrorism Portal*, <http://www.satp.org/satporgtp/countries/india/states/jandk/data_sheets/casualtiesmilitency.htm>.
10. 'Attacks on Hindus', *South Asia Terrorism Portal* <http://www.satp.org/satporgtp/countries/india/states/jandk/data_sheets/attack_hindu.htm?>.
11. 'BJP nominee's son-freed at last but scared', *Daily Excelsior*, 21 September 1999.
12. 'Kupwara turning into Afghanistan', *Daily Excelsior*, 17 September 1999.
13. 'RR unearths ISI plan to give Doda control to LET', *Daily Excelsior*, 17 September 1999.
14. 'Kupwara turning into Afghanistan', *Daily Excelsior*'.
15. Ibid.
16. Ibid.
17. Shujaat Bukhari, 'New strategies to fight militancy in J&K', *The Hindu*, 31 September 1999.
18. Muzamil Jaleel, 'Hurriyat in a hurry to keep the Muftis down', *Indian Express*, 13 September 1999.
19. Dulat, *Kashmir: The Vajpayee Years*, pp. 36–38.
20. Kanchan Gupta, 'The truth behind Kandahar', *The Pioneer*, 24 December 2008.
21. Zahid Hussain, *Frontline Pakistan: The Struggle with Militant Islam*, New York: Columbia University Press, 2008, p. 63.
22. Ritu Sarin, 'The hijack confession: Why reading between the lines could help', *Indian Express*, 19 December 2001.
23. Jaswant Singh, 'Troubled Neighbour, Turbulent Times: 1999', *A Call to Honour: In Service of Emergent India*, Part III, New Delhi: Rupa, 2007.
24. Seema Mustafa, 'Hurriyat criticizes Pakistan', *Asian Age*, 26 August 1999.

CHAPTER XIV: THE RISE OF JIHAD

1. Lawrence Wright, *The Looming Tower: Al Qaeda and the Road to 9/11*, New York: Knopf Books, 2005, p. 95. For a brilliant description of Pakistan's duplicity and the CIA's connivance, see Steve Coll, *Ghost Wars: The Secret History of the CIA, Afghanistan, and bin Laden from the Soviet Invasion to September 10, 2001*, London: Penguin Books, 2004.
2. Bruce Riedel, 'Hafiz Saeed, Pakistani extremist with a $10 million price on his head, is al Qaeda's Ally', *Brookings Institution*, 3 April 2012.
3. Kamal Siddiqi, 'Muridke complex: a nursery for Taiba men', *Dawn*, 7 May 2000.
4. For a full description including this quote, see Radha Kumar, 'Untying the Kashmir Knot'.

5   Ibid.
6   'From teacher to a terrorist mastermind: the astonishing story of JeM chief Masood Azhar', *Firstpost*, 14 January 2016.
7   Praveen Swami, 'Pakistan moves secret Jaish base used for Pathankot attack, reports say', *Indian Express*, 3 May 2016.
8   Ayesha Siddiqa, 'Terror's training grounds', 17 November 2010, carried on Siddiqa's blogsite <http://ayesha-siddiqa.blogspot.in/>.
9   Jayshree Bajoria, 'Profile: Lashkar-e-Taiba (Army of the Pure)', *Council on Foreign Relations*, 5 December 2008.
10 Transcript of John Quinones interview with Rhys Partridge, 'Traveler: Pearl's kidnapper almost got me', ABC News, 28 February 2003 <http://abcnews.go.com/Primetime/story?id=132138>.
11 'Dismantling The Financial Infrastructure Of Global Terrorism', Hearing Before The Committee On Financial Services, U.S. House Of Representatives, October 3, 2001, Washington D.C.: U.S. Government Printing Office, 2002.
12 'Omar Takes Responsibility for Strikes Inside India', *News International*, 18 February 2002.
13 Ahmed Rashid, 'The Taliban: Exporting Extremism', *Foreign Affairs*, November/December 1999.
14 Eleven years of the Laskhar-e-Taiba', <www.markazdawa.org.pk>, retrieved on 3 May 2002.
15 'Abu Amir Haroon-ur-Rasheed (Swat), Abu Abdullah Iftikhar (Faisalabad), Abu Sangar Yar Shams-ur-Rahman (Afghan), Abu Marsad Hafiz Abdur Rahman (Sheikhupura), Qari Abu Zar Ata-ur-Rahman (Gujranwala), Abu Mansoor Shoaib Najeeb (Sahiwal), Abu Abdulah Arshad Javed (Faisalabad), Abu Zul Qarnain Muhammad Akhtar Sajid (Bahawalnagar), Abu Awais Ghazanfar Abbas (Khanewal)', <www.markazdawa.org.pk>.
16 Bhashyam Kasturi, 'The Indian Army's Experience of Counter-Insurgency Operations in J&K', *Aakrosh: Asian Journal on Terrorism and Internal Conflict*, 29 April 2012, For a detailed analysis of the army's counter-insurgency policy, see Rajesh Rajagopalan, *Fighting like a Guerrilla, the Indian Army and Counterinsurgency*, Routledge, 2008.
17 Human Rights Watch report, 'India's Secret Army in Kashmir: New Patterns of Abuse Emerge in the Conflict', May.
18 Masood Hussain, 'Mufti disbands SOG, merges force with police', *Economic Times*, 25 February 2003; Yusuf Jameel, 'J&K: Security forces conduct cordon, search ops in 10 villages of Shopian, *Asian Age*, 19 August 2017.
19 According to Indian government figures. Kashmiris put the figure at double that, but in general casualty figures taken during crisis tend to over-enumerate, whether official or unofficial.
20 'Disquiet in the valley', *Times of India*, 9 December 1999.
21 Mohammed Wajihuddin, 'The Village that Death Stalked', *Times of India*, 28 November 2009, reviewing Ashoke Pandit's documentary *A Village of Widows*.
22 Jeffrey Goldberg, 'Inside Jehad University', *New York Times*, 25 June 2000; Ghulam Husnain, 'Inside Jehad', *Time Magazine*, Asian Edition, 5 February 2001.
23 Ahmed Rashid, 'The Taliban'; Jessica Stern, 'Pakistan's Jehad culture', *Foreign Affairs*, November/December 2000.
24 The chat room was shut down in early 2001, after news of the web site was carried in the US, UK and Indian newspapers.

CHAPTER XV: SUDDENLY IN 2000

1. 'An Islamic leader's advice to Kashmiris', *United News of India*, 24 February 1999.
2. Vikram Jit Singh, 'Surrendered militant bares sex, sleaze of secessionists', *Indian Express*, 15 March 1999.
3. 'Free Gilgit, Baltistan from clutches of Pakistan', *Daily Excelsior*, 8 April 1999.
4. 'Pakistan changed PoK's demographics', *Deccan Herald*, 25 April 1999.
5. A. K. Dhar and G. Sudhakar Nair, 'J&K groups warn Pakistani mercenaries', *The Pioneer*, 14 May 1999.
6. Harish Khare, 'Hurriyat looks forward to "new initiative" after polls', *The Hindu*, 24 September 1999.
7. Amit Baruah, 'Kashmir issue cannot be sidelined, says Musharraf', *The Hindu*, 1 November 1999.
8. Special Correspondent, 'Pak rulers allow Lashkar to hold 3-day terror camp', *Asian Age*, 2 November 1999.
9. Rahul Bedi, 'Pakistan attack on Uri post beaten back', *Asian Age*, 9 November 1999.
10. As told to me by Mishra. I later checked with members of the Hurriyat and JKLF, who substantiated what he had told me.
11. Dhar and Nair, 'J&K groups warn Pakistani mercenaries', *The Pioneer*, 14 May 1999.
12. 'No plans to contest polls under present dispensation: Hurriyat', *Indian Express*, 13 May 1999.
13. Seema Mustafa, 'The Hurriyat is open to talks with Delhi, attacks Pak', *Asian Age*, 28 September 1999.
14. Seema Mustafa, 'Hurriyat signals new line to Delhi', *Asian Age*, 10 November 1999.
15. Seema Mustafa, 'Advani takes hard line with Hurriyat', *Asian Age*, 8 December 1999.
16. Sukumar Muralidharan, 'From demand to dialogue', *Frontline*, Vol. 17, No. 15, 22 July–4 August 2000.
17. Ibid.
18. Fazal Haq Qureshi interview with author, 14 August 2000.
19. Ishfaq Tantry, 'Had differences with Lone, but never wanted him killed: Geelani in his book', *The Tribune*, 17 May 2015.
20. Murali Krishnan and Priya Sahgal, 'Stammer, and speak: villains of the peace talk with bullets, but it need not spell the end of dialogue. Sincerity is the key to resolving the Kashmir issue', *Outlook*, 14 August 2000.
21. Qureshi interview with author.
22. 'Statement by Home Minister L. K. Advani on the Situation in Jammu & Kashmir on August 9, 2000 in Parliament', *South Asia Terrorism Portal* <http://www.satp.org/satporgtp/countries/india/document/papers/lk_advani_on_jk_situation.htm>.
23. Human Rights Watch World Report, 2002, India, p. 226.
24. Mukhtar Ahmad, 'Hurriyat team to visit Pak on Jan 15', *Rediff.com*, 21 December 2000.
25. Speech by External Affairs Minister Jaswant Singh in Lok Sabha, 'Jammu And Kashmir is not a territorial dispute', *Outlook*, 8 August 2001.
26. Speech by Prime Minister Atal Bihari Vajpayee in Lok Sabha, 'We talked with a firm voice', *Outlook*, 8 August 2001.
27. For an overview of changing conditions post 9/11 and the Bush administration's Pakistan policy, see Sumit Ganguly, *The Kashmir Question: Retrospect and Prospect*, Abingdon: Routledge, 2003.
28. 'Case by case clearance for Hurriyat leaders, says Govt', *The Hindu*, 8 January 2001.
29. Ibid.

30 Ramesh Vinayak, 'Outsiders should go back', *India Today*, 3 June 2002.
31 Ishfaq Tantry, 'Had differences with Lone, but never wanted him killed', *The Tribune*, 17 May 2015.
32 Tara Sahay Sarkar, 'The Terrorists are Desperate', Election Interview with Inspector General JK Police, K Rajendra Kumar, *Rediff.com*, 8 October 2002, <http://www.rediff.com/election/2002/oct/08inter.htm>.

CHAPTER XVI: NEW BEGINNINGS

1 A. G. Noorani, 'Vajpayee & Mehbooba: myths and falsehoods', *Greater Kashmir*, 18 May 2017.
2 'First significant step', *The Guardian*, 22 January 2004.
3 L. K. Advani, 'Dealing with the Kashmir issue', *My Country, My Life*, New Delhi: Rupa Publications, 2008.

CHAPTER XVII: THE PEACE PROCESS, 2004–2008

1 'Why is India Talking to Hurriyat Now?' *Rediff.com*, 1 September 2005.
2 Shamim Meraj, 'Dateline Kashmir: 2005, a wrap up', *News18.com*, 30 December 2005.
3 Mirwaiz Farooq interview with author, 25 May 2017.
4 'Hurriyat leaders return from Pak, PoK visit', *Rediff.com*, 17 June 2005 <http://www.rediff.com/news/report/bus/20050616.htm>.
5 'Pak shouldn't have let Hurriyat in: BJP', *Rediff. com*, 12 June 2005.
6 'PM hold talks with Hurriyat', *Rediff. com*, 6 September 2005.
7 Javaid Malik, 'Delhi to re-engage separatists', *Greater Kashmir*, 24 July 2017.
8 'Fatalities in terrorist violence, 1988–2017', South Asia Terrorism Portal <http://www.satp.org/satporgtp/countries/india/states/jandk/data_sheets/annual_casualties.htm>.
9 B. Muralidhar Reddy, 'Hurriyat leaders call on Musharraf', *The Hindu*, 7 January 2006.
10 'Manmohan to meet Hurriyat leaders next week', *Reuters*, 28 April 2006.
11 Sandeep Dikshit, 'Hurriyat has reneged on its promise: Manmohan', *Indian Express*, 19 October 2007.
12 Steve Coll, 'The Back Channel: India and Pakistan's secret Kashmir talks', *New Yorker*, 2 March 2009.
13 G. Parthasarathy and Radha Kumar, *Frameworks for a Kashmir Settlement*, New Delhi: Delhi Policy Group, 2006.
14 European Parliament Committee on Foreign Affairs, *Report on Kashmir: Present Situation and Future Prospects* (2005/2242(INI)), 2007; Rapporteur: Baroness Nicholson of Winterbourne, European Parliament A6-0158/2007, 25 April 2007.
15 Vijaita Singh, 'Had enough proof against Aseemanand', *The Hindu*, 9 March 2017.
16 A. G. Noorani, 'Vajpayee & Mehbooba' *Greater Kashmir*, 19 May 2017.
17 'India Fatalities: 1994–2018', South Asia Terrorism Portal, <http://www.satp.org/satporgtp/countries/india/database/indiafatalities.htm>.
18 Mir Ehsan, 'Shopian: wedding Plans cut short as militants shoot 21-year-old', *Indian Express*, 16 December 2009.
19 'Moderate Hurriyat welcomes Manmohan's peace offer', *The Hindu*, 26 October 2009.
20 Ibid.
21 Ishfaq ul Hassan, 'Mirwaiz suspends aide for rejecting backdoor talks', *DNA*, 23 December 2009.

22   Praveen Swami, 'Hurriyat holds secret meeting with Chidambaram', *The Hindu*, 17 November 2009.
23   Riyaz Wani, 'Hurriyat closes ranks after Qureshi attack, dialogue move gets boost', *Indian Express*, 13 December 2009.
24   Masood Haider, 'Zardari seeks US mediation on Kashmir issue', *Dawn*, 10 December 2009.
25   Nisar Ahmed Thokar, 'Talks useless for now: UJC', *Greater Kashmir*, 10 December 2009.
26   Sanjeev Pargal, 'Two more PoK visitors turn out to be ISI agents', *Daily Excelsior*, 27 November 2009.

CHAPTER XVIII: INTIFADA, 2010

1   Nitin Gokhale and Surabhi Malik, 'Machil Fake Encounter Case: Army Orders Court Martial Against Two Officers, 4 Other Personnel', NDTV.com, 25 December 2013, <https://Www.Ndtv.Com/India-News/Machil-Fake-Encounter-Case-Army-Orders-Court-Martial-Against-Two-Officers-4-Other-Personnel-545678>; Rajat Pandit, 'Machil Fake Encounter: 5 Armymen Sentenced To Life Imprisonment', *Times of India*, 14 November 2014.
2   Peerzada Ashiq, 'Six Army men sentenced to life in Machil fake encounter case', *The Hindu*, 7 September 2015; 'Macchil fake encounter case: Tribunal suspends life imprisonment of five army personnel; grants them bail', *Firstpost*, 26 July 2017.
3   'Surgical strikes: Nine soldiers awarded gallantry medals for destroying terror launch pads', *Firstpost*, 7 September 2017.
4   'Manmohan announces over Rs. 1,000-crore sops for J&K', *The Hindu*, 8 June 2010.
5   Peerzada Ashiq, 'Kashmir separatists unveil grand agitation programme on streets, social networking sites', *Hindustan Times*, 24 June 2010.
6   Praveen Swami, 'Kashmir's bizarre new "normal"', *The Hindu*, 23 July 2010.
7   Shabir Choudhry, 'Another round of jihad is to start soon in Kashmir', *countercurrents.org*, 10 February 2010 <https://www.countercurrents.org/choudhry100210.htm>.
8   'Pakistan up to something big, army informs Antony', *Economic Times*, 12 December 2010.
9   Anil Anand and Josy Joseph, 'India likely to face a bloody summer', *DNA*, 27 January 2010.
10 Sankarshan Thakur, 'Centre unhappy with "reluctant" Omar: crowd control not army job', *The Telegraph*, 7 July 2010.
11 Toufiq Rashid, 'Kashmiris locked up, hurt, humiliated by curfew', *Hindustan Times*, 16 September 2010.
12 Maseeh Rahman, 'Kashmir riots over Qur'an "burning" leave 13 dead', *The Guardian*, 13 September 2010; 'Quran-Burn Reports Spark Kashmir Clashes, 15 Die', CBS/AP, 13 September 2010; 'Fifteen killed in Kashmir violence', *The Hindu*, 13 September 2010, Sanjeev Pargal, 'Free for all: all Govt offices, vehicles set ablaze in Mendhar, 3 killed', *Daily Excelsior*, 15 September 2010.
13 Sameer Arshad, 'J&K stone-throwers an illiterate, frustrated lot', *Times of India*, 19 January 2011.
14 Izhar Wani, 'In Kashmir, YouTube generation defines new struggle', AFP, 21 July 2010.
15 Justine Hardy, 'Children of a violent past see no future', *Times of India*, 27 February 2010.
16 'If I react with a bit of emotion, good. For too long, politics has been dehumanised

in this country', *Indian Express*, 12 December 2009.
17 Nirupama Subramanian, 'Understanding what young Kashmiris want', *The Hindu*, 7 December 2010; Mercy Corps, Youth Entrepreneurship in Kashmir: Challenges and Opportunities (report of the Mercy Corps Start-up Kashmir Youth Entrepreneurship Development Project, <https://www.mercycorps.org/sites/default/files/youth_entrepreneurship_in_kashmir.pdf>.
18 Praveen Swami, 'Inside Kashmir's new Islamist movement', *The Hindu*, 19 August 2010.
19 '"Quit JK": Geelani to handover letter to army commander today', *Greater Kashmir*, 27 August 2016.
20 Sanjeev Pargal, 'Masrat Alam admits taking Rs 40 lakh to fuel protests', *Daily Excelsior*, 14 December 2010.
21 Ibid.
22 Ishfaq-ul-Hassan, 'Stone-pelting in Kashmir was a "joint" exercise', *DNA*, 10 February 2011. Replying to a question in parliament in 2016, Minister of State Hansraj Ahir presented figures showing 115 civilian deaths in 2010, along with injuries to 1,047 civilians and 5,188 security personnel: PTI, 'J&K: More civilians, security forces injured in 2016 than in 2010', *Economic Times*, 18 July 2017.
23 Shujaat Bukhari, 'Chidambaram hints at resuming talks with J&K separatists', *The Hindu*, 14 October 2009, Updated on 17 December 2016.
24 'Police being trained to play greater role than army: Omar', *Indian Express*, 24 November 2009.
25 'Entrusting law & order to J&K police ultimate aim', *Daily Excelsior*, 31 January 2010.
26 'Bold steps needed to control situation in Kashmir', *The Express Tribune*, 30 June 2010.
27 '3 teams to monitor Kashmir's strife-torn districts', *Hindustan Times*, 31 July 2010.
28 'Civil society calls for efforts to resolve Kashmir', *Rising Kashmir*, 24 July 2010.
29 Bukhari, 'Chidambaram hints at resuming talks with J&K separatists', *The Hindu*.
30 M. Saleem Pandit, 'Demoralized & helpless, J&K cops refuse field duty', *Times of India*, 22 July 2010.
31 Swami, 'Kashmir's Bizarre New "normal"'.
32 Peerzada Ashiq, 'Kashmir separatists unveil grand agitation', *Hindustan Times*.
33 'Breather for valley, Omar, but PDP ignores PM call for meet', *Indian Express*, 11 July 2010.
34 Shujaat Bukhari, 'Kashmir situation needs a human touch', *The Hindu*, 2 September 2010.
35 'Full text of the joint memorandum presented by Mirwaiz Umar Farooq and Yasin Malik', *The Hindu*, 20 September 2010 <http://www.thehindu.com/news/resources/Full-text-of-the-joint-memorandum-submitted-by-Mirwaiz-Umar-Farooq-and-Yasin-Malik/article16010278.ece>.
36 Bukhari, 'Chidambaram hints at resuming talks with J&K separatists' *The Hindu*.
37 Zulfiqar Ali, 'Pakistani militants "hijacking" Kashmir cause', *BBC*, 28 September 2010.

CHAPTER XIX: 'TALKING TO THE PEOPLE'
1 'Choice of Kashmir interlocutors a dampener, says Mehbooba Mufti', NDTV.com, 14 October 2010.
2 'J&K interlocutors: Padgaonkar, Ansari, Radha Kumar', *Outlook*, 13 October 2010.
3 'Omar asks Delhi for fourth interlocutor', *Economic Times*, 15 October 2010.

4   Smita Gupta, 'Kashmir team catches Congress by surprise', *The Hindu*, 14 October 2010.
5   Vinay Kumar, 'Three interlocutors chosen for J&K', *The Hindu*, 13 October 2010.
6   'No red lines for J&K interlocutors: Chidambaram', *Economic Times*, 20 October 2010.
7   'BJP asks PMO to clarify Padgaonkar's Pak comment', *Outlook*, 24 October 2010.
8   '"Back channel diplomacy" underway with India on Kashmir: Pak', *Economic Times*, 11 December 2010.
9   'Incidents involving All Parties Hurriyat Conference', South Asia Terrorism Portal, 13 October 2010, <http://www.satp.org/satporgtp/countries/india/states/jandk/terrorist_outfits/Hurriyat_tl.htm>.
10 'Humane approach with people: Lt Gen Hasnain', *Daily Excelsior*, 16 December 2010.
11 PTI, '104 armymen punished for human rights violations in JK: Gen VK Singh', *DNA*, 24 October 2010.
12 Shuja ul Huq, 'Documents suggest Major Avtar Singh was involved in at least 5 cases of killings, abductions', *India Today*, 12 June 2012; Zahid Rafiq, 'From Kashmir to California: in the footsteps of a wanted killer', *Christian Science Monitor*, 12 June 2012.
13 Ishfaq-ul-Hassan, 'Ghani Bhat says can't implement UN Resolution on Kashmir', *DNA*, 14 October 2010.
14 'Militants want to submit peace plan to interlocutors', *The Hindu*, 31 October 2010.
15 'Interlocutors' claim baseless: UJC', *Kashmir Observer*, 2 November 2010.
16 'Appointment of J-K interlocutors a "dirty trick": Geelani', *Hindustan Times*, 25 October 2010.
17 Ishfaq-ul-Hassan, 'Stone-pelting in Kashmir was a "joint" exercise', *DNA*, 'J&K: More civilians, security forces injured in 2016 than in 2010', *Economic Times*.
18 M. Salim Pandit, 'J&K interlocutors hint at accommodating "Azaadi" debate', *Times of India*, 28 October 2010.
19 'Interlocutors now talk of "azaadi" in Kashmir', *Economic Times*, 27 October 2010.
20 Ishfaq Ahmad Shah, '3000 arrested, released in summer unrest: K. Panel', *Rising Kashmir*, 23 January 2010; 'All but 50 J&K stone pelters released: Padgaonkar', *Zee News*, 24 December 2010.
21 'Jammu and Kashmir Timeline-2011', 17 February 2011, <http://www.satp.org/satporgtp/countries/india/states/jandk/timeline/year2011.htm>.
22 'Valley group admits militants responsible for disappearances', *The Hindu*, 12 December 2011.
23 'H. M. gives nod to case against Syed Ali Shah Geelani', OneIndia.com, 24 October 2010.
24 'Attempt to open dialogue being foiled: Mufti', *Outlook*, 26 November 2010.
25 Vinay Kumar, 'We aim to evolve a dialogue structure: J&K interlocutor', *The Hindu*, 28 November 2010.
26 Ishfaq-ul-Hassan, 'Omar Abdullah announces new package for surrendered militants', *DNA*, 21 June 2010.
27 Asem Mohiuddin, 'Former militants form association', *Rising Kashmir*, 17 July 2011.
28 Muzamil Jaleel, 'Ex-militants turning up as hired guns in valley', *Indian Express*, 20 March 2011.
29 Sanjeev Pargal, 'Govt. wants to make return of Kashmiri youth legal: Omar', *Daily Excelsior*, 27 November 2010.
30 'J-K rehabilitation policy receives 600 applications', *Hindustan Times*, 6 March 2011.

31 M. Saleem Pandit, 'Home Ministry official in Srinagar to discuss militant rehab', *Times of India*, 10 May 2011.
32 Sameer Arshad, 'J&K stone-throwers an illiterate, frustrated lot' *Times of India*, 20 January 2011.
33 Ishfaq Tantry, 'HC's landmark judgement', *Rising Kashmir*, 2 April 2011.
34 Shujaat Bukhari, 'Omar's rehabilitation policy may hit a roadblock', *The Hindu*, 24 November 2010.
35 J&K Interlocutors' Report, October 2011, p. 97.
36 Another delegation to visit Kashmir next month', *Indian Express*, 22 November 2010.
37 Umer Maqbool Dar, 'New political panel on Kashmir in the making', *Greater Kashmir*, 26 December 2010.
38 Abid Bashir, 'Mind your mandate: coalition to interlocutors', *Rising Kashmir*, 26 December 2010; Shah, '3000 arrested, released in summer unrest: K. Panel', *Rising Kashmir*.
39 'A New Compact for Jammu and Kashmir: Interlocutors creating confusion: Kamal', *Greater Kashmir*, 21 December 2010.
40 Ibid.
41 '697 J-K leaders killed in militancy in past 2 decades', *Hindustan Times*, 12 December 2010.
42 Peerzada Ashiq, 'Srinagar shuts down against stone-throwers', *Hindustan Times*, 15 December 2011.
43 'HC's strike call: schools, govt offices remain open in Kashmir', *Indian Express*, 24 November 2010; 'Protest against shutdowns, Geelani tones down strike schedule', *The Hindu*, 7 November 2010.
44 Riyaz Wani, 'Salahuddin blasts "hartal policy"', says ready for talks', *Indian Express*, 14 January 2011.
45 Shujaat Bukhari, 'Stop force and stone throwing will stop: Kupwara People', *The Hindu*, 22 November 2010.
46 Vinay Kumar, 'Interlocutors should not give "ball-by-ball" commentary: Chidambaram', *The Hindu*, 1 November 2010.
47 Cordelia Jenkins, 'In Kashmir, CRPF battles stress, suicide', *Livemint*, 29 March 2011.
48 Maneesh Chibber, 'Train forces to respect rights, says J&K panel', *Indian Express*, 8 January 2011.
49 'Centre to withdraw 10,000 paramilitary personnel in J&K', *Daily Excelsior*, 13 February 2011.
50 'Farooq seeks "forgiveness" for "ethnic cleansing"', *The Hindu*, 7 January 2011.
51 'Will Indian army's charm offensive work in Kashmir?' *Reuters*, 24 February 2011; 'Hundreds of youth turn up for police jobs in Srinagar', *Daily Excelsior*, 12 January 2011.
52 'Indian army launches human rights campaign in Kashmir', *IANS*, 26 March 2011.
53 M. Saleem Pandit, 'J&K custodial death: 3 cops suspended', *Times of India*, 1 August 2011.
54 Vijaita Singh, '2 of 6 valley men framed by cops were postgraduates, fought own case', *Indian Express*, 10 February 2011.
55 'Centre asks states not to target residents of Jammu And Kashmir', *The Hindu*, 3 February 2011.
56 Mahim Prat Singh, 'Madhya Pradesh discriminating against Kashmiri students', *The Hindu*, 3 July 2011.
57 Vijay Kumar, 'Interlocutors working on agenda of autonomy & self-rule: JK BJP', *The Hindu*, 20 December 2010.

58. K. Balchand, 'BJP rejects Manmohan's call for restraint in J&K', *The Hindu*, 24 January 2011.
59. Masood Hussain, 'J&K: PDP, NC against BJP's negative agenda', *Economic Times*, 25 December 2010.
60. Asem Mohiuddin, 'B'pora abuzz with demands for K solution', *Rising Kashmir*, 13 November 2010.
61. Census of India 2011, summary of Jammu and Kashmir table data, <https://www.census2011.co.in/census/state/jammu+and+kashmir.html>.
62. Muzaffar Raina, 'Militant support for fight for girls—Omar govt on drive to improve sex ratio', *The Telegraph*, 17 May 2011.
63. Census of India 2011, 'Jammu and Kashmir districts—religion 2011' <http:/www.census2011.co.in/data/religion/state/1-jammu-and-kashmir.html>.
64. Sanjeev Pargal, 'Poonch says no to azadi; accession final, seeks Council', *Daily Excelsior*, 18 December 2010.
65. 'Interlocutors meet delegations; Kargil for united J&K', *Daily Excelsior*, 10 November 2010.
66. 'JKNPP bats for re-organization of J-K', *Indian Express*, 18 July 2011.
67. 'Interlocutors continue "Mission Kashmir", visit Uri', *Daily Excelsior*, 11 November 2010.
68. 'Interlocutors meet delegations; Kargil for united J&K'.
69. Afaq Hussain, Riya Sinha, 'Truckloads of goodwill', *The Hindu*, 21 October 2016, last updated on 2 December 2016.
70. Lalit K. Jha, 'Kashmiri Pandit diaspora seeks separate homeland in valley', *PTI*, 6 February 2011.
71. 'J&K Gujjars to interlocutors: include our demands in report', *The Hindu*, 17 July 2011.
72. 'Backed by Pak army chief, a Kashmir deal was nearly reached: Kasuri', NDTV.com 20 November 2011 <https://www.ndtv.com/india-news/backed-by-pak-army-chief-a-kashmir-deal-was-nearly-reached-kasuri-445603>.
73. 'Time for dialogue to resolve Kashmir problem: Hurriyat', *IANS*, 9 February 2011.
74. Zahid Rafiq, 'Will truth set Kashmir free? Candid Bhat believes so', *Tehelka*, 7 January 2011.
75. 'Sajjad backs Bhat's admission on Lone, Farooq's killing', *Indian Express*, 10 January 2011.
76. 'J-K locals condemn killing of two sisters by Lashkar militants', *ANI*, 3 February 2011.
77. Peerzada Ashiq, 'Geelani turns dove, bats for peaceful struggle', *Hindustan Times*, 5 May 2011.
78. 'Osama dead: Hizbul Mujahideen owns Osama bin Laden mansion in Abbottabad', *Economic Times*, 4 May 2011.
79. 'New Indo-Pak thaw playing differently to separatists?', *Greater Kashmir*, 4 April 2011.
80. 'Valley shuts to protest Maulana killing', *Indian Express*, 9 April 2011.
81. Toufiq Rashid, 'Separators blame "black sheep" for Maulvi's killing', *Hindustan Times*, 13 April 2011.
82. 'Breakthrough in Showkat's assassination, 3 arrested', *Daily Excelsior*, 16 April 2011.
83. 'Yasin Malik was the next target of assassins: LeT', *Rising Kashmir*, 25 August 2011.
84. Randeep Singh Nandal, 'Blast Kills J&K Cleric Who Preached Peace', *Times of India*, 8 April 2011.
85. 'Jamiat chief's murder: BJP seeks PM's role in probe', *Rising Kashmir*, 14 April 2011.
86. Muzaffar Raina, 'Hurriyat talks axe on member', *The Telegraph*, 20 April 2011.
87. Randeep Singh Nandal, 'J&K interlocutors queer the pitch for peace', *Times of India*, 21 April 2011.

88 'Militant groups warn public against taking part in civic polls in J&K', *Times of India*, 5 April 2011.
89 'People of Jammu & Kashmir give befitting reply to stone-pelters', *Economic Times*, 13 April 2011, Updated on 24 April 2011.
90 Randeep Singh Nandal, '82% turnout in J&K panchayat poll', *Times of India*, 18 April 2011.
91 Randeep Singh Nandal, 'Valley's panchayat polls usher in change', *Times of India*, 19 June 2011,
92 'People of Jammu & Kashmir give befitting reply to stone-pelters',
93 Government of Jammu and Kashmir', Report of the committee on devolution of powers to the panchayats', July 2011 <http://jkgad.nic.in/pdf/report_pris.pdf>.
94 Abdul Qayoom Khan, 'Empowerment of panchayats and implications of 73rd and 74th constitutional amendment in Jammu & Kashmir state', *Greater Kashmir*, 18 October 2012.
95 H. S. Gill, 'Local governance in Jammu and Kashmir: historical perspective and future trends', *Centre for Land Warfare Studies* (CLAWS), Issue Brief No. 914, 7 October 2012.
96 '148 J&K panchayat members quit following threats from terrorists', *DNA*, 21 May 2015.
97 Randeep Singh Nandal, 'In valley, It's OK to slam govt but not separatists', *Rising Kashmir*, 8 July 2011.
98 Ibid.
99 'Not stones, it will rain "words" in Kashmir next month', *Indian Express*, 1 August 2011.
100 'Kashmir literary festival off over fears of violence', *AFP*, 29 August 2011.
101 Abantika Ghosh, 'Kashmir's foreign soccer coach gets death threat', *Times of India*, 27 March 2011.
102 Bashaarat Masood, 'At youth meet, call to build a "better" Kashmir', *Indian Express*, 27 March 2011.
103 'India Inc keeps word, to hire Jammu and Kashmir youth', *Times of India*, 11 March 2011.
104 Shujaat Bukhari, 'Make LoC irrelevant, says former PoK premier', *The Hindu*, 20 September 2011.
105 'Geelani rebukes Mehmood, says UN resolutions only solution', *Kashmir Despatch*, 19 September 2011.
106 'Sultan meets Omar, Radha Kumar at wedding', *Daily Excelsior*, 19 September 2011.
107 Shabir Choudhry, 'Protest against ISI in Muzaffarabad', *faxts.com*, 7 December 2009.
108 Amir Mir, 'Lashkar-e-Zil behind Azad Kashmir suicide hits', *News International*, 10 January 2010.
109 Marvi Memon, 'Concerns of AJK', *News International*, 25 January 2010.
110 Tanveer Ahmed, 'The state vs the activist', countercurrents.org, 15 April 2010 <https://www.countercurrents.org/tahmed150410.htm>.
111 M. Ilyas Khan, 'The Kashmiri fighters who lost their cause', *BBC*, 23 February 2011.
112 See Immigration and Refugee Board of Canada, Azad Kashmir and the Northern Areas, 1 August 1997, available at: <http://www.refworld.org/docid/3ae6a83ac.html>.
113 'As China opens its One Belt One Road summit, anti-CPEC protests erupt in PoK', *Times of India*, 15 May 2017.

114 'CSC on autonomy seeks another extension', *Daily Excelsior*, 27 December 2011.

CHAPTER XX: 2016 AND AFTER: LOSING KASHMIR?

1. Manu Joseph, 'Face of hope reflects calm in Kashmir', *New York Times*, 29 February 2012.
2. 'Tax revenues in Jammu And Kashmir touch a high of Rs 4,800 crore', *Economic Times*, 20 February 2012.
3. Nazir Ganaie, 'Dukhtaran brigade raid café's, gift shops', *Kashmir Observer*, 14 February 2012.
4. Sanjeev Pargal, 'Govt announces 16 new ULBs: 12 for Kashmir, 4 for Jammu', *Daily Excelsior*, 20 February 2012.
5. Full text of the Agenda of Alliance carried on *DNA*, 1 March 2015.
6. Mail Today Bureau, 'Omar Abdullah hits out at MoS Jitendra Singh's Article 370 remark', *India Today*, 28 May 2014.
7. Government of India, Ministry of Defence press release on ceasefire violations, 11 December 2015, New Delhi: Press Information Bureau, Government of India.
8. Pranay Kotasthane, Pavan Srinath, Nitin Pai and Varun Ramachandra, 'The India–Pakistan conflict escalation framework', *The Takshashila Institution*, July 2015 <http://takshashila.org.in/wp-content/uploads/2015/07/India-Pakistan-conflict-escalationframework_TDD.pdf>.
9. 'Statement read out by Foreign Secretaries of India and Pakistan in Ufa, Russia', Media Briefing, Government of India, Ministry of External Affairs, 10 July 2015. The full text of the statement can be accessed at <http://www.mea.gov.in/media-briefings.htm?dtl/25452/Statement_read_out_by_Foreign_Secretaries_of_India_and_Pakistan_in_Ufa_Russia_July_10_2015>.
10. Radha Kumar, 'India and Pakistan: at tilt with destiny', *Delhi Policy Group Issue Brief*, August 2015.
11. 'Beef ban: Supreme Court suspends J-K High Court order for 2 months', *India Today*, 5 October 2015.
12. Mudasir Ahmed, 'After the warm glow of Modi's "package", Kashmir fears the big political Big Chill', *The Wire*, 20 November 2015.
13. 'Resolution passed by Rajya Sabha on situation in the Kashmir Valley today', New Delhi: *Press Information Bureau*, Government of India, Ministry of Home Affairs, 10 August 2016.
14. 'Mehbooba for instituting institutionalised mechanism for dialogue', *Greater Kashmir*, 4 September 2017.
15. 'Am upset we shut doors on MPs: Bhat', *The Tribune*, 8 September 2016.
16. Radha Kumar, 'Now is the time for political dialogue towards a lasting solution in Kashmir', *The Wire*, 9 September 2016.
17. '280 youth join militancy in last three years: Govt', *Rising Kashmir*, 6 February 2018.
18. Shaurya Karanbir Gurung, '82 join militants in J&K in 2018', *Economic Times*, 11 July 2018.
19. 'To open schools withdraw cases first: Geelani', *Kashmir Monitor*, 28 October 2016.
20. M. Saleem Pandit, 'Call it Islamic struggle or die: Hizbul Mujahideen to Hurriyat', *Times of India*, 13 May 2017.
21. Athar Parvaiz, 'How much have NIA sweeps in valley reduced stone-pelting?' *Kashmir Observer*, 26 August 2017.
22. Muzaffar Raina, 'PM salve on Valley TV ulcer', *The Telegraph*, 16 August, 2017
23. Neeta Sharma, 'Centre's Interlocutor Dineshwar Sharma Has 'Hopes For Kashmir': 10 Facts', NDTV.com, October 24, 2017.

24. Ashiq Hussain, 'Army chief should do his job, not give sermons on education: J-K govt', *Hindustan Times*, January 13, 2018
25. 'CFA violations: 2009–2017', *South Asia Terrorism Portal*, <http://www.satp.org/satporgtp/countries/india/states/jandk/data_sheets/CFAViolations.htm>.
26. Arun Sharma and Sushant Singh, 'Ceasefire violation: Four soldiers, including Army Captain, killed in Pakistani shelling', *Indian Express*, 5 February 2018.
27. 'UN Security Council sanctions monitoring team arrived in Pakistan', *Pak Tribune*, 26 January 2018.
28. 'Rajiv Gandhi, Benazir Bhutto were ready to resolve Kashmir dispute: Asif Ali Zardari', *Economic Times*, 6 February 2018.
29. 'Two BJP Ministers Who Rallied In Support Of Kathua Gangrape Accused Resign', *Outlook*, 13 April 2018.
30. Sanjay Khajuria, 'Kathua minor rape-murder: Lawyers stop cops from filing chargesheet', *Times of India*, 9 April 2018.
31. 'The General Talk of Peace', *Greater Kashmir*, 16 April 2018.
32. V. Sudarshan, 'The shadow of death returns to the Valley', *The Hindu*, 21 June 2018; Peerzada Ashiq, 'Who killed Shujaat Bukhari?', *The Hindu*, 7 July 2018.
33. Prem Shankar Jha, 'Shujaat Bukhari, A Hero Martyred', *The Wire*, 16 June 2018.
34. Shaurya Karanbir Gurung, 'Abducted jawan Aurangzeb killed for being buddy to Army officer', *Economic Times*, 16 June 2018.
35. 'Fatalities in Terrorist Violence 1988 – 2018', *South Asia Terrorism Portal*, <http://www.satp.org/satporgtp/countries/india/states/jandk/data_sheets/annual_casualties.htm>.
36. 'Failed Ramzan Ceasefire, Killing Of Shujaat Bukhari: What Made BJP End Alliance With PDP', News18.com, 19 June 2018; 'Jammu Kashmir govt collapses as BJP pulls out of ruling alliance with PDP', *Asian Age*, 19 June 2018.
37. 'Ceasefire Revocation, Shujaat Bukhari's Murder, the BJP-PDP Split: What Kashmir Thinks', A report by the Concerned Citizens' Group, *The Wire*, 2 July 2018.
38. Ibid.
39. Office of the United Nations High Commissioner for Human Rights, Report on the Situation of Human Rights in Kashmir: Developments in the Indian State of Jammu and Kashmir from June 2016 to April 2018, and General Human Rights Concerns in Azad Jammu and Kashmir and Gilgit-Baltistan, 14 June 2018.
40. 'UN report on Kashmir: 'Prejudiced, mischievous, misleading'—BJP, Congress react in one voice', *Financial Express*, 14 June 2018.
41. Shahbaz Rana, 'Pakistan formally placed on FATF grey list', *Express Tribune*, 30 June 2018.
42. Nirupama Subramanian, 'Pakistan elections: No contest, assured victory', *Indian Express*, 23 July 2018.

CHAPTER XXI: A DOOM ONLY PARTIALLY FORESEEN

1. 'Daily Fatalities', *South Asia Terrorism Portal*, https://www.satp.org/datasheet-terrorist-attack/fatalities/india-jammukashmir.
2. Poonam Agarwal, 'Pulwama: CRPF Wanted Air Transit for Attacked Convoy, Was Ignored, *The Quint*, 21 February 2019; Express Web Desk, 'Pulwama attack: Did not refuse air transit facility for CRPF jawans, MHA clarifies', *Indian Express*, 17 February 2019. In 2023, former Jammu and Kashmir Governor Satyapal Malik alleged he 'had been told to keep quiet' when he spoke to the prime minister on the security failures that led to the deaths of 40 troopers, PTI, '2019 Lok Sabha elections were fought on bodies of our soldiers: Satya Pal Malik', *The Hindu*, 22 May 2023.

NOTES

3   Suhasini Haider and Dinaker Peri, 'IAF plane shot down: pilot taken captive by Pak. Army', *The Hindu*, 27 February 2019.

4   Ministry of Home Affairs, Government of India, Notification No. S.O. 1069(E) dated 28th February 2019, *Gazette of India - Extraordinary*, II:3(ii), February 28, 2019; Shakir Mir, '2019 is the Year that Changed Kashmir to the Detriment of India', *The Wire*, 31 December 2019.

5   Hakeem Irfan Rashid, 'Abdullahs request PM Modi not to take 'precipitous steps', *Economic Times*, August 2, 2019; Karan Thapar interview with Not Feel Indian, Today They'd Rather Have the Chinese Rule Them": Farooq Abdullah', *The Wire*, 23 September 2020.

6   PTI, 'Forces' deployment a security measures, no knowledge of change in constitutional provisions: Jammu and Kashmir governor', *Times of India*, 3 August 2019.

7   Agence-France Presse (AFP), 'About 4,000 people arrested in Kashmir since August 5: govt sources to AFP', *The Hindu*, 18 August 2019; G. Kishan Reddy, Minister of State in The Ministry of Home Affairs, Government of India, Reply to Lok Sabha Unstarred Question No. 2417, 3 December 2019, Digital Sansad, https://sansad.in/getFile/loksabhaquestions/annex/172/AU2417.pdf?source=pqals; The Wire Staff, '5,161 People Detained in J&K Since August 5 Decision, Says Centre', *The Wire*, 20 November 2019.

8   Azaan Javaid, 'J&K has 2 sets of cell-phone numbers—those on 'white list' work, ones on 'black list' don't', *The Print*, 26 September 2019.

9   Niha Masih, Shams Irfan and Joanna Slater, 'India's Internet shutdown in Kashmir is the longest ever in a democracy', *The Washington Post*, 16 December 2019.

10 Compiled from Correspondent, 'Internet Services Suspended in Kashmir: A Brief History of Data Shutdowns in The State', News 18, 7 August 2019, https://www.news18.com/news/tech/internet- services-suspended-in-kashmir-a-brief-history-of-data-shutdowns-in-the-state-2258401.html; *Voices from Kashmir: Narratives that lost connection* (initiative by internetshutdowns.in), 27 January 2020, https://sflc.in/using-2g-fight-pandemic-digital-world; Government of Jammu and Kashmir, Department of Disaster Management, Relief, Rehabilitation and Reconstruction, Order No.66-JK (DMRRR) of 2020, https://jkgad.nic.in/commonshowOrder.aspx?actCode=O35860.

11 Ministry of Law and Justice (Legislative Department), The Constitution (Application to Jammu And Kashmir) Order, 2019, C.O. 272, *The Gazette of India – Extraordinary*, II:3(i), August 5, 2019; Declaration under Article 370(3) of the Constitution, C.O. 273, *The Gazette of India – Extraordinary*, II:3(i), August 6, 2019; The Jammu and Kashmir Reorganisation Act, 2019, 34 of 2019, *The Gazette of India – Extraordinary*, II:1, August 9, 2019.

12 The Wire Staff, 'Government Shuts Down J&K Human Rights Commission, Information Commission', *The Wire*, 24 October 2019; PTI, 'JK state laws governing commissions lik SHRC have been repealed, SC told', *Economic Times*, 18 March 2023, https://legal.economictimes.indiatimes.com/news/industry/jk-state-laws-governing-commissions-like-shrc-have-been-repealed-sc-told/98742105, 18 Mar 2023.

13 Under the PSA a person could be arrested and kept in detention for up to one year if the grounds were maintenance of public order, and two years if the grounds were smuggling, Jammu and Kashmir Public Safety Act, VI of 1978, s.18.a and 18.b, https://jkhome.nic.in/pdf/PSA0001.pdf; under the preventive detention act the period of detention was limited to three months. Government Of India Ministry of Law, The Preventive Detention Act, 1950, IV of 1950, *The Gazette of India –*

Extraordinary, IV, 26 February 1950.

14 The Government of Jammu And Kashmir, Civil Secretariat: Department of Law, Justice and Parliamentary Affairs, The Jammu and Kashmir Juvenile Justice (Care and Protection of Children) Act, 2013, VII of 2013, *The Jammu and Kashmir Government Gazette*, 126:4-5: III; 25 April 2013; The Juvenile Justice (Care and Protection) of Children Act 2015, 2 of 2016, *The Gazette of India – Extraordinary*, II:1, January 1, 2016.

15 Livelaw News Network14, 'Illegal Detention of Children in Kashmir: Two Child Right Experts Move SC, Seek Urgent Intervention of Court' [Read Petition] https://www.livelaw.in/top-stories/illegal-detention-of-children-kashmir--148066?infinitescroll=1, https://www.livelaw.in/top-stories/illegal-detention-of-children-kashmir--148066?infinitescroll=1, https://www.indiatoday.in/india/story/children-among-minors-detained-kashmir-article-370-abrogation-reports-1605322-2019-10-01. Also see Supreme Court of India, Writ Petition (C) No.1166/2019, https://indiankanoon.org/doc/193384604/,https://www.livelaw.in/top-stories/kashmir-sc-to-consider-plea-against-alleged-illegal-detention-of-juveniles-on-december-13-150617?infinitescroll=1; Anjana Prakash, 'Jammu and Kashmir Police Has Violated the JJ Act in Detaining Children', *The Wire*.

16 Mudasir Ahmed, 'J&K Leader's Ability to Convince People to Vote During Boycotts Cited as Reason for PSA Charge', *The Wire*, 8 February 2020; HT Newsdesk, 'J&K HC quashes PSA detention of NC leader Sagar', *Hindustan Times*, 16 June 2020.

17 Muzaffar Raina, 'Crisis in Kashmir: Bond of silence that buys freedom', *The Telegraph*, 19 October 2019.

18 Naseer Ganai, 'Kashmiri Author and Journalist Gowhar Geelani, Booked Under UAPA, Moves HC', *Outlook* magazine, April 24, 2020; Mudasir Ahmed, 'Kashmiri Photojournalist Charged Under UAPA for Unspecified Social Media Posts', *The Wire*, 20 April 2020.

19 The Unlawful Activities (Prevention) Amendment Act, 2019, 28 of 2019, *The Gazette of India – Extraordinary*, II:1, 8 August 2019.

20 Free Speech Collective, '16 Indian Journalists Have Been Charged Under UAPA, 7 Are Currently Behind Bars', *The Wire*, 6 October 2023.

21 Azaan Javaid, 'Muharram restrictions have Kashmir on edge, 200 detained as clashes with police break out', *The Print*, 28 August 2020.

22 The Wire Staff, 'NIA Raid Could Endanger Families of Disappeared Persons in Kashmir: APDP', *The Wire*, 28 October 2020.

23 Jehangir Ali and Kabir Agarwal, 'Forensic Evidence Shows Attempts Were Made to Infect Phones in Kashmir With Pegasus', *The Wire*, 23 July 2021.

24 Bureau, 'PM Modi: Centre's rule is temporary, elections in Jammu and Kashmir', *The Hindu Businessline*, 8 August 2019. Full speech on YouTube, Prime Minister Narendra Modi's address to the Nation on Article 370, August 8, 2019, https://www.youtube.com/watch?v=Cb8DIUBXvjA. Reference to precautionary measures, end of terrorism, investment flow and elections, 19.40-21.40, to the people of Jammu, Kashmir and Ladakh bearing the brunt, 34.38-34.47.

25 Press Trust of India, 'Kashmir economy suffered loss of Rs. 17,878 cr. in 4 months after Article 370 abrogation', *Indian Express*, December 17, 2019. For category-wise figures, including job losses, see The Forum for Human Rights in Jammu and Kashmir, *Jammu and Kashmir: The Impact of Lockdowns on Human Rights*, August 2019-July 2020', p. 45.

26 The Government of India, Niti Aayog and Institute for Competitiveness, 'Export

Preparedness Index 2020', Delhi: Niti Aayog, pp. 29–32.

27 Central Administration Division, The Government of Jammu and Kashmir, S.O. 166, Civil Secretariat: Jammu, 18 May 2020; Shakir Mir, 'JK Govt's New Domicile Certificates Rule a Move to Undercut Resistance from Kashmiri Officials?', *The Wire*, 19 May 2020.

28 Ministry of Home Affairs (Department of Jammu, Kashmir and Ladakh Affairs), S.O. 3807(E): The Jammu and Kashmir Reorganisation (Adaptation of Central Laws) Third Order, 2020, *Gazette of India – Extraordinary*, II:3(ii), 26 October 2020.

29 Riyaz Wani, 'Why are nomads being evicted from Jammu and Kashmir?', *Down to Earth* magazine, December 1, 2020; Naseer Ganai, 'Eviction During Pandemic: No Relief for Nomads of J&K', *Outlook* magazine, 26 May 2021; PTI, 'Land eviction drive: Protests in parts of J&K', *The Times of India*, 3 February 2023.

30 India.com news desk, 'Srinagar PDP Office Sealed by J&K Police, Several Workers Arrested: Mehbooba Mufti', India.com, 29 October 2020.

31 The Government of Jammu and Kashmir, Revenue Department, Notification s.o. 668, s.12, Jammu: Civil Secretariat, 9 December 2022; Nazir Masoodi, 'Concern over New Rule on Land Lease in Jammu and Kashmir', NDTV.com 16 December 2022.

32 PTI, 'Traders protest against opening of Reliance retail store in Jammu', *The Print*, 16 October 2022.

33 The Forum for Human Rights in Jammu and Kashmir: *Jammu and Kashmir: The Impact of Lockdowns on Human Rights, August 2019-July 2020*, Chapters 6: Impact on Children and Youth; 7: Impact on Health; 8: Impact on Industry and Employment, pp. 32–48.

34 Athar Parvaiz, 'In A First, Outside Companies Earn 100 Percent Mining Rights in Kashmir', *Kashmir Observer*, 7 February 2020.

35 Reserve Bank of India, *Handbook of Statistics on Indian States* (2022), Table 15: State-Wise Unemployment Rate Usual Status (Adjusted) (Rural Overall), Table 16: State-Wise Unemployment Rate – Usual Status (Adjusted) (Urban Overall), New Delhi: Department of Economic Affairs, Ministry of Finance, Government of India (January, 2023); *Economic Survey 2022-23*, Statistical Appendix, Table 8.12: Unemployment Rate (UR) (in per cent) according to current weekly status for different States (persons, all ages).

36 *Economic Survey 2022-23*, op. cit., Statistical Appendix, Table 1.11B: Growth of Per Capita Net State Domestic Product at Current Prices (2011-12 Series) As on 01.08.2022; Table 8.16: Children under 5 years who are wasted (weight-for-height) (%) across states and UTs of India; Table 8.17: Children under 5 years who are underweight (weight-for-age) (%) across states and UTs of India Some health indices, such as maternal and child mortality, improved, but these pertained to health care delivery rather than impoverishment.

37 S.P. Vaid, 'View: Amit Shah engagements, priorities show he means business in J&K', *Economic Times*, 3 November 2020; Yawar Hussain, 'The Home Minister's Visit', *Kashmir Life*, 8 October 2022; Ministry of Home Affairs, press release, 'Under the leadership of Shri Modi a people-oriented governance has been put at the grassroots level in Jammu and Kashmir', Delhi: Press Information Bureau, Government of India, 23 June 2023; PTI, 'All-round development in J&K since Article 370 abrogation: Amit Shah', *Deccan Herald*, 24 June 2023.

38 Special Correspondent, '2 NC leaders, including MP's son, arrested', *The Hindu*, 25 December 2020; Devesh K. Pandey, 'ED files chargesheet against Farooq Abdullah in J&K cricket association case', *The Hindu*, 26 July 2022; PTI, 'Court Frames Terror Charges Against PDP Leader Waheed Parra', *The Hindu*, 26 July 2021.

39   Shakir Mir, 'J&K: Are 'Security Restrictions' Being Used to Give BJP DDC Candidates an Upper Hand?', *The Wire*, 24 November 2020; Naveed Iqbal and Deeptiman Tiwary, 'Security blanket for DDC polls in J&K: Candidates and campaign in lockdown', *Indian Express*, 19 November 2020.

40   Reuters, '75 political leaders detained in Kashmir after DDC elections', *Deccan Herald*, 26 December 2020.

41   The Jammu and Kashmir Delimitation Commission, Notification and Order, *Jammu and Kashmir Official Gazette*, 134: II-C, March 14, 2022; Shakir Mir, 'J&K Delimitation: Will It Really Help BJP? Will It Further Alienate Kashmiris?', *The Quint*, 7 May 2022; Radha Kumar, 'With delimitation over, a look at the slate for J&K', *The Hindu*, 13 May 2022.

42   The Jammu and Kashmir Reorganisation (Amendment) Act, 2021, 2 of 2021, *Gazette of India – Extraordinary*, II:1, 25 February 2021.

43   M. Saleem Pandit, 'J&K govt sets up special task force to fire employees with anti-national attitude', *Times of India*, 22 April 2021.

44   The Hindu Bureau, 'Five J&K Government Employees Sacked for "Anti-National Activities"', *The Hindu*, October 15, 2022; Express News Service, 'J&K Admin Terminates 3 Employees for Involvement in Anti-national Activities', *Indian Express*, February 27, 2023.

45   Ceasefire violations stood at 4,645 in 2020, almost three times the 2018 figure of 1,629. Between 2014-2020, there were 11,424 ceasefire violations, as compared to 523 in 2004-2013. 'Datasheet: Terrorist attacks, Jammu and Kashmir', *South Asia Terrorism Portal*, https://www.satp.org/datasheetterrorist-attack/fatalities/india-jammukashmir; Deeptiman Tiwary, Naveed Iqbal, 'After three-month thaw, an uptick in militancy in Kashmir; June, July see 16 encounters', *Indian Express*, 22 July 2021, *India Today*, 'Ceasefire Violations along India-Pakistan border were highest in 2020, reveals RTI', 11 May 2021.

46   'Security Forces Data: Attacks on Police Personnel, Jammu & Kashmir', *South Asia Terrorism Portal*, https://www.satp.org/security-force-data-details/Police/india-jammukashmir; Security Forces Data: Attacks on CRPF Personnel, Jammu & Kashmir, https://www.satp.org/security-force-data-details/CRPF/india-jammukashmir. Data for 2023 was not yet available).

47   Express News Service, '4 militants killed in encounter with security forces in J&K's Poonch', *Indian Express*, July 18, 2023; Nirupama Subramaniam, 'The challenge in Poonch: A new terror push in Jammu, likely alienation of Gujjar-Bakerwals', *Indian Express*, April 27, 2023; Yogesh, 'Poonch attack carried out with active local support; steel coated bullets, IED used to blow army vehicles: DGP Dilbagh Singh', *SNS Kashmir*, April 29, 2023; Jehangir Ali, 'Outrage as 2 Civilians Found Dead Outside Rajouri Army Camp, J&K Police Begins Probe', *The Wire*, December 16, 2022; Outlook Web Desk, 'J&K's Rajouri Village's Death Toll Rises to Six as Child Succumbs to Injuries, Village Holds Tearful Cremation', *Outlook India*, January 3, 2023; Anees Zargar, 'Five Killed, near Dozen Injured in Back to Back Attacks in Rajouri Village', NewsClick, January 2, 2023.

48   HT Correspondent, 'Kashmiri Pandits in Jammu protesting killing of a Kashmiri Sarpanch at Anantnag', *Hindustan Times*, 9 June 2020; Kusum Arora and Irfan Lone, 'Despite Persistent Security Threats, J&K Sarpanchs Say Govt Has Little Concern for Their Safety', *The Wire*, 19 June 2020; Azaan Javaid, 'Day after Kashmir killings, a village in shock & families surprised by BJP connection,' *The Print*, 30 October 2020; The Scroll Staff, 'J&K: Jeweller allegedly shot dead by suspected militants over domicile certificate', Scroll.in, 2 January 2021; Hari Kumar and Mujib Mashal, 'As Targeted Killings Spike, Hindus are Desperate to Flee Kashmir', *New York Times*, 3

June 2022; Ayesha Jain and Anthony Rozario, "Situation crawling back to '90's': Fear grips Kashmiri Hindus over killing spree', *The Quint*, 3 June 2022; Safwat Zargar, 'A Kashmiri actor was shot dead inside her home. Her family can't fathom why', Scroll.*in*, 30 May 2022; Azaan Javaid, 'Threatened by militants with beheading, 10 J&K panches & sarpanches resign', *The Print*, 5 March 2021; The Forum for Human Rights in Jammu and Kashmir, 'Three years as a Union Territory: Human Rights in Jammu and Kashmir, August 2021-July 2022', pp. 2-4.

49 Peerzada Ashiq, 'Hindu teacher shot dead at Kulgam school as Kashmir sees 7th targeted killing this month', *The Hindu*, May 31, 2022; Forum for Human Rights in Jammu and Kashmir, *Three Years as a Union Territory: Human Rights In Jammu and Kashmir, August 2021-July 2022*, Chapter 4: Kashmiri Pandits, pp. 19-27.

50 Peerzada Ashiq, 'Kashmiri Pandits Flee Kashmir Valley', *The Hindu*, 3 June 2022.

51 Fayaz Wani, 'Targeted Killings Trigger Fear, Kashmiri Pandits Leave Valley', *New Indian Express*, October 26, 2022; Nazir Masoodi, 'Last Kashmiri Pandit in Terror-Hit Village, A Woman, Migrates To Jammu', NDTV.com, 28 October 2022.

52 Sunil Bhat, '"Will Turn Transit Colonies to Graveyard': Kashmir Fight's Fresh Threat to Kashmiri Pandits', *India Today*, 19 December 2022.

53 Hakeem Irfan Rashid, 'No positive outcome of talks with Amit Shah and MHA officials: Ladakh bodies', *Economic Times*, 4 March 2024; Rekha Chowdhary, 'Ladakhi Politics since the Formation of Union Territory', *Economic & Political Weekly*, 58:18, 6 May 2023; Bilal Kuchay, 'Ladakh Buddhists who hailed India's Kashmir move not so sure now' Aljazeera.com, 14 October 2020; Kabir Agarwal, "What Did We Do?': Kargil Seethes at Centre's Bifurcation Decision', *The Wire*, 17 August 2019.

54 The Hindu Bureau, 'China pitched four tents in 'buffer zone' in Ladakh, says councillor', *The Hindu*, 12 July 2023; Vijay Gokhale, 'Stabilizing the Border: A Possible Way Ahead in the Post-Galwan Situation', Carnegie India, December 15, 2023, HTTPS://CARNEGIEINDIA.ORG/2023/12/15/STABILIZING-BORDER-POSSIBLE-WAY-AHEAD-IN-POST-GALWAN-SITUATION-PUB-91244; Matthew P. Funaiole, Brian Hart, Joseph S. Bermudez Jr., and Jennifer Jun, 'China Is Deepening Its Military Foothold along the Indian Border at Pangong Tso', CSIS China Power Project, 28 November 2022, https://chinapower.csis.org/analysis/china-satellite-imagery-military-pangong-tso/.

AFTERWORD

1 2023 INSC 1058, In Re: Article 370 of the Constitution, https://main.sci.gov.in/pdf/LU/article_370.pdf.

2 AIR 2017 SC 25, State Bank of India vs Santosh Gupta and Anr., judgement authored by R.F. Nariman, https://indiankanoon.org/doc/105489743/. While holding that Article 370 had acquired permanence, the judgment also held that parliament overrode the state legislature.

3 2023 INSC 1058, op. cit., paragraphs 497 and 503, pp. 337, 342.

4 See Chapter 17, pp. 244-247, for a discussion of the Aziz-Lambah Framework and its genesis.

5 Editorial, 'Degrees of irresponsibility', *Indian Express*, 10 January 2014; Steve Coll, 'The Back Channel, *New Yorker*, March 2009; The Council on Foreign Relations, 'Summer Thaw in India-Pakistan Freeze? Interview with Radha Kumar by Jayshree Bajoria and Greg Bruno', 13 May 2010, https://www.cfr.org/interview/summer-thaw-india-pakistan-freeze; Ashley J. Tellis, 'Are India-Pakistan Peace Talks Worth a Damn?', Carnegie Endowment for International Peace, 20 September 2017, https://carnegieendowment.org/2017/09/20/are-india-pakistan-peace-talks-worth-damn-pub-73125.

BIBLIOGRAPHY

Abdullah, Sheikh, *The Blazing Chinar*, Srinagar: Gulshan Books, 2016.
Advani, L. K., *My Country, My Life*, New Delhi: Rupa Publications, 2008.
Akbar, M. J., *Kashmir: Behind the Vale*, New Delhi: Roli Books, 2002.
al-Biruni, *India*, edited by Qeyumuddin Ahmad, New Delhi: National Book Trust, 2005.
Ali, Agha Shahid, *The Country Without a Post Office*, New York: W. W. Norton and Company, 1997.
Ali, Rao Farman, *History of Armed Struggles in Kashmir*, Srinagar: J. K. Books, 2017.
Ankit, Rakesh, *The Kashmir Conflict: From Empire to the Cold War, 1945-66*, Abingdon: Routledge, 2016.
Ahmad, Khalid Bashir, *Kashmir: Exposing the Myth Behind the Narrative*, New Delhi: Sage Publications, 2017.
Bazaz, Prem Nath, *Kashmir in Crucible*, New Delhi: Pamposh Publications, 1967.
Bhattacharjea, Ajit, *Sheikh Mohammad Abdullah: Tragic Hero of Kashmir*, New Delhi: Roli Books, 2008.
Bhutto, Benazir, *Daughter of Destiny: An Autobiography*, London: Simon and Schuster, 2007.
Bose, Sumantra, *Kashmir: Roots of Conflict, Paths to Peace*, Cambridge: Harvard University Press, 2005.
Brown, William Alexander, *Gilgit Rebellion: The Major who Mutinied Over Partition of India*, Barnsley: Pen & Sword Books, 2014.
C. Bilqees Taseer, *The Kashmir of Sheikh Muhammad Abdullah*, Lahore: Ferozsons Books, 1986.
Choudhary, Zafar, *Kashmir Conflict and Muslims of Jammu*, Srinagar: Gulshan Books, 2015.
Coll, Steve, *Ghost Wars: The Secret History of the CIA, Afghanistan, and bin Laden from the Soviet Invasion to September 10, 2001*, London: Penguin Books, 2004.
Dasgupta, Chandrashekhar, *War and Diplomacy in Kashmir, 1947-8*, New Delhi: Sage Publications, 2004.
Dayal, Rajeshwar, *A Life of Our Times*, Hyderabad: Orient Longman, 1998.
Dewan, Parwez, *A History of Kashmir*, New Delhi: Manas Publications, 2011.
Dixit, J. N., *India-Pakistan in War and Peace*, London: Routledge, 2002.
Dulat, A. S. with Sinha, Aditya, *Kashmir: the Vajpayee Years*, New Delhi: Harper Collins, 2015.
Gandhi, M. K., *Collected Works of Mahatma Gandhi*, Vol. 90, New Delhi: Publications Division, Government of India, 1999
Ganguly, Sumit, *The Kashmir Question: Retrospect and Prospect*, Abingdon: Routledge, 2003.
Gopal, Sarvepalli, *Selected Works of Jawaharlal Nehru*, New Delhi: Navrang Publishers, 1994.
Grover, Verinder and Arora, Ranjana, *50 Years of Indo-Pak Relations: Chronology of All Important Events and Documents from 1947–1997*, New Delhi: Deep and Deep Publications, 1990.
Gupta, Sisir Kumar, *Kashmir: A Study in India-Pakistan Relations*, Mumbai: Asia Publishing House, 1966.
Habibullah, Wajahat, *My Kashmir: The Dying of the Light*, New Delhi: Penguin Viking, 2001.
Hingorani, Aman M., *Unravelling the Kashmir Knot*, New Delhi: Sage Publications, 2016.
Hitchens, Christopher, *The Trial of Henry Kissinger*, London: Verso Books, 2001

Hussain, Zahid, *Frontline Pakistan: The Struggle with Militant Islam*, New York: Columbia University Press, 2008.
Jagmohan, *My Frozen Turbulence in Kashmir*, New Delhi: Allied Publishers, 1991.
Jha, Prem Shankar, *Kashmir 1947: Rival Versions of History*, New Delhi: Oxford University Press, 1996.
Kalhana, *Rajatarangini*, translated by Marc Aurel Stein, Vol. I, Stein's Introduction and Books I-VII, New Delhi: Motilal Banarsidass, 1900.
Kaw, M. K., ed., *Kashmir and Its People: Studies in the Evolution of Kashmiri Society*, New Delhi: A. P. H. Publishing, 2004.
Khan, Muhammad Ibrahim and Khan, Sardar Ibrahim, *The Kashmir Saga*, Mirpur: Verinag Publishers, 1990.
Kissinger, Henry, *White House Years*, London: Simon and Schuster, 1979.
Korbel, Josef, *Danger in Kashmir*, Princeton: Princeton University Press, 1954.
Kux, Dennis, *The United States and Pakistan, 1947–2000: Disenchanted Allies*, Baltimore: John Hopkins University Press, 2001.
Lavoy, Peter R., ed., *Asymmetric Warfare in South Asia: The Causes and Consequences of the Kargil Conflict*, Cambridge: Cambridge University Press, 2009.
Levy, Adrian and Scott-Clark, Cathy, *The Meadow: Kashmir 1995 – Where the Terror Began*, London: HarperPress, 2012.
Madhok, Balraj, *Kashmir: The Storm Center of the World*, Houston: A. Ghosh Publishers, 1992.
Maini, K. D., *Poonch: The Battlefield of Kashmir*, Srinagar: Gulshan Books, 2012.
Malhotra, Inder, *Indira Gandhi: A Personal and Political Biography*, London: Hodder and Stoughton, 1989.
Musharraf, Pervez, *In the Line of Fire: A Memoir*, New York: Free Press Books, 2006.
Nehru, Jawaharlal, *An Autobiography: Towards Freedom*, New Delhi: Jawaharlal Nehru Memorial Fund and Oxford University Press, 1982.
Noorani, A. G., *The Kashmir Dispute: 1947–2012*, New Delhi: Tulika Books, 2003.
Parthasarathy, G. and Kumar, Radha, *Frameworks for a Kashmir Settlement*, New Delhi: Delhi Policy Group, 2006.
Peer, Basharat, *Curfewed Night*, New Delhi: Penguin Random House India, 2009.
Perkovich, George, *India's Nuclear Bomb: The Impact on Global Proliferation*, Oakland: University of California Press, 2001, pp. 400–3.
Prasad, H. Y. Sharada and Hasan, Mushirul, eds., *Selected Works of Jawaharlal Nehru*, Volume 22, New Delhi: Jawaharlal Nehru Memorial Fund, 2005.
Puri, Balraj, *Kashmir: Towards Insurgency*, Tracts for the Times, New Delhi: Sangam Books, 1993.
———, *Simmering Volcano: A Study of Jammu's Relations with Kashmir*, New Delhi: Sterling Publishers, 1983.
Qasim, Mir, *My Life and Times*, New Delhi: Allied Publishers, 1992.
Qureshi, Hashim, *Kashmir: The Unveiling of Truth*, Lahore: Jeddojuhd Publications, 1999.
Schaffer, Howard B., *The Limits of Influence: America's Role in Kashmir*, Washington D. C.: Brookings Institution Press, 2009.
Schofield, Victoria, *Kashmir in Conflict*, London: I. B. Tauris and Co., 2000.
Singh, Karan, *Autobiography*, New Delhi: Oxford University Press, 1994.
Singh, Tavleen, *Kashmir: A Tragedy of Errors*, New Delhi: Penguin Books India, 2000.
Snedden, Christopher, *Kashmir: The Unwritten History*, New Delhi: HarperCollins India, 2013.
Strachey, John, *India*, London: K. Paul, Trench, 1888.
Swami, Praveen, *India, Pakistan and the Secret Jihad: The Covert War in Kashmir, 1947-2004*,

Kiribati: Routledge, 2007.
Talbott, Strobe, *Engaging India: Diplomacy, Democracy and the Bomb*, Washington D. C.: Brookings Institution Press, 2004.
Taseer, C. Bilqees, *The Kashmir of Sheikh Muhammad Abdullah*, Lahore: Ferozsons Books, 1986.
Teng, Mohan Krishen, Bhatt, Ram Krishen Kaul and Kaul, Santosh, eds., *Kashmir: Constitutional History and Documents*, New Delhi: Light & Life Publishers, 1977.
US Department of State, *Soviet-American Relations: The Détente Years, 1969–1972*, Washington, DC: G. P. O., 1972.
Verghese, B. G., *First Draft: Witness to the Making of Modern India*, New Delhi: Tranquebar Press, 2010.
Whitehead, Andrew, *A Mission in Kashmir*, New Delhi: Penguin Books India, 2007.
Wink, Andre, *Al-Hind: the Making of the Indo-Islamic World*, Vol. I, New Delhi: Oxford University Press, 1990.
Wright, Lawrence, *The Looming Tower: Al Qaeda and the Road to 9/11*, New York: Knopf Books, 2005.
Zutshi, Chitralekha, *Kashmir's Contested Pasts: Narratives of Sacred Geographies and the Historical Imagination*, New Delhi: Oxford University Press, 2014.
———, *Languages of Belonging: Islam, Regional Identity, and the Making of Kashmir*, New Delhi: Permanent Black, 2003.

REPORTS

Amin, Agha Humayun, 'The 1947-48 Kashmir War: the war of lost opportunities', accessed through *Internet Archive*.
Bamzai, Sandeep, 'Nehru's Pacifism and the Failed Recapture of Kashmir,' Observer Research Foundation Special Report, 13 August 2016.
Bass, Gary J., 'The Indian way of humanitarian intervention', Yale Journal of International Law, Volume 40, Issue 2, 2015.
Davis, R. A., 'Kashmir in the balance', *International Defense Review*, Vol. 24, No. 4, April 1991.
Human Rights Watch Arms Project, *India: Arms and Abuses in Indian Punjab and Kashmir*, September 1994, Vol. 6, No. 10.
Kotasthane, Pranay, Srinath, Pavan, Pai, Nitin and Ramachandra, Varun, 'The India–Pakistan conflict escalation framework,' The Takshashila Institution, July 2015.
Mahmud, Ershad, paper on 'Azad Kashmir: Emergence, Progress and Irritants'.
Meier, Oliver, 'Involving India and Pakistan: nuclear arms control and non-proliferation after the nuclear tests', BITS Research Report No. 99:2, Berlin Information Center for Trans-Atlantic Security.
Ministry of External Affairs, Government of India, Annual Report 1990-91.
Padgaonka, Dileep, Ansari, M. M. and Kumar, Radha, 'A New Compact for Jammu and Kashmir: J&K Interlocutors' Report', October 2011.

INDEX

Abbas, Ghulam, 29, 40, 77, 82, 83, 84, 94, 125
Abdullah, Farooq, 154, 158, 159, 165, 174, 181, 199, 204, 206, 212, 244, 262, 265, 270, 278, 279, 298, 350, 355, 454, 457
Abdullah, Omar, 312, 313, 317, 320, 322, 326, 333, 345, 376, 379, 390, 391, 399, 449, 452
Abdullah, Sheikh, 29, 67, 75, 77, 78, 85, 102, 109, 112, 120, 187, 312, 368, 370, 384, 426, 431, 432, 434, 435
Adil, Musaddiq, 143
Advani–Hurriyat talks, 287, 290, 295
Advani, L. K., 183, 242, 264, 432, 445
Afghanistan, 2, 3, 5, 6, 8, 11, 15, 16, 27, 31, 63, 153, 154, 166, 167, 169, 172, 199, 203, 239, 243, 244, 246, 247, 248, 250, 254, 255, 257, 277, 285, 303, 308, 311, 312, 316, 392, 410, 411, 442, 443, 460
Afghan jihad, 154, 155, 167, 219, 246, 247, 250, 255, 257, 437
  Azzam's Arab recruitment campaign for, 255
Afghan Pathans, 61
Afghanistan, 2, 3, 5, 6, 8, 15, 16, 27, 31, 154, 156, 166, 167, 169, 172, 203, 239, 243, 244, 246, 248, 250, 254, 257, 277, 285, 303, 308, 311, 316, 410, 411
  Soviet Union withdrawal from, 166
Aftab, Abu Khalid, 255
Agenda of Alliance, 403, 405, 452
Agrarian Reforms (Amendment) Act of, 147
Agra summit, 273, 274, 275, 276
Agreement on Prohibition of Attack against Nuclear Installations and Facilities, 173 1988, 173
Ahmad, Hadhrat Mirza Bashiruddin Mahmud, 32
Ahmad–Haidar press conferences, 211
Ahmad, Shamshad, 106, 208, 227, 434, 440
Ahmed, Aziz, 58, 84
Ahmed, Lieutenant General, 234
Aiyar, Mani Shankar, 310
Akbar, emperor, 430

Akhtar, Sheeraza, 313
Aksai Chin, 20, 103, 104, 307
al-Afghani, Syed Jamaluddin, 31
Alam, Masrat, 318, 447
Alam, Sardar Muhammad, 65
al-Biruni, 6, 7, 8, 9, 429, 460
Al Fatah, 123, 126, 143, 144, 184
All Assam Gana Sangram Parishad, 161
Allen, Ethan, 220, 276
All Parties Hurriyat Conference (APHC), 222
Almeida, Cyril, 234, 442
Al Qaeda, 227, 247, 248, 392, 410, 443, 462
  interest in Kashmir, 248
Al-Rahmat Trust, 249
Al-Umar Mujahideen, 184, 189, 244
Amarnath conflict, 312, 321
Amarnath Yatra, 308, 418
Amin, Major Agha Humayun, 56
Amritsar–Lahore–Nankana Sahib bus, 222
Anantnag communal riots, 161
Andrabi, Asiya, 328, 374, 398, 404, 410
Anglo-Sikh Wars, 15, 16
Anjuman-i-Hamdard Islam, 28
Anjuman-i-Nusrat-al-Islam, 28, 30
Annan, General Kofi, 213
Ansari, Maulvi Abbas, 163, 193, 287, 373
Ansari, M. M., 462
Ansari, Moulana Iftikhar Hussain, 159
anti-Hindu riots of 1986, 164
anti-Zia 'Movement for the Restoration of Democracy', 165
Antony, A. K., 314
Anwar, Major Khurshid, 51
Anwar, Tariq, 160
Apparao, Jayashree, 78
April agreement, 82
April resolution, 73, 74
Arab–Israeli conflict, 134
Armed Forces (Special Powers) Act (AFSPA), 305, 306, 317, 350, 354, 355, 385, 386, 401, 408, 415
Article 249 of the Indian Constitution, 162

Article 352 of the Indian Constitution, 89
Article 370 of Constitution, 86, 89, 90, 91, 95, 96, 97, 101, 110, 120, 142, 150, 151, 204, 265, 282, 340, 384, 387, 389, 401, 418, 425, 426,
Articles 356 and 357 of the Indian Constitution, 110
Articles 371A of the Indian Constitution, 384
Ashoka, Emperor, 4
Asian Games, 216
assembly elections
  1920s, 34
  1962, 121
  1967, 121
  1972, 140
  1977, 145
  1983, 163
  1996
attack on India's Parliament, 249
Auchinleck, General Claude, 54
autonomy, 43, 86, 88, 89, 91, 92, 96, 103, 110, 120, 121, 122, 124, 128, 129, 142, 143, 146, 147, 151, 156, 194, 197, 204, 205, 221, 259, 265, 266, 267, 270, 282, 296, 301, 307, 309, 356, 357, 384, 386, 387, 389, 390, 407, 426, 450, 452
Awami Action Committee, 108, 163, 184, 185
Awami League, 128, 129, 131, 135
Ayub, Gohar, 208, 213
Ayyangar, Gopalaswami, 38, 141
Azad Army, 50, 55, 56, 57, 58, 68, 79, 80, 83, 113
Azad, Ghulam Nabi, 158, 160, 294, 297, 422
'Azad Kashmir', 43, 49, 151, 152, 433
Azad Muslim Conference and League, 40
Azhar, Masood, 244, 246, 247, 443
Aziz–Lambah backchannel, 296, 301, 302, 315, 389
Aziz, Sartaj, 208, 216, 219, 220, 227, 229, 235, 403, 441
Aziz, Sheikh Abdul, 143
Azzam's Arab recruitment campaign for, 255

Baalu, T. R., 330
Babri Masjid dispute, 161, 183
Badhwar, Inderjit, 164, 437
Bahawalpur, 244, 249, 251
Bajpai, Sir Girija Shankar, 80

Bajwa, General, 413, 414
Bakshi, 67, 96, 97, 98, 99, 100, 101, 102, 107, 108, 109, 110, 120, 121, 122, 126, 145, 151
Bakula, Kushak, 101
Balawaristan National Front, 392, 394
Balawaristan National Students Organization, 394
Bali, G. C., 59
Banerjee, Sir Albion, 28
Basic Democrats, 112, 124
Baweja, Harinder, 165, 198, 437, 439
Bazaz, Prem Nath, 460
Beg, Mirza Afzal, 96, 101
Beg-Parthasarathi, 'Agreed Conclusions', 435
Bhandara, M. P., 321
Bharatiya Janata Party (BJP), 160, 163, 175, 183, 184, 192, 195, 199, 207, 215, 228, 239, 249, 264, 265, 270, 281, 288, 290, 291, 294, 305, 306, 334, 339, 348, 353, 357, 375, 384, 395, 399, 400, 401, 403, 413–16, 422, 426
Bhat, Fayaz Ahmad, 321
Bhatt, Abdul Ghani, 176, 193, 268, 298
Bhattacharjea, Ajit, 460
Bhutto, Benazir, 460
Bhutto–Swaran Singh talks, 115
Bhutto, Zulfikar Ali, 84, 106
Blood, Archer, 133
'Bloody Tuesday', 268
Bogra, Mohammad Ali, 98, 128
Boundary Commission, 52
BRICS (Brazil, Russia, India, China and South Africa), 402
British volunteers, 257
Brown, Major William Alexander, 63, 71
Buddhism, 4, 5, 7, 63
Butt, Bashir Ahmed, 157
Butt, Maqbool, 126, 132, 158

Cadogan, Alexander, 71
Casablanca meeting, 206
ceasefire line, 76, 77, 79, 85, 107, 113, 115, 118, 123, 126, 127, 136, 137, 155, 230, 433
Central Asia, 5, 6, 7, 11, 14, 15, 17, 63, 71, 251, 284, 285, 298, 363
Central Reserve Police Force (CRPF), 123
Centre for Dialogue and Reconciliation, 285, 292

INDEX

Chandrapida, King, 6
Chandra, Satish, 219, 229, 440
Chapter VII of the UN Charter, 133
Chavan, S. B., 191
Chidambaram–Hurriyat backchannel, 315
Chidambaram, P., 314
China–Pakistan Economic Corridor (CPEC), 394
China's People's Liberation Army (PLA), 103
Choudhary, Zafar, 114, 430
Clinton, Bill, 439
Communist Party of India Marxist (CPM), 160, 307, 317, 330, 360, 395
confidence-building measure (CBM), 170, 173, 210, 217, 283, 284, 292, 293, 295, 298, 300, 302, 306, 315, 333, 335, 337, 344, 345, 247, 363, 364, 385, 386, 402, 411, 414
Constitution Act, 38, 40, 152, 436
Constitutional Reforms Commission's political recommendations, 34
Cripps Mission, 42
cross-border guerrillas, 319, 397
cross-border insurgency and violence, 209, 424

Dalai Lama, 103, 105
Damodara, 3
Dar, Aijaz, 166
Dardistan, 2
Dar initiative, 268
Dar, Majid, 267, 339
Dar, Shabir Ahmed, 262
Darul Uloom, 30
Datta Khel, 64, 433
Dayal, Rajeshwar, 107, 434
Defence of India Rules, 109
Delhi Agreement, 88, 89, 90, 96, 101, 110, 149, 150, 426, 434
Delhi–Hurriyat track, 299, 315
Delhi–Lahore bus, 217
Delhi Pact of 1950, 84
Democratic Alliance, 215, 391
Democratic Freedom Party, 184
Desai, Morarji, 145
Dev, Ranjit, 21, 28
Dhar, D. P., 99, 108, 134
Dhar, P. N., 137
Dixit, J. N., 104, 204, 434, 439
Dixon, Sir Owen, 87

Dixon's partition-cum-plebiscite proposal, 87
Dobrynin, Anatoly, 134, 435
Doda, 119, 223, 239, 266, 268, 273, 301, 308, 361, 442
Dogra feudalism, 25
Dogra, Girdhari Lal, 96
Dogra, Prem Nath, 93
Dogras, 21, 22, 23, 27, 43, 53, 54, 92, 98, 119
Dogra Sabha, 28
Dogri language, 23
Doraiswamy, K., 188
Doval, Ajit, 397, 403
Drabu, Haseeb, 400
Drass, 65, 66, 114, 225, 226, 234
Drass–Kargil link road, 234
Dukhtaran-e-Millat, 177, 185, 328, 374, 398
Dulat, A. S., 460
Dulles, John Foster, 73
Durrani, Ahmed Shah, 14

East Pakistan, 100, 105, 114, 128, 129, 130, 131, 132, 133, 134, 135, 136, 435
East Pakistani conflict, 136
eight-point programme, 330, 335
Ekta Yatra campaign, 183
ethnic conflict, 59, 60, 266

Faesal, Shah, 398
Faiz, Ahmed Faiz, 58, 84
Farooq, Mirwaiz Mohammad, 108, 174, 177
Farooq, Mirwaiz Omar, 198
Federally Administered Tribal Areas (FATA), 129
Fein, Sinn, 247, 263
Fernandes, George, 176, 265, 269
First Anglo-Afghan War, 16
Forward Policy, 104
Franchise Committee, 431
frontiers of Kashmir, 20
funding sources, 249

Gajendragadkar Commission, 123, 146
Gandhi, Indira, 121, 122, 124, 127, 132, 133, 134, 135, 136, 137, 140, 141, 143, 144, 146, 147, 148, 154, 155, 156, 157, 159, 160, 161, 164, 166, 192, 435, 436, 461
Gandhi, Rajiv, 162, 163, 168, 171, 172, 179, 283, 370, 399, 453
Gandhi, Sonia, 269, 292, 334

Gauhar, Altaf, 116
Gawkadal Massacre, 175
Geelani, Syed Ali Shah, 157, 205, 222, 449
General Council of the Muslim Conference, 39
geopolitics of Kashmir, 19, 150
Ghulam Abbas of Jammu, Chaudhry, 29
Gilgit, 4, 11, 17, 18, 19, 22, 27, 34, 35, 43, 44, 45, 63, 64, 65, 66, 71, 75, 76, 77, 80, 82, 85, 87, 106, 132, 148, 155, 221, 235, 251, 259, 260, 262, 285, 298, 301, 303, 305, 307, 334, 363, 385, 388, 389, 390, 391, 392, 393, 394, 415, 426, 433, 444, 454, 460
    Pakistan, acquisition of, 71
Gilgit-Baltistan, 43, 44, 155, 221, 251, 260, 298, 301, 303, 307, 385, 389, 391–93, 415, 426
Gilgit and Hunza Scouts, 65
Glancy Commission's social recommendations, 34
Glancy, B. J., 33
Golden Temple insurgency, 160, 161, 166, 170, 190
Gonanda I, King, 3
Good Friday/Belfast Agreement, 220
Government of India Act, 1919, 33
Government of India Act, 1935, 36
Gowda, H. D. Deve, 207
Gracey, General Douglas, 54
Grafftey-Smith, Sir Laurence Barton, 68
Great Game of 1830s, 15
Green Revolution, 129, 154
guerrilla infiltration in Kashmir, 112
Gujjar caste, 29
Gujral Doctrine, 207
Gujral, Inder Kumar, 122
Gujral–Sharif meeting, 214
'Gul-e-Curfew', 161
Gul, Hamid, 168, 169, 180, 233, 319, 437
Gupta, Kanchan, 242, 244, 442
Gurdaspur, 46, 47
Gurmani, M. A., 81, 82, 83
Guru, Abdul Ahad, 188

Habibullah, Wajahat, 460
Haidar, Salman, 208, 276, 440
Haji Pir pass, 117
Hamidullah, Choudhry, 41
Hamoodur Commission, 135

Handwara murder, 126
Haqqani-run Jamia Uloomul Islamia, 249
hard-line policy, 406
Harkat-ul-Ansar, 203, 238, 244, 246, 250
Harkatul Mujahideen, 240, 244, 250, 251, 252, 253
Hasan, Mubashir, 127
Hasnain, S. A., 336
Hassan, Khwaja Ahmed, 218
Hazari, Lieutenant General K. K., 229
Hazratbal crisis, 191, 192
    Criticism over handling of, 192
    Government-guerrilla agreement, 190
    release of hostages and surrender of arms, 190
Hekmatyar, Gulbuddin, 172
Henderson, Loy, 93
hijack plan, 127
Hindu communalism, 93
Hinduism, 4, 429
Hindu–Muslim violence, 59
Hindu Progressive Party, 37, 38
Hizbul–Home Ministry meeting, 270
Hizbul Mujahideen, 167, 175, 176, 177, 179, 187, 224, 240, 259, 267, 372, 376, 396, 451, 453
Holbrooke, Richard, 199

Ibn-e-Baz, Abdul Aziz, 247
Ibrahim, Dawood, 186, 256
Ibrahim, Sardar, 49, 50, 62, 77, 80, 83, 124, 261, 433, 461
India–China War, 2, 20
Indian embassy, Kabul, attacks on, 311
Indian National Congress, 30, 36
India–Pakistan negotiations, 106, 168, 214
    Advani–Hurriyat talks, 287, 290, 295,
    Aziz–Lambah backchannel, 296, 301, 302, 315, 316, 389, 390
    Centre for Dialogue and Reconciliation– Delhi Policy Group initiative,
    Chidambaram–Hurriyat backchannel, 292
    Dar initiative, 268
    Delhi-Lahore bus, 217
    Gujral–Sharif meeting, 214
    Hizbul–Home Ministry meeting, 270
    Lahore Declaration, 217, 225, 229, 236, 245,
    Mishra–Naik discussions, 221
    Nehru–Bogra talks, 100

INDEX

'people-to-people' initiatives, 222
roadmap to consensus, 383
SAARC, 171
Shafi's proposals, 266
Singh–Hurriyat talks, 296, 300
Singh–Musharraf 'four-point formula', 298
Srinagar–Muzaffarabad bus service, 291
three-track formula, 294
Vajpayee–Musharraf peace process (Agra summit), 298
Verma–Gul meetings, 169, 170, 172
India–Pakistan Question, 72, 79
India–Pakistan summit in Simla in June 1972, 136
India's counter-insurgency, 116, 237
Indira–Abdullah accord, 205
Indo-Pak War, 1965, 114, 117, 121,
  impact on Kashmir, 118
  India's counter-insurgency, 116
  war aims, 117
Indus Waters Treaty, 105, 308
Inquilabi, Azam, 143, 144
Inquilabi, Shafqat, 392
Instrument of Accession, 54, 73, 74, 81, 86, 89, 96
Instrument of Accession to India, 54
interest in Kashmir, 248
Irish Republican Army (IRA), 247
Islamic Gateway, 238, 239
Islamic State (ISIS), 253
Ittehad-ul-Muslimeen, 162, 185, 193, 287

Jahangir, 13, 14, 218
Jaipur Literary Festival, 381
Jaish-e-Mohammad, 244, 246, 251, 274, 404
Jaitley, Arun, 289, 357
Jaleel, Muzamil, 241, 381, 442, 449
Jamaat-e-Islami, 140, 144, 145, 154, 157, 162, 163, 179, 180, 181, 185, 218, 259, 268, 269, 271, 272, 325, 396, 417
Jamaat-ud-Dawa, 249, 252, 316, 331, 412
Jamali, Mir Zafarullah Khan, 282
Jamiat Ahle Hadees, 185, 373
Jamiatul Tulaba, 144, 157
Jammu and Kashmir National Liberation Front (JKNLF), 126
Jammu and Kashmir Panchayat Act of 1989, 377
Jammu and Kashmir Resettlement Bill, 148

Jammu and Kashmir State Council, 26
Jammu Autonomy Forum in 1967, 123
Jammu Kashmir Liberation Front (JKLF), 153, 158, 165, 166, 168, 174, 175, 179, 181, 182, 184, 185, 187, 188, 189, 193, 194, 197, 198, 205, 218, 241, 255, 262, 271, 294, 313, 331, 337, 343, 352, 361, 371, 374, 390, 408, 417
Jammu Muslims, 29, 62, 120
Jammu's population, 46
Jammu–valley divide, 33, 44
Janata Dal coalition, 179, 183
Janata Party, 144, 145, 146, 160
Janbaz Force, 201, 206
Jan Sangh, 90, 92, 93, 95, 101, 103, 121, 140, 143, 156, 160
Jayaprakash Narayan, 120, 121, 144, 435
Jha, L. K., 146
Jinnah, Fatima, 112
Jinnah, Muhammad Ali, 81
Jodhpur–Karachi train (the Thar Express), 222
Johnson Line, 103
Joint Resistance Leadership, 408
Joshi, Murli Manohar, 184

Kachru, Dwarkanath, 66
Karamat, General Jahangir, 218
Kargil, vii, 46, 65, 66, 67, 69, 114, 221, 225, 226, 227, 228, 229, 230, 231, 232, 234, 235, 236, 237, 240, 241, 245, 246, 248, 259, 260, 261, 264, 266, 272, 305, 307, 344, 361, 362, 363, 424, 441, 442, 450, 459, 461
Kargil Committee, 229, 231, 237,
Kargil War, 227, 228, 235, 247, 256, 260, 264
lessons from, 231
Karra, Mohiuddin, 127, 159
Kashmir accord, 142
Kashmir Bar Association, 185, 342
Kashmir for Kashmiris' movement, 26
Kashmiri guerrillas, 166, 172
Kashmiri Muslims, 24, 31, 39, 119, 237, 413
Kashmir insurgency, 180, 192, 212, 246, 442
Kashmiri Pandits, exodus of, 12, 26, 27, 174, 306, 307, 355, 356, 365, 423, 458
Kashmiri Pandit Yuvak Sabha, 37
Kashmiriyat, 13, 165, 281, 401, 433
Kashmir's accession to Pakistan, 59, 123, 151
Kashmir's security map, 5

Kashmir state election, 400
Kashyapa, Sage, 2, 3
Kasmira Mahatmya, 2
Kasuri, Khurshid, 228, 305, 371, 428
Kathwari, Farooq, 220, 276
Kaul, B. M., 99
Kaushal, M. B., 269
Khalil, Fazlur Rahman, 250
Khan, Abdul Ghaffar Khan, 37
Khan, Amanullah, 126, 132, 153, 158, 166, 181, 279, 392
Khan, Arif Mohammad, 158
Khan, Brigadier Hayat, 153
Khan, General Ayub, 79
Khan, General Yahya, 117, 118, 126, 128
Khan, Ghulam Jilani, 233
Khan, Imran, 234, 411
Khan, Liaquat Ali, 51
Khan, Rahim Yar, 251
Khan, Riaz, 334
Khan, Sardar Abdul Qayyum, 49
Khan, Sardar Ibrahim, 49, 261
Khan, Sardar Qayyum, 206
Khan, Wali, 153
Khan, Zafrullah, 72, 81, 94, 106
Khatoon, Habba, 13
Khayal, G. N., 176
Khilafat Movement, 30
Khoda, Kuldeep, 325
Khudai Khidmatgars, 50, 51
Khurshid, 51, 124, 125, 126, 132, 199, 228, 259, 305, 310, 371, 428, 435
Kissinger–Zhou Enlai conversations, 134
Korbel, Josef, 461
Kosygin, Aleksey, 113
Kushanas, 4, 5

Laden, Osama bin, 219, 247, 372, 451
Lahore Declaration, 217, 225, 229, 236, 440
Lahore Process, 222, 223, 227, 228, 230, 262
Lalitaditya of Magadha, King, 6
Lambah, Satinder, 334
Lashkar-e-Jhangvi, 8, 251, 252, 392
Lashkar-e-Zil, 392, 452
Lawrence, Sir Walter, 25
Liberation League, 152
Liberation Tigers of Tamil Eelam (LTTE), 179
Line of Control (LoC), 417
list of 'martyred commanders', 256
'Livingston Proposal' of 1998, 220, 441

Lodhi, Maleeha, 412
Lone, Abdul Ghani, 176
Lone, Bashir Ahmad, 317
Lone, Sajad Gani, 332
Longowal, Harcharan Singh, 161

Machil investigation, 336
Madhav, Ram, 400
Madhok, Balraj, 461
Mahajan, Meher Chand, 52
Mahaz-e-Azadi, 157, 185
Mahmud of Ghazni, 6
Maini, K. D., 147, 436
Malhotra, Inder, 461
Malhotra, V. K., 294
Malik, Major General Akhtar Hussain, 113
Malik, Yasin, 13, 168, 179, 187, 197, 198, 241, 255, 279, 294, 330, 333, 337, 343, 357, 367, 374, 439, 448, 451
Mandal agitation, 183
Manekshaw, Field Marshal Sam, 55
Mansour, Mullah, 244
Mao, 94, 103, 117
Markaz ud Dawa'ah wal Irshad, 238, 247
    attack on India's Parliament, 249
    funding sources, 249
Martyrs' Day, 32
Masoodi, Maulana, 146
massive retaliation, 402
Mast Gul, 203
Mattoo, Amitabh, 327
Mazar-e-Shuhada, 32
Mehra, Brigadier, 317
Mehta, Asoke, 120
Menon, V. K. Krishna, 104
Menon, V. P., 75
Mhatre, Ravinder, 158
Mihirakula, 7, 8
military coup against, 231
Ministry of Kashmir Affairs, 79, 81, 83, 84, 125, 389
Mir, Ghulam Hassan, 297
Mir Syed Ali bin Shahabuddin Hamadani, 11
Mirwaiz's murder, 177
Mishra, Brajesh, 284, 288, 289, 291, 295, 296
Mishra–Naik discussions, 221
Mishra–Naik talks, 231
Mishra, R. K., 219, 274, 298
Modi, Narendra, 457
    Agenda of Alliance, 403, 405

hard-line policy, 406
massive retaliation, 402
'no talks with the Hurriyat', 403
talks with Hurriyat, Tehreek and allied groups, 405
unilateral cessation of hostilities, 413
Mohammad, Bakshi Ghulam, 96, 98
Mohammad, Mir, 12
Mo-i-Muqaddas crisis, 108, 113
Mookerjee, Syama Prasad, 84, 90
Mufti, Mehbooba, 292, 328, 332, 333, 336, 391, 397, 405, 415, 448, 457
Mujahideen-e-Lashkar-e-Tayyaba
British volunteers, 257
funding sources, 249
list of 'martyred commanders', 256
members, 29, 34, 35, 37, 38, 39, 41, 51, 58, 69, 70, 71, 75, 77, 81, 86, 98, 101, 107, 108, 112, 120, 123, 124, 127, 131, 132, 133, 134, 135, 138, 143, 144, 152, 160, 163, 168, 173, 193, 202, 212, 223, 224, 232, 244, 247, 250, 262, 263, 268, 271, 272, 277, 278, 279, 280, 281, 286, 287, 289, 303, 304, 306, 315, 329, 332, 343, 350, 352, 359, 375, 377, 391, 392, 394, 395, 420, 425, 444, 451
Mukti Bahini, 134, 135, 138
mulkis, 25
Mullick, B. N., 99
Mumbai attacks of 26 November 2008, 309
Musharraf, General, 218, 219, 229, 231, 245, 260
Muslim Conference, 30, 35, 36, 37, 38, 39, 40, 41, 42, 43, 44, 48, 49, 62, 82, 83, 84, 126, 152, 176, 185, 193, 336
Muslim-Hindu-Sikh violence, 48
Muslim Khawateen Markaz, 185
Muslim Scouts, 64
Muslim Sudhans, 62
Muttawakil, Mullah Wakil Ahmed, 243
Muzaffarabad invasion, 52, 53, 58

Nagas, 2, 3, 263
Naik, Niaz, 169, 219, 228
Nanda, Gulzarilal, 151
Naqash, Mohammad Yousuf, 315
Naqshbandi, Khwaja Bahawuddin, 32
National Cadet Corps, 123
NATO, 100, 303, 410
Naya Kashmir' agenda, 151

Naya (new) Kashmir manifesto, 85
Nehru, B. K., 148, 159
Nehru–Bogra talks, 100
Nehru, Jawaharlal, 461
Nilamata Purana, v, 2, 6, 7, 12, 429
Nimitz, Chester, 80
Nixon–Kissinger conversations, 133
Nixon, President, 133
Noel-Baker, Philip, 71
non-aggression pact, 154, 155
Non-Aligned Movement's Durban summit, 216
Noon, Feroze Khan, 105
Noorani, A. G., 142, 312, 434, 435, 440, 441, 445, 446
Nooruddin Wali of Kaimoh, Sheikh, 12
Northern Irish peace process, 263
Northern Tier alliance, 99
North West Frontier Province (NWFP), 30
Northern tier alliance, 95, 99
no talks with the Hurriyat, 403
no-war pact proposal, 105
nuclear weapons programme, 138, 173

October coup, 260
Operation Balakote, 193
Operation Gibraltar, 113, 114
Operation Grand Slam, 116
Organisation of Islamic Cooperation (OIC), 409

Padgaonkar, Dileep, 332, 333
Pakistan-administered, 43, 50, 60, 77, 79, 81, 82, 83, 87, 94, 99, 106, 110, 119, 123, 124, 125, 126, 132, 151, 152, 153, 166, 167, 175, 201, 205, 206, 212, 238, 244, 259, 279, 294, 296, 298, 303, 305, 307, 331, 334, 347, 348, 362, 363, 385, 388, 389, 390, 391, 393, 394, 415
Pakistan-administered Kashmir, 43, 50, 60, 77, 79, 81, 82, 83, 87, 94, 110, 119, 123, 124, 125, 126, 132, 151, 152, 153, 166, 167, 175, 201, 205, 206, 212, 238, 244, 279, 294, 296, 298, 303, 305, 307, 331, 334, 347, 348, 362, 363, 385, 388, 389, 390, 391, 393, 394, 415
Pakistan–China alliance, 105
Pakistan-held territories of the former princely state, 43, 102, 119, 148, 303, 341, 394

Pakistan–India Peoples' Forum for Peace and Democracy, 274
Pakistan People's Party (PPP), 118
Palestine, British mandate of, 71
Panchayati Raj Act of 1993, 377
Pant, K. C., 289
Parbat, Hari, 157
Parthasarathy, G., 461
partition idea for Kashmir, 75
   April resolution, 73, 74
   Dixon's partition-cum-plebiscite proposal, 87
   Instrument of Accession, 54, 73, 74, 81, 86, 89, 96, 198   Korbel's, 75, 77, 81
   Noel-Baker, 71, 72, 73
Patel, Sardar, 52
Patil, Shivraj, 291
PDP–BJP coalition, 403
Pearl, Daniel, 244, 254
'people-to-people' initiatives, 222
pipeline diplomacy, 285
Plebiscite Front, 101, 102, 110, 111, 112, 114, 115, 121, 123, 126, 127, 140, 141, 152, 159
plebiscite, UN-organized, 68
policy towards Kashmir, 58
Poonch, 22, 27, 37, 41, 44, 46, 48, 49, 50, 51, 54, 56, 57, 58, 59, 60, 61, 66, 67, 75, 76, 77, 80, 81, 82, 83, 87, 111, 114, 115, 116, 117, 118, 119, 125, 135, 147, 148, 159, 202, 221, 239, 261, 293, 294, 321, 348, 349, 362, 363, 392, 393, 423, 432, 436, 450, 458, 461
Praja Parishad, 53, 86, 90, 91, 92, 101, 121, 145
Praja Sabha, 33, 34, 36, 37, 40, 41
Praja Socialist Party, 120
President's Rule, 162, 174, 179, 206
Prime Minister's Reconstruction Plan (PMRP), 327
public safety act (PSA), 418
Public Safety Ordinance, 147
Punjab, 4, 6, 8, 14, 15, 16, 21, 22, 23, 32, 36, 37, 39, 40, 46, 47, 48, 52, 53, 59, 82, 105, 116, 129, 135, 155, 159, 161, 172, 175, 180, 190, 192, 208, 217, 233, 242, 246, 247, 248, 250, 256, 257, 310, 319, 347, 352, 357, 363, 364, 369, 370, 393, 400, 404, 417, 432, 438, 462
Punjab State People's Conference, 39

Puri, Balraj, 461

Qasim, Mir, 461
Qazi, Ashraf Jehangir, 265
Quit India Movement, 42
Qureshi, Ashraf, 127
Qureshi, Fazal Haq, 123, 143, 267, 315, 335, 444
Qureshi, Shah Mehmood, 310

Radcliffe, Sir Cyril, 46
Rahman, Mujibur, 128, 129
Rajatarangini, 7, 10, 429, 461
Rangarajan Committee's proposal for employment of Kashmiri youth, 383
Rao, P.V. Narasimha, 179, 186, 263
Rao–Clinton summit, 198, 199
Rao, N. T. Rama, 161
Rashtriya Swayamsevak Sangh, 53
Rasool, Ghulam, 123, 193, 262, 373
Rauf, Abdul, 250
Rawalpindi Conspiracy, 84
Razakaars, 114, 115, 119, 131, 135
Reading Room, 28, 32
Reshi, Khurshid Ahmad, 259
regional autonomy, 120, 121, 146, 147
release of hostages and surrender of arms, 190
Rinchen, Prince Lhachen Gyalbu, 10
roadmap to consensus, 383
Round Table Conference, 30
Roy, B. C., 92

SAARC, 171, 173, 208, 214, 282, 283, 284, 316, 426
sadr-i-riyasat, 89, 90, 92, 93, 95, 97, 98, 99, 108, 110, 141, 142, 204
Sadiq, G. M., 101, 108
Saifuddin, Suhabhatt Malik, 11
Salafi movement, 31
Salafization strategy, 177
Saltoro Ridge, 156
Samjhauta blasts, 304
Samjhauta (Conciliation) Express, 222
Sanghvi, Vir, 329
Saraf, Muhammad, 126
Saraf, Shyam Lal, 96
Saxena, Governor Girish, 178
Sayeed, Mufti Mohammad, 4, 140, 162, 173, 174, 241, 436, 437

Sayeed, Rubaiya, 174, 176, 244
self-governance in Jammu and Kashmir, 302
Sen Gupta, Bhabani, 207
September 11 attacks in New York and Washington, 276
Sethi, Krishan Dev, 48
Shafiq-ur-Rehman, 238
Shafi's proposals, 266
Shah, Amit, 405, 421, 457, 459
Shaheed, Arif, 180, 437
Shah, Ghulam Mohammad, 146
Shah, Jalil Ahmed, 271
Shah, Mirwaiz Yusuf, 29, 35, 40
Shah, Shabir, 143, 157, 176, 184, 185, 197, 204, 205, 222, 262, 342, 439, 441
   People's League, 143, 144, 157, 176, 184, 185, 197, 201, 222, 439
Shah, Yusuf, 13, 29, 35, 40, 108, 165, 167, 181, 268, 270, 316, 352, 406, 430
Shaksgam valley, 111
Shalimar Garden, 4, 14
Shamsuddin, Khwaja, 107, 108
Shamzai, Nizamuddin, 250
Shanghai Cooperation Organisation, 402
Sharif, Nawaz, 173, 200, 207, 226, 227, 399, 442
   military coup against, 231
   Ufa statement, 411
Sharma, Dineshwar, 407, 453
Shastri, Lal Bahadur, 111
Sheikh, Omar, 252
Shekhar, Chandra, 173, 179
Shia–Sunni clashes, 260
Shikoh, Dara, 14
Shirani, Maulana Mohammad Khan, 259
Sholay analogy, 380
Shopian stoning agitation of 2009, 328
Shourie, Arun, 188, 438
Siachen Glacier, 155, 156
Siachen talks, 171
Sikander, 11, 12, 238
Silk Route, 2
Simla Agreement, 137, 138, 163, 172, 180, 198, 199, 209, 228, 273, 435
Simon Commission, 30
Sindh, 5, 15, 16, 30, 116, 129, 257, 284
Singh, Brigadier Rajinder, 55
Singh, Ghansara, 64
Singh–Hurriyat talks, 296, 300
Singh, Jaswant, 221, 225, 231, 243, 244, 245, 273, 275, 442, 445
Singh, Jitendra, 401, 452
Singh, Karan, 28, 50, 85, 86, 90, 92, 93, 96, 97, 98, 99, 395, 432, 434
Singh, Maharaja Gulab, 21, 26, 27
Singh, Maharaja Hari, 26, 27, 32, 33, 39, 64, 83, 85, 178, 368
Singh, Maharaja Ranbir, 18, 23
Singh, Major Avtar, 336, 448
Singh, Manmohan, 290, 295, 423
Singh–Musharraf 'four-point formula, 298
Singh, Natwar, 290
Singh, Pratap, 18, 19, 22, 24, 25, 26, 27, 430
Singh, Rajnath, 357, 375, 397, 414, 415
Singh, Ranjit, 14, 16, 26
Singh, Swaran, 105, 106, 107, 113, 115
Singh, Tavleen, 160, 163, 436
Singh, V. K., 326, 408
Singh, Zorawar, 22
Sipah-e-Sahaba, 251, 252
Sitharaman, Nirmala, 334
Skardu, 22, 65, 66, 67, 69, 230, 305, 363, 394
Snedden, Christopher, 462
South Asian Free Trade Agreement, 283
Southeast Asia Treaty Organization (SEATO), 100
Soviet Union, 63, 102, 113, 117, 134, 138, 154, 166, 167, 246
Special Operations Group (SOG), 242
Srinagar jail, 338, 340
Srinagar–Muzaffarabad bus service, 291, 292
Srinagar–Rawalpindi road, 22
Srinagar round table, 300
Standstill Agreement, 47
State Autonomy Report, 266
Stevenson, Adlai, 93
St. John, Colonel Oliver, 18
stoning protests, 325, 328, 339, 342, 352, 359, 364, 388, 407
Strachey, Sir John, 24
Subrahmanyam, K., 229
Suhrawardy, Hussein, 128
Swami Vivekananda, 1
Swatantra Party, 103

Tajamul Islam, 157
Talbott, Strobe, 226, 441
Tamman, Hayat Mohammad Khan, 153
Tashkent Agreement, 118, 119
Tashkent Declaration, 117, 124, 435

Tehreek-i-Hurriyat Kashmir, 185
terrorist attacks, 182, 186, 223, 300, 304, 308, 379, 423, 426
Tharoor, Shashi, 395
Thimayya, Major General, 65
Thimpu SAARC summit, 316
Thinkers' Forum, 391
three-track formula, 294
Tibetan empire, 5
Tiger Hill (Point 4660), 226
Tota, Bashir Ahmed, 143
Treaty of Amritsar, 14, 42, 430
Treaty of Lahore, 14
Treaty of Peace, Friendship and Cooperation, 134, 135, 154

Udhampur, 23, 46, 59, 61, 119, 135, 223, 239
U-li-to, 6, 429
UN-brokered ceasefire agreement, 76
UN Commission resolution, 82
unilateral cessation of hostilities, 413
United Movement, 394
Unlawful Activities (Prevention) Act, 386, 419
UN Military Observer Group in India, 77
UN Military Observer Group in India and Pakistan (UNMOGIP), 77
UN Security Council, 69, 70, 71, 72, 73, 87, 102, 117, 412, 424, 453
UN Trusteeship, 71

US–India Track II Neemrana Dialogue, 302

Vajpayee, Atal Bihari, 160, 199, 215, 442, 445
Vajpayee–Musharraf peace process, 298
Vasudeva, King, 5
Verghese, B. G., 462
Verma, A. K., 168, 437
Verma–Gul meetings, 169
Village Defence Committees, 224
Vohra, N. N., 281, 286, 309

Wani, Abdul Hamid, 143
Wani, Burhan, 396
war aims, 117
War Council, 81, 82, 389
Wilson, Harold, 115

Yalta conference, 70
Yechury, Sitaram, 330
Young Men's League, 123, 124
Young Men's Muslim Association, 28, 29, 31
Yuva Sabha, 28

Zainagirs, 12
Zain-ul-Abidin, Sultan, 12
Zardari, Asif Ali, 233, 453
Zargar, Mushtaq Ahmed, 244
Zhou Enlai, 103, 111, 116, 134
Zia-ul-Haq, General, 153
Zubaydah, Abu, 248